P9-EEU-494

Drama
and
Revolution

Drama and Revolution

Bernard F. Dukore

CITY UNIVERSITY OF NEW YORK

HOLT, RINEHART AND WINSTON, INC.

NEW YORK CHICAGO SAN FRANCISCO ATLANTA DALLAS
MONTREAL TORONTO

Preface

This anthology aims to trace revolution in world drama. Representing examples of various periods of world drama, with emphasis on the modern, it includes Greek tragedy (*Prometheus Bound*) as well as contemporary guerilla theatre (*Justice*). This anthology also aims to cover dramatic representations of important world revolutions. Beginning with a play focusing on the archetypal revolutionist, it continues with dramatizations of particular revolutions: the Reformation, the American Revolution, the French Revolution, communist revolution (both western and eastern), the Irish Revolution, revolution in the third world, the Black Revolution, and the Brown Revolution. Following each selection is a commentary analyzing that work from the viewpoint of the revolution that is its subject, plus a bibliography consisting of other plays dealing with that revolution and of critical or background works.

Obviously, no anthology of ten plays can cover dramatic representations of all revolutions, historical and fictive. At the end of this volume, therefore, is a selective Supplementary Bibliography of plays dealing with revolutions not represented in this anthology. Selections in this volume were governed by the two aims cited in the previous paragraph, by considerations of space, and (admittedly) by editorial bent. Two omissions, a Shakespearean and a Soviet play, require additional explanation. Because plays by Shakespeare are so easily available else-where, considerations of space prevailed. Brecht's *Saint Joan of the Stock-yards* was selected rather than a Soviet play dealing with communist revolution simply because Brecht's work is far superior to any of the latter.

Finally, I should like to call the reader's attention to a companion volume, *Documents for Drama and Revolution.* Designed to supplement the plays in this anthology, *Documents* contains contemporary writings on revolutions that are the subjects of plays in this volume (composed in some instances by the authors of those plays), as well as (where pertinent and available) on the plays themselves and (where relevant) on the revolutionary form of theatre they represent.

Bernard F. Dukore

New York, New York
July, 1970

Contents

The Archetypal Revolutionist

PROMETHEUS BOUND
Aeschylus

PROMETHEUS BOUND
Aeschylus
Translated by Philip Vellacott

CHARACTERS

STRENGTH
VIOLENCE
HEPHAESTUS, *the God of Fire*
PROMETHEUS
CHORUS *of the Daughters of Oceanus*
OCEANUS, *the God of the Sea*
IO, *a Priestess of Argos*
HERMES, *Messenger of Zeus*

A rocky mountain-top, within sight of the sea.
    Enter STRENGTH *and* VIOLENCE, *dragging in* PROMETHEUS. HEPHAES-
    TUS *follows.*

STRENGTH   Here we have reached the remotest region of the earth,
        The haunt of Scythians, a wilderness without a footprint.
        Hephaestus, do your duty. Remember what command
        The Father laid on you. Here is Prometheus, the rebel:
        Nail him to the rock; secure him on this towering summit
        Fast in the unyielding grip of adamantine chains.
        It was your treasure that he stole, the flowery splendour
        Of all-fashioning fire, and gave to men—an offence
        Intolerable to the gods, for which he now must suffer,
        Till he be taught to accept the sovereignty of Zeus
        And cease acting as champion of the human race.
HEPHAESTUS   For you two, Strength and Violence, the command of Zeus
        Is now performed. You are released. But how can I

Copyright © 1961 by Philip Vellacott. From Aeschylus, *Prometheus and Other Plays*, published by Penguin Books.

3

Find heart to lay hands on a god of my own race,
And cruelly clamp him to this bitter, bleak ravine?
And yet I must; heart or no heart, this I must do.
To slight what Zeus has spoken is a fearful thing.
[*to* PROMETHEUS] Son of sagacious Themis, god of mountainous
    thoughts,
With heart as sore as yours I now shall fasten you
In bands of bronze immovable to this desolate peak,
Where you will hear no voice, nor see a human form;
But scorched with the sun's flaming rays your skin will lose
Its bloom of freshness. Glad you will be to see the night
Cloaking the day with her dark spangled robe; and glad
Again when the sun's warmth scatters the frost at dawn.
Each changing hour will bring successive pain to rack
Your body; and no man yet born shall set you free.
Your kindness to the human race has earned you this.
A god who would not bow to the gods' anger—you,
Transgressing right, gave privileges to mortal men.
For that you shall keep watch upon this bitter rock,
Standing upright, unsleeping, never bowed in rest.
And many groans and cries of pain shall come from you,
All useless; for the heart of Zeus is hard to appease.
Power newly won is always harsh.
STRENGTH   What is the use
    Of wasting time in pity? Why do you not hate
    A god who is an enemy to all the gods,
    Who gave away to humankind your privilege?
HEPHAESTUS   The ties of birth and comradeship are strangely strong.
STRENGTH   True; yet how is it possible to disobey
    The Father's word? Is not that something you dread more?
HEPHAESTUS   You have been always cruel, full of aggressiveness.
STRENGTH   It does no good to break your heart for him. Come now,
    You cannot help him: waste no time in worrying.
HEPHAESTUS   I hate my craft, I hate the skill of my own hands.
STRENGTH   Why do you hate it? Take the simple view: your craft
    Is not to blame for what must be inflicted now.
HEPHAESTUS   True—yet I wish some other had been given my skill.
STRENGTH   All tasks are burdensome—except to rule the gods.
    No one is free but Zeus.
HEPHAESTUS   I know. All this [*indicating* PROMETHEUS] is proof
    Beyond dispute.

STRENGTH   Be quick, then; put the fetters on him
Before the Father sees you idling.

HEPHAESTUS   Here, then, look!
The iron wrist-bands are ready. [*he begins to fix them*]

STRENGTH   Take them; manacle him;
Hammer with all your force, rivet him to the rock.

HEPHAESTUS   All right, I'm doing it! There, that iron will not come loose.

STRENGTH   Drive it in further; clamp him fast, leave nothing slack.

HEPHAESTUS   This arm is firm; at least he'll find no way out there.

STRENGTH   Now nail his other arm securely. Let him learn
That all his wisdom is but folly before Zeus.

HEPHAESTUS   There! None—but he—could fairly find fault with my
work.

STRENGTH   Now drive straight through his chest with all the force you
have
The unrelenting fang of the adamantine wedge.

HEPHAESTUS   Alas! I weep, Prometheus, for your sufferings.

STRENGTH   Still shrinking? Weeping for the enemy of Zeus?
Take care; or you may need your pity for yourself.
[HEPHAESTUS *drives in the wedge.*]

HEPHAESTUS   There! Now you see a sight to pain your eyes.

STRENGTH   I see
Prometheus getting his deserts. Come, fix these girths
Around his ribs.

HEPHAESTUS   I must. Don't drive me with commands.

STRENGTH   I swear I *will* command you—yes, and hound you on.
Come lower down now; force his legs into this ring.

HEPHAESTUS   That's quickly done.

STRENGTH   Now nail those shackles fast. Hit hard!
Our work has a stern judge.

HEPHAESTUS   Your speech matches your looks.

STRENGTH   [*jeering*]   Be soft, then. But if I am hard and pitiless,
Don't cast it at me.

HEPHAESTUS   Come, his legs are safe; let's go.
[*Exit* HEPHAESTUS.]

STRENGTH   [*to* PROMETHEUS]   Stay there, and swell with upstart arrogance;
and steal
The privileges of gods to give to mortal men.
How are your mortals going to cut *this* knot for you?
You're wrongly named, Prometheus, Wise-before-the-event!
Wisdom is just the thing you want, if you've a mind

To squirm your way out of this blacksmith's masterpiece!
[*Exeunt* STRENGTH *and* VIOLENCE.]

PROMETHEUS   O divinity of sky, and swift-winged winds, and leaping
   streams,
O countless laughter of the sea's waves,
O Earth, mother of all life!
On you, and on the all-seeing circle of the sun, I call:
See what is done by gods to me, a god!

See with what outrage
Racked and tortured
I am to agonize
For a thousand years!
See this shameful prison
Invented for me
By the new master of the gods!
I groan in anguish
For pain present and pain to come:
Where shall I see rise
The star of my deliverance?

What am I saying? I know exactly every thing
That is to be; no torment will come unforeseen.
My appointed fate I must endure as best I can,
Knowing the power of Necessity is irresistible.
Under such suffering, speech and silence are alike
Beyond me. For bestowing gifts upon mankind
I am harnessed in this torturing clamp. For I am he
Who hunted out the source of fire, and stole it, packed
In pith of a dry fennel-stalk. And fire has proved
For men a teacher in every art, their grand resource.
That was the sin for which I now pay the full price,
Bared to the winds of heaven, bound and crucified.

Ah! Who is there?
What sound, what fragrant air
Floats by me—whence, I cannot see?
From god, or man, or demigod?
Have you come to this peak at the world's end
To gaze at my torment? Or for what?
See me, a miserable prisoner,
A god, the enemy of Zeus,

Who have earned the enmity of all gods
That frequent the court of Zeus
Because I was too good a friend to men.

Ah, ah! I hear it again, close to me!
A rustling—is it of birds?
And the air whispering with the light beat of wings!
Whatever comes, brings fear.
[*Enter the* CHORUS *in a winged ship or carriage.*]

CHORUS   Fear nothing. We are all your friends.
We have flown to this mountain on racing wings,
Winning reluctant leave from our father;
And the winds carried us swiftly along.
For the echo of ringing steel
Shivered through the depths of our cave,
Shaking quiet bashfulness out of our thoughts;
And barefoot as we were
We came at once in our winged carriage.

PROMETHEUS   Alas, alas! Children of fertile Tethys,
Daughters of Oceanus, whose unsleeping tide
Encircles the whole earth, look at me.
See in how cruel a grip,
Pinned on the craggy peak of this ravine,
I must endure my fearful watch.

CHORUS   I look, Prometheus; and sudden fear fills my eyes
To see your body withering on this rock,
Outraged with fetters of adamant.
A new master holds the helm of Olympus;[1]
These are new laws indeed
By which Zeus tyrannically rules;
And the great powers of the past he now destroys.

PROMETHEUS   Would that Zeus had sunk me under the earth,
Down below Hades, haven of the dead,
Into the immensity of Tartarus,
Fastening me in cruel fetters inextricably,
That no god or any other creature
Might feel glad to see me suffer.
Instead I am the miserable sport of every wind,
And my torments bring joy to my enemies.

---

[1] Home of Zeus and the other "Olympian gods," who were so named because of their home.

CHORUS   What god is cruel-hearted enough
    To find joy in such a sight?
    Who does not suffer with you in your pain—
    Save Zeus? He, firm in inflexible anger,
    Treads down the race of Ouranos,[2] and will not relent
    Till his passion is sated, or till some cunning plot
    Wrests from his hand his impregnable empire.
PROMETHEUS   I swear to you that I, humiliated as I am,
    Bound hand and foot in these strong straps,
    Shall yet be needed by the lord of immortals
    To disclose the new design, tell him who it is
    Shall rob him of his power and his glory.
    The honied spells of his persuasive tongue shall not enchant me,
    Nor shall I cower under his fierce threats, or tell this secret,
    Until he free me from these brutal bonds
    And consent to compensate me for his outrage.
CHORUS   You are defiant, Prometheus, and your spirit,
    In spite of all your pain, yields not an inch.
    But there is too much freedom in your words.
    My heart is shaken with a piercing terror;
    I tremble at your fate: how are you to reach
    The end of these troubles and rest in a safe port?
    For the son of Cronos[3] is unapproachable in temper,
    And no words can soften his heart.
PROMETHEUS   Zeus, I know, is ruthless,
    And keeps law within his own will.
    Nevertheless his temper shall in time turn mild,
    When my words come true and he is broken.
    Then at last he will calm his merciless anger,
    And ask for a pact of friendship with me;
    And I shall welcome him.
CHORUS   Now disclose everything and explain to us
    Upon what charge Zeus had you seized
    And treated with such ignominy and brutality.
    Tell us, if telling involves no harm for you.
PROMETHEUS   To speak of this is painful for me; to keep silence
    Is no less pain. On every side is suffering.
    When first among the immortal gods anger broke out
    Dividing them into two factions, of which one
    Resolved to unseat the power of Cronos, and make Zeus

[2] Mankind.
[3] Zeus.

Absolute king—mark that!—while the opposing side
Resolved no less that Zeus should never rule the gods—
At that time I, offering the best of all advice,
Tried to convince the Titan sons of Heaven and Earth,
And failed. They despised cunning; in their pride of strength
They foresaw easy victory and the rule of might.
I knew the appointed course of things to come. My mother,
Themis, or Earth (one person, though of various names),
Had many times foretold to me, that not brute strength,
Not violence, but cunning must give victory
To the rulers of the future. This I explained to them,
With reasons—which they found not worth one moment's heed.

Then, of the courses open to me, it seemed best
To take my stand—my mother with me—at the side
Of Zeus, willing and welcome. It was I who gave
That counsel through which ancient Cronos and his crew
Lie buried now in the black abyss of Tartarus.
That was the help I gave the king of the gods; and this
Is my reward—this is his black ingratitude.
To look on all friends with suspicion—this disease
Would seem to be inherent in a tyrant's soul.

Now, for your question, on what charge Zeus tortures me,
I'll tell you. On succeeding to his father's throne
At once he appointed various rights to various gods,
Giving to each his set place and authority.
Of wretched humans he took no account, resolved
To annihilate them and create another race.
This purpose there was no one to oppose but I:
I dared. I saved the human race from being ground
To dust, from total death.
For that I am subject to these bitter pains—
Agony to endure, heart-rending to behold.
I pitied mortal men; but being myself not thought
To merit pity, am thus cruelly disciplined—
A sight to fix dishonour on the name of Zeus.

CHORUS Only a heart of iron, a temper carved from rock,
Prometheus, could refuse compassion for your pains.
Had I known, I could have wished never to see this sight;
Now I have seen, sorrow and anger rack my heart.

PROMETHEUS Indeed my friends feel pity at the sight of me.

CHORUS Did your offence perhaps go further than you have said?

PROMETHEUS   Yes: I caused men no longer to foresee their death.
CHORUS   What cure did you discover for their misery?
PROMETHEUS   I planted firmly in their hearts blind hopefulness.
CHORUS   Your gift brought them great blessing.
PROMETHEUS   I did more than that:
     I gave them fire.
CHORUS   What? Men, whose life is but a day,
     Possess already the hot radiance of fire?
PROMETHEUS   They do; and with it they shall master many crafts.
CHORUS   This then was the offence for which you suffer here—
PROMETHEUS   Suffer the unrelenting savagery of Zeus.
CHORUS   And is no end of this ordeal appointed you?
PROMETHEUS   No, none; until such time as he sees fit to choose.
CHORUS   He never will. What hope is there? Oh, you were wrong—
     Do you not see? To say that you were wrong grieves me,
     And tortures you. So let us talk no more of it.
     Instead, try now to think of some deliverance.
PROMETHEUS   Oh, it is easy for the one who stands outside
     The prison-wall of pain to exhort and teach the one
     Who suffers. All you have said to me I always knew.
     Wrong? I accept the word. I willed, willed to be wrong!
     And helping humans I found trouble for myself.
     Yet I did not expect such punishment as this—
     To be assigned an uninhabited desert peak,
     Fastened in mid-air to this crag, and left to rot!

          Listen: stop wailing for the pain I suffer now.
     Step to the ground; I'll tell you what the future holds
     For me; you shall know everything from first to last.
     Do what I ask you, do it! Share the suffering
     Of one whose turn is now. Grief is a wanderer
     Who visits many, bringing always the same gift.
CHORUS   Your appeal falls on willing ears, Prometheus.
     Come, sisters, leave your seats
     In the ship that flies on the holy highway of birds;
     Step lightly down to the rocky ground.
     —We are eager to hear to the end
     The story of all you have undergone, Prometheus.
     [*The* CHORUS *leave their ship. As they group themselves on the
     ground* OCEANUS *arrives seated on a winged four-footed creature.*]
OCEANUS   Here at last!
     Prometheus, I have come a long way to visit you,

Guiding this swift-winged creature
By will, without any bridle.
Believe me, I am sorry for your misfortunes.
Being related to you, I suppose,
Makes me sympathize with you;
But apart from relationship, there is no one
Whom I hold in greater respect.
That is true, and I will prove it to you;
For I am incapable of mere flattery.
Come, now, tell me what I should do to help you.
You shall never say, Prometheus,
That you have any firmer friend than Oceanus.

PROMETHEUS   What's that? Who is it? Ah! So you too have come
To observe my torment? How was it you dared to leave
Your Ocean-river and your rock-roofed natural caves
To visit Earth, mother of iron? Are you here
To gaze at what I suffer, and add your grief to mine?
Behold a spectacle—me here, the friend of Zeus,
By whose help he established his sole sovereignty:
See with what pains I am now disciplined by him.

OCEANUS   I see, Prometheus; and although your mind is subtle
I want at least to give you the best advice I can.
A new king rules among the gods. Then know yourself,
And take upon yourself new ways to suit the time.
If in this way you fling out edged and angry speeches,
It may be Zeus—throned though he is so far above—
Will hear you; and, for result, your present load of troubles
Will seem a childish trifle. Oh, my unhappy friend,
Throw off your angry mood and seek deliverance
From all your suffering. What I say may seem perhaps
Well worn; but your plight is the inescapable
Reward, Prometheus, of a too proud-speaking tongue.
You still will not be humble, will not yield to pain;
You mean to add new sufferings to those you have.
Come now, accept my guidance: we are ruled by one
Whose harsh and sole dominion none may call to account.
Acknowledge this, and cease to kick against the goad.
Now I will go and try if there is any way
Within my power to set you free. Meanwhile, keep quiet,
Don't rage and storm. You are intelligent: full well
You know that punishment falls on the unruly tongue.

PROMETHEUS   I envy you your luck in not being under censure

Even for having dared to sympathize with me.
Now leave it, give it no more thought. Do what you many,
You never will persuade him; he is immovable.
Look out yourself, lest you meet trouble on your way.
OCEANUS You are a far more prudent counsellor of others
Than of yourself; experience makes this plain to me.
But I'm resolved to go, so say no more against it.
I'm sure—yes, sure that Zeus will grant me what I ask,
And for my sake will loose your bonds and set you free.
PROMETHEUS I thank you, and shall always thank you. Your goodwill
Is all that one could ask. But stir no hand for me;
Your trouble will be wasted, and bring me no good,
Whatever you intend to try. Do nothing, and
Keep clear of danger. If I suffer, I do not therefore
Wish that as many as possible should suffer too;
Far from it. The fate of Atlas grieves me—my own brother,
Who in the far West stands with his unwieldy load
Pressing upon his back, the pillar of heaven and earth.
I pity Typhon, that earth-born destroying giant,
The hundred-headed, native of the Cilician caves;
I saw him, all his fiery strength subdued by force.
Against the united gods he stood, his fearful jaws
Hissing forth terror; from his eyes a ghastly glare
Flashed, threatening to annihilate the throne of Zeus.
But Zeus's sleepless weapon came on him; he felt
The fiery vapour of the crashing thunderbolt,
Which blasted him out of his lofty boasts, and struck
His very heart, and burnt his strength to sulphurous ash.
Now, crushed under Mount Etna's roots, near the sea-strait,
He lies, a helpless sprawling hulk; while on the peak
Hephaestus hammers red-hot iron; and thence one day
Rivers of flame shall burst forth, and with savage jaws
Devour the bright smooth fields of fertile Sicily;
Such rage shall Typhon, though charred with the bolt of Zeus,
Send boiling out in jets of fierce, fire-breathing spume
Unquenchable. But you are not without experience;
You have no need of my instruction. Save yourself
As you know how. Meanwhile I'll drink my painful cup
To the dregs, till Zeus relaxes from his angry mood.
OCEANUS Have you not learnt, Prometheus, anger's a disease
Which words can heal?

PROMETHEUS   Yes, if you soothe the spirit when
          The moment's ripe—not roughly baulk a swelling rage.
OCEANUS   Tell me, Prometheus: do you see some risk entailed
          Even in my having dared to sympathize with you?
PROMETHEUS   Superfluous labour and light-minded foolishness.
OCEANUS   Let me be guilty then of foolishness. Sometimes
          A wise man gains his point by being thought not wise.
PROMETHEUS   In this case it is I who will be thought not wise.
OCEANUS   Your way of speaking plainly sends me home again.
PROMETHEUS   Why, yes. In pitying me I fear you may well gain
          An enemy.
OCEANUS   Who? The new-enthroned almighty lord?
PROMETHEUS   Take care; he may turn angry.
OCEANUS   Your fate is a lesson
          To me, Prometheus.
PROMETHEUS   Go! Get out! Be what you are!
OCEANUS   I'm anxious to be going; there's no need to shout.
          This four-legged beast's already beating with his wings
          The smooth path of the air. Yes, he'll be pleased enough
          To lie down comfortably in his own stall at home.
          [*Exit* OCEANUS.]
CHORUS   I weep, Prometheus, for your deadly plight.
          Tears flow from my eyes,
          Fall in a gentle stream,
          And wash my cheek like a spring of water.
          In this pitiful sight
          Zeus, ruling by laws of his own invention,
          Provides an example
          Of his proud power over the gods of the past.
          Now every country cries aloud in grief:
          The peoples of Europe mourn
          For you and the Titan race,
          Your glorious, ancient rule and honour;
          And all the settled tribes
          That graze the fields of holy Asia
          Weep loudly for you and share your suffering;

          The Amazons of the land of Colchis,
          Virgins fearless in battle,
          The Scythian hordes who live at the world's end
          On the shores of Lake Maeotis;

The warlike princes of Arabia,
Holding their cliff-perched fortress near Mount Caucasus,
Whose battle-cry strikes terror
In the ranks of sharpened spears, weep for you.

Only once before have I seen
A Titan god so tormented,
Vanquished in bonds invincible,
Atlas, alone in excellence of strength,
Who holds the vault of the sky upon his back, and groans;

And the wave of the wide Ocean
Roars in unison with him,
The depths of waters weep,
The cavernous darkness of the dead world mutters under,
And the holy fountains of flowing rivers
Weep in pity for his pain.

PROMETHEUS   You must not think it is through pride or stubbornness
That I am silent; thought and anger gnaw my heart,
To see myself so outraged. Why, who else but I
Assigned to these new gods their honours, first and last?
All that you know, and I'll not speak of. What I did
For mortals in their misery, hear now. At first
Mindless, I gave them mind and reason.—What I say
Is not in censure of mankind, but showing you
How all my gifts to them were guided by goodwill.—
In those days they had eyes, but sight was meaningless;
Heard sounds, but could not listen; all their length of life
They passed like shapes in dreams, confused and purposeless.
Of brick-built, sun-warmed houses, or of carpentry,
They had no notion; lived in holes, like swarms of ants,
Or deep in sunless caverns; knew no certain way
To mark off winter, or flowery spring, or fruitful summer;
Their every act was without knowledge, till I came.
I taught them to determine when stars rise or set—
A difficult art. Number, the primary science, I
Invented for them, and how to set down words in writing—
The all-remembering skill, mother of many arts.
I was the first to harness beasts under a yoke
With trace or saddle as man's slave, to take man's place
Under the heaviest burdens; put the horse to the chariot,
Made him obey the rein, and be an ornament

To wealth and greatness. No one before me discovered
The sailor's waggon—flax-winged craft that roam the seas.
Such tools and skills I found for men: myself, poor wretch,
Lack even one trick to free me from this agony.

CHORUS   Humiliation follows pain; distraught in mind
You have lost your way; like a bad doctor fallen ill
You now despair of finding drugs to cure yourself.

PROMETHEUS   Now hear the rest of what I have to tell, what crafts,
What methods I devised—and you will wonder more.
First in importance: if a man fell ill, he had
No remedy, solid or liquid medicine,
Or ointment, but for lack of drugs they pined away;
Until I showed them how to mix mild healing herbs
And so protect themselves against all maladies.
Then I distinguished various modes of prophecy,
And was the first to tell from dreams what Fate ordained
Should come about; interpreted the hidden sense
Of voices, sounds, sights met by chance upon the road.
The various flights of crook-clawed vultures I defined
Exactly, those by nature favourable, and those
Sinister; how each species keeps its mode of life;
What feuds, friendships, associations kind with kind
Preserves; how to interpret signs in sacrifice,
Smoothness of heart and lights, what colours please the gods
In each, the mottled shapeliness of liver-lobes.
The thigh-bones wrapped in fat, and the long chine, I burnt,
Leading men on the highway of an occult art;
And signs from flames, obscure before, I now made plain.

So much for prophecy. Next the treasures of the earth,
The bronze, iron, silver, gold hidden deep down—who else
But I can claim to have found them first? No one, unless
He talks like a fool. So, here's the whole truth in one word:
All human skill and science was Prometheus' gift.

CHORUS   Then do not, after helping men to your own hurt,
Neglect to save yourself from torment. I have hopes
That you will yet be freed and rival Zeus in power.

PROMETHEUS   Fate fulfils all in time; but it is not ordained
That these events shall yet reach such an end. My lot
Is to win freedom only after countless pains.
Cunning is feebleness beside Necessity.

CHORUS   And whose hand on the helm controls Necessity?

PROMETHEUS   The three Fates; and the Furies, who forget nothing.
CHORUS   Has Zeus less power than they?
PROMETHEUS   He cannot fly from Fate.
CHORUS   What fate is given to Zeus, but everlasting power?
PROMETHEUS   This is a thing you may not know; so do not ask.
CHORUS   It is some holy truth you cloak in mystery.
PROMETHEUS   Turn your thoughts elsewhere; now is not the time to speak
    Of that: it is a secret which by every means
    Must be kept close. By keeping it I shall escape
    This ignominious prison and these fearful pains.
CHORUS   May Zeus, who disposes all things,
    Never exert his power to crush my will;
    May I never grow weary
    In worshipping the gods with pure offerings of bulls
    Beside the inexhaustible stream of my father Oceanus.
    May I not offend in word; but let this resolve
    Remain unfading in my heart.

    It is a pleasant thing to spend the length of life
    In confidence and hope,
    And to nourish the soul in light and cheerfulness.
    But I shudder when I see you, Prometheus,
    Racked by infinite tortures.
    For you have no fear of Zeus,
    But pursuing your own purpose
    You respect too highly the race of mortals.

    See, my friend, how thankless were all your benefits.
    Tell me, what strength is there, and where,
    What help to be found in men who live for a day?
    Did you not note the helpless infirmity,
    Feeble as a dream,
    Which fetters the blind tribes of men?
    For human purposes shall never trespass
    Outside the harmony of Zeus's government.

    This is the truth I have learnt from your downfall, Prometheus.
    What strikes my ear is the difference
    Between today's sounds of sorrow
    And the songs we sang to grace your marriage,
    The song for the bath and the song for the bed,
    When you wooed and won with gifts
    My sister Hesione for your wedded bride.

[*Enter* IO]

IO   What land is this? What race lives here?
Who is this that I see held in fetters of rock
At the mercy of wind and storm?
For what sin do you suffer such a death?
Tell me, where has my miserable wandering brought me?
[*suddenly she shrieks in pain and terror*]
The gadfly stings me again. Oh, oh!
I see the ghost of Argus,[4]
The earth-born herdsman with a thousand eyes—
Gods! Keep him away!
He was killed, but no earth can hide him;
He follows me with his crafty gaze;
He escapes from his grave to hound me without mercy,
And drives me starving along the sandy shores;
While the clear music of wax-bound pipes
Fills my ears with a tune that longs for sleep.

Where, where, where
Will my endless, endless journeys bring me?
Son of Cronos, what have I done?
What sin did you find in me,
To put on me such a yoke of torment,
Plague me to misery and madness
With this driving, stinging terror?
Burn me with fire, let the earth swallow me,
Throw me as food for sea-serpents—
Lord God, will you grudge me this prayer?
I have wandered so far,
I have been punished enough with wandering;
I cannot tell how to escape from pain.
Do you hear my voice? It is Io, the girl with horns!

PROMETHEUS   I hear indeed the frenzied daughter of Inachus
Who fired the heart of Zeus with love, and suffers now
Through Hera's hate her long ordeal of cruel pursuit.

IO   You spoke my father's name: how do you know it?
Tell me who you are—you, as pitiable as I.
You know who I am, and you named truly

---

[4] Hera, Zeus's wife, became aware that Zeus was infatuated with Io. Before Zeus could satisfy his desire, she turned Io into a cow and had her watched by Argus, a monster with many eyes (Io first says a thousand, later ten thousand), who never closed more than two at a time when he went to sleep. Zeus had Hermes kill Argus but then Hera sent a gadfly to torment Io.

The heaven-sent tormentor
Which ravages and drives me with stings.
I have run without rest
In a leaping frenzy of pain and hunger,
The victim of Hera's calculating resentment.
Are there any in all this suffering world
Who endure what I endure?
Tell me clearly what remains for me to suffer,
What resource, what cure can save me.
Speak, if you know; give help and guidance
To the tortured, exiled virgin.

PROMETHEUS   I'll tell you plainly everything you wish to learn,
Not weaving mysteries, but in such simple speech
As one should use in speaking to a friend. I am
Prometheus, who bestowed on man the gift of fire.

IO   O universal benefactor of mankind,
Ill-starred Prometheus, why are you thus crucified?

PROMETHEUS   I was lamenting all my pains. I have ceased now.

IO   Will you not tell me—

PROMETHEUS   Ask; I can tell everything.

IO   Who was it, then, that clamped you fast in this ravine?

PROMETHEUS   The will of Zeus decreed; Hephaestus' hand obeyed.

IO   What were the sins for which you suffer punishment?

PROMETHEUS   What I have told you is enough.

IO   Then reveal this:
Where is the end of my cursed wandering, and when?

PROMETHEUS   Not to know this is better for you than to know.

IO   Do not hide from me what it is my doom to suffer.

PROMETHEUS   It is not that I grudge you what you ask of me.

IO   Why then do you hesitate to tell me the whole truth?

PROMETHEUS   Not from ill will. I shrink from shattering your heart.

IO   Come, do not take more thought for me than I would wish.

PROMETHEUS   Since you're determined, I must tell you. Listen then.

CHORUS   Not yet. Let us too share this pleasure. Let us ask Io to tell us
first the story of her affliction,
And hear the ruin of her life from her own lips.
Then let her learn from you what she must yet endure.

PROMETHEUS   It is for you, Io, to grant them their request;
And more especially, since they are your father's sisters.
Tears and lamenting find their due reward when those
Who listen are ready too with tears of sympathy.

IO   I cannot disobey; you shall hear everything
You want to know, in plain words; though even to speak

Of those events from which my troubles first arose,
And my unhappy transformation, makes me weep.

At night in my own room visions would visit me,
Repeating in seductive words, 'Most blessed maid,
Why live a virgin for so long? Love waits for you—
The greatest: Zeus, inflamed with arrows of desire,
Longs to unite with you in love. Do not reject,
My child, the bed of Zeus. Go out to the deep grass
Of Lerna, where your father's sheep and cattle graze,
That the eye of Zeus may rest from longing and be satisfied.'

By such dreams every troubled night I was beset,
Until I dared to tell my father. Then he sent
Messengers many times to Pytho and Dodona
To learn what he must do or say to please the gods.
They came back with reports of riddling oracles,
Obscurely worded, hard to interpret. But at last
Was given a clear utterance unmistakably
Commanding Inachus to turn me from his house
And city, to wander homeless to the ends of the earth;
If he refused, the fiery thunderbolt of Zeus
Would fall and extirpate his race to the last man.

Such was the oracle of Loxias. My father
Yielded, and sent me forth, and locked his door against me—
He as unwilling as myself; but he was forced
To do this by the cruel bridle-rein of Zeus.
At once my shape was changed, my mind distorted. Horned,
As you now see, stung by the gadfly's stabbing goad,
Convulsed and mad, I rushed on, to the crystal stream
Of Cerchnea and the spring of Lerna; I was followed
By Argus, a giant herdsman of ungoverned rage,
Who watched my every step with his ten thousand eyes.
A sudden, unexpected stroke robbed him of life.
I, gadfly-maddened, still am driven from land to land,
Lashed by this God-appointed scourge.

That is my story.
If you can say what still remains to be endured,
Tell me; and do not out of pity comfort me
With lies. I count false words the foulest plague of all.

CHORUS What a pitiful, terrible fate!

Never did I dream that so strange a story
Would ever come to my ears;
That anguish, cruelty, terror,
So bitter to see and to endure,
Would ever chill my spirit with a wound so sharp.
Alas, Fate, Fate!
I see the lot of Io, and tremble.
PROMETHEUS   You shed your tears too early, like a frightened woman.
Keep them until you hear what is to follow now.
CHORUS   Speak, then, and tell her all. It comforts those in pain
To know beforehand all the pain they still must bear.
PROMETHEUS   Your first request to me was easily obtained;
You wished to hear Io's ordeal from her own lips.
Now hear the rest—what sufferings at Hera's hands
Are yet in store for this young maid. Now lay to heart
My words, daughter of Inachus, and learn the goal
Of all your journeys.

From this place turn first toward the rising sun, and pass
Over the unploughed plains until you reach the land
Of nomad Scythians, living high above the ground
In houses built on strong-wheeled carts, and wattled roofs.
They are armed with powerful bows; keep well away from them,
And take your path by the loud-roaring rocky shore,
And so pass through that country. Next, on your left hand,
Is the country of the Chalybes, craftsmen in iron.
Beware of them; they are savage, and no stranger can
Approach them safely. After this you reach the river
Hybristes,[5] whose wild torrent justifies its name.
Do not attempt to cross—it is too dangerous—
Until you come to Caucasus itself, the peak
Of all that range, where from the very brows the river
Floods forth its fury. You must cross the topmost ridge
Close to the stars, and take the pathway leading south.
There you will find the warlike race of Amazons,
Haters of men. This race in time to come shall found
The city of Themiscyra, on the Thermodon,
Where the rough jaw of Salmydessus fronts the sea,
An enemy to sailors, stepmother to ships.
The Amazons will most gladly guide you on your way.

[5] Violent.

Next, where a narrow creek gives entrance to a lake,
You will come to the Cimmerian Isthmus. Boldly then
Leave land, and cross the Maeotic Strait. Ages to come
Shall tell the story of your passage, and the place
Shall be called Bosporus⁶ to commemorate you. Thus
From Europe you will reach the Asian continent.

Does it not seem to you that this king of gods
In all matters alike is given to violence?
A god, lusting for union with this mortal maid,
He dooms her to such journeys! You are unfortunate,
Io, in your lover. All that I have told so far
Hardly begins—believe me!—all there is to tell.

IO [*weeping*]   Oh, oh! I cannot bear it!

PROMETHEUS   More cries and groans? When you shall hear the rest, what
then?

CHORUS   Have you still more to tell her of distress and pain?

PROMETHEUS   I have, a stormy sea of deadly misery.

IO   Why should I go on living? Why not hurl myself
At once down from this rocky cliff, be dashed in pieces,
And find relief from all my pain? Better to die
Once, than to suffer torment all my living days.

PROMETHEUS   Then you would find it hard to bear *my* agonies,
Since I am fated not to die. Death would have brought
Release; but now no end to suffering is in sight
For me, until Zeus be deposed from sovereignty.

IO   What? Is it possible that Zeus should be deposed?

PROMETHEUS   You would be glad, I think, to see that come about.

IO   How could I help it, after all he has made me suffer?

PROMETHEUS   Learn it as truth: it shall be so.

IO   By whom shall Zeus
Be stripped of power?

PROMETHEUS   By his own foolish purposes.

IO   How will it happen? Tell me, if it does no harm.

PROMETHEUS   He plans a union that will turn to his undoing.

IO   With mortal or immortal? Tell me, if you may.

PROMETHEUS   Why ask with whom? That is a thing I may not tell.

IO   Then is it she who will unseat him from his throne?

PROMETHEUS   She is to bear a son more powerful than his father.

IO   Is there no way by which Zeus can escape this fate?

⁶ Ford of the cow.

PROMETHEUS   None, but with my help. I could save him, once set free.
IO   But if Zeus be unwilling, who can set you free?
PROMETHEUS   A child of yours is named as my deliverer.
IO   What do you say? My child shall free you from these chains?
PROMETHEUS   Yes, in the thirteenth generation after you.[7]
IO   I find it hard to interpret this last prophecy.
PROMETHEUS   Then do not seek to learn your own appointed lot.
IO   You offered me this favour; do not now refuse.
PROMETHEUS   I'll grant you one or two other prophecies.
IO   What are they? Offer me my choice.
PROMETHEUS   Then choose between
          The remainder of your journey, and my deliverer.
CHORUS   Of these two favours, if you please, grant one to her,
          And one to me, Prometheus; do not grudge the telling.
          Reveal to Io all her future wandering,
          And tell me who shall set you free. I long to know.
PROMETHEUS   Since you are eager, I will not refuse to tell
          Everything you desire. First, Io, I will name
          The many lands where Fate will toss you in your journey;
          Write what I tell you in your book of memory.

          When you have crossed the stream that bounds two
             continents
          Press on, over the surge of the sea, toward the east
          Where the sun stalks in flame, to the Gorgonean land,
          Cisthene. There live Phorcys' aged virgin daughters,
          In shape like swans, possessing one eye and one tooth
          Between the three; beings on whom no ray of sun
          Ever looks down, nor moon at night. And close to them
          Their three winged sisters, loathed enemies of humankind,
          The snake-haired Gorgons, whom no man can see and live.
          This is but the beginning. Now hear yet another
          Grim sight you must encounter: beware the silent hounds
          Of Zeus, the sharp-beaked griffins; and beware the tribe
          Of one-eyed Arimaspian horsemen, on the banks
          Of the Plutonian river whose waters wash down gold.
          Do not go near them. Then you will reach a remote region
          Where near the sun's bright fountains live a dark-skinned race.
          There is the Ethiopian river; follow its course
          Down, till your reach the cataract where from the Bybline hills
          The Nile pours forth his holy stream to quench men's thirst.

[7] Prometheus is to be freed by Heracles, son of Zeus and Alcmena.

And he will guide you to the delta of the Nile
Where, Io, you and your descendants shall at last
By Fate's appointment found your far-off colony.

    If any point is indistinct or hard to follow
Ask further, and make sure that you have understood.
I have more time to spare than I would wish to have.
CHORUS   If anything passed over still remains to tell
Of Io's painful journeys, speak. If not, grant now
To us the favour which, you remember, we asked of you.
PROMETHEUS   Io has heard the whole course of her wandering.
And, lest she think I may have given her idle words,
I'll speak of what she suffered before coming here,
To prove my words. Most of the details I'll omit,
And come directly to your recent wanderings.

    On reaching the Molossian plains, and the rock-wall
Which towers above Dodona, where Thesprotian Zeus
Has his oracular seat, where grow the speaking oaks—
A marvel past belief—by which you were addressed
Plainly and unambiguously as the destined bride
Of Zeus—does that truth touch you?—from that place you rushed,
Plagued by the gadfly's sting, along the sea-shore path
To the wide Adriatic, whence back yet again
The storm of frenzy drove you on your wild flight here.
And that bay of the sea shall for all future time—
Mark this—be called Ionian, to perpetuate
For all mankind the story of Io's wanderings.
I tell you this as proof that my prophetic mind
Sees more than meets the eye. Now to you all I'll tell
The rest, resuming at the point where I broke off.

    Where the Nile's outflow lays its bank of silt, there stands
On the last edge of land the city of Canopus;
And here at last Zeus shall restore your mind, and come
Upon you, not with terror, with a gentle touch;
His hand laid on you shall put life into your womb,
And you shall bear a dark-skinned son to Zeus, and name him
From his begetting, 'Child of a touch', Epaphos.
He shall possess the harvest-wealth of all those lands
Watered by the broad-flowing Nile. Five generations
From him, a family of fifty sisters shall return
Against their will to Argos, desperate to escape

From kindred marriage with their cousins. The young men
Follow in passionate pursuit close on their track,
As hawks hunt doves; lusting for an unlawful love.
But God shall grudge them the enjoyment of their brides.
And Argive soil shall welcome them, when in the night
Bold resolution goes on guard, and women's hands
Make war and slaughter, and male pride is overthrown.
For each shall plunge her sharp sword in his throat, and kill
Her husband. May such love come to my enemies!
But sweet desire shall charm one girl, and blunt the edge
Of her resolve, and she shall spare her husband's life,
And choose to be called coward, but not murderess;
And she shall live in Argos and give birth to kings.

And from her children's children shall be born in time
(To trace each step would take too long) a fearless hero
Famed as an archer, who shall free me from these bonds.
Such is the oracle as my mother told it me,
Titanian Themis, born in the old time. But how
All this shall come about, would take me long to tell,
And you in listening would gain nothing.
[Io *interrupts with a wild cry of pain.*]

IO   The stroke of madness burns me again,
My brain is convulsed, the gadfly
Stings me with his immortal arrow.
My heart beats wildly in my body;
My eyeballs roll and turn;
Insanity falls on me like a raging storm
And drives me off course;
I can't govern my tongue; words rush out at random,
Beating against waves of deadly ruin!
[*Exit* Io]

CHORUS   He was a wise man indeed
Who first weighed this thought in his mind
And gave it utterance in speech,
That the best rule by far
Is to marry in your own rank;
That a man who works with his hands should never crave
To marry either a woman pampered by wealth
Or one who prides herself on her noble family.

O Fates, who bring all things to fulfilment,
May you never see me sharing the bed of Zeus;

May I never be joined in marriage with any god!
For I tremble when I look at the girlhood of Io,
Denied the love of a man,
Tormented in ever-restless exile
By the cruelty of Hera.

When marriage is with an equal
For me it holds no fear or danger.
But may the love of the greater gods
Never cast on me its irresistible glance.
That is a fight which cannot be fought,
The straight road to despair.
What would become of me I cannot say;
For I see no way to escape the design of Zeus.

PROMETHEUS   I swear that Zeus, for all his obstinacy, shall yet
Be humbled, so disastrous shall this marriage prove
Which he proposes—a marriage that shall hurl him out
Of throne and sovereignty into oblivion.
And then the curse his father Cronos cursed him with,
The day he lost his ancient throne, shall all come true.
There is no god but I who can reveal to him
The way to avert this ignominy. I know it all.
So now let him sit on, serenely confident
In his celestial thunders, brandishing in his hand
His fierce fire-breathing thunderbolt—that will not save him:
His fall will be sure, shameful, unendurable!
Such an antagonist he is even now himself
Preparing against himself, a wonder irresistible,
One who will find a flame hotter than lightning-strokes,
A crash to overwhelm the thunder; one whose strength
Shall split Poseidon's trident-spear, that dreaded scourge
That shakes both sea and land. This is the reef on which
His power shall strike and founder, till he learns how great
A chasm lies between ruling and being ruled.

CHORUS   These threats against Zeus surely voice but your own wish.
PROMETHEUS   I speak what shall prove true—and my own wish as well.
CHORUS   Must we expect one who shall bring Zeus to his knees?
PROMETHEUS   Yes; Zeus's neck shall bow beneath worse pains than mine.
CHORUS   Why are you not afraid to fling such taunting words?
PROMETHEUS   Why should I fear? My destiny is not to die.
CHORUS   Zeus might invent for you some still worse agony.
PROMETHEUS   Then let him do it! I am prepared for everything.
CHORUS   A wise man will speak humbly, and fear Nemesis.

PROMETHEUS   Bow! Pray! As always, fawn upon the powerful hand!
　　　For great Zeus I care less than nothing. Let him do
　　　And govern as he wills, for the short time he has.
　　　He will not govern long among the gods.—Why, look!
　　　Here comes his runner, the new tyrant's lickspittle.
　　　No doubt he brings some message.
　　　[*Enter* HERMES.]
HERMES   I speak to you—the master-mind, with heart more sour
　　　Than sourness; you who honoured creatures of a day
　　　And sinned against immortals; you, the thief of fire:
　　　The Father bids you tell him what this marriage is
　　　Through which you boast that he shall fall from power. Now speak
　　　No clever riddles, but set forth the detailed truth.
　　　Do not, Prometheus, make me travel all this way
　　　Again; Zeus is not mollified by such replies.
PROMETHEUS   This underling of gods makes a high-sounding speech
　　　Crammed with importance.—You and all your crew are young;
　　　So is your power; and you imagine that you hold
　　　An unassailable citadel. But I have seen
　　　Two dynasties already hurled from those same heights;
　　　And I shall see the third, today's king, fall to earth
　　　More shamefully than his precursors, and more soon.
　　　Do you think I quake and cower before these upstart gods?
　　　Not much, nor little—not one slightest thought! Now you
　　　Trot back the way you came; you'll find out nothing here.
HERMES   Conduct like this, both obstinate and insolent,
　　　Has once already brought you to a painful plight.
PROMETHEUS   Understand this: I would not change my painful plight,
　　　On any terms, for your servile humility.
HERMES   Being bondslave to this rock is preferable, no doubt,
　　　To being the trusted messenger of Father Zeus.
PROMETHEUS   You use the fitting language of the insolent.
HERMES   It seems you find your present state a luxury.
PROMETHEUS   You think so? May I one day see my enemies,
　　　And you among them, in such luxury as this!
HERMES   What, I? Do you blame me too for your sufferings?
PROMETHEUS   In one word, I detest all gods who could repay
　　　My benefits with such outrageous infamy.
HERMES   It's plain that your insanity is far advanced.
PROMETHEUS   Perhaps—if to hate enemies is insanity.
HERMES   Now you, free and in power, would be unbearable.
PROMETHEUS   Alas!

HERMES   Alas? That word is one which Zeus has never known.
PROMETHEUS   But Time, as he grows older, teaches everything.
HERMES   Time has not taught *you* self-control or prudence—yet.
PROMETHEUS   No—or I would not argue with an underling.
HERMES   It seems you'll tell nothing of what Zeus wants to know.
PROMETHEUS   And yet I owe him much—that I would gladly pay.
HERMES   You banter with me—do you think I am a child?
PROMETHEUS   Are you not then a child, or worse than childish, if
    You still expect to get an answer out of me?
    There is no torture, no ingenuity, by which
    Zeus can persuade me to reveal my secret, till
    The injury of these bonds is loosed from me. Therefore
    Let scorching flames be flung from heaven; let the whole earth
    With white-winged snowstorms, subterranean thunderings,
    Heave and convulse: nothing will force me to reveal
    By whose hand Fate shall hurl Zeus from his tyranny.
HERMES   Consider now whether this course seems profitable.
PROMETHEUS   I have long ago considered all this, and resolved.
HERMES   Come, bring yourself, perverse fool, while there is still time,
    To weigh your situation, and so turn to sense.
PROMETHEUS   You waste your breath; you may as well exhort the waves.
    Never persuade yourself that I, through fear of what
    Zeus may intend, will show a woman's mind, or kneel
    To my detested enemy, with womanish hands
    Outspread in supplication for release. No, never!
HERMES   My words lead only to more words, without effect;
    Beg as I may, nothing can soothe or soften you.
    Like an unbroken colt you try your strength, and take
    The bit between your teeth, and fight against the reins.
    Yet all your violence springs from feeble reckoning;
    For obstinacy in a fool has by itself
    No strength at all. Consider now what punishments
    Will burst inevitably upon you like a storm
    Of mountainous waves, if you refuse to listen to me.

    First, Zeus will split this rugged chasm with the shock
And flame of lightning, and entomb you underground
Still clamped on this embracing rock. When a long age
Has passed, you will return into the light; and then
The dark-winged hound of Zeus will come, the savage eagle,
An uninvited banqueter, and all day long
Will rip your flesh in rags and feast upon your liver,

Gnawing it black. And you may hope for no release
From such a torment, till some god be found to take
Your pains upon him, and of his own will descend
To sunless Hades and the black depths of Tartarus.

So think again; this is no fabricated boast,
But truth as Zeus has spoken it, who cannot lie,
But will accomplish every word his mouth has uttered.
Look every way; consider; and be sure of this:
Wise counsel always is worth more than stubbornness.

CHORUS   To us it seems that Hermes' words are sensible.
He bids you quit resistance and seek good advice.
Do so; a wise man's folly forfeits dignity.

PROMETHEUS   I knew what Hermes had to say
Before he made his brag. It is no dishonour
For an enemy to suffer at his enemy's hands.
So let the pronged locks of lightning be launched at me,
Let the air be roused with thunder and convulsion of wild winds,
Let hurricanes upheave by the roots the base of the earth,
Let the sea-waves' roaring savagery
Confound the courses of the heavenly stars;
Let him lift me high and hurl me to black Tartarus
On ruthless floods of irresistible doom:
I am one whom he cannot kill.

HERMES   Thoughts and words like these
Are what one may hear from lunatics.
This prayer of his shows all the features of frenzy;
And I see no signs of improvement.
[*to the* CHORUS] You, however, who sympathize with his sufferings,
Get away quickly from this place,
Lest the intolerable roar of thunder stun your senses.

CHORUS   If you want to persuade me, use a different tone
And give other advice. You speak too hastily,
Bidding me do what I could not think of doing.
Would you have me practise cowardice?
I will stay with Prometheus, come what must.
I was taught to hate those who desert their friends;
And there is no infamy I more despise.

HERMES   Then remember my warning;
And when you are caught by calamity
Don't lay the blame on Fortune, or say that Zeus
Plunged you in suffering unforeseen;

Not Zeus but yourselves will be to blame.
You know what is coming; it is neither sudden nor secret.
Only your own folly will entangle you
In the inextricable net of destruction.
[*Exit* HERMES]

PROMETHEUS   Now it is happening: threat gives place to performance.
The earth rocks; thunder, echoing from the depth,
Roars in answer; fiery lightnings twist and flash.
Dust dances in a whirling fountain;
Blasts of the four winds skirmish together,
Set themselves in array for battle;
Sky and sea rage indistinguishably.
The cataclysm advances visibly upon me,
Sent by Zeus to make me afraid.

O Earth, my holy mother,
O Sky, where sun and moon
Give light to all in turn,
You see how I am wronged!
[*The rock collapses and disappears, as the* CHORUS *scatter in all directions.*]

COMMENTARY

Prometheus Bound (463–456 B.C.)   Like Job, Prometheus is a victim who suffers at the hands of a god. Like Jesus Christ, he is a savior of mankind who is crucified for his efforts to save man. Like Milton's Satan (in *Paradise Lost*), he is a god who rebels against the divine ruler of the universe. It is in this last role that Prometheus is relevant, indeed crucial, in the context of this anthology. "Prometheus, the rebel," as Strength characterizes him in Aeschylus' *Prometheus Bound*, is not only the archetypal revolutionist but also the archetype of the revolutionary hero-victim.

The archetypal rebel, Prometheus refuses to submit to tyranny. "Bow! Pray! As always, fawn upon the powerful hand!" proudly exclaims this god scornfully. This *god*. A suffering hero, a crucified savior, a revolutionist, Prometheus is not a man who revolts against the gods: he is himself a god. Like many revolutionaries who rebel in behalf of the less privileged, Prometheus—in behalf of less privileged mankind—revolts against his fellow gods.

The revolt of Prometheus against Zeus is only one of three revolutions with which the play is concerned. A past revolution, Zeus against Cronos, and a possible future one, Zeus's son against Zeus, also figure importantly in the play's fabric. Centering upon the seizure of power, these two revolutions also symbolize the revolt of the younger generation against the older. In *Prometheus Bound*, revolution is a recurring condition and in all three revolutions Prometheus is a key figure.

For many years, Cronos ruled the universe. When his son Zeus revolted against him, Prometheus—whose name, as Strength indicates, means "Wise-before-the-event" (that is, Foreknowledge or Forethought) —offered his services to Cronos. Proud of his strength, Cronos refused the knowledge offered by Prometheus, who then helped Zeus to seize the rule of the universe.

"Ruthless," "merciless," "unapproachable in temper," Zeus is kept offstage, perhaps because of credibility, perhaps because the presence of such a tyrant would reduce the conflict to melodramatic terms. Instead of representing the figure of Zeus, Aeschylus represents the power of Zeus. He does this through three groups of characters. Prometheus (in contrast to Zeus, onstage throughout the entire play) and Io (the only mortal in the play) represent a pair of victims of Zeus. Although the immediate cause of Io's plight is Zeus's remorseless wife Hera, it is Zeus's lust that is the ultimate cause of Io's sufferings. The other two pairs serve Zeus, one group willingly, the second unwillingly. By means of this quartet of

servants, the playwright suggests multitudes under Zeus's will. The cruel
and pitiless Strength eagerly complies with Zeus's commands, as does the
arrogant Hermes, "the new tyrant's lickspittle." The compassionate
Hephaestus is reluctant to serve the new master of the gods, but nevertheless he obeys him. Similarly ineffectual in translating his pity into action
is the bumbling Oceanus, who like Hephaestus fears that Zeus might
punish him if he opposes him or gives comfort to his enemy. Both accomo-
date the tyrant, and thereby serve him as effectively as those who enthusiastically obey him. Represented by his victims and by his underlings,
Zeus is in his absence a powerful presence.

The mighty ruler of the gods, regarding the race of man contemptuously, had planned to destroy it. Of all the gods, only Prometheus
opposed his wish. He stole fire from Hephaestus, God of Fire, and gave
it to man. In defiance of Zeus, he saved mankind. Fire is both a key to
and a symbol of knowledge and power, of crafts and of arts. With fire,
says Prometheus, man "shall master many crafts" and be taught "every
art." Before Prometheus helped men, they lived in caves, knew nothing
even about the seasons, could not understand the world about them, or
plan their lives. "At first/Mindless," as Prometheus says, "I gave them
mind and reason." He taught men astronomy, mathematics, writing, sailing, medicine, natural science, metallurgy, and how to tame animals to
help them. In brief, "All human skill and science was Prometheus' gift."
The "universal benefactor of mankind," as Io calls him, Prometheus is in
that sense a second father to man.[1] For his transgression, Zeus punishes
him, condemning him to suffer until he learns to accept Zeus's sovereignty.

But the foreknowing Prometheus knows that Zeus is to be deposed
by a son more powerful than he, and he knows who the mother is to be.
Only if Prometheus gives Zeus the name of the woman (Thetis) who is to
bear his son can Zeus avert his fate. Having achieved his rule by revolution against his father, Zeus is in danger of being deposed by revolution
by his own son. In both revolutions Prometheus and what he represents,
knowledge, is the key. With the aid of his knowledge, Prometheus can
enable Zeus to avoid being overthrown by his son. What Prometheus gave
to man he also gives to the gods: knowledge. With this gift, man averts

---

[1] According to another myth, he and his brother Epimetheus created man.
Planning to make man better than the animals, Epimetheus first fashioned man. True
to his name, which means Afterknowledge or Afterthought, he realized that he erred
in making animals better in many respects: for instance, he gave them strength and
various coverings, such as furs and feathers, to keep them warm. Prometheus then
corrected his brother's job by making man superior to the animals: he made him
stand upright, like the gods, and gave him fire.

destruction. With this gift, Zeus can avoid destruction. Power and force are helpless without knowledge, which is necessary not only for successful revolution but also for the successful avoidance of revolution.

The end of *Prometheus Bound* is not the end of Aeschylus' story of the conflict between Prometheus and Zeus. As the bound Prometheus prophesies, he will be freed. *Prometheus Bound* is one play of a trilogy whose other two parts are lost. In *Prometheus Unbound,* the next play, Heracles, a descendant of Io, at Zeus's command sets Prometheus free.[2] Rebel and tyrant are reconciled, mankind is allowed to exist and grow stronger through Prometheus' gift, and Prometheus tells Zeus the name of the woman he must not impregnate if he is to survive as ruler of the universe.

In *Prometheus Bound,* reconciliation is thirteen generations into the future. At present, Prometheus and Zeus are antagonistic. But Zeus is not an unchanging divinity whose characteristics are fixed for all time. Instead, he is a "new master of the gods" and, as Hephaestus observes, "Power newly won is always harsh." At the beginning of his reign at the time of this play, Zeus will eventually learn from experience and submit to the unyielding rebel who will not die and who knows that time is on his side.

Paralleling Zeus's acrimony toward Prometheus is Prometheus' bitterness toward Zeus. Prometheus will delight, he says, in seeing his enemy brought to his knees. "These threats against Zeus surely voice but your own wish," says the Chorus when Prometheus prophesies what will happen to Zeus if the latter does not come to terms with him. "I speak what shall prove true," replies Prometheus, who adds honestly, "and my own wish as well." Still, in the light of his sufferings, who can blame Prometheus for having what Hermes calls a "heart more sour/Than sourness"? It is not surprising that Prometheus feels anger at his oppressor, nor that he refuses to submit to force or threats. Though the Chorus rebukes him for his stubbornness, it parallels him in this regard when it is put to the test: "If you want to persuade me," says the Chorus to Hermes when he threatens it and demands that it abandon Prometheus, "use a different tone/And give other advice. . . ./Would you have me practise cowardice?" What is surprising—and admirable—is that unlike

---

[2] The other play in the trilogy is *Prometheus the Firebringer*. According to some it is the trilogy's first play, according to others the last. The former regard the trilogy as dramatizing first the offence, then the punishment, and finally the reconciliation. The latter believe that *Prometheus the Firebringer* dramatizes the establishment by Zeus of the Festival of the Promethia in honor of Prometheus and the celebration of the reconciliation between the former enemies.

Zeus, Prometheus is not vindictive. When Zeus sues for friendship, as Prometheus predicts he will, the bound god will not humble his erst-while oppressor; instead, he says, "I shall welcome him." Prometheus will win, but Zeus will not lose.

Bibliography

(A) Other Plays About Prometheus:

Johann Wolfgang von Goethe, *Prometheus* (only two acts completed), 1773
Percy Bysshe Shelley, *Prometheus Unbound*, 1819
Robert Lowell, *Prometheus Bound*, 1967

(B) Works About Aeschylus and Prometheus Bound:

Havelock, E. A. *Prometheus*. Seattle: University of Washington Press, 1968.
Kitto, H. D. F. *Greek Tragedy*. Garden City, N.Y.: Doubleday Anchor, 1954.
Murray, Gilbert. *Aeschylus: The Creator of Tragedy*. London: Oxford University Press, 1962.
Norwood, Gilbert. *Greek Tragedy*. New York: Hill and Wang, 1960.
Podlecki, Anthony J. *The Political Background of Aeschylean Tragedy*. Ann Arbor: University of Michigan Press, 1966.
Rosenmeyer, Thomas G. *The Masks of Tragedy*. Austin: University of Texas Press, 1963.
Thomson, George. *Aeschylus and Athens*. New York: Grossett and Dunlap Universal Library, 1968.

The
Reformation

MASTER OLOF
August Strindberg

MASTER OLOF
A Play In Five Acts
August Strindberg
Translated by Walter Johnson

CHARACTERS

MASTER OLOF   (*Olaus Petri*)
GERT BOOKPRINTER
KING GUSTAV I   (*Gustav Vasa*)[1]
BISHOP HANS BRASK   *of Linköping*
BISHOP MÅNS SOMMAR   *of Strängnäs*
LARS SIGGESON SPARRE,   *national marshal, lord high constable*
LARS ANDERSSON   (*Laurentius Andreae*), *later chancellor*
LAURENTIUS PETRI   (*Lars Pedersson*), *Master Olof's brother, later archbishop*
HANS WINDRANK,   *a sea captain*
A SMÅLÄNNING   (*native of Småland*)
A GERMAN
A DANE
BROTHER MÅRTEN *and* BROTHER NILS,   *Dominicans or Black Friars*
KNIPPERDOLLINK
THE ABBESS
THE TAVERNKEEPER
AN UNDERTAKER'S ASSISTANT
PUPIL I *and* PUPIL II
THE SEXTON *and the* SEXTON'S WIFE
THE SERVANT
THE OVERSEER
THE BURGHER *and the* BURGHER'S WIFE
KRISTINA,   *Master Olof's mother*

[1] Reign: 1523–1560.

A NOBLEMAN
KRISTINA,   *Gert's daughter, Master Olof's wife*
THE PROSTITUTE
MINOR CHARACTERS

SETTINGS

ACT I: *In Strängnäs*
ACT II: *A tavern in the wall of the Great Church in Stockholm; a small room in the Great Church*
ACT III: *A room in Stockholm Castle; Olof's study*
ACT IV: *A room in the house of Olof's mother*
ACT V: *The churchyard of St. Clara's convent; a part of the Great Church.*

Act I

IN STRÄNGNÄS

A crosswalk outside the study hall. Trees. At a distance the cloister church. At the back a wall above which can be see fruit trees in bloom. OLOF *is sitting on a stone bench; in front of him stand pupils reading their parts in* The Comedy of Tobias.[1]

PUPIL I   "Alas for us, poor children of Israel; we are caught in the toils of our enemies."

PUPIL II   "Dear brother, we should lament! The days of our tribulations have come—both our lands and our tithes are gone; never again can we look to the future with happy expectation. I have said and dreamt for a long time that the promise of Abraham was forgotten long ago."

LARS ANDERSSON   (*who has entered*)   What are you doing?

OLOF   I'm playing.

---

[1] The oldest surviving Swedish play on a Biblical subject. Master Olof may have been the author.

LARS   You're playing!

OLOF   Yes. I'm playing a little comedy about the children of Israel and the Babylonian captivity.

LARS   Haven't you anything better to do? A greater task awaits you.

OLOF   I'm still too young.

LARS   Don't say you're too young.

OLOF   No, I suspect there are enough who do.

LARS   (*unrolls a paper which he has taken out; observes* OLOF *for a while; then he reads*)   And the Lord spoke to Jeremiah: "Before I formed thee in the belly, I knew thee; and before thou camest forth out of the womb, I sanctified thee, and I ordained thee a prophet unto the nations."

      And Jeremiah said: "Ah, Lord God! behold, I cannot speak; for I am a child."

      And the Lord said: "Say not I am a child; for thou shalt go to all that I shall send thee, and whatsoever I command thee thou shalt speak. . . .

      "For, behold, I have made thee this day a defenced city, and an iron pillar, and brasen walls against the whole land, against the kings of Judah, against the princes thereof, against the priests thereof, and against the people of the land.

      "And they shall fight against thee; but they shall not prevail against thee; for I am with thee . . . to deliver thee."[2]

OLOF   (*jumps up*)   Did the Lord say that?

LARS   (*continues*)   "Thou therefore gird up thy loins and arise, and speak unto them all that I command thee."[3]

OLOF   Why don't you go?

LARS   I'm too old.

OLOF   You're afraid!

LARS   Yes, for I don't have the strength; but you do—may God give you the faith.

OLOF   I once had the flame of faith, and it burned beautifully, but the gang of monks put it out with their holy water when they tried to drive the devil from my body.

LARS   That was a fire of straw that had to flicker out; now the Lord will make you a fire of logs, which will burn up the seed of the Philistines. Do you really know what you want to do, Olof?

OLOF   No, but I feel as if I were suffocating when I think about our poor people yearning for deliverance. They cry for water, living water, but no one has any to give them.

[2] Jeremiah, 1:4–7, 18–19.
[3] Jeremiah, 1:17.

LARS   Tear down the rotten old house first—you can! The Lord Himself will build a new one!

OLOF   But they won't have a roof for a while.

LARS   They'll get fresh air, at least.

OLOF   But to rob a whole people of their faith! They'd despair!

LARS   Yes, they'll despair.

OLOF   They'll curse me and revile me and bring me before the authorities.

LARS   Are you afraid?

OLOF   No! But they'll be offended—

LARS   Olof! You were born to offend; you were born to strike. The Lord will heal.

OLOF   I feel how the current pulls; I still have hold of the sluice gate, but, if I let go, the current will carry me on.

LARS   Let go—those who hold back will come.

OLOF   If I get too far into the whirlpool, stretch out your hand to me, Lars.

LARS   That's beyond my power. You have to go into the whirlpool even if you perish.

OLOF   What storms you've stirred up in my soul; a little while ago I sat playing in the shadow of the trees, and it was Pentecost eve, and it was spring and there was peace. Now—why don't the trees tremble? Why doesn't the sky darken? Put your hand on my forehead; feel how my blood's throbbing! Don't leave me, Lars. I see an angel who comes to me with a cup; she walks on the evening sky over there; her path is blood red, and she has a cross in her hand.—No, I can't do it; I'll go back to the quiet valley; let others struggle; I'll look on.—No, I'll follow them and heal the wounded; I'll whisper words of peace in the ears of the dying. Peace!—No, I want to fight, too, but in the last ranks. Why should I go first?

LARS   You're the most daring.

OLOF   Not the strongest?

LARS   The strong will follow; and the strongest is at your side. He's the One who summons you to battle!

OLOF   Help me, God! I go!

LARS   Amen.

OLOF   And you'll follow me.

LARS   You're to go alone with God.

OLOF   Why do you draw back?

LARS   I wasn't born to be a fighter; I can only supply you with weapons. God's pure words shall be your weapons. You shall place them in the hands of the people; for the door of the papal armory has been broken open, and every human being must fight for the freedom of his own spirit.

OLOF   But where are my enemies? I'm eager for the struggle, but I see
no enemies!

LARS   You don't have to summon them—they'll come! Good-bye. You can
begin when you please. God be with you.

OLOF   Don't go; I have to talk with you!

LARS   Here comes the vanguard—get your weapons ready! (LARS *exits*.)

(*A crowd of burghers—among them women and children—goes up to
the church door to the right. They stop, remove their hats, and
cross themselves.*)

GERT   (*disguised as a burgher*)   They haven't rung the bell for vespers
on Pentecost eve[4]—that's mighty strange.

BURGHER   And the church door's closed. Maybe the priest is sick.

GERT   Or hasn't got up.

BURGHER   What did you say?

GERT   I mean he's sick!

BURGHER   But he has so many acolytes that one of them could conduct
mass.

GERT   They're too busy, I suspect.

BURGHER   Doing what?

GERT   That's hard to tell.

BURGHER   Take care, my good man. You seem to have a touch of
Lutheranism. Bishop Hans of Linköping's in town, and the king,
too.

GERT   Is Brask in town?

BURGHER   He certainly is. But we'd better try the door first to see if the
church is closed.

GERT   (*runs up the steps and knocks on the door*)   The house of God is
closed on Pentecost eve. The most reverend priests don't grant an
audience with God today, so you praiseworthy burghers will have
to go home and go to bed without mass. Look, good people—here's
a door, it's just a wooden door, but that makes no difference since
it's lined with copper. Look at this door! If I tell you that God lives
on the other side—for it is His house, if I tell you that the bishop's
diakonis or *sekretarius* or *kanonikus*[5] or any other man that ends
in *-us*, for it's only men of the spirit who end in *-us*, if I tell you
that a man like that has the key to this door hanging on a nail in
his bedroom, I'm not saying that he has locked God away from us
and hung the key on a nail in his bedroom, I'm simply saying that
we can't get in to attend divine services tonight, we who have

---

[4] The seventh Sunday after Easter, commemorating the descent of the Holy
Spirit on the apostles.

[5] Deacon, Secretary, Canon.

worked hard for six days making shoes and coats, and we who have brewed and baked and butchered all week long for the right worshipful priests so that on the seventh day they'd have the strength to conduct divine services for us. I don't blame the right worshipful chapter, for they're only human beings like us, and God alone could work for six days and rest on the seventh.

BURGHER   You're blaspheming God, master!

GERT   Oh well, He doesn't hear it when the door's shut.

A WOMAN   Mary, Mother of Jesus! He's an Antichrist!

GERT   (*knocks on the door*)   Hear how empty it sounds. The Bible says that the veil before the holy of holies was rent, and that must be true, but if the priests have sewn it together since, the Bible doesn't say, and it doesn't need to be a lie for all that.

(*The people rush toward* GERT; *the children scream.*)

BURGHER   Woe unto you, Luther, for you are one of them! We have sinned; so the Lord has closed His house. Unclean spirit, can't you hear how even the children scream at sight of you?

GERT   You're stepping on their toes, my friends.

WOMAN   Don't touch him; he's possessed by the devil!

BURGHER   Down with him! Down with him!

GERT   Don't touch me, for in this place I'm in God's sanctuary!

BURGHER   God doesn't protect the cast-out angel!

GERT   If God doesn't, the holy church does, and I'm within its consecrated walls.

BURGHER   Drag him outside the church walls!

GERT   If you don't fear God, at least fear the holy father's ban!

WOMAN   Drag him from the door; it's his unclean spirit that has bewitched the church!

BURGHER   Yes! Yes! God doesn't open His church to the devil!

(*They rush toward* GERT *just as the bishop's* SECRETARY *enters; he is preceded by a deacon who asks for their attention.*)

SECRETARY   (*reads*)   "Inasmuch as our cathedral city has not fulfilled its obligations to the bishop's chair and as the city continues to resist fulfillment of the same, the cathedral chapter has found it fitting, in accordance with its rights and with the approval of the curia, to close the doors of the church and to discontinue masses and offerings until the grievance named is corrected, reminding each and every one who does not conduct himself accordingly that he will have all our disfavor.

> "*Datum vigilia assumptionis Mariae*[6]
> "The Chapter of Strängnäs."

(*Exits*)

[6] Written on the Feast of the Assumption.

GERT   What about that, good people?

BURGHER   No mass on Pentecost eve! That's a disgrace!

GERT   Watch out! Don't say anything against the priests—it's certainly not their fault.

BURGHER   Whose fault is it?

GERT   The church's! That invisible, almighty church! It's the church that has closed the church, you see.
(*The people express their displeasure.*)

OLOF   (*has come up and now rings the vesper bell by means of a rope that hangs down from the tower*)   If you're serious about your divine services, I'll celebrate mass for you!

BURGHER   Thank you, Master Olof, but don't you know what that may lead to?

OLOF   Let us fear God rather than man! (*The people kneel.*) "Dear friends, brothers and sisters in Jesus Christ! Since we are now gathered together . . ."

BURGHER   Master Olof . . .

OLOF   What?

BURGHER   We want our regular mass and not human innovations.

GERT   It will have to be in Latin, Master Olof. Otherwise, we won't understand what you're saying.

BURGHER   It has to be in the sacred language; otherwise, anyone at all could conduct mass.

OLOF   Yes, that's just how it's going to be. Each and every one by himself and with God.

PEOPLE   A Luther! A Luther! Antichrist!

BURGHER   Really, Master Olof. You, who are so young and enthusiastic, have been infected by that German devil. I'm an old man and have seen the world. For your own good turn back while you're still young. Grant us our wish and conduct the old mass.

OLOF   No, that trickery is done for. You should pray in spirit and in truth, not with words you don't understand.

BURGHER   Don't you think, my young friend, that our Lord understands Latin?

GERT   But He certainly doesn't understand Swedish at all!

BURGHER   Master Olof! Are you going to let the people go without a word of edification? Don't you see how they long for their God? Sacrifice your own sinful will, and don't let them go like sheep without a shepherd.

OLOF   You call my will sinful?

BURGHER   You are a hard man.

OLOF   Don't say that! Do you know what the ringing of these bells is going to cost me?

BURGHER   Your vanity!

GERT   And your peace! That was the signal bell that called to battle. It's starting right now! Soon the bells of Stockholm will answer, and then the blood of Huss,[7] and of Ziska,[8] and of the thousands of German peasants will be on the heads of the princes and the Catholics.

WOMAN   God save us! Is he mad?

BURGHER   Do you know that man, Master Olof?

OLOF   No!

GERT   Olof! You know me! Don't deny me! Are you afraid of these poor miserable people who don't want what's best for them—people who have never heard the word freedom?

OLOF   Who are you?

GERT   If I were to tell you, you'd tremble! It's true, of course, you have to tremble to awaken from your sleep. I'm the cast-out angel, who will reappear ten thousand times; I'm the deliverer who came too early; I'm called Satan because I loved you more than my own life; I've been called Luther; I've been called Huss; now I'm called Anabaptist![9]

PEOPLE   (*draw away from him and cross themselves*)   Anabaptist!

GERT   (*unmasks himself; is much older than he has seemed*)   Now, do you recognize me, Olof?

OLOF   Father Gert!

BURGHER   He calls him father!

PEOPLE   (*draw away*)   Anabaptist! Anabaptist!

WOMAN   Don't you see? He's the man who was excommunicated—

BURGHER   Gert Bookprinter. Brask's printer.

ANOTHER BURGHER   The one who printed Luther!

WOMAN   Woe upon us and our city; woe upon our priests when they associate with Antichrist!

BURGHER   He denies baptism!

WOMAN   He denies God! (*The people leave.*)

OLOF   Father Gert, you said dangerous things.

[7] John Huss (*c.* 1369–1415), Bohemian Protestant. Like Luther, he condemned the sale of indulgences and the primacy of the Pope, and insisted on the supremacy of the Bible. He was burned at the stake for heresy.

[8] John Ziska (*c.* 1370–1424), Bohemian Protestant. The leading Protestant commander in the Hussite wars (1419–36), which broke out after Huss's death. In these wars against the Pope and Emperor, thousands of Bohemian and German peasants were killed.

[9] The Anabaptists maintained that infant baptism was without scriptural foundation. Opposed to the union of church and state, they advocated the renunciation of private property and the establishment of religious communalism.

GERT   Do you think *that* was dangerous, Olof? God bless you for that.
OLOF   Dangerous for you, I mean.
GERT   Not for anyone else?
OLOF   Let's hope not.
GERT   You have known Luther?
OLOF   Yes, I have. I want to do his work in my own country.
GERT   Is that all?
OLOF   What do you mean?
GERT   It's too little. Luther is dead. He started. We'll go farther.
OLOF   Where would you lead me?
GERT   Far. Far. Olof!
OLOF   I'm afraid of you, Father Gert!
GERT   Yes, yes! You'll be very much afraid, for I'll lead you up on a high
       mountain and from there you'll see the whole world. You see, Olof,
       it's Pentecost. That was the time the Holy Spirit descended and
       filled the Apostles with His Spirit, no, filled all mankind. You can
       receive the Holy Spirit; I've received the Holy Spirit because I
       believed. The spirit of God came down to me, I feel it; and that's
       why they've locked me up as insane, but now I'm free; now I'll
       speak the word, for you see, Olof, now we're on the mountain top!
       Do you see how the people crawl on their knees up to the two
       men who sit on their thrones? The greater one has two keys in
       one hand, a thunderbolt in the other. That's the pope. Now he
       lifts the thunderbolt, and a thousand souls are damned, and the
       others kiss his foot and sing *Gloria Deo*[10]—and the man on the
       throne turns and smiles. Now look at the other man! He has a
       sword and a scepter. Bow down before the scepter, or the sword
       will bite! He wrinkles his brows, and all the people tremble. Then
       he turns to his neighbor on the other throne, and they both smile.
       These are the two pillars of Baal.[11] But then there's a murmur in
       the air like the murmur of human voices. "Who murmurs?" cries
       the pope and shakes his thunderbolt. "Who murmurs?" and the
       emperor shakes his sword. No one answers. But there's still a
       murmur in the air, and it sighs and it calls: "Think!" And the pope
       is startled, and the emperor turns pale and asks: "Who cried
       'think'? Bring him here, and I'll take his life," and the pope cries:
       "Bring him here, and I'll take his soul!" It was the air that cried;
       it was no one who cried; but the voice rises, and a storm wind
       rushes forward and crosses the Alps and roars over the Fichtel

[10] Glory to God.
[11] Chief god of the Canaanites.

Mountains and awakens the Baltic and echoes against the shores, and increased a thousandfold the cry goes out over the world: "Freedom! Freedom!" And the pope throws his keys into the sea, and the emperor sheathes his sword, for they can do nothing against that cry! Olof! You want to strike the pope, but you forget the emperor; the emperor who murders his people without counting them, because they dare to sigh when they're trodden underfoot. You want to strike the pope in Rome, but, like Luther, you want to give them a new pope in the Holy Scriptures. Listen to me! Don't bind the spirits with any bond! Don't forget the great day of Pentecost; don't forget your great goal: spiritual life and spiritual freedom. Don't listen to that death cry: "Lo, everything is good!" because then the millennium, the millennium of freedom, will never come into being, and that's just what is beginning now! (OLOF *remains silent.*)

GERT Are you getting dizzy?

OLOF You're going too far, Gert!

GERT There'll come a day when people will call me a papist! Aim for the sky, and you'll hit the horizon.

OLOF Back, Gert! You'll bring disaster on yourself and the kingdom. Don't you see how the country still trembles with fever from the wounds of recent wars? And you want to sow civil war. That's godless!

GERT No, now that the knife's in the flesh, cut away so you can save the body.

OLOF I'll report you as a traitor.

GERT You shouldn't—you've offended the church beyond help today, and besides—

OLOF Speak out, Gert; just now you look like Satan.

GERT I'll give you my secret; do with it as you wish. You see, the king's going to Malmö today; the day after tomorrow, let's say, Stockholm will be in revolt.

OLOF What's that?

GERT Do you know Rink and Knipperdollink?

OLOF (*frightened*) The Anabaptists!

GERT Yes! Why be so amazed? Why, they're just a couple of louts. A furrier and a shopkeeper who deny the value of baptism for an irresponsible child and are simple enough to oppose a deliberate false vow, extorted from an irresponsible being.

OLOF There's something else.

GERT What could that be?

OLOF They're possessed!

GERT   By the spirit, yes! It's the storm that calls through them! Take care you don't get in their way!

OLOF   They must be stopped! I'll go to the king!

GERT   We ought to be friends, Olof. Doesn't your mother live in Stockholm?

OLOF   You know she does.

GERT   Do you know my daughter Kristina's living with your mother?

OLOF   Kristina?

GERT   Yes, for the time being. If we win, your mother will be safe because of my daughter. If the Catholics win, my daughter will be safe because of your mother. And you are concerned about Kristina, aren't you?

OLOF   Gert! Gert! Where did you get so wise?

GERT   In the insane asylum!

OLOF   Leave me. You'll lead me into misfortune.

GERT   Yes, if it's misfortune to be robbed of all earthly happiness, to be dragged to prison, to suffer poverty, to be ridiculed and reviled because of the truth. Then you're not worthy of such a great misfortune. I thought you'd understand me, I counted on your help, for you still have the fire, but the world's tempting you, I see. Follow the current and be happy.

OLOF   A man certainly can't reshape his time.

GERT   Luther did!

OLOF   One man can't set himself against the current.

GERT   Fool! Lead the current. For we are the current; the old people are stagnant puddles; you certainly won't have to struggle against them. Don't let them rot or dry up; give them outlets, and they'll follow the current.

OLOF   I understand; you've planted a thought in my soul, but I must strangle it at birth, or it will kill me.

GERT   Believe me, you shall be a Daniel, who shall speak the truth to princes. They will try to destroy you, but the Lord will protect you.[12] Now I can safely leave; I see the lightning flashing in your eye, and the tongue of fire flickering over your head. Happy Pentecost, Master Olof! (*As he goes*) Here comes the king of flies; don't let him sully your pure soul.

OLOF   Jesus help me!

(BISHOPS HANS BRASK and MÅNS SOMMAR *enter*.)

MÅNS   (*goes toward* OLOF; BRASK *remains behind, observing everything about him*)   Canon! Who rang the bells for vespers?

---

[12] Daniel, 6.

OLOF (*gently and firmly*) I did.

MÅNS Weren't you aware of the orders?

OLOF I knew it was forbidden.

MÅNS You dared to defy them?

OLOF Yes, when the people were left as sheep without a shepherd, I wanted to gather them.

MÅNS Why, you're reproaching us for our actions! You're really insolent.

OLOF The truth is always insolent.

MÅNS So you want to play the apostle of truth, young man; you'll get no thanks for that.

OLOF I ask only ingratitude.

MÅNS Save your truths; they're not much in demand.

OLOF (*violently*) Advice worthy of the father of lies! (*Gently*) Forgive me.

MÅNS Do you know whom you're talking to?

OLOF (*heatedly*) To *servus servi servorum*[13] Måns Sommar!

BRASK (*comes up to them*) Who is this man?

MÅNS He's one of the servants of the church.

BRASK What's his name?

MÅNS Olaus Petri.

BRASK (*stares fixedly at* OLOF) Are you Master Olof?
  (OLOF *bows and looks at* BRASK.)

BRASK I like you! Will you be my secretary?

OLOF Thank you, Your Grace, but I have no recommendation.

BRASK Bishop Måns, what do you say?

MÅNS They say Dr. Luther praised him highly.

BRASK That's what I've heard. Merely youthful enthusiasm. We'll train him.

OLOF I'm afraid it's too late.

BRASK A young twig can be bent.

MÅNS Your Grace should not foster serpents. Our canon is strongly inclined to the heresy and has dared to defy our orders today.

BRASK Really?

MÅNS We proclaimed the suspension of mass on entirely legal grounds, and he has dared to conduct mass, and what's worse a Lutheran mass, and thereby has stirred up the people.

BRASK Be careful, young man! Do you know that excommunication strikes the man who preaches Luther's doctrines?

OLOF I know. But I fear no god but God!

---

[13] Servant of the servants of the servants (of God). In the sixteenth century, *servus servorum* was one of the Pope's titles.

BRASK   Consider your words! I wanted to help you, but you push me away!

OLOF   You wanted to buy my talents to save your own sickly cause, and I was shameless enough not to sell myself!

BRASK   By St. George, I think you've lost your mind!

OLOF   If I have, don't use the same cure on me as on Gert Bookprinter, the one you put in the insane asylum. He became too sane, I'm afraid.

BRASK   (*to* MÅNS)   Do you know Gert?

MÅNS   No, Your Grace.

BRASK   He's a mad fellow who used my press to print Lutheran documents when I put anti-Lutheran ones in his hands. And then he raved about the Apocalypse and the millennium. (*To* OLOF)   Have you seen him?

OLOF   He was just here, and you can expect little good from him.

BRASK   Has he been let out?

OLOF   He'll soon be in Stockholm, and then you'll certainly hear about him. Be careful, Lord Bishop!

BRASK   Huh! There's no danger yet.

OLOF   The Anabaptists are in Stockholm!

BRASK   What's that?

OLOF   The Anabaptists are in Stockholm!

BRASK   The Anabaptists?

KING GUSTAV   (*enters hastily*)   What's going on? The city's stirred up. The people are rushing along the streets demanding mass. What's the meaning of this?

BRASK   Mischief, Your Majesty!

KING   Bishop Måns!

MÅNS   The city has not paid its tithes.

KING   So you refuse to conduct divine services. God's death!

BRASK   Your Majesty should consider . . .

KING   Bishop Måns! Answer me!

MÅNS   Your Majesty should consider that matters like these which fall under the jurisdiction of the church . . .

KING   I command you to do your job!

BRASK   The bishops of Sweden take orders only from their superiors, the pope and the canonical law.

KING   (*subdued*)   I know, but the pope can't keep his eye on you all the time?

BRASK   That's our business.

KING   (*flares up, but calms down*)   You're right, Your Reverence. It shall be your business.

BRASK   To change the subject. They say Stockholm's on the verge of revolt.

KING   Who says so?

MÅNS   Our canon.

KING   Your schoolmaster? Where is he? (*To* OLOF) Are you the one? What's your name?

OLOF   Olaus Petri.

KING   Master Olof! You're a heretic, aren't you? And have plans against the holy church? That's dangerous business!

BRASK   He tore off his mask today. He was audacious enough to break the chapter's prohibition of mass openly. Because of that we demand Your Majesty's approval of his being duly punished.

KING   That's a matter for the cathedral chapter and does not concern me. But what did you say about a revolt in Stockholm?

OLOF   The Anabaptists!

KING   Is that all?

BRASK   Your Majesty, don't you know how those mad fools have behaved in Germany? We suggest that Your Majesty return with your soldiers yourself.

KING   That's my affair!

BRASK   But civil war!

KING   That will be my business! Olof, I appoint you secretary to the Council of Stockholm. Go there at once.[14] Speak to the people. I'll rely on you.

BRASK   For the sake of our country, I beg Your Majesty to consider how foolish it is to talk to fools.

KING   You can't subdue the spirit by swords. Consider that, my lords!

BRASK   The church has never . . .

KING   Yes, not with keys, either. (*To* OLOF) Go to my chancellor and you'll get your official appointment.

BRASK   You'd better wait a moment, canon.

KING   Our secretary doesn't obey your orders ahead of mine.

BRASK   The rights of the church shall be satisfied first—Olaus Petri!

KING (*corrects him*)   Secretary . . .

BRASK   Secretary Olaus Petri, don't leave the city before the chapter has handed down its judgment.

KING   The chapter doesn't hand down judgment before it has investigated!

BRASK   That's our affair!

---

[14] In 1524, Olof was made the King's Secretary to the Council of the City of Stockholm, where he preached until 1531.

KING It won't be your affair, Bishop Brask! The bishop of Linköping does not judge a canon in Strängnäs. Bishop Måns, speak up!

MÅNS After what has happened . . . hm!

BRASK Further arguments should be superfluous.

KING Bishop Brask, be silent or step aside when I speak privately to Bishop Måns—privately! Speak up, Lord Måns!

MÅNS I can't see anything else—but—since His Reverence Bishop Brask—

KING Now it's a question of Master Olof. You can postpone the investigation, my lords. Please leave us.
(*The* BISHOPS *go.*)

KING Will you be my man?

OLOF Your Majesty's secretary?

KING No. You'll be my right hand on the condition that the left doesn't know for the time being what the right is doing. Go to Stockholm.

OLOF The chapter will demand my return and excommunicate me.

KING Before they've had time to go that far, you may blame me. Until then, stand on your own feet as well as you can.

OLOF What does Your Majesty wish?

KING Talk to the fanatics in Stockholm.

OLOF And then?

KING Oh, that's far off. I don't dare to think of it yet—let them preach; it can't hurt the stupid fools to hear a new word even if it's crazy; but there must be no acts of violence; then the sword will join in the game. Farewell, Olof. (*Exits*)

OLOF The emperor doesn't want to agree with the pope!
(PUPILS, *who have been on a walk at the back, come forward.*)

PUPIL I May we go on with the play now, Master Olof?

OLOF There'll be no more playing, children.

PUPIL I Are you leaving us, Master Olof?

OLOF Yes, and apparently for always.

PUPIL I You could stay over Pentecost so we could put on our comedy.

PUPIL II And so I may play the angel Gabriel.

PUPIL I Do as we wish, Master Olof. You were the only one who was kind to us and let us get out of the terrible fasts.

PUPIL II Master Olof, don't leave us!

OLOF Children, you don't know what you ask. The day will come when you'll thank God that I left you. No. May that day never come! Let's make our parting brief. Good-bye, Nils; good-bye, Vilhelm.
(*He embraces them; they kiss his hand.*)
(LARS *has entered; observes them closely.*)

PUPIL I Won't you ever come back, Master Olof?

LARS   (*steps forward*)   Are you ready to leave?

OLOF   (*to the boys*)   No, I'll never come back.

PUPILS   (*as they exit*)   Good-bye, Master Olof; don't forget us!
    (OLOF *looks after them.*)

LARS   I have met the king.

OLOF   (*absent-mindedly*)   Have you?

LARS   Do you know what he said?

OLOF   No.

LARS   "I've acquired a pointer, who can raise the game; we'll see if he
    comes back when I whistle."

OLOF   Look! They're sitting among the graves, playing and picking
    flowers and singing Pentecost songs.

LARS   (*takes him by the arm*)   Child!

OLOF   (*startled*)   What did you say?

LARS   I thought you had taken such a firm grip on the plow today that
    it was too late to look back.
    (OLOF *waves to the* PUPILS.)

LARS   Are you still dreaming?

OLOF   That was the last fair morning dream that went; forgive me—now
    I am awake!
    (*They go to the right. When* OLOF *comes to the wing, he turns once
    more to look at the* PUPILS. *The* BLACK FRIARS MÅRTEN *and* NILS *have
    stepped forward from the very wing through which the* PUPILS *have
    made their exit.*)
    (OLOF *gives a cry of involuntary amazement and draws his hand
    across his forehead.*)
    (LARS *takes him by the arm, and they go.*)

CURTAIN

Act II

STOCKHOLM

SCENE I

*A beer tavern in the wall of the Great Church. At the back a counter with
    beer cans and stoups, etc. To the right of the counter a table,
    behind which can be seen an iron door. At this table are sitting two
    disguised monks—MÅRTEN and NILS—drinking beer. At the rest*

of the tables are sitting farmers, sailors, and German soldiers. The street door is to the right. A fiddler is sitting on a barrel. The soldiers are shaking dice. Everyone is intoxicated and noisy. HANS WINDRANK, *a native of Småland, a* GERMAN BURGHER, *and a* DANE *are sitting at one table.*

GERMAN (*to the* DANE) So you're defending that bloody scoundrel Christian![1]

DANE Good gracious! He's a human being.

GERMAN No, he's a monster! A bloodhound! A cowardly, false Dane!

DANE Heavens! You mustn't talk about blood! Do you remember the Käpplinge murders when the German[2]—

WINDRANK Listen, gentlemen. We should get together and have fun; so I'll talk about America.

GERMAN Do you blame us Lübeckers for what the Germans did?

DANE Good gracious! I only said the Germans—

WINDRANK Listen, you gentlemen shouldn't quarrel. (*Calls to the tavern keeper*) Four mugs of brandy. Now we'll be agreeable and peaceful, and I'll talk about America . . .
(*The brandy is put on the table.*)

GERMAN (*tastes the brandy*) A marvelous drink. Just think, gentlemen, how civilization has progressed. Today the grain's growing in the field . . .

WINDRANK And tomorrow it's changed to liquor. I wonder who made that discovery.

GERMAN I beg your pardon—it's a German invention—I say invention —because they discover America.

WINDRANK And Germans never make discoveries.

GERMAN God's death!

WINDRANK There, there. You're surely not German.

DANE (*to the* GERMAN) Can you tell me who invented the idea that the Germans gave Sweden its present king? (*Laughter*)

GERMAN The Lübeckers gave Sweden its liberator when it stood on the verge of destruction.

WINDRANK A toast to the king!

DANE A toast to Lübeck!

GERMAN (*flattered*) I can't find words really . . .

WINDRANK You're certainly not the king.

GERMAN I beg of you, it was my Danish brother's . . .

---

[1] Christian II the Tyrant (reign: 1520–21).

[2] In 1389, a group of German burghers from Stockholm burned to death several Swedish burghers in Käpplinge Island.

DANE You're not a Lübecker when you're a burgher in Stockholm, are you?

WINDRANK (*to the* SMÅLÄNNING) Why aren't you drinking, our silent brother?

SMÅLÄNNING I'll drink your liquor, but I'll do this to the toast.
(*Crushes the tin mug and throws it on the floor*)

WINDRANK (*reaches for his knife*) You refuse to drink a toast to the king?

SMÅLÄNNING I have drunk from his cup so long I haven't the slightest desire to drink his toast.

WINDRANK God's blood!

GERMAN (*in a lively fashion*) Quiet! Quiet! Let's hear the man!

DANE (*in the same fashion*) Good gracious!

SMÅLÄNNING God help me when I get home!

WINDRANK (*touched*) What is it, poor fellow? You look sad. Don't you have any money? Look here, and we'll see. (*Takes up his purse*) I have half my wages left. What's wrong with you?

SMÅLÄNNING Let's not talk about it. More brandy! Brandy! I have money, too! Look! Gold! (*The brandy is brought.*) But it isn't mine. But I'm going to drink up every penny! And you're going to be decent and help me!

WINDRANK But it's not your money—how come?

GERMAN Who has wronged you, my good fellow? I can see it's something bad.

SMÅLÄNNING I'm ruined! You see, I bought two hundred oxen on credit, and when I got to Stockholm, the king's bailiff took charge and said I couldn't sell them at a price higher than his! The king fixes the price. The king's the one who has ruined me.

GERMAN Oh, no!

SMÅLÄNNING Oh, I know a lot more. They say he'll take the monks and priests away from us soon just to give everything to the lords.

DANE The lords?

SMÅLÄNNING Yes, indeed! King Christian should have clipped a little closer! God bless him!

WINDRANK Goodness, is the king like that? I thought he had the lords by the ear.

SMÅLÄNNING He? No, he lets them hatch with the right to cut oaks on my land—if I had any left! You see, I did have a bit of land once, but then a lord came along and said my great-grandmother had borrowed it from his great-grandfather, and that was that.

GERMAN Can the king be like that? I certainly didn't think that.

SMÅLÄNNING Oh, yes, indeed! And the lords' boys run around with their guns in our woods shooting wild game just for the hell of it; but if we farmers were starving to death and should shoot an animal, we wouldn't have to die of hunger—they'd hang us—not in an oak, God save us; that would disgrace the royal tree—no, in a pine! You see, the pine isn't born with a crown, so it isn't royal . . . That's why the ballad goes:

"And we hanged the farmers up
 In the pine trees' highest top"

It doesn't say crown—you notice.

GERMAN   But the pine raises its head all the same, and is as straight as can be.

SMÅLÄNNING   Drink, gentlemen. I mean it sincerely. That's a blessed drink! If I only didn't have a wife and children at home! Oh, well. That doesn't matter. Oh, I know a lot more, but I won't say anything.

WINDRANK   What do you know?

GERMAN   Maybe it's something funny?

SMÅLÄNNING   You see—if you'd count all the pine trees in Småland, they'd outnumber the oaks, I think.

GERMAN   You think so?

WINDRANK   I don't like it when anyone says anything again the king. Of course, I don't know what he does and says, and it's none of my business, either. But I do know this: he's all in favor of shipping. Yes, he's the one who's equipped ships for trade with Spain, and he made me a sea captain, so I certainly haven't anything to complain about.

GERMAN   And he's done that out of spite just to ruin Lübeck's commerce, Lübeck's—to which he owes so much.

SMÅLÄNNING   He'll get to enjoy it. The oxen still have their horns even if they've been cut. Thanks for your company.—I have to go.

GERMAN   Oh, no. Another little mug, so we can talk.

SMÅLÄNNING   No thanks, though it's good of you; I don't dare to drink any more for then I'm afraid I'd be in for it. You see, I have a wife and children at home, and now I'm going home to tell them we're ruined—no—I don't dare to. (*Changes his mind*) Thank you, Mr. German—we'll have some more.

GERMAN   Fine, that's right. (*They drink.*)

SMÅLÄNNING (*empties his mug and jumps up*)   The devil, how bitter it is! (*Staggers out*)

GERMAN (*to the* DANE)   Well! Wait till that fellow wakes up!
    (DANE *nods in agreement. The noise has increased; the fiddler plays. Then the organ can be heard from the church.*)

WINDRANK   Strange all the same that the king lets them have a tavern in the church wall.

GERMAN   So you have scruples, captain! The king doesn't know about this.

WINDRANK   Well, it doesn't sound good, that organ music with this singing. You see I've always been religious; I got that from home.

GERMAN   (*ironically*)   Lucky the man who's been brought up like that! You had a mother—

WINDRANK   (*touched*)   Yes—yes!

GERMAN   Who tucked you into bed at night and taught you: "There went an angel 'round our house."

WINDRANK   Yes, yes!

GERMAN   She was a splendid woman.

WINDRANK   (*is getting drunk*)   Oh, if you only knew!

GERMAN   God has heard her prayers. You're crying. You are a good man.

DANE   Good gracious!

GERMAN   If your mother could see you now! With tears in your eyes!

WINDRANK   Oh, I'm a weak sinner, I know, but you see—I have a heart —the devil take me. If a poor soul would come along and he were hungry, I'd take the shirt off my back.

GERMAN   Shouldn't we have one more mug?

WINDRANK   No, I don't think so.

(*Sharp blows can be heard on the iron door. General excitement.*)

WINDRANK   Oh, oh!

GERMAN   You're surely not afraid! That's not the door to heaven.

WINDRANK   I'll never drink again. I promise.(*Dozes off*)

GERMAN   (*to the* DANE)   Isn't brandy a blessed drink that can move a rascal like that to enthusiasm, even to thoughts of temperance?

DANE   You're right. There just isn't another drink like it.

GERMAN   It opens the heart wide and closes the head tight; that is to say, it makes us good people, for the good people are the ones who have a big heart and a little head.

DANE   Yes, I go still further; brandy makes us religious, because it kills reason, and reason's the rock that keeps religion from entering the heart.

GERMAN   Brandy's a sacred drink! Strange that . . .

DANE   Enough said!

(*Blows on the iron door can again be heard.*)

WINDRANK   (*who has been asleep, wakes up*)   Help! I'm dying!

GERMAN   Too bad about such a beautiful soul.

(*The door is opened violently, overturning the table with the stoups and mugs, at which* MÅRTEN *and* NILS *are sitting. A woman dressed in a black and red skirt with a nun's veil over her head rushes in; for a moment* GERT *can be seen in the doorway behind her. Then the door is closed violently.*)

PROSTITUTE (*looks about in amazement*) Save me! The people want to kill me!

A GERMAN SOLDIER A prostitute with a nun's veil? (*Laughs*)
[*Laughter*]

MÅRTEN (*crosses himself*) A prostitute! Who brought her into this respectable company? Keeper, take her out if you don't want to hurt the reputation of your place and the sanctity of the church.

PROSTITUTE Isn't there anyone who'll help me? (*The* KEEPER *has taken her by the arm to lead her out to the street.*) Don't drive me out among the raging people! I wanted to steal into the Lord's house to get a crumb of His mercy; I wanted to start a new life—but the monks drove me away and set the people on me; then Father Gert came along and saved me by bringing me here.

MÅRTEN You can all hear she has desecrated the sanctuary of God. She wants to conceal her garb of shame with the veil of holiness.

GERMAN And the veil wasn't long enough!

MÅRTEN (*goes up to her to tear off her veil*) Tear off your mask, and show your vileness! (*He recoils when he sees her face.*)

PROSTITUTE It's you, Mårten, is it? You murderer!

GERMAN Old acquaintances!

MÅRTEN A shameful lie! I've never seen her before! I'm Brother Mårten, and Brother Nils is my witness!

NILS (*drunk*) I can testify—that Brother Mårten has never seen that woman.

PROSTITUTE And still, Nils, you were the one who showed me Mårten's letter of absolution when I was driven out of the cloister and they let him stay.

NILS Yes, that's the truth, that is.

MÅRTEN (*beside himself with fury, pulls* NILS *by the arm*) You're lying, you, too! You can all see he's drunk!

GERMAN Good people, I testify that the holy brother's drunk and therefore he's lying.

PEOPLE (*with disgust*) A drunken priest!

GERMAN Oh, well! The binge gives absolution to the lie. Isn't that right, Father Mårten?

KEEPER I have to say this: you'll have to behave here; if this goes on, I'll lose my customers and probably be dragged before the chapter. So please take out the miserable creature who's causing all this commotion.

MÅRTEN   Take her out, or I'll have you excommunicated! Don't you know
we're within the walls of the holy church even if the chapter has
opened this room for the bodily refreshment of travelers?

GERMAN   Good people, this is a holy room, and God obviously lives here.
(PEOPLE *drag the* PROSTITUTE *toward the door.*)

PROSTITUTE   Christ, help me!

OLOF (*has appeared in the door, now forces his way forward, takes the*
PROSTITUTE *by the hands, and draws her away from the drunken
people*)   Tell me. Who is this woman?

MÅRTEN   She's not a woman—

OLOF   What's that?

MÅRTEN   She's not a man—though she's disguised!

OLOF   You say *she.* Isn't she a woman?

MÅRTEN   She's a prostitute!

OLOF (*startled; lets go her hand*)   A prostitute!

GERMAN   Don't let go of her, Master Olof, or she'll run away!

OLOF   Why do you lay hands on her? What is her crime?

GERMAN   She goes to church!

OLOF   I see. (*Looks about*)

MÅRTEN   What are you looking for?

OLOF (*becomes aware of* MÅRTEN)   A priest.

MÅRTEN   I'm a black friar.

OLOF   So! I guessed that! You're the one who set the people on her!

MÅRTEN   I'm the one who protects the church from vileness and wants
to keep it pure from vice. She's an excommunicated woman who
sells her body, which should be the temple of God. (*The woman
falls to her knees before* OLOF.)

OLOF (*takes her hand*)   You see, black friar, I dare to take her hand
and match her against you! She has sold her body, you say! How
many souls have you bought? I, too, am a priest! No, I'm a human
being, for I'm still not so presumptuous that I've locked the house
of God, and, as a sinful man, I give my hand to a fellow human
being who can't be without sin. Let him who is without sin come
forward to cast the first stone.[3] Come here, Brother Mårten, you
angel of light, who have clad yourself in the black garb of
innocence and have shaved your head so no one will see how you've
grown gray in sin. Maybe you don't have a stone ready? Woe unto
you! What have you done with the stones you were going to give
to the people when they asked for bread?[4] Have you already given

[3] John, 8:7.
[4] Matthew, 7:9.

all of them away? Come here, respectable burgher. (*To* WINDRANK, *who's sleeping on the floor*) You, who sleep the sleep of beasts, why don't you wake up so you can throw your knife? See how he blushes? Because of shame over the bad company you've given him or because of sensual pleasure? (*The* PEOPLE *murmur disapprovingly.*) You murmur! From shame because of what I've said or because you're ashamed of yourselves? Why don't you cast stones? True, you haven't any. Oh, well. Open the door. Call the people and drag the woman out. If you don't believe fifty men can tear her to pieces, be assured that five hundred women can! Well! You don't say anything! Woman! Rise! They have acquitted you. Go and sin no more, but don't show yourself to the priests, for they'd throw you to the women.

MÅRTEN (*who has tried to interrupt* OLOF *several times but has been held back by the* GERMAN, *takes out a paper*)   The man to whom you're listening is a heretic. You heard that in what he said, but he has been excommunicated, too.[5] Look here! Read it yourselves! (*He takes a candle from one of the tables and throws it into the middle of the floor.*) "As that light is extinguished which we here cast out, so may joy and comfort and all the good he may have from God be extinguished for him."

PEOPLE (*cross themselves and draw back;* OLOF *stands alone with the* PROSTITUTE *in the middle of the stage*)   Anathema!

MÅRTEN (*to the* PROSTITUTE)   Now you hear what Master Olof's absolution is worth.

OLOF (*who has been reticent*)   Woman, do you still dare to rely on my words? Aren't you afraid of men? Don't you hear the lightning of excommunication hissing about our heads? Why don't you go over to these twenty righteous men who are still within the protection of the holy church? Answer me! Do you believe God has cast me out as these have?

PROSTITUTE   No!

OLOF (*takes the proclamation of excommunication*)   Well, then! The great bishop of the little city of Linköping has sold my soul to Satan for my lifetime—his power doesn't extend beyond that—because I urged the people to turn to God at a forbidden time. Here's the contract; since the church has bound me to Hell by this, I release myself from the same (*he tears the parchment to pieces*), and from the ban of the church! God help me, amen!

PEOPLE (*howl*)   Anathema!

---

[5] Olof was excommunicated in 1524.

MÅRTEN   Pull him down! Strike him! He's excommunicated!

OLOF (*places himself in front of the* PROSTITUTE)   Listen to the devils crying for their sacrifice! (*To the* PEOPLE) Don't touch me!

MÅRTEN   Down with him!

(*A soldier lifts his weapon; the iron door is opened, and the Aanabaptists, led by* KNIPPERDOLLINK, *rush in shouting; they are carrying smashed crucifixes, saints' images, and rent choir robes. All the people in the tavern are crowded toward the exit.*)

KNIPPERDOLLINK (*who has been in the lead, as he opens the door wide*)   In here, people; here's another holy house. What's this? A tavern in the temple! Look! The abomination has gone so far that they desecrate the sanctuary. But I'll cleanse it with fire! Set fire to the church and put the saints on the fire!

OLOF (*steps forward*)   Consider what you're about to do!

KNIPPERDOLLINK   Are you afraid the heat will make the beer kegs burst, you Belial?[6] Are you the papal tavern keeper, who doesn't hesitate to erect a chapel for vice in the church wall?

OLOF   I'm the secretary of the city council; in the name of the king I command you to observe law and order!

KNIPPERDOLLINK   So you're the man the king has sent out to fight against our sacred cause! Forward, forward, men of God, and seize him first. After that we'll cleanse the house of God from idolatry.

MÅRTEN   Go on, good people! He's a heretic and has been excommunicated.

KNIPPERDOLLINK (*to* OLOF)   Heretic! So you're not one of the Catholics?

OLOF   Since I've been excommunicated, I don't belong to the church any more.

KNIPPERDOLLINK   Then you're on our side. (OLOF *remains silent.*) Answer me! Are you for or against us?

MÅRTEN   He's Olaus Petri—the king has sent him.

KNIPPERDOLLINK   Are you Olaus Petri?

OLOF   Yes.

KNIPPERDOLLINK   But you're a heretic!

OLOF   I'm proud that I am.

KNIPPERDOLLINK   And are in the king's service!

OLOF   Yes. (*The Anabaptists shout and surround* OLOF.)

GERT (*rushes in*)   Stop it! What are you doing?

KNIPPERDOLLINK   Gert! Who is this man?

GERT   He's ours! Let go of him, friends. There are the devil's messengers! (GERT *points at* MÅRTEN *and* NILS, *who steal out through the door.*

---

[6] An ancient Phoenician god. The personification of evil.

The Anabaptists run after them, raining blows on them. GERT *turns by the door to* OLOF. *The* PROSTITUTE *has withdrawn into a corner.* WINDRANK *is still sleeping under the table.* OLOF *stops thoughtfully in the center of the room.*)

GERT   (*throws himself on a bench, exhausted*)   It's heavy work, Olof.

OLOF   What have you done?

GERT   We've done some cleaning, to start with.

OLOF   That will cost you dearly.

GERT   We still have the upper hand. The whole city's on the move. Rink's at work up in St. George's chapel. Listen, has the king sent you against us?

OLOF   Yes.

GERT   That was very sensible.

OLOF   Tomorrow I'll preach in the new pulpit.

GERT   Well! How are you attending to your royal job? You're still standing here with your arms folded!

OLOF   Bring your friends with you to church tomorrow.

GERT   Will it be a Catholic sermon?

OLOF   I was excommunicated today.

GERT   (*jumps up and embraces* OLOF)   God bless you, Olof! That was the baptism of your rebirth!

OLOF   I still don't understand you. Why do you behave like wild animals? Why, you desecrate everything holy!

GERT   (*picks up a broken saint's image*)   Is this fellow holy? A St. Nicholas,[7] I think. Has Jesus Christ come and lived in vain when people still worship pieces of wood? Is what I can smash a god? Look at it!

OLOF   But the people consider him holy.

GERT   So was the golden calf, so was Zeus, and Thor and Odin, too![8] And still they were struck down. (*Catches sight of the* PROSTITUTE) Who's that woman? Oh, yes, the one I tried to get into your safe-keeping. Olof! Tell me one thing! Has the king bought you?

OLOF   Leave me, Gert! I hate you!

GERT   Who's that pig sleeping over there?

OLOF   When I stand before you, I become very small. Leave me. I want to do my work and not yours.

[7] The Great Church was originally called the Church of St. Nicholas.

[8] The golden calf, which the Israelites worshipped, is the symbol of apostasy (Exodus, 32:2–5; I Kings, 12:28–30). Zeus (Greek mythology) is ruler of the Olympian gods. Thor (Teutonic mythology) is god of yeomen and peasants and in Scandinavia is associated with law and justice. He is the son of Odin, one-eyed chief of the gods and god of war and wisdom.

GERT   Listen . . .

OLOF   You want to confuse our destinies.

GERT   Listen . . .

OLOF   You've thrown an invisible net about me; you proclaim that I'm an Anabaptist. How can I defend myself to the king?

GERT   Which king?

OLOF   King Gustav.

GERT   Oh! That one! Good-bye, Olof . . . So you're going to preach tomorrow . . . Why doesn't the woman go? . . . Good-bye. (*Goes*)

OLOF   Is he doing the errands of God or of the devil?

PROSTITUTE   (*approaches* OLOF; *kneels*)   Let me thank you.

OLOF   Thank God alone for having saved your soul, and don't believe that you have atoned for your sins today. Get strength to bear the curse for your lifetime. God has forgiven you—people never will. (OLOF *takes her by the hand and leads her out through the door.*)

MÅRTEN   (*appears in the doorway and after him* OLOF'S MOTHER *and* KRISTINA, GERT'S *daughter*)   We've come to the wrong place, I think.

MOTHER   (*when she becomes aware of* OLOF *and the* PROSTITUTE, *is beside herself*)   Olof! Olof!

KRISTINA   Who is that woman? She looks so unhappy.

MÅRTEN   Let's leave this dreadful den.

OLOF (*turns and runs toward the door, which is slammed shut by* MÅRTEN) Mother! Mother! (*He runs out through the other doorway; the stage becomes dark.*)

CURTAIN

INTERLUDE

(*The door to the church is opened again carefully and the* ORGANBLOWER-SEXTON *with a lantern and his* WIFE *climb in carefully.*)

SEXTON   Katrina, darling! Hold the lantern while I padlock the door.

WIFE   Bengt, dear, we ought to take a look at this mess first. I never could have believed we were so close to the tavern. Why, it's terrible! See, large barrels with beer in them!

SEXTON   And brandy, too. How it smells! I'll get a headache if I stay any longer.

WIFE   Merciful God, what a godless life they've led in here!

SEXTON   Katrina, darling!

WIFE   Yes, dear.

SEXTON   You know, I feel sick already. It's so cold and damp down here!

WIFE   Maybe we ought to go home.

SEXTON   I think I'll have to sit down and rest on this bench.

WIFE   Don't sit here in the damp and cold; let's go into the church.

SEXTON   No, you know, I think it was still colder there.

WIFE   Maybe you have a fever.

SEXTON   Yes, I almost think so. I'm so hot.

WIFE   Maybe you want something to drink.

SEXTON   Maybe that wouldn't be so bad.

WIFE   I'll see if there's any water.

SEXTON   There's not likely to be any in a hole like this.

WIFE   You certainly can't drink beer when you have a fever.

SEXTON   You know, I think the fever's gone; I feel frozen.

WIFE   I'll look for some mild beer.

SEXTON   If it's going to do any good, it had better be strong. Look: there's a keg of Rostock Number 4 stamped A.W.

WIFE   (*searching*)   I don't see any. Here's an Amsterdam Number 3.

SEXTON   Can't you see the fourth shelf from the top to the right?
(WIFE *searching*)

SEXTON   There's a metal tap to the left, right next to the funnel.

WIFE   I can't see any.

SEXTON   Well, I ought to know!

WIFE   I found it!
(SEXTON *gets up to help her but happens to step on* WINDRANK.)

WINDRANK   (*awakens*)   Oh, oh! Jesus Christ! St. Peter and St. Paul and Ferdinand and Isabella and St. George and the dragon and all the rest, and in came the doom in *dejom pote potentum ernos ternon*[9] Jesus Christ, the great dipper certainly is, an angel went 'round our house, the fellow was a great singer, in came Nils *in puttri*. Amen! Amen! Who's stepping on my stomach?

SEXTON   Please be merciful enough to say if you're a man or an evil spirit!

WINDRANK   I used to be a spirit, but at the moment I'm a pig!

SEXTON   What sort of spirit are you if I may ask?

WINDRANK   I'm a sea spirit! But you don't have to tramp on my bellows for all that.

SEXTON   Look, sir; my bread and butter is tramping the bellows . . . of the great organs.

WINDRANK   So it's the organ-tramper I have the honor—

---

[9] Windrank's Latin is poor.

SEXTON   Sexton, really, but I have a little clothing shop in the church wall, too.

WINDRANK   So you're an organ-tramper, a sexton, and a dealer in clothes—

SEXTON   In one person. Without confusion or transformation . . .

WINDRANK   That's a respectable trinity!

SEXTON   One doesn't joke about things like that.

WINDRANK   Oh! Oh! I'm drowning. Help!

SEXTON   What in God's name?

WINDRANK   There's a flood—ugh!

SEXTON   Katrina, darling! Where are you, angel? (*Runs up*) Christ, you've given my wife heart failure! She has run away from the beer keg . . . and taken the tap with her! Get up, get up, and let's get out of this godless den!

WINDRANK   My friend, now that I've just got into my proper element, I'll most likely stay.

SEXTON   By all means; the clock's striking twelve, and the ghostly hour begins.

WINDRANK   (*jumps up*)   That's another matter! (*The* SEXTON *is leading* WINDRANK.) Listen, sexton. I'm beginning to be attacked by strong doubts of the trinity.

SEXTON   Well, I declare!

WINDRANK   I mean your trinity!

SEXTON   What do you mean by that, captain . . .

WINDRANK   There are four of you all the same!

SEXTON   Four? Which?

WINDRANK   What about the tapster? Mayn't he be along?

SEXTON   Sh! Sh! That's only at night! (*They both fall down on the smashed St. Nicholas.*)

WINDRANK   Oh! Oh! Ghosts! Help, Mary, Mother of God!

SEXTON   (*gets up and lifts up the image*)   By my soul, it's so one's hair could stand straight on end. Here lies St. Nicholas smashed and swimming in beer. That's going pretty far, when they drag sacred things down into the dirt—the world won't last long, I guess; when the like of that happens to dry wood—

WINDRANK   (*who has recovered*)   To wet, you mean!

SEXTON   Silence, blasphemer! St. Nicholas is my patron saint. I was born on his day.

WINDRANK   That's why the two of you both like beer, I suppose.

SEXTON   It's the fashion to be a heretic now.

WINDRANK   Yes, it must be in the air, for I'm a very religious man otherwise. But don't be sad; I'll glue St. Nicholas together for you.

SEXTON   (*calls into the church*)   Katrina!

WINDRANK   Sh, sh! What the hell, don't call up the ghosts!
SEXTON   Shame! (*They leave.*)

CURTAIN

SCENE II

*A door. A smaller one leading into the pulpit. Stoles and choir robes on
the walls. Prayer stools and some small chests. The sun is shining
in through a window. The bells are ringing. An uninterrupted
murmur can be heard at the left wall. The* SEXTON *and his* WIFE
come in, stop by the door, and pray silently.

SEXTON   There. Hurry up and dust a little, Katrina, darling.
WIFE   Oh, well. It doesn't have to be so particular; it's only that Master
Olof who's preaching today. I can't understand how the chapter
can permit anything like that.
SEXTON   He has the king's permission, you see.
WIFE   Yes! Yes!
SEXTON   And he's had a basket put on the wall![10] Just new-fangled no-
tions. I declare, that Luther!
WIFE   There'll be the same trouble as yesterday, I suppose. I thought
they'd tear down the whole church.
SEXTON   (*carries a glass of water up into the pulpit*)   He'll most likely
need something to wet his throat today, the poor fellow.
WIFE   I don't think it matters in the least.
SEXTON   (*up in the pulpit*)   Katrina! Here comes Master Olof!
WIFE   That's terrible; they haven't rung the sermon bell yet. No, no, they
probably won't ring it for that fellow.
(OLOF *enters, serious and solemn—goes to a prayer stool and
kneels.* SEXTON *comes down and brings a robe which he holds out
to* OLOF.)
OLOF   (*gets up*)   God's peace.
(WIFE *curtseys and goes.* SEXTON *holds out the robe.*)
OLOF   Let it hang.
SEXTON   Aren't you going to wear a robe, master?
OLOF   No.

[10] The pulpit was shaped like a basket. He was popularly called "Master
Olof of the basket."

SEXTON But it's always done. What about the cloth?

OLOF I don't need it.

SEXTON Well, I declare!

OLOF Please leave me, my friend.

SEXTON Shall I leave? I usually . . .

OLOF Do me that favor.

SEXTON Well! Yes, indeed! But first I'll tell you I've put the missal to the right as you come up, and I've put a marker where you're to stop, and I've put the water right next to it. Don't forget to turn the hourglass, master, for things could drag on too long . . .

OLOF Don't worry. There'll be those who'll tell me when to stop!

SEXTON Yes, Lord preserve us! Beg your pardon. We have our customs here, see.

OLOF Tell me, what's that mournful murmur?

SEXTON A devout brother's praying for a poor soul. (*Goes*)

OLOF "Thou therefore gird up thy loins, and arise, and speak unto them all that I command thee"[11]—God help me! (*Throws himself onto a prayer stool; finds a piece of paper on it. Reads*) "Don't appear in the pulpit today; they're after your life!"—the tempter wrote that! (*Tears the paper to pieces*)

MOTHER (*enters*) You've gone astray, my son!

OLOF Who knows?

MOTHER *I* know! But, as your mother, I give you my hand. Turn back!

OLOF Where would you lead me?

MOTHER To the fear of God and virtue.

OLOF If the decision of the pope's chancery is fear of God and virtue, it's too late.

MOTHER It's not merely the doctrine; it's the life you're leading, too.

OLOF I know you mean the company I had last night, but I'm too proud to answer you. It wouldn't do any good, anyway.

MOTHER Oh, that I should get this reward for sacrificing so you could go away to study.

OLOF Your sacrifice won't be in vain, God willing. You're the one I have to thank for this day when I at last can step forward openly to speak the words of truth!

MOTHER Do you talk about truth, you, who have made yourself the prophet of lies?

OLOF That was a harsh word, mother!

MOTHER Have I and my people before me lived and believed and died in a lie?

[11] See Act I, note 3.

OLOF It *wasn't* a lie, but it has become a lie. When you were young, mother, you were right. When I get old, well, then I may be wrong. One doesn't grow with time.

MOTHER I don't understand you.

OLOF That's my only great sorrow. Everything I do and say from the purest of motives must seem like sin and ungodliness to you.

MOTHER Olof! I know you've made up your mind, I know you've gone astray—I can't do anything about that, for you know more than I do. God will surely bring you back, but I beg you not to rush into damnation today. Don't cut your life short!

OLOF What do you mean? Surely they won't kill me in the pulpit!

MOTHER Haven't you heard that Bishop Brask is negotiating with the pope for the introduction of the law that condemns heretics to the stake?

OLOF The inquisition?

MOTHER Yes! That's it!

OLOF Leave me, mother; I have to preach today!

MOTHER You mustn't!

OLOF Nothing will prevent me!

MOTHER I have prayed that God would change your heart—I'll tell you something, but you may not repeat it—I was weak with age, and my knees wouldn't support me—I sought out a servant of the Lord and asked him, who's closer to God, to read masses for your soul. He refused, because you've been excommunicated! Oh, it's terrible! God forgive me; I bribed his clear conscience with gold, with devil's gold, just to save you!

OLOF What are you saying, mother? It's not possible!

MOTHER (*takes* OLOF *by the hand and leads him to the left wall*): Listen! He's praying for you in the chapel!

OLOF So that was the mumbling! Who is he?

MOTHER Friar Mårten—

OLOF You're having that devil pray for me! Forgive me, mother—thank you, for you meant well, but—

MOTHER (*weeps; on her knees*) Olof! Olof!

OLOF Don't ask me! A mother's prayers can tempt the angels in heaven to desert their cause. The psalm's almost ended; I have to go. The people are waiting.

MOTHER You'll be the death of me, Olof!

OLOF (*violently*) The Lord will awaken you! (*Kisses her hand*) Don't say any more; I don't know what I'd answer.

MOTHER Listen! The people are murmuring.

OLOF I'm coming! I'm coming! The God who held His hand over Daniel in the lion's den will protect me, too.[12] (OLOF *goes. During the following scenes in the sacristy a powerful speaking voice can be heard, but the words cannot be made out. When the sermon has proceeded for a while, there is murmuring which quickly becomes shouts.*)

KRISTINA (*enters*)   Did you see him, mother?

MOTHER   Did you come, child? Why, I asked you to stay at home.

KRISTINA   Why mayn't I go into the house of the Lord? You're concealing something from me.

MOTHER   Go home, Kristina!

KRISTINA   Mayn't I hear Olof preach? Why, they're the words of God, aren't they, mother?

(MOTHER *remains silent.*)

KRISTINA   You don't answer! Why? Didn't Olof have permission to preach? Why do the people out there look so strange? They were muttering when I came.

MOTHER   Don't ask me. Go home, and thank God for your ignorance.

KRISTINA   Am I a child, that I mustn't be told . . .

MOTHER   Your soul is still pure and mustn't be sullied. You haven't anything to do with this struggle.

KRISTINA   Struggle? I felt there was something like that.

MOTHER   Yes, there's a struggle here, so go, go. You know what our lot is when men wage war.

KRISTINA   Tell me what it's about. Ignorance makes me unhappy. I can see a terrifying darkness and moving shadows. Give me light so that I may really know. Perhaps I know these ghosts.

MOTHER   You'll tremble when you see who they are.

KRISTINA   Let me tremble, then, rather than be tormented by this horrible calm!

MOTHER   Don't call the lightning from the clouds—it would crush you!

KRISTINA   You frighten me! But tell me the truth; I must know—or I'll ask someone else!

MOTHER   Have you decided to enter the convent?

KRISTINA   Father wants me to.

MOTHER   You're hesitating.

(KRISTINA *remains silent.*)

MOTHER   There's a bond that holds you?

KRISTINA   You know that.

MOTHER   I know, and you have to break it.

KRISTINA   That will soon be impossible.

[12] Daniel, 6.

MOTHER   I'll save you, child—you still can be saved; I'll give the Lord my greatest sacrifice if only one soul can be saved from damnation. My son!

KRISTINA   Olof?

MOTHER   Olof's lost, and I, his mother, have to tell you that.

KRISTINA   Lost?

MOTHER   He's a prophet of lies! The devil has captured his soul.

KRISTINA   (*violently*)   That isn't true!

MOTHER   Would to God it weren't!

KRISTINA   Why, why do you tell me this now for the first time?—but that's right, it's a lie! (*Goes to the door and opens it slightly*) See mother; there he stands. Is it the evil spirit who speaks through his mouth? Is it a fire from Hell that glows in his eyes? Does one utter lies with trembling lips? Can darkness radiate light? Don't you see the radiance about his head? You're wrong! I know that! I don't know what he's preaching, I don't know what he's denying, but he *is* right! He's right, and God is with him!

MOTHER   You don't know the world, child; you don't know the tricks of the devil. Watch out! (*She draws* KRISTINA *away from the door.*) You mayn't listen to him; your soul's weak; he's the apostle of Antichrist!

KRISTINA   Who is Antichrist?

MOTHER   He's Luther!

KRISTINA   You've never told me who Luther is, but if Olof is his apostle, Luther is great.

MOTHER   Luther is possessed by the devil!

KRISTINA   Why didn't anyone tell me that before? Now I don't believe it!

MOTHER   I'm telling you now—I wanted to protect you from the evil of the world, so I kept you in ignorance . . .

KRISTINA   I don't believe you! Let me go; I have to see him; I have to hear him; because he doesn't talk like the others.

MOTHER   Jesus, my Saviour! You, too, are possessed by the unclean spirit!

KRISTINA   (*at the door*)   "You should not bind the souls of men," he said. "You are free, because God has made you free!" Look, the people tremble at his words; they're getting up; they're murmuring. "You don't want freedom; woe unto you; that is a sin against the Holy Ghost."

SEXTON   (*enters*)   I don't think it's wise for you ladies to stay here; the people are getting restless. This won't end well for Master Olof.

MOTHER   Mary, Mother of God! What are you saying?

KRISTINA   Don't be afraid; the spirit of God is with him!

SEXTON   Well, I don't know about that, but he certainly can preach. As old a sinner as I am, I couldn't keep from weeping up where I was sitting in the organ loft. I don't understand how a heretic and an Antichrist can preach like that. Well, I'll say this, that Luther! (*Shouts out in the church*) There! Now there'll be something terrible again, and the king had to be away, too.

MOTHER   Let's leave. If God is with him, they can't hurt him. If it's the devil—then Thy will be done, Lord, but forgive him.

(*Shouts outside. They leave. The stage is empty for a moment and only* OLOF's *voice [now stronger than ever] can be heard—interrupted by shouts and throwing of stones.* KRISTINA *comes back alone and shuts the door from the inside and throws herself onto a prayer stool. Heavy blows on the door can be heard; there is a tumult in the church. Then it becomes quiet, and* OLOF *comes down with a bloody forehead and disheveled appearance.*)

OLOF   (*without seeing* KRISTINA, *throws himself in a chair*)   In vain! They don't want to! I loosen the prisoner's bonds, and he strikes me; I tell him, "You're free!" and he doesn't believe me. Is that word so great that there isn't room for it in a human brain? If there were only one who believed—but now I'm alone—a fool, whom no one understands . . .

KRISTINA   (*goes up to him*)   Olof! I believe in you!

OLOF   Kristina!

KRISTINA   You are right!

OLOF   How do you know?

KRISTINA   I don't know, but I believe. I heard you just now.

OLOF   And you don't curse me?

KRISTINA   You're preaching the word of God, aren't you?

OLOF   Yes!

KRISTINA   Why hasn't anyone told us this before? Why do they speak a language we don't understand?

OLOF   Girl, who put those words on your tongue?

KRISTINA   Who? I hadn't thought about that.

OLOF   Your father?

KRISTINA   He wants me to enter a convent.

OLOF   Has it gone that far? And what do you want to do?

KRISTINA   (*looks at* OLOF's *injured forehead*)   They've hurt you, Olof; for goodness' sake, let me bandage your forehead.

OLOF   (*sits down*)   Kristina, have I destroyed your faith?

KRISTINA   (*takes her handkerchief, tears it, and bandages* OLOF *during the following speech*)   My faith? I don't understand—tell me, who is Luther?

OLOF   I mustn't say.

KRISTINA   Always the same answer! That's what my father says, your mother says it, and you, too! Don't people dare to tell me the truth? Is truth dangerous?

OLOF   Look! (*Pointing at his forehead*) Truth is dangerous!

KRISTINA   So you want to have me shut up in a convent cell to a living death in ignorance.

(OLOF *remains silent.*)

KRISTINA   You want me to weep my life away, my youth, and pray the long eternal prayers until my soul falls asleep. No—I don't want that, now that I've awakened; people are struggling around me, they're suffering and are in despair; I have seen that, but I mayn't have a part in it, not even look on, not even know what they're struggling about; people have kept me in a beastlike sleep. Don't you think I have a soul, which can't be satisfied with bread or empty prayers that have been put into my mouth? "Don't bind the spirits," you said. If you only knew how those words struck me— they brought daylight, and the wild shouts out there sounded like the morning songs of the birds . . .

OLOF   Kristina! You're a woman; you weren't born to fight.

KRISTINA   But at least let me suffer—just so I don't have to stay asleep. You see, God awakened me all the same. You'd never have dared to tell me who Antichrist is, you'd never have let me know who Luther is, and when your mother frightened me by saying you were a Luther, I blessed Luther! Whether he's a heretic or a believer, I don't know, I don't care, for neither Luther nor the pope nor Antichrist can bring peace to my immortal soul when I don't have faith in the eternal God!

OLOF   Kristina! If you want to, you can be by my side and help me, for you are the one I love.

KRISTINA   Now I can say yes to you, because I know what I want, and without appealing to my father, for I am free! I *am* free!

OLOF   Do you know what lies ahead of you, too?

KRISTINA   Now I do. And you won't have to destroy any false dreams— they're gone; I've dreamt about the knight who'd come to offer me a kingdom and who'd talk about flowers and love—Olof, I want to be your wife. Here's my hand. I'll tell you, though, that you were never the knight of my dreams. Thank God he never came— he'd have gone, too—like a dream.

OLOF   You'll be mine, Kristina, and you'll be happy, for you were the one who was always with me when I was in trouble and temptation, and now you'll be by my side. You were the fair maiden of my dreams, imprisoned in the tower by the stern lord of the castle. Now you're mine!

KRISTINA   Beware of dreams, Olof! (*Blows on the door*)

OLOF   Who is it?

GERT *(outside)*   Gert!

OLOF   What will he say? My promise!

KRISTINA   Are you afraid? Shall I open?
   (OLOF *opens the door.*)

GERT *(startled)*   Kristina? Olof! You've broken your promise!

OLOF   No.

GERT   You're lying! You've stolen my child, my only comfort!

KRISTINA   Olof isn't lying!

GERT   You were in church, Kristina?

KRISTINA   I've heard what you didn't want me to hear.

GERT   The Lord begrudged me my only joy.

OLOF   The current you wanted to free takes its sacrifices where it will.

GERT   You have stolen my child!

OLOF   Give her to me, Father Gert.

GERT   Never!

OLOF   Isn't she free?

GERT   She's my child!

OLOF   Don't you preach freedom? She's mine! God has given her to me, and you can't take her from me!

GERT   God be praised, you're a—priest!

OLOF AND KRISTINA   A priest!

GERT   So—you can't marry!

OLOF   If I do anyway?

GERT   Do you dare?

OLOF   Yes!

GERT   Do you want a husband who has been excommunicated, Kristina?

KRISTINA   I don't know what that means.

OLOF   You see, Gert.

GERT   God, Thy punishment is heavy.

OLOF   The truth is for everyone.

GERT   Your love is greater than mine. That was only selfishness. God bless you! Now I'm alone. (*Embraces them both*) There, there. Go home, Kristina, and calm them. I want to talk with Olof. (KRISTINA *goes.*) Now you're mine!

OLOF   What's that?

GERT   My kinsman!—did you get my letter?

OLOF   So you were the one who advised me not to preach!

GERT   The very opposite, though I did express myself a little strangely.

OLOF   I don't understand.

GERT   No, no. You're still too young, so you need a Providence. To a man like you one has to say, "Don't do that," when one wants to get something done.

OLOF   Why weren't you in church with your followers?

GERT   Only the sick need doctors; we were at work elsewhere. You've done good work today, and I see you got your wages. I've set you free today, Olof.

OLOF   You?

GERT   The king ordered you to calm the rebels, and look at what you've done.

OLOF   I'm beginning to understand, Father Gert.

GERT   I'm glad. Yes, you've really stirred things up.

OLOF   Yes, I have.

GERT   What do you think the king will say about that?

OLOF   I'll answer for that!

GERT   Good!

OLOF   And the king will approve what I've done, because he wants a reformation, but doesn't dare to do it himself yet.

GERT   Fool!

OLOF   I see you want to set me against the lawful king.

GERT   Listen, how many masters do you think you can serve? (OLOF *remains silent.*)

GERT   The king's here!

OLOF   What's that?

GERT   He just got back.

OLOF   And the Anabaptists!

GERT   In jail, of course.

OLOF   And you stand here absolutely calm.

GERT   I'm old, I've raged like you, too, but I only got tired. Rink and Knipperdollink were my vanguard. They had to fall, that's plain; now my work begins. (*Drums are beaten out on the street.*)

OLOF   What was that?

GERT   The royal drums accompanying the prisoners to jail. Come over here and see.

OLOF   (*gets up on a bench and looks out through the window*) What in the world! Women and children dragged off by soldiers!

GERT   Oh, well, they threw stones at the king's guards. That certainly won't do.

OLOF   Are they going to take fools or sick people to prison?

GERT   There are two kinds of fools: you put one kind into insane asylums and give them pills and cold baths; you cut off the heads of the other kind. That's a radical cure, but then that kind's dangerous.

OLOF   I'll go to the king; he can't want these atrocities.

GERT   Watch out for your head, Olof!

OLOF   Watch out for yourself, Father Gert!

GERT   I'm in no danger. I'm certified to the insane asylum.

OLOF   I can't bear to see this; I'll go to the king, even if it costs my life! (*Goes toward the door*)

GERT   This is a matter the king doesn't decide. Turn to the law.

OLOF   The king is the law.

GERT   Yes, unfortunately! If the horse knew his strength, he wouldn't be crazy enough to wear the harness—someday when he gets wise, he'll run away from his oppressor—then they'll say he's crazy . . . Let's pray to God to save the minds of these poor people.

CURTAIN

Act III

SCENE I

A room in Stockholm Castle. In the background a gallery, which is later divided by means of a curtain. An old SERVANT *is walking in the gallery.*

OLOF (*enters*)   Is the king receiving today?

SERVANT   Yes.

OLOF   Do you know why they've let me wait in vain four days in a row?

SERVANT   No, I don't. I don't know anything about that.

OLOF   It seems strange I haven't been received.

SERVANT   What did you want?

OLOF   That doesn't concern you.

SERVANT   No, no. I understand that, but I thought I perhaps could throw some light on it.

OLOF   Are you usually in charge of the king's audiences?

SERVANT   No, not at all, but you see anyone who hears as much as I do knows a little about everything. (*Pause*)

OLOF   Will it be long?

(SERVANT *pretends that he doesn't hear.*)

OLOF   Do you know if the king is coming soon?

SERVANT (*with his back to* OLOF)   What?

OLOF   Don't you know whom you're talking to?

SERVANT   No, I don't.

OLOF   I'm the king's secretary.

SERVANT   Goodness, are you Master Olof? I knew your father, Peter Smith—you see, I'm from Örebro, too.

OLOF   Can't you be polite anyway?

SERVANT   Oh, yes. That's how it goes when a person gets up in the world —he forgets his poor ancestors.

OLOF   If my father actually honored you with his acquaintance—maybe he did—but I don't believe he put you in his place as father when he died.

SERVANT   Well, well. There you see. Your poor mother! (*Goes to the left. Pause. Then* LARS SIGGESON SPARRE *enters from the right*).

SPARRE   (*throws his coat to* OLOF *without looking at him*)   Is the king coming soon?

OLOF   (*takes the coat and throws it on the floor*)   I don't know!

SPARRE   Get me a chair.

OLOF   That's not my job!

SPARRE   I haven't any idea what the doorkeeper's duties are.

OLOF   I'm not the doorkeeper!

SPARRE   It doesn't concern me what you are; I don't carry a list of the servants. But be polite!
(OLOF *says nothing.*)

SPARRE   Are you going to do anything? I think the devil's got you!

OLOF   Excuse me! It isn't part of my job as secretary to wait on people!

SPARRE   So! Master Olof! So it amuses you to sit by the door acting like a servant to reveal yourself later as God! I thought you were a proud man. (*He picks up the coat and puts it on the bench.*)

OLOF   Lord Marshal!

SPARRE   No! You're a vain upstart! Please come here and sit down, Mr. Secretary. (*Shows him a place; then goes into a side room.* OLOF *sits down. A young* NOBLEMAN *greets* OLOF *from the gallery.*)

NOBLEMAN   Good morning, Mr. Secretary. No one here yet? Well, how are things in Stockholm? I've come directly from Malmö.

OLOF   Things are pretty bad here.

NOBLEMAN   Yes, so I've heard. The mob's cutting up as usual when the king turns his back. And those stupid priests! Forgive me, you're a freethinker, aren't you, Mr. Secretary?

OLOF   I don't understand.

NOBLEMAN   Don't be embarrassed. You see, I've had my training in Paris. Francis I,[1] oh *Saint-Sauver!*[2] He's a man who'll go far! Do you

[1] King of France (reign: 1515–47).
[2] Saint Savior!

know what he said to me at a *bal masqué*[3] at the carnival recently? (OLOF *says nothing.*) "*Monsieur,*" he said, "*la religion est morte, est morte,*"[4] said he; but that doesn't keep him from attending mass!

OLOF So-o!

NOBLEMAN And do you know what he said when I asked him why he did? "*Poésie! Poésie!*"[5] he said. Isn't he divine?

OLOF What did you say then?

NOBLEMAN "Your Majesty," I said, in French, of course, "happy the country which has a king who can look beyond the narrowness of his time so that he sees what the spirit of the time demands, but who all the same doesn't force the sleeping masses to accept a higher point of view for which they'd need centuries to get ready." Wasn't that nicely said?

OLOF Yes, indeed. But I suspect it lost something in translation. Things like that ought to be said in French.

NOBLEMAN (*not paying attention*) You're absolutely right! You know, you ought to make your fortune. You're so far ahead of your time.

OLOF I don't think I'll get that far. Unfortunately, my training was neglected; I got it in Germany, you know, and the Germans haven't got beyond religion yet.

NOBLEMAN Yes, yes. Can you tell me why they're making all that fuss about that reformation in Germany? Luther's an enlightened man, I know, I believe it, but he could keep it to himself or at least not throw out sparks among the crude masses, which will always be like casting pearls before swine. If one looks at the time, if one absorbs the great movements of thought a little, one can easily see the causes of the disturbances in balance that now are dominant in the great civilized countries. I'm not talking about Sweden, for it isn't civilized. Do you know what the center of gravity is, the one whose destruction leads to the dissolution of everything, and without whose stabilizing force everything's turned upside down? It's the aristocracy! The aristocracy is the intelligentsia! The feudal system's on its way out—*hoc est*[6] the world, education's on the decline, culture's dying! Yes, yes! So you don't believe that! But if you had the slightest historical sense, you'd see it. The aristocracy did the crusades, the aristocracy did this, the aristocracy did that. Why is Germany torn to pieces? Well, the peasants revolt against the aristocracy. Cut off their own heads. Why is France

[3] Masked ball.
[4] Religion is dead, dead.
[5] Poetry.
[6] Thus is.

strong? *La France*, well, because France is the aristocracy and the aristocracy is France; they're identical concepts; they're inseparable. Why, I ask again, is Sweden just now shaken to its very foundations? Well, the aristocracy is crushed. Christian II was a man of genius, he knew how to conquer a country, he sawed off not a leg or an arm; no, he knocked off the head! Oh, well! Sweden will be saved; the king knows how. The aristocracy will be restored, and the church crushed. What do you say to that?

OLOF (*gets up*) Nothing! (*Pause*) Are you a freethinker?

NOBLEMAN Of course.

OLOF So you don't believe Balaam's ass could talk?[7]

NOBLEMAN Good heavens, no!

OLOF But I do!

NOBLEMAN Really!

LARS ANDERSSON (*enters*) God's peace, Olof.

OLOF (*embraces him*) Welcome, Lars.

NOBLEMAN (*goes*) Rabble!

LARS How do you like it here?

OLOF It's stuffy.

LARS Well, yes.

OLOF And the ceiling's so low.

LARS That's why they have a hard time walking upright.

OLOF During the last ten minutes I've become such a courtier that I've learned to keep still when an ass talks.

LARS That doesn't do any harm.

OLOF What does the king think?

LARS He doesn't say. (*People have begun to gather.*)

OLOF How does he look?

LARS Like a question mark with several exclamation points after it.
(BRASK *enters; everyone gives way to him* LARS SPARRE *thas returned, goes up to the* BISHOP, *and greets him.* OLOF *greets* BRASK, *who looks amazed.*)

BRASK (*to* SPARRE) Is this the clerks' room?

SPARRE It shouldn't be, but our king is so infinitely gracious.

BRASK Condescending, you mean.

SPARRE Exactly!

BRASK Many audiences today.

SPARRE Mostly formal calls after His Majesty's happy return.

BRASK It's a pleasure, Lord Marshal, to express my sincere felicitations to the king on the happy solution to the problem.

[7] Numbers, 22–24.

SPARRE You're much too courteous, Lord Bishop, to take the trouble to make such a long journey at your age.

BRASK Yes, yes. And I can't always rely on my health.

SPARRE So your health isn't too good, my lord. It's always sad not to have one's full strength, especially when one occupies such a high and responsible position.

BRASK You're looking well, Lord Marshal.

SPARRE Yes, God be praised! (*Pause*)

BRASK (*sits down*) Isn't there a draft, Lord Marshal?

SPARRE Yes—there is. Perhaps we should have the doors closed.

BRASK No, no, thank you; I don't think that's necessary. (*Pause*)

SPARRE The king certainly is taking his time.

BRASK Yes.

SPARRE Probably it isn't worth waiting.

BRASK Probably.

SPARRE May I call your servants, my lord?

BRASK Since I've waited this long, I think I'll stay. (*Pause*)

SERVANT His Majesty!

KING (*enters*) Welcome, my lords. (*Sits down at a table*) If you'll step out into the antechamber, my lords, I'll receive you one at a time. (*All go except* BRASK.) Our marshal will stay.

BRASK Your Majesty!

KING (*with raised voice*) Lord Sparre! (BRASK *goes.* SPARRE *stays. Pause*) Speak up. What shall I do?

SPARRE Your Majesty! The state has lost its main support, so it's tottering; the state has an enemy that has become more powerful than it is. Raise the support, the aristocracy, and crush the enemy, the church.

KING I don't dare!

SPARRE Your Majesty has to!

KING What's that?

SPARRE In the first place: Brask's negotiating with the pope for the introduction of the inquisition; Lübeck's insisting on its shameless demands, and threatens war; the treasury's empty; there are rebellions in every part of the country . . .

KING Enough! But the people are with me!

SPARRE Excuse me, no! The Dalesmen, for example: a spoiled tribe, who argue with the Lübeckers over the honor of having given Sweden a king; they're ready to revolt at the first chance and come up with demands like these: "No foreign fashions with fancifully cut multicolored clothes such as those which have just been introduced at the king's court may be used!"

KING   God's death!

SPARRE   "Everyone who eats meat on Fridays or Saturdays shall be burned alive or otherwise killed." Further: "No new faith or Lutheran doctrine may be forced upon us." What a faithless, spoiled people!

KING   They showed they were men once, all the same!

SPARRE   When fire was threatening them, it wasn't strange that they carried water themselves. And how often haven't they broken faith and promise! No! They've heard their praises sung so often they call their crude insolence old-fashioned Swedish honesty.

KING   You're a nobleman!

SPARRE   Yes, and I'm convinced the yeomen have finished playing their part: the expulsion of the enemy by crude strength. Your Majesty! Crush the church, for it keeps the people in bondage; take the church's gold and pay the kingdom's debt—and return to the ruined aristocracy what the church has got from the lords through trickery.

KING   Call Brask!

SPARRE   Your Majesty!

KING   Bishop Brask! (SPARRE *goes.* BRASK *enters.*)

KING   Please speak out, Lord Bishop.

BRASK   I want to extend our congratulations for . . .

KING   Thanks, Lord Bishop. Go on.

BRASK   Unfortunately, there have been rumors of complaints from various parts of the kingdom about the unpaid loans of silver from the church that Your Majesty has made.

KING   And you're demanding payment now! Are all the chalices really needed for communion?

BRASK   Yes.

KING   Let them drink out of pewter, then!

BRASK   Your Majesty!

KING   Is there anything else?

BRASK   The worst of all—heresy.

KING   That doesn't concern me; I'm not the pope.

BRASK   I'll tell Your Majesty this: the church will insist on what's coming to it, even if it should get into conflict—

KING   With whom?

BRASK   With the state!

KING   The devil take your church! Now it's said!

BRASK   I know!

KING   And you waited only to hear it directly from me?

BRASK   Yes!

KING   Watch out! You travel with two hundred men in your retinue and dine on silver while the people eat bark.

BRASK   You take too narrow a view of the matter, Your Majesty.

KING   Do you know Luther, then? You're an enlightened man. What sort of phenomenon is he? What do you say about the movements under way throughout Europe?

BRASK   A step forward in reverse! Luther's role is simply to purge what is old, centuries-old, and tried, so that it may be purified and through conflict go forward in victory.

KING   I'm not interested in your learned arguments.

BRASK   But Your Majesty takes criminals under his protection and interferes with the rights of the church! Master Olof has seriously offended the church.

KING   Well, excommunicate him.

BRASK   We have, but he's in Your Majesty's service anyway.

KING   What else do you want to do to him? Tell me that. (*Pause*)

BRASK   Moreover, he's said to have gone so far as to have married secretly against canonical law.[8]

KING   Well! That has gone fast!

BRASK   It doesn't concern Your Majesty, perhaps; but what if he stirs up the people?

KING   Then I'll take charge! Anything else?

BRASK   (*after a pause*)   For the sake of Heaven, don't plunge the country into ruin! It's not yet ready for a new faith. We are frail reeds that can be bent, but the faith, the church, never!

KING   (*gives him his hand*)   You're probably right. Let's be enemies, Bishop Hans, rather than false friends!

BRASK   Fine! But never do what you'll regret. Every stone you tear from the church the people will throw at you!

KING   Don't force me to extremes, bishop, for then we'll get the same terrible spectacles as in Germany.[9] For the last time: Will you make concessions if the welfare of the country is at stake?

BRASK   The church—

KING   The church first, I see. Farewell! (BRASK *leaves.* SPARRE *enters.*)

KING   The bishop confirmed what you said. Yes, that was the idea. Get masons that can tear down; the walls may stand, the crosses may remain on the roofs and the bells in the towers, but I'll smash the cellars; one starts with the foundation, you see.

---

[8] Olof was married on February 12, 1525 (Luther did not marry until June of that year).

[9] See Act I, note 8.

SPARRE   But the people will be convinced they're being robbed of their faith; they must be enlightened.

KING   We'll let Master Olof preach.

SPARRE   Master Olof's a dangerous fellow.

KING   He's needed now.

SPARRE   He has been behaving like an Anabaptist instead of fighting them.

KING   I know. That will come later. Send him in!

SPARRE   Chancellor Lars is better.

KING   Bring in both of them.

SPARRE   Or Olof's brother, Lars Perti.

KING   Won't do yet. He's too faint-hearted to fight. His time will come.
(SPARRE *brings in* OLOF *and* CHANCELLOR LARS [ANDERSSON].)

KING (*to the* CHANCELLOR)   Do you want to help me, Lars?

LARS   With the church?

KING   Yes; It's to be torn down!

LARS   I'm not the man for that. But if Your Majesty turns to Master Olof!

KING   So you don't want to?

LARS   I can't. But I can give you a weapon! (*Hands the* KING *a copy of the new translation of the Bible*)[10]

KING   The Holy Scriptures! That's a good weapon! Do you want to handle this, Olof?

OLOF   Yes, with God's help!

KING (*signals to* LARS *to leave; he exits*)   Are you calm yet, Olof? (OLOF *does not answer.*) I gave you four days in which to think it over. How have you handled your assignment?

OLOF (*violently*)   I have spoken to the people—

KING   So you're still running a temperature! You intend to defend the crazy fools they call Anabaptists?

OLOF (*courageously*)   Yes!

KING   Easy! You got married in a hurry?

OLOF   Yes!

KING   You've been excommunicated?

OLOF   Yes!

KING   And you're just as daring anyway. And if you're sent to the gallows with the other agitators, what would you say?

OLOF   I'd regret I didn't get to carry out my mission, but I'd thank God for what I've been allowed to do.

KING   That's good. Do you dare to go up to the old owl's nest Uppsala

---

[10] The Swedish translation of the New Testament (1526) was a joint effort in which Olof played a major role.

and tell the professors that the pope isn't God and hasn't anything to do with Sweden?[11]

OLOF   Merely that?

KING   Do you want to tell them the Bible alone is the word of God?

OLOF   Nothing more?

KING   You may not mention Luther by name!

OLOF   (*after consideration*)   Then I don't want to.

KING   You'd rather go to your death?

OLOF   No. But my king needs me.

KING   It isn't noble of you, Olof, to make use of my misfortune. Say what you want; but you'll have to excuse me if I take back something later.

OLOF   One doesn't bargain about the truth.

KING   God's death! (*Changing his tone of voice*) Do as you want!

OLOF   (*kneeling*)   May I speak the whole truth?

KING   Yes!

OLOF   Then my life won't be wasted if I cast merely one spark of doubt into the souls of the sleeping people. So there's to be a reformation!

KING   (*after a pause*)   Yes! (*Pause*)

OLOF   (*frightened*)   What will happen to the Anabaptists?

KING   You're asking me? They're going to die!

OLOF   Would Your Majesty permit one question?

KING   Tell me, what do these crazy fools want?

OLOF   The tragedy is that they themselves don't really know. And if I were to say it . . .

KING   Speak up! (GERT *enters suddenly, acting as if he were insane.*) Who are you that dare to force your way in?

GERT   I ask most humbly that Your Majesty certify the correctness of this statement.

KING   Wait till you're called!

GERT   Yes, I can, but the guards don't want to wait for me! See, I ran away from prison because I didn't belong there.

KING   Were you with the Anabaptists?

GERT   Yes, I happened to be with them, but I have a certificate that I belong in the insane asylum, Department 3 for Incurables, Cell 7.

KING   (*to* OLOF)   Call the guards!

GERT   No, that's unnecessary; all I ask is justice, and the guards don't handle that.

---

[11] In December, 1524, Olof went with the king to Uppsala, where he debated Dr. Peder Galle, professor of theology, who defended Catholicism and the rights of the church.

KING (*stares fixedly at* GERT) Didn't you take part in the outrage committed in the city churches?

GERT Of course. A sane person surely can't behave in such a crazy way.
    We merely wanted to make a few minor changes in the style, you
    see; the ceiling was too low, we thought.

KING What did you really want?

GERT Oh! We want so much, though we haven't had time for half of it
    yet; yes, we want so much and so fast that one's thoughts don't
    keep up with it, and that's why we're a little behind. Yes, and we
    wanted to repaper a little in the church and take out the windows
    because it smelled musty. Yes, and we wanted still more, but we'll
    have to let it go just now.

KING (*to* OLOF) That's a dangerous disease; it can't be anything else.

OLOF Who knows?

KING Now I am tired. I'll give you fourteen days to prepare yourself.
    Your hand on helping me.

OLOF I'll do my share.

KING Order that they take Rink and Knipperdollink to Malmö.

OLOF And then?

KING They may escape! Have that fool taken to the insane asylum.
    Farewell. (*Exits*)

GERT (*shakes his fist at the* KING) Shall we go?

OLOF Where?

GERT Home! (OLOF *doesn't say anything.*) Do you want to take your
    father-in-law to the insane asylum, Olof?

OLOF Want to? It's my duty!

GERT Aren't there higher duties than obeying an order?

OLOF Are you starting that again?

GERT What will Kristina say when you've put her father away with
    madmen?

OLOF Don't tempt me.

GERT Do you see how hard it is to serve the king? (OLOF *says nothing.*)
    Poor boy, I won't trouble you. Here's absolution for your conscience. (*Shows* OLOF *a paper*)

OLOF What is it?

GERT A health certificate. You see, one has to be a madman among the
    sane and sane among the madmen.

OLOF How did you get it?

GERT Don't you think I deserve it?

OLOF I don't know.

GERT That's true; you don't dare yet.

SERVANT (*enters*) Please go; we have to sweep in here.

GERT Probably it ought to be aired out, too?

SERVANT Yes, indeed.

GERT Don't forget to open the windows.

SERVANT No, indeed. That's certainly needed; we don't usually have such company.

GERT Listen, man, I have greetings from your father.

SERVANT Really!

GERT Maybe you don't know him.

SERVANT Yes, indeed!

GERT You know what he said?

SERVANT No.

GERT You should wet your broom, he said; otherwise you'll get dust on you.

SERVANT I don't understand.

GERT That's your excuse. (*Exits*)

SERVANT Riffraff!

CURTAIN

SCENE II

OLOF's *study. The sunlight is streaming through the windows at the back. Trees outside.* KRISTINA *is standing by a window watering flowers; she chats with the birds in a cage as she does so.* OLOF *is sitting writing; with an expression of impatience he looks up from the papers toward* KRISTINA *as if he wanted her to be quiet. This is repeated several times until* KRISTINA *knocks down a flower pot.* OLOF *stamps gently on the floor.*

KRISTINA Poor plant! See, Olof, four buds broke off!

OLOF I see.

KRISTINA No, you don't. Come over here.

OLOF Dear, I haven't time.

KRISTINA You haven't even looked at the goldfinches I bought you this morning. Don't you think they sing beautifully?

OLOF Oh, yes.

KRISTINA Oh, yes?

OLOF I have such a hard time working when they screech!

KRISTINA They certainly don't screech, Olof, but apparently you prefer a screaming night owl! What does the owl on your signet ring mean?

OLOF   The owl's an old symbol of wisdom.

KRISTINA   That's stupid, I think—the wise man certainly doesn't love the dark.

OLOF   The wise man hates the dark and the night, but he makes night day with his sharp eyes.

KRISTINA   Why are you always right, Olof? Can you tell me why?

OLOF   Because I know it pleases you to admit I'm right, dear.

KRISTINA   Now you're right again. What are you writing?

OLOF   I'm translating.

KRISTINA   Read a little of it to me.

OLOF   I don't think you'd understand this.

KRISTINA   Understand! Isn't it Swedish?

OLOF   Yes, but it's too abstract for you.

KRISTINA   Abstract? What does that mean?

OLOF   You wouldn't understand me if I told you, but if you don't understand what I'm going to read, you'll know what abstract means.

KRISTINA   (*picks up a half-finished piece of knitting*)   Read while I knit.

OLOF   Listen carefully, and forgive me if it bores you.

KRISTINA   I'll understand you; I want to.

OLOF   (*reads*)   "Matter conceived in its abstraction from form is completely without predictability, undefined, and indistinguishable. Because not from pure nonbeing but only from reality's nonbeing, that is to say, out of being as a possibility, can anything originate. The possible being is just as little nonbeing as reality. Every existence is therefore a realized possibility. Matter is thus for Aristotle a far more positive substratum than for Plato, who explains matter as a pure nonbeing. From this one can see how Aristotle could conceive matter in contrast to form as a positive negative."

KRISTINA   (*throws her knitting aside*)   Stop! Why can't I grasp that? Don't I have the same mental faculties as you? I'm ashamed. Olof, that you have such a poor wife she can't understand what you're saying; no, I'll stay with my knitting; I'll clean and dust your study; I'll learn to read the wishes in your eyes at least. I'll be your slave, but I'll never, never, understand you! Oh, Olof, I'm not worthy of you! Why did you marry me? You overestimated me in a moment of infatuation. You'll regret it, and we'll both be unhappy!

OLOF   Kristina! Calm yourself, dear. Sit down by me. (*Picks up her knitting*)   Will you believe me if I tell you it's impossible for me to do work like this? I'll never be able to. So aren't you more skillful than I, and I less than you?

KRISTINA   Why can't you?

OLOF   For the same reason you didn't understand what I read; I've never learned. Will you be happy again if I tell you that you can learn to understand this book—which you ought to distinguish very carefully from me—while I never can learn your work?

KRISTINA   Why not?

OLOF   I'm not made for it, and I don't want to.

KRISTINA   But if you wanted to?

OLOF   You see, dear, that's just my weakness—I never can want to. Believe me, you're stronger than I; you control your will; I can't control mine.

KRISTINA   Could I learn to understand that book?

OLOF   I'm sure of it. But you mustn't.

KRISTINA   Am I still to be kept in ignorance?

OLOF   No, no, don't misunderstand me. The minute you understand what I understand, you'd lose your respect for me . . .

KRISTINA   As a god . . .

OLOF   If you wish! But, believe me, you'd lose what makes you greater than I: the strength to subdue your will, and then you'd be less than I, and I wouldn't respect you. Believe me: our happiness lies in overestimating each other; let's keep that illusion.

KRISTINA   Now I can't understand you, but I'll have to believe in you, Olof. You're right.

OLOF   Please, Kristina, I need to be alone.

KRISTINA   Do I disturb you?

OLOF   I'm busy with very serious matters. I'm expecting the decision today, you know. The king has abdicated because they don't want to accept his proposals.[12] I'll either have reached my goal today or have to begin the struggle over again.

KRISTINA   Mayn't I be happy today, Olof, on midsummer eve?

OLOF   Why are you so happy today?

KRISTINA   Shouldn't I be happy when I've been released from bondage, when I've become your wife?

OLOF   Forgive me, if my joy is heavier to bear, for my happiness has cost me—a mother.

KRISTINA   I know; I feel it keenly, too. When she finds out we're married, your mother will forgive you but curse me. Who'll have the

---

[12] In 1527, at Västerås, Gustav threatened to abdicate if the Parliament did not agree to his demands, which included the restoration of the church's surplus wealth to the crown, nobles, and people; the transfer to the crown of the bishops' castles; a ban on appeals to Rome; and a prohibition on purchasing episcopal offices from Rome. The Parliament agreed.

heavier burden? But that doesn't matter; it's for your sake! I know
this: great struggles lie before you, daring thoughts are born in
your brain, and I can never take part in the struggle, can never
help you with advice, never defend you against those who defame
you, but I have to look on anyway, and the whole time live in my
little world, busy myself with these little things, which I think you
don't appreciate, but which you'd miss. Olof, I can't weep with
you; help me by smiling with me; step down from your heights
which I can't attain; turn home now and then from the struggles
you wage up on the mountains; I can't come up to you; come
down to me for a moment. Olof, forgive me if I'm talking childishly.
You're a man sent by God, I know, and I've felt the blessing of
your words, but you're more than that; you're a human being—
you're my husband or should be! You won't fall from your heights
if you put away your solemn talk and let the clouds disappear
from your forehead for once. Are you too great to look at a flower
or to listen to a bird! I put the flowers on your table to rest your
eyes; you let the maid carry them out, because you get a headache;
I wanted to interrupt the lonely silence of your studies so I gave
you the song of the birds; you call it screeching; I asked you to
come to dinner a while ago; you didn't have time; I want to talk
with you; you don't have time; you despise this little reality, and
still you've given it to me. You don't want to raise me; at least
don't trample me down! I'll take away everything that disturbs
you. You won't be disturbed by me—or my rubbish. (*She throws
the flowers out of the window, takes the bird cage, and is going.*)

OLOF   Kristina, dear child, forgive me! You don't understand me!

KRISTINA   Always the same; you don't understand me! Oh, now I know!
That moment in the sacristy made me old—so old I became a
child again.

OLOF   Dear, I'll look at your birds and babble with your flowers.

KRISTINA   (*carries the cage away*)   Oh, no! I'm done with babbling now
—it'll be serious here; don't be afraid of my noisy happiness. I just
pretended for your sake, but since it doesn't suit you and your
serious calling . . . (*She bursts into tears.*)

OLOF   (*embraces and kisses her*)   Kristina! Kristina! Now you're right.
Forgive me.

KRISTINA   Olof, you gave an unfortunate gift when you gave me freedom.
I can't manage it. I have to have someone to obey.

OLOF   You will, but let's not say anything more about this. We'll go to
dinner; I'm quite hungry.

KRISTINA   (*happily*)   Can you really be hungry? (*Looks out through the*

window and makes a movement of amazement) Go ahead, Olof.
I'll come right away; I want to straighten up a little first.

OLOF (*goes*)   Don't make me wait for you as long as you've had to
for me.

(KRISTINA *extends her hands as if in prayer and stations herself to
wait for someone who will come through the street door. Pause.*)

MOTHER (*enters, goes past* KRISTINA *without turning to her*)   Is Master
Olof at home?

KRISTINA (*who has gone up to her in a friendly fashion, stops with
amazement and then assumes the same tone as the* MOTHER)   No.
Won't you sit down? He'll soon be here.

MOTHER   Thank you. (*Sits down. Pause*) Bring me a glass of water.
(KRISTINA *does.*) Leave me.

KRISTINA   As his wife it's my duty to keep you company.

MOTHER   I didn't know a priest's housekeeper calls herself wife.

KRISTINA   I'm Master Olof's wife in the sight of God. So you don't know
we're married!

MOTHER   You're a prostitute! That I do know.

KRISTINA   I don't understand that word.

MOTHER   You're the kind of woman that Master Olof talked to that evening in the tavern.

KRISTINA   The one who looked so unhappy. Well, I'm not happy!

MOTHER   No, I should think not! Get out of my sight; your presence is
an insult to me!

KRISTINA (*kneels*)   For your son's sake, don't abuse me!

MOTHER   With a mother's power I order you to leave my son's house,
whose threshold you've desecrated.

KRISTINA   As his wife I'll open my door to anyone I please. I would have
closed it to you if I could have guessed what you'd say.

MOTHER   Big words, indeed! I order you to go!

KRISTINA   With what right do you dare to force your way into this house
and drive me out of my home? You bore a child, you brought
him up; that was your duty, your destiny, and you can thank God
that you've been permitted to fulfill it so well, for not everyone
is that fortunate; you're approaching your grave; step aside before
it's over; or have you brought up your son so badly that he's still
a child and still needs your guidance? If you want gratitude, look
for it, but in another way. Do you think it's the child's lot to
sacrifice his life simply to show you gratitude? His calling says,
"Go there!" You call, "Ungrateful boy, come here!" Is he to go
astray, is he to sacrifice his powers, which belong to the community,
to humanity, simply to satisfy your personal little selfishness, or
do you think your having given him life and upbringing even

deserves gratitude? Wasn't that the purpose and function of your life? Shouldn't you thank God that you've had such a great mission? Or did you do it simply to demand gratitude for half a lifetime? Don't you know that by the word gratitude you tear down what you once built up? And what right do you have to interfere with me? Is marriage the mortgaging of my free will to the one whom nature has made the mother or father of my husband, who unfortunately couldn't exist without both? You're not my mother, and I never vowed to be faithful to you when I married Olof, and I have enough respect for my husband so that I won't let anyone insult him, even his mother! That's why I've said all this!

MOTHER   Now I see the fruits of the doctrines my son is spreading!

KRISTINA   If you want to abuse your son, you'll do it in his presence! (*She goes to the door and calls.*) Olof!

MOTHER   So you're already that sly!

KRISTINA   Already? I've always been, I think, even if I didn't know it until I needed it.

OLOF (*enters*)   Mother! Welcome!

MOTHER   Thank you, my son; farewell!

OLOF   Are you going? What does this mean? I'd like to talk to you.

MOTHER   That won't be necessary. She has said everything. You don't need to show me the door.

OLOF   Mother, what in God's name are you saying? Kristina, what is this?

MOTHER (*wants to leave*)   Farewell, Olof, I'll never forgive you for this!

OLOF (*wants to have her stay*)   Stay and give me an explanation at least!

MOTHER   It's shameful! You send her to tell me you don't owe me anything, that you don't need me any more! That's hard to take! (*She goes.*)

OLOF   What did you say to her, Kristina?

KRISTINA   I don't remember, but there were a lot of things I had never dared to think, but that I must have dreamed while my father kept me in bondage.

OLOF   You're like a different person, Kristina!

KRISTINA   You know, I'm beginning to find myself a little strange.

OLOF   You were unfriendly to my mother!

KRISTINA   Yes, I must have been. Don't you think I've become hard, Olof?

OLOF   Did you tell her to leave?

KRISTINA   Forgive me, Olof; I wasn't polite to her.

OLOF   For my sake you could have spoken a little more gently. Why didn't you call me right away?

KRISTINA   I wanted to see if I could manage by myself. Olof, will you sacrifice me for your mother if she asks you to?

OLOF   I won't answer a question like that offhand!

KRISTINA   I'll answer! It pleases you to bend before your mother's will and wishes because you're strong; but it humiliates me, because I'm weak. I'll never do it!

OLOF   If I ask you to?

KRISTINA   You can't ask that! Do you want me to hate her? . . . Tell me, Olof, what does prostitute mean?

OLOF   You certainly ask strange questions.

KRISTINA   Would you stoop to answering it?

OLOF   Will you forgive me if I don't?

KRISTINA   Always this eternal silence! Don't you dare to tell me everything yet? Am I still a child? Put me in the nursery, then, and talk to me as if I were an infant.

OLOF   It's an unfortunate woman.

KRISTINA   No. It's something else.

OLOF   Has anyone dared to call you that?

KRISTINA   (*after a pause*)   No.

OLOF   You're not telling the truth, are you, Kristina?

KRISTINA   I'm lying, I know. Oh, I've become bad since yesterday.

OLOF   Something happened yesterday that you haven't told me.

KRISTINA   Yes. I thought I could bear it all by myself, but I can't any more.

OLOF   Tell me! Please!

KRISTINA   But you mustn't call me weak. A mob pursued me to the door and shouted this terrible word that I don't understand. People don't laugh at an unfortunate woman!

OLOF   Yes, dear, that's exactly what they do.

KRISTINA   I didn't understand their word, but I understood enough of their gestures to get angry!

OLOF   And you've been so considerate, anyway! Forgive me if I've been unkind to you . . . It's the name that brute strength gives to its victims. You'll soon hear more about this, but never come to the defense of an "unfortunate woman," for people will throw dirt at you! (*A messenger with a letter enters.*) At last! (*Reads the letter hastily*) Read it, Kristina; I want to hear the happy news from your lips.

KRISTINA   (*reads*)   "You have won, young man! I, your enemy, am the first to tell you this, and without humility I turn to you, for you bore the weapons of the spirit when you spoke for the new faith! I do not know if you are right, but I believe you deserve a bit of advice from an old man. Stop now, for your enemies are gone. Do not struggle with spirits of the air; that would cripple your arm and you would die yourself. 'Do not rely on princes' is the advice of a once powerful man, who now steps aside and leaves in the hands of the Lord the fate of His ruined church. Johannes Brask."

KRISTINA   You have won!

OLOF (*happy*)   God, I thank Thee for this hour! (*Pause*) No. I'm afraid, Kristina. This good fortune is too great. I'm too young to have reached my goal already. Nothing more to do: a dreadful thought! No struggle any more: that's death itself!

KRISTINA   Rest for a moment, and be happy it's over.

OLOF   Can there be any end? An end to this beginning. No! No! I'd like to begin again. It wasn't victory I wanted; it was the struggle.

KRISTINA   Don't tempt God, Olof. I've a feeling there's a lot left to do, a lot.

NOBLEMAN (*enters with a document*)   Good day, Mr. Secretary. Pleasant news! (KRISTINA *goes.*)

OLOF   Welcome! I've already heard something.

NOBLEMAN   Thanks for the excellent defense against that stupid Galle. You crushed him like a man—only a little too much; not so much fire; a little poison doesn't hurt.

OLOF   You have news from the king?

NOBLEMAN   Yes. I'll give you the decisions most briefly (*Unfolds the document, reads*) Number one: Mutual agreement to resist and punish all rebellions.

OLOF   Go on, please.

NOBLEMAN   Number two: The right of the king to take possession of the bishops' castles and strongholds, to determine their incomes . . .

OLOF   Number three.

NOBLEMAN   This is the best of all, the very kernel of the whole business. Number three: The right of the lords to repossess their estates that have come into the control of churches and cloisters since King Charles VIII's confiscations in 1454 . . .

OLOF   Number four.

NOBLEMAN   . . . in so far as the heir can support his claim through right of birth by means of twelve men's oaths at the *Thing*.[13] (*Folds the paper*)

OLOF   Is that all?

NOBLEMAN   Yes. Isn't this fine?

OLOF   Nothing more?

NOBLEMAN   Oh, yes, then there are a few minor matters, but they're not particularly important.

OLOF   What are they?

---

13 Local assembly.

NOBLEMAN   (*reads*)   There's a fifth provision about the right of preachers to preach the word of God, but they had that before.

OLOF   Nothing else?

NOBLEMAN   Yes, there's this ordinance: "That lists shall be made of the income of all bishops, cathedrals, and canons, and that the king shall determine . . ."

OLOF   That's beside the point.

NOBLEMAN   ". . . how much thereof they may retain and how much they shall give him for the needs of the crown; that priestly offices"— this ought to interest you—"priestly offices, not only higher but lower as well shall henceforth be filled only with the king's approval so that . . ."

OLOF   Be so good as to read what it says about the faith . . .

NOBLEMAN   The faith—it's not mentioned. Yes, let me see—"The Bible shall after this day be studied in all schools."

OLOF   Is that all?

NOBLEMAN   All! No, that's true. I have special orders from the king to you, very sensible, that as long as the people are stirred up about these new matters, you may not in any way disturb the old, not do away with mass, holy water, or other customary uses as well as in general not undertake any new liberties, because the king will not close his eyes to your future undertakings as he did in the past when he didn't have the power to do anything else.

OLOF   Oh! What about the new faith he let me preach!

NOBLEMAN   Let it mature slowly. It'll come. It'll come.

OLOF   Is there anything else?

NOBLEMAN   (*gets up*)   No. Now just take it calmly, and you'll go far. Oh! I almost forgot the best news! Rector, I have the honor to congratulate you. Here is your letter of appointment. Rector in the Great Church with 3,000 *dalers* at your age! My word, you can really take it easy and enjoy life even if you never get any higher. It's fine to have reached one's goal when one's so young. Congratulations. (*Goes*)

OLOF   (*throws his letter of appointment on the floor*)   This was what I've struggled and suffered for. An appointment! A royal appointment! I served Belial[14] instead of God! Woe unto you, false king, who sold your Lord and God! Woe unto me who sold my life and my work to Mammon![15] God in Heaven, forgive me! (*Throws himself on a bench and weeps.* KRISTINA *and* GERT *enter.* KRISTINA *comes forward.* GERT *remains in the background.*)

[14] See Act II, note 6.
[15] Wealth or material possessions.

KRISTINA (*picks up the letter of appointment, reads it, and then goes joyously up to* OLOF)   Olof! Now I want to congratulate you with a happy heart! (*She wants to caress him, but he jumps up and pushes her aside.*)

OLOF   Leave me! You, too!

GERT (*comes up*)   Well, Olof. The faith . . .

OLOF   The lack of faith, you mean!

GERT   But the pope's defeated! Shall we take on the emperor soon?

OLOF   We began at the wrong end.

GERT   Finally!

OLOF   You were right, Gert. I'm ready. War! But open and honest!

GERT   You've been living in childish dreams until today.

OLOF   I know. Now comes the flood. Let it come! Woe unto them and us!

KRISTINA   Olof, for heaven's sake, stop!

OLOF   Go your way, child. Here you'll drown, or you'll drag me down.

GERT   My child! What were you doing out in the storm? (KRISTINA *goes. Ringing of bells. Cheering. Music. Beating of drums outside*)

OLOF (*goes to the window*)   Why are the people cheering?

GERT   Because the king's treating them to a Maypole and music out beyond North Gate.

OLOF   And they don't know he's given them the sword instead of birch branches!

GERT   Know? If they only knew!

OLOF   Poor children! They're dancing to his pipes and going to their deaths to the music of his drums—must all die that one may live?

GERT   One shall die that all may live!
    (OLOF *makes a gesture of repugnance and amazement.*)

CURTAIN

Act IV

A room in OLOF'S MOTHER'S *home. To the right a four-poster bed in which the* MOTHER *is lying, ill.* KRISTINA *is sitting on a chair sleeping.* LARS PERTI *fills the night lamp with oil and turns the hourglass.*

LARS (*to himself*)   Midnight! It's to be decided now. (*He goes up to his* MOTHER'S *bed and listens.* KRISTINA *moans in her sleep.* LARS *goes up to her, awakens her, and says*) Kristina!
    (KRISTINA *startled*)

LARS   Go to bed, child. I'll keep watch.

KRISTINA   No, I want to! I have to talk with her before she dies . . . Olof ought to be here soon!

LARS   So you're keeping watch for Olof's sake.

KRISTINA   Yes. You mustn't tell him I fell asleep. Promise!

LARS   Poor child . . . You're not happy.

KRISTINA   Who said I should be happy?

LARS   Does Olof know you're here?

KRISTINA   No. He'd never have let me come. He wants me to be like a saint on a pedestal. The smaller and weaker I am, the greater his pleasure in placing his strength at my feet . . .

MOTHER   (*awakens*)   Lars!

(KRISTINA *holds* LARS *back and goes up to the bed.*)

MOTHER   Who are you?

KRISTINA   Your nurse.

MOTHER   Kristina! . . .

KRISTINA   Is there something you want?

MOTHER   From you, nothing!

KRISTINA   Madame!

MOTHER   Don't embitter my last moments. Go.

LARS   (*steps up*)   What is it, mother?

MOTHER   Take that woman away. Bring my father confessor; I'm dying.

LARS   Isn't your son worthy of your last confession?

MOTHER   He doesn't deserve to be! Has Mården come?

LARS   Mården's an evil person!

MOTHER   God, Thy punishment is too great! My children come between Thee and me. Are they going to deny me the comfort of religion in my last moments? You've taken my life. Do you want to destroy my soul—your mother's soul? (*She becomes unconscious.*)

LARS   You heard, Kristina. What am I going to do? Is she to die, deceived by a scoundrel like Mården, and probably thank us for it? Or is her last prayer to be a curse? No! Let them come! What do you think, Kristina?

KRISTINA   I don't dare to think anything.

LARS   (*goes out, but comes back immediately*)   It's terrible! They've fallen asleep playing dice and drinking. And they are to prepare mother for death!

KRISTINA   Tell her the truth.

LARS   She doesn't believe the truth; it would be like a lie on our heads.

MOTHER   My son! Grant your mother's last request!

LARS   (*goes*)   God forgive me!

KRISTINA   Olof would never do this!

(LARS *comes in with* MÅRTEN *and* NILS *and then takes* KRISTINA *out with him.*)

MÅRTEN (*goes up to the bed*) She's asleep.

NILS (*places a box on the floor; opens it, and takes out a vessel of holy water, an incense burner, a container of oil, palms, and candles*) So we can't start the job yet.

MÅRTEN If we've waited this long, we can wait a little longer, just so that devil of a priest doesn't come.

NILS Master Olof, you mean . . . Do you think his brother noticed anything out there?

MÅRTEN I don't care—just so the old lady hands over the money. Then I'm free!

NILS You're a pretty big rascal all the same.

MÅRTEN Yes, but I'm tired of it. I'd like to get a little peace and quiet. Do you know what life is?

NILS No.

MÅRTEN Pleasure! The flesh is God! Doesn't it say so somewhere?

NILS The word became flesh, you mean.

MÅRTEN Oh, is that it? Yes!

NILS You could've been a mighty able fellow, with your brains.

MÅRTEN Yes, I certainly could. That's what they were afraid of, and that's why they whipped the spirit out of my body in the monastery, for I did have a spirit just the same. But now I'm only a body, and now it's to have its day.

NILS Well, they must have whipped the conscience out of you at the same time.

MÅRTEN Yes, almost . . . But give me that recipe for spiced Rochelle that you started before we fell asleep out there.

NILS Did I say Rochelle? I meant claret. That is, it could be either. Well, for every half gallon of wine, you add half a pound of cardamom, well cured—

MÅRTEN Shut up—she's stirring! Get the book!

NILS (*reads softly during the following speeches*)

> *Aufer immensam, Deus aufer iram;*
> *Et cruentatum cohibe flagellum:*
> *Nec scelus nostrum proferes ad aequam*
> > *Pendere lancem.*[1]

MOTHER Is it you, Mårten?

MÅRTEN It's Brother Nils invoking the holy Virgin.

(NILS *lights up the incense burner while he reads.*)

---

[1] Oh God, take away your great wrath;/And fend off your bloodstained whip:/Do not bring our guilt to the punishment it deserves.

MOTHER   What a wonderful comfort to hear the word of God in the sacred language!

MÅRTEN   No more acceptable sacrifice is ever given to God than the prayers of pious souls.

MOTHER   My heart is lighted like incense by holy reverence.

MÅRTEN   (*sprinkles her with holy water*)   Thy God purifies thee of the mire of sin.

MOTHER   Amen . . . Mårten, I'm dying; our king's ungodliness forbids me to strengthen the power of the holy church to save souls by giving it earthly gifts; take my property, pious man, and pray for me and my children. Pray that the Almighty will turn their hearts from falsehood so that we may meet again in heaven.

MÅRTEN   (*accepts the bag of money*)   Madame, your sacrifice is pleasing to the Lord, and for your sake God will hear my prayers.

MOTHER   I'd like to sleep a little so I'll be strong enough to receive the last sacrament.

MÅRTEN   No one shall disturb your last moments; not even those who used to be your children.

MOTHER   That's hard, Father Mårten, but that's how God wants it. (*Dozes*)

MÅRTEN   (*opens the bag and kisses the money*)   What treasures of joy are hidden in these hard pieces of gold! Ah!

NILS   Shall we go?

MÅRTEN   I certainly could, since I've done my job, but it's a shame to let the old woman die unsaved.

NILS   Unsaved?

MÅRTEN   Yes.

NILS   Do you believe that?

MÅRTEN   I don't know what to believe. The one dies saved through this, the other through that. They all insist they've found the truth.

NILS   What if you were to die right now, Mårten?

MÅRTEN   That isn't possible!

NILS   But if?

MÅRTEN   I'd go to Heaven like all the rest. Only, I'd like to settle a few little matters with Master Olof first! You see, there's one pleasure that's greater than all the others. That's revenge!

NILS   What harm has he done you?

MÅRTEN   He dared to look right through me, he stripped me, he sees what I think!

NILS   So you hate him!

MÅRTEN   Isn't that reason enough? (*Someone knocks on the outer door.*) Somebody's coming! Go on, read for Hell's sake! (NILS *rattles off the verses above. The door is opened from outside; a key can be heard inserted into the lock.*)

(OLOF *enters, looking bewildered and upset.*)

MOTHER (*awakens*) Father Mårten!

OLOF (*goes up to the bed*) Here's your son, mother. You didn't let me know you were sick!

MOTHER Farewell, Olof! I'll forgive you the evil you've done to me if you don't disturb me while I'm preparing for heaven. Father Mårten! Give me the extreme unction so I may die in peace.

OLOF So that's why you didn't call me! (*Sees the money bag* MÅRTEN *has neglected to conceal; snatches it from him*) You're dealing in souls here. And this is the price. Leave this room and this death bed; it's my place to be here, not yours!

MÅRTEN You intend to keep us from performing our duties!

OLOF I'm showing you the door!

MÅRTEN We're here professionally, not with papal but with royal authority, as long as we haven't been suspended.

OLOF I'll cleanse the temple of the Lord even if the pope and the king don't want it!

MOTHER Olof! You want to plunge my soul into damnation; you want to let me die with a curse!

OLOF Be calm, mother; you shall not die in a lie; seek your God through prayer. He isn't as far away as you think.

MÅRTEN A man has to be a prophet of the devil if he doesn't want to spare his own mother the agonies of purgatory!

MOTHER Christ, help my soul!

OLOF Get out of this room or I'll use force! Take this nonsense away! (*Kicks the accessories aside*)

MÅRTEN If you give me the money your mother has given the church, I'll go.

MOTHER Was that why you came, Olof—you want my gold? Give it to him, Mårten. Olof, you may have all of it if you'll only let me be in peace—you'll get still more! You'll get everything!

OLOF (*in despair*) In God's name, take the money and go! Please!

MÅRTEN (*snatches the bag and goes out with* NILS) Madame Kristina! Where the devil is, we have no power! (*To* OLOF) Heretic, you're damned for all eternity. Lawbreaker, you'll get your punishment even in this life! Watch out for the king! (*They go.*)

OLOF (*kneels at his* MOTHER's *bed*) Mother, listen to me before you die! (MOTHER *has become unconscious.*)

OLOF Mother, mother, if you're still alive, talk to your son! Forgive me, for I cannot do otherwise! I know that you've suffered for a lifetime for my sake; you've prayed God that I would walk His paths; the Lord has heard your prayer. Would you want me to make your whole life pointless, do you want me to destroy what has cost you so much effort and so many tears by obeying you? Forgive me!

MOTHER   Olof! My soul doesn't belong to this world any more—it's from the other side I'm speaking to you—turn back, break the unclean bond your body has made, take up again the faith I gave you, and I'll forgive you.

OLOF   (*with tears of despair*)   Mother! Mother!

MOTHER   Swear you'll do it!

OLOF   (*after a pause*)   No!

MOTHER   God's curse rests on you! I see Him. I see God with His eyes filled with wrath! Help me, holy Virgin!

OLOF   That isn't the God who is love!

MOTHER   It's the avenging God! You are the one who has enraged Him, you are the one who casts me into the fire of His wrath—cursed be the hour I gave you birth! (*Dies*)[2]

OLOF   Mother! Mother! (*He takes her hand.*) She's dead! Without forgiving me! If your soul still lingers in this room, look down on your son; I want to do as you wished; what is holy for you will be holy for me. (*He lights the large wax candles, which the monks have left, and places them about the bed.*) You shall have the consecrated candles to light you on the way (*he places a palm in her hand*), and with the palm of peace you shall forget the last struggle with what is earthly. Mother, if you see me, you will forgive me. (*The sun has begun to rise and throw a reddish glow on the curtains.*)

OLOF   (*jumps up*)   Morning sun, you make my candles pale. You have more of love than I. (*He goes up to the window and opens it.*)

LARS   (*enters slowly; is amazed*)   Olof!

OLOF   (*embraces him*)   Brother! It's over!

LARS   (*goes up to the bed, kneels, rises*)   She's dead. (*Prays silently*) You were alone with her!

OLOF   You were the one who let in the monks.

LARS   You drove them out!

OLOF   Yes; you should have.

LARS   Did she forgive you?

OLOF   She died with a curse! (*Pause*)

LARS   (*points at the candles*)   Who arranged these? (*Pause*)

OLOF   (*irritated and ashamed*)   I was weak for a moment.

2 Olof's mother, Kristina Larsdotter, died in 1545.

LARS   So you're a human being all the same. Thank you for that.

OLOF   Are you sneering at my weakness?

LARS   I'm praising it.

OLOF   I curse it! God in Heaven, am I not right?

LARS   You're wrong!

KRISTINA   (*who has just entered*)   You're all too right!

OLOF   Kristina! What are you doing here?

KRISTINA   It was so quiet and lonely at home.

OLOF   I asked you not to come here.

KRISTINA   I thought I could be of some use, but I understand . . . I'll stay home another time.

OLOF   You've been up all night!

KRISTINA   That isn't hard. I'll go now if you tell me to.

OLOF   Go in and rest, while Lars and I talk.
        (KRISTINA *walks absent-mindedly about extinguishing the candles.*)

OLOF   What are you doing, dear?

KRISTINA   Why, it's broad daylight. (LARS *gives* OLOF *a look.*)

OLOF   My mother's dead, Kristina.

KRISTINA   (*goes up to* OLOF *with mild but cold sympathy to receive a kiss on her forehead*)   I'm sorry for your sake. (*Goes. Pause.* LARS *and* OLOF *look first after* KRISTINA, *then at each other.*)

LARS   As your brother and friend, Olof, I beg you not to rush on as you have.

OLOF   That's what you always say. But the person who puts the axe to the tree doesn't stop until the tree falls. The king has deserted our cause; now I'll take charge of it.

LARS   The king is wise.

OLOF   He's a miser, a traitor, and a patron of the lords! First he uses me like a dog; then he kicks me aside.

LARS   He sees farther than you do. If you were to go to three million people and say: "Your faith is false; believe what I say," do you think it would be possible for them to discard their deepest, profoundest convictions, which have sustained them both in sorrow and in joy? No, things would be badly arranged for the human spirit if it didn't take longer to throw the old faith overboard.

OLOF   That isn't so! All the people doubt; hardly one priest knows what to believe, even if he believes anything; everything is ready for the new faith; but you're to blame, you weaklings, who don't dare to take it on your consciences to cast out doubt where there's only a feeble faith.

LARS   Beware, Olof! You want to play the role of God!

OLOF   Yes, one has to, for He's not likely to descend among us again!

LARS   You tear down and tear down, Olof, so that there soon will be nothing, but when we ask, "What are you giving us instead?" you answer, "Not that, not that," but you never answer, "This"!

OLOF   Presumptuous! Do you think a person can give away faith? Has Luther given us anything new? No! He has simply knocked down the screens that stood in the way of light. What I want that's new is doubt of the old, not because it's old but because it's rotten.
(LARS *gestures toward his* MOTHER.)

OLOF   I know what you mean. She was too old, and I thank God she died. Now I'm free, now for the first time; so it was the will of God.

LARS   You're either out of your mind or you're a wicked person.

OLOF   Don't reproach me for that. I respect my mother's memory as much as you do, but, if she hadn't died now, I don't know how far I'd have gone in my compromises. Brother, have you seen in the spring how last year's fallen leaves cover the ground and want to smother the young plants that should come up? What do they do? They either shove the dry leaves aside or go straight through them because they *have* to come up.

LARS   You're right in a way . . . Olof, you've broken the laws of the church during a time of lawlessness and unrest; what was then forgiven must be punished now; don't force the king to appear worse than he is; don't let your unlawful acts and your willfulness force him to punish a man whom he admits he is grateful to.

OLOF   He reigns willfully; he has to learn to bear it in others. Tell me, you're in the king's service. You intend to work against me?

LARS   Yes!

OLOF   So we're enemies! I need them, for the old ones have gone.

LARS   Olof, our blood ties!

OLOF   I don't recognize them except in their very source, the heart.

LARS   You did weep over mother!

OLOF   Weakness, perhaps old affection and gratitude, but not blood ties. What are they?

LARS   You're exhausted, Olof.

OLOF   Yes, I'm weary. I've been up all night.

LARS   You came very late.

OLOF   I was out.

LARS   Your work shuns daylight.

OLOF   Daylight shuns my work.

LARS   Beware of false apostles of freedom.

OLOF   (*struggling against sleep and weariness*) That's a contradiction! Don't talk with me; I haven't the strength any more. I talked so

much at the meeting—that's true, you don't know about our group
. . . *Concordia res parvae crescunt*[3] . . . We're going to complete
the reformation—Gert is a farsighted man—I'm very little compared to him. Good night, Lars. (*He falls asleep in a chair.*)

LARS (*looks at him with sympathy*) Poor brother! God protect you!
(*Knocks on the house entrance can be heard.*) What is it? (*He
goes to the window.*)

GERT (*outside*) Open for God's sake!

LARS (*goes out*) I hope it's not a matter of life and death, Father Gert.

GERT (*outside*) Let me in, in the name of the Lord!

KRISTINA (*comes in with a blanket*) Olof! Why are they knocking? He's
asleep. (*Tucks the blanket about* OLOF) Why am I not sleep so
that you would flee to me when you're tired of the struggle?
*The rumbling of a heavy cart, which stops outside the house, can
be heard.*

OLOF (*startled out of his sleep*) Is it five o'clock already?

KRISTINA It's only three.

OLOF Wasn't that a baker's cart I heard?

KRISTINA I don't know. But it doesn't sound that heavy. (*Goes to the
window*) Look, Olof, what is it?

OLOF (*goes to the window*) The hangman's cart! No! It isn't the hangman's cart.

KRISTINA A hearse!

LARS The plague!

ALL The plague!

GERT (*who has entered*) The plague has broken out! Kristina, my child,
leave this house. The angel of death has placed his mark on its gate!

OLOF Who sent the cart over here?

GERT The one who drew the black cross on the gate. The dead may not
remain in the houses for a minute.

OLOF It's Mårten, who's the angel of death. So the whole thing's a lie.

GERT If you look out of the window, you'll see the cart's filled. (*Blows
on the entrance*) Listen! They're waiting.

OLOF Without a funeral! That shan't be!

LARS Without ceremonies, Olof!

GERT Kristina, leave this terrible house with me; I'll take you out of
town to a healthier place.

KRISTINA I go with Olof. If you had loved me a little less, father, you'd
have harmed me less.

---

[3] Small matters grow with peace.

GERT   Olof, you have the right; tell her to go with me.

OLOF   I freed her from your selfish tyranny once; I won't return her to it.

GERT   Kristina, leave this house, at least.

KRISTINA   Not one step before Olof tell me to.

OLOF   I don't order you to do anything, Kristina; remember that.
(*The* UNDERTAKER'S ASSISTANTS *enter.*)

UNDERTAKER'S ASSISTANT   I was to fetch a body. Quickly!

OLOF   Be on your way!

UNDERTAKER'S ASSISTANT   The king's orders!

LARS   Olof! Think it over. The law demands it.

GERT   Delay won't do. The crazy people have been stirred up against you, Olof. This was the first house to be marked. "God's punishment on the heretic!" they're shouting.

OLOF   (*kneels by his* MOTHER'S *bed*)   Forgive me, mother! (*Gets up*) Do your duty. (*The* UNDERTAKER'S ASSISTANTS *go up and begin to get their ropes ready.*)

GERT   (*aside to* OLOF)   We shout, "God's punishment on the king!"

CURTAIN

Act V

SCENE I

The churchyard of St. Clara's convent. At the back a half-razed convent building out of which workmen are carrying lumber and debris. To the left a burial chapel; lights can be seen through the windows; when the door is opened later, a strongly lighted figure of Christ can be seen above the sarcophagus in the chapel. Graves here and there have been opened. The moon is beginning to come up behind the convent ruins. WINDRANK *is sitting on watch at the chapel door. Singing can be heard from the chapel.*

NILS   (*enters and goes up to* WINDRANK)   Good evening, Windrank.

WINDRANK   Please don't talk to me.

NILS   What's up?

WINDRANK   Didn't you hear what I said?

NILS   So your embarrassing dismissal from the ship hit you so hard you're thinking of entering a cloister!

WINDRANK   52, 53, 54, 55, 56, 57 . . .

NILS   Are you crazy?

WINDRANK   58, 59, 60. Please leave, for Christ's sake!

NILS   Have a little nightcap with me.

WINDRANK   64, 65. I thought so! Go away, tempter! I'm not drinking any more—not before the day after tomorrow.

NILS   It's medicine for the plague. You want to watch out for the smell of corpses here.

WINDRANK   70. Is it really good for the plague?

NILS   Excellent!

WINDRANK   (*takes a drink*)   Well, just a little.

NILS   Just a little. But tell me, don't you get dizzy after you count to a hundred?

WINDRANK   Sh-h! sh-h! A new era's to start!

NILS   Era?

WINDRANK   Yes, the day after tomorrow.

NILS   And that's why you're counting!

WINDRANK   No, that's only because I have such a hard time keeping my mouth shut. Don't say anything, for God's sake! Please leave, or I'll be ruined! 71, 72, 73.

NILS   Who's in there?

WINDRANK   74, 75.

NILS   Is it a funeral?

WINDRANK   76, 77. Please go to Hell!

NILS   Another little drink and it'll be easier to count.

WINDRANK   Another little drink. All right (*Drinks. Singing can be heard.*)

NILS   The nuns of St. Clara are coming to celebrate the memory of the saint for the last time.

WINDRANK   What sort of nonsense is that in our enlightened times?

NILS   They have the king's permission. You see, the plague broke out in St. Clara's parish, and they think it comes from the ungodly tearing down of St. Clara's convent.

WINDRANK   And now they're going to sing the plague away! It must hate music; it wouldn't amaze me if it fled from their screeching.

NILS   Who's invading this last sanctuary? The saint's remains were to be interred here before the building's torn down.

WINDRANK   Then there'll most likely be a fight! (*The singing has come nearer; a procession of Dominican monks and Franciscan nuns enters; at the head of the procession is* MÅRTEN. *They stop but continue singing. Workmen are making noise at the back.*)

Cur super vermes luteos furorem
Sumis, O magni fabricator orbis!
Quid sumus quam fex, putris, umbra, pulvis
Glebaque terrae![1]

MÅRTEN (*to the* ABBESS) You see, sister, how they've laid waste the dwelling place of the Lord.

ABBESS The Lord who delivered us into the hands of the Egyptians will redeem us in due time.

MÅRTEN (*to the workmen*) Stop your work, and don't disturb our holy task.

FOREMAN Our orders are to work day and night until this den has been torn down.

ABBESS Alas, disbelief has made its way so far down among the people.

MÅRTEN We're celebrating this festival with the king's permission.

FOREMAN Fine, go ahead.

MÅRTEN On that basis I order you to stop all this noise. I'll turn to your workmen whom you've forced to undertake this infamous thing; I'll appeal to them if they still have enough respect for what's holy . . .

FOREMAN You shouldn't, for I'm the one who gives orders here; besides, I'll tell you: they're happy enough to tear down these old hornets' nests that they themselves have had to pay for, and they're grateful, too, I think, to earn a little in this time of famine. (*Goes away*)

MÅRTEN Let's forget the evil and tumult of this world, and go into the sanctuary to pray for them.

ABBESS Lord, Lord, Thy holy places are laid waste; Zion is laid waste! Jerusalem is in ruins!

WINDRANK 100! No one's to come in!

CONSPIRATORS (*in the burial chapel*) We swear!

MÅRTEN Who has invaded the chapel?

WINDRANK It isn't a chapel any more; it's the king's storehouse.

ABBESS So that was why that godless man permitted our festival!
(*The chapel door is opened; the conspirators—*OLOF, LARS ANDERS-SON, GERT, *the* GERMAN, *the* DANE, *the* SMÅLÄNNING, *and others come out.*)

OLOF (*heatedly*) What sort of buffoonery is this?

MÅRTEN Make way for the servants of St. Clara!

OLOF Do you believe your idols can ward off the plague God has sent

---

[1] Why do you pour out Your wrath/Upon poor, earthly worms, oh great Creator of the world!/What are we but dregs, rottenness, shadow, dust,/And clod of earth!

you by way of punishment? Do you believe the Lord finds those pieces of bone you carry in that box so pleasing that He'll forgive your horrible sins? Away with the abomination! (*He snatches the box from the* ABBESS *and throws in into a grave.*) From dust you came and dust you shall be[2] even if your name was St. Clara da Spoleto and you only ate an ounce and half of bread a day and slept among the swine at night! (*The nuns scream.*)

MÅRTEN   If you don't fear what's holy, fear your earthly king! You see, he still has so much respect left for the divine that he fears the wrath of the saints! (*Shows* OLOF *a document*)

OLOF   Do you know what the Lord did to the king of the Assyrians when he permitted the worship of idols?[3] He struck him and his people; that's why the just must suffer with the unjust! In the name of the one almighty God, I abolish this worship of Baal, even if all the kings of this earth would permit it; the pope wanted to sell my soul to Satan, but I tore the contract to pieces, you remember! Should I now fear a king who wants to sell his people to Baal? (*He tears the order to pieces.*)

MÅRTEN   (*to the monks and the nuns*)   You are witnesses that he defames the king!

OLOF   (*to the men with him*)   You are my witnesses before God that I have led His people from an ungodly king!

MÅRTEN   Listen, men of faith! It's because of that heretic that the Lord has struck us with the plague; it was God's punishment that it struck his mother first!

OLOF   Listen, you papal unbelievers! It was the Lord's punishment of me because I served Sennacherib against Judah! I will atone for my sin; I will lead Judah against the king of Assyria and Egypt! (*The moon has risen, it is red, and a red glow falls on the stage. The people are frightened.*)

OLOF   (*steps up on a grave*)   Heaven is weeping blood over your sins and your worship of idols! Punishment will come, for those in power have sinned! Don't you see how the graves open their jaws for prey . . .
(GERT *takes* OLOF *by the arm, whispers to him, and is leading him away. General panic*)

ABBESS   Give us back our box so we may leave this place of desolation!

MÅRTEN   Rather let the remains of the saint rest in this consecrated earth than expose them to the desecrating hands of the heretic!

---

[2] Genesis, 3:19.
[3] 2 Kings, 18–19.

OLOF   You're afraid of the plague, you cowards! Wasn't your faith in the holy relics greater than that? (GERT *whispers to* OLOF *again. The procession has dispersed so that only a few of its participants are on stage.*)

OLOF (*to* MÅRTEN)   Now you can be satisfied, you hypocrite! Go and tell the one you serve they're burying a silver box, and he'll tear it out of the ground with his nails; tell him the moon which otherwise is silver is changed to gold so that for once your master may turn his eyes to heaven; tell him that your blasphemous acts have succeeded in arousing an honest man's indignation . . . (*as* MÅRTEN *and the procession go*)

GERT   Enough, Olof! (*To all the conspirators except* OLOF *and* LARS) Leave us! (*They whisper among themselves and leave.*)

GERT (*to* OLOF *and* LARS ANDERSSON)   It's too late to turn back!

OLOF   What is it, Gert? Speak up!

GERT (*takes out a book*)   To both of you, servants of God, a whole people come forward to make their confession. Do you acknowledge your oaths?

OLOF AND LARS   We have sworn!

GERT   This book is the fruit of my quiet labor! On every page you'll read a cry of distress, the sighs of thousands who have been blind enough to believe it was God's will that they should suffer the oppression of one man; they have thought it their duty not to dare to believe in their deliverance.
(OLOF *is reading.*)

GERT   You will hear cries of distress from farthest Norrland to the sound —from the ruins of the church the aristocrats are building new castles for themselves and new prisons for the people—you will read how the king sells law and justice when he lets murderers escape punishment if they'll work at the salt boilers; you will read how he taxes vice when he lets prostitutes pay for the privilege of plying their trade; yes, even the fish in the rivers, even the sea water he has brought under his control, but it's over now; the eyes of the people have been opened; it's fermenting, and soon the oppression will be crushed, and they will be free.

OLOF   Who has written this book?

GERT   The people! They're folk songs, you see; this is how they sing when they're under the yoke. I've traveled about in the cities and out in the country; I have asked them: Are you happy? Here are recorded the answers. I have held court! Here are the decisions! Do you think that the will of millions depends on one person? Do you think that God has given this country with its human souls and possessions to one person so that he can deal with them as he wishes?

Don't you rather believe that he should carry out what all the
people want? You don't answer! Oh, well, you tremble at the
thought that it can end. Listen to my confession! Tomorrow the
oppressor shall die, and you will all be free!

OLOF AND LARS   What are you saying?

GERT   You didn't understand what I said at our meetings.

OLOF   You have deceived us!

GERT   Not at all. You're free. Two voices less make no difference. Everything's ready!

LARS   Have you considered the consequences?

GERT   Fool, it was just because of the consequences I did this!

OLOF   If you were right, Gert? What do you say, Lars?

LARS   I wasn't born to be in the vanguard.

OLOF   Everyone's born to be in the vanguard, but it isn't everyone who's
willing to sacrifice his life!

GERT   Only the one who has the courage to be laughed at and ridiculed
goes foremost. What is their hate compared to their deadly ridicule?

OLOF   If we don't succeed?

GERT   Risk even that! You don't know that Thomas Münster has set up
a new spiritual kingdom in Mühlhausen.[4] You don't know that all
Europe is in revolt. Who was Dacke[5] if not a defender of the
oppressed? What have the Dalesmen done in their revolts but
defend their freedom against the one who has broken both faith
and promise? He breaks them without being punished, but, when
they want to defend themselves, others shout about treason and
revolt!

OLOF   So that's where you wanted to lead me, Gert!

GERT   Hasn't the current led you this far? You want to, but you don't
dare. Tomorrow the bomb will explode in the Great Church. That
will be the signal for the people to rise and elect a ruler to their
liking!

OLOF   (*puts his fist to the book*)   If that is what everyone wants, no one
can prevent it! Gert, let me go to the king with this book and show
him what his people want, and he'll give them justice.

GERT   Child! He'd be frightened for a moment, maybe he'd return a
silver stoup to some church; then he'd point to Heaven and say:
It's not my will that makes me sit here dealing with you unjustly;
it's God's.

OLOF   Let the will of God be done!

----

[4] Thomas Münzer or Müntzer, a German Anabaptist who led the Thuringian
peasants in the Peasants' War. He was beheaded in 1525.

[5] Nils Dacke, leader of the Småland rebellion against Gustav Vasa (1542–
1543).

GERT   How?

OLOF   Let him die that all may live! They may call me murderer, ungrateful, traitor—well, let them! I sacrificed everything, even honor and conscience and faith—could I give more to these poor souls who cry for deliverance? Let's go before I regret it!

GERT   Even if you did, it's too late. You don't know Mårten's a spy; the sentence over the agitator has probably been handed down.

OLOF   Well, then, I shan't! And why should I regret an action that carries out the judgment of God? Forward in the name of the Lord! (*They go.*)

PROSTITUTE   (*has entered, kneels beside a grave which she strews with flowers*)   Hast Thou punished me enough now, Lord, so that Thou canst forgive me?

KRISTINA   (*comes in hastily*)   Tell me, ma'am, have you seen Master Olof?

PROSTITUTE   Are you his friend or enemy?

KRISTINA   You're insulting me . . .

PROSTITUTE   Forgive me. I haven't seen him since I last prayed.

KRISTINA   You look troubled. I recognize you! You were the one Olof talked to one evening in the Great Church.

PROSTITUTE   You shouldn't talk to me so anyone sees it. Don't you know who I am?

KRISTINA   Yes, I do.

PROSTITUTE   You do! They've told you?

KRISTINA   Olof did.

PROSTITUTE   My God! And you don't despise me?

KRISTINA   You're an unhappy mistreated woman, Olof said. Why should I despise misfortune?

PROSTITUTE   Then you're not happy yourself.

KRISTINA   No. We share the same fate.

PROSTITUTE   Then I'm not the only one! Tell me, to what unworthy man did you give your love?

KRISTINA   Unworthy?

PROSTITUTE   Forgive me, no one a person loves is unworthy. To whom did you give your love?

KRISTINA   You know Master Olof?

PROSTITUTE   Say that it isn't true! Don't rob me even of my faith in him; that's the only thing I have left since God took my child.

KRISTINA   You had a child! Then you have been happy!

PROSTITUTE   I thank God He never let my son know how unworthy his mother was.

KRISTINA   Have you committed a crime that you talk like that?

PROSTITUTE   I have just buried it.

KRISTINA   Your child? What are you saying? And I who pray to God every day that He will give me a being, just one, that I may love.

PROSTITUTE   Poor child! Pray to God He will protect you.

KRISTINA   I don't understand you, madame.

PROSTITUTE   Don't call me that; you know who I am.

KRISTINA   Don't people pray in the churches for those who are expecting?

PROSTITUTE   Not for us!

KRISTINA   Us?

PROSTITUTE   They pray for the others—they curse us!

KRISTINA   What do you mean by the others? I don't understand.

PROSTITUTE   Do you know Master Olof's wife?

KRISTINA   Why, I'm his wife!

PROSTITUTE   You! Why didn't I see that? Can you forgive me for a moment's doubt? Would sin look like you and him? Go! You're a child who doesn't know about evil. You oughtn't to talk with me any more. God bless you! Farewell! (*She wants to go.*)

KRISTINA   Don't leave me. Whoever you are, stay, for God's sake. They've broken into our house, and I can't find my husband. Go with me, to your home, anywhere. You're a good woman; you can't be a criminal . . .

PROSTITUTE   (*interrupts*)   If I tell you that the vulgarity of the mob can't hurt you half as much as my company, you'll forgive me for leaving . . .

KRISTINA   Who are you?

PROSTITUTE   I'm an outcast, in whom the curse God hurled at woman when Eve fell has been fulfilled. Don't ask me any more, for, if I told you more, your contempt would tempt me to self-defense, which would be still more contemptible. Here comes someone who probably would be noble enough to escort you if you promised him your honor and eternal peace for his trouble, for he's not likely to ask for less for his protection at such a late hour. Forgive me, I don't want my bitterness to hurt you.

WINDRANK   (*comes in, drunk*)   It's a hell of a thing one can't be left alone even when he's among the dead. Listen, women, please don't ask me anything, for I don't guarantee that I'll answer. I'm going to tell everything the day after tomorrow, because it'll be too late then. Maybe you're nuns who've lost your home. Yes, yes! Although you women are only women, I don't think I have the right to be impolite even though the sun has set; there's an old law, of course, that no one may be seized after sunset, but the law's a tramp, who doesn't, out of politeness, want to be applied to women. Hush! Hush, my tongue; why, you're going like a spinning wheel; but that's because of that damned brandy! But why should they drag me into things like that? It's certainly true I'll be well paid and will be a wealthy man, but you mustn't think I'm doing it for the sake of money. But it's done now! But I don't want to; I don't want to! I want to sleep at night and not be disturbed by ghosts. If I should go and tell? No, then they'll seize me! If anyone else should go and tell? Maybe one of you nuns would!

KRISTINA *(who has conferred with the* PROSTITUTE*)* If you have something on your conscience that's troubling you, go ahead and tell us.

WINDRANK Should I tell? That's just what I want to get out of. But it's terrible; I can't stand it any longer. And I'm the one who has to do it. Why should I be the one? I don't want to!

KRISTINA My friend, you intend to commit . . .

WINDRANK A murder? Who told you? Thank God you know! By all means, go ahead and tell—right now; otherwise, I'll get no peace, no peace in eternity.

KRISTINA *(who has been amazed, recovers her self-control)* Why are you going to murder him?

WINDRANK Oh, there's a lot, a lot! Just look at how he's tearing down your convents!

KRISTINA The king!

WINDRANK Yes, exactly, the liberator and father of our country. Of course, he's an oppressor, but he certainly shouldn't be murdered for that.

KRISTINA When is it going to happen?

WINDRANK Tomorrow, mind you, in the Great Church, in the church itself.

(The PROSTITUTE *goes at a silent signal from* KRISTINA.*)*

KRISTINA Why did they select you to commit an act like that?

WINDRANK Well, see, I have a few connections with some of the servants in the church, and I am so poor. But it doesn't matter who fires the gun, just so some sensible person aims it, and besides we have several ideas in reserve though I'm to start firing. But why don't you go and tell?

KRISTINA That has already been done.

WINDRANK Well, God be praised! Good-bye, my money!

KRISTINA Tell me: who are you, you conspirators?

WINDRANK No, that I simply won't tell.

*(*NILS, *soldiers, and people cross the stage.)*

KRISTINA You see, they're already searching for you.

WINDRANK I wash my hands!

NILS (*goes up to* WINDRANK *without seeing* KRISTINA)   Have you seen
    Olaus Petri?
WINDRANK   Why?
NILS   We're looking for him.
WINDRANK   No, I haven't seen him. Are there others you're looking for?
NILS   Oh, yes, several.
WINDRANK   No, I haven't seen anyone at all.
NILS   We'll be right back for you. (*Goes*)
KRISTINA   Is it the conspirators they're looking for?
WINDRANK   Yes, that's it. I'll be going. Good-bye.
KRISTINA   Tell me before you go . . .
WINDRANK   Haven't time.
KRISTINA   Is Master Olof one of you?
WINDRANK   Of course!
    (KRISTINA *falls, unconscious, on a grave.*)
WINDRANK (*becomes sober and is genuinely moved*)   God in Heaven,
    she's his wife! (*Goes up to* KRISTINA) I think I've killed her! Hans!
    Hans! Now you can go and hang yourself! Why did you get mixed
    up with the big shots? (*Calls*) Come here and help a poor woman!
OLOF (*is brought in by soldiers who carry torches, sees* KRISTINA, *tears
    himself loose and falls to his knees beside her*)   Kristina!
KRISTINA   Olof! You're alive! Let's leave this place and go home!
OLOF (*crushed*)   It's too late!

CURTAIN

SCENE II

A part of the Great Church. OLOF *and* GERT *in prison garb in pillories by
    the door. The organ is playing. The church bells are ringing. The
    divine services are over, and the people are leaving. The* SEXTON
    and his WIFE *are standing to one side downstage.*

SEXTON   Chancellor Lars got mercy, but not Master Olof![6]
WIFE   The chancellor has always been a peaceful man, who hasn't stirred

    [6] In his trial for treason (1539–40), Olof was sentenced to death.

up much fuss; I can't understand how he could want to be in on such a horrible thing.

SEXTON The chancellor has always been strange though he hasn't said much. And he was reprieved, but it cost him his whole fortune. I can't help feeling sorry for Master Olof. I've always liked him all the same, even though he has been difficult.

WIFE Should they make a young boy like that pastor?

SEXTON Well, he was pretty young; but that's probably what was wrong with him; but he'll most likely get over it in time.

WIFE Nonsense—why, he's going to die today!

SEXTON Yes, good Lord, I almost forgot, but it seems to me that's crazy.

WIFE Do you know if he has repented?

SEXTON I doubt it—he's still pretty stiff-necked, I guess.

WIFE But he'll soften up when he sees his confirmands, whom he can't confirm.

SEXTON I must say the king's pretty small when he turns that side. Having the pastor do penance in the church the very day his pupils are confirmed! It's almost as horrible as when he made Dean Göran drink a toast of friendship with the hangman or when he had the bishops ride through town with birchbark baskets on their heads.

WIFE And his brother Lars is to prepare him for death.

SEXTON See, here come the confirmands. They look sad; I don't blame 'em. I think I'll have to go in my room and cry . . .

(*The confirmands—girls and boys—march past* OLOF *with flowers in their hands. They are distressed and walk with their eyes cast down. People follow them. Curious ones among them point at* OLOF; *others reprove them.* VILHELM, *the pupil from Strängnäs, comes last in the procession, stops shyly before* OLOF, *falls to his knees, and puts his flowers at* OLOF's *feet.* OLOF *does not notice this because he has pulled his hood over his face. Some of the people murmur disapprovingly, others approvingly.* MÅRTEN *steps up to take away the flowers but is pushed back by the people. Soldiers make a path for* ARCHBISHOP LARS PETRI, *who appears in the ceremonial garb of his office. The people leave.* LARS, OLOF, *and* GERT *are alone. The organ becomes silent. The bells continue ringing.*)

LARS (*to* OLOF) Olof! The king has rejected the burghers' plea for mercy! Are you prepared to die?

OLOF I can't think that far!

LARS They have assigned me to prepare you.

OLOF Better do it fast! The blood's still surging in my veins.

LARS Have you repented?

OLOF   No!

LARS   Do you want to enter eternity with an unforgiving heart?

OLOF   Put aside your formulary if you want me to listen. I don't think I can die now; there's too much of the power of life left in me!

LARS   I think so, too, and it's for a new life in this world I'm preparing you.

OLOF   So I'm to live?

LARS   If you'll admit that what you've done was an error, and if you'll retract what you've said about the king.

OLOF   How can I? That would be death!

LARS   This is what I had to tell you. Decide for yourself.

OLOF   A man doesn't compromise about a conviction!

LARS   Even an error can become a conviction. I'll go, so you can think it over. (*Goes*)

GERT   What we had planted was not ready for harvest. A lot of snow must fall if the seed planted in autumn shall grow, yes, centuries will pass before anyone will see even a sprout. The conspirators have been caught, they say, and they offer thanks to God; they're mistaken; the conspirators are everywhere, in the rooms of the royal palace, in the churches, and on the squares, but they don't dare to do what we dared. But the day will come! Farewell, Olof! You ought to live longer, for you are young; I shall die with great satisfaction: The name of every new martyr will be a battle cry for a new host. Never believe that a lie has lighted a fire in a human soul; never doubt the emotions that have shaken you to the very core of your being when you have seen anyone suffer because of spiritual or physical oppression. Even if the whole world says you're wrong, believe your heart if you have the courage! The day you deny yourself, you're dead, and eternal damnation will be a favor to the one who has committed the sin against the Holy Ghost.

OLOF   You speak with certainty about my being set free!

GERT   The burghers have offered five hundred ducats to ransom you. When it cost only two thousand to get Birgitta declared a saint, five hundred ought to be enough to declare you innocent. The king doesn't dare to take your life!

LARS SPARRE   (*enters, accompanied by the hangman and soldiers*)   Take Gert Bookprinter away!

GERT   (*as he is taken away*)   Farewell, Olof! Take care of my daughter, and never forget the great day of Pentecost!

SPARRE   Master Olof! You're a young man who has been led astray. The king forgives you because you are very young, but demands as surety a retraction in which you take back what you have done above and against his orders.

OLOF   So the king still needs me?

SPARRE   There are many who need you. But don't count on mercy before you have met the condition. Here is the king's order: your chains can be removed this very moment if you wish, but even this order can be torn to pieces.

OLOF   The one who's satisfied with five hundred ducats isn't likely to bother about a retraction—

SPARRE   That's a lie! The hangman is expecting you, too! But I beg you to listen to a few words from an old man. I, too, have been young, and have been driven by powerful passions; that's part of being young, but it's intended that the passions be conquered. I did what you've done; I went about blurting out truths, but I got no thanks, at best only ridicule; I wanted to build a little heaven on earth (*with emphasis*) on other bases than you, of course; but I soon brought my mind under control, and banished my false dreams. I don't want to maintain that you're a man who wants to become famous by attracting attention to yourself—I don't believe that— you mean well, but meaning well can do a lot of harm. You're so hot-blooded you're blinded because you don't control yourself; you preach freedom and plunge thousands into the slavery of license. Go back, young man, and atone for the wrong you've done; restore what you've torn down, and the people will bless you.

OLOF   (*bewildered and shaken*)   You speak the truth, I hear, but who has taught you to speak it?

SPARRE   Experience! You lack that!

OLOF   Have I lived and fought for a lie? Will I have to declare my whole youth and the best years of my manhood lost, pointless, wasted? I'd rather die with my delusions!

SPARRE   You should have let your dreams go a little sooner! But calm yourself. Life is still ahead of you; the past has been a school, a hard one to be sure, but all the sounder. So far you have lived for fancies and follies; you have neglected some things reality demands of you. Outside this door stand your creditors with their bills. Here are their papers. The clergy of the new church demand that you live to complete what you have begun so beautifully. The burghers of the city demand their secretary in their town hall; the congregation demands its pastor, and the confirmands their teacher. Those are the legal creditors. But there's yet another out there, the one to whom you owe most, but who doesn't demand anything—your young wife. You have torn her from her father and are casting her out into the storms of life; you have robbed her of her childhood faith, you have made her mind anxious; your folly has made a crude mob drive her out of her home, and she doesn't demand even love from you; she asks only that she may suffer a lifetime at your side; you see, even we are concerned about others, though you call us selfish. Let me open this door which will lead you out into the world again; humble your spirit while it is still flexible, and thank God who still gives you time to serve humanity!

OLOF (*weeps*)   I am lost!

SPARRE (*signals to the hangman, who removes* OLOF's *chains and prison garb; then the marshal opens the door to the sacristy, and deputies of the council, the clergy, and the burghers enter*)   Olaus Petri, formerly pastor of the Great Church of Stockholm, do you hereby apologize for your offenses, do you retract what you have said against and above the king's orders, and will you keep your oath to the king of Sweden and serve him faithfully?

  (OLOF *remains silent.*)

  (LARS PETRI *enters with* KRISTINA; *they approach* OLOF. *The people make gestures of appeal.*)

OLOF (*coldly and firmly*)   Yes!

SPARRE   In the name of the king, you are free!

  (OLOF *and* KRISTINA *embrace each other. The people take* OLOF *by the hand and congratulate him.*)

OLOF (*coldly*)   Before I leave this room, let me be alone with my God! I must! Here I struck my first blow, and here . . .

LARS   Here you have won your greatest victory—today! (*All but* OLOF *leave.*)

  (OLOF *kneels.*)

VILHELM (*comes in very quietly. Becomes amazed to find* OLOF *alone and free*)   Master Olof, I've come to say farewell.

OLOF (*rises*)   Vilhelm, you didn't desert me! Let me weep with you over the memory of the happy moments of my youth.

VILHELM   Before you die, I want to thank you for all the good you've done for us. I was the one who gave you these flowers, but you haven't seen them . . . They've been crushed under foot, I see . . . I wanted to remind you of the time we played under the lindens in the monastery gardens of Strängnäs; I thought it would do you good to know we haven't thanked God you didn't come back as you said we could. We never forgot you, because you freed us from the cruel punishments, and you opened the heavy monastery doors and gave us freedom and the blue sky and a happy life again. Why you're going to die we don't know, but you could never do anything but what is right. If you're to die because you have supported a few oppressed people, as they say, it shouldn't pain you if it hurts us very, very much. You told us once how they burned Huss at the stake because he had dared to say the truth to the mighty, you told us how he stepped onto the pile and commended himself into the hands of God, prophesying about the swan who would come and sing new songs in praise of the new freedom. I've thought of you going to your death like that— with your face radiant and your eyes raised to the sky while the people shout: So dies a martyr!

(OLOF *crushed, leans on the pillory.*)

GERT'S VOICE (*far off in the church*)   Renegade!

(OLOF *collapses on the pillory, completely crushed.*)

CURTAIN

COMMENTARY

Master Olof (1872)[1] In 1516, Olof Petersson (in Latin, Olaus or Olavus Petri) enrolled in the University of Wittenberg, where Martin Luther regularly lectured on the Bible. He was in Wittenberg when Luther posted his ninety-five theses (October 31, 1517), and he received his master's degree there in February, 1518. The chief Swedish theologian of the Lutheran Reformation, Master Olof was the man most responsible for the creation of Protestantism in Sweden. In addition, he had a major role in translating the New Testament into Swedish, and he wrote (in Swedish) a Postil and a catechism.

Master Olof is foremost a play about revolution: religious revolution, different degrees and kinds of revolt, the relationship between religious rebellion and political power, the rebel coopted and castrated by the establishment. The play traces two revolutions: the religious revolt against the Roman church, which succeeds, and the political rebellion against the king, which fails. Not only does Strindberg portray a vast political and religious panorama, from radical Anabaptist vandals to Catholic reactionaries, he sketches a vast social panorama, from the king to commoners. He also depicts the varying responses to a revolutionist. Olof's mother curses him; his wife, though understanding as little as his mother, nevertheless supports him; his brother urges conciliation and turns against him; his enemies slander and misrepresent him; members of the masses oppose him; other members of the masses believe in him. Strindberg vividly dramatizes parallel and contrasting characters and scenes: Olof and a prostitute, both excommunicated, both threatened by an angry populace; Olof and Gert, preaching freedom but keeping Kristina (Olof's wife, Gert's daughter) in intellectual bondage; Olof comforting a prostitute threatened with stoning and later trying to comfort his dying, respectable mother; Olof treating his wife as the King treats him but, unlike his wife, turning against his ruler; and so forth. In human terms, Strindberg dramatizes the revolutionary ferment of sixteenth century Sweden.

In the play's first scene—which significantly takes place on the eve of Pentecost, the seventh Sunday after Easter, commemorating the

---

[1] Strindberg completed a prose version of *Master Olof* in 1872. Unable to obtain a production, he wrote a new prose version in 1875. Still unable to obtain a production, he rewrote the play in verse in 1876 and added a verse epilogue the following year. This version too was rejected. For accounts of differences among the three versions, see Johnson and Valency (bibliography following introduction). The first version, whose translation is printed here, was the first to be produced, in 1881.

descent of the Holy Spirit on the apostles—Olof realizes his calling, that he is "to go alone with God" and with "God's pure words . . . [as his] weapons," help "every human being . . . fight for the freedom of his own spirit." Throughout the play, Strindberg depicts the abuses of the sixteenth century Roman church and the goals of the Lutheran reformers. Because the city of Strängnäs has not paid its tithes, the powerful bishop, ignoring the needs of the people, orders the church doors closed and the mass discontinued. He refuses to allow divine services to be conducted even on Pentecost eve, though the king commands him to do so. Like the real Olof, who preached according to the doctrine in Jeremiah 17:5 and 7, "Cursed be the man that trusteth in man" and "Blessed is the man that trusteth in the Lord," Strindberg's Olof, offering to conduct services in defiance of the bishop's ban, replies to a warning against possible consequences, "Let us fear God rather than man!" Preaching the Lutheran doctrine of the personal relationship between man and God, Olof wants "Each and every one [to be] by himself and with God," and to this end he aims to substitute Swedish for Latin in church, since then any man could conduct services, not only an ordained priest.

Master Olof is not about villainous defenders of the *status quo* versus virtuous, heroic reformers. If Strindberg had written such a melodrama, he would have treated antagonists like the king and Bishop Brask far less sympathetically. In such a melodrama, he might have cast the strong-willed, visionary Gert in the role of revolutionary hero, rather than focusing on the weak-willed Olof, who is almost a revolutionist in spite of himself. In this play, Strindberg depicts various degrees of and attitudes toward revolution, and no single character holds a monopoly on truth.

Gert, the one major character in this play that Strindberg invented, is significantly surnamed Bookprinter, the means of making knowledge available to the people. Olof conducts religious services in the vernacular, but bookprinting may reach more people. The protoanarchist Gert wants to free people of all bondage. "You want to strike the pope in Rome," says Gert, "but, like Luther, you want to give them a new pope in the Holy Scriptures." Hoping to lay the foundations for "the millennium of freedom," Gert would go farther than religious reform: he wants to change the entire political and social structure. "You want to strike the pope," he tells Olof, "but you forget the . . . [king,] who murders his people without counting them, because they dare to sigh when they're trodden underfoot." And yet, while Gert urges Olof to "go farther" as a revolutionist, he himself draws back when his daughter becomes involved. Daringly radical regarding mankind in general, he fearfully tries to play it safe with his daughter, whom he forbids to marry Olof. When Olof tauntingly inquires, "Isn't she free?" Gert can only reply helplessly, "She's my child."

At first less radical than Gert, Olof is an enthusiastic idealist who does not realize that the king is using him for his own political goals. Only gradually does Olof come to understand the full significance of his actions and the implications of his ideals, all of which come from others. Olof is not an original thinker but an effective activator of others' thoughts. His religious ideas derive from Luther, his decision to act from Lars Andersson. Appropriately, Olof's initial response to Andersson's promptings is "I'm still too young." In the ways of practical politics, he *is* a child. Too naive to understand that he is to be used as a political tool in a power struggle between church and state, Olof is foolishly confident that the king will approve his actions "because he wants a reformation, but doesn't dare do it himself yet." Equally naive is Olof's expectation that the people will quickly accept the truths he preaches. He is therefore bitterly disappointed when they reveal their essential conservatism, their fear of change, and their hostility to the radical. "They don't want to [be free]!" exclaims Olof. "I loosen the prisoner's bonds, and he strikes me; I tell him, 'You're free!' and he doesn't believe me." Only gradually does Olof succeed in persuading them to embrace change. Only gradually do they turn from hostility to reverence. The play dramatizes Olof's education to political and social realities. Strong in many ways, Olof is able to withstand physical abuse and is a source of spiritual strength in others. Yet he is spiritually weak and crumbles at crucial moments, in regard to both his mother (when she dies, he provides her with a Catholic ceremony) and the king (discussed below).

Unlike Olof, Gustav Vasa is a practical politician who will be as idealistic as he realistically can allow himself to be. He wants to strengthen Sweden by strengthening the monarchy, and he will permit other reforms only insofar as they can support his own—the creation of a powerful and independent kingdom. At the start of *Master Olof*, King Gustav rules a Sweden only recently independent and still split by over a century of foreign exploitation and internal disorder. Since Gustav is unable to repay the crown's debts to the Roman church, his most powerful political opponent, he wishes to make the church's financial resources dependent upon him. His support of Lutheranism is not religiously but economically and politically inspired. Lars Sparre articulates the king's motives when he urges Gustav Vasa, "Crush the church, for it keeps the people in bondage; take the church's gold and pay the kingdom's debt—and return to the ruined aristocracy [which supports the king] what the church has got from the lords through trickery." Ironically, although the king makes use of the religious reformation for the purpose of a political reformation, the former would not have been possible if he had not done so.

At the end of the third act, after Gustav Vasa has concluded the Treaty and Ordinance of Västerås, Olof realizes the insufficiency of his revolutionary efforts. Not only does the king not embrace Lutheranism, he denies the charge of having introduced a new faith in the land and even warns Olof not to make trouble. In the words of the nobleman who reports Gustav's message, the king "will not close his eyes to your future undertakings as he did in the past when he didn't have the power to do anything else." The Västerås agreements bring the church under his control. Although Bishop Brask is correct when he says he has been defeated, he is inaccurate when he congratulates Olof on his victory, for only Gustav is the victor.

"You were right, Gert," admits Olof. Unless the king is defeated, Olof recognizes, victory over the pope is meaningless, since a church controlled by the former is in his view no freer than one controlled by the latter. Gert reveals to Olof how the newly powerful king has been misusing his powers—instituting new taxes, oppressing the people, and assisting vice and corruption in order to bring more revenue to the crown. Convinced that his efforts to persuade the king to bring justice to the people would achieve only a token gesture ("He'd be frightened for a moment," argues Gert, "maybe he'd return a silver stoup to some church"), Olof agrees to join Gert in a revolution of the people against the king.

But the revolution fails. Olof is tried, convicted, and sentenced to death. In his supreme hour of trial, the man who fostered a new faith loses faith in himself, the man who helped the people realize their manhood submits to emasculation, the revolutionist collapses. Ironically, while this spiritual leader had been able to withstand such physical abuse as stoning, he fails at the spiritual testing point. Olof retracts his statements against the king, apologizes for all offenses charged against him, swears to keep his oath to serve the king faithfully, and saves his skin. Earlier, Gert had unsuccessfully tried to encourage him: "Even if the whole world says you're wrong, believe your heart if you have the courage! The day you deny yourself, you're dead, and eternal damnation will be a favor to the one who has committed the sin against the Holy Ghost." To keep his body alive, Olof permits the destruction of his spirit. In the play's moving, ironic, final scene, a humble man, ignorant of Olof's capitulation, praises what Olof means to the Swedish people, and thus provides (for Olof as well as for us) a telling contrast with and condemnation of what Olof has become. Instead of replying, Olof, *"crushed, leans on the pillory."* When Gert's voice booms "Renegade!" he *"collapses on the pillory, completely crushed."* Almost four centuries later, the Mexican revolutionist Emiliano Zapata, one of the heroes of the Chicano movement,[2] would say, "It is better to die on your feet than to live on your knees." Olof chooses the latter.

[2] See Commentary on *Justice.*

Bibliography

A. *Plays About the Reformation:*

Hertzivigius, *Lutherus*, 1617.
John Osborne, *Luther*, 1961.
Z. Rivander, *Lutherus redivivus*, 1593.

B. *Works About Strindberg and* Master Olof:

Andersson, Hans. *Strindberg's Master Olof and Shakespeare*. Uppsala: Almqvist and Wiksell, 1952.
Bulman, Joan. *Strindberg and Shakespeare*. London: Cape, 1933.
Johnson, Walter. *Strindberg and the Historical Drama*. Seattle: University of Washington Press, 1963.
Valency, Maurice. *The Flower and the Castle*. New York: Macmillan, 1963.

The
American
Revolution

MY KINSMAN, MAJOR MOLINEUX
Robert Lowell

MY KINSMAN, MAJOR MOLINEUX
Robert Lowell

CHARACTERS

ROBIN
BOY (*his brother*)
FERRYMAN
MAN WITH MASK (*Colonel Greenough*)
CLERGYMAN
MAN IN PERIWIG
PROSTITUTE
MAJOR MOLINEUX
TWO REDCOATS
TWO BARBERS
TAVERN KEEPER
MAN WITH LIBERTY BOWL
WATCHMAN
CITIZENS OF BOSTON

The Scene

Boston, just before the American Revolution.
To the left of the stage, ROBIN, *a young man barely eighteen, in a coarse
grey coat, well-worn but carefully repaired, leather breeches, blue
yarn stockings, and a worn three-cornered hat. He carries a heavy
oak-sapling cudgel and has a wallet slung over his shoulder. Beside
him, his brother, a* BOY *of ten or twelve, dressed in the same respectable but somewhat rustic manner. On the far left of the stage,
the triangular prow of a dory; beside it, a huge* FERRYMAN *holding
an upright oar. He has a white curling beard. His dress, although
eighteenth century, half suggests that he is Charon. Lined across*

*the stage and in the style of a primitive New England sampler,
are dimly seen five miniature houses: a barber shop, a tavern, a
white church, a shabby brick house with a glass bay window, and
a pillared mansion, an official's house, on its cornice the golden lion
and unicorn of England. The houses are miniature, but their doors
are man-size. Only* ROBIN, *his* BROTHER, *and the* FERRYMAN *are lit up.*

ROBIN Here's my last crown, your double price
for ferrying us across the marsh
at this ungodly hour.

FERRYMAN A crown!
Do you want me to lose my soul?
Do you see King George's face?
judging us on this silver coin?
I have no price.

ROBIN You asked for double.

FERRYMAN I'll take the crown for your return trip. (*Takes the coin*) No
one returns.

ROBIN No one?

FERRYMAN No one.
Legs go round in circles here.
This is the city of the dead.

ROBIN What's that?

FERRYMAN I said this city's Boston,
No one begs here. Are you deaf?
(*The little houses on stage light up, then dim out*)

ROBIN (*To the* FERRYMAN) Show me my kinsman's mansion. You
must know him—Major Molineux,
the most important man in town.

FERRYMAN The name's familiar . . . Molineux . . .
Wasn't he mixed up with the French?
He's never at home now. If you'll wait
here, you'll meet him on his rounds.
All our important people drift
sooner or later to my ferry landing,
and stand here begging for the moon.
You'll see your cousin. You're well-placed.

ROBIN I know it. My kinsman's a big man here.
He told me he would make my fortune;
I'll be a partner in his firm,
either here or in London.

FERRYMAN   Settle
 for London, that's your city, Boy.
 Majors are still sterling silver across
 the waters. All the English-born
 suddenly seem in love with London.
 Your cousin's house here is up for sale.
ROBIN   He cares for England. *Rule Britannia,*
 that's the tune he taught me. I'm
 surprised he's leaving.
FERRYMAN   He's surprised!
 He seemed to belong here once. He wished
 to teach us *Rule Britannia,* but
 we couldn't get it through our heads.
 He gave us this to keep us singing.
 (*The* FERRYMAN *holds up a boiled lobster*)
ROBIN   You're joking, it's a lobster.
FERRYMAN   No.
 Look, it's horny, boiled and red,
 It is the Major's spitting image.
 (*On the other side of the stage,* TWO BRITISH REDCOATS *are seen marching slowly in step with shouldered muskets. Rule Britannia played faintly*)
FERRYMAN   (*Pointing to* SOLDIERS)   Here are the Major's chicken lobsters.
ROBIN   Our soldiers!
FERRYMAN   We call them lobsterbacks.
 They are the Major's privates. Wherever
 they are gathered together, he is present.
 You'll feel his grip behind their claws.
 What are you going to do now:
 run home to Deerfield, take a ship
 for England, Boy, or chase the soldiers?
ROBIN   Why, I'm staying here. I like
 soldiers. They make me feel at home.
 They kept the Frenchmen out of Deerfield.
 They'll tell me where my kinsman lives.
FERRYMAN   The French are finished. The British
 are the only Frenchmen left.
 Didn't you say your cousin's name
 was Molineux?
ROBIN   He's Norman Irish.
 Why are you leaving?

FERRYMAN   Money. The soldiers
         make me pay them for the pleasure
         of shuttling them across the marsh.
         Run, Boy, and catch those soldiers' scarlet
         coat-tails, while they're still around.
         (*The* FERRYMAN *goes off pushing his boat*
         ROBIN *and the* BOY *advance towards the* SOLDIERS)
ROBIN   I need your help, Sirs.
FIRST SOLDIER   (*Smiling*)   We are here
         for service, that's our unpleasant duty.
ROBIN   I liked the way
         the soldiers smiled. I wonder how
         anyone could distrust a soldier.
BOY   We've lost our guide.
ROBIN   We'll find another.
BOY   Why did that boatman gnash his teeth
         at Cousin Major?
ROBIN   He was cold.
         That's how big city people talk.
         Let's walk. We're here to see the city.
         (*As* ROBIN *and the* BOY *start moving, the miniature houses light
         up one by one and then go dark. A* BARBER *comes out of the barber
         shop; he holds a razor, and a bowl of suds. A* TAVERN KEEPER *enters
         holding a newspaper*)
BARBER   (*Cutting away the suds with his razor*)
         That's how we shave a wig.
TAVERN KEEPER   You mean
         a Tory.
BARBER   Shave them to the bone!
TAVERN KEEPER   (*Pointing to newspaper*)
         Here's the last picture of King George;
         He's passed another tax on tea.
BARBER   Health to the King, health to the King!
         Here's rum to drown him in the tea!
         (*Drenches the newspaper with his mug*)
         (*A* CLERGYMAN, *white-whigged, all in black, comes out of the church*)
CLERGYMAN   What an ungodly hour! The city's
         boiling. All's rum and revolution.
         We have an everlasting city,
         but here in this unsteady brightness,
         nothing's clear, unless the Lord
         enlighten us and show the winner!

(*A* PROSTITUTE *comes out of the bay-window house. She wears a red skirt and a low, full-bosomed white blouse*)

PROSTITUTE Here in the shadow of the church,
I save whatever God despises—
Whig or Tory, saint or sinner,
I'm their refuge from the church.
(*The pillared mansion lights up. A* MAN *comes out in a blue coat and white trousers like General Washington's. He wears a grayish mask covered with pocks. His forehead juts out and divides in a double bulge. His nose is a yellow eagle's beak. His eyes flash like fire in a cave. He looks at himself in a mirror*)

MAN WITH MASK My mind's on fire. This fire will burn
the pocks and paleness from my face.
Freedom has given me this palace.
I'll go and mingle with the mob.
(*Now the houses are dark.* ROBIN *rubs his eyes in a daze, stares into the darkness, then turns to his brother*)

BOY Who are these people, Brother Robin?
We're in the dark and far from Deerfield.

ROBIN We're in the city, little brother.
Things will go smoother when we find
our kinsman, Major Molineux.

BOY Our kinsman isn't like these people.
He is a loyal gentleman.

ROBIN We'll see. He swore he'd make my fortune,
and teach you Latin.

BOY I want something.

ROBIN Let's see the city.

BOY I want a flintlock.
(*A* MAN *enters from the right. He wears a full gray periwig, a wide-skirted coat of dark cloth and silk stocking rolled up above the knees. He carries a polished cane which he digs angrily into the ground at every step. "Hem, hem," he says in a sepulchral voice as he walks over to the barber shop. The* TWO BARBERS *appear,* ONE *with a razor, the* OTHER *with a bowl of suds*)

MAN IN PERIWIG Hem! Hem!

ROBIN Good evening, honored sir.
Help us. We come from out of town.

MAN IN PERIWIG A good face and a better shoulder!
Hem, hem! I see you're not from Boston.
We need good stock in Boston. You're lucky!
meeting me here was providential.

I'm on the side of youth. Hem, hem!
I'll be your guiding lamp in Boston.
Where do you come from?

ROBIN   Deerfield.

MAN IN PERIWIG   Deerfield!
Our bulwark from the savages!
Our martyred village! He's from Deerfield,
Barber. We can use his muscle.

BARBER   You can feel it.

MAN IN PERIWIG   (*Seeing the* BOY)   Look, a child!

BARBER   Shall I shave him?

MAN IN PERIWIG   Yes, shave him.
Shave him and teach him to beat a drum.

BOY   I want a flintlock.

MAN IN PERIWIG   A gun! You scare me!
Come on Apollo, we must march.
We'll put that shoulder to the wheel.
Come, I'll be your host in Boston.

ROBIN   I have connections here, a kinsman . . .

MAN IN PERIWIG   Of course you have connections here.
They will latch on to you like fleas.
This is your town! Boy! With that leg
You will find kinsmen on the moon.

ROBIN   My kinsman's Major Molineux.

MAN IN PERIWIG   Your kinsman's Major Molineux!
Let go my coat cuff, Fellow. I have
authority, authority!
Hem! Hem! Respect your betters. Your leg
will be acquainted with the stocks
by peep of day! You fellows help me!
Barber, this man's molesting me!

FIRST BARBER   (*Closing in*)   Don't hit His Honor, Boy!

SECOND BARBER   His Honor
is a lover of mankind!

BOY   Brain him with your cudgel, Robin!

ROBIN   Come, Brother, we will see the city;
they're too many of them and one has a razor.
(ROBIN *and the* BOY *back off. Barber shop goes dark*)

BOY   Who was that fellow, Brother Robin?

ROBIN   He is some snotty, county clerk,
chipping and chirping at his betters.
He isn't worth the Major's spit.

BOY   You should have brained him with your stick.

ROBIN   Let's go, now. We must see the city
    and try to find our kinsman's house.
    I am beginning to think he's out
    of town. Look, these men will help us.
    (*The tavern lights up. A sign with King George III's head hangs in
    front. There's a poster nailed to the door. The* MAN WITH THE MASK
    strolls over and sits in the chair)

CROWD   Health to the rattlesnake. A health
    to Colonel Greenough! He's our man!

MAN WITH MASK   A shine, men, you must shine my shoes
    so bright King George will see his face
    flash like a guinea on the toe.

CROWD   Health to the rattlesnake![1]

TAVERN KEEPER   (*Turning to* ROBIN)   You boys
    are from the country, I presume.
    I envy you, you're seeing Boston
    for the first time. Fine town, there's lots
    to hold you, English monuments,
    docks, houses, and a fleet of tea-ships
    begging for buyers. I trust you'll stay;
    nobody ever leaves this city.

ROBIN   We come from Deerfield.

TAVERN KEEPER   Then you'll stay;
    no Indians scalp us in our beds;
    our only scalper is this man here.
    (*General laughter*)

ROBIN   Our massacre was eighty years
    ago. We're not frontiersmen now,
    we've other things to talk about.

BARBER   He has other things to talk about.
    This boy's a gentleman. He is
    no redskin in a coonskin cap.

ROBIN   I'm on our village council. I've
    read Plutarch.

TAVERN KEEPER   You are an ancient Roman.
    You'll find you like our commonwealth.
    I crave the honor of your custom.

---

[1] A rattlesnake appeared on two early flags of the United States, the Gadsden Flag and the Navy Jack, both 1775. Beneath the rattlesnake was the motto "Don't tread on me."

I've whiskey, gin and rum and beer,
and a spruce beer for your brother.

BOY   I want a real beer.

BARBER   Give them beer.
(*Shouting*)

TAVERN KEEPER   Two real beers for the Deerfield boys,
they have the fighting Deerfield spirit.

ROBIN   I'm sure you'll trust me for your money.
I have connections here in Boston,
my kinsman's Major Molineux.
I spent our money on this journey.

MAN   His kinsman's Major Molineux;
sometimes a boy is short of money!
(*Laughter*)

MAN   (*Bringing out a silver Liberty Bowl*)   I've something stronger
than beer.
Here is the Bowl of Liberty.
The Major dropped this lobster in
the bowl. It spikes the drink.
MAN *puts down his mug and lifts a lobster out of bowl.*
(*Cheers*)

ROBIN   I know
the lobster is a British soldier.

MAN   Yes, there they are.
(*The* TWO REDCOATS *march on stage as before. Silence. The* MAN
WITH THE MASK *starts writing on a bench. The* SOLDIERS *saunter
over to him*)

FIRST SOLDIER   What are you writing, Colonel Greenough?

MAN WITH MASK   My will.

FIRST SOLDIER   Things aren't that desperate.

MAN WITH MASK   I'm adding up my taxes, Redcoat.
Just counting up the figures kills me.
. My bankers say I'm burning money.
I can't afford your bed and board
and livery, Soldiers. We'll have to part.

SECOND SOLDIER   I've had enough. We ought to throw
them all in jail.

FIRST SOLDIER   Go easy.

ROBIN   (*Walking shyly up to* SOLDIERS)   Sir,
I need your guidance, I'm looking for
my kinsman, Major Molineux.

FIRST SOLDIER   Watch your words!

SECOND SOLDIER   Damn your insolence!

FIRST SOLDIER   We'll haul you to the Major's court.

(*Shots and screams off stage.* SOLDIERS *leave on the run*)

MAN   (*Pointing to* ROBIN)   He's one of us.

SECOND MAN   He is a spy.

CROWD   Both boys are spies or Tories.

TAVERN KEEPER   (*Drawing* ROBIN *over to the poster*)   Look,
    do you see this poster? It says,
    "Indentured servant, Jonah Mudge:
    ran from his master's house, blue vest,
    oak cudgel, leather pants, small brother,
    and his master's third best hat.
    Pound sterling's offered any man
    who nabs and lodges him in jail."
    Trudge off, Young Man, you'd better trudge!

CROWD   Trudge, Jonah Mudge, you'd better trudge!

BOY   They're drunk. You'd better hit them, Robin.

ROBIN   They'd only break my stick and brains.

BOY   For God's sake stand and be a man!

ROBIN   No, they're too many, little brother.
    Come, I feel like walking.
    We haven't seen the city yet.
    (*Lights go off.* ROBIN *and* BOY *stand alone*)

BOY   We haven't seen our kinsman, Robin.
    I can't see anything.

ROBIN   You'd think
    the Major's name would stand us for
    a beer. It's a funny thing, Brother, naming
    our kinsman, Major Molineux,
    sets all these people screaming murder.
    Even the soldiers.
    (*The house with the bay-window lights up. A woman's red skirt
    and bare shoulders are clearly visible through the window. She is
    singing*)

WOMAN   Soldiers, sailors.
    Whig and Tories, saints and sinners,
    I'm your refuge from despair.

ROBIN   (*Knocks*)   Sweet, pretty mistress, help me. I
    am tired and lost. I'm looking for
    my kinsman, Major Molineux.
    You have bright eyes.

WOMAN   I know your kinsman.
          Everybody is my kinsman here.
ROBIN   Yes, I am sure. You have kind eyes.
          My kinsman is a blood relation.
WOMAN   You're my blood relation too then.
          What a fine back and leg you have!
          You're made right.
ROBIN   Oh, I will be made
          when I find my kinsman. You
          must know him, he's a man of some
          importance in your city, Lady.
WOMAN   The Major dwells here.
ROBIN   You're thinking of some other major,
          Lady; mine is something more
          important than a major, he's
          a sort of royal governor,
          and a man of fortune. Molineux
          tea ships sail from here to China.
          He has a gilded carriage, twenty
          serving men, two flags of England
          flying from his lawn. You could hide
          your little house behind a sofa
          in his drawing-room.
WOMAN   I know,
          your kinsman is a man of parts,
          that's why he likes to camp here. Sometimes
          his greatness wearies him. These days
          even kings draw in their horns,
          and mingle with the common people.
          Listen, you'll hear him snoring by
          the roof.
ROBIN   I hear a hollow sound.
          My kinsman must be happy here.
          I envy him this hideaway.
WOMAN   You mean to say you envy him
          the mistress of his house. Don't worry,
          a kinsman of the Major's is
          my kinsman. I knew you right away.
          You have your kinsman's leg and shoulders.
          He wears an old three-cornered hat
          and leather small-clothes here in the rain.

Why, you *are* the good old gentleman,
only you're young! What is this cloth?
You've good material on your leg.
(*The* WOMAN *feels the cloth of* ROBIN's *trousers*)

ROBIN It's deerskin. I'm from Deerfield, Lady.

WOMAN You must be starved. I'll make you happy.

ROBIN I'll wait here on your doorstep, Lady.
Run up and tell the Major that
his Deerfield cousins are in town.

WOMAN The Major'd kill me, if I woke him.
You see, he spilled a little too much
rum in his tea.

ROBIN I'll leave a note then. I must go,
my little brother needs some sleep.
(WOMAN *takes* ROBIN's *hat and twirls it on her finger*)
What are you doing with my hat?

WOMAN I'm showing you our Boston rites
of hospitality. The Major
would kill me, if I turned you out
on such a night. I even have
a downstairs bedroom for your brother.
I find a playroom comes in handy.

BOY I want to go with Robin.

WOMAN Oh, dear,
children keep getting me in trouble.
We have a law.
(*A bell is heard off stage*)
Mother of God!
(*The* WOMAN *ducks into her house*
Her light goes out)

BOY Why did the lady slam her door?

ROBIN The bell reminded her of something.
She has to catch up on her sleep.

BOY Has the Major left his mansion?
Is he really sleeping here?

ROBIN How can I tell you? Everyone
answers us in riddles.

BOY She said,
the Major dwells here.

ROBIN That's her city
way of being friendly, Brother.

BOY   Robin, the Major could afford
   to buy the lady better clothes.
   She was almost naked.
ROBIN   She
   was dressed unwisely.
BOY   Isn't Eve
   almost naked in our Bible?
ROBIN   Don't ask so many questions, brother.
   I wish I knew the naked truth.
   (*A* WATCHMAN *enters, dishevelled and yawning. He holds a lantern
   with a bell tied to it and a spiked staff*)
WATCHMAN   Stop, we don't allow this sort
   of talk about the Bible here.
ROBIN   You are mistaken, Sir. I said
   I wished I knew the naked truth.
WATCHMAN   You're in New England. Here we fine
   mothers for bearing naked children.
   You're leading this child into perdition.
   We have a fine for that. What's in
   your wallet, Boy?
ROBIN   Nothing.
WATCHMAN   Nothing! You've been inside then!
ROBIN   Watchman, I'm looking for my kinsman.
WATCHMAN   And you thought you'd find him in this house
   Doing his martial drill.
ROBIN   You know him!
   My kinsman's Major Molineux.
   I see you know him, he will pay you
   if you will lead us to his house.
WATCHMAN   (*Singing*)

> *Your aunt's the lord high sheriff,*
> *your uncle is King George;*
> *if you can't pay the tariff,*
> *the house will let you charge.*

ROBIN   I asked for Major Molineux.
WATCHMAN   Keep asking! We are cleaning house.
   The Major's lost a lot of money
   lately, buying bad real estate.
   He can't afford his country cousins.
   Move, you filthy, sucking hayseed!
   or I'll spike you with my stick!

BOY   Why don't you hit him, brother?
WATCHMAN   I'll have
    you in the stocks by daybreak, Boy.
ROBIN   We'll go, Sir. I'm your countryman
    learning the customs of the city.
WATCHMAN   (*Goes off singing*)

> *Baggy buttocks, baggy buttocks,*
> *The Queen of England's willing*
> *To serve you for a shilling*
> *And stick you in the stocks.*

ROBIN   We're learning
    how to live. The man was drunk.
BOY   Our Deerfield watchmen only drink
    at Communion. Something's wrong,
    these people need new blood.
ROBIN   Perhaps
    they'll get it. Here's a clergyman,
    he'll tell us where to find our kinsman.
    (*The* CLERGYMAN *comes across the stage. He is awkwardly holding*
    a large English flag on a staff)
ROBIN   Help me, I beg you, Reverend Sir.
    I'm from Deerfield, I'm looking for
    my kinsman, Major Molineux.
    No one will tell me where he lives.
CLERGYMAN   I have just left the Major's house.
    He is my patron and example.
    A good man—it's a pity though
    he's so outspoken; other good men
    misunderstand the Major's meaning.
    He just handed me this British
    flag to put above my pulpit—
    a bit outspoken!
ROBIN   Our country's flag, Sir!
CLERGYMAN   Yes, a bit outspoken. Come
    I'll lead you to your kinsman's house.
    (*The* MAN WITH THE MASK *strides hurriedly across the stage, and*
    unrolls a rattlesnake flag, which he hands to the CLERGYMAN, *who*
    has difficulty in managing the two flags)
MAN WITH MASK   I have a present for you, Parson:
    our Rattlesnake. "Don't tread on me!"
    it says. I knew you'd want to have one.

Hang it up somewhere in church;
there's nothing like the Rattlesnake
for raising our declining faith.

CLERGYMAN   I thank you, Sir.

MAN WITH MASK   You'd better hurry.
Think of the man who had no garment
for the wedding. Things are moving.
MAN WITH MASK *hurries off stage*

CLERGYMAN   (*To himself*)   God help us, if we lose! (*Turns to go*)

ROBIN   Sir, you're leaving! You promised me
you'd lead me to my kinsman's house.
Please, let me help you with the flags.

CLERGYMAN   I'll see you later. I have to hurry.
I have a sick parishioner,
a whole sick parish! I have a notion
one of these flags will cure us. Which?
Everyone's so emphatic here.
If you should meet your kinsman, tell him
I'm praying for him in my church.
(CLERGYMAN *goes out*)

(*A loud "hem, hem" is heard. The* MAN IN THE PERIWIG *comes jauntily forward followed by the* TWO BARBERS. *He goes to the house with the bay-window and raps with his cane. The light inside the house goes on. A rattlesnake flag has been nailed to the door. No one sees* ROBIN *and the* BOY)

FIRST BARBER   Look, Your Honor, Mrs. Clark
has taken on the Rattlesnake.

MAN IN PERIWIG   Good, this pricks my fainting courage.
"Don't tread on me!" That's rather odd
for Mrs. Clark.

FIRST BARBER   Come on, your Honor.

SECOND BARBER   There's always a first time.

FIRST BARBER   Then a second.

MAN IN PERIWIG   Thank God, I've but one life to give
my country.[2]
Lay on, Macduff![3] I owe this to
my reputation, boys.

---

[2] Nathan Hale's last words, before the British hanged him as a spy (September 22, 1776) were, "I only regret that I have but one life to lose for my country."
[3] Shakespeare, *Macbeth*, V, vii.

FIRST BARBER   He owes
>his reputation to the boys.

SECOND BARBER   Between the devil and the deep
>blue sea, Your Honor!

FIRST BARBER   His Honor likes
>the sea. Everyone loves a sailor.

MAN IN PERIWIG   Hurry! I'm in torture! Open!
>I have authority hem, hem!
>(MAN IN PERIWIG *knocks loudly. The* WOMAN *stands in doorway*)

WOMAN   (*Singing*)
>*Where is my boy in leather pants,*
>*who gives a woman what she wants?*

MAN IN PERIWIG   (*Singing in falsetto*)

>*Woman, I have a royal Crown*
>*your countryman gave the ferryman*
>*a-standing on the strand;*
>*but money goes from hand to hand:*
>*the crown is on the town,*
>*the money's mine, I want to dine.*
>*Whatever we do is our affair,*
>*the breath of freedom's in the air.*

FIRST BARBER   The lady's ballast's in the air.

SECOND BARBER   Two ten pound tea chests. The lady needs
>a little uplift from the clergy.

MAN IN PERIWIG   I'm breaking on the foamy breakers!
>Help! help!
>I wish my lady had a firm,
>hard-chested figure like a mast,
>but what has love to do with fact?
>A lover loves his nemesis;
>the patriotic act.
>(*The* MAN IN THE PERIWIG *gives the lady the crown and passes in.*
>*The lights go out*)

BARBER   Once to every man and nation
>comes the time a gentleman
>wants to clear his reputation.

TAVERN KEEPER   Once to every man and nation
>comes the time a man's a man.

BARBER   His Honor's perished on the blast.
>(*The* BARBER *saunters off along with* TAVERN KEEPER. *The* BOY *turns*
>*to* ROBIN, *who is lost in thought*)

ROBIN   I think the Major
  has left. By watching I have learned
  to read the signs. The Rattlesnake
  means Major Molineux is out.
  A British flag means he's at home.
BOY   You talk in riddles like the town.
ROBIN   Say what you mean; mean what you say:
  that's how we used to talk in Deerfield.
  It's not so simple here in the city.
  The pillared mansion lights up. ROBIN *and the* BOY *approach it. The*
  Lion and Unicorn of England are gone. Instead, a large Rattle-
  snake flag is showing
  Brother, we've reached our destination.
  This is our kinsman's house. I know it
  from the steel engraving that
  he gave us when he came to Deerfield.
  Our journey's over. Here's our mansion.
BOY   Robin, it has a Rattlesnake.
ROBIN   That means the Major's not at home.
  (*The* MAN WITH THE MASK *comes out of the mansion. Half his face*
  is now fiery red, the other half is still mottled)
MAN WITH MASK   I am the man on horseback.
ROBIN   No,
  you're walking, Sir.
MAN WITH MASK   I am a king.
ROBIN   The king's in England. You must be sick.
  Have you seen your face? Half's red,
  the other half is pocked and mottled.
MAN WITH MASK   Oh I'm as healthy as the times.
  I am an image of this city.
  Do you see this colored handkerchief?
  (MAN WITH MASK *draws out a small British flag*)
ROBIN   Our British flag, Sir.
MAN WITH MASK   Yes, it doesn't
  help my illness any more,
  when I try to cool my burning brow,
  or blow my nose on it.
ROBIN   I know
  a man who used to own this house.
  Let's see if he's still here. Perhaps,
  my friend can help to heal your sickness.

MAN WITH MASK   My face will be entirely red soon;
      then I'll be well. Who is your friend?
ROBIN   A kinsman, Major Molineux.
MAN WITH MASK   I have a fellow feeling for him.
      The Major used to own this house:
      now it's mine. I'm taking over,
      I've just signed the final deed.
      Do you see my nameplate on the gate?
ROBIN   The Rattlesnake?
MAN WITH MASK   The Rattlesnake.
ROBIN   If I pick up the Rattlesnake,
      will it help me find my kinsman?
      I think he needs my help. We are
      his last relations in the world.
MAN WITH MASK   The last shall be the first, my Boy.
ROBIN   What do you mean? You talk like Christ.
MAN WITH MASK   The first shall be the last, my Boy.
      The Major has a heavy hand;
      we have been beaten to the ground.
ROBIN   My kinsman has an open hand.
MAN WITH MASK   Ridden like horses, fleeced like sheep,
      worked like cattle, clothed and fed
      like hounds and hogs!
ROBIN   I want to find him.
MAN WITH MASK   Whipping-posts, gibbets, bastinadoes
      and the rack! I must be moving.
ROBIN   Wait, I'll take up the Rattlesnake.
      Please, help me find my kinsman.
      (ROBIN *takes hold of the* MAN WITH THE MASK's *shoulder. The* MAN
      steps back and draws his sword)
MAN WITH MASK   Move!
      You've torn my cloak. You'd better keep
      a civil tongue between your teeth.
      I have a mission.
      (ROBIN *raises his cudgel. He and the* MAN WITH THE MASK *stand a*
      moment facing each other)
BOY   Brain him, Robin.
      Mangle the bastard's bloody face.
      He doesn't like our kinsman, Robin.
ROBIN   I only asked for information.
MAN WITH MASK   For information! Information

is my trade. I was a lawyer
before I learned the pleasures of
the military life. The Major
was my first teacher. Now I know you!
I met you at the tavern. You
were short of cash then. Take this crown:
drink to the Major, then a health
to Greenough, and the Rattlesnake.
To Greenough!

ROBIN   You're a fighter.

MAN WITH MASK   I hate war, wars leave us where
they find us, don't they, boy?
Let's talk about my health.

ROBIN   Where can
I find my kinsman?

MAN WITH MASK   He owned this house.
Men used to find him here all day,
before the storms disturbed his judgment,
He's out now ranging through the town,
looking for new accommodations.
Wait here. You'll meet him on his walk. (*Strides off singing*)

The king is in his counting house;
we're counting up his money.

BOY   Why was that fellow's face half red now?
He's changing color.

ROBIN   I don't know.
He is someone out of "Revelations"—
Hell revolting on its jailers.
(*The church lights up a little.* ROBIN *walks over to it, and looks in a window*)
Our church is empty, brother. Moonbeams
are trembling on the snow-pure pews,
the altar's drowned in radiant fog,
a single restless ray has crept
across the open Bible.
(*Turns to a gravestone by the church*)
        I'm lonely.
What's this? A gravestone? A grave? Whose grave?
I think the Major must have died:
everything tells me he is gone
and nothing is forever.

(*Turns back to the church*)
> Brother,
the moon's the only worshipper!
(*The* CLERGYMAN *comes out of the church. He lays a white clay pipe on the steps and holds up a little colored celluloid whirligig*)

CLERGYMAN   The wind has died.

ROBIN   What are you doing?

CLERGYMAN   I'm playing with this whirligig,
and waiting to see which way the wind
will veer. It's quite amusing, Son,
trying to guess the whims of the wind.
I am waiting for a sign.
A strange thing for a modern churchman.

ROBIN   My father says the Church is a rock.

CLERGYMAN   Yes, yes, a rock is blind. That's why
I've shut my eyes.

ROBIN   I see my father. He's the Deerfield
minister, and Church of England.
You remind me of my father.

CLERGYMAN   Be careful, son. Call no man father:
that's what we tell the Roman clergy;
sometimes I think we go too far,
they get their people out for Mass.

ROBIN   Father. When I shut
my eyes, I dream I'm back in Deerfield.
The people sit in rows below
the old oak; a horseman stops to water
his horse and to refresh his soul.
I hear my father holding forth
thanksgiving, hope and all the mercies—

CLERGYMAN   Those village
pastors! Once they used to preach
as if the world were everlasting;
each Sunday was longer than a summer!
That's gone now. We have competition:
taverns, papers, politics
and trade. It takes a wolfhound now
to catch a flock!

ROBIN   Why are you waiting
for the wind?

CLERGYMAN   (*Taking up two little flags*)   Do you see
these two flags? One's the Union Jack,

the other is the Rattlesnake.
The wind will tell me which to fly.

ROBIN I'm thinking of the absent one.
My kinsman, Major Molineux
is absent. The storms have hurt his house
lately. No one will help me find him.

CLERGYMAN Perhaps the wind will blow him back.

ROBIN I met a strange man, Colonel Greenough;
Half of his face was red, and half
was pocked. He said, "Wait here, and you
will meet your kinsman on his walk."

CLERGYMAN You'd better wait here then. That red
and pocked man tends to speak the truth.

ROBIN Why was his face two-colors, Father?

CLERGYMAN He is an image of the city.
If his whole face turns red as blood,
We'll have to fly the Rattlesnake.

ROBIN Say more about my kinsman, Father.
You said he was your friend and patron.

CLERGYMAN Poor Molineux! he served the clergy
somewhat better than this city.
He had a special pew, you know.
He used to set a grand example.

ROBIN He used to! You speak as if he were dead!

CLERGYMAN Men blamed me, but I liked to watch
his red coat blazing like the sunset
at Sunday morning service here.
He was an easy-going fellow,
a lover of life, no Puritan.
He had invention, used to send
two six foot Privates here to help
with the collection. Yes, I had
to like him. He had his flaws, of course.

ROBIN A red coat blazing like the sunrise,
that's how the Major was in Deerfield;
the gold lion of England shone
on his gilded carriage. He had a little
white scar like a question mark
on his right cheek. He got it killing
Frenchmen. He seemed to hold the world
like a gold ball in the palm of his hand.

Ours for the asking! All! We are
his last relations in the world!
CLERGYMAN   No one will dispute your claim.
ROBIN   The Major said he was the King's
intelligence in Massachusetts.
CLERGYMAN   No one will dispute his claim.
What shall we do with people? They
get worse and worse, but God improves.
God was green in Moses' time;
little by little though, he blossomed.
First came the prophets, then our Lord,
and then the Church.
ROBIN   The Church?
CLERGYMAN   The Church
gets more enlightened every day.
We've learned to disregard the Law
and look at persons. Who is my neighbor?
Anyone human is my neighbor. Sometimes
my neighbor is a man from Sodom.
(*Great noise of shouting.* ALL FORMER CHARACTERS, *except the* MAN
WITH THE MASK, *parade across the stage.* MOST OF THEM *wave
Rattlesnake flags*)
ROBIN   Father, I see two clergymen,
they're waving flags.
CLERGYMAN   I see my sign. (*Snaps the whirligig with his thumb*)
Look, the wind has risen! Whenever
the spirit calls me, I must follow.
CROWD   Hurrah for the Republic!
Down with Major Molineux!
(*The* PEOPLE *sing a verse of Yankee Doodle, and draw* COLONEL
GREENOUGH *on stage in a red, white and blue cart. He stands up and
draws his sword. One can see that his face is now entirely red*)
MAN WITH MASK   The die is cast! I say, the die is cast.
ROBIN   Look at the Colonel,
his whole face is red as blood!
MAN WITH MASK   Major Molineux is coming.
CLERGYMAN   Are you sure we're strong enough?
MAN WITH MASK   Every British soldier in Boston
is killed or captured.
CROWD   Don't tread on me!
Don't tread on me! Don't tread on me!

ROBIN   What can I do to help my kinsman?

CLERGYMAN   Swap your flag and save your soul.

ROBIN   I want to save my kinsman, Father.

CLERGYMAN   No, no, Son, do as I do. Here, hold
this flag a moment, while I speak.
(*The* CLERGYMAN *hands* ROBIN *his Rattlesnake flag, tosses away the
whirligig, breaks his clay pipe, then takes a chair and stands on it
while he addresses the* CROWD *with both hands raised. Throughout
the crowd scene,* ROBIN *stands unconsciously holding the flag and
suffering*)
How long, how long now, Men of Boston!
You've faced the furious tyrant's trident,
you've borne the blandishments of Sodom.
The Day of Judgment is at hand,
now we'll strip the scarlet whore,
King George shall swim in scarlet blood,
Now Nebuchadnezzar shall eat grass and die.
How long! How long! O Men of Boston,
behave like men, if you are men!
(*The* PEOPLE *cheer and take the* CLERGYMAN *on their shoulders*)
You've drawn the sword, Boys, throw away
the scabbard!
(*The* CLERGYMAN *draws a sword and throws down the scabbard.
Many of the* PEOPLE, *including the* PROSTITUTE, *draw swords and
throw the scabbards rattling across the stage. They draw* MAJOR
MOLINEUX *on stage in a red cart. He is partly tarred and feathered;
one cheek is bleeding; his red British uniform is torn; he shakes
with terror*)

ROBIN   Oh my kinsman, my dear kinsman,
they have wounded you!

MAN WITH MASK   Throw the boy from Deerfield out,
he has no garment for our wedding.

CLERGYMAN   No, let him stay, he is just a boy.
(ROBIN, *unthinking, holds the flag in front of him, while his eyes
are fixed in horror and pity on the figure of the Major. The* BOY,
unconsciously, too, mingles among the CROWD *without thinking.
Someone asks him to give some dirt to throw at the* MAJOR *and he
unthinkingly picks up some from a basket, and hands it to the*
TAVERN KEEPER, *who throws it at the* MAJOR)

ROBIN   (*With a loud cry, but unconsciously waving the flag in his grief*)
Oh my poor kinsman, you are hurt!

CROWD   Don't tread on me! Don't tread on me!
(*The* MAJOR *slowly staggers to his feet. Slowly he stretches out his right arm and points to* ROBIN)

MAJOR MOLINEUX   *Et tu, Brute!*[4]

TAVERN KEEPER   The Major wants to teach us Latin. (*The* CROWD *laughs, and* ROBIN, *once more without thinking, laughs too, very loudly*)
(TAVERN KEEPER *goes up to the* MAJOR *and hands him a Rattlesnake flag*)
Your're out of step, Sir. Here's your flag.
(*The* MAJOR *lurches a few steps from the cart, grinds the Rattlesnake underfoot, then turns and addresses the crowd*)

MAJOR MOLINEUX   Long live King George! Long live King George!
I'll sing until you cut my tongue out!

CROWD   Throw the Major in the river,
in the river, in the river!
(*With a grating sound, the* FERRYMAN *appears at the side of the stage, pushing the prow of his dory. The* MAJOR *staggers towards the* FERRYMAN)

MAJOR MOLINEUX   (*To* FERRYMAN)   Help me in my trouble. Let
me cross the river to my King!
(*The* FERRYMAN *stiffens.* THE MAN WITH THE MASK *throws him a silver crown*)

MAN WITH MASK   Ferryman, here's a silver crown,
take him or leave him, we don't care.

FERRYMAN   (*Still more threatening*)   The crown's no longer currency.
(*The* FERRYMAN *kicks the crown into the water*)

MAJOR MOLINEUX   Boatman, you rowed me here in state;
save me, now that I'm fallen!

FERRYMAN   There's no returning on my boat.

MAJOR MOLINEUX   (*Stretching out his hands and grappling the* FERRYMAN)
Save me in the name of God!
(*The* FERRYMAN *pushes the* MAJOR *off and hits him on the head with his oar. The* MAJOR *screams, and lies still*)

FERRYMAN   He's crossed the river into his kingdom;
all tyrants must die as this man died.
(*One by one, the* PRINCIPAL CHARACTERS *come up and look at the* MAJOR)

CLERGYMAN   He's dead. He had no time to pray.

---

[4] Caesar's words to his friend Brutus when the latter stabs him. Shakespeare, *Julius Caesar*, III, i.

I wish he'd called me. O Lord, remember
his past kindness to the Church;
all tyrants must die as this man died.
MAN IN PERIWIG (*Taking the* MAJOR's *empty scabbard*)
I have the Major's sword of office;
hem, hem, I have authority.
FIRST BARBER   His Honor has the hollow scabbard.
MAN IN PERIWIG   They build men right in England. Take him
all in all, he was a man;[5]
all tyrants must die as this man died.
TAVERN KEEPER (*Holding a poster*)
Look, this poster says the town
of Boston offers a thousand guineas
to anyone who kills the Major.
I'll take his wallet for the cause.
All tyrants must die as this man died.
PROSTITUTE (*Taking the* MAJOR's *hat*)
I'll need this hat to hide my head.
They build men right in England. Take him
all in all, he was a man;
all tyrants must die as this man died.
MAN WITH MASK (*Plunging his sword in the* MAJOR)
Sic semper tyrannis![6]
FERRYMAN   His fare is paid now;
the Major's free to cross the river.
(*The* FERRYMAN *loads* MAJOR MOLINEUX's *body on his boat, and
pushes off*)
CLERGYMAN (*Coming up to* MAN WITH MASK)   Your hand! I want
to shake your hand, Sir. A great day!
MAN WITH MASK   Great and terrible! There's nothing
I can do about it now. (*Turns to* ROBIN)
Here, boy, here's the Major's sword;
perhaps, you'll want a souvenir.
(CROWD *starts to leave.* ROBIN *and* BOY *alone*)
BOY   The Major's gone. We'll have to go
Back home. There's no one here to help us.
ROBIN   Yes, Major Molineux is dead.
(*Stats sadly towards the river*)

---

[5] Hamlet says of his father, "He was a man, take him for all in all,/ I shall
not look upon his like again." Shakespeare, *Hamlet*, I, ii.

[6] "Thus always to tyrants!"—the motto of the state of Virginia; also, the
words spoken by John Wilkes Booth when he shot Abraham Lincoln in 1865.

CROWD   Long live the Republic! Long live the Republic!

BOY   Look, Robin, I have found a flintlock.

> (ROBIN *looks wistfully at the* CROWD, *now almost entirely gone. He pauses and then answers in a daze*)

ROBIN   A flintlock?

BOY   Well, that's all I came to Boston for, I guess.
Let's go, I see the ferryman.

ROBIN   (*Still inattentive*)   I'm going.

> (ROBIN *takes his brother's hand and turns firmly towards the city*)

BOY   We are returning to the city!

> (ALL THE PEOPLE *are gone now, the lights start to go out. A red sun shows on the river*)

ROBIN   Yes, brother, we are staying here.
Look, the lights are going out,
the red sun's moving on the river.
Where will it take us to? . . . It's strange
to be here on our own—and free.

BOY   (*Sighting along his flintlock*)
Major Molineux is dead.

ROBIN   Yes, Major Molineux is dead.

CURTAIN

COMMENTARY

My Kinsman, Major Molineux (1964)   Set on the eve of the American Revolution, *My Kinsman, Major Molineux* takes place in Boston. At that time Boston was a hotbed of revolutionary activity and Bostonians frequently clashed with British troops, sometimes tarring and feathering representatives of King George III. They engaged in the first of several "tea parties" in American harbors (on December 16, 1773, dressed as Indians, Bostonians registered their objection to a tea tax by dumping 340 chests of tea into Boston harbor). To punish the Bostonians for the Boston Tea Party, Parliament passed the Boston Port Bill, which declared that "the opposition to the authority of Parliament had always originated in the colony of Massachusetts, and . . . the colony itself had ever been instigated to such conduct by the seditious proceedings of the town of Boston," and which closed Boston harbor until the East India Company was reimbursed for the tea the Bostonians destroyed. (In response, Bostonians refused to buy tea from that company.) Other vengeful measures, collectively known as the Coercive Acts, provided that English troops be quartered in Boston, that the number of town meetings be restricted, and that agents of the Crown charged with crimes be tried in England or in other colonies. As is the case today in clashes between rebels and the Establishment, antagonisms were thereby exacerbated. Instead of making Bostonians more docile, the intransigent attitudes and repressive actions of the King and his Prime Minister, Lord North, had—predictably—opposite effects: they caused the rebellious colonists to harden their positions and they radicalized those colonists who had hitherto been neutral. By the time of the battle of Concord (April 19, 1775), wherein "the shot heard round the world" was fired, reconciliation between England and the colonies was difficult—perhaps impossible—to achieve.

This is the milieu of *My Kinsman, Major Molineux.*[1] In Lowell's play, the American Revolution is presented in dream-like terms as the nightmare of a boy entering manhood. Arriving from Deerfield, Robin is at first unaware of, then bewildered by, and finally engulfed in the hostility of the Bostonians toward the British. As America rejects its parent country and achieves freedom, the eighteen-year-old Robin, urged several times by his younger brother to "be a man," rejects his parent surrogate, his kinsman Major Molineux. Robin gives dirt to the Tavern Keeper, who

---

[1] Its source, however, Nathaniel Hawthorne's short story of that title, takes place some forty-five years earlier than the play.

throws it at the British major, and Robin waves the American flag before him—albeit *"unthinkingly"* and *"unconsciously."*[2] At the death of Major Molineux, a youth and a country achieve independence and manhood— as symbolized by the dawn of the next day ("the red sun's moving on the river," observes Robin, "It's strange/to be here on our own—and free").

Lowell's drama focuses on the American Revolution. Instead of treating its causes and conditions discursively, however, *My Kinsman, Major Molineux* suggests them by a succession of visual and verbal images. A man removes a boiled lobster—symbolizing the British soldiers, called "lobsterbacks" and "redcoats"—from a "Bowl of Liberty" and is cheered when he announces that the dead lobster "spikes his drink." One of the sights of Boston, says the Tavern Keeper, is "a fleet of tea-ships/begging for buyers." The British soldiers, complains the Ferryman, do not pay him but instead "make me pay them for the pleasure/of shuttling them across the marsh." "Here's rum to drown him in the tea!" cries a barber as he pours his drink over the newspaper announcing King George's tea tax. "I'm adding up my taxes, Redcoat," says the Man with the Mask,

> Just counting up the figures kills me.
> My bankers say I'm burning money.
> I can't afford your bed and board
> And livery, Soldiers. We'll have to part.

People become hostile when Robin mentions that he seeks his kinsman, for Major Molineux is "a sort of royal governor" and has "two flags of England/flying from his lawn." Behind the claws of the oppressive lobster-backs is the grip of Major Molineux who, says the Ferryman, "wished/to teach us *Rule Britannia,* but/we couldn't get it through our heads." Oppressed by the British Major, according to the Man with the Mask, Bostonians "have been beaten to the ground."

> Ridden like horses, fleeced like sheep,
> worked like cattle, clothed and fed
> like hounds and hogs.
>
> . . . .
>
> Whipping-posts, gibbets, bastinadoes
> And the rack!

In the play, the revolutionary mob, composed like its colonial counter-parts of people of all social classes, violently turns on the British. The Man

---

[2] A prominent Bostonian at the time of the American Revolution was named William Molineux. Unlike his namesake in the play, however, the real Molineux opposed taxation without representation, was a member of the subversive "Sons of Liberty," demanded that British troops be removed from Boston, and was arrested on suspicion of treason. He died on October 22, 1774.

with the Mask, who "is an image of the city," is dressed *"like George Washington,"* has a profile like the American eagle, and *"wears a grayish mask covered with pocks."* As the bloody revolution approaches, his face (mask) changes. In his next appearance, half of it is *"fiery red, the other half is still mottled."* Using the British flag to wipe his feverish brow and to blow his nose, he predicts that when his face is entirely red he will be well. Near the end of the play, as a crowd sings "Yankee Doodle," they draw him onstage in a red, white, and blue cart. His face now completely red ("red as blood!" says Robin), he announces that "every British soldier in Boston is killed or captured," whereupon the crowd cries "Don't tread on me!" three times. The motto of the first official American flag, first raised by John Paul Jones on December 3, 1775, "Don't tread on me" was written below the picture of a rattlesnake. In *My Kinsman, Major Molineux*, the rattlesnake flag of America vies with the Union Jack of Great Britain. "I have a sick parishioner," says the Clergyman, "a whole sick parish! I have a notion/one of these flags will cure us." Afraid to choose, he decides to go the way the wind is blowing: "The wind will tell me which to fly." The flag at the pillared mansion of Major Molineux indicates the outcome of the contest. "The Rattlesnake/means Major Molineux is out./A British flag means he's at home." Revealing the triumph of the Yankee rebels, the flag of the republic becomes their "nameplate" on the gate.

Written by an American descended from early New England colonists, this play of the American Revolution dramatizes the nightmare of revolution, but not its legitimacy. During World War II, Robert Lowell refused to be drafted into the U. S. Army because he objected to the Allied bombing of European cities, which inflicted casualties on civilians. A quarter-century later, Lowell became an outspoken critic of the Vietnamese War. In *My Kinsman, Major Molineux*, he views revolution ambiguously. "I hate war," says the Man with the Mask, apparently the leader of the revolutionary activities, "wars leave us where/they find us . . ." The most demagogic and belligerent jingoism in the play is voiced not by a patriot but by the opportunistic Clergyman who, seeing the Rattlesnake victorious over the Union Jack, harangues the crowd about "the furious tyrant's trident," prophesies that "King George shall swim in scarlet blood," and calls upon the mob to finish what they started. In contrast, the brief appearance of Major Molineux demonstrates not villainy or cowardice but integrity and loyalty. By grinding the Rattlesnake flag underfoot and crying "Long live King George!" twice he provokes the mob to murder him. Although five people proclaim over Molineux's body, "all tyrants must die as this man died," two of them describe him with a misquotation from *Hamlet*—"Take him for all in all, he was a man"—in which the

154 THE AMERICAN REVOLUTION

Danish Prince *affectionately* refers to his father. "Thank God I've but one life to give/my country," says the Man in the Periwig, and he adds, "Lay on, Macduff!"—thus combining Nathan Hale with Macbeth, the former a "good," the latter an "evil" revolutionist. "*Sic semper tyrannis!*" cries the Man with the Mask as he plunges his sword into the Major. The motto of the state of Virginia—"Thus always to tyrants!"—the phrase was also used by John Wilkes Booth when he shot Abraham Lincoln. How are we to regard these allusions in the play? Possibly, Lowell would like us to recognize precisely their ambiguity. The Man with the Mask may speak for the author when in response to the Clergyman's exclamation, "A great day!" he says soberly, "Great and terrible! There's nothing/I can do about it now."

Bibliography

A. Plays About the American Revolution:

Maxwell Anderson, *Valley Forge*, 1934
John Daly Burk, *Bunker Hill, or The Death of General Warren*, 1797
William Dunlap, *André*, 1798
Clyde Fitch, *Nathan Hale*, 1898
Sidney Kingsley, *The Patriots*, 1943
Kenneth Koch, *George Washington Crossing the Delaware*, 1962
Robert Munford, *The Patriots*, 1777

B. Works About My Kinsman, Major Molineux:

Brustein, Robert. *Seasons of Discontent*. New York: Simon and Shuster, 1967.
Hochman, Baruch. "Robert Lowell's *The Old Glory*," *Tulane Drama Review*, XI (Summer, 1967).

The
French
Revolution

DANTON'S DEATH
Georg Büchner

DANTON'S DEATH
Georg Büchner
Translated by Theodore H. Lustig

CHARACTERS

GEORGES DANTON
LEGENDRE
CAMILLE DESMOULINS
HÉRAULT-SÉCHELLES
LACROIX   } *deputies*
PHILIPPEAU
FABRE D'EGLANTINE
MERCIER
THOMAS PAYNE

ROBESPIERRE
SAINT-JUST   } *members of the Committee*
BARÈRE   *of Public Safety*[1]
COLLOT D'HERBOIS
BILLAUD-VARENNES

CHAUMETTE, *Attorney for the City of Paris*
DILLON, *a general*
FOUQUIER-TINVILLE, *Public Prosecutor*
AMAR   } *members of the Committee*
VOULAND   *of Security*[2]
HERMAN } *presidents of the*
DUMAS *Revolutionary Tribunal*[3]
PARIS, *a friend of Danton's*
SIMON, *a prompter*

[1] Established by the French National Convention on Apr. 6, 1793, partly to take measures for external and internal defense. Its duties became more extended and it became a virtual dictatorship.

[2] Established by the French National Convention on Oct. 2, 1792, it directed the administration of justice and of the revolutionary police.

[3] Established on March 10, 1793 to judge counterrevolutionaries, this body allowed no appeal of its decisions.

From *Classical German Drama*, translated by Theodore H. Lustig. Copyright © 1963 by Bantam Books, Inc. All rights reserved.

LAFLOTTE
JULIE,   *Danton's wife*
LUCILE,   *Camille Desmoulins's wife*
ROSALIE ⎫
ADELAIDE ⎬ *grisettes*[4]
MARION   ⎭
> MEN *and* WOMEN *of the people,* GRISETTES, DEPUTIES,
> EXECUTIONERS, *etc.*

Act I

SCENE 1. HÉRAULT-SÉCHELLES *and several* LADIES *seated at a card table.* DANTON *and* JULIE *sit apart,* DANTON *on a footstool at* JULIE's *feet.*

DANTON   Look how nicely that pretty lady deals the cards! She really has a knack for it. They say that she always deals a heart to her husband and diamonds to everyone else. You women could make a man fall in love with a lie!

JULIE   Do you believe in me?

DANTON   Who knows! We know so little about each other. We are thick-skinned. We reach out for each other, but it is no good; we only manage to rub against each other and to irritate the coarse leather. We are very lonely.

JULIE   You know me, Danton.

DANTON   Yes, what we call knowing! You have dark eyes, curly hair and a delicate complexion, and you always say "dear Georges" to me! But (*Pointing to her eyes and her forehead.*) there . . . there . . . what is behind that? Look, our senses are not very refined. To know each other, we would have to crack open each other's skulls and pull the thoughts out of the fibres of our brains.

A LADY (*to* HÉRAULT)   What are you doing with your fingers?

HÉRAULT   Nothing.

THE LADY   Don't tuck your thumb in like that! It looks terrible!

HÉRAULT   Oh, but you see, that has a special meaning.

DANTON   Julie, I love you like the grave.

JULIE (*turning her head away*)   Oh!

DANTON   No, don't turn away! Listen to me! They say that there is peace

---

[4] Working-class girls who were part-time prostitutes.

in the grave, that being buried is the same as resting. If that is true, I'm buried when I lie in your lap. Sweet grave, your lips are funeral bells, your voice my deathknell, your breast the mound above my grave and your heart my coffin.

THE LADY   You have lost!

HÉRAULT   It was a romantic adventure that cost money, as they always do.

THE LADY   You must have declared your love with your fingers, like a deaf mute.

HÉRAULT   And why not? Some people even insist that deaf mutes are easier to understand than anyone else. I was arranging a love affair with a card queen. My fingers were bewitched princes in the shape of spiders, and you, Madame, were the Good Fairy. But it didn't work out; the queen was constantly pregnant and gave birth to one knave after the other. I wouldn't allow my daughter to play games like this, with gentlemen and ladies most indecently tumbling over each other, and little knaves turning up shortly after.

(CAMILLE DESMOULINS *and* PHILIPPEAU *enter.*)

HÉRAULT   Philippeau, how sad your eyes are! Did you tear a hole in your red cap? Did Saint Jacob give you a stern look? Or was it raining during the guillotine performance? Or did you have a bad seat and couldn't see anything?

CAMILLE   You are parodying Socrates.[1] Do you know what the Divine One asked Alcibiades one day when he saw him downcast and brooding? "Have you lost your shield on the field of battle? Did someone beat you in a race or in a fight? Did someone else sing better or play the zither better than you?" Oh, what classical minds we Republicans have! Compare it with the romanticism of our guillotine!

PHILIPPEAU   Twenty more victims died today. We were wrong; they sent the Hébertists[2] to the scaffold only because they were not systematic enough; perhaps also because the Decemvirs[3] thought themselves lost if there were men who even for one single week had been feared more than they.

HÉRAULT   They would like to make us into antediluvians. Saint-Just

---

[1] Greek philosopher of the fifth century B. C. The socratic method of learning and teaching consists of asking a series of questions in order to establish or refute a proposition. At the battle of Potidaea, Socrates is said to have saved the life of Alcibiades.

[2] Followers of the extremist and anti-clerical Jacques-René Hébert, who with some of his followers was executed on March 24, 1794.

[3] I.e., the Committee of Public Safety. The nickname derives from ten Roman magistrates who drew up a code of laws and who had absolute power while in office.

would not mind at all if we walked again on all fours; then the attorney from Arras could start all over inventing hats, school benches, and a God for us, in accordance with the system of mechanics established by the watchmaker from Ghent.

PHILIPPEAU   If that would do it, they would be quite willing to add some zeros to the record Marat set. How long are we supposed to remain dirty and bloody like new-born babes, have coffins for cradles and play with heads? We must go forward! The Clemency Committee must become reality and the expelled deputies must be readmitted!

HÉRAULT   The Revolution has reached the period of consolidation.—The Revolution must end, the Republic must begin.—In the fundamental principles of the state, right must take the place of duty, contentment the place of virtue, and defense the place of punishment. Everyone must count, and must be allowed to follow his natural inclination. Whether he is reasonable or unreasonable, educated or uneducated, good or evil—that is not the government's concern. All of us are fools and no one has the right to force his particular brand of foolishness on anyone else. Everyone should be allowed to enjoy himself according to his taste, as long as it is not at the expense of others, nor by interfering with their preferred form of enjoyment.

CAMILLE   The form of government must be a transparent gown which closely hugs the body of the People. The pulsing of the veins, the flexing of the muscles, each twitching of the sinews must show through it. The body may be beautiful or ugly, it has the right to be as it happens to be. We have no right to tailor it a little dress to suit our fancy. We shall slap the hands of those people who would like to drape a nun's veil over the naked shoulders of that most enticing of sinners, France. We want nude gods, we want Bacchantes, Olympic games, and love, sung by melodious lips, that makes our limbs unbend—oh, wicked love! We shall not stop the Romans from sitting in a corner and cooking turnips, but let them not insist on treating us to gladiatorial games! Let the divine Epicurus and Venus with the glorious behind stand guard at the doors of the Republic instead of St. Marat and St. Chalier. Danton, you are the one to mount the attack in the Convention!

DANTON   I am, you are, he is. If I am still alive, said the old woman. After one hour, sixty minutes have passed, is that not true, my boy?

CAMILLE   What does that mean? It is self-evident!

DANTON   Oh, everything is self-evident. And who, if I may ask, is to get all these beautiful things started?

PHILIPPEAU   We—and all honest men.

DANTON   That "and" is a very long word! It keeps us rather far apart! The way is long, and Honesty may lose its breath before we get together! However . . . one can lend money to honest men, one can become godfather to their children and give them one's daughters in marriage—but that is all!

CAMILLE   If that is your opinion why did you start the fight?

DANTON   I detest those people. I have never been able to look at such blown-up paragons of virtue without giving them a kick. That is the way I am. (*He rises.*)

JULIE   You are going?

DANTON   (*to* JULIE)   I must go. Their talk of politics rubs me the wrong way. (*As he leaves.*) Standing between pillar and post, I shall make you a prophecy: the statue of liberty has not yet been poured, but the furnace is glowing and we all have a chance to burn our fingers.
(*He leaves.*)

CAMILLE   Let him go! Do you think he will be able to keep out of it once we start to act?

HÉRAULT   That's true, but he will do it only as a pastime, like playing chess.

SCENE 2. *A street.* SIMON *and his* WIFE.

SIMON   (*beating his wife*)   You procurer! You shriveled quicksilver pill! You worm-eaten apple of sin!

WIFE   Help! Help!

PEOPLE   (*running in*)   Get them apart! Pull them apart!

SIMON   No! Leave me alone, Romans! I want to break your bones, you vestal virgin!

WIFE   I—a vestal virgin? That I would like to see!

SIMON   From your putrid shoulders I tear your robe, and naked in the sun your corpse shall lie. You whore! Every wrinkle of your body is a seat of lechery! (*The* CITIZENS *separate them.*)

FIRST CITIZEN   What's wrong?

SIMON   Where is the virgin? Tell me! No, I can't call her that! The girl! No, not that, either! The woman, the wife! No, no, not even that! There is only one word! Oh, it strangles me! I don't have enough breath to speak it.

SECOND CITIZEN   A good thing that, too; it would reek of brandy.

SIMON   Old Virginius![4] Veil your bald head! The Raven of Shame is sitting on it, trying to peck at your eyes. Hand me a knife, Romans! (*He collapses.*)

WIFE   Oh, he's really not a bad man, only he can't hold his drink. The brandy quickly trips him up by giving him another leg.

SECOND CITIZEN   He walks on three legs, then.

WIFE   No, he falls, on his face.

SECOND CITIZEN   That's right. First he walks on all three legs, then he shifts his weight onto the third until that falls too.

SIMON   You are the vampire's tongue that licks the warm blood of my heart.

WIFE   Just leave him alone. This is the moment where he always gets sentimental. He'll get over it.

FIRST CITIZEN   What is the matter?

WIFE   You see, I was sitting on a stone in the sun, warming myself, you see—because we don't have any firewood, you see—

SECOND CITIZEN   Why don't you use your husband's nose?

WIFE   —and my daughter had gone down, just around the corner— she is a good girl and takes care of her parents.

SIMON   Ha, she confesses!

WIFE   Judas! Would you have a single pair of pants to put on if the young gentlemen didn't take off theirs when they're with her? You brandy barrel, wouldn't you die of thirst if the fountain stopped flowing, eh? We work with all our limbs, why not with that one? Her mother worked with it when she brought her into the world, and it hurt. So why shouldn't she work with it for her mother? And does it hurt? You blockhead!

SIMON   Ha, Lucretia![5] A knife, give me a knife, Romans! Ha, Appius Claudius![6]

FIRST CITIZEN   A knife—yes. But not to use on that poor whore. What has she done? Nothing! It's her hunger that whores and goes begging. A knife—yes, but to use on those who buy the flesh of our wives and daughters! Your stomach rumbles and theirs is stuffed. Your jackets are torn, but they have warm coats. Your

---

[4] Father of Virginia. Appius Claudius, one of the Decemvirs (see note 3), fell in love with her and used his powerful office to have her declared a slave of one of his dependants. Virginius then stabbed her.

[5] After having been raped by Sextus, son on Tarquinius Superbus, she revealed the incident to her husband and then killed herself.

[6] See note 4.

hands are callused, theirs are soft as velvet. Which means you work and they do not; which means that you have earned what you possess and they have stolen it; which means that you must beg and prostitute yourselves if you want to regain a few pennies of the property that they have stolen from you; which means that they are scoundrels and that we must kill them!

THIRD CITIZEN   There is no blood in their veins but the blood they have sucked from ours. They told us, "Kill the Aristocrats, they are wolves!" And we strung them up on the lanterns. They told us, "The Veto[7] is eating your bread," and we killed the Veto. They told us, "The Girondists[8] are starving you," and we guillotined the Girondists! But they stole the clothes from the dead and we are still running around on naked feet and freezing. We shall peel the skin off their legs and make pants from it! We shall melt their fat and put it into our soup! Go to it! Kill everyone who does not have a hole in his coat!

FIRST CITIZEN   Kill everyone who knows how to read and write!

SECOND CITIZEN   Kill everyone who walks with his toes turned out!

ALL   (*shouting*)   Kill them! Kill them!

(*A* YOUNG MAN *is dragged in by several people.*)

SEVERAL VOICES   He has a handkerchief! He is an Aristocrat! On the lantern with him! On the lantern!

SECOND CITIZEN   What? He doesn't blow his nose with his fingers? String him up! (*A lantern is being let down.*)

YOUNG MAN   Oh, but gentlemen!

SECOND CITIZEN   There are no gentlemen here! Up with him!

SOME VOICES   (*sing*)

If you're buried in the ground
Worms will eat you without sound.
Hanging in the air is better
Than to rot beneath a mound.

YOUNG MAN   Mercy!

THIRD CITIZEN   It's just a little game with a piece of hemp around your neck! It only lasts a moment. We are much more charitable than you people. Our whole life, we are murdered by work, we hang on the

---

[7] The King's veto.

[8] The party of the middle class which wanted to establish a bourgeois republic and, largely to maintain and increase lucrative business contracts, supported a war which would spread the revolution throughout Europe. They opposed the egalitarian wishes of the working classes and peasants.

rope for sixty years and kick our legs, but we'll cut ourselves loose! On the lantern with him!

YOUNG MAN   Go ahead then! It won't make the light any brighter for you.

PEOPLE AROUND HIM   Bravo! Bravo!

SOME VOICES   Let him go! (*He escapes.* ROBESPIERRE *appears with a retinue of women and* SANS-CULOTTES.[9])

ROBESPIERRE   What is going on, Citizens?

THIRD CITIZEN   What do you think? Those few drops of blood that dripped in August and September weren't enough to give the people red cheeks. The guillotine works too slowly. We need a downpour!

FIRST CITIZEN   Our women and children are crying for bread and we are going to feed them Aristocrats' meat. Let's go! Kill everyone who doesn't have a hole in his coat!

ALL   Kill them! Kill them!

ROBESPIERRE   In the name of the law!

FIRST CITIZEN   What is the law?

ROBESPIERRE   The will of the people.

FIRST CITIZEN   We are the people! And our will is not to have any law. Which means that in the name of the law there is no law, which means, kill them!

SEVERAL VOICES   Listen to Aristides! Listen to the Incorruptible!

A WOMAN   Listen to the Messiah who was sent to choose and to judge! He will kill those who are evil with his sharp sword. His eyes are the eyes of selection, his hands the hands of justice!

ROBESPIERRE   Poor, virtuous People! You are doing your duty, you sacrifice your enemies. You great People! You manifest yourself with thunder and lightning. But your blows, People, must not wound your own body, or else you will murder yourself in your wrath. Your enemies know that you can be vanquished only by your own strength. Your legislators are on guard and will guide your hands. Their eyes are unerring, your hands are inescapable. Follow me to the Jacobins! Your brothers will open their arms to receive you and we shall sit in bloody judgment over our enemies.

MANY VOICES   To the Jacobins![10] Long live Robespierre! (*All leave except* SIMON *and his* WIFE.)

[9] Political extremists whose name means literally "without breeches." So called because they rejected short breeches as aristrocatic apparel; instead, they wore other clothing, particularly pantaloons.

[10] An extremist group which demanded execution of suspected enemies of the Republic. Established a virtual dictatorship in 1793.

SIMON   Woe! All alone! (*He attempts to get up.*)
WIFE   There! (*She helps him.*)
SIMON   Oh, mine own Baucis![11] You are gathering fiery coals on my head!
WIFE   There! Stand on your feet now!
SIMON   You are turning from me? Can you forgive me, Portia?[12] Did I
    beat you? It was not my hand, not my arm that beat you—it was
    madness!
            Then Hamlet did it not, Hamlet denies it.
            His madness is poor Hamlet's enemy.[13]
        Where is our daughter? Where is my little Sanna?
WIFE   There, around the corner.
SIMON   To her! Come with me, virtuous spouse!
    (*Both leave.*)

SCENE 3. *The Jacobin Club.*

A MAN FROM LYON   Our brothers in Lyon have sent us to pour into your
    breasts their bitter discontent. We are not sure if the tumbril on
    which Ronsin rode to the guillotine was the hearse of Liberty; but
    we are certain that since that day the feet of Chalier's murderers
    are once again firmly planted on the ground as if there was no
    grave big enough to hold them. Have you forgotten that Lyon is
    a blemish upon the ground of France that must be covered with
    the bones of traitors? Have you forgotten that this whore of kings
    can wash away her scabs only in the water of the Rhone? Have
    you forgotten that Pitt's navy[14] will have to run aground on the
    corpses of aristocrats carried to the Mediterranean by this revolu-
    tionary river? Your clemency is murdering the revolution. The
    breath inhaled by an aristocrat is the death rattle of Liberty! Only
    cowards die for the Republic; a Jacobin will kill for her! Remember
    this: if we do not find in you the energy possessed by the men of

    [11] From Greek legend, a faithful wife.
    [12] Wife of Brutus (one of Julius Caesar's assassins). After Brutus' death, she
killed herself.
    [13] Inaccurate quotation of Shakespeare's *Hamlet*, V, ii, 228–231.
    [14] I.e., the British navy. William Pitt the younger was then Prime Minister of
England, which was at war with the French Republic.

the tenth of August,[15] of September[16] and of the thirty-first of May,[17] only one choice will be left us, the same that was left to that great patriot Gaillard[18]—the dagger of Cato![19] (*Applause and tumultuous shouts.*)

A JACOBIN   We shall empty the cup of Socrates with you![20]

LEGENDRE   (*jumping upon the platform*)   There is no need for us to turn our eyes to Lyon. People who wear garments of silk, ride in carriages, occupy the boxes in the theatre, and talk like the dictionary of the Academy seem to have carried their heads firmly anchored to their shoulders for some time now. They are even witty and say that Marat and Chalier should be given the benefit of a double martyrdom by guillotining them in effigy. (*Strong movement among the crowd.*)

SEVERAL VOICES   Those people are already dead—their tongues have guillotined them.

LEGENDRE   The blood of these saints may come upon them! I ask the members of the Committee of Public Safety who are present here, since when are your ears so deaf . . .

COLLOT D'HERBOIS   (*interrupts him*)   And I ask you, Legendre, whose voice is it that gives expression to such thoughts, so that they come to life and dare to speak? The time has come to pull off the masks! The cause accuses its effect, the shout its echo, the premise its conclusion. The Committee of Public Safety is better versed in logic, Legendre! Rest assured that the busts of the saints will not be touched; like the head of Medusa they will turn the traitors into stone.

ROBESPIERRE   I demand the floor!

THE JACOBINS   Listen to him! Listen to the Incorruptible!

ROBESPIERRE   We only waited, before speaking, to hear the cry of discontent which now sounds from all sides. Our eyes were open. We saw the enemy arming, making ready to rise up, but we did not sound the alarm. We let the people guard itself, and it was not

---

[15] On August 10, 1792, the Tuileries Palace was attacked.

[16] During the "September massacres" (September 2–6, 1792), for which Danton was partly responsible, about 1200 royalists, aristocrats, and priests were executed.

[17] On May 31, 1793, the Jacobins triumphed over the Girondists. The Jacobins surrounded the Convention, demanded the arrest of Girondist leaders, the lowering of the price of bread, and the restriction of voting rights to Sans-Culottes.

[18] Gaillard stabbed himself after the Hébertists were arrested.

[19] A conspirator against Julius Caesar, Cato killed himself after the republicans were defeated.

[20] Poison hemlock. Described in Plato's *Phaedo*.

asleep, it clanged its arms! We let the enemy come out of hiding and approach; now he stands in the open, without cover in the bright light of day, and every blow we strike will find its mark. He will be dead the moment you lay eyes on him. I have told you before that the internal enemies of the Republic are divided into two groups, like two armies. Under flags of different colors, on different roads, they march toward the same goal. One of these factions no longer exist. In their conceit and madness they attempted to push the tried and tested patriots aside as worn-out weaklings, and thus to rob the Republic of her strongest arms. They declared war on God and on Property, as a diversion in favor of the kings. They parodied the sublime drama of the Revolution in order to confute it by their studied excesses. If Hébert had triumphed, the Republic would have disintegrated into chaos, and despotism would have reigned supreme. The sword of the law descended upon the traitor. But what do the foreigners care, as long as they have other criminals at their disposal ready to help them reach the selfsame end? We have accomplished nothing if we do not exterminate that other faction, too.

That faction is the other's opposite. These men exhort us to be weak. Their war cry is, "Have mercy!" They want to tear the weapons from the people's hands and sap the strength with which they handle them, in order to deliver them naked and unnerved to the kings. Republic's weapon is the Terror, its strength is Virtue. Virtue, because without it Terror is corrupt; Terror, because without it Virtue is powerless. Terror flows from Virtue, for it is nothing but swift, stern, and inflexible justice. They say that the Terror is the weapon of a despotic government, that our government, therefore, is despotism. Indeed! But only if the sword a fighter wields for freedom is like the sabre that a satellite swings fighting for the tyrant whom he serves. If a despot governs his animal-like subjects through terror, he exercises only the right of a despot. If you shatter the enemies of freedom through terror, you are no less right, you, the founders of the Republic. The revolutionary government is the dictatorship of freedom against tyranny. From certain quarters, we hear the shout, "Have pity on the Royalists!" Have pity on scoundrels? No! We reserve our pity for the innocent, for the weak and the unfortunate, we pity mankind! Only the peaceful citizen has a right to protection by society. In a republic, only republicans are citizens; royalists and foreigners are enemies. It is merciful to punish the oppressors of mankind; to forgive them would be barbaric. All these signs of a false sensitivity seem very much like sighs heaved toward Austria or England. But they are not content with wresting the arms from the hands of the People; they want to poison the most sacred sources of its power by Vice. This is the most subtle, the most dangerous, and most despicable attack on liberty. Vice is the mark of Cain borne by the aristocracy. In a republic, vice is not only a moral but a political offense. The depraved are freedom's political enemies, and they are all the more dangerous, the greater the services they seem to have rendered it. The most dangerous citizen is the one who uses up a dozen red caps before doing one single good deed.

You will understand what I mean when you think of the people who used to live in garrets and who are now riding in carriages, wenching with former marquises and baronesses. We may well ask: have not the people been robbed, do we not shake the gold-plated hands of the kings when we, the legislators of the People, parade the vices and the luxuries of erstwhile courtiers before the People, when we see these counts and barons of the Revolution marry rich women, give sumptuous banquets, gamble, surround themselves with servants, and wear luxurious clothes? We may well prick up our ears when we hear their new ideas, their precious discourse, and their pretty speeches. Not long ago, someone impertinently parodied Tacitus;[21] I could reply with quotations from Sallust[22] and with a travesty on Catiline,[23] but I believe there is no need to add more details to the picture—the portraits are complete. Let us not make peace nor even make a truce with those who have thoughts only for robbing the people, with those who hope to get away with robbery, with those for whom the Republic is a game of fortune and the Revolution nothing but a trade. Terrified by the examples they have seen passing before their eyes in a roaring cataract, they are now carefully trying to cool the fires of justice. It almost seems as if they said to themselves: "We are not virtuous enough to be terrible. Have pity on our weakness, philosophic legislators! I do not dare admit to you that I'm depraved; I rather say: do not be cruel!"

Be confident, virtuous People! Have faith, Patriots! Tell your brothers in Lyon that the sword of Justice will not rust in the

[21] Roman rhetorician (*c.* 55 A.D.–*c.* 117 A.D.).

[22] Roman historical writer (86–35 B.C.) whose subject was the conflict between democratic power and the nobility.

[23] Roman revolutionist whose conspiracy (65 B.C.) failed and who was killed three years later.

hands of those to whom you have confided it! We shall set the
Republic a great example! (*General applause.*)
MANY VOICES   Long live the Republic! Long live Robespierre!
PRESIDENT   The meeting is adjourned.

SCENE 4. *A street.* LACROIX, LEGENDRE.

LACROIX   What have you done, Legendre! Do you have any idea at whose
head you are aiming with your busts?
LEGENDRE   The heads of a few fops and elegant women. That's all.
LACROIX   You are committing suicide! You are a shadow that murders its
original and thus itself.
LEGENDRE   I don't understand.
LACROIX   I thought Collot had made himself quite plain.
LEGENDRE   What of it? He was drunk again.
LACROIX   Fools, children and—well?—drunks speak the truth. Whom
do you think Robespierre meant when he mentioned Catiline?
LEGENDRE   Well?
LACROIX   It's so simple. They sent the atheists and ultra-revolutionaries
to the scaffold. But that didn't help the people, they are still walking the streets barefoot, bent on making shoes from aristocrats'
hides. So the temperature of the guillotine must not be allowed to
drop; let the thermometer show only a few degrees less and the
Committee of Public Safety will find that their beds have been
moved to the Place de la Révolution.
LEGENDRE   What do my busts have to do with all that?
LACROIX   Don't you understand yet? You have given official recognition
to the counterrevolution; you have forced the Decemvirs to show
some energy, you have guided their hands. The people are like the
Minotaur;[24] they must have their corpses every week, or they will
eat the Committee itself.
LEGENDRE   Where is Danton?
LACROIX   Who knows? He is trying to find the Venus of Medici[25] piece-
meal in all the grisettes of the Palais-Royal. He is putting a mosaic

[24] A monster with the body of a human and the head of a bull. Until Theseus
destroyed it, it devoured young Athenians whom it received as a tribute.
[25] A sculpture of the third century B.C.

together, as he calls it. God only knows with which part of the body he is busy right now. What a shame that Nature has dismembered beauty, like Medea her brother, and deposited the fragments in different bodies.[26] Let's go to the Palais-Royal.
(*Both leave.*)

SCENE 5. *A room.* DANTON, MARION.

MARION   No, let me sit like this—at your feet. I want to tell you a story.
DANTON   I could think of a better use for your lips.
MARION   No, let me sit like this—just this once!—My mother was a wise woman. She used to tell me that chastity was a great virtue. When people came to the house and started to talk about all sorts of things, she always sent me out of the room. When I asked her later what the people had wanted, she used to reply that I ought to be ashamed of myself. When she gave me a book to read, I always had to skip some pages. But she let me read the Bible as much as I wanted; there everything was sacred. Still, there were some things in it that I did not understand, but I didn't like to ask anybody about it; I just brooded about it. Then spring came, and things were going on all around me in which I had no part. I became enveloped in a peculiar atmosphere, and it almost suffocated me. I looked at my limbs and sometimes I seemed to be two, and then again I melted into one. At that time, a young man used to come to the house. He was handsome and often said crazy things. I didn't quite know what he wanted, but he made me laugh. My mother asked him to come more often, and that suited both of us. Finally, we didn't see why we couldn't just as well lie next to each other between two bed sheets as sit next to each other on two chairs. I liked that better than his conversation and couldn't understand why I should be deprived of the greater and be allowed only the smaller pleasure. We did it secretly. And thus it went. But I became like the sea, devouring everything, and churning deeper and deeper. Only one difference existed for me—all men blended

[26] With Medea's help, Jason obtained the Golden Fleece. Pursued by her father, King Æetes, she and Jason fled. Medea killed her brother, cut his body into small pieces, and threw them into the sea. In order to give his son a proper burial, Æetes had to retrieve the pieces. This slowed him down long enough to allow Medea and Jason to escape.

into one body. That's how I was, and who can jump out of his skin? He finally noticed it. One morning he came and kissed me as if he wanted to choke me. His arms knotted around my neck and I was terribly afraid. Then he let go of me, laughed and said he had almost done something foolish; I should keep my dress and wear it; it would wear out eventually anyway and he didn't want to spoil my fun too soon; after all, he said, it was the only thing I had. Then he left. Again I didn't know what he meant. That evening I sat by the window. I am very sensitive; I am connected with the world around me only by my senses; I drowned in the waves of the sunset. Then a crowd came down the street, the children were running ahead, and women looked out of the windows. I looked down; they were carrying him past in a basket, the moon fell on his pale forehead and his hair was damp. He had drowned himself. And I started to cry. That was the only break in my life. Other people have Sundays and weekdays, they work for six days and pray on the seventh, they become emotional once a year on their birthday and think a little once a year on New Year's Day. I don't understand any of this; there are no intermissions or changes in my life. My life is only one thing: an uninterrupted yearning and holding, a furnace, a river. My mother died of a broken heart. People point their fingers at me. That's stupid. It's all the same, whether one enjoys bodies, pictures of Christ, flowers, or children's toys. It's all the same feeling. The one who enjoys most, prays the most.

DANTON   Why can't I absorb your beauty completely, why can I not encircle all of it?

MARION   Danton, your lips have eyes.

DANTON   I wish I were a part of the ether, so that I could bathe you, so that I could break myself on every wave of your beautiful body. (LACROIX, ADELAIDE *and* ROSALIE *enter.*)

LACROIX (*remains standing in the doorway*). This really makes me laugh! It is too funny!

DANTON· (*cross*) Well?

LACROIX   I was just thinking of the street.

DANTON   So?

LACROIX   There were two dogs on the street, a great Dane and a tiny, long-haired lap dog. They had a hard time.

DANTON   What about it?

LACROIX   The thought just occurred to me and I had to laugh. It really was an edifying sight! The girls were watching from the windows. One shouldn't even let them sit in the sunshine; the mosquitoes might carry on right on their hands, and that makes them think. Legendre and myself have been chasing through almost all of the cells, and the little nuns of the Revelation through the Flesh were hanging on to our coattails, they wanted us to bless them. Legendre is helping one of them do penance, but he will have to fast a month for it. Here are two of the Priestesses of the Body.

MARION   Good day, Demoiselle Adelaide! Good day, Demoiselle Rosalie!

ROSALIE   We haven't had the pleasure for a long time.

MARION   I have missed you.

ADELAIDE   My God, we are so busy day and night.

DANTON   (*to* ROSALIE)   Eh, little girl, your hips have really become supple!

ROSALIE   Oh yes, I'm improving every day.

LACROIX   What is the difference between an Adonis of antiquity and one of our time?

DANTON   And Adelaide has become interestingly modest. What a stimulating change! Her face looks like a fig leaf that she is holding in front of her whole body. A fig tree like this, standing on such a busy thoroughfare, offers the most delightful shade.

ADELAIDE   I would be a cow path if Monsieur—

DANTON   I understand. Don't be angry, Mademoiselle!

LACROIX   Now listen to me! A modern Adonis is not torn apart by a wild boar but by sows. He is wounded, not in the thigh, but in his groin. And not roses grow from his blood, but blossoms of quicksilver.

DANTON   Mademoiselle Rosalie is a restored torso: only the hips and feet date back to antiquity. She is a magnetic needle: what the pole "head" repels, the pole "foot" attracts. In the middle is the equator, and everyone who passes the line is baptized with quicksilver sublimate.

LACROIX   They are two Sisters of Charity. They serve in a hospital, that is, each in her own body.

ROSALIE   You ought to be ashamed to make us blush!

ADELAIDE   You really ought to have better manners!

(ADELAIDE *and* ROSALIE *leave.*)

DANTON   Good night, my pretty children!

LACROIX   Good night, you quicksilver mines!

DANTON   I feel sorry for them. They have been cheated out of their dinner.

LACROIX   Listen, Danton. I'm coming from the Jacobins.

DANTON   Is that all?

LACROIX   The people from Lyon read a proclamation. They felt all that was left for them to do was to wrap themselves in the toga. They all made faces as if each was about to say to his neighbor: Paetus, it does not hurt![27] Legendre shouted that there were men about who were prepared to smash the busts of Chalier and Marat. I believe he is trying to paint his face red again. He has completely lost touch with the Terror; even the children pull his coattails on the street.

DANTON   And Robespierre?

LACROIX   He shook his finger from the rostrum and said that Virtue has to rule through Terror. That phrase gave me a pain in the neck.

DANTON   It planes planks for the guillotine.

LACROIX   And Collot shouted like mad, he said the masks should be torn off.

DANTON   The faces would come off, too, if they were.

(PARIS *enters.*)

LACROIX   What's new, Fabricus?[28]

PARIS   I went from the Jacobins to Robespierre and demanded an explanation. He tried to make a face like Brutus sacrificing his sons.[29] He talked about duty in general and said that he would do anything for the defense of liberty, that he would be willing to sacrifice everything, himself, his brother, his friends.

DANTON   That was plain, I would say. One only has to reverse the order and he stands at the bottom, holding the ladder for his friends. We have to be grateful to Legendre; he has made them talk.

LACROIX   The Hébertists are not yet dead and, physically, the people still suffer. That is a terrible lever. The scale with blood must not be allowed to rise or it will become the lantern on which the Committee of Public Safety will hang. He needs ballast on the other side of the scales, he needs a heavy head.

DANTON   I know, I know very well—the Revolution is like Saturn; she devours her own children. (*After some reflection.*) Yet, they will not dare.

LACROIX   You are a dead saint, Danton. But the Revolution has no use for relics; the bones of the kings were thrown out on the street and the statues out of the churches. Do you think for a moment that they will let you stand as a monument?

DANTON   But my name! The People!

LACROIX   Your name! You are a moderate, like myself, like Camille,

---

[27] The Roman emperor Claudius sentenced Paetus' wife Arria to be executed. Instead, she killed herself and, expiring, said, "Paetus, it does not hurt."

[28] A Roman (third century B.C.) who revealed to Pyrrhus a plan to poison him.

[29] When his sons tried to restore the Tarquins (see note 5), Brutus had them killed.

Philippeau and Hérault. The mob knows no difference between weakness and moderation; they kill the stragglers. The tailors in the division of the Red Caps will feel the entire history of Rome in the point of their needles, if the Man of September should look like a moderate compared with them.

DANTON   That's very true. Besides, the masses are like children. They have to break everything to see what's inside.

LACROIX   What's more, Danton, we are wicked men, as Robespierre calls us. That is, we are able to enjoy ourselves. The masses are virtuous, which is to say that they enjoy nothing because work has dulled their organs of enjoyment; neither do they drink—because they have no money. Nor do they go to a brothel—because they reek of cheese and herring, and the girls find that disgusting.

DANTON   He hates anyone who enjoys life as a eunuch hates men.

LACROIX   They call us scoundrels, and (*Bending down until his mouth almost touches* DANTON's *ears.*)—between ourselves—there is a kernel of truth in that. Robespierre and the masses will remain virtuous, Saint-Just will write a novel and Barère will tailor a Carmagnole[30] and drape the robe of blood around the shoulders of the Convention and—I can see it all!

DANTON   You are dreaming. They never had courage without me and they will not have any against me. The Revolution is not yet finished and they may need me again. They are likely to keep me in storage in their arsenal.

LACROIX   We must act.

DANTON   We shall see.

LACROIX   We shall see—when we are lost.

MARION   (*to* DANTON)   Your lips have grown cold. Your words have smothered your kisses.

DANTON   (*to* MARION)   To waste all this time! It was not worth it! (*To* LACROIX.)   I'll go to Robespierre tomorrow. I shall make him so angry that he won't be able to keep silent. So—tomorrow! Good night, my friends, good night! I thank you!

LACROIX   Off with you, my good friends, off with you! Good night, Danton! The thighs of Mademoiselle will be your guillotine, her Mound of Venus your Tarpeian Rock![31]

(*He and* PARIS *leave.*)

---

[30] A revolutionary song.

[31] In ancient Rome, criminals sentenced to death were hurled from the Tarpeian Rock of the Capitoline Hill.

SCENE 6. *A room.* ROBESPIERRE, PARIS, *and* DANTON.

ROBESPIERRE I tell you, anyone who tries to stop me when I draw my
   sword is my enemy—no matter what his intentions. Anyone who
   prevents me from defending myself kills me as much as if he had
   attacked me.
DANTON Where self-defense ends, murder begins. I see no reason that
   forces us to continue killing.
ROBESPIERRE The social revolution has not been completed. Leaving
   a revolution half-finished means digging your own grave. The
   aristocracy is not yet dead, the healthy forces of the people must
   take the place of this class that is decadent in every way. Vice
   must be punished, Virtue must rule by Terror.
DANTON I don't quite understand this word, "punishment." You and
   your virtue, Robespierre! You have never taken money, you don't
   have any debts, you never sleep with a woman, you always wear
   a decent suit of clothes and you never get drunk. Robespierre, you
   are outrageously righteous! I would be ashamed of myself for
   chasing around between heaven and earth for thirty years with
   the same moral expression on my face just for the miserable
   pleasure of being able to look down on everybody else. Is there
   really nothing in you that tells you sometimes, very quietly and
   secretively: you are a liar, you are a liar!
ROBESPIERRE I have a clear conscience.
DANTON Conscience is a mirror, and only monkeys torment themselves
   in front of it. Everyone decks himself out as well as he can and
   tries to have his fun in his own way. It's hardly worthwhile to get
   into each other's hair about that! Let everyone defend himself if
   somebody else spoils his pleasure. Do you have any right to make
   the guillotine into a washtub for other people's dirty linen, and
   their heads into a ball of soap to wash their dirty clothes, merely
   because your coat is always immaculately clean? Yes, you have a
   right to defend yourself if they spit on your coat or tear holes in it.
   But if they leave you alone, what do you care? If they don't mind
   walking around the way they are, what right have you to lock
   them into their graves? Are you heaven's policeman? If you can't
   bear to look at it as easily as your Good Lord, why—hold a
   handkerchief before your eyes!
ROBESPIERRE Are you denying Virtue?

DANTON Virtue and Vice. All men love pleasure, some are crude and some refined; Jesus was the most refined of all. That is the only difference between men I have been able to discover. Everyone acts according to his nature, that is, he does what does him good. It is cruel, Incorruptible, is it not, to make you walk without your shoes like this?

ROBESPIERRE Danton, at times Vice is high treason.

DANTON You must not banish Vice, for heaven's sake, do not do that! It would be most ungrateful; you owe Vice too much—by contrast, that is. But even if one thinks the way you do, our blows must be of benefit to the Republic. We must not punish the innocent along with the guilty.

ROBESPIERRE And who says that one man was punished who was innocent?

DANTON Did you hear that, Fabricius? Not one man has died innocent! (*He turns to leave; while he is walking to the door, to* PARIS.) We must not waste one single moment. We must show ourselves. (*Both leave.*)

ROBESPIERRE (*alone*) Go! Go! He wants to halt the steeds of the Revolution in front of a brothel like a coachman his well-trained horses. They will be strong enough to drag him to the scaffold. Make me walk without shoes! If one thinks the way I do!—but wait! Stop! Is that perhaps it?—They will say that his towering stature had cast too long a shadow on me, and that I therefore had made him step aside. And if they're right? Is it really necessary? Yes, it is! For the sake of the Republic! He must go. It's ridiculous how my thoughts keep an eye on each other.—He must go. If a man who is part of moving masses stops, he resists as much as if he tried to halt their march. He'll perish under their feet.

We will not allow the ship of the Revolution to run aground on the mud banks of these people's shallow calculations. We must chop off the hand which dares to stop it—even if he tries to hold on with his teeth!

Let us wipe out this crowd that has stolen the clothes of dead aristocrats and has inherited their leprosy! No virtue! Virtue one of my shoes! If one thinks the way you do!—How that keeps coming back to me. Why can I not forget it? His bleeding finger keeps pointing there, at that one spot! No matter how many bandages I wrap around it, the blood still oozes out. (*After a pause.*) I don't know which part of myself is lying to the other. (*He steps to the window.*)

The night snores across the face of the earth and tosses in a wild dream. Thoughts and desires, barely suggested, confused and shapeless, which timidly hid from the light of day, now take on form, dress up and creep into the quiet house of dreams. They open doors, look out of windows and almost become flesh. The sleeping limbs stretch in their sleep and lips begin to murmur words.—And is not waking just a clearer dream? Are we not sleepwalkers? Do we not act awake just as we do in dreams, if more distinctly, more decisively and more effectively? Who can blame us? The mind performs more acts of thought in sixty minutes than our bodies' leaden organism is able to enact in years. The sin is in our thoughts. Whether the thought becomes an act, whether the body imitates the mind—is merely accident.

(SAINT-JUST *enters.*)

ROBESPIERRE   Heh, who is that in the dark? Light, bring light!

SAINT-JUST   Do you know my voice?

ROBESPIERRE   Oh, it is you, Saint-Just! (A MAID SERVANT *brings a candle.*)

SAINT-JUST   Were you alone?

ROBESPIERRE   Danton just left.

SAINT-JUST   I met him on the way, in the Palais-Royal. He had put on his revolutionary face and talked in epigrams. He called the Sans-Culottes by their first names and the grisettes ran after him looking at his calves. People stopped and whispered to each other what he had said. We are going to lose the advantage of the attack. Do you still hesitate? In that case, we shall act without you. We are determined.

ROBESPIERRE   What do you propose to do?

SAINT-JUST   We are going to call the Legislative Committee and the Committees of Security and Public Safety into solemn session.

ROBESPIERRE   Very ceremonious.

SAINT-JUST   We must bury such an important corpse with all the decencies, like priests and not like murderers. It must not be mutilated—all its limbs must go into the grave together.

ROBESPIERRE   Be a little more explicit!

SAINT-JUST   We must bury him in all his armor and kill his horses and his slaves above his grave. Lacroix—

ROBESPIERRE   An unmitigated scoundrel, former law clerk, now Lieutenant General of France. Go on!

SAINT-JUST   Hérault-Séchelles.

ROBESPIERRE   A handsome face.

SAINT-JUST   He was the illuminated letter at the head of the Constitution. Since we no longer have any need for decorations of this kind, he will be erased.—Philippeau. Camille.

ROBESPIERRE   He, too?

SAINT-JUST   (*handing him a paper*)   I thought so. Read this!

ROBESPIERRE   Aha! "Le Vieux Cordelier"![32] Is that all? He is a child. He
laughs at you.

SAINT-JUST   Read this—here! (*He points to a passage in the paper.*)

ROBESPIERRE   (*reads*)   "Robespierre, the Bloody Messiah, on his Calvary
between the two thieves, Couthon and Collot, on which he sacrifices rather than is sacrificed. Below him stand the Saintly Sisters
of the Guillotine like Mary and Magdalen. Saint-Just, embracing
him like John, announces the Master's apocalyptic revelations to
the Convention. He carries his head like a monstrance."

SAINT-JUST   I'll make him carry his like St. Denis.[33]

ROBESPIERRE   (*continues reading*)   "Is it possible that the clean frock-
coat of the Messiah is France's shroud and that his thin fingers,
twitching all over the rostrum, are the knives of the guillotine?
And you, Barère, who said that money could be coined on the
Place de la Révolution! But—I do not want to rummage in that old
bag. He is like a widow who has had half a dozen husbands and
has buried them all. Who can help that sort of thing? He simply
has that special, hippocratic gift to see death in the face of people
six months before they die. Who wants to sit with corpses and
smell the stink?"—So you, too, Camille? Away with them! And
quickly! Only the dead don't return. Is the indictment ready?

SAINT-JUST   It was easy. You gave enough hints at the Jacobins.

ROBESPIERRE   I wanted to frighten them.

SAINT-JUST   I only had to follow through. The forgers will supply the egg,
the foreigners the apple. I give you my word, the meal will be
deadly for them.

ROBESPIERRE   Quick then, tomorrow! No long drawn-out death struggle!
I have become sensitive these last few days. Make it quick!
(SAINT-JUST *leaves.*)

ROBESPIERRE   (*alone*)   Yes, a Bloody Messiah who sacrifices and is not
sacrificed. He redeemed them with His blood, I save them with
theirs. He made them sin, I take the sin upon myself. He had the
voluptuous pleasure of pain—I suffer the torments of the hangman. Whose abnegation was greater, His or mine? And still, this
thought contains some kind of foolishness. Why do we always look

---

[32] "The Old Cordelier." The Cordeliers, founded in 1790 in the Paris district
of that name, denounced to the people abuses of power and infractions of the rights
of man. In 1793, they helped overthrow the Girondists.

[33] First bishop of Paris, who was martyred. He is usually represented as
holding his head in his hands.

at Him? Truly, in each of us the Son of Man is crucified and each
of us sweats blood struggling in his own Garden of Gethesemane,
but none of us saves any other with his wounds. My dear Camille!
They leave me, all of them—all is an empty desert—I am alone.

Act II

SCENE 1. *A room.* DANTON, LACROIX, PHILIPPEAU, PARIS, CAMILLE
DESMOULINS.

CAMILLE   Quick, Danton, we have no time to lose!
DANTON   (*getting dressed*)   But time loses us. How boring always to put
on first the shirt and then on top of it the trousers, to creep to bed
at night and out of it again next morning, and always to put one
foot in front of the other. And there's no prospect that these things
will ever change. How sad to think that millions before us did it
just like we, that millions coming after us will keep on doing it,
and that, to top it all, we consist of two parts doing both the same,
so that all that is done is duplicated—how sad to contemplate all
this.
CAMILLE   You talk like a child.
DANTON   The dying often become childish.
LACROIX   Your hesitations are your ruin, and you pull all your friends
with you into the abyss. Give notice to the cowards that the time
has come to rally round you; call those who sit on the Mountain[1]
and the others below! Denounce the tyranny of the Decemvirs,
speak of daggers, refer to Brutus—and you will frighten the
galleries and bring to your side even those who are threatened as
associates of Hébert! Give your wrath free rein! At least don't let us
die disarmed and humiliated like the miserable Hébert!
DANTON   You called me a "dead saint," remember? There was more truth
in that than you suspected. I have been talking to all the Sections;
they showed respect, but looked like undertakers. I am a relic, and
one throws relics into garbage cans; you were quite right.
LACROIX   Why did you let it come to this?
DANTON   To this? Yes, I believe I was bored in the end. To wear the
same coat and the same expression all the time! Pitiful! To be such

[1] Pun on the Montagnards, a political faction.

a poor instrument that one string can only produce one sound—
it is unbearable! I wanted to have an easy life, and I succeeded;
the Revolution lets me rest, although a little differently than I
thought. Besides, on whom can we rely? True, our whores would
be a match for the Pious Sisters of the Guillotine; but that is all!
You can figure it out on your fingers: the Jacobins have declared
that Virtue is the order of the day, the Cordeliers call me Hébert's
hangman, the City Council is doing penance and the Convention—
now there might be the answer! But it would take another thirty-
first of May, they would not willingly give in. Robespierre is the
dogma of the Revolution, and you do not erase a dogma. Nor
would it work. We did not make the Revolution, the Revolution
made us! But even if it worked—I'd rather be guillotined than
order others to the guillotine. I am fed up with it. Why should men
fight each other? We should sit down side by side and have some
peace. When we were created, someone made a mistake; there is
something missing in us—I don't have a name for it, but we are not
going to dig it out of each other's entrails. So why cut open our
bellies? Go on—we're miserable alchemists!

CAMILLE   Put a little more solemnly, you might say: How long will
humanity continue gulping its own limbs to satisfy its endless
hunger? Or: Shall we shipwrecks continue forever sucking the
blood out of each other's veins to still our unquenchable thirst? Or:
how long shall we who do our algebra with flesh, continue writing
our accounts with lacerated limbs while we search for the unknown
X that is eternally refused us?

DANTON   You are a powerful echo.

CAMILLE   A pistol shot makes as much noise as a clap of thunder. So
much the better for you; you should always have me around!

PHILIPPEAU   And we leave France to her hangmen?

DANTON   What of it? It does not seem to bother anyone. They are unfortunate. What more could they ask, if they want to feel sentimental, noble, virtuous or witty, and above all for constant enter-
tainment? What does it matter whether they die under the guillotine or of a fever or old age? All things considered, it is preferable
that they should take their bow and leave the stage while they are
in good health; as they withdraw, they still can make some pretty
gestures and even hear the audience applaud. That is quite gracious
and very suitable for us. We always have been on the stage, although at last we're stabbed in earnest.

It is a good thing that our life-span is reduced a little. Our
coats are much too big for us, we do not fill them. Life becomes an

epigram and that will do. For who has enough breath and wit to write an epos of fifty or sixty cantos? It's time that we stopped drinking the tiny bit of elixir allowed us from washtubs, and that we started using liqueur glasses instead. At least we'll get a mouthful that way while we could hardly make a few drops roll together in the clumsy vessel.

And finally, I would have to shout; that is far too much trouble. Life is not worth the effort we make to preserve it.

PARIS   Flee then, Danton!

DANTON   Can you take your country with you on the soles of your shoes? Finally—and that is the most important thing: they will not dare. (*To* CAMILLE.) Come, my friend; I tell you, they won't dare. Adieu, adieu!

(DANTON *and* CAMILLE *leave.*)

PHILIPPEAU   There he goes.

LACROIX   And does not believe one word of all he said. Nothing but laziness! He'd rather put his head under the guillotine than make a speech.

PARIS   What can we do?

LACROIX   Go home and study how to make a decent exit, like Lucretia.

SCENE 2. *A promenade. People strolling.*

A CITIZEN   My good Jacqueline—I meant to say Corn . . . I mean Cor . . .

SIMON   Cornelia, Citizen, Cornelia.[2]

CITIZEN   My good Cornelia has presented me with a little boy.

SIMON   Borne the Republic a son!

CITIZEN   The Republic—that sounds a bit too general; you might say . . .

SIMON   That's just it! The individual and the general must . . .

CITIZEN   Ah yes, that's what my wife says, too.

STREET-SINGER (*sings*).

> *What is this, what is this*
> *That a man would hate to miss?*

CITIZEN   Only, about the names—I just can't make up my mind.

SIMON   Call him Pike Marat!

---

[2] A virtuous Roman matron whose sons advocated economic reform for farmers and relief for the poor.

STREET-SINGER (*continues to sing*).

> *To grief and sorrow we are born,*
> *We must toil from early morn*
> *Till the sun goes down.*

CITIZEN   I would like to give him three names; there is something about the number three; and also names that would be useful and proper. Now I have it: Plow, Robespierre. But what about the third one?

SIMON   Pike.

CITIZEN   Many thanks, neighbor. Pike—Plow—Robespierre—they are nice names, they have a pretty sound.

SIMON   I can tell you, your Cornelia's breast will swell like the udder of the Roman she-wolf—no, that won't do at all. Romulus[3] was a tyrant, that won't do. (*They pass.*)

A BEGGAR (*sings*)   "A handful of earth and a little moss . . ." Dear Gentlemen, beautiful Ladies!

FIRST GENTLEMAN   Scoundrel! Go and work! You don't look exactly starved!

SECOND GENTLEMAN   There! (*He gives him some money.*) His hands are like velvet! What impudence!

BEGGAR   Sir, where did you get your coat?

SECOND GENTLEMAN   I work! Work, that's what paid for it! You could have one just like it. I'll give you work. Come around and see me. I live—

BEGGAR   Sir, why did you work?

SECOND GENTLEMAN   So I could buy this coat, you fool!

BEGGAR   So you have slaved in order to have some pleasure. For to have a coat like that gives you pleasure. Rags would do the same thing.

SECOND GENTLEMAN   Of course, there's no other way.

BEGGAR   I'd have to be a fool! The one offsets the other. The sun is warm at the corner and that makes it easy. (*Sings.*)
"*A handful of earth and a little moss . . .*"

ROSALIE (*to* ADELAIDE)   Hurry up, there are soldiers coming! We haven't had anything warm in our stomachs since yesterday.

BEGGAR   ". . . as last greeting on my grave they toss."
Gentlemen, kind ladies!

SOLDIER   Halt! Where are you going, girls? (*To* ROSALIE.) How old are you?

ROSALIE   As old as my little finger.

SOLDIER   You're pretty sharp.

---

[3] The founder of Rome, Romulus and his twin brother Remus were abandoned in infancy and suckled by a wolf.

ROSALIE And you're very dull.

SOLDIER Then you be my whetstone! (*Sings.*)

> *My dear Christine, Christine, my dear,*
> *The damage hurts you much, I fear.*
> *Much I fear, much I fear.*

ROSALIE (*sings in reply*)

> *Oh no, dear soldier, that's not true.*
> *I'd like some more, some more like you,*
> *More like you, more like you.*
> (DANTON *and* CAMILLE *enter.*)

DANTON Isn't this merry? I smell something in the air—it feels as if the sun was breeding obscenities. Don't you feel like jumping right into the middle, pulling down your trousers and copulating from behind like dogs in the street? (*They pass.*)

YOUNG GENTLEMAN Ah, Madame, the sound of bells, the evening sun seen through the trees, the distant glimmer of a star . . .

MADAME The perfume of flowers! Yes, these natural pleasures, the pure enjoyment of nature! (*To her daughter.*) You see, Eugenie, only virtue has eyes for this.

EUGENIE (*kisses her mother's hand*) Oh, Mamma, I can see only you!

MADAME You are a good child!

YOUNG GENTLEMAN (*whispers into* EUGENIE's *ear*) Do you see the pretty young lady with the old gentleman over there?

EUGENIE I know her.

YOUNG GENTLEMAN I'm told her hairdresser set her hair—*à l'enfant.*[4]

EUGENIE (*laughing*) Wicked tongues!

YOUNG GENTLEMAN The old gentleman walks next to her; he sees the little bud swell, takes it for a walk in the sunshine, and thinks that he was the thundershower that started it.

EUGENIE Oh, how naughty! I feel like blushing!

YOUNG GENTLEMAN That would make me blanch.
    (*They leave.*)

DANTON (*to* CAMILLE) Don't ask me to be serious! I simply cannot understand why people don't stop in the street and laugh in each other's faces. It seems to me they ought to be laughing from the windows and even from their graves, and the sky ought to split and the earth roll with laughter.
    (*They leave.*)

---

[4] Pun: the hairstyle is childlike and also appropriate to a lady who is with child.

FIRST GENTLEMAN   I assure you, it is an extraordinary discovery! It puts all technical knowledge into a completely different light. Mankind is rushing toward its supreme destiny with giant strides.

SECOND GENTLEMAN   Did you see the new play? A Tower of Babylon! A maze of vaults, little stairs, corridors, and everything so airy and bold as if thrown high into the air. One gets dizzy with every step. A bizarre face. (*He stops, embarrassed.*)

FIRST GENTLEMAN   What's the trouble?

SECOND GENTLEMAN   Oh nothing! Please, give me your hand, sir! This puddle—there. Thank you so much. I almost didn't make it. That might have become dangerous!

FIRST GENTLEMAN   You weren't afraid, were you?

SECOND GENTLEMAN   Well, the earth has such a thin crust. I'm always afraid I might drop right through when there are holes like that. One has to step carefully—it's easy to break through! But you must go to the theatre, I really recommend it.

SCENE 3. *A room.* DANTON, CAMILLE, LUCILE.

CAMILLE   I tell you, if you don't serve it to them in wooden copies spread all over the theatres, concert halls, and art exhibitions, they have neither eyes nor ears for it. If someone carves a marionette that shows the thread by which it is made to move, and that creaks in the joints at every step in five-footed iambics—oh, what character, how impressive! When somebody takes a trite little emotion, an aphorism or some idea, dresses it up in coat and pants, makes hands and feet for it, paints its face and lets it squirm its way through three whole acts, until finally it either gets married or shoots itself —that is perfection! When someone fiddles an opera that reflects the floating and sinking of the human soul as accurately as a water-filled clay pipe the song of the nightingale—ah, what art!

   Take the people out of the theatre and into the street—that is miserable reality. They cannot see their creator for all his pitiful imitators. They see nothing and hear nothing of the creation which glows and roars and shines around and within them and is born anew every moment. They go to the theatre, read poetry and novels, grimace like the caricatures about which they read—and to God's creatures they say: how common! The Greeks knew whereof they spoke when they told the story about Pygmalion's statue which came to life but did not procreate.

DANTON   And all the artists have the same attitude toward Nature as David when he cold-bloodedly drew pictures of the September victims just as their bodies were being thrown from the prison into the street; he said: I am catching the last spasm of life in these scoundrels!

(DANTON *is called out of the room.*)

CAMILLE   What do you say, Lucile?

LUCILE   Nothing. I like to see you talk.

CAMILLE   Do you hear me, too?

LUCILE   Why, of course!

CAMILLE   Am I right? Do you know what I said?

LUCILE   No, I really don't.

(DANTON *comes back.*)

CAMILLE   What is the matter?

DANTON   The Committee of Public Safety has decided on my arrest. I have been warned and have been offered a hide-out. They want my head—so be it. I'm tired of all the trouble. Let them take it! What does it matter? I'll know how to die courageously. It's easier than living.

CAMILLE   Danton, there is still time!

DANTON   Impossible. But I didn't think . . .

CAMILLE   You are so lazy!

DANTON   I'm not lazy, I'm tired. The soles of my feet are burning.

CAMILLE   Where are you going?

DANTON   Oh, if I knew that!

CAMILLE   Seriously, where to?

DANTON   For a walk, my boy, for a walk.

(*He leaves.*)

LUCILE   Oh, Camille!

CAMILLE   Be calm, dear child!

LUCILE   When I think that this head . . . Oh, Camille! It isn't true, is it? Am I mad?

CAMILLE   Be calm! Danton and I are not one.

LUCILE   The world is huge, there are so many things in it. Why do they want just this one thing? Why do they want to take it from me? That would be terrible. What do they want to do with it?

CAMILLE   I repeat what I told you, don't worry! I talked to Robespierre only yesterday, and he was friendly. It's true, there is some tension between us, there are differences of opinion, but that is all.

LUCILE   You must go and talk to him!

CAMILLE   We sat on the same bench in school. He was always gloomy, always alone. I was the one who sought him out and sometimes made him laugh. He has always been loyal to me. I'll go and talk to him.

LUCILE   So soon, my friend? Yes, go! Come, just this! (*She kisses him.*) And this! And now go quickly! (CAMILLE *leaves.*) These are hard times. That is the way it goes. Who can resist it? We must bear it. (*She sings.*)

Oh, parting, oh parting, oh parting!
Who ever has thought of it first?

How did this song get into my head just now? It is not good that it should find its way all by itself like that—when we left, I felt as if he would never be able to turn back and would leave me farther and farther behind, farther and farther. How empty this room is! The windows are open as if a body had been lying here. I can't stand it any longer inside.
(*She leaves.*)

SCENE 4. *An open field.* DANTON.

DANTON   I don't want to walk any farther. I don't want to break this silence with the chitchat of my marching feet, the gasping of my lungs. (*He sits down. After a pause.*) I have been told of an illness which robs you of your memory. Death is supposed to be somewhat like that. But sometimes I have hopes that death is still more powerful, that it takes everything. If this were true! Then, like a Christian, I would run to save an enemy—my memory. That place may well be safe, yes, for my memory; but not for me. For me, the grave is safer; at least it lets me forget, it kills my memory. But there, my memory would stay alive and kill me! My memory or I? The answer is so simple! (*He gets up and turns back.*) I flirt with Death. It is quite pleasant to ogle Death like this, through my lorgnette and from a comfortable distance. But when I think about it, this whole business makes me laugh. I have a feeling of stability that tells me tomorrow will be like today, and so the day after tomorrow, and thus always as it is now. It is a false alarm; they want to frighten me. But they won't dare!
(*He leaves.*)

SCENE 5. *A room. It is night.* DANTON.

DANTON (*at a window*)   Will it never stop? Will the light never fade, the sound never rot? Will there never be darkness and peace, so that we need no longer see and hear each other's beastly sins? September!

JULIE (*calls from the next room*)   Danton! Danton!

DANTON What?

JULIE (*enters*)   What were you shouting?

DANTON Did I shout?

JULIE You talked of beastly sins, and then you groaned, "September!"

DANTON Did I? No, no, I did not talk. I barely thought these things; they were but very quiet, secret thoughts.

JULIE You are trembling, Danton!

DANTON Isn't it enough to make you tremble when the walls start to speak? When my body is so shattered that my thoughts flicker and roam and talk with the lips of the stones? That's strange.

JULIE Georges, dearest Georges!

DANTON It's very strange, Julie. I'd rather not think at all any more if my thoughts immediately turn into words. For some thoughts, Julie, there should be no ears. They should not cry like babes as soon as they are born. It is not fitting.

JULIE May God preserve your reason, Georges! Georges, do you recognize me?

DANTON Why not? Of course I do! You are a human being, you're a woman and, finally, you are my wife, and then there are five continents, Europe, Asia, Africa, America, and Australia, and two times two is four. You see, I am in full possession of my senses. Didn't something shout, "September"? Didn't you say something like that?

JULIE Yes, Danton. I could hear it through all the rooms of the house.

DANTON When I stepped to the window . . . (*He looks out.*) The city is quiet, all the lights are out . . .

JULIE A child is crying not far away.

DANTON When I stepped to the window . . . it shouted and it screamed through all the streets, "September!"

JULIE You had a dream, Danton. Now calm yourself!

DANTON A dream? Yes, I was dreaming. But it was something different, I'll tell you all about it in a minute . . . oh, my poor head . . . it is so weak . . . in just a minute. There—now I remember: the earth groaned under me with its mighty thrust and I gripped it like a wild steed, burying enormous hands in its mane and pressing gigantic feet into its ribs, my head turned to one side, my hair flying above the abyss. Thus I was dragged along. In my fright I cried out—and awoke. Then I stepped to the window—and there I heard the shout, Julie.

Why just this word? Why this and not another? What does it matter to me? Why does it reach for me with its bloodstained hands? I did not strike it. Julie, help me, my senses are dull! Wasn't it in September, Julie?

JULIE   The kings were within forty hours of Paris . . .

DANTON   The fortifications had been taken, the aristocrats were in the city . . .

JULIE   The Republic was lost.

DANTON   Yes, it was lost. We would have been fools to leave the enemy at large at our rear. Two enemies together on one plank, we or they—the stronger of the two pushed off the weaker one. Was that not fair?

JULIE   Of course.

DANTON   We beat them and that was not murder, it was civil war.

JULIE   You saved the country.

DANTON   Yes, I did. It was self-defense, we had no choice. The Man on the Cross took the easy way out; trouble is bound to come but woe betide the man who causes it! We must. This was a "must." Who can condemn the hand on which the curse of "must" has fallen? Who spoke the "must"? Who was it? Was it that part of ourselves which lies, whores, steals, and murders?

We're puppets, and unknown powers manipulate our wires. Ourselves we're nothing, nothing! We are the swords wielded by ghosts who fight each other, their hands remain unseen as in a fairy tale. Now I am calm.

JULIE   Quite calm, my dearest?

DANTON   Yes, Julie; come to bed.

SCENE 6. *Street before* DANTON's *house.* SIMON, CITIZEN SOLDIERS.

SIMON   How far is the night?

FIRST CITIZEN   What about the night?

SIMON   How far is the night?

FIRST CITIZEN   As far as from sundown to sunup.

SIMON   Scoundrel, what time is it?

FIRST CITIZEN   Look at your dial. It's the hour when the pendulum swings under the bed covers.

SIMON   We must go up! Forward, Citizens! We answer for it with our heads. Dead or alive? He has powerful limbs. I'll go ahead, Citizens. A path for liberty! Take care of my wife! I'll leave her a cluster of oak leaves.

FIRST CITIZEN   With acorns on them? It seems enough acorns fall into her lap every day as it is!

SIMON   Forward, Citizens! You'll deserve well of the country!

SECOND CITIZEN   I wish the country deserved well of us. For all the holes we rip into other peoples' bodies not one in our pants has yet been mended.

FIRST CITIZEN   Do you want the fly of your pants sewn up? Ha, ha, ha!

THE OTHERS   Ha, ha, ha!

SIMON   Forward, forward! (*They push into* DANTON's *house.*)

SCENE 7. *The National Convention. A group of* DEPUTIES.

LEGENDRE   Will the butchering of deputies never end? Who is safe if Danton falls?

A DEPUTY   What can we do?

ANOTHER DEPUTY   He must get a chance to appear before the Convention. The result is certain. What could they do against his voice?

ANOTHER   Impossible. There is a decree which prevents it.

LEGENDRE   It must be repealed or an exception must be granted. I shall move that this be done, and I count on your support.

THE PRESIDENT   The meeting will come to order.

LEGENDRE   (*mounts the rostrum*)   Four members of the National Convention were arrested last night. Danton is one of them, this much I know.[5] I don't know who the others are. Whoever they may be, I demands that they be heard before these bars.

Citizens, I assure you that Danton is, in my oninion, as untainted as I am myself, and I do not believe that anyone can bring an accusation against me. I do not wish to attack any members of the Committees of Public Safety and Security, but there are

[5] Danton was arrested on March 31, 1794.

sound reasons for my concern that private hatred, private passions may in the end rob Liberty of defenders who in the past have rendered her the greatest services. The man whose energy saved France in 1792 deserves to be heard. He must have a chance to defend himself if he is accused of high treason. (*Violent commotion.*)

SOME VOICES   We second Legendre's motion.

A DEPUTY   We sit here in the name of the people. We cannot be pushed off our seats without the consent of our constituents.

ANOTHER   Your words smell of cadavers. You must have taken them out of the mouths of the Girondists. Are you asking for privileges? The sword of Justice is suspended over the heads of all of us.

ANOTHER   We cannot permit our Committees to push legislators from the sanctuary of the law to the guillotine.

ANOTHER   Crime has no sanctuary, only crowned criminals find sanctuaries—on their thrones.

ANOTHER   Only scoundrels claim the right of sanctuary.

ANOTHER   Only murderers do not recognize it.

ROBESPIERRE   We have not seen this assembly in such confusion for some time. That it exists proves that most important matters are before us now. We shall decide today whether a few men shall be allowed to defeat the nation. How could you go so far in denying your own principles that you would grant some individuals today what yesterday you refused Chabot, Delaunay, and Fabre? Why such a distinction in favor of some few? The speeches which men make to praise themselves and all their friends mean nothing to me. We have had adequate experience to know what they are worth. We do not ask whether a man has one or another patriotic achievement to his credit; we look at his entire political career. Legendre does not seem to know the names of the arrested men. The whole Convention knows them. His friend Lacroix is one of them. Why does Legendre pretend not to know that? Because it would take audacity to come to Lacroix's defense. He named no one but Danton because he thinks that privileges attach to his name. But no, we want no privileges, we want no idols! (*Applause*) In what respect is Danton superior to Lafayette, to Dumouriez, to Brissot, Fabre, Chabot, or Hébert? What could be said of them that would not be true of him? And did you spare them for all that? Why does he deserve to be treated with greater respect than his fellow citizens? Perhaps because some dupes, and also some who were not duped, gathered around him because they hoped that in his retinue they were bound to find fortune and power? The more he deceived the real patriots who put their trust in him, the more he now must feel the wrath of all the friends of liberty.

They are trying to make you wince at the misuse of a power which you have exercised yourselves. They shout about the despotism which the Committees exercise, as though the confidence which the people placed in you and which you transferred to the Committees, were not an ample guaranty of their patriotism. They will have you believe that everyone is trembling with fear. But I tell you that anyone who trembles now is guilty. For innocence has never trembled at the sight of public vigilance. (*General applause.*)

They have tried to frighten me, too. They gave me to understand that the fate now closing in on Danton might engulf me, too. They wrote me, Danton's friends besieged me, all in the hope that the memory of a long association and blind faith in fake virtues would be able to temper my zeal and my passion for freedom. But I tell you that nothing will stop me, not even the thought that Danton's present peril might become my own. All of us need a little courage and some measure of greatness. Only criminals and small minds fear the prospect of seeing men of their own kind fall at their side, because when they can no longer hide behind a crowd of accomplices they are exposed to the glaring light of truth. But if there are some souls like these in this assembly, there are heroic men here, too. The number of scoundrels is not great. We need to strike only at a few heads, and the nation will be saved. (*Applause.*) I demand that Legendre's motion be rejected. (*The* DEPUTIES *rise to signify general approval.*)

SAINT-JUST There are, it seems, some sensitive ears in this assembly which cannot stand the sound of the word "blood." A few general observations will perhaps convince them that we are not any more cruel than Nature and Time. Nature follows her laws calmly and irresistibly. Man is destroyed if he comes into conflict with them. A slight change in the composition of the air, a sudden flaring-up of the tellurian fires, a change of equilibrium in masses of water, an epidemic, the eruption of a volcano or a flood may be the death of thousands. What is the result? An infinitesimal, hardly noticeable change of physical nature which would have passed with hardly a trace, if we did not see the corpses in its path. I therefore ask: should spiritual Nature be more considerate in accomplishing its revolutions than physical Nature? Should an idea not be permitted to destroy what obstructs it as much as a physical law? Should an event which changes the entire structure of morality, that is the structure of humanity, not be allowed to find its way through blood? The Spirit of the Universe makes use of our arms in the realm of the mind just as it uses floods and volcanoes in the physical sphere. What difference whether men perish in epidemics or in revolutions?

Mankind progresses slowly; its paces can be measured only in centuries, and behind each of these century-long paces rise the funeral mounds of generations. To make the simplest inventions and to establish the most modest principles has cost the lives of millions who fell by the wayside. Is it not then a simple truth that when history quickens the pace more people are likely to lose their breath? We are quickly led to the simple conclusion that, since all men were created under the same circumstances, all men are equal, excepting only those differences which Nature itself has made between them. Therefore, while anyone may have superior traits, none may have privileges, either as individuals or in a smaller or a larger group.

Each part of this proposition has demanded its victims when translated into reality. The fourteenth of July,[6] the tenth of August,[7] the thirty-first of May[8] are punctuation marks. It took four years to bring it to success, to give it life while under normal circumstances a century would have been necessary, and generations would have been the punctuation marks. Is it then so remarkable that the great river of the Revolution leaves corpses at every cliff and at every bend?

There are some conclusions we must add to our proposition. Should a few hundred corpses really prevent us from drawing them? Moses led his people through the Red Sea and into the desert until the old, corrupted generation had perished, and only then he founded his new state. Legislators! We have neither a Red Sea nor a desert, but we have war and the guillotine. The Revolution is like the daughters of Pelias: she tears mankind to pieces to make it young again. Mankind will emerge from the cauldron of blood as the earth emerged from the waves of the Flood, with strong and healthy limbs as they were at the time of Creation. (*Sustained applause. In their enthusiasm, some* DEPUTIES *rise from their seats.*) We call upon all secret enemies of tyranny,

[6] On July 14, 1789, Parisians stormed and seized the Bastille, the prison that was the symbol of royal tyranny.

[7] See Act I, note 15.

[8] See Act I, note 17.

who here in Europe and all over the globe carry the dagger of Brutus[9] hidden under their cloaks, to share with us this sacred moment. (*The* DEPUTIES *and the public intone the "Marseillaise."*)

Act III

SCENE 1. *A large room in the Palais Luxembourg.* CHAUMETTE, PAYNE, HÉRAULT-SÉCHELLES *and other prisoners.*

CHAUMETTE (*pulling* PAYNE's *sleeve*) Listen, Payne, it may well be, after all. It passed through my mind a little while ago . . . I have a headache today. You might help me a little with your logic . . . I feel very strange.

PAYNE   Come then, Anaxagoras,[1] you philosopher, I shall catechize you! *There is no God*, for either God created the world or He did not. If He did not create it, the world carries its cause of its creation within itself; in that case, there is no God, for God becomes God only by virtue of His being the source of all existence. Now, God cannot have created the world, for either creation is perpetual like God or it has had a beginning. In the latter case, God must have created the world at a definite point in time, which means that God, after having rested for an eternity, must suddenly have become active, and thus must have experienced a change within Himself, which would make it possible to apply to Him the notion of *Time*. Both of these assumptions contradict the essence of God. Therefore, God cannot have created the world. Since we know, on the other hand, that the world, or at least that our ego exists, and since our existence, according to our previous conclusions, must carry its origin within itself or in something that is not God, therefore then, there can be no God. *Quod erat demonstrandum.*[2]

CHAUMETTE   Indeed, I can see light again! Thank you! Thank you very much!

MERCIER   Just a minute, Payne! What if creation is, in fact, perpetual?

PAYNE   In that case it is no longer creation, for it would be one with God,

---

[9] Brutus was one of the conspirators who stabbed Julius Caesar.

[1] Chaumette's nickname. Anaxagoras was a Greek philosopher (fifth century B.C.).

[2] Which was to be demonstrated.

or an attribute of God, as Spinoza[3] said. In that event, God would be in everything, in you, my good friend, in our philosopher Anaxagoras and in me. That wouldn't be bad at all, but you must admit that there wouldn't be much to the heavenly majesty if the dear Lord can, in each of us, get a toothache or the clap, be buried alive, or at least have the very unpleasant premonitions of it.

MERCIER   But there must be some first cause.

PAYNE   Who denies that? But who can affirm that this cause is what we think of as God, that is as perfection? Do you consider the world perfect?

MERCIER   No.

PAYNE   So how do you want to deduce from an imperfect effect a perfect cause? Voltaire didn't dare to get himself into trouble with God any more than with kings; that's why he came to that conclusion. Somebody who has nothing but a reasoning mind and does not even have the ability or courage to use it consistently is only a dilettante.

MERCIER   I on the other hand ask: can a perfect cause have a perfect effect, that is, can something perfect create something perfect? Is that not impossible because something that was created can never have its cause within itself—which, as you said, is part of being perfect?

CHAUMETTE   Be quiet! Stop it!

PAYNE   Calm yourself, philosopher! You are right. If God really has to create, but can create only something imperfect, He'd do better to leave it alone. Isn't it very human to be unable to think of God otherwise than as a creator? Just because we have to keep being active and always on the move, to tell ourselves over and over again: we exist! But do we have to ascribe this sorry urge to God as well? Must we, the moment our mind tries to immerse itself into the essence of an eternal being, harmonious and at rest within itself, must we, I say, immediately assume that it cannot do otherwise than reach across the table for the bread and knead little figures because of a prodigious need to love, as we discreetly whisper into each other's ears? Must we really do all that just so that we can call ourselves sons of God? I'll be content with a less imposing father. At least I won't have to complain behind his back that he brought me up beneath his station, in a pig sty or as a galley slave.

　　　Do away with imperfection, for only then can you demon-

---

[3] Dutch philosopher (1632–1677).

strate God; Spinoza tried it. You can deny evil but you can't deny pain. Only reason can prove the existence of God, the emotions revolt against it. Remember this, Anaxagoras: why do I suffer? This is the bedrock on which atheism stands. The faintest twitch of pain, be it but in one single atom, fissures creation from one end to the other.

MERCIER   And morality?

PAYNE   First you deduce God from morality and then morality from God! What about your morality? I don't know if there is any absolute good or evil but that is no reason for me to change my conduct. I act according to my nature. What agrees with it is good for me, and I do it; what is against my nature is bad for me, and I don't do it, I fight against it if it gets in my way. One can very well be, as they call it, "virtuous" and fight against so-called vice, without despising one's opponents, which is a very sad feeling.

CHAUMETTE   Very true.

HÉRAULT   Yes, Anaxagoras, you philosopher, but one could also say that God, in order to be everything, must also be His own opposite, which means that He must be both perfect and imperfect, both good and evil, blessed and suffering. Of course, the result would be zero, one would counterbalance the other and we would arrive at Nothingness. Be happy, for you are gaining your ends. You may keep right on worshipping Madame Momoro[4] as Nature's masterpiece. At least she's left the rosaries you need for your devotions in your groin.

CHAUMETTE   My most sincere thanks to you, gentlemen!
      (*He leaves.*)

PAYNE   He is still unconvinced. In the end, he'll accept extreme unction, will point his feet toward Mecca[5] and have himself circumcised, to make sure that no possible route will be barred.
      (DANTON, LACROIX, CAMILLE, *and* PHILIPPEAU *are led in.*)

HÉRAULT   (*quickly walks to* DANTON *and embraces him*)   Good morning! Good night, I should say! I can't ask you, how did you sleep? The question is rather, how *will* you sleep?

DANTON   Well, one had better go to bed laughing.

MERCIER   (*to* PAYNE)   This bulldog with the wings of a dove! He is the evil genius of the revolution. He even defied his mother, but she was stronger than he.

PAYNE   His life and his death are equally great misfortunes.

---

[4] Chaumette's mistress, an opera singer.
[5] The holy city of the Moslems.

LACROIX (*to* DANTON) I did not expect them to get you so soon.

DANTON I knew about it. I had been warned.

LACROIX And you said nothing?

DANTON Why should I? A stroke is the best death. Would you like to be ill first? And—I did not think that they would dare. (*To* HÉRAULT) It is better to lie in the earth than to get corns treading it. I'd rather have it as a pillow than as a footstool.

HÉRAULT At least we won't have calluses on our hands when we pat the cheeks of that beautiful lady, Decay.

CAMILLE (*to* DANTON) Don't try so hard! You can stick your tongue out as far as it will go, it won't be long enough to lick the death sweat off your forehead. Oh, Lucile! This is too pitiful!
(*The prisoners crowd around the new arrivals.*)

DANTON (*to* PAYNE) What you did for the good of your country I have been trying to do for mine. I have been less fortunate; they now send me to the scaffold. All right, I shall not stumble.

MERCIER (*to* DANTON) You are drowning in the blood of the Twenty-two.

A PRISONER (*to* HÉRAULT) The power of the people and the power of reason are the same thing.

ANOTHER (*to* CAMILLE) Well, Attorney General of the Lanterns, the improvements you made in lighting the streets did not make France any brighter.

ANOTHER Leave him alone! These are the lips which formed the word "mercy." (*He embraces* CAMILLE; *several other prisoners follow his example.*)

PHILIPPEAU We are priests who have prayed with the dying. Now we have caught the disease ourselves, we will die of the same epidemic.

SEVERAL VOICES The blow that falls on you kills all of us.

CAMILLE Gentlemen, I regret exceedingly that our labors were to no avail. I mount the scaffold because I shed tears over the fate of some unfortunates.

SCENE 2. *A room.* FOUQUIER-TINVILLE *and* HERMAN.

FOUQUIER Is everything ready?

HERMAN It will be very difficult; if Danton were not one of them, it would be easier.

FOUQUIER He has to lead the dance.

HERMAN He will scare the jury. He is the scarecrow of the Revolution.

FOUQUIER The jury will have to be determined.

HERMAN   I have thought of a way, but it would be against the rules of legal procedure.

FOUQUIER   Go ahead!

HERMAN   We won't choose them by lot but pick the most robust.

FOUQUIER   That should be possible. It will be a nice bonfire. There are nineteen of them, and they are a very cleverly mixed company. Four counterfeiters, a few bankers and foreigners—that is a very tempting dish. That's what the people need. Yes, reliable men! Who, for example?

HERMAN   Leroi. He's deaf and won't hear a thing of what the accused will say. Danton can shout until he's hoarse for all he cares.

FOUQUIER   Excellent! Go on!

HERMAN   Vilatte and Lumière. The one sits in the tavern all day, the other one is always asleep. Both will open their mouths only to pronounce the word "guilty." Then there's Girard, who acts according to the principle that no one must escape who has been put before the bars of the Tribunal. Renaudin . . .

FOUQUIER   He, too? He assisted some clerics once.

HERMAN   Never mind! A few days ago he came to see me and demanded that all the condemned men be bled before the execution to weaken them a little. He found their usually defiant attitude most vexing.

FOUQUIER   Ah, excellent! I shall rely on you, then.

HERMAN   Leave it to me!

SCENE 3.   *A hallway in the Palais Luxembourg.* LACROIX, DANTON, MERCIER *and other prisoners are walking back and forth.*

LACROIX   (*to a prisoner*)   What? So many unfortunates in such miserable condition?

THE PRISONER   Didn't the tumbrils ever tell you that Paris is a slaughterhouse?

MERCIER   Lacroix, it's true, is it not, that Equality swings its scythe above the heads of all of us, the lava of the Revolution flows, the guillotine makes Republicans! This kind of talk brings applause from the galleries and the Romans rub their hands in delight. But they do not hear that every one of these words is a victim's death rattle. Follow your phrases just for once to the point where they become reality. Take a look around! All you see you have said! This is a pantomimic translation of your words. These miserable beings, their hangmen and the guillotine are your speeches come to life. You constructed your systems, like Bajazet[6] his pyramids, from human heads.

DANTON You are right. These days, all our work is done in human flesh. That is the curse of our time. My body, too, will now be used. It's just a year ago that I created the Revolutionary Tribunal. I apologize to God and humanity for doing it; I meant to forestall another September massacre and hoped to save innocent lives. But this slow formal murder is more horrible and just as inescapable. I had hoped, gentlemen, that what I did would serve to let all of you leave this place.

MERCIER Oh, we shall leave it all right!

DANTON Now I am one of you. Heaven knows how it will end.

SCENE 4. *The Revolutionary Tribunal.*[7]

HERMAN (*to* DANTON) Your name, Citizen!

DANTON The Revolution calls my name. Soon I shall live in the Void and my name in the Pantheon of History.

HERMAN Danton, the Convention accuses you of having conspired with Mirabeau and Dumouriez, with Orléans, with the Girondists and with foreigners, and with the faction of Louis XVII.

DANTON My voice, which has so often sounded to defend the cause of the people, will easily refute this calumny. Let those miserable creatures who accuse me appear here, confront me—and I shall cover them with shame. Let the Committees come before this court, I shall reply only in their presence. I shall need them as accusers and as witnesses. Let them show themselves!

Besides, what do I care about you and your verdict? I have already told you that I shall soon find sanctuary in the Void. Life is a burden to me; tear it from me! I yearn to shake it off!

HERMAN Danton, audacity is the earmark of the criminal; the innocent are calm.

DANTON No doubt, personal audacity is reprehensible. But that national audacity which I have often demonstrated, with which I so often fought for freedom, that audacity is the greatest of virtues. That is my kind of audacity and I use it now for the benefit of the Republic

[6] Turkish conqueror of Asia Minor (in the fourteenth century).

[7] On April 2, 1794, Danton made his first speech before the Revolutionary Tribunal.

and against my miserable accusers. How can I be calm when I must stand here and listen to these despicable slanders? Do not expect a cold, detached defense from a revolutionary like me! Men of my cast are invaluable in revolutions, for the genius of liberty hovers over their heads. (*Signs of applause among the public.*)

I am accused of having conspired with Mirabeau, with Dumouriez and with Orléans, of having scraped at the feet of contemptible despots. I am asked to answer these charges before the bars of inescapable and inflexible justice. Wretched Saint-Just, you will be responsible to posterity for this calumny!

HERMAN   I demand that you give your replies calmly. Think of Marat; he stood before his judges with respect.

DANTON   They lay hands upon my whole life. My whole life, therefore, stands up and faces them. I shall bury them under the weight of each one of my actions. I am not proud of them. Fate guides our arms, but only powerful natures become its instruments. I declared war on the monarchy on the Field of Mars; I defeated the monarchy on the tenth of August and I killed it on the twenty-first of January.[8] I flung all other kings a royal head as gauntlet. (*Repeated signs of applause.* DANTON *takes the Bill of Particulars.*) Just glancing at this slanderous document makes me tremble to the core of my being. Who are those who had to appeal to Danton that he show himself on that memorable day, that tenth of August? Who are those privileged men from whom he borrowed his energy? Let my accusers appear! I demand it in full possession of my mental powers. I shall unmask those shallow scoundrels and fling them back into the Nothingness from which they never should have crawled.

HERMAN   (*ringing the bell*)   Don't you hear the bell?

DANTON   The voice of a man who defends his honor and his whole life must be stronger than the sound of your bell. In September, I nourished the young cubs of the Revolution with the torn bodies of aristocrats. It was my voice which forged arms for the people from the gold of aristocrats and of the rich. My voice was the gale which buried the statellites of the despots under waves of bayonets. (*Loud applause.*)

HERMAN   Your voice is getting hoarse, Danton. You are too excited. You may complete your defense at the next session. You do need rest. The court is adjourned.

DANTON   Now you know Danton. Only a few more hours and he will fall asleep in the arms of glory.

---

[8] On January 21, 1793, Louis XVI was executed.

SCENE 5. *A prison cell in the Palais Luxembourg.* DILLON, LAFLOTTE *and a* JAILER.

DILLON   Brute! Don't stick your nose right in my face! It won't make me see any better. Ha, ha, ha.

LAFLOTTE   Keep your mouth shut! Your half-moon has a halo. Ha, ha, ha.

JAILER   Ha, ha, ha! Do you think, sir, that you can read by its light? (*He points to a piece of paper he holds in his hand.*)

DILLON   Give me that!

JAILER   Sir, my half-moon is at low tide.

LAFLOTTE   Your trousers look like as if the tide was high.

JAILER   No, no, the moon is in the clouds. (*To* DILLON.) It is hiding before your sun, sir. You'll have to give me something to make it come out again if you want to have enough light to read by.

DILLON   There, you scoundrel! Off with you! (*He gives him some money. The* JAILER *leaves.* DILLON *reads.*) Danton has frightened the Tribunal. The jury vacillates and the public grumbles. The crowd around the Palace of Justice reached all the way to the bridges. A handful of money, an arm—hm, hm! (*He walks up and down, filling his glass from a bottle now and then.*) If I only had my feet on the street! I am not going to let them kill me just like that. Yes, if I were only on the street!

LAFLOTTE   And on the tumbril, that's the same.

DILLON   Do you think so? There are a few steps in between, a distance long enough to measure with the bodies of Decemvirs. The time has come for honest people to raise their heads.

LAFLOTTE   (*aside*)   All the better. They are easier to hit that way. Go on, old man. A few more glasses, and I shall be afloat.

DILLON   Scoundrels! Idiots! In the end they'll guillotine themselves! (*He paces rapidly up and down.*)

LAFLOTTE   (*aside*)   One could begin once more really to love life, like one's own child, if one has brought it forth oneself. That doesn't happen so often, to have a chance of committing incest with fate and to become one's own father. Father and child in one! A cozy Oedipus![9]

DILLON   One cannot feed people with corpses. Let Danton's and Camille's women throw assignats[10] among the people! That would be better than heads!

[9] According to Greek myth, Oedipus killed his father and married his mother.
[10] Paper currency issued by the republic.

LAFLOTTE (*aside*) I wouldn't tear my eyes out afterward. I might need
  them to cry for this good general.
DILLON To lay hands on Danton! Who is still safe? Fear will unite them.
LAFLOTTE (*aside*) He's lost anyhow. What of it then, if I step on his
  corpse to climb out of my grave?
DILLON Only to be on the streets! I would find enough people, old
  soldiers, Girondists, and former noblemen. We would break open
  the jails, we must come to an understanding with the prisoners.
LAFLOTTE (*aside*) Of course, it does smell a little of perfidy. What does
  it matter? I would like to try that. I have been in a rut. My conscience would bother me, and that would be a change. After all, it
  isn't too bad to smell one's own stink. I'm bored with the prospect
  of the guillotine, after waiting so long. I've tried it out in my mind
  at least twenty times and there is no spice left; it has become most
  ordinary.
DILLON We'll have to send a letter to Danton's wife.
LAFLOTTE (*aside*) And then—I'm not afraid of death, I am afraid of
  pain. It might hurt; who can guarantee that it won't? They say
  it's just a moment, but pain measures time on a subtler scale, it
  counts in minute fractions of seconds. No! Pain is the one and only
  sin, and suffering the only vice. I shall stay virtuous!
DILLON Listen, Laflotte, what happened to that rascal? I have money,
  and it must work. We'll have to forge the iron now, my plan is
  made.
LAFLOTTE Immediately! I know the jailer, I shall talk to him. You can
  count on me, General, we shall get out of this hole— (*Aside, while
  he walks to the door.*) —and enter another one: I, the biggest hole
  there is, the wide world, and you the smallest one, the grave.

SCENE 6. *The Committee of Public Safety.* SAINT-JUST, BARÈRE,
COLLOT D'HERBOIS, BILLAUD-VARENNES.

BARÈRE What does Fouquier write?
SAINT-JUST They have finished the second session. The prisoners demand
  that several members of the Convention and of the Committee of
  Public Safety appear before the court. They appeal to the people
  against the refusal to hear their witnesses. The excitement seems
  to be indescribable. Danton parodied Jupiter and shook his mane.[11]

---

[11] Jupiter is the Roman name for the Greek Zeus, king of the gods. The
lion is king of the beasts.

COLLOT   It will be that much easier for Samson[12] to grab it.

BARÈRE   We must not show ourselves. The fishwives and ragpickers may not find us very imposing.

BILLAUD   The people have an instinct for being kicked, even though it be with mere glances. They love insolent faces like his, although their expressions are worse than a nobleman's coat-of-arms; for they reflect the subtle aristocracy of those who are contemptuous of all humanity. Everyone who dislikes being looked down upon should help bash in these faces.

BARÈRE   His skin is as horny as Siegfried's. The blood he shed in September has made him invulnerable.[13] What does Robespierre say?

SAINT-JUST   He pretends having something to say. The jury will have to declare themselves adequately informed and close the debate.

BARÈRE   Impossible! We cannot do that.

SAINT-JUST   We have to get rid of them, at any price, and if we have to throttle them with our own hands. Be bold! Danton taught us the word, his lesson shall not have been in vain. The Revolution will not stumble over their corpses; but if Danton stays alive, he will tug at her dress, and there is something about him that makes you think he could rape Liberty.

(SAINT-JUST *is called out. A* JAILER *enters.*)

JAILER   There are prisoners dying at St. Pelagie. They want a doctor.

BILLAUD   That's quite unnecessary. That much less trouble for the executioner.

JAILER   There are pregnant women among them.

BILLAUD   So much the better. We won't need coffins for the babies then.

BARÈRE   Every time an aristocrat comes down with consumption we save the Tribunal a session. Medicine would be downright counter-revolutionary.

COLLOT   (*takes a piece of paper and reads*)   A petition! And signed by a woman!

BARÈRE   Probably one of those who would like to be forced to choose between a crouch under the guillotine and the couch of a Jacobin. Like Lucretia, they die after they have lost their honor, only they wait a little longer than the Roman lady; they die in child-birth, or of cancer or old age. It may not even be unpleasant to chase a Tarquin out of a virgin's virtuous republic!

COLLOT   This one is too old. Madame demands death, and she knows

---

[12] A famous executioner of the time.

[13] Siegfried became invulnerable when he killed the dragon Fafnir and bathed in its blood. During the bath, a leaf fell on his shoulder and left him with one vulnerable spot.

how to express herself quite well: prison, she says, weighs upon her like the lid of a coffin. And she's been in prison only four weeks! The answer is very simple. (*He reads the words as he writes them down.*) "Citizeness, it has not yet been long enough that you have longed for death."

(*The* JAILER *leaves.*)

BARÈRE   Well said. But I don't like to see the guillotine starting to laugh, Collot. People won't be afraid of it any more. One should not become so familiar!

(SAINT-JUST *comes back.*)

SAINT-JUST   I have just received word from an informer. There is a conspiracy in the prisons, and a young fellow called Laflotte has discovered it all. He shared a room with Dillon, and Dillon got drunk and babbled.

BARÈRE   He will cut his throat with the bottle. That has happened before.

SAINT-JUST   According to Laflotte, Danton's and Camille's women are to throw money among the people, Dillon is to break out, the prisoners are to be liberated and the Convention is to be blown up.

BARÈRE   That sounds like fairy tales.

SAINT-JUST   But we will sing them to sleep with these fairy tales! I have the information in my hands, and if you add to that the impudence of the accused, the grumbling of the people and the consternation of the jury—I shall make a report.

BARÈRE   Go ahead, Saint-Just, and spin your periods so that each comma is a blow struck with a sword, each period a severed head!

SAINT-JUST   The Convention must decree that the Tribunal is to bring the trial to conclusion without delay, and that it is empowered to exclude from the debate any one of the accused who does not conduct himself with due respect to the court or who causes scenes which disrupt the proceedings.

BARÈRE   You have the instincts of a revolutionary! This sounds very moderate and yet it will do the trick. They can't remain silent; Danton, for one, must shout.

SAINT-JUST   I count on your support. There are some people in the Convention who are as sick as Danton and afraid of the same medicine. They have become bold again and will scream about irregular procedure . . .

BARÈRE (*interrupting him*)   I shall tell them that the Roman consul who uncovered Catiline's conspiracy and sentenced the criminals to death on the spot was also accused of having violated the rules of procedure. And who were his accusers?

COLLOT (*with great fervor*)   Go, Saint-Just! The lava of the Revolution flows. Liberty will suffocate in her embrace those weaklings who make bold to impregnate her mighty womb! As Jupiter appeared to Semele, the people, in their majesty, will appear to them with thunder and lightning and turn them into ashes. Go, Saint-Just! We shall assist you in hurling the thunderbolt upon the heads of the cowards!

(SAINT-JUST *leaves.*)

BARÈRE Did you hear him say "medicine"? They will finish by making a specific against venereal disease out of the guillotine. They do not fight the Moderates, they battle against Vice.

BILLAUD Our road has been the same so far.

BARÈRE Robespierre would like to transform the Revolution into an auditorium for lectures on Morals, and to use the guillotine as his lectern.

BILLAUD Or as his prayer stool.

COLLOT On which he should, however, lie—not kneel.

BARÈRE That will be easy. The world would have to be upside down if so-called scoundrels were to be hanged by so-called righteous people.

COLLOT (*to* BARÈRE) When will you come to Clichy again?

BARÈRE When the doctor stops coming to see me.

COLLOT It's true, isn't it, that above that place hangs a comet whose burning rays are shriveling your marrow?

BILLAUD It won't be long until the charming Demaly will use her adorable hands to pull it out of its casing and make him wear it down his back like a pigtail.

BARÈRE Psh! The Virtuous One must never know a thing about this.

BILLAUD He is an impotent free-mason.

(BILLAUD *and* COLLOT *leave.*)

BARÈRE (*alone*) The monsters! "It has not yet been long enough that you have longed for death." Those words should have withered the tongue that formed them.

And I? When the Septembrists[14] pushed into the prisons, one of the prisoners took his knife and, mingling with the murderers, plunged it into the breast of a priest. He was saved! Who can argue against it? Whether I join assassins or sit as a member of the Committee of Public Safety, whether I take the blade of a penknife or the blade of the guillotine—it is the same; the circumstances are a little more involved, but fundamentally the situation is the

---

[14] Name given to the executioners in the September massacres (see Act I, note 16).

same. Now, if it was permissible to kill one man, was he allowed
to kill two—three—or still more? Where does it end? And here
we arrive at the famous question of the grains of barley: do two
grains make a pile? Or three, or four, or how many? Come, conscience, come little chicken, cluck, cluck, cluck, here is some food
for you! But—was I like that prisoner? I was suspect, and that
amounts to the same thing. My death was certain.
(*He leaves.*)

SCENE 7. *The Conciergerie.* LACROIX, DANTON, PHILIPPEAU, CAMILLE.

LACROIX   Well shouted, Danton! If you had tried as hard to save your life
a little earlier, things would be different now. When death so im-
pudently snuggles up to you, so that you can smell his foul breath,
and becomes more and more insistent—you see now, don't you?
CAMILLE   If at least death came like a man and raped you and wrestled
his prize from your hot limbs in a hard-fought struggle! But like
this, with all the formalities, like a wedding with an old woman
where the contract is signed, the witnesses called, the Amen spoken,
and then the bed covers lifted and it crawls in with its cold
limbs . . .
DANTON   If only it were a battle where arms and teeth become enmeshed!
I feel as if I had fallen into the gears of a mill, as if my limbs were
being systematically wrenched off by cold, brute force. To be
killed so mechanically!
CAMILLE   And then to lie there, all alone, cold and stiff, in the dank
fumes of decay . . . perhaps death tortures life slowly out of your
fibres . . . to be conscious, perhaps, that you're rotting away!
PHILIPPEAU   Be calm, my friends! We are like autumn flowers whose
seed ripens only after the winter has passed. We differ from flowers
that are transplanted only in that we start stinking a little in the
attempt. Is that so bad?
DANTON   An edifying prospect! From one dung heap to another! That is
the theory of the divine school classes again, is it not? From first
grade into second, from second to third and so on? I am tired of
school benches—like an ape I have calluses on my rear end from
sitting on them.
PHILIPPEAU   Then what do you want?

DANTON Rest.

PHILIPPEAU You'll find it in God.

DANTON I'll find it in Nothingness. Can you immerse yourself into anything more restful than Nothingness? So if God is supreme peace,
is not Nothingness God? But I'm an atheist. And there is this
damned maxim that something cannot become nothing! I am something, that is the trouble! Creation has spread itself so widely that
there is not an empty spot. It's teeming everywhere. Nothingness
has committed suicide, Creation is its wound, we are drops of its
blood and the world is the grave in which it rots. This sounds crazy,
and yet there is much truth in it.

CAMILLE The world is like the Wandering Jew, Nothingness is like death
—but death is impossible. Oh, not to be able to die, not to be able
to die, as the song goes!

DANTON All of us have been buried alive, put to rest in triple and quad-
ruple coffins like kings, under the sky, in our homes, in our coats
and shirts. For fifty years we claw at the coffin lid. Yes, if one
could only believe in complete destruction, that would be a help!
There is no hope in death. Death is only a more simple life, a more
complicated and higher organized form of decay. That's the whole
difference. But I happen to be used to this particular sort of decay
and the devil knows how I'll adjust to another.

Oh, Julie! If I had to go by myself! If she left me alone!
Even if I disintegrated utterly, if I dissolved entirely, I would be
a handful of tormented dust and every atom of me could find rest
only with her. I cannot die. No, I cannot die! We must scream!
And they will have to press each drop of life out of my limbs.

LACROIX We must stand by our demands. Our accusers and the Committee must appear before the Tribunal.

SCENE 8. *A room.* FOUQUIER, AMAR, VOULAND.

FOUQUIER I don't know any more what to tell them. They now demand
a commission.

AMAR We have caught them, the scoundrels. This is what you want.
(*He hands* FOUQUIER *a piece of paper.*)

VOULAND That will satisfy them.

FOUQUIER Yes, indeed, we needed this.

AMAR Now hurry up, so both we and they get this business off our necks.

SCENE 9. *The Revolutionary Tribunal.*

DANTON The Republic is in danger—and he has no instructions! We appeal to the people. My voice is still strong enough to speak the funeral oration for the Decemvirs. I repeat, we demand a commission; we shall make important revelations. I shall retreat into the citadel of reason, bring into play the guns of truth and squash my enemies. (*Signs of applause.* FOUQUIER, AMAR, *and* VOULAND *enter.*)

FOUQUIER In the name of the Republic, silence! Respect for the law! The Convention has passed the following resolution: "Whereas there have been discovered signs of insurrection in the prisons, and whereas Danton's and Camille's women are throwing money among the people; and whereas further General Dillon is to escape from prison and to put himself at the head of the rebels with the aim to liberate the accused, and whereas, finally, the accused themselves have attempted to create disorders and to insult the Tribunal, be it resolved that the Tribunal is empowered to continue the inquiry without interruption and to exclude from participation in the proceedings any of the accused who shall fail to accord due respect to the law."

DANTON I ask those present here, did we mock this Tribunal, the people or the National Convention?

MANY VOICES No, no!

CAMILLE The wretches! They want to kill my Lucile!

DANTON Some day the truth will be known. I foresee a great misfortune for France. That is a dictatorship! It has already torn away the veils; it carries its head high, and it advances over our bodies. (*Pointing to* AMAR *and* VOULAND.) Look at the cowardly murderers! There they are, the vultures of the Committee of Public Safety! I accuse Robespierre, Saint-Just and their hangmen of high treason. They want to drown the Republic in blood. The ruts made by their tumbrils are the highroads on which the foreigners are to push straight into the heart of the fatherland.

How much longer are graves to be the footprints of liberty? You ask for bread, and they throw you heads. You are thirsty, and they make you lick the blood off the steps that lead to the guillotine. (*Violent commotion among the spectators, shouts of approval, many voices shout "Long live Danton, down with the Decemvirs!" The prisoners are led out of the room by force.*)

SCENE 10. *Square in front of the Palace of Justice. A crowd of people.*

SOME VOICES   Down with the Decemvirs! Long live Danton!

FIRST CITIZEN   Yes, that is the truth. Heads instead of bread, blood instead of wine!

SOME WOMEN   The guillotine is a very bad mill, and Samson is a miserable baker. We want bread! We want bread!

SECOND CITIZEN   It's Danton who has eaten your bread. His head will give bread to all of you. He was right.

FIRST CITIZEN   Danton was with us on the tenth of August, Danton was with us in September. Where were those who now accuse him?

SECOND CITIZEN   And Lafayette was with you in Versailles and yet he was a traitor.

FIRST CITIZEN   Who says that Danton is a traitor?

SECOND CITIZEN   Robespierre.

FIRST CITIZEN   And Robespierre is a traitor.

SECOND CITIZEN   Who says so?

FIRST CITIZEN   Danton.

SECOND CITIZEN   Danton wears beautiful clothes, Danton has a beautiful house, Danton has a beautiful wife, he bathes in Burgundy, eats game from silver plates and sleeps with your wives and daughters when he's drunk. Danton used to be as poor as you are. Where did all this come from? The Veto bought it for him, so he would save his crown for him. The Duke of Orléans gave it to him so he would betray all of you. What does Robespierre own? You know him, all of you!

ALL   Long live Robespierre! Down with Danton! Down with the traitor!

Act IV

SCENE 1. JULIE, A BOY.

JULIE   This is the end. He makes them tremble. They kill him out of fear. Go! I have seen him for the last time. Tell him that I cannot see him in this condition. (*She gives him a lock of hair.*) There, give him this and tell him that he will not go alone—he'll understand. And then come quickly back, for I want to read his glances in your eyes.

SCENE 2. *A Street.* DUMAS, A CITIZEN.

CITIZEN How can they sentence all these innocent men to death after such a trial?

DUMAS It is indeed extraordinary. But those revolutionaries have a sense which other people lack, and that sense never betrays them.

CITIZEN The instinct of the tiger. You have a wife.

DUMAS Soon I will have had a wife.

CITIZEN So it is true?

DUMAS The Revolutionary Tribunal will pronounce the divorce and the guillotine will separate us from bed and board.

CITIZEN You are a monster!

DUMAS Idiot! Do you admire Brutus?

CITIZEN Deeply.

DUMAS Must one be a Roman consul and have a toga to cover one's head if one wishes to sacrifice what one holds dearest to the fatherland? I shall dry my eyes with the sleeves of my red coat. That's all the difference there is!

CITIZEN It is horrible!

DUMAS Go away, you don't understand me.

(*Both leave.*)

SCENE 3. *The Conciergerie.* LACROIX *and* HÉRAULT *sitting on one,* DANTON *and* CAMILLE *sitting on another bed.*

LACROIX Hair and nails are growing in such a way one really has to be ashamed of oneself.

HÉRAULT Be a little careful. You are sneezing sand all over my face.

LACROIX And don't you step on my toes, my friend. I have corns.

HÉRAULT You also seem to be suffering from vermin.

LACROIX Oh, if only I could get completely rid of the worms.

HÉRAULT   Well, sleep well! We'll see how we get along with each other. There isn't much room. Don't scratch me with your nails while you're asleep! There. Don't tug at this shroud so much; it's cold down there!

DANTON   Yes, Camille, tomorrow we'll be like worn-out shoes that are thrown into the lap of that beggarwoman, Earth.

CAMILLE   The cow-hide from which the angels cut themselves the slippers they use to patter around on earth, according to Plato. Looks like it, too. Oh, my Lucile!

DANTON   Calm, now, my boy.

CAMILLE   Can I be calm? Do you think, Danton? Can I? They must not touch her! The light of beauty which radiates from her sweet body is inextinguishable. Even the earth would not dare to fall on top of her; it would form a vault around her, the dampness of the grave would sparkle on her eyelashes like dew, crystals would shoot from her limbs like flowers, and clear springs would sing her lullaby.

DANTON   Sleep now, sleep!

CAMILLE   Listen, Danton. Between the two of us, it is quite miserable, to have to die. It is good for nothing. I want to steal from life's beautiful eyes their last glances; I want to keep my eyes open.

DANTON   You are going to keep them open anyhow, my boy. Samson doesn't close one's eyes. Sleep is more charitable. Sleep now, sleep!

CAMILLE   Lucile, your kisses are dancing on my lips, each kiss turns into a dream, and my eyes close around it to hold it tight.

DANTON   Will the clock not stop ticking? With every tick the walls are closing in on me, until they are as close together as the sides of a coffin. As a child I once read a story like that, and my hair stood on end. Yes, as a child! It really wasn't worth their trouble to feed me and to keep me warm until I was a man! It just made work for the gravedigger.

I feel as if I smelled already. My dear body, I will hold my nose and try to think that you are a woman, sweaty and smelly from dancing, and I will pay you compliments. We used to entertain each other differently in the past.

Tomorrow you'll be like a broken fiddle, and gone the melody you used to play. Tomorrow you will be an empty bottle, the wine drained, but I won't be drunk from it and go to bed sober. Lucky people who can still get drunk! Tomorrow you will be a pair of seat-worn pants that is thrown into the wardrobe to be eaten by moths, no matter how much you stink.

Oh, there is nothing to be done about it! Yes, it is miserable having to die. Death apes birth: we are as helpless and as naked when we die as new-born babies. Of course, we get a shroud as a

diaper. What good is that? We can whimper as much in the grave
as we did in the cradle.

Camille!—He is asleep. (*He bends over him.*) A dream
plays on his eyelids. I do not want to wipe the golden dew of sleep
from his eyes. (*He rises and steps to the window.*) I will not go
alone! Thank you, Julie! Yet, I would have liked to die differently,
without any effort, as a star shoots across the sky, as a sound of
music expires, kissing itself to death with its own lips, as a ray of
light buries itself in clear water.

The stars are sprinkled through the night like shimmering
tears. The eyes from which they dropped must be full of great
sorrow.

CAMILLE   Oh! (*He sits up and feels for the ceiling.*)

DANTON   What is it, Camille?

CAMILLE   Oh, oh!

DANTON (*shakes him*)   Do you want to scratch the ceiling down?

CAMILLE   Oh, it is you! You—hold me! Talk to me!

DANTON   Your whole body is trembling, drops of sweat are on your forehead.

CAMILLE   This is you, and I am here—there! This is my hand! Yes, now I
remember. It was terrible, Danton!

DANTON   What was terrible?

CAMILLE   I was lying here, between dream and waking, when suddenly
the ceiling disappeared and the moon sank down, quite near, very
close, so close that I could touch it. The heavens dropped down
with all their lights until my head hit against them, I touched the
stars and I was suffocated like a drowning man under a sheet of
ice. It was terrible, Danton!

DANTON   The lamp throws a round spot of light on the ceiling; that is
what you saw.

CAMILLE   Perhaps. At any rate, it does not take much to make us lose
the little bit of reason that is left. Madness had gripped me by my
hair! (*He rises.*) I don't want to sleep any more, I don't want to
go mad. (*He takes a book.*)

DANTON   What are you reading?

CAMILLE   *Night Thoughts.*[1]

DANTON   Do you want to die ahead of time? I shall read *La Pucelle.*[2]
I don't want to steal out of life as from a prayer stool but rather
as from the bed of one of the Sisters of Mercy. Life is a whore;
she sleeps with everybody.

---

[1] *Night Thoughts on Life, Death, and Immortality,* by Edward Young.
[2] *The Maid* (Joan of Arc), by Voltaire.

SCENE 4. *Square in front of the Conciergerie. A* JAILER, *two* DRAY-MEN *with tumbrils,* WOMEN.

JAILER   Who called you here?

FIRST DRAYMAN   My name isn't "Here." A silly name that is.

JAILER   Idiot, who gave the order?

FIRST DRAYMAN   Nobody gave me an order. All I got was ten sous per head.

SECOND DRAYMAN   That scoundrel wants to steal my bread.

FIRST DRAYMAN   You call that bread? (*Pointing to the prisoners' windows.*) That's food for worms.

SECOND DRAYMAN   So are my children worms, and they want their share. Business is bad, and yet we are the best draymen around.

FIRST DRAYMAN   How is that?

SECOND DRAYMAN   Who is the best drayman?

FIRST DRAYMAN   The one who drives farthest the quickest.

SECOND DRAYMAN   Well, you ass, who drives farther than the one who drives out of this world, and who drives quicker than the one who can do it in a quarter of an hour? It's exactly a quarter of an hour from here to the Place de la Révolution.

JAILER   Hurry up, rascals! Closer to the door! Make room there, girls!

FIRST DRAYMAN   Stay where you are! One doesn't drive around a girl but straight into the middle.

SECOND DRAYMAN   That I'll believe. You'll drive in with your tumbril and horses, the tracks are so well-worn. But you'll have to stay in quarantine when you come out. (*They drive up.*)

SECOND DRAYMAN (*to the* WOMEN)   What are you staring at?

A WOMAN   We're waiting for old customers.

SECOND DRAYMAN   Do you think my tumbril is a brothel? This is a decent cart; the King himself and all the gentlemen of Paris have been driven to dinner in it.

LUCILE *enters. She sits on a stone under the prisoners' windows.*

LUCILE   Camille! Camille! (CAMILLE *appears at a window.*) Oh, Camille, you make me laugh with your long coat of stone and the iron mask in front of your face. Can't you bend down? Where are your arms? —I'll call you sweetly, my darling bird. (*She sings.*)

Two little stars gleam in the sky,
They are brighter than the moon.
The one glows at my sweetheart's window,
The other at her bedroom door.

Come, dear friend, come! Quietly up the stairs—they're all asleep. The moon has kept me company in my long wait. But you can't get through the door, in your absurd costume. This is going too far, this is no joke! Now stop it! And you do not move, why don't you speak to me? You frighten me. Listen, the people say that you must die and they are making very serious faces. Die! Their faces make me laugh! Die! What kind of a word is that? Tell me, Camille! To die! I'll think about it. There—there it is! I'll run after it. Come, my sweet friend, help me catch it! Come, come!

(*She runs away.*)

CAMILLE (*shouts*) Lucile! Lucile!

SCENE 5. *The Conciergerie.* DANTON, *at a window which opens into the adjoining room;* CAMILLE, PHILIPPEAU, LACROIX, HÉRAULT.

DANTON Now you are quiet, Fabre.

A VOICE (*from the other room*) I'm dying.

DANTON And do you know what we are going to do now?

THE VOICE Well?

DANTON Something you have been doing all your life—*des vers!*[3]

CAMILLE (*to himself*) Madness gleamed behind her eyes. Many people have gone mad before—that is the way it goes. What can we do about it? We wash our hands of it. And it is best that way.

DANTON I am leaving everything in terrible confusion. None of them knows anything about governing. It might yet work out if I could leave my whores to Robespierre and my legs to Couthon.

LACROIX We would have made a whore of liberty!

DANTON What of it! Liberty and whores are the most cosmopolitan things under the sun. Now Liberty will prostitute herself most decently on the marital couch of the advocates from Arras. Yet, I have an idea that she may act the part of Clytemnestra against him.[4] I don't give him more than six months—I shall drag him along!

CAMILLE Heaven may send her a comfortable fixed idea. The usual fixed

---

[3] The plural "*vers*" has a double meaning: "verses" (poetry) and "worms" [translator's note].

[4] In Greek legend, Clytemnestra committed adultery with Aegisthus and killed her husband, Agamemnon.

ideas, which we call "common sense," are unbearably boring. He would be the most fortunate of men who could imagine himself to be God Father, Son, and Holy Ghost.

LACROIX   Those idiots will shout "Long live the Republic," when we come by.

DANTON   Does it matter? The deluge of the Revolution may deposit our bodies wherever it decides. Our fossilized bones will still be good for bashing in the heads of kings.

HÉRAULT   Yes, if there happens to be a Samson to use our jaw bones.[5]

DANTON   They bear the mark of Cain.[6]

LACROIX   There is no more convincing proof that Robespierre is a Nero[7] than the fact that he was never more friendly toward Camille than two days before his arrest. Isn't that true, Camille?

CAMILLE   Suppose that it is true, what does it matter? (*To himself.*) How lovely is this child of hers, her madness! Why must I leave just now? Together we could have laughed with it and rocked and kissed it.

DANTON   Once history opens her vaults, the aroma of our corpses may still be enough to suffocate the tyrants.

HÉRAULT   We stank enough while we were alive. These are phrases for posterity, Danton. They don't really have anything to do with us.

CAMILLE   He makes a face as if it were to petrify and be dug up by posterity as an antique. It's really not worth the trouble to purse your lips, to put on a little rouge and to talk with a refined accent! We ought to take off our masks for once; then we would see, as in a gallery of mirrors, everywhere the same age-old, toothless and indestructible blockhead—no more and no less. The differences aren't very great. We are all villains and angels, fools and geniuses, all in one. These four are not as huge as we usually think, there's room for all of them in the same body. Sleep, digest, make children, that everybody does. And all the rest is nothing but variations on a theme, played in different keys. There's really no need to walk on tiptoes and make faces, no need to be so bashful in front of each other! We've all been eating more than our fill at the same table, now we have a bellyache. Why do you hold the napkins in front of your faces? Go ahead, scream and moan to express what you feel! Only don't make such virtuous, witty, heroic, and inspired

[5] With the jawbone of an ass, Samson killed a thousand Philistines. See Judges, 15:15–16.

[6] God put a mark on Cain, who killed his brother Abel. See Genesis, 4:13–15.

[7] Roman emperor (reigned 54–68 A.D.), notorious for his cruelty.

grimaces! After all, we know each other, save yourselves the trouble.

HÉRAULT   Yes, Camille, let us sit next to each other and scream. Nothing is more stupid than to bite your lips when something hurts. The Greeks and their gods used to scream, the Romans and the Stoics grimaced heroically.

DANTON   They were all good Epicureans, one as much as the other. They tailored themselves quite a cozy self-respect. It's not a bad idea to drape the toga and look over your shoulder to see if you cast a long shadow. Why make such a fuss? What does it matter whether we tie laurel leaves, a wreath of roses, or vine leaves in front of our genitals or whether we carry the ugly thing open and let the dogs lick it?

PHILIPPEAU   Friends, one need not stand very high above the surface of the earth to lose sight of all the confusion, the flutter and the glittering; your eyes will be completely filled with the sight of a few great, divine lines. There is an ear which hears all the confused shouting and the cries of distress—which stupefy us—as a stream of perfect harmonies.

DANTON   Yes, but we are the poor musicians and our bodies the instruments. Are those ugly sounds which are amateurishly squeezed out of them destined only to rise higher and higher and, finally fading into silence, to die in heavenly ears like a voluptuous breath?

HÉRAULT   Are we like sucking pigs which are whipped to death for the table of princes so that their meat will be tastier?

DANTON   Are we children, who are roasted in the fiery Moloch[8] arms of this world and tickled with a few rays of light, so the gods may laugh at their laughter?

CAMILLE   Is the ether, with its golden eyes, nothing but a dish with golden carps that stands on the table of the blissful gods, and the blissful gods laugh forever and the fish die forever and the gods delight forever in the play of colors during their death struggle?

DANTON   The world is chaos. Nothingness is the World-God, still unborn. (*The* JAILER *enters.*)

WARDER   Gentlemen, you may now go. The carriages are at the door.

PHILIPPEAU   Good night, my friends! Let us calmly spread over us the great blanket, under which all hearts cease to beat and all eyes close. (*They embrace each other.*)

HÉRAULT   (*taking* CAMILLE'*s arm*)   Be glad, Camille. We are going to

[8] Canaanite god to whom humans were sacrificed.

have a beautiful night. The clouds hang in the still evening sky like a fading Olympus[9] with paling figures of the sinking gods. (*They leave.*)

SCENE 6. *A room.* JULIE *alone.*

JULIE   Crowds were running around in the streets. Now all is quiet. I don't want to let him wait even one moment. (*She takes a vial from her garment.*) Come, you beloved priest, whose Amen sends us to bed. (*She steps to the window.*) It is so pleasant to take leave. All that is left to do now is close the door behind me. (*She drinks.*)

It would be nice to stand like this forever. The sun has gone down. The earth had such sharp features in its light, but now her face is serene and solemn like that of a dying woman. How beautifully the evening light plays around her forehead and cheeks. Paler and paler, like a corpse it floats downstream on the ether's current. Won't any arm reach out to grasp her golden locks, to pull her out of the river and bury her?

I leave quietly. I won't kiss her, so that not one breath, not one sigh may disturb her slumber. Sleep, sleep! (*She dies.*)

SCENE 7. *The Square of the Revolution. The tumbrils drive up and stop in front of the guillotine.* MEN *and* WOMEN *sing and dance the Carmagnole. The Prisoners intone the Marseillaise.*

A WOMAN WITH CHILDREN   Make room there! Make room! My children are crying from hunger. To keep them quiet I have to let them get a good look. Room there!

A WOMAN   Eh, Danton, now you can seduce the worms!

ANOTHER WOMAN   Hérault, I'll have myself a wig made from your beautiful hair.

HÉRAULT   My forest isn't thick enough to cover a *mons Veneris* that's been deforested as much as yours.

---

[9] In Greek mythology, Mount Olympus was the home of the Olympian gods.

CAMILLE   Damned witches! Before you're through you'll shout "Ye mountains, fall upon us!"

A WOMAN   The mountain has fallen on you, or rather you've fallen off
the mountain.

DANTON (*to* CAMILLE)   Never mind them, my boy. You're hoarse from
shouting.

CAMILLE (*gives the* DRAYMAN *some money*)   There, old Charon,[10] your
tumbril is a good serving platter! Gentlemen, I will be served as the
first course. This is a classical banquet. We lie on our cushions
and spill a little blood as libation. Farewell, Danton! (*He mounts
the steps of the scaffold, followed, one after the other, by the other
prisoners,* DANTON *last.*)

LACROIX (*to the crowd*)   You kill *us* on the day you lost your reason;
you will kill *them* the day you regain it.

SEVERAL VOICES   We've heard that before. What a bore!

LACROIX   The tyrants will break their necks stumbling over our graves.

HÉRAULT (*to* DANTON)   He thinks his corpse will be a hotbed for liberty.

PHILIPPEAU (*on top of the scaffold*)   I forgive you. I hope that your hour
of death may not be harsher than mine.

HÉRAULT   I thought so! He simply has to pull out his shirt once more to
show the people down there that his linen is clean.

FABRE   Farewell, Danton! I die a double death.

DANTON   Adieu, my friend. The guillotine is the best doctor.

HÉRAULT (*trying to embrace* DANTON)   Oh, Danton, I can't even think
of a joke any more. That means the time has come. (*A hangman
pushes him back.*)

DANTON (*to the hangman*)   Do you want to be more cruel than death?
You can't prevent our heads from kissing at the bottom of the
basket![11]

SCENE 8. *A street.*

LUCILE   There is something serious about this, after all. I want to think
about it a little. Something is dawning on me.
                   Dying—dying! Everything is allowed to live, this tiny

---

[10] In Greek mythology, the ferryman who transported the souls of the dead
across the river Styx.

[11] On April 5, 1794, Danton was executed.

mosquito there and the bird. Why not he? The whole stream of life would stop if only this one drop were spilled. The blow would open a wound in the earth.

Everything moves, the clocks tick, the bells ring, people run around, the water flows, and so everything goes on until—no! It must not happen. I'll sit down on the ground and scream so that everything is frightened to a standstill, stops dead—that nothing moves. (*She sits down, covers her eyes and lets out a scream. After a pause, she rises again.*) That doesn't work either. Everything is exactly as it always is, the houses, the street, the wind blows, the clouds move. It seems that we must live with it. (SEVERAL WOMEN *come down the street.*)

FIRST WOMAN   A handsome man, that Hérault.

SECOND WOMAN   When he stood by the triumphal arch on Constitution Day, I sort of thought that he would look quite well on the guillotine, I thought. That must have been a premonition.

THIRD WOMAN   Yes, one should be able to see people in all situations. It's a good thing that dying is getting to be such a public affair. (*They pass on.*)

LUCILE   Oh, Camille! Where shall I look for you now?

SCENE 9. *Place de la Révolution. Two* EXECUTIONERS *working at the guillotine.*

FIRST EXECUTIONER (*stands on the guillotine and sings*)
    And when home I go
    The moon shines so. . . .

SECOND EXECUTIONER   Hey! Are you going to finish soon?

FIRST EXECUTIONER   In a minute! (*He sings.*)
    The moon shines in my father's window,
    Fellow, where have you been so long?
    There! Give me my coat! (*Both leave, singing.*)
    And when home I go
    The moon shines so . . .

LUCILE (*entering and sitting down on the steps of the scaffold*)   I shall sit on your lap, you silent angel of death. (*She sings.*)
    There is a reaper, he's called Death,
    Has power from Almighty God.

Dear cradle who has rocked my Camille to sleep, who suffocated
him with your roses. Bell of Death who sang at his grave with your
sweet voice. (*She sings.*)
Their number is legion, no one knows
How many his sickle has known.
(*A patrol enters.*)
CITIZEN   Halt, who goes there?
LUCILE (*lost in thought, suddenly comes to a decision*)   Long live the
King!
CITIZEN   In the name of the Republic!
(*She is surrounded by the guard and taken away.*)
CURTAIN

COMMENTARY

Danton's Death (1835)   While he was preparing for his examinations at the medical school of the University of Strasbourg, Georg Büchner, who was twenty-one and who was to live only two more years, was on his guard against the police, who might at any moment have arrested him for radical political activities. It was at this time that the undergraduate political activist wrote his first play, *Danton's Death*. Borrowing passages from actual speeches, embroidering and inventing, Büchner aimed, as he said in a letter to his family, to recreate history and to transplant readers and spectators into the midst of the life of the French Revolution.

"After the Revolution" might be a suitable subtitle for *Danton's Death*, which dramatizes postrevolutionary loss of idealism in the face of bitter political and human realities. At the time of the play, March 24– April 5, 1794, the lower classes had replaced the bourgeoisie as the major force of the French Revolution. Demagogues exploited the frustrations and fears of the poor, who were bitter and angry because the revolution had not significantly improved their lives. The revolution, which had overthrown the monarchy and abolished the aristocracy, shed the civil libertarian ideals of the middle class and became still more radical. Differences of opinion as to the goals and methods of the revolution became hardened positions. Counterrevolution, a legitimate fear, became an excuse to destroy political opposition, denunciation and execution became the means. One kind of tyranny replaced another.

In the face of demagoguery, political machinations, and bloodshed, weary politicians—even such erstwhile bloodletters as Georges Danton —have begun to wonder whether continued struggle is worthwhile. Told by his followers that they "and all honest men" will accomplish the task of transforming the revolution into a republic, Danton wearily exclaims, "that 'and' is a very long word! It keeps us rather far apart!" A revolutionary politician can help and bless honest men, Danton realizes, but he is not one of them. His innocence gone, Danton is on the brink of despair. But he does not lose his footing. Although he is disillusioned by the turns of events of the French Revolution, he does not lose his faith in the initial goals of that revolution, or in revolution as a means of effecting social progress. "The deluge of the Revolution may deposit our bodies where it decides," says Danton shortly before he is taken away to be killed. "Our fossilized bones will still be good for bashing in the heads of kings. . . . Once History opens her vaults, the aroma of our corpses may still be enough to suffocate the tyrants." Even the dead victim of revolution may be useful in destroying tyranny. For all of Danton's despair, he ultimately affirms his belief in revolution.

Although *Danton's Death* is not an antirevolutionary play, it is an anti-extremist play. In *Danton's Death*, extremism in pursuit of virtue is a vice. Büchner's play dramatizes the conflict between the extremist Robespierre and the moderate Danton. Robespierre is not only a political extremist who ruthlessly and tyranically fights counterrevolution, he is a stoic demagogue who opposes luxurious living and sexual indulgence. Believing himself to be an agent of God and the Revolution, he opposes vice and the enemies of the revolution. In the name of God, he kills men. "Terror flows from Virtue," says Robespierre, "for it is nothing but swift, stern, and inflexible justice." To Robespierre, who often equates evil with counterrevolution, vice may sometimes be "high treason," and is therefore punishable by terror, which he regards as the strength behind the weapon. Anyone who tries to prevent him from drawing his sword in defense of the revolution, Robespierre declares, is an enemy whom he must kill. Danton, on the other hand, is an epicurean voluptuary who lives lavishly and visits prostitutes. In contrast to Robespierre, who pursues his goals with fanatical zeal, Danton is weary of political machinations and of killing for political ends. Although Danton once murdered as fiercely as Robespierre now does, he has recanted, for he wants an end to killing and a beginning to the enjoyment of life. "I'd rather be guillotined than order others to the guillotine," the disillusioned Danton tells his unyielding opponent. "I am fed up with it. Why should men fight each other? We should sit down side by side and have some peace." Because Danton is a moderate who opposes the extremist measures of Robespierre, he is in danger. As Lacroix, one of his followers, warns him, "The mob knows no difference between weakness and moderation; they kill the stragglers."

Lacroix's analysis of the mob is accurate, but the Parisian lower classes cannot be described so simply. Although the mob is incapable of distinguishing between moderation and weakness, although they are unable to comprehend the soul-searching of an intellectual, although they are swayed by political demagogues who flatter them, the mob, like Danton, is a victim rather than a villain. Their bellies are empty, their women reduced to prostitution to earn money for their families, their hands callused, their clothing torn and ragged. The Parisian lower classes have been lied to and manipulated by politicians who have not kept their promises to improve their lot. When told to kill the aristocrats who were feeding on them, the mob did so. When told to kill politicians charged with counterrevolution, they helped send them to the guillotine. But they are still cold and hungry, for none of the changes the commoners helped make have helped them. As one citizen—echoing Danton's feeling of the futility of murder—sadly observes, "For all the holes we rip into other people's bodies not one in our pants has yet been mended." Danton correctly points out that the Jacobins have given the people executions as an opiate and have substituted blood and decapitated heads for wine and loaves of bread. Nevertheless, as the mob is quick to notice, Danton does not want for food, drink, and women. Compared to them, Danton lives very well. "Danton wears beautiful clothes," says a citizen, "Danton has a beautiful house, Danton has a beautiful wife, he bathes in Burgundy, eats game from silver plates, and sleeps with your wives and daughters when he's drunk. Danton used to be as poor as you are. Where did all this come from?" These charges are only partly exaggerative; essentially, as the scenes of Danton's luxurious life reveal, the charges are accurate.

Although the people are frequently deceived, they are, paradoxically, perceptive. Similar paradoxes characterize the two chief antagonists as well, for as Desmoulins observes, "We are all villains and angels, fools and geniuses, all in one." A murderer, Robespierre wants to end exploitation and "wipe out this crowd that has stolen the clothes of dead aristocrats and has inherited their leprosy!" A humane moderate, Danton—whose former murders in the name of ideals return to him in nightmares—is condemned by the Revolutionary Tribunal which he himself a year earlier was instrumental in creating. Using the Revolutionary Tribunal to kill his political opponents, Robespierre will be executed—as Danton warns him—less than six months later by the Revolutionary Tribunal. In *Danton's Death*, former revolutionary extremists are killed by present revolutionary extremists, who will be killed by other revolutionary extremists. Those who employ the guillotine perish by the guillotine.

"We're puppets," says Danton, "and unknown powers manipulate our wires." Fatalism and the absence of free will are frequent themes of Danton's speeches. "Life is not worth the effort we make to preserve it," says Danton. "They want my head—so be it. I'm tired of all the trouble. Let them take it! What does it matter?" Danton's point of view is frequently regarded as the point of view of the play. An apparent buttress to this interpretation is Büchner's statement in a letter to his fiancée in November, 1833, that the French Revolution revealed to him the "gruesome fatalism of History." The individual, he felt, was "mere froth on the wave, greatness sheer chance, the mastery of genius a marionette play, a ridiculous struggle against brazen law; to recognize it, the supreme achievement, to control it impossible." But is this the argument of the play as revealed in the play? Not necessarily. Again and again, Büchner seems to demonstrate not that the events are inevitable but that they are avoidable. In the first act Danton tries to prevent himself from getting involved in political machinations, but before the act ends he becomes involved and he acts (meeting and trying to persuade Robespierre), though he is ineffective. In the second act he is given the opportunity to act (to flee the country) but, unable to believe that his enemies would dare arrest him, and at the same time feeling it not worth the effort to save his life, he chooses not to act. In the third act he acts vigorously (defending himself before the tribunal) but by that time it is too late. By contrast, his enemies, at the end of each of these acts, act quickly, decisively, and effectively. In the fourth act, Danton is executed. Because he has—successively—acted ineffectively, refused to act, and acted too late, his enemies' actions determine what happens to him.

Danton's Death is not a dramatization of the futility of human action in the face of a determined outcome but of the folly of human inaction when timely action could have prevented that outcome. "Well shouted, Danton!" says Lacroix after Danton defends himself before the Revolutionary Tribunal. "If you had tried as hard to save your life a little earlier, things would be different now." The play reveals the necessity of acting decisively and of not underestimating one's political opponents, particularly during and immediately after a revolution.

Bibliography

A. Plays About the French Revolution:

Fritz Hochwalder, *The Public Prosecutor*, 1949

Stanisława Przybyszewska, *The Danton Affair, 1793, Thermidor*: entire trilogy, 1929

Romain Rolland, *The Wolves*, 1898; *Danton*, 1900; *The Fourteenth of July*, 1902; *The Game of Love and Death*, 1924; *Robespierre*, 1938

Arthur Schnitzler, *The Green Cockatoo*, 1899

Eugene Scribe, *Before, During, and After*, 1828

Tom Taylor, *A Tale of Two Cities*, adapted, with Charles Dickens' help, from Dickens' novel, 1860

B. Works About Georg Büchner and Danton's Death:

Baxandall, Lee. "Georg Büchner's *Danton's Death*," *Tulane Drama Review*, VI (Spring, 1962).

"From Georg Büchner's Letters," *Tulane Drama Review*, VI (Spring, 1962).

Knight, A. H. J. *Georg Büchner*. Oxford: Blackwell, 1951.

Lindenberger, Herbert. *Georg Büchner*. Carbondale: Southern Illinois University Press, 1964.

Peacock, Ronald. *The Poet in the Theatre*. New York: Hill and Wang, 1960.

Spalter, Max. *Brecht's Tradition*. Baltimore: Johns Hopkins Press, 1967.

Communist
Revolution
in the West

ST. JOAN OF THE STOCKYARDS
Bertolt Brecht

SAINT JOAN OF THE STOCKYARDS
Bertolt Brecht
Translated by Frank Jones

CHARACTERS

PIERPONT MAULER
CRIDLE
LENNOX } *Meat Kings*
GRAHAM
MEYERS

JOAN DARK
MARTHA
MAJOR PAULUS SNYDER } *Black Straw Hats*
JACKSON

SLIFT, *a stockbroker*

MULBERRY, *a landlord*

MRS. LUCKERNIDDLE, *a worker's wife*

GLOOMB, *a worker*

MRS. SWINGURN, *a worker's wife*

A WAITER

AN OLD MAN

A BROKER

A FOREMAN

AN APPRENTICE

TWO DETECTIVES

FIVE LABOR LEADERS

TWO POLICEMEN

And, as groups: WHOLESALERS, STOCKBREEDERS, SMALL SPECULATORS, BROKERS, WORKERS, NEWSBOYS, PASSERS-BY, JOURNALISTS, VOICES, MUSICIANS, SOLDIERS, POOR FOLK

227

1. The Meat King Pierpont Mauler gets a Letter from His Friends in New York

Chicago stockyards.

MAULER (*reading a letter*)   "As we can plainly see, dear Pierpont, there has been a real glut in the meat market for some little time. Also tariff walls to the south of us are resisting all our attacks. In view of this it seems advisable, dear Pierpont, to let the packing business go." I have this hint today from my dear friends in New York. Here comes my partner. (*Hides letter.*)

CRIDLE   Well, my dear Pierpont! Why so gloomy?

MAULER   Remember, Cridle, how some days ago—
We were walking through the stockyards, it was evening—
We stood beside our brand-new packing machine.
Remember, Cridle, the ox that took the blow,
Standing there blond, huge, dumbly gazing up
Toward Heaven: I feel the stroke was meant for me.
Oh, Cridle! Oh, our business is bloody.

CRIDLE   So—the old weakness, Pierpont!
Almost incredible: you, giant of packers,
Lord of the stockyards, quaking at the kill,
Fainting with pain, all for a fair-haired ox!
Don't tell a soul of this but me, I beg you.

MAULER   O loyal Cridle!
I oughtn't to have visited the stockyards!
Since I went into this business—that's seven
Years—I'd avoided them; and now—oh, Cridle,
I cannot bear it any longer! I'm giving up today.
You take this bloody business, with my share!
I'll let you have it cheap: you above all,
For no one else belongs to it like you.

CRIDLE   How cheap?

MAULER   No long palaver can be held
On such things by old friends like you and me.
Let's say ten million.

CRIDLE   That would not be expensive but for Lennox,
Who fights with us for every case of meat
And ruins our market with his cutthroat prices

And will break us all if he does not go broke.
Before he falls, and only you can fell him,
I shall not take your offer. Until then
Your cunning brain must be in constant practice.
MAULER   No, Cridle! That poor ox's outcry
          Will nevermore go mute within me. Therefore
          This Lennox must fall fast, for I myself
          Have willed to be a decent man henceforth
          And not a butcher. Cridle, come with me,
          And I will tell you what to do to make
          Lennox fall fast. But then you must
          Relieve me of this business, which hurts me.
CRIDLE   If Lennox falls.
          (*Exeunt.*)

2. The Collapse of the Great Packing Plants

In front of the Lennox Plant.

THE WORKERS   We are seventy thousand workers in Lennox's packing
          plant and we
          Cannot live a day longer on such low wages.
          Yesterday our pay was slashed again
          And today the notice is up once more:
          ANYONE NOT SATISFIED
          WITH OUR WAGES CAN GO.
          All right then, let's all go and
          Shit on the wages that get skinnier every day.
          (*A silence.*)
          For a long time now this work has made us sick
          The factory our hell and nothing
          But cold Chicago's terrors could
          Keep us here. But now
          By twelve hours' work a man can't even
          Earn a stale loaf and
          The cheapest pair of pants. Now
          A man might just as well go off and
          Die like a beast.

(*A silence.*)
What do they take us for? Do they think
We are going to stand here like steers, ready
For anything? Are we
Their chumps? Better lie and rot!
Let's go right now.
(*A silence.*)
It must be six o'clock by now!
Why don't you open up, you sweatshop bosses? Here
Are your steers, you butchers, open up!
(*They knock.*)
Maybe they've forgotten us?
(*Laughter.*)
Open the gates! We
Want to get into your
Dirt-holes and lousy kitchens
To cook stuffed meat
For the eaters who possess.
(*A silence.*)
We demand at least
Our former wages, even though they were too low, at least
A ten-hour day and at least—

A MAN (*crossing stage*) What are you waiting for? Don't you know
That Lennox has shut down?
(NEWSBOYS *run across stage.*)

THE NEWSBOYS Meat king Lennox forced to shut down his plants!
Seventy thousand workers without food or shelter! M. L. Lennox
a victim of bitter competitive struggle with Pierpont Mauler, well-
known meat baron and philanthropist.

THE WORKERS Alas!
Hell itself
Shuts its gate in our faces!
We are doomed. Bloody Mauler grips
Our exploiter by the throat and
We are the ones who choke!

P. MAULER *A street.*

THE NEWSBOYS Chicago Tribune, noon edition! P. Mauler, meat baron
and philanthropist, to attend opening of the P. Mauler Hospitals,
largest and most expensive in the world! (P. MAULER *passes, with
two* MEN.)

A PASSER-BY (*to another*)   That's P. Mauler. Who are the men walking
    with him?

THE OTHER   Detectives. They guard him so that he won't be knocked
    down.

TO COMFORT THE MISERY OF THE STOCKYARDS, THE BLACK STRAW HATS LEAVE
    THEIR MISSION-HOUSE. JOAN'S FIRST DESCENT INTO THE DEPTHS

    (*In front of the Black Straw Hats Mission.*)

JOAN (*at the head of a Black Straw Hat* SHOCK TROOP)
    In gloomy times a bloody confusion
    Ordered disorder
    Planful wilfulness
    Dehumanized humanity
    When there is no end to the unrest in our cities:
    Into such a world, a world like a slaughterhouse—
    Summoned by rumors of threatening deeds of violence
    To prevent the brute strength of the short-sighted people
    From shattering its own tools and
    Trampling its own bread-basket to pieces—
    We wish to reintroduce
    God.
    A figure of little glory,
    Almost of ill repute,
    No longer admitted
    To the sphere of actual life:
    But, for the humblest, the one salvation!
    Therefore we have decided
    To beat the drum for Him
    That He may gain a foothold in the regions of misery
    And His voice may ring out clearly among the slaughterhouses.
    (*To* THE BLACK STRAW HATS.)
    And this undertaking of ours is surely
    The last of its kind. A last attempt
    To set Him upright again in a crumbling world, and that
    By means of the lowest.
    (*They march on, drums beating.*)

FROM DAWN TO DARK THE BLACK STRAW HATS WORKED IN THE STOCKYARDS,
    BUT WHEN EVENING CAME THEY HAD ACCOMPLISHED JUST ABOUT
    NOTHING

In front of the Lennox Plant.

A WORKER   They say there's another spell of dirty dealing going on at the livestock market. Till it's over we'll have to bide our time, I guess, and live on air.

A WORKER   Lights are on in the offices. They're counting up the profits.
(THE BLACK STRAW HATS *arrive. They put up a sign: "Bed for a Night, 20 cents; With Coffee, 30 cents; Hot dogs, 15 cents."*)

THE BLACK STRAW HATS (*singing*)   Attention, your attention!
We see you, man that's falling
We hear your cry for help
We see you, woman calling.
Halt the autos, stop the traffic!
Courage, sinking people, we're coming, look our way!
You who are going under,
See us, oh, see us, brother, before you say you're beat!
We bring you something to eat,
We are still aware
That you are standing out there.
Don't say it can't be helped, for things are changing
The injustice of this world cannot remain
If all the people come and join us marching
And leave their cares behind and help with might and main.
We'll bring up tanks and cannon too
And airplanes there shall be
And battle ships over the sea
All to conquer a plate of soup, brother, just for you.
For you, yes, you, poor folk,
Are an army vast and grand.
So even in times like these
We've all got to lend you a hand!
Forward march! Eyes right! Rifles ready to fire!
Courage, you sinking people, we're coming, look our way!
(*During the singing the* BLACK STRAW HATS *have been distributing their leaflet, "The Battle Cry," spoons, plates and soup. The* WORKERS *say "Thank you" and listen to* JOAN's *speech.*)

JOAN   We are the Soldiers of the Lord. On account of our hats we are called the Black Straw Hats. We march with drums and flags wherever unrest prevails and acts of violence threaten, to remind men of the Lord whom they have all forgotten, and to bring back their souls to Him. We call ourselves soldiers because we are an army and when we are on the march we have to fight crime and misery, those forces that want to drag us down. (*She begins to ladle out the soup herself.*) That's it, just eat some hot soup and then everything will look real different, but please give a little thought to Him who bestows it upon you. And when you think that way you will see that this is really the complete solution: Strive upward, not downward. Get in line for a good position up above, not here below. Want to be the first man up, not the first man down. Surely you realize now what sort of trust you can place in the fortunes of this world. None at all. Misfortune comes like the rain, that nobody makes, and still comes. Tell me, where does all your misfortune come from?

AN EATER   From Lennox & Co.

JOAN   Maybe Mr. Lennox has more worries right now than you have. After all, what are you losing? His losses run into millions!

A WORKER   There's not much fat floating in this soup, but it contains plenty of wholesome water and there's no lack of warmth.

ANOTHER WORKER   Shut up, revellers! Listen to the heavenly text, or they'll take away your soup!

JOAN   Quiet! Tell me, dear friends, why are you poor?

WORKER   Aw, *you* tell *us*.

JOAN   All right, I will tell you: it is not because you aren't blest with worldly goods—that is not for all of us—but because you have no sense of higher things. That is why you are poor. These low pleasures for which you work so hard, a bite to eat, nice homes, the movies, they are just coarse sensual enjoyments, but God's word is a far finer, more inward, more exquisite pleasure, maybe you can't think of anything sweeter than whipped cream, but God's word, I tell you, is still sweeter, honestly it is, oh, how sweet God's word is! It's like milk and honey, and in it you dwell as in a palace of gold and alabaster. O ye of little faith, the birds of the air have no *Help Wanted* ads and the lilies of the field have no jobs, and yet He feeds them, because they sing His praises. You all want to get to the top, but what kind of top, and how do you propose to get there? And so it's we Straw Hats who ask you, quite practically: What does a man need to rise?

WORKER   A starched collar.

JOAN   No, not a starched collar. Maybe you need a starched collar to get ahead on earth, but in God's eyes you need much more than that around you, a quite different sort of splendor, but before Him you don't even have a rubber collar on because you have utterly neglected your entire inner natures. But how are you going to get to the top—whatever, in your ignorance, you call the top—by brute

force? As if force ever caused anything but destruction! You
believe that if you rear up on your hind legs there'll be heaven on
earth. But I say to you: that way not paradise but chaos is created.

WORKER (*enters, running*)   A position has just opened up! It pays, and
it's calling you over

To Plant Number Five!

It looks like a urinal on the outside.

Run!

(*Three* WORKERS *put down full plates of soup and run.*)

JOAN   Hey, you, where are you off to? Talk to you about God, *that* you
don't want to hear, eh!

A BLACK STRAW HAT GIRL   The soup's all gone.

THE WORKERS   The soup's all gone.

Fatless it was and scant,

But better than nothing.

(*All turn away and stand up.*)

JOAN   Oh, keep your seats, no harm's done, the grand soup of heaven
never gives out, you know.

THE WORKERS   When will you finally

Open your roachy cellars,

You butchers of men?

(*Groups form.*)

A MAN   How am I to pay for my little house now, the cute damp thing

With twelve of us in it? Seventeen

Payments I've made and now the last is due:

They'll throw us onto the street and never again

Will we see the trampled ground with the yellowish grass

And never breathe again

The accustomed pestilent air.

A SECOND MAN (*in a circle*)   Here we stand with hands like shovels

And necks like trucks wanting to sell

Our hands and necks

And no one will buy them.

THE WORKERS   And our tool, a gigantic pile

Of steam hammers and cranes,

Barred in behind walls!

JOAN   What's up? Now they're simply leaving! Finished eating, have you?

We hope it does you good. Thanks. Why have you listened till now?

A WORKER   For the soup.

JOAN   We're moving on. Sing!

THE BLACK STRAW HATS (*singing*)   Go straight to the thick of the fight

Where there's the toughest work to do.

Sing with all your might! It may still be night,

But already the morning is coming in might!
Soon the Lord Jesus will come to you, too.

A VOICE FROM THE REAR   There's still work to be had at Mauler's! (*Exeunt*
WORKERS, *all but a few* WOMEN.)

JOAN (*gloomily*)   Pack up the instruments. Did you see how they hurried
Away as soon as the soup was gone?
This thing gets no higher up
Than the rim of a dish. It believes
In nothing that it does not
Hold in its hand—if it believes in hands.
Living from minute to minute, uncertainly,
They can no longer raise themselves
From the lowest ground. Only hunger
Is a match for them. They are touched
By no song, no word
Penetrates their depths.
(*To the* BYSTANDERS.)   We Black Straw Hats feel as though we
were expected to satisfy a starving continent with our spoons.
(*The* WORKERS *return. Shouting in distance.*)

THE WORKERS (*in front*)   What's that yelling? A huge stream of people
from the packing houses!

A VOICE (*in back*)   Mauler and Cridle are shutting down too!
The Mauler works are locking us out!

THE RETURNING WORKERS   Running for jobs, we met halfway
A stream of desperate men
Who had lost their jobs and
Asked us for jobs.

THE WORKERS (*in front*)   Alas! From over there, too, a troop of men!
You can't see the end of it! Mauler
Has shut down too! What's to become of us?

THE BLACK STRAW HATS (*to* JOAN)   Come along with us now. We're
freezing and wet and we have to eat.

JOAN   But now I want to know who's to blame for all this.

THE BLACK STRAW HATS   Stop! Don't get mixed up in that! They're sure
To give you an earful. Their minds are stuffed
With low ideas! They're lazybones!
Gluttonous, shirkers, from birth onward
Void of all higher impulse!

JOAN   No, I want to know. (*To the* WORKERS.) Tell me now: why are
you running around here without any work?

THE WORKERS   Bloody Mauler's locked in battle
With stingy Lennox; so we go hungry.

JOAN   Where does Mauler live?

THE WORKERS   Over there where livestock is bought and sold,
  In a big building, the livestock market.
JOAN   There I will go, for
  I have to know this.
MARTHA   (*one of the* BLACK STRAW HATS)   Don't get mixed up in that!
  Ask many questions
  And you'll get lots of answers.
JOAN   No, I want to see this Mauler, who causes such misery.
THE BLACK STRAW HATS   Then, Joan, we take a dark view of your further
  fate.
  Do not mix in the quarrels of this world!
  He who meddles in a quarrel becomes its victim!
  His purity swiftly perishes. Soon
  His small warmth perishes in the cold
  That reigns over everything. Goodness abandons him
  Who flees the protective hearth.
  Striving downward
  From level to level toward the answer you never will get,
  You will disappear in dirt!
  For only dirt is stuffed into the mouths
  Of those who ask without caution.
JOAN   I want to know.
  (*Exeunt* BLACK STRAW HATS.)

3.   Pierpont Mauler Feels a Breath from Another World

In front of the livestock market. Lower level, JOAN *and* MARTHA
waiting; upper level, the meat packers LENNOX *and* GRAHAM, *con-
versing.* LENNOX *is white as chalk.*

GRAHAM   How you have felt the blows of brutal Mauler,
  My good friend Lennox! There's no hindering
  The rise of this monstrosity: to him
  Nature is goods, even the air's for sale.
  What we have inside our stomachs he resells to us.
  He can squeeze rent from ruined houses, money
  From rotten meat; throw stones at him,
  He's sure to turn the stones to money; so

Unruly is his money-lust, so natural
To him this lack of nature that he himself
Cannot deny its driving force within him
For I tell you: himself, he's soft, does not love money,
Cannot bear squalor, cannot sleep at night.
Therefore you must approach him as though you could hardly
    speak,
And say: "Oh, Mauler, look at me and take
Your hand off my throat—think of your old age—"
That will frighten him, for sure. Maybe he'll cry . . .

JOAN (*to* MARTHA)   Only you, Martha, have followed me this far.
All the others left me with warnings
As if I were bound for the end of the world.
Strange warning from their lips.
I thank you, Martha.

MARTHA   I warned you too, Joan.

JOAN   And went with me.

MARTHA   But will you really recognize him, Joan?

JOAN   I shall know him!

CRIDLE (*coming out on upper level*)   Well, Lennox, now the under-
bidding's over.
You're finished now and I'll close up and wait
Until the market recovers. I'll clean my yards
And give the knives a thorough oiling and order some
Of those new packing machines that give a fellow
A chance to save a tidy sum in wages.

GRAHAM   Damnable times!
Waste lies the market, flooded out by goods.
Trade, that was once so flourishing, lies fallow.
Scuffling over a market that's long been glutted,
You wrecked your own prices by underbidding one another: thus
Do buffaloes, fighting for grass, trample to shreds the grass they
fight for.
(MAULER *comes out, with his broker,* SLIFT, *among a crowd of*
PACKERS, *two* DETECTIVES *behind him.*)

THE MEAT PACKERS   Now everything's a matter of holding out.

MAULER   Lennox is down. (*To* LENNOX.)   Admit it, you are out.
And now I ask you, Cridle, to take over
The packing plant as stated in our contract,
Presuming Lennox finished.

CRIDLE   Agreed, Lennox is out. But also finished
Are good times on the market; therefore, Mauler,
You must come down from ten million for your stock!

MAULER   What? The price stands
      Here in the contract! Here, Lennox, see if this
      Is not a contract, with a price right on it!
CRIDLE   Yes, but a contract made in better times!
      Are bad times also mentioned in the contract?
      What can I do alone with a stockyard now
      When not a soul will buy a can of meat?
      Now I know why you couldn't bear to watch
      More oxen dying: it was because their flesh
      Cannot be sold!
MAULER   No, it's my heart
      That swells, affected by the creature's shrieks!
GRAHAM   Oh, mighty Mauler, now I realize
      The greatness of your actions: even your heart
      Sees far ahead!
LENNOX   Mauler, I wanted to talk with you . . . again . . .
GRAHAM   Straight to his heart, Lennox! Straight to his heart!
      It's a sensitive garbage pit!
      (*He hits* MAULER *in the pit of the stomach.*)
MAULER   Ouch!
GRAHAM   You see, he has a heart!
MAULER   Well, Freddy, now I'll make a settlement with Cridle
      So he can't buy a single can from you,
      Because you hit me.
GRAHAM   You can't do that, Pierpy! That's mixing
      Personal matters with business.
CRIDLE   O.K., Pierpy, with pleasure. Just as you please.
GRAHAM   I have two thousand workers, Mauler!
CRIDLE   Send them to the movies! But really, Pierpy, our agreement isn't
      valid. (*Figuring in a notebook.*) When we contracted for your
      withdrawal from the business, the shares—of which you hold one-
      third, as I do—stood at 390. You gave them to me for 320; that was
      cheap. It's expensive today; they're at a hundred now, because the
      market's blocked. If I'm to pay you off I'll have to throw the
      shares onto the market. If I do that they'll go down to 70, and
      what can I use to pay you then? Then I'll be done for.
MAULER   If that's your situation, Cridle, I must certainly
      Get my money out of you right away,
      Before you're done for.
      I tell you, Cridle, I am so afraid
      I'm all of a sweat, the most I can let you have
      Is six days! What am I saying? Five days
      If that's your situation.

LENNOX Mauler, look at me.

MAULER Lennox, you tell me if the contract says anything about bad
    times.

LENNOX No. (*Exit.*)

MAULER (*watching him go*) Some worry seems to be oppressing him,
    And I, on business bent (would I were not!)
    Did not perceive it! Oh, repulsive business!
    Cridle, it sickens me.
    (*Exit* CRIDLE. *Meanwhile* JOAN *has called one of the* DETECTIVES *over
    to her and said something to him.*)

THE DETECTIVE Mr. Mauler, there are some persons here who want to
    talk to you.

MAULER Unmannerly lot, eh? With an envious look, eh?
    And violent, no doubt? I
    Cannot see anyone.

THE DETECTIVE They're a pair from the Black Straw Hat Organization.

MAULER What kind of an organization is that?

THE DETECTIVE They have many branches and are numerous and re-
    spected among the lower classes, where they are called the Good
    Lord's Soldiers.

MAULER I've heard of them. Curious name:
    The Good Lord's Soldiers . . . but
    What do they want of me?

THE DETECTIVE They say they have something to discuss with you.
    During this the market uproar has resumed: "Steers 43," "Hogs
    55," "Heifers 59," *etc.*)

MAULER All right, tell them I will see them.
    But tell them also they may say nothing that I
    Do not ask about first. Nor must they break out
    Into tears or songs, especially sentimental ones.
    And tell them it would be most profitable to them
    For me to get the impression
    That they are well-meaning people, with nothing to their discredit,
    Who want nothing from me that I do not have.
    Another thing: do not tell them I am Mauler.

THE DETECTIVE (*going over to* JOAN) He consents to see you, but
    You must ask no questions, only answer
    When he asks you.

JOAN (*walking up to* MAULER) You are Mauler!

MAULER No, I'm not. (*Points to* SLIFT.) That's him.

JOAN (*pointing to* MAULER) You are Mauler.

MAULER No, he is.

JOAN You are.

MAULER   How do you know me?

JOAN   Because you have the bloodiest face. (SLIFT *laughs.*)

MAULER   You laugh, Slift? (*Meanwhile* GRAHAM *has hurried off. To*
JOAN.) How much do you earn in a day?

JOAN   Twenty cents, but food and clothing are supplied.

MAULER   Thin clothes, Slift, and thin soup too, I guess!
Yes, those clothes are probably thin and the soup not rich.

JOAN   Mauler, why do you lock the workers out?

MAULER (*to* SLIFT)   The fact that they work without pay
Is remarkable, isn't it? I never heard
Of such a thing before—a person working
For nothing and none the worse. And in their eyes
I see no fear
Of being down and out.
(*To* JOAN.) Extraordinary folk, you Black Straw Hats.
I shall not ask you what particularly
You want of me. I know the fool mob calls me
Mauler the Bloody, saying it was I
Who ruined Lennox or caused unpleasantness
For Cridle—who, between ourselves, is one
Of little merit. I can say to you:
Those are just business matters, and they won't
Be interesting to you. But there's something else, on which
I would like to hear your views. I am thinking of giving up
This bloodstained business, as soon as possible; once for all.
For recently—this *will* interest you—I saw
A steer die and it upset me so
That I want to get rid of everything, and have even sold
My interest in the plant, worth twelve million dollars. I gave it to
that man
For ten. Don't you feel
That this is right, and to your liking?

SLIFT   He saw the steer die and made up his mind
To butcher wealthy Cridle
Instead of the poor steer.
Was that right?
(*The* PACKERS *laugh.*)

MAULER   Go on, laugh. Your laughter's nothing to me.
Some day I'll see you weep.

JOAN   Mr. Mauler, why have you shut down the stockyards?
This I must know.

MAULER   Was it not an extraordinary act to take my hand

Out of a mighty concern, simply because it is bloody?
Say this is right, and to your liking.
All right then, don't say it, I know, I admit, some people
Did poorly out of it, they lost their jobs,
I know. Unhappily, that was unavoidable.
A bad lot anyway, a tough mob, better not go near them, but
　　tell me:
My act in withdrawing my hand from the business,
Surely that is right?

JOAN　I don't know whether you ask in earnest.

MAULER　That's because my damned voice is used to faking,
　　And for that reason too I know: you
　　Do not like me. Say nothing.
　　To the OTHERS.
　　I seem to feel a breath from another world wafted toward me.
　　(*He takes everybody's money from them and gives it to* JOAN.)
　　Out with your money, you cattle butchers, give it here!
　　(*He takes it out of their pockets, gives it to* JOAN.)
　　Take it to give to the poor folk, Joan!
　　But be assured that I feel no obligation in any way
　　And sleep extremely well. Why am I helping here? Perhaps
　　Just because I like your face, because it is so unknowing, although
　　You have lived for twenty years.

MARTHA　(*to* JOAN)　I don't believe in his sincerity.
　　Forgive me, Joan, for going away now too:
　　It seems to me you also
　　Should really drop all this!
　　(*Exit.*)

JOAN　Mr. Mauler, you know this is only a drop in the bucket. Can you
　　not give them real help?

MAULER　Tell the world I warmly commend your activities and
　　Wish there were more like you. But
　　You mustn't take this thing about the poor this way.
　　They are wicked people. Human beings do not affect me:
　　They are not guiltless, and they're butchers themselves.
　　However, let's drop the matter.

JOAN　Mr. Mauler, they are saying in the stockyards that you are to
　　blame for their misery.

MAULER　On oxen I have pity; man is evil.
　　Mankind's not ripe for what you have in mind:
　　Before the world can change, humanity
　　Must change its nature.

Wait just one more moment.
(*In a low tone, to* SLIFT.)   Give her more money away from here,
    when she's alone.
Say "for the poor folk," so that she can take it
Without blushing, but then see what she buys for herself.
If that's no help—I'd rather it were not—
Then take her with you
To the stockyards and show her
Those poor of hers, how wicked and gross they are, full of treach-
    ery and cowardice
And how they themselves are to blame.
Maybe that will help.
(*To* JOAN.)   Here is Sullivan Slift, my broker; he will show you
    something.
(*To* SLIFT.)   I tell you, it's almost intolerable in my eyes
That there should be people like this girl, owning nothing
But a black hat and twenty cents a day, and fearless.
(*Exit.*)

SLIFT   I would not care to know what you want to know;
Still, if you wish to know it, come here tomorrow.

JOAN   (*watching* MAULER *go*)   That's not a wicked man, he is the first
To be scared from the tanglewoods of meanness by our drums,
The first to hear the call.

SLIFT   (*departing*)   I give you a fair warning: do not take up with those
    people
Down in the yards, they're a lowdown lot, really
The scum of the earth.

JOAN   I want to see it.

4. The Broker Sullivan Slift Shows Joan Dark the
    Wickedness of the Poor: Joan's Second Descent into
    the Depths

The stockyards district.

SLIFT   Now, Joan, I will show you
The wickedness of those
For whom you feel pity and
How out of place the feeling is.

(*They are walking alongside a factory wall inscribed "Mauler and Cridle, Meat Packing Company." The name Cridle has been painted out in crosswise strokes. Two* MEN *come through a small gate.* SLIFT *and* JOAN *hear their conversation.*)

FOREMAN (*to a young* APPRENTICE)   Four days ago a man named Lucker-niddle fell into our boiler, we couldn't stop the machinery in time so he got caught in the bacon-maker, a horrible thing to happen; this is his coat and this is his cap, take them and get rid of them, all they do is take up a hook in the cloakroom and make a bad impression. It's a good plan to burn them, right away would be best. I entrust the things to you because I know you're a reliable man. I'd lose my job if the stuff were found anywhere. Of course as soon as the plant opens again you can have Luckerniddle's job.

THE APPRENTICE   You can count on me, Mr. Smith. (*The* FOREMAN *goes back in through the gate.*) Too bad about the fellow that has to go out into the world as bacon, but I feel bad about his coat too, it's still in good shape. Old Man Bacon has his can to wear now and won't need this any more, but I could use it very well. Shit, I'll take it. (*Puts it on and wraps his own coat and cap in newspaper.*)

JOAN (*swaying*)   I feel sick.

SLIFT   That's the world as it is. (*Stopping the* YOUNG MAN.) Wherever did you get that coat and cap? Didn't they belong to Luckerniddle, the man that had the accident?

APPRENTICE   Please don't let it get around, sir. I'll take the things off right away. I'm pretty nearly down and out. That extra twenty cents you get in the fertilizer-cellars fooled me into working at the bone-grinding machine last year. There I got it bad in the lungs, and a chronic eye inflammation too. Since then my working capacity has gone down and since February I've only been employed twice.

SLIFT   Keep the things on. And come to Canteen No. Seven at noon today. You'll get a free lunch and a dollar there if you tell Luckerniddle's wife where your cap and coat came from.

APPRENTICE   But, sir, isn't that sort of raw?

SLIFT   Well, if you don't need the money . . . !

APPRENTICE   You can rely on me, sir. (JOAN *and* SLIFT *walk on.*)

MRS. LUCKERNIDDLE (*sitting in front of the factory gate, lamenting*)   You in there, what are you doing with my husband?
Four days ago he went to work, he said:
"Warm up some soup for me tonight!" And to this
Day he hasn't got back! What have you done with him
You butchers! Four days I have been standing here
In the cold, nights too, waiting, but nobody tells me

Anything, and my husband doesn't come out! But I tell
You, I'm going to stand right here until I get to see him!
You'll rue the day if you've done him any harm!

SLIFT (*walking up to the* WOMAN)   Your husband has left town, Mrs. Luckerniddle.

MRS. LUCKERNIDDLE   Oh, don't give me that again.

SLIFT   I'll tell you something, Mrs. Luckerniddle, he is out of town, and it's very embarrassing to the factory to have you sitting around here talking foolishness. So we'll make you an offer which could not be required of us by law. If you give up your search for your husband, you may have lunch in our canteen every day for three weeks, free.

MRS. LUCKERNIDDLE   I want to know what's become of my husband.

SLIFT   We're telling you, he's gone to Frisco.

MRS. LUCKERNIDDLE   He has not gone to Frisco, he's had some accident because of you, and you're trying to hide it.

SLIFT   If that's what you think, Mrs. Luckerniddle, you cannot accept any meals from the factory, but you will have to bring suit against the factory. But think it over thoroughly. I shall be at your disposal in the canteen tomorrow. (SLIFT *goes back to* JOAN.)

MRS. LUCKERNIDDLE   I must have my husband back. I have nobody but him to support me.

JOAN   She will never come.
Twenty dinners may mean much
To one who is hungry, but
There is more for him.
(JOAN *and* SLIFT *walk on. They stop in front of a factory canteen and see two* MEN *looking in through a window.*)

GLOOMB   There sits the overseer who's to blame for my getting my hand in the tin-cutting machine—stuffing his belly full. We must see to it that this is the last time the swine gorges at our expense. You'd better give me your club, mine will probably splinter right off.

SLIFT   Stay here. I want to talk to him. And if he approaches you, say you're looking for work. Then you'll see what kind of people these are. (*Going up to* GLOOMB.) Before you get carried away into doing something—that's the way it looks to me—I'd like to make you a profitable proposition.

GLOOMB   I have no time right now, sir.

SLIFT   That's too bad, because there would have been something in it for you.

GLOOMB   Make it short. We cannot afford to let that swine go. He's got to get his reward today for that inhuman system he plays overseer to.

SLIFT   I have a suggestion to make for your own benefit. I am an inspector in the factory. Much inconvenience has been caused by your place remaining vacant. Most people think it too dangerous, just because you have made all this to-do about your fingers. Now it would be just fine if we had someone to fill that post again. If you, for example, could find somebody for it, we would be ready to take you on again right away—in fact, to give you an easier and better-paid job than you've had up to now. Perhaps even a foreman's position. You seem a clever man to me. And that fellow in there happens to have got himself disliked lately. You understand. You would also have to take charge of production speed, of course, and above all, as I say, find somebody for that place at the tin-cutting machine, which, I admit, is not safe at all. Over there, for instance, there's a girl looking for work.

GLOOMB   Can a man rely on what you say?

SLIFT   Yes.

GLOOMB   That one over there? She looks weak. It's no job for anyone who tires easily. (*To the* OTHERS.) I've thought it over, we'll do the job tomorrow night. Night's a better time for that kind of fun. So long. (*Goes over to* JOAN.) Looking for a job?

JOAN   Yes.

GLOOMB   Eyesight good?

JOAN   No. Last year I worked at a bone-grinding machine in the fertilizer cellars. I got it bad in the lungs there and a chronic eye inflammation too. Since then my work-capacity has gone down badly. I've been out of a job since February. Is this a good place?

GLOOMB   The place is good. It's work that even weaker people, like yourself, can do.

JOAN   Are you sure there's no other place to be had? I've heard that working at that machine is dangerous for people who tire easily. Their hands get unsteady and then they grab at the blades.

GLOOMB   That isn't true at all. You'll be surprised to see how pleasant the work is. You'll fan your brow and ask yourself how people could ever tell such silly stories about that machine. (SLIFT *laughs and draws* JOAN *away.*)

JOAN   Now I'm almost afraid to go on—what will I see next! (*They go into the canteen and see* MRS. LUCKERNIDDLE, *who is talking to the* WAITER.)

MRS. LUCKERNIDDLE (*figuring*)   Twenty lunches . . . then I could . . . then I'd go and then I'd have . . . (*She sits down at a table.*)

WAITER   If you're not eating you'll have to leave.

MRS. LUCKERNIDDLE   I'm waiting for somebody who was going to come in here today or tomorrow. What's for lunch today?

WAITER Peas.

JOAN There she sits.

> I thought she was firmly resolved, and feared
> That still she might come tomorrow, and now she has run here faster than we
> And is here already, waiting for us.

SLIFT Go and take her the food yourself—maybe she'll think again. (JOAN *fetches a plate of food and brings it to* MRS. LUCKERNIDDLE.)

JOAN Here so soon?

MRS. LUCKERNIDDLE It's because I've had nothing to eat for two days.

JOAN You didn't know we were coming in today, did you?

MRS. LUCKERNIDDLE That's right.

JOAN On the way over here I heard someone say that something happened to your husband in the factory and the factory is responsible.

MRS. LUCKERNIDDLE Oh, so you've reconsidered your offer? So I don't get my twenty meals?

JOAN But you got along with your husband very well, didn't you? People told me you have nobody except him.

MRS. LUCKERNIDDLE Well, I've had nothing to eat for two days.

JOAN Won't you wait till tomorrow? If you give up your husband now, no one will ask after him any more. (MRS. LUCKERNIDDLE *is silent.*) Don't take it. (MRS. LUCKERNIDDLE *snatches the food from her hands and begins to eat greedily.*)

MRS. LUCKERNIDDLE He's gone to Frisco.

JOAN And basements and storerooms are full of meat

> That cannot be sold and is going rotten
> Because no one will take it away.

(*The* WORKER *with the cap and coat enters, rear.*)

SLIFT Just take a seat beside that woman over there. (*The* MAN *sits down.*) That's a good-looking cap you have there. (*The* WORKER *hides it.*) Where did you get it?

WORKER Bought it.

SLIFT Well, where did you buy it?

WORKER Not in any store.

SLIFT Then where did you get it?

WORKER I got it off a man that fell into a boiling vat.

MRS. LUCKERNIDDLE (*feels sick. She gets up and goes out. On the way out she says to the* WAITER) Leave the plate where it is. I'm coming back. I'm coming here for lunch every day. Just ask that gentleman. (*Exit.*)

SLIFT For three whole weeks she will come and feed, without looking up, like an animal. Have you seen, Joan, that their wickedness is beyond measure?

JOAN   But what mastery you have
                Over their wickedness! How you thrive on it!
                Do you not see that their wickedness hasn't a chance?
                Certainly she would have liked
                To be true to her husband, as others are,
                And to ask after the man who supported her
                For some time longer, as is proper.
                But the price was too high: it amounted to twenty meals.
                And would that young man on whom
                Any scoundrel can rely
                Have shown the coat to the dead man's wife
                If things had gone as he would like?
                But the price appeared too high to him.
                And why would the man with only one arm
                Have failed to warn me? if the price
                Of so small a scruple were not so high for him?
                Why, instead, did he sell his wrath, which is righteous, but too
                    dear?
                If their wickedness is beyond measure, then
                So is their poverty. Not the wickedness of the poor
                Have you shown me, but
                The poverty of the poor.
                You've shown the evil of the poor to me:
                Now see the woes of evil poverty.
                O thoughtless rumor, that the poor are base:
                You shall be silenced by their stricken face!

5. Joan Introduces the Poor to the Livestock Exchange

The Livestock Exchange.

THE PACKERS   We have canned meat for sale!
                Wholesalers, buy canned meat!
                Fresh, juicy, canned meat!
                Mauler and Cridle's bacon!
                Graham's sirloins, soft as butter!
                Wilde's Kentucky lard, a bargain!
THE WHOLESALERS   And silence fell upon the waters and
                Bankruptcy among the wholesalers!
THE PACKERS   Due to tremendous technical advances

Engineers' hard work and entrepreneurs' farsightedness
We have now succeeded
In lowering prices for
Mauler and Cridle's bacon
Graham's sirloins, soft as butter
Wilde's Kentucky lard, a bargain
BY ONE-THIRD!
Wholesalers, buy canned meat!
Seize your opportunity!

THE WHOLESALERS   And silence fell upon the mountaintops
And hotel kitchens covered their heads
And stores looked away in horror
And middlemen turned pale!
We wholesalers vomit if we so much as
See a can of meat. This country's stomach
Has eaten too much meat from cans
And is fighting back.

SLIFT   What news from your friends in New York?

MAULER   Theories. If they had their way
The meat ring would be lying in the gutter
And stay there for weeks till there wasn't a peep left in it
And I'd have all that meat around my neck!
Madness!

SLIFT   I'd have to laugh if those men in New York really had
Tariffs lowered now, opened things up below the border
And started a bull-market—just supposing!—and we
Were to miss the bus!

MAULER   What if they did? Would you be harsh enough
To hack your pound of flesh from misery
Like this? Look at them, watching for a move,
As lynxes do! I couldn't be so harsh.

WHOLESALERS   Here we stand, wholesalers with mountains of cans
And cellars full of frozen steers
Wanting to sell the steers in cans
And no one will buy them!
And our customers, the kitchens and stores,
Are stuffed to the ceiling with frozen meat!
Screaming for buyers and eaters!
No more buying for us!

PACKERS   Here we stand, packers with slaughterhouses and packing space
And stables full of steers; day and night the machines
Run on under steam; brine, tubs and boiling vats

Wanting to turn the lowing ravenous herds
Into canned meat and nobody wants canned meat.
We're ruined.
STOCKBREEDERS   And what about us, the stockbreeders?
Who'll buy livestock now? In our barns stand
Steers and hogs eating expensive corn
And they ride to town in trains and while they ride
They eat and eat and at stations
They wait in rent-devouring boxcars, forever eating.
MAULER   And now the knives motion them back,
Death, giving livestock the cold shoulder,
Closes his shop.
PACKERS   (*shouting at* MAULER, *who is reading a newspaper*)   Traitorous
Mauler, nest befouler!
Do you think we don't know who's selling livestock here—
Oh so secretly—and knocking the bottom out of prices?
You've been offering meat for days and days!
MAULER   Insolent butchers, cry in your mothers' laps
Because the hunted creature's outcry ceases!
Go home and say that one of all your number
Could not hear oxen bellow any longer
And would rather hear your bellow than their bellow!
I want my cash and quiet for my conscience!
A BROKER   (*bellowing from the Exchange entrance, rear*)   Terrific drop
in stock exchange quotations!
Colossal sales of stocks. Cridle, formerly Mauler,
Whirl the whole meat ring's rates down with them
Into the abyss.
(*Uproar arises among the* MEAT-PACKERS. *They rush at* CRIDLE, *who
is white as chalk.*)
PACKERS   What's the meaning of this, Cridle? Look us in the eye!
Dumping stocks, with the market the way it is?
BROKERS   At 115!
PACKERS   Are your brains made of dung?
It's not yourself alone you're ruining!
You big shit! You criminal!
CRIDLE   (*pointing to* MAULER)   There's your man!
GRAHAM   (*standing in front of* CRIDLE)   This isn't Cridle's doing, some-
one else
Is fishing these waters and we're supposed to be the fish!
There are people who want to take care of the meat-ring, now,
And do a final job! Defend yourself, Mauler!

PACKERS (*to* MAULER) The story is, Mauler, that you're squeezing your
money
Out of Cridle, who, we hear, is groggy already, and Cridle
Himself says nothing and points to you.

MAULER If I leave my money in this Cridle's hands an hour longer—a
man who's confessed to me personally that he's unsound—who
among you would still take me seriously as a businessman? And I
want nothing so much as for *you* to take me seriously.

CRIDLE (*to the* BYSTANDERS) Just four weeks ago I made a contract with
Mauler. He wanted to sell me his shares—one-third of the total—
for ten million dollars. From that time on, as I've just found out,
he has been secretly selling quantities of livestock, cheap, to make
a still worse mess of prices that are sagging already. He could ask
for his money whenever he wanted to. I intended to pay him by
disposing of part of his shares on the market—they were high then
—and reinvesting part. Then the drop came. Today Mauler's shares
are worth not ten but three million. The whole plant is worth ten
million instead of thirty. That's exactly the ten million I owe
Mauler, and that's what he wants overnight.

PACKERS If you're doing this, making things hard for Cridle,
Whose affiliates we are not, then you're well aware
That this concerns us too. You're stripping
All business bare: the fault is yours
If our cans of meat are as cheap as sand,
Because you ruined Lennox with cheap cans!

MAULER You shouldn't have gone and slaughtered so many cattle,
You raving butchers! Now I want my money;
Though you should all go begging, I must have
My money! I have other plans.

STOCKBREEDERS Lennox smashed! And Cridle groggy! And Mauler
Pulls all his money out!

SMALL SPECULATORS Oh, as for us, the little speculators,
Nobody cares. They scream when they see
The colossus topple, but don't see where it falls,
Whom it strikes down. Mauler! Our money!

PACKERS Eighty thousand cans at 50, but fast!

WHOLESALERS Not a single one! (*Silence. The drumming of the* BLACK
STRAW HATS *and* JOAN's *voice are heard.*)

JOAN Pierpont Mauler! Where is Mauler?

MAULER What's that drumming? Who
Is calling my name?

Here, where every man
Shows his bare chops all smeared with blood!
(*The* BLACK STRAW HATS *march in. They sing their war-chant.*)
BLACK STRAW HATS (*singing*)   Attention, pay attention!
    There is a man who's falling!
    There is a cry for help!
    There is a woman calling!
    Halt the autos, stop all traffic!
    Men falling all around us and no one looks their way!
    Is there no sight in your eye?
    Say hello to your brother, not just any guy!
    Get up from where you've dined—
    Is there no thought in your mind
    For the starving folk nearby?
    I hear you say: it will always be the same,
    The injustice of the world will still remain.
    But we say this to you: You've got to march
    And leave your cares and help with might and main
    And bring up tanks and cannon too
    And airplanes there shall be
    And battleships over the sea
    To conquer a plate of soup, poor brother, just for you.
    You've all got to lend us a hand
    And it must be today
    For the army of the good
    Is not a vast array.
    Forward march! Eyes right! Rifles ready to fire!
    Men falling all around us and no one looks their way!
    (*Meanwhile the Exchange battle has continued. But laughter, prompted by exclamations, is spreading toward the front of the scene.*)
PACKERS   Eighty thousand cans at half price, but fast!
WHOLESALERS   Not a single one!
PACKERS   Then we're finished, Mauler!
JOAN   Where is Mauler?
MAULER   Don't go, Slift! Graham, Meyers,
    Stay there in front of me.
    I don't want to be seen here.
STOCKBREEDERS   Not a steer to be sold in Chicago any more
    This day spells ruin for all of Illinois
    With mounting prices you prodded us on into raising steers
    And here we stand with steers

And no one will buy them.

Mauler, you dog, you are to blame for this disaster.

MAULER   Enough of business. Graham! My hat. I've got to go.

A hundred dollars for my hat.

CRIDLE   Oh, damn you to hell. (*Exit.*)

JOAN   (*behind* MAULER)   Now, you stay here, Mr. Mauler, and listen to what I have to say to you. It is something you all may hear. Quiet! Yes, indeed, you hardly think it right for us Black Straw Hats to turn up like this in the dark hidden places where you do your business! I've been told about the kind of things you do here, how you make meat more and more expensive by your carryings-on and subtle trickery. But if you ever supposed you could keep it all concealed, then you're on the wrong track, now and on the Day of Judgment, for then it will be revealed, and how will you look then, when our Lord and Saviour has you walk up in a row and asks with His big eyes, "Well, where are my steers? What have you done with them? Did you make them available to the people at prices within their reach? What has become of them, then?" And when you stand there embarrassed, groping for excuses, the way you do in your newspapers, which don't always print the truth either, then the steers will bellow at your backs in all the barns where you keep them tucked away to make prices go sky-high, and by their bellowing they will bear witness against you before Almighty God! (*Laughter.*)

STOCKBREEDERS   We stockbreeders see nothing funny in that!

Dependent on weather, summer and winter, we stand

Considerably nearer the Lord of old.

JOAN   And now an example. If a man builds a dam against the unreasonable water, and a thousand people help him with the labor of their hands, and he gets a million for it, but the dam breaks as soon as the water rises and everybody working on it and many more are drowned—what kind of man is he who builds a dam like that? You may call him a businessman or a rascal, depending on your views, but we tell you he's a numskull. And all you men who make bread dear and life a hell for human beings, so that they all become devils, you are numskulls, wretched, stingy numskulls and nothing else!

WHOLESALERS   (*shouting*)   Because of your unscrupulous

Juggling with prices and filthy lust for profit

You're bringing on your own ruin!

Numskulls!

PACKERS   (*shouting back*)   Numskulls yourselves!

Nothing can be done about crises!

      Unshakable above our heads
      Stands economic law, the not-to-be-known.
      Terrible is the cyclic recurrence
      Of natural catastrophes!

STOCKBREEDERS Nothing to be done about your hold on our throats?
      That's wickedness, calculated wickedness!

JOAN And why does this wickedness exist in the world? Well, how could it be otherwise? Naturally, if a man has to smash his neighbor's head for a ham sandwich so that he can satisfy his elementary needs, brother striving with brother for the bare necessities of life, how can the sense of higher things help being stifled in the human heart? Why not think of helping your neighbor simply as serving a customer? Then you'll understand the New Testament in a flash, and see how fundamentally modern it is, even today. Service! Why, what does service mean if not charity—in the true meaning of the word, that is! Gentlemen, I keep hearing that the poor haven't enough morals, and it's true, too. Immorality makes its nest down there in the slums, with revolution itself for company. I simply ask you: Where are they to get morals from, if they have nothing else? Where can they get anything without stealing it? Gentlemen, there is such a thing as moral purchasing-power. Raise moral purchasing-power, and there's your morality. And I mean by purchasing-power a very simple and natural thing—that is, money, wages. And this brings me back to the practical point: if you go on like this you'll end by eating your own meat, because the people outside haven't got any purchasing power.

STOCKBREEDERS (*reproachfully*) Here we stand with steers
      And nobody can afford them.

JOAN But you sit here, you great and mighty men, thinking that no one will ever catch you at your tricks, and refusing to know anything about the misery in the world outside. Well then, just take a look at them, the people whom your treatment has brought to this condition, the people you will not admit to be your brothers! Come out now, you weary and heavy-laden, into the light of day. Don't be ashamed! (JOAN *shows to the Exchange* CROWD *the* POOR PEOPLE *she has brought along with her.*)

MAULER (*shouting*) Take them away! (*He faints.*)

A VOICE (*rear*) Pierpont Mauler has fainted!

THE POOR PEOPLE He's the one to blame for everything! (*The* PACKERS *attend to* MAULER.)

PACKERS Water for Pierpont Mauler!
      A doctor for Mauler!

JOAN If you, Mauler, showed me the wickedness
Of the poor, now I show you
The poverty of the poor, for they live far away from you
And that puts beyond their reach goods they cannot do without—
The people out of sight, whom you
Hold down in poverty like this, so weakened and so urgently
In need of unobtainable food and warmth that they
Can be just as far away from any claim
To higher things than the lowest gluttony, the beastliest habits.
(MAULER *comes to.*)

MAULER Are they still here? I implore you, send them away.

PACKERS The Black Straw Hats? You want them sent away?

MAULER No, those others, behind them.

SLIFT He won't open his eyes before they get out.

GRAHAM Can't bring yourself to look at them, eh? But it was you
Who brought them to this state.
Shutting your eyes won't rid you of them,
Far from it.

MAULER I beseech you, send them away! I'll buy!
Listen, all of you: Pierpont Mauler's buying!
So that these people may get work and go.
Eight weeks' production in cans of meat—
I'll buy it!

PACKERS He's bought! Mauler has bought!

MAULER At today's prices!

GRAHAM (*holding him up*) And what about back stocks?

MAULER (*lying on the floor*) I'll buy 'em.

GRAHAM At 50?

MAULER At 50!

GRAHAM He's bought! You heard it, he has bought!

BROKERS (*shouting through megaphones, rear*) Pierpont Mauler keeps
the meat market going. According to contract, he's taking over the
meat-ring's entire stock, at 50, as of today, besides two months'
production, starting today, also at 50. The meat-ring will deliver
at least four hundred tons of canned meat to Pierpont Mauler on
November 15.

MAULER But now, my friends, I beg you, take me away.
(MAULER *is carried out.*)

JOAN That's fine, now have yourself carried out!
We work at our mission jobs like plough-horses
And this is the kind of thing you do up here!
You had your man tell me I shouldn't say a thing.

Who are you, I'd like to know,
To try to muzzle the Lord in His goodness? You shouldn't even
Muzzle the ox that's yoked to the thresher!
And speak I will.
(*To the* POOR PEOPLE.)
You'll have work again on Monday.

POOR PEOPLE　We've never seen such people anywhere. But we'd prefer
them to the two that were standing beside him. They have a far
worse look than he does.

JOAN　Now sing, as a farewell song, "Who Ever Feels the Lack of Bread."

BLACK STRAW HATS (*singing*)　Who ever feels the lack of bread
Once he's given the Lord his bond?
A man will never be in need
If he stays within God's grace.
For how shall snow fall on him there?
And how shall hunger find that place?

WHOLESALERS　The fellow's sick in his head. This country's stomach
Has eaten too much meat from cans and it's fighting back.
And he has meat put into cans
That no one will buy. Cross out his name!

STOCKBROKERS　Come on, up with those prices, you lousy butchers!
Until you double livestock prices
Not an ounce will be delivered, for you need it.

PACKERS　Keep your filth to yourselves! We will not buy.
For the contract which you saw agreed on here
Is a mere scrap of paper. The man who made it
Was not in his right mind. He couldn't raise
A cent from Frisco to New York
For that kind of business.
(*Exeunt* PACKERS.)

JOAN　Well, anyone who is really interested in God's word and what He
says and not just in what the ticker tape says—and there must be
some people here that are respectable and conduct their business
in a God-fearing way, we have nothing against that—well, he's
welcome to visit our Divine Service Sunday afternoon in Lincoln
Street at two P.M. Music from three o'clock, no entrance charge.

SLIFT (*to the* STOCKBREEDERS)　What Pierpont Mauler promises he fulfills.
Breathe freely now! The market's getting well!
You who give bread and you to whom it's given,
At last the doldrums have been overcome!
They menaced confidence, and even concord.
You who give work, and you to whom it's given,

>You're moving in and opening wide the gates!
>Sensible counsel, sensibly adopted,
>Has got the upper hand of foolishness.
>The gates are opening! The chimney's smoking!
>It's work you've both been needing all the time.

STOCKBREEDERS (*placing* JOAN *up on the steps*)   Your speech and presence
>made a great impression
>On us stockbreeders and many a man
>Was deeply moved, for we
>Have terrible sufferings too.

JOAN   You know, I have my eye
>On Mauler, he has woken up, and you,
>If there's something you need to help you out,
>Then come with me, that he may aid you also,
>For from now on he shall not rest
>Till everyone is helped.
>For he's in a position to help: so
>Let's go after him.
>(*Exeunt* JOAN *and* BLACK STRAW HATS, *followed by the* STOCK-
>BREEDERS.)

6. The Cricket Caught

The City. The broker SULLIVAN SLIFT's *house, a small one with two
entrances.*

MAULER (*inside the house, talking to* SLIFT)   Barricade the door, turn on
>all the lights there are—then take a good look at my face, Slift,
>and see if it's true that anybody could tell by it.

SLIFT   Tell what by it?

MAULER   My business!

SLIFT   A butcher's? Mauler, why did you fall down when she talked?

MAULER   What did she say? I did not hear it,
>For behind her stood such people with such ghastly faces
>Of misery—misery that comes
>Before a wrath that will sweep us all away—
>That I saw nothing more. Slift,
>I will tell you what I really think

About this business of ours.
It can't go on this way, nothing but buying and selling
And one man coldly stripping off another's skin:
There are too many people howling with pain
And they are on the increase.
That which falls into our bloody cellars
Is past all consolation:
When they get hold of us they'll slap us against the pavement
Like rotten fish. All of us here,
We're not going to die in our beds. Before
We get that far they will stand us up against walls
In throngs, and cleanse the world of us and
Our hangers-on.

SLIFT   They have upset you! (*Aside.*) I'll make him eat a rare steak. His old weakness has come over him again. Maybe he'll come to his senses after enjoying some raw meat. (*He goes and broils* MAULER *a steak on a gas stove.*)

MAULER   I often ask myself why
I'm moved by that fool talk, worlds away,
The cheap, flat chitter-chatter they study up . . .
Of course, it's because they do it for nothing, eighteen hours a
     day and
In rain and hunger.

SLIFT   In cities which are burning down below
And freezing up on top, there are always people
Who'll talk of this and that—details that aren't
In perfect order.

MAULER   But what is it they're saying? In these cities, incessantly
On fire, in the downward rush
Of howling humanity,
Surging toward hell without respite
For years on end, if I hear a voice like that—
Foolish, of course, but quite unlike a beast's—
I feel as if I'd been cracked on the backbone with a stick
Like a leaping fish.
But even this has only been evasion until now, Slift,
For what I fear is something other than God.

SLIFT   What is it?

MAULER   Not what is above me
But what is below me! What stands in the stockyards and cannot
Last through the night and will still—I know—
Rise up in the morning.

SLIFT   Won't you eat a little meat, my dear Pierpont? Think, now you
can do it with a clear conscience again, for from this day onward
you won't have anything to do with cattle-murder.

MAULER   Do you think I should? Perhaps I could.
I ought to be able to eat now, oughtn't I?

SLIFT   Have a bite to eat and think over your situation. It's not very satis-
factory. Do you realize that today you bought up everything there
is in cans? Mauler, I see you engrossed in the contemplation of
your noble nature, allow me to give you a concise account of your
situation, the external, the unimportant one. The main point is
that you've taken one hundred and fifty tons of stocks away from
the meat-ring. You'll have to get rid of these in the next few weeks
on a market that can't swallow one more can even today. You've
paid 50 for them, but the price will go down at least to 30. On
November 15, when the price is 30 or 25, the meat-ring will deliver
four hundred tons to you at 50.

MAULER   Slift! I'm done for!
I'm finished. I've gone and bought up meat.
Oh, Slift, what have I done!
Slift, I've loaded myself with all the meat in the world.
Like Atlas I stumble, cans by the ton on my shoulders,
All the way down to join the people who sleep
Under bridges. Only this morning
Many men were about to fall, and I
Went to see them fall and laugh at them
And tell them not a soul
Would be fool enough to buy meat in cans now
And while I stand there I hear my own voice saying:
I'll buy it all.
Slift, I've gone and bought meat, I'm done for.

SLIFT   Well, what do you hear from your friends in New York?

MAULER   That I ought to buy meat.

SLIFT   You ought to do what?

MAULER   Buy meat.

SLIFT   Then why are you yammering because you have bought it?

MAULER   Yes, they told me I ought to buy meat.

SLIFT   But you have bought meat!

MAULER   Yes, that is so, I did buy meat, but I bought it
Not because of the letter that said I should
(That's all wrong anyhow, just armchair theory)
Not from any low motives, but because
That person gave me such a shock, I swear

I barely riffled through the letter, it only came this morning.
Here it is. "Dear Pierpont——

SLIFT (*reads on*)   —today we are able to inform you that our money
    is beginning to bear fruit. Many Congressmen are going to vote
    against tariffs, so it seems advisable to buy meat, dear Pierpont.
    We shall write you again tomorrow."

MAULER   This bribery, too, is something
    That shouldn't happen. How easily a war
    Might start from a thing like that, and thousands bleed
    For filthy lucre. Oh, my dear Slift, I feel
    That nothing good can come of news like this.

SLIFT   That would depend on who had written the letters.
    Bribing, abolishing tariffs, making wars—
    Not everybody can do that. Are these people all right?

MAULER   They're solvent.

SLIFT   But who are they? (MAULER *smiles.*)
    Then prices might go up after all?
    Then we'd be off the hook.
    That might be a prospect if it wasn't for the farmers—
    By offering all their meat, only too eagerly,
    They'd bring prices crashing down again. No, Mauler,
    I don't understand that letter.

MAULER   Think of it this way: a man has committed theft
    And is caught by a man.
    Now if he doesn't knock the other man down
    He's done for; if he does, he's out of the woods.
    The letter (which is wrong) demands (so as to be right)
    A misdeed like that.

SLIFT   What misdeed?

MAULER   The kind I could never commit. For from now on
    I wish to live in peace. If they want to profit
    By their misdeeds—and they will profit—
    They need only buy up meat wherever they see it,
    Beat into the stockbreeders' heads the fact
    That there's too much meat around and mention
    The Lennox shutdown and take
    Their meat away from them. This above all:
    Take the stockbreeders' meat from them . . . but then
    They'll be duped all over again . . . no, I'll have nothing
    To do with that.

SLIFT   You shouldn't have bought meat, Pierpont.

MAULER   Yes, it's a bad business, Slift.

      I'm not going to buy so much as a hat or a shoe
      Until I get out of this mess, and I'll be happy
      If I have a hundred dollars when I do.
      (*Sound of drums.* JOAN *approaches, with the* STOCKBREEDERS.)

JOAN   We'll lure him out of his den the way you catch a cricket. You stand over there, because if he hears me singing he'll try to get out the other way, to avoid meeting me again: I'm a person he doesn't care to see. (*She laughs.*) And so are the people who are with me. (*The* STOCKBREEDERS *take up a position in front of door, right.* JOAN, *in front of door, left.*) Please come out, Mr. Mauler, I must talk to you about the terrible condition of the stockbreeders of Illinois. I also have several workers with me—they want to ask you when you're going to reopen your factory.

MAULER   Slift, where's the other exit? I don't want to run into her again, still less the people she has with her. I'm not opening any factories now, either.

SLIFT   Come out this way. (*They go through the interior to door, right.*)

STOCKBREEDERS   (*in front of door, right*) Come on out, Mauler, our troubles are all your fault, and we are more than ten thousand Illinois stockbreeders who don't know whether they're coming or going. So buy our livestock from us!

MAULER   Shut the door, Slift! I'm not buying.
      With the whole world's canned meat around my neck,
      Now should I buy the cattle on the dog-star?
      It's as if a man should go to Atlas when
      He can barely drag the world along, and say:
      "They need another carrier on Saturn."
      Who's going to buy the livestock back from me?

SLIFT   The Grahams, if anybody will—they need it!

JOAN   (*in front of door, left*) We're not leaving the place until the stockbreeders get some help.

MAULER   Most likely the Grahams, if anybody, they need livestock. Slift, go out and tell them to let me have two minutes to think things over. (SLIFT *goes and returns.*)

SLIFT   (*to the* STOCKBREEDERS) Pierpont Mauler wishes to give careful consideration to your request. He asks for two minutes' thinking time. (*Re-enters the house.*)

MAULER   I'm not buying. (*He starts figuring.*) Slift, I'm buying. Slift, bring me anything that looks like a hog or a steer, I'll buy it, whatever smells of lard, I'll buy it, bring every grease-spot, I'm the buyer for it, and at today's price too, at 50.

SLIFT   Not a hat will you buy, Mauler, but
      All the cattle in Illinois.

MAULER   Yes, I'll still buy that. Now it's decided, Slift.
     Take A. (*He draws an A on the closet door.*)
     A man makes a mistake, let that be A,
     He did it because his feelings overcame him,
     And now he goes on to do B, and B's wrong too
     And now the sum of A and B is right.
     Ask the stockbreeders in, they're very nice people,
     Badly in need and decently clothed and not
     The sort of folk that scare you when you see them.
SLIFT   (*stepping out in front of the house; to the* STOCKBREEDERS)   To
     save Illinois and avert ruin from its farmers and stockbreeders,
     Pierpont Mauler has decided to buy up all the livestock on the
     market.
STOCKBREEDERS   Long live Pierpont Mauler! He's saved the livestock trade!
     (*They enter the house.*)
JOAN   (*calling after them*)   Tell Mr. Mauler that we, the Black Straw
     Hats, thank him for this in the name of the Lord. (*To the* WORKERS.)
     If the people who buy cattle and the people who sell cattle are
     satisfied, then there'll be bread once more for you too.

7. The Expulsion of the Money-Changers from the Temple

The Black Straw Hats' Mission. The BLACK STRAW HATS, *sitting at
a long table, are counting out from their tin boxes the widows' and
orphans' mites they have collected.*

BLACK STRAW HATS   (*singing*)   Gather the pennies of widows and orphans
     with song!
     Great is the need
     They have no roof or bread
     But Almighty God
     Won't let them go hungry long.
PAULUS SNYDER   (*Major of the* BLACK STRAW HATS, *getting up*)   Very little,
     very little. (*To some* POOR FOLK *in the background, among them*
     MRS. LUCKERNIDDLE *and* GLOOMB.) You here again? Don't you ever
     leave this place? There's work at the stockyards again, you know!
MRS. LUCKERNIDDLE   Where? The yards are shut down.
GLOOMB   We were told they would open up again, but they haven't.

SNYDER   Well, don't go too near the cash-box. (*He motions them still further back.* MULBERRY, *the landlord, enters.*)

MULBERRY   Say, what about my rent?

SNYDER   My dear Black Straw Hats, my dear Mulberry, my honored listeners! As to this troublesome problem of financing our operations—anything that's good speaks for itself, and needs propaganda more than anything—hitherto we have aimed our appeals at the poor, indeed the poorest, on the assumption that they, being most in need of God's help, were the people most likely to have a bit left over for Him, and that their sheer numbers would produce the desired effect. To our regret, it has been borne in upon us that these very classes manifest an attitude of reserve toward God that is quite beyond explanation. Of course, this may be due to the fact that they have nothing. Therefore, I, Paulus Snyder, have issued an invitation in your name to Chicago's wealthy and prosperous citizens, to help us launch a major offensive next Saturday against the unbelief and materialism of the city of Chicago, primarily against the lower orders. Out of the proceeds we shall also pay our dear landlord, Mr. Mulberry, the rent he is so kindly deferring for us.

MULBERRY   It would certainly be welcome, but please don't worry about it.

(*Exit.*)

SNYDER (*to the* POOR PEOPLE)   Well, now go happily about your work and be sure to clean the front steps. (*Exeunt* BLACK STRAW HATS.) Tell me, are the locked-out workers in the stockyards still standing there patiently, or have they begun to talk like rebels?

MRS. LUCKERNIDDLE   They've been squawking pretty loud since yesterday, because they know the factories are getting orders.

GLOOMB   Many are saying already that they won't get any more work at all if they don't use force.

SNYDER (*to himself*)   A good sign. The meat kings will be more likely to come and listen to our appeal if they're driven in by stones. (*To the* POOR PEOPLE.) Couldn't you split our wood, at least?

POOR PEOPLE   There isn't any more, Major. (*Enter* CRIDLE, GRAHAM, SLIFT, MEYERS.)

MEYERS   You know, Graham, I keep asking myself where that livestock can be hiding out.

GRAHAM   That's what I'm asking too, where can that livestock be hiding out?

SLIFT   So am I.

GRAHAM   Oh, you too? And I guess Mauler is too, eh?

SLIFT   I guess he is.

MEYERS   Somewhere some swine is buying everything up.
Someone who knows quite well that we're committed
By contract to deliver meat in cans
And so need livestock.

SLIFT   Who can it be?

GRAHAM   (*hitting him in the stomach*)   You cur, you!
Don't play any tricks on us there, and tell Pierpy not to either!
That's a vital spot!

SLIFT   (*to* SNYDER)   What do you want of us?

GRAHAM   (*hitting him again*)   What do you think they want, Slift?
(SLIFT, *with exaggerated mockery, makes the gesture of handing
out money.*)   You said it, Slift!

MEYERS   (*to* SNYDER)   Fire away.   (*They sit down on the prayer benches.*)

SNYDER   (*in the pulpit*)   We Black Straw Hats have heard that fifty
thousand men are standing around in the stockyards without work.
And that some are beginning to grumble and say: "We'll have to
help ourselves." Aren't your names beginning to be called as the
ones to blame for fifty thousand men being out of work and standing idly in front of the factories? They'll end by taking the factories
away from you and saying: "We'll act the way the Bolsheviks did
and take the factories into our own hands so that everybody can
work and eat." For the story is getting around that unhappiness
doesn't just come like the rain but is made by certain persons who
get profit out of it. But we Black Straw Hats try to tell them that
unhappiness does come down like the rain, no one knows where
from, and that they are destined to suffering and there's a reward
for it shining at the end of the road.

PACKERS   Why mention rewards?

SNYDER   The reward we speak of is paid out after death.

PACKERS   How much will it cost?

SNYDER   Eight hundred dollars a month, because we need hot soup and
loud music. We also want to promise them that the rich will be
punished—when they're dead, of course. (*The* FOUR *laugh noisily.*)
All that for a mere eight hundred a month!

GRAHAM   You don't need that much, man. Five hundred.

SNYDER   Well, we could get along with seven hundred and fifty, but
then——

MEYERS   Seven hundred and fifty. That's better. Let's make it five
hundred.

GRAHAM   You do need five hundred, certainly. (*To the* OTHERS.) They've
got to get that.

MEYERS (*front*) Out with it, Slift, you fellows have that livestock.

SLIFT Mauler and I have not bought one cent's worth of livestock, as true as I'm sitting here. The Lord's my witness.

MEYERS (*to* SNYDER) Five hundred dollars, eh? That's a lot of money. Who's going to pay it?

SLIFT Yes, you'll have to find someone who will give it to you.

SNYDER Yes, yes.

MEYERS That won't be easy.

GRAHAM Come on, Slift, cough it up; Pierpy has the livestock.

SLIFT (*laughingly*) A bunch of crooks, Mr. Snyder. (*All laugh except* SNYDER.)

GRAHAM (*to* MEYERS) The man has no sense of humor. Don't like him.

SLIFT The main point is, man, where do you stand? On this side of the barricades, or the other?

SNYDER The Black Straw Hats stand above the battle, Mr. Slift. This side. (*Enter* JOAN.)

SLIFT Why, here's our sainted Joan of the Livestock Exchange!

THE PACKERS (*shouting at* JOAN) We're not satisfied with you, can't you tell Mauler something from us? You're supposed to have some influence with him. They say he eats out of your hand. Well, the market is so short of livestock that we have to keep an eye on him. They say you can bring him round to doing whatever you want. Have him get that livestock out. Listen, if you'll do this for us we're willing to pay the Black Straw Hats' rent for the next four years.

JOAN (*has seen the* POOR PEOPLE *and is shocked*) Why, what are you doing here?

MRS. LUCKERNIDDLE (*coming forward*) The twenty dinners are all eaten now.
Please don't get angry because I'm here again.
It's a sight I would be glad enough to spare you.
That's the awful thing about hunger: no sooner
Is it satisfied than back it comes again.

GLOOMB (*coming forward*) I know you, it was you I tried to talk
Into working on that slicer that tore my arm off.
I could do worse things than that today.

JOAN Why aren't you working? I did get work for you.

MRS. LUCKERNIDDLE Where? The stockyards are closed.

GLOOMB We were told they would open up again, but they haven't.

JOAN (*to the* PACKERS) So they're still waiting, are they?
The PACKERS *say nothing.*
And I thought they had been provided for!

It's been snowing on them now for seven days
And the very snow that kills them cuts them off
From every human eye. How easily
I forgot what everyone likes to forget for the peace of his mind!
If one man says things are all right again, no one looks into them.
(*To the* PACKERS.) But surely Mauler bought meat from you?
He did it at my request! And now you still refuse to open up your
    factories?

CRIDLE, GRAHAM, MEYERS   That's quite right, we wanted to open up.

SLIFT   But first of all you wanted to leap at the farmers' throats!

CRIDLE, GRAHAM, MEYERS   How are we to do any slaughtering when
there's no livestock?

SLIFT   When Mauler and I bought meat from you we took it for granted
you would start employment going again so that the workers would
be able to buy meat. Now who will eat the meat we got from you?
For whom did we buy meat if consumers can't pay for it?

JOAN   Look, if you people have control of all the equipment your em-
ployees use in your all-powerful factories and plants, then the least
you could do would be to let them in, if they're kept out it's all up
with them, because there is a sort of exploitation about the whole
thing, and if a poor human creature is tormented till the blood
comes, and can think of no way out but to take a club and bash
his tormentor's head in, then it scares the daylights out of you, I've
noticed that, and then you think religion's fine and it's supposed
to pour oil on the troubled waters, but the Lord has His pride too,
and He won't pitch in and clean your pigsties for you all over again.
And I run around from pillar to post, thinking: "If I help you
people on top, the people under you will also be helped. It's all
one in a way, and the same strings pull it," but I was a prize fool
there. If a man wants to help folks that are poor it seems he'd better
help them get away from you. Is there no respect left in you for
anything that wears a human face? Some day, maybe, you won't
rate as human beings either, but as wild animals that will simply
have to be slaughtered in the interest of public order and safety!
And still you dare to enter the house of God, just because you own
that filthy Mammon, everybody knows where you got it and how,
it wasn't come by honestly. But this time, by God, you've come to
the wrong people, we'll have to drive you out, that's all, yes, drive
you out with a stick. Come on, don't stand there looking so stupid,
I know human beings shouldn't be treated like steers, but you
aren't human beings, get out of here, and fast, or I'll lay hands on
you, don't hold me back, I know what I'm doing, it's high time I

found out. (JOAN *drives them out, using as a stick a flag held upside down. The* BLACK STRAW HATS *appear in the doorways.*) Get out! Are you trying to turn the house of God into a stable? Another Livestock Exchange? Get out! There's nothing for you here. We don't want to see such faces here. You're unworthy and I'm showing you the door. For all your money!

THE FOUR   Very well. But forty months' rent goes with us—simply, modestly, irretrievably. We need every cent of it anyway: we're facing times as terrible as the livestock market has ever seen. (*Exeunt.*)

SNYDER (*running after them*)   Please stay, gentlemen! Don't go, she has no authority at all! A crazy female! She'll be fired! She'll do whatever you want her to do.

JOAN (*to the* BLACK STRAW HATS)   Well, that certainly wasn't very smart at a time like this, what with the rent and all. But we can't think about that now. (*To* LUCKERNIDDLE *and* GLOOMB.) Sit down back there, I'll bring you some soup.

SNYDER (*returning*)   Go on, make the poor your guests
And regale them with rainwater and fine speeches
When there's really no pity for them up above,
Nothing but snow!
You followed your very first impulses,
Utterly without humility! It is so much easier
Simply to drive the unclean out with arrogance.
You're squeamish about the bread we have to eat,
Much too curious how it's made, and still
You want to eat it! Now, woman above the world,
Get out in the rain and face the snowstorm in righteousness!

JOAN   Does that mean I'm to take off my uniform?

SNYDER   Take off your uniform and pack your bags! Get out of this house and take along the riff-raff you brought us. Nothing but riff-raff and scum followed you in here. Now you'll be in that class yourself. Go and get your things.

JOAN (*goes out and comes back dressed like a country servant, carrying a little suitcase*)   I'll go find rich man Mauler, he is not
Without fear or good will, and ask his help.
I won't put on this coat or black straw hat
Ever again or come back to this dear house
Of songs and awakenings till
I bring in rich man Mauler as one of us,
Converted from the ground up.
What if their money has eaten away

Their ears and human faces like a cancer
Making them sit apart but loftily
Beyond the reach of any cry for help!
Poor cripples!
There must be *one* just man among them!
(*Exit.*)

SNYDER   Poor simpleton!
You're blind to this: set up in huge formations
The givers and the takers of work
Confront one another:
Warring fronts: irreconcilable.
Run to and fro between them, little peacemaker, little mediator—
Be useful to neither and go to your doom.

MULBERRY   (*entering*)   Have you the money now?

SNYDER   God will still be able to pay for the definitely scanty shelter He
has found on earth, I said scanty, Mr. Mulberry.

MULBERRY   Yes, pay, that's the ticket, that's the problem! You said the
right word then, Snyder! If the Lord in His goodness pays, good.
But if He doesn't pay, not so good. If the Lord in His goodness
doesn't pay His rent, He'll have to get out, and what's more, He'll
have to go on Saturday night, eh, Snyder?
(*Exit.*)

8. Pierpont Mauler's Speech on the Indispensability of Capitalism and Religion

MAULER   Well, Slift, today's the day
When our good friend Graham and all his crew
Who wanted to wait for the lowest livestock prices
Will have to buy the meat they owe us.

SLIFT   It will cost them more, because anything
The Chicago market can show in the way of lowing cattle
    Is ours now.
Every hog they owe us
They'll have to buy from us, and that's expensive.

MAULER   Now, Slift, let loose all your wholesalers!
Let them torment the livestock market with demands
For everything that looks like hogs and cattle
And so make prices go up and up.

SLIFT   What news of your Joan? There's a rumor
Around the Livestock Exchange that you slept with her.
I did my best to scotch it. She hasn't been heard of
Since that day she threw us all out of the temple:
It's as though black roaring Chicago had swallowed her up.

MAULER   I liked her action very much,
Throwing you all out like that. Yes, that girl's afraid of nothing.
And if I'd been along on that occasion
She'd have thrown me out with the rest and that's
What I like about her and that house of hers,
The fact that people like me are impossible there.
Force the price up to 80, Slift. That will make those Grahams
Rather like mud you stick your foot into
Merely to see its shape again.
I won't let an ounce of meat go by:
This time I'll rip their skins off for good and all,
In accordance with my nature.

SLIFT   I'm delighted, Mauler, that you've shaken off
Your weakness of the past few days. And now
I'll go and watch them buy up livestock.
(*Exit.*)

MAULER   It's high time this damn town had its skin ripped off
And those fellows taught a thing or two
About the meat market: what if they do yell "Crime!"
(*Enter* JOAN, *carrying a suitcase.*)

JOAN   Good morning, Mr. Mauler. You're a hard man to find. I'll just leave my things over there for the time being. You see, I'm not with the Black Straw Hats any more. We had an argument. So I thought, well, I'll go and see how Mr. Mauler's doing. Having no more of that wearing mission work to do, I can pay more attention to the individual. So, to begin with, I'm going to occupy myself with you a little, that is, if you'll let me. You know, I've noticed that you are much more approachable than many other people. That's a fine old mohair sofa you have there, but why do you have a sheet on it?— and it isn't made up properly, either. So you sleep in your office? I thought surely you would have one of those great big palaces. (MAULER *says nothing.*) But you're quite right, Mr. Mauler, to be a good manager in little things too, being a meat king. I don't know why, but when I see you I always think of the story about the Lord when He visited Adam in the Garden of Eden and called out, "Adam, where are you?" Do you remember? (*Laughs.*) Adam is standing behind a bush with his arms up to the elbows in a doe, and he hears the voice of God just like that, with blood all over him. And so he acts as if he wasn't there. But God doesn't give up, and calls out again, "Adam, where are you?" And then Adam says, faintly and blushing crimson: "This is the time you pick to visit me, right after I've killed a doe. Oh, don't say a word, I know I shouldn't have done it." But your conscience is clear, Mr. Mauler, I hope.

MAULER   So you're not with the Black Straw Hats any more?

JOAN   No, Mr. Mauler, and I don't belong there either.

MAULER   Then what have you been living on? (JOAN *says nothing.*) I see. Nothing. How long ago did you leave the Black Straw Hats?

JOAN   Eight days ago.

MAULER   (*turns away and weeps*)   So greatly changed, and in a mere eight days!
Where has she been? To whom has she been talking? What was it
That drew those lines around her mouth?
The city she has come from
Is a thing I do not yet know.
(*He brings her food on a tray.*) I see you very much changed.
Here's something to eat, if you like, I'm not hungry myself.

JOAN   (*looking at the food*)   Mr. Mauler, after we drove the rich people out of our house—

MAULER   Which amused me very much, and seemed the right thing to do—

JOAN   The landlord, who lives on the rent we pay, gave us notice to get out next Sunday.

MAULER   Indeed! So the Black Straw Hats are poorly off financially?

JOAN   Yes, and that's why I thought I'd go and see Mr. Mauler. (*She begins to eat hungrily.*)

MAULER   Don't you fret. I'll go into the market and get you the money you need. Yes, I'll do that, I'll get hold of it whatever it costs me, even if I have to slice it right out of the city's skin. I'll do it for you. Money's expensive, of course, but I'll produce it. That will be to your liking.

JOAN   Yes, Mr. Mauler.

MAULER   So you go and tell them: "The money is on the way. It will be there by Saturday. Mauler will get hold of it. He just left for the livestock market to dig it up." That matter of the fifty thousand didn't go so well, not exactly as I wanted it. I was unable to get them work immediately. But for you I'll make an exception, and your Black Straw Hats shall be spared, I'll get the money for you. Run and tell them.

JOAN   Yes, Mr. Mauler!

MAULER   There, I've put it in writing. Take it.
    I too am sorry that the men are waiting for work
    In the stockyards and not very good work at that.
    Fifty thousand men
    Standing around in the stockyards, not even leaving at night.
    JOAN *stops eating.*
    But that's the way this business goes:
    It's to be or not to be—a question whether
    I am to be the best man in my class or go
    The dark and dreary way to the stockyards myself.
    Also, the scum is filling up the yards again
    And making trouble.
    And now—I'll tell you the simple truth—I would have liked
    To hear you say that what I do is right
    And my business is natural: so
    Tell me for sure that it was on your advice
    I ordered meat from the meat-ring and from
    The stockbreeders too, thus doing good; then,
    Because I know well that you are poor and right now
    They're trying to take away the very roof over your heads,
    I'll add a contribution for that too, as token
    Of my goodwill.

JOAN   So the workers are still waiting in front of the slaughterhouses?

MAULER   Why are you set against money? and yet look
    So very different when you haven't any?
    What do you think about money? Tell me,
    I want to know; and don't get wrong ideas,
    The way a fool will think of money as
    Something to be doubted. Consider the reality,
    The plain truth, not pleasant maybe, but still
    True for all that: everything is unsteady and the human race
    Is exposed to luck, you might say, to the state of the weather,
    But money's a means of making some improvement—even if only
    For certain people—apart from that, what a structure!
    Built up from time immemorial, over and over again
    Because it keeps collapsing, but still tremendous: demanding sacrifice,
    Very hard to set up, continually set up
    With many a groan, but still inescapably
    Wresting the possible from a reluctant planet,
    However much or little that may be; and accordingly defended

At all times by the best. Just think, if I—
Who have much against it, and sleep badly—
Were to desert it, I would be like a fly
Ceasing to hold back a landslide. There and then
I would become a nothing and it would keep on going over me.
For otherwise everything would have to be overturned
And the architect's design fundamentally altered
To suit an utterly different, incredible, new valuation of man,
Which you people don't want any more than we do, for it would take effect
With neither us nor God, who would have no function left
And be dismissed accordingly. Therefore you really ought to
Collaborate with us, and even if you make no sacrifices—
We don't ask that of you—still sanction the sacrifices:
In a word, you really ought
To set God up once more—
The only salvation—and
Beat the drum for Him so that He may
Gain a foothold in the regions of misery and His
Voice may ring out among the slaughterhouses.
That would suffice.
(*Holding out the note to her.*)
Take what you get, but know the reason
Before you take it! Here's the voucher, this is four years' rent.

JOAN Mr. Mauler, I don't understand what you have been saying
And do not wish to either.
(*Rising.*) I know I should be overjoyed to hear
That God is going to be helped, only
I belong to those for whom
This does not mean real help. And to whom
Nothing is offered.

MAULER If you take the money to the Straw Hats you can also
Stay in their house again: this living
On nothing is not good for you. Believe me,
They're out for money, and so they should be.

JOAN If the Black Straw Hats
Accept your money they are welcome to it,
But I will take my stand among the people waiting in the stockyards,
Until the factories open up again, and
Eat nothing but what they eat and if
They are offered snow, then snow,

And the work they do I will do also, for I have no money either
And no other way to get it honorably, anyhow—
And if there is no more work, then let there be none
For me either, and
You, who live on poverty and
Cannot bear to see the poor and condemn
Something you do not know and make arrangements
So as not to see what sits condemned,
Abandoned in the slaughterhouses, disregarded,
If you want to see me again
Come to the stockyards.
(*Exit.*)

MAULER   Tonight then, Mauler,
Get up every hour and look out of the window
To see if it's snowing, and if it is
It will be snowing on the girl you know.

9. Joan's Third Descent into the Depths: The Snowfall

Stockyards district.

JOAN   Listen to the dream I had one night
A week ago.
Before me in a little field, too small
To hold the shade of a middle-sized tree, hemmed in
By enormous houses, I saw a bunch
Of people: I could not make out how many, but
There were far more of them than all the sparrows
That could find room in such a tiny place—
A very thick bunch indeed, so that
The field began to buckle and rise in the middle
And the bunch was suspended on its edge, holding fast
A moment, quivering: then, stirred
By the intervention of a word—uttered somewhere or other,
Meaning nothing vital—it began to flow.
Then I saw processions, streets, familiar ones, Chicago! you!
I saw you marching, then I saw myself:
I, silent, saw myself striding at your head
With warlike step and bloodstains on my brow

And shouting words that sounded militant
In a tongue I did not know; and while many processions
Moved in many directions all at once
I strode in front of many processions in manifold shapes:
Young and old, sobbing and cursing,
Finally beside myself! Virtue and terror!
Changing whatever my foot touched,
Causing measureless destruction, visibly influencing
The courses of the stars, but also changing utterly
The neighborhood streets familiar to us all—
So the procession moved, and I along with it,
Veiled by snow from any hostile attack,
Transparent with hunger, no target,
Not to be hit anywhere, not being settled anywhere;
Not to be touched by any trouble, being accustomed
To all. And so it marches, abandoning the position
Which cannot be held: exchanging it for any other one.
That was my dream.
Today I see its meaning:
Before tomorrow morning we
Will start out from these yards
And reach their city, Chicago, in the gray of dawn,
Displaying the full range of our wretchedness in public places,
Appealing to whatever resembles a human being.
What will come after, I do not know.

Livestock Exchange.

MAULER (*to the* PACKERS) My friends in New York have written me
        to say
    That the tariff in the south
    Was repealed today.
PACKERS This is awful, the tariff law gone and here we are
    Without any meat to sell! It's been sold already
    At a low price and now we are asked to buy meat when it's
        going up!
STOCKBREEDERS This is awful, the tariff law gone and here we are
    Without any livestock to sell! It's already been sold
    At a low price!
SMALL SPECULATORS Awful! Eternally inscrutable
    Are the eternal laws
    Of human economics!

Without warning
The volcano erupts and lays the country waste!
Without an invitation
The profitable island rises from the barren seas!
No one is told, no one is in the know! But the last in line
Is bitten by the dogs!

MAULER   Well, seeing that livestock is being demanded
In cans at an acceptable price
I now request you to hand over quickly
The canned meat I am supposed to get from you
According to contract.

GRAHAM   At the old price?

MAULER   As the contract specified, Graham.
Four hundred tons, if I remember correctly
A moment when I was not myself.

PACKERS   How can we take likestock now, with prices rising?
Someone has made a corner in it,
Nobody knows who—
Release us from the contract, Mauler!

MAULER   Unfortunately I must have those cans. But there is
Still livestock enough, a bit expensive, granted, but
Livestock enough. Buy it up!

PACKERS   Buy livestock now? The hell with it!

A little tavern in the stockyards district. MEN *and* WOMEN WORKERS,
JOAN *among them.—A group of* BLACK STRAW HATS *enter.* JOAN
rises and makes frantic gestures at them during what follows.

JACKSON   (*after a hurried song*)   Brother, why won't you eat the bread
that Jesus gives?
See how happy and glad are we.
It's because we have found the Lord Jesus, Lord of all our lives.
Hurry, come to Him heartily!
Hallelujah!
(*One of the* BLACK STRAW HAT GIRLS *talks to the* WORKERS, *making
side remarks to her* COMRADES.)

BLACK STRAW HAT   (It's no use, is it?)   Brothers and sisters, I too used to
stand sadly by the wayside, just as you are, and the old Adam in
me cared for nothing but meat and drink, but then I found my
Lord Jesus, and then it was so light and glad inside me, but now
(They aren't listening at all!) if I just think real hard about my
Lord Jesus, who redeemed us all by His suffering in spite of our

many wicked deeds, then I stop feeling hungry and thirsty, except
for our Lord Jesus' word. (No use.) Where the Lord Jesus is,
there is not violence, but peace, not hate but love. (It's quite
hopeless!)

BLACK STRAW HATS   Hallelujah! (JACKSON *passes the box around. Nothing
is put into it.*) Hallelujah!

JOAN   If only they wouldn't stay here in the cold
Making all that nuisance and talking, talking!
Really, now I can hardly bear
To hear the words
That once were dear and pleasant to me! If only a voice,
Some remnant inside them, would say:
There's snow and wind here, be quiet here!

A WOMAN   Oh, let them be. They have to do this to get a bit of warmth
and food. I wish I was in their shoes.

MRS. LUCKERNIDDLE   That was nice music!

GLOOMB   Nice and short.

MRS. LUCKERNIDDLE   But they really are good people.

GLOOMB   Good and brief, short and sweet.

WOMAN WORKER   Why don't they give us a real talk, and convert us?

GLOOMB (*making a gesture of paying out money*)   Can you keep the
pot boiling, Mrs. Swingurn?

WOMAN WORKER   The music is very pretty but I was expecting them to
give us a plate of soup, maybe, seeing they had brought a pot
along.

WORKER (*surprised at her*)   No kidding, you thought that?

JOAN   Are there no people here with any enterprise?

A WORKER   Yes, the Communists.

JOAN   Aren't they people who incite to crime?

THE WORKER   No.

Livestock Exchange.

PACKERS   We're buying livestock! Yearlings!
Feeders! Calves! Steers! Hogs!
Offers, please!

STOCKBREEDERS   There isn't any! We've sold whatever was salable.

PACKERS   Isn't any? The depots are bursting with cattle.

STOCKBREEDERS   Sold.

PACKERS   To whom? (*Enter* MAULER. *Milling around him.*)
Not a steer to be found in Chicago!
You'll have to give us more time, Mauler.

MAULER You'll deliver your meat as agreed. (*Going over to* SLIFT.)
    Squeeze 'em dry.
A STOCKBREEDER Eight hundred Kentucky steers at 400.
PACKERS Impossible. 400! Are you crazy?
SLIFT I'll take them. At 400.
STOCKBREEDERS Eight hundred steers sold to Sullivan Slift for 400.
PACKERS It's Mauler! What did we say? He's the one!
    You crooked hound! He makes us deliver canned meat
    And buys up livestock! So we have to buy from him
    The meat we need to fill his cans!
    You filthy butcher! Here, take *our* flesh, hack yourself off a slice!
MAULER If you're an ox you shouldn't be surprised when people's
    appetites grow with looking at you.
GRAHAM (*makes as if to attack* MAULER) He's got it coming, I'll settle
    his hash!
MAULER All right, Graham, now I demand your cans.
    You can stuff yourself into them.
    I'll teach you the meat business, you
    Traders! From now on I get paid, and well paid,
    For every hoof, every calf from here to Illinois[1]
    And so I'll offer five hundred steers at 56 to start with.
    (*Dead silence.*)
    And now, in view of the weak demand, seeing nobody here
    Needs livestock,
    I want 60! And don't forget my cans, either!

*Another part of the stockyards. Placards are inscribed: "Solidarity
with Locked-out Stockyard Workers!" "All out for General Strike!"
In front of a shed two* MEN *from the central union office are speaking to a group of* WORKERS. *Enter* JOAN.

JOAN Are these the people who lead the movement of the unemployed?
    I can help, too. I've learned to speak in streets and meeting-halls,
    even big ones, I have no fear of insults and I think I can explain
    a good thing well. Because, as I see it, something's got to be done
    right away. I have some suggestions to make, too.
A LABOR LEADER Listen, all. So far the meat gang hasn't shown the least
    inclination to open up its factories. At first it seemed that the ex-
    ploiter Pierpont Mauler was all out for a reopening because he
    wants from the meat gang huge quantities of canned meat that they

---

[1] *Sic.* [Translator's note.]

owe him by contract. Then it became clear that the meat they need
for packing is in Mauler's own hands and he won't even consider
letting it go. Now we know that if things are left up to the meat
gang we workers will never all get back into the slaughterhouses,
and never at the old wages. With things in this pass we've got to
realize that nothing can help us but the use of force. The city
utilities have promised to join the general strike by the day after
tomorrow at the latest. Now this news must be spread in all parts
of the stockyards; if it isn't, there's a danger that the masses will
be led by some rumor or other to leave the yards, and then be
forced to yield to the meat gang's terms. So these letters, stating
that the gasworks, waterworks and power stations are going to help
us by going on strike, must be handed out to delegates who will be
awaiting our password in different parts of the stockyards at ten
o'clock tonight. Stick that in your overalls, Jack, and wait for the
delegates in front of Mother Schmitt's canteen. (*A* WORKER *takes
the letter and leaves.*)

SECOND WORKER   Give me the one for the Graham works, I know them.

LEADER   26th Street, corner Michigan Park. (WORKER *takes letter and
leaves.*) 13th Street by the Westinghouse Building. (*To* JOAN.)
Well, and who may you be?

JOAN   I was fired from the job I had.

LEADER   What job?

JOAN   Selling magazines.

LEADER   Who were you working for?

JOAN   I'm a peddler.

A WORKER   Maybe she's a stool-pigeon.

THE OTHER LEADER   Who can tell what she will do with the letter we
give her?

FIRST LEADER   Nobody. (*To* JOAN.)
A net with a torn mesh
Is of no use:
The fish swim through at that spot
As though there were no net.
Suddenly all its meshes
Are useless.

JOAN   I used to sell papers on 44th Street. I'm no stool-pigeon. I'm for
your cause heart and soul.

SECOND LEADER   Our cause? Why, isn't it your cause?

JOAN   It certainly isn't in the public interest for the factory owners to
put all those people in the street just like that. Why, it makes you
think the poverty of the poor is useful to the rich! You might say

poverty is all their doing! (*The* WORKERS *laugh uproariously.*) It's inhuman, that's what it is! I even have people like Mauler in mind when I say that. (*Renewed laughter.*) Why do you laugh? I don't think you have any right to be malicious and to believe without proof that a man like Mauler can be inhuman.

SECOND LEADER   Not without proof! You can give the letter to her, all right.

FIRST LEADER   Go to Storehouse Five at the Graham plant. When you see three workers come up and look around them, ask if they are from the Cridle plant. This letter is for them.

Livestock Exchange.

SMALL SPECULATORS   Quotations going down! The packing plants in peril!
　　　What will become of us, the stockholders?
　　　The man with small savings who gave his last cent
　　　For the middle class, which is weakened anyway?
　　　A man like Graham ought to be
　　　Torn to shreds before he makes waste paper
　　　Out of the note with our share marked on it, the one
　　　We earned from his bloody cellars.
　　　Buy that livestock, buy it at any price!
　　　(*Throughout this scene the names of firms suspending payment are being called out. "Suspending payment: Meyer & Co.," etc.*)

PACKERS   We can do no more, the price is over 70.

WHOLESALERS   Mow 'em down, they won't buy, the high-hats.

PACKERS   Two thousand steers demanded at 70.

SLIFT (*to* MAULER, *beside a column*)   Shove 'em up.

MAULER   I see that you have not stood by your part
　　　Of the contract I drew up with you that day
　　　In the wish to create employment. And now I hear
　　　They're still standing around out there in the yards. But
　　　You're going to regret it: out with the canned meat
　　　Which I have bought!

GRAHAM   There's nothing we can do: meat has completely
　　　Vanished from the market!
　　　I'll take five hundred steers at 75.

SMALL SPECULATORS   Buy them, you greedy hounds!
　　　They won't buy! They'd rather hand over
　　　The packing plants.

MAULER   We shouldn't push it up any higher, Slift.
　　　They're powerless now.

They are meant to bleed, but they mustn't perish;
If they go out we're goners too.

SLIFT   There's life in them yet, put it up a notch.
Five hundred steers at 77.

SMALL SPECULATORS   77. Did you hear that? Why
Didn't you buy at 75? Now
It's gone to 77 and still climbing.

PACKERS   We get 50 from Mauler for the cans and can't pay Mauler 80
for the livestock.

MAULER   (*to a group of* MEN)   Where are the people I sent to the stockyards?

A MAN   There's one.

MAULER   Well, let's have it.

FIRST DETECTIVE   (*reports*)   Those crowds, Mr. Mauler, you can't see the
end of them. If you called the name of Joan, ten or maybe a
hundred would answer. The mob sits there and waits, without a
face or a name. Besides, nobody can hear just one man's
voice and there are far too many people running around asking
after relatives they've lost. Serious unrest prevails in the sections
where the unions are at work.

MAULER   Who's at work? The unions? And the police let them agitate?
Damn it all! Go and call the police right away, mention my name,
ask them what we're paying taxes for. Insist that the troublemakers
get their heads cracked, speak plainly to them. (*Exit* FIRST
DETECTIVE.)

GRAHAM   Oh, give us a thousand at 77, Mauler;
If it knocks us out, it's the end of us.

SLIFT   Five hundred to Graham at 77. All the rest at 80.

MAULER   (*returning*)   Slift, this business no longer entertains me.
It might take us too far.
Go up to 80, then let it go at 80.
I'll hand it over and let them go.
Enough's enough. The town needs a breathing-spell.
And I have other worries.
Slift, this throat-squeezing isn't as much fun
As I thought it would be.
(*Seeing the* SECOND DETECTIVE.) Did you find her?

SECOND DETECTIVE   No, I saw no woman in a Black Straw Hat uniform.
There are a hundred thousand people standing around in the stockyards; besides, it's dark and that biting wind drowns your voice.
Also, the police are clearing the yards and shots are being fired
already.

MAULER   Shots? At whom? Oh, yes, of course.
It seems strange—you can't hear a thing in this place.
So she's not to be found, and shots are being fired?
Go to the phone booths, look for Jim and tell him
Not to call, or people will say again
That we demanded the shooting.
(*Exit* SECOND DETECTIVE.)
MEYERS   Fifteen hundred at 80!
SLIFT   Not more than five hundred at 80!
MEYERS   Five thousand at 80, you cutthroat!
MAULER (*returning to the column*)   Slift, I feel unwell. Let up, will you?
SLIFT   I wouldn't think of it. There's life in them yet. And if you start to
weaken, Mauler, I'll shove them up higher.
MAULER   Slift, I need a breath of air. You carry on
The business. I can't. Carry it on
The way I would. I'd rather give it all away
Than have more things happen because of me!
Go no higher than 85! But manage it
The way I would. You know me.
(*Exit.*)
SLIFT   Five hundred steers at 90!
SMALL SPECULATORS   We heard that Mauler was willing
To sell at 85. Slift has no authority.
SLIFT   That's a lie! I'll teach you
To sell meat in cans and then
Not have any meat!
Five thousand steers for 95!
(*Uproar.*)

Stockyards. Many PEOPLE *waiting,* JOAN *among them.*

PEOPLE   Why are you sitting here?
JOAN   I have to deliver a letter. Three men are supposed to come by here.
(*A group of* REPORTERS *comes up, led by a* MAN.)
MAN (*pointing to* JOAN)   That's the one. (*To* JOAN.) These people
are reporters.
REPORTERS   Hello, are you Joan Dark, the Black Straw Hat?
JOAN   No.
REPORTERS   We have heard from Mauler's office that you've sworn not to
leave the stockyards before the plants open up. We have it, you can
read it here, in big front-page headlines. (JOAN *turns away.*) Our

Lady of the Stockyards Avers God Solidly Behind Stockyard Workers.

JOAN   I said no such thing.

REPORTERS   We can assure you, Miss Dark, that public opinion is on your side. All Chicago sympathizes with you, except a few unscrupulous speculators. Your Black Straw Hats will reap terrific success from all this.

JOAN   I'm not with the Black Straw Hats any more.

REPORTERS   That can't be. For us, you belong to the Black Straw Hats. But we don't want to disturb you, we'll keep well in the background.

JOAN   I would like you to go away. (*They sit down some distance off.*)

WORKERS (*in the stockyards, rear*)   Before our need is at its worst
They will not open the factories.
When misery has mounted
They will open up.
But they must answer us.
Do not go before they answer.

COUNTER-CHORUS (*also rear*)   Wrong! Let misery mount,
They will not open up,
Not before profits mount.
If you wait for the answer
You will get the answer:
Out of cannon and machine guns
They will answer you.
And we advise you to wait
For this answer: do not go.

JOAN   I see this system and on the surface
It has long been familiar to me, but not
In its inner meaning! Some, a few, sit up above
And many down below and the ones on top
Shout down: "Come on up, then we'll all
Be on top," but if you look closely you'll see
Something hidden between the ones on top and the ones below
That looks like a path but is not a path—
It's a plank and now you can see it quite clearly,
It is a seesaw, this whole system
Is a seesaw, with two ends that depend
On one another, and those on top
Sit up there only because the others sit below,
And only as long as they sit below;

They'd no longer be on top if the others came up,
Leaving their place, so that of course
They want the others to sit down there
For all eternity and never come up.
Besides, there have to be more below than above
Or else the seesaw wouldn't hold. A seesaw, that's what it is.
(*The* REPORTERS *get up and move upstage, having received some news.*)

A WORKER (*to* JOAN) Say, what have you to do with those fellows?

JOAN Nothing.

WORKER But they were talking with you.

JOAN They took me for someone else.

OLD MAN (*to* JOAN) You sure look frozen. Like a swig of whiskey?
(JOAN *drinks.*) Stop! Stop! That's no mean shot you took!

A WOMAN Scandalous!

JOAN Did you say something?

WOMAN I said, scandalous! Guzzling all the old man's whiskey!

JOAN Shut your trap, you silly old thing. Hey, where's my shawl? They've
gone and swiped it again. That's the last straw! Going and stealing
my shawl, on top of everything else! Now who's got my shawl?
Give it here pronto. (*She grabs a sack off the head of the* WOMAN
standing next to her. The WOMAN *resists.*) Oh, so it's you. No lies!
Gimme that sack.

THE WOMAN Help, she's killing me!

A MAN Shut up! (*Someone throws her a rag.*)

JOAN For all you people care, I might be sitting around in this draft
nekkid.
It wasn't as cold as this in my dream.
When I came to this place with brave plans,
Fortified by dreams, I still never dreamed
That it could be so cold here. Now the only thing I miss
Of all I have is my nice warm shawl.
You may well be hungry, you have nothing to eat,
But they're waiting for me with a bowl of soup.
You may well freeze
But I can go into the warm room any time,
Pick up the flag and beat the drum
And speak about HIM who lives in the clouds. After all,
What did you leave? What I left
Was no mere occupation, it was a calling,
A noble habit, but a decent job as well
And daily bread and a roof and a livelihood.

Yes, it seems almost like a play,
Something undignified, for me to stay in this place
Without extremely pressing need. And yet
I may not go, and still—
I'll be frank about it—fear tightens round my throat
At the thought of this not eating, not sleeping, not knowing
Where you are,
Habitual hunger, helpless cold and—
Worst of all—wanting to get away.

WORKER   Stay here! Whatever happens,
Do not break ranks!
Only if you stand together
Can you help each other!
Realize that you have been betrayed
By all your public sponsors
And your unions, which are bought.
Listen to no one, believe nothing
But test every proposal
That leads to genuine change. And above all learn:
It will only work out by force
And only if you do it yourselves.
(*The* REPORTERS *return.*)

REPORTERS   Hey there, gal, you've had sensational success: we've just
found out that the millionaire Pierpont Mauler, who has vast
quantities of livestock in his hands now, is releasing livestock to
the slaughterhouses in spite of rising prices. This being so, work
will be resumed in the yards tomorrow.

JOAN   Oh, what good news! The ice has thawed in their hearts. At least
The one just man among them
Has not failed us. Appealed to as a man,
He has answered as a man.
There *is* kindness in the world.
(*Machine guns rat-a-tat in the distance.*)
What's that noise?

REPORTER   Those are army machine guns. The army has orders to clear
the stockyards because the agitators who are inciting to violence
will have to be silenced now that the slaughterhouses are to be
reopened.

A WORKER   You just take it easy and stay here. The stockyards are so big
it'll take the army hours to get this far.

JOAN   How many people are there in them now, anyway?

REPORTER   There must be a hundred thousand.

JOAN   So many?
   Oh, what an unknown school, an unlawful space
   Filled up with snow, where hunger is teacher and unpreventably
   Need speaks about necessity.
   A hundred thousand pupils, what are you learning?
WORKERS (*rear*)   If you stay together
   They will cut you to pieces.
   We advise you to stay together!
   If you fight
   Their tanks will grind you to pulp.
   We advise you to fight!
   This battle will be lost
   And maybe the next
   Will also be lost.
   But you are learning to fight
   And realizing
   That it will only work out by force
   And only if you do it yourselves.
JOAN   Stop: no more lessons
   So coldly learned!
   Do not use force
   To fight disorder and confusion.
   Certainly the temptation is tremendous!
   Another night like this, another wordless
   Oppression like this, and nobody
   Will be able to keep quiet. And certainly
   You have already stood together
   On many a night in many a year and learned
   To think coldly and terribly.
   Certainly acts of violence and weakness
   Are matching one another in the dark
   And unsettled business is piling up.
   But the meal that's cooking here—who
   Will be the ones to eat it?
   I'm leaving. What's done by force cannot be good. I don't belong
   with them. If hunger and the tread of misery had taught me
   violence as a child, I would belong to them and ask no questions.
   But as it is, I must leave. (*She remains seated.*)
REPORTERS   Our advice to you is, leave the stockyards right now. You
   made a big hit, but that's over and done with.
   (*Exeunt. Shouting, rear, spreading forward. The* WORKERS *rise.*)

A WORKER They're bringing the men from headquarters. (*The two*
    LEADERS *of the workers are brought forward, handcuffed.*)
A WORKER (*to his handcuffed* LEADER) Never mind, William, not every
    day is dark.
ANOTHER (*shouting after the* GROUP) Bloody brutes!
WORKERS If they think they're stopping anything that way, they're on
    the wrong track. Our men have taken care of everything.

IN A VISION JOAN SEES HERSELF AS A CRIMINAL, OUTSIDE THE FAMILIAR
    WORLD.

JOAN The men who gave me the letter! Why are they
    Handcuffed? What is in the letter?
    I could do nothing
    That would have to be done by force and
    Would provoke force. A person like that would stand
    Against his fellow man, full of deceit
    And beyond the range of any settlement
    That human beings usually make.
    Not belonging, he would lose his way
    In a world no longer familiar to him. The stars
    Would hurtle over his head breaking
    The ancient rules. Words
    Would change meaning for him. Innocence
    Would abandon one who was constantly persecuted.
    He can look at nothing without suspicion.
    I could not be like that. So I'm leaving.
    For three days Joan was seen
    In Packingtown, in the stockyards swamps
    Going down, downward from level to level
    To clear the mud away, to manifest
    To the lowest. Three days walking
    Down the slope, growing weaker on the third
    And finally swallowed by the swamp. Say:
    "It was too cold."
    (*She gets up and goes. Snow begins to fall.*)
A WORKER I thought right away that she'd take off when the real snow
    came. (*Three* WORKERS *come by, look around for someone, fail to*
    find him, and leave.)
    As it grows dark, a writing appears.
    "The snow is starting to fall,

Will anyone stay at all?
They'll stay today as they've stayed before—
Stony ground and folk that are poor."

PIERPONT MAULER CROSSES THE BOUNDARY OF POVERTY

A Chicago street corner.

MAULER (*to one of the* DETECTIVES) No further, let's turn back now,
what do you say?
Admit it: you laughed. I said, "Let's turn back now,"
And you laughed. They're shooting again.
Seems to be some resistance, eh? But this is what
I wanted to impress upon you: think nothing of it
If I turned back a couple of times
As we came nearer the stockyards. Thinking
Is nothing. I'm not paying you to think.
I probably have my reasons. I'm known down there.
Now you are thinking again. Seems I've taken
A couple of nitwits along. Anyway,
Let's turn back. I hope the person I was looking for
Has listened to the voice of sense and left that place
Where hell appears to be breaking loose.
A NEWSBOY *goes by.*
Give me those papers! let's see how the livestock market is going!
He reads and turns pale.
Well, something's happened here that changes things:
It's printed here, black on white, that livestock
Is down to 30 and not a head is being sold,
That's what it says here, black on white, the packers
Are ruined and have left the livestock market.
And it also says that Mauler and Slift, his friend,
Are the worst hit of all. That's what it says and it means
That things have reached a point that certainly was not striven for,
But is greeted with sighs of relief. I can help them no further—
I freely offered
All my livestock for the use of any man that wanted it
And nobody took it and so I am free now
And without pretensions and hereby
I dismiss you in order to cross
The boundary of poverty, for I no longer require your services.
Henceforth nobody will want to knock me down.

THE TWO DETECTIVES   Then we may go.
MAULER   You may indeed, and so may I, wherever I want.
      Even to the stockyards.
      And as for the thing made of sweat and money
      Which we have erected in these cities:
      It already seems as though a man
      Had made a building, the largest in the world and
      The most expensive and practical, but—
      By an oversight, and because it was cheap—he used dog-shit
      As its material, so that it would have been very difficult
      To stay there and in the end his only glory was
      That he had made the biggest stink in the world.
      And anyone who gets out of a building like that
      Should be a cheerful man.
A DETECTIVE   (*departing*)   So, he's finished.
MAULER   Bad luck may crush the man of humble size;
      Me it must waft to spiritual skies.

A No-Man's-Land in the Stockyards. JOAN, *hurrying toward the city, over-
      hears two passing* WORKERS.

FIRST WORKER   First they let the rumor leak out that work would start up
      again, full blast, in the stockyards; but now that a part of the
      workers have left the yards to come back tomorrow morning,
      they're suddenly saying that the slaughterhouses won't be opened
      at all, because Mauler has ruined them.
SECOND WORKER   The Communists were right. The masses shouldn't have
      broken ranks. All the more so because all the factories in Chicago
      would have all called a general strike for tomorrow.
FIRST WORKER   We didn't know that.
SECOND WORKER   That's bad. Some of the messengers must have failed
      us. A lot of people would have stayed put if they'd known about it.
      Even in the teeth of the cops' violence.
      (*Wandering to and fro,* JOAN *hears voices.*)
A VOICE   He who does not arrive
      Can plead no excuse. The fallen man
      Is not excused by the stone.
      Let not even the one who does arrive
      Bore us with reports of difficulties
      But deliver in silence
      Himself or what is entrusted to him.
      (JOAN *has stood still and now runs in another direction.*)

A VOICE (JOAN *stands still*)   We gave you orders
>   Our situation was critical
>   We did not know who you were
>   You might carry out our orders and you might
>   Also betray us.
>   Did you carry them out?
>   (JOAN *runs farther and is halted by another voice.*)

A VOICE   Where men are waiting, someone must arrive!
>   (*Looking around for an escape from the voices,* JOAN *hears voices on all sides.*)

VOICES   The net with a torn mesh
>   Is of no use:
>   The fish swim through it at that point
>   As though there were no net.
>   Suddenly all its meshes
>   Are useless.
>   (JOAN *falls to her knees.*)

JOAN   Oh, truth, shining light! Darkened by a snowstorm in an evil hour!
>   Lost to sight from that moment! Oh, how violent are snowstorms!
>   Oh, weakness of the flesh! What would you let live, hunger?
>   What outlasts you, frost of the night?
>   I must turn back! (*She runs back.*)

10.   Pierpont Mauler Humbles Himself and is Exalted

The Black Straw Hats' Mission.

MARTHA (*to another* BLACK STRAW HAT)   Three days ago a messenger from Pierpont Mauler, the meat king, came to tell us that he wishes to pay our rent and join us in a big campaign for the poor.

MULBERRY   Mr. Snyder, it's Saturday evening. I'm asking you to pay your rent, which is very low, or get out of my building.

SNYDER   Mr. Mulberry, we expect Mr. Pierpont Mauler any minute now and he has promised us his support.

MULBERRY   Dick, old man, Albert, old man, put the furniture out in the street. (*Two* MEN *begin to move the furniture out.*)

BLACK STRAW HATS   Oh! They're taking the prayer bench!
>   Their greedy grasp even threatens

Pipe organ and pulpit.
And louder still we cry:
Please, rich Mr. Mauler, come
And save us with your money!

SNYDER   Seven days now the masses have been standing
In rusting stockyards, cut off from work at last.
Freed from every kind of shelter they stand
Under rain and snow again, sensing above them
The zenith of an unknown decision.
Oh, dear Mr. Mulberry, give us hot soup now
And a little music and they'll be ours. In my head I see
The Kingdom of Heaven ready and waiting.
Just give us a band and some decent soup,
Really nourishing, and God will settle things
And all of Bolshevism, too,
Will have breathed its last.

BLACK STRAW HATS   The dams of faith have burst
In this Chicago of ours
And the slimy flood of materialism surges
Menacingly round the last of its houses.
Look, it's tottering, look, it's sinking!
Never mind—keep going—rich man Mauler's on the way!
He's started out already with all his money!

A BLACK STRAW HAT   Where can we put the public now, Major? (*Enter three* POOR PEOPLE, MAULER *among them.*)

SNYDER   (*shouting at them*) Soup, that's all you want! No soup here! Just the Word of God! We'll get rid of them straight off when they hear that.

MAULER   Here are three men coming to their God.

SNYDER   Sit down over there and keep quiet. (*The three sit down. A* MAN *enters.*)

MAN   Is Pierpont Mauler here?

SNYDER   No, but we're expecting him.

MAN   The packers want to speak to him and the stockbreeders are screaming for him.
(*Exit.*)

MAULER   (*facing* AUDIENCE) I hear they're looking for a man named Mauler.
I knew him: a numskull. Now they're searching
High and low, in heaven and in hell,
For that man Mauler who was dumber all his life
Than a dirty drink-sodden tramp.

(Rises and goes over to BLACK STRAW HATS.*)*
I knew a man who once was asked
For a hundred dollars. And he had about ten million.
And he came along without the hundred but threw
The ten million away
And gave himself.
(He takes two of the BLACK STRAW HATS *and kneels with them on the prayer bench.)*
I wish to confess my sins.
No one who ever knelt here, friends,
Was as humble as I am.

BLACK STRAW HATS   Don't lose confidence,
  Don't be souls of little faith!
  He's sure to come—already he's approaching
  With all his money.

A BLACK STRAW HAT   Is he here yet?

MAULER   A hymn, I pray you! For my heart
  Feels heavy and light at once.
  (They intone a hymn. The BLACK STRAW HATS *join in abstractly, eyes on the door.)*

SNYDER *(bent over the account books)*   I won't tell how this comes out.
  Quiet!
  Bring me the housekeeping record and the unpaid bills. I've got
    to that stage.

MAULER   I accuse myself of exploitation,
  Misuse of power, expropriation of everybody
  In the name of property. For seven days I held
  The city of Chicago by the throat
  Until it perished.

A BLACK STRAW HAT   That's Mauler!

MAULER   But at the same time I plead that on the seventh day
  I rid myself of everything, so that now
  I stand before you without possessions.
  Not guiltless, but repentant.

SNYDER   Are you Mauler?

MAULER   Yes, and torn to pieces by remorse.

SNYDER *(with a loud cry)*   And without any money? *(To the* BLACK STRAW HATS.*)* Pack up the stuff, I hereby suspend all payments.

MUSICIANS   If that's the man you were waiting for
  To get the cash to pay us with
  Then we can go. Good night.
  (Exeunt.)

CHORUS OF BLACK STRAW HATS (*gazing after the departing* MUSICIANS)
 We were awaiting with prayers
 The wealthy Mauler, but into our house
 Came the man converted.
 His heart
 He brought to us, but not his money.
 Therefore our hearts are moved, but
 Our faces are long.
 (*Confusedly the* BLACK STRAW HATS *sing their last hymns as they
 sit on their last chairs and benches.*)
BLACK STRAW HATS By the waters of Lake Michigan
 We sit down and weep.
 Take the proverbs off the walls
 Wrap the songbooks in the cover of the defeated flag
 For we can pay our bills no more
 And against us rush the snowstorms
 Of approaching winter.
 (*Then they sing "Go Into the Thick of the Fight."* MAULER *joins in,
 looking over a* BLACK STRAW HAT's *shoulder.*)
SNYDER Quiet! Everybody out now—(*To* MAULER.)—especially you!
 Where is the forty months' rent from the unconverted
 Whom Joan expelled? Look what she's driven in instead! Oh, Joan,
 Give me my forty months' rent again!
MAULER I see you would like to build your house
 In my shade. Well, for you a man
 Is what can help you; likewise, for me
 A man was only plunder. But even
 If man were only what is helped,
 There would be no difference. Then you'd need drowning men,
 For then it would be your business
 To be straws for them to clutch at. So all remains
 Within the mighty orbit of wares, like that of the stars.
 Such teaching, Snyder, would embitter many.
 But I can see that as I am
 I'm the wrong man for you.
 (MAULER *makes to go, but the* MEAT KINGS *stop him at the door;
 they are all white as chalk.*)
PACKERS Forgive us, noble Mauler, for seeking you out,
 Disturbing you amid the involved emotions
 Of your colossal head.
 For we are ruined. Chaos is around us
 And over us the zenith of an unknown intention.

What are you planning for us, Mauler?
What will the next step be? We're sensitive
To the blows you rain on our necks.
(*Enter the* STOCKBREEDERS *in great commotion, equally pale.*)
STOCKBREEDERS   Damnable Mauler, is this where you've sneaked off to?
     You pay for our livestock, instead of getting converted!
     Your money, not your soul! You would not need
     To lighten your conscience in a place like this
     If you hadn't lightened our pockets! Pay for our livestock!
GRAHAM (*stepping forward*)   Permit us, Mauler, to give a brief account
     Of the seven-hour battle which began this morning and ended
     By plunging us all into the abyss.
MAULER   Oh, everlasting slaughter! Nowadays
     Things are no different from ancient times
     When they bloodied each other's heads with iron bars!
GRAHAM   Remember, Mauler, by our contract to deliver
     Meat to you, you forced us to buy meat
     In these of all times, and it had to be
     From you, as only you had meat to sell.
     Well, when you went away at noon, that Slift
     Pulled the rope even tighter around our necks.
     With harsh cries he kept on raising prices
     Until they stood at 95. But then
     A halt was called by the ancient National Bank.
     Bleating with responsibility, the old crone dumped
     Canadian yearlings on the chaotic market, and prices stood
          quivering.
     But Slift—that madman!—scarcely had he seen
     The handful of widely-traveled steers but he grabbed them at 95,
     As a drunkard who's already swilled an oceanful
     And still feels thirsty greedily laps up one
     Tiny drop more. The old crone shuddered at the sight.
     But some people leaped to the beldame's side to hold her up—
     Loew and Levi, Wallox and Brigham, the most reputable firms—
     And mortgaged themselves and all their possessions down to the
          last eraser,
     As a promise to bring forth the last remaining steer
     From the Argentine and Canada within three days—they even
          offered
     To get hold of unborn ones, ruthlessly,
     Anything that was steerlike, calfly, hoggish!
     Slift yells: "Three days? No! Today, today!"
     And shoves the prices higher. And in floods of tears

The banks threw themselves into the death-struggle,
Because they had to deliver the goods and therefore buy.
Sobbing, Levi himself punched one of Slift's brokers
In the belly, and Brigham tore his beard out
Screaming: NINETY-SIX! At that point
An elephant might have wandered in
And been crushed underfoot like a berry.
Even office-boys, seized with despair, bit one another
Without saying a word, as horses in olden times
Would bite each others' flanks among their fighting riders!
Unsalaried clerks, famous for lack of interest in business,
Were heard gnashing their teeth that day.
And still we bought and bought; we had to buy.
Then Slift said: ONE HUNDRED! You could have heard a pin
　　drop.
And as quietly as that the banks collapsed,
Like trampled sponges—formerly strong and firm,
Now suspending payment like respiration. Softly
Old Levi spoke, and all of us heard him: "Now
Our packing plants are yours, we can no longer
Fulfill our contracts," and so,
Packer after packer, they sullenly laid
The shut-down, useless packing plants at your feet—
Yours and Slift's—and went away;
And the agents and salesmen snapped their brief cases shut.
And at that moment, with a sigh as of liberation—
Since no more contracts compelled its purchase—
Livestock sank into the bottomless pit.
For unto prices it was given
To fall from quotation to quotation
As water hurtles from crag to crag
Deep down into the infinite. They didn't stop before 30.
And so, Mauler, your contract became invalid.
Instead of gripping our throats you have strangled us.
What does it profit a man to grip the throat of a corpse?

MAULER　So, Slift, that was how you managed the fight
　　I left on your hands!

SLIFT　Tear my head off.

MAULER　What good is your head?
　　I'll take your hat, that's worth five cents!
　　What is to become
　　Of all that cattle no one has to buy?

THE STOCKBREEDERS　Without becoming excited

We request you to tell us
Whether, when and with what
You wish to pay
For the bought but unpaid-for cattle.

MAULER   At once. With that hat and this boot.
Here is my hat for ten million, here
My first shoe for five. I need the other.
Are you satisfied?

THE STOCKBREEDERS   Alas, when moons ago
We led the frisky calf
And clean young steers,
Carefully fattened, by ropes to the station in far-off Missouri
The family yelled after us
And even after the rolling trains,
With voices broken by toil they yelled:
"Don't drink the money away, fellows, and
Let's hope prices will rise!"
What'll we do now? How
Can we go home? What
Shall we tell them
Showing the empty ropes
And empty pockets?
How can we go home in such a state, Mauler?
(MAN WHO WAS THERE BEFORE enters.)

MAN   Is Mauler here? There's a letter from New York for him.

MAULER   I *was* the Mauler to whom such letters were addressed. (*Opens it, reads it aside.*) "Recently, dear Pierpont, we wrote to tell you to buy meat. Today, however, we advise you to arrive at a settlement with the stockbreeders and limit the quantity of livestock, so as to give prices a chance to recover. In that event we shall gladly be of service to you. More tomorrow, dear Pierpont.—Your friends in New York." No, no, that won't work.

GRAHAM   What won't work?

MAULER   I have friends in New York who claim to know a way out. It doesn't seem feasible to me. Judge for yourselves. (*Gives them the letter.*)
How completely different
Everything seems now. Give up the chase, my friends.
Your property is gone: you must grasp that, it is lost.
But not because we are no longer blest with earthly
Goods—not everyone can be that—
Only because we have no feeling for higher things.
That's why we're poor!

MEYERS Who are these friends of yours in New York?

MAULER Horgan and Blackwell. Sell. . . .

GRAHAM Would that be Wall Street? (*Whispering spreads through the gathering.*)

MAULER The inward man, so cruelly crushed within us. . . .

PACKERS *and* STOCKBREEDERS Noble Mauler, consent to bring yourself
>   To descend to us from your lofty
>   Meditations! Think of the chaos
>   That would swoop on everything, and take up—
>   Since you are needed, Mauler—
>   The burden of responsibility again!

MAULER I don't like to do it.
>   And I won't do it alone, for the grumbling in the stockyards
>   And the rat-tat-tat of machine guns
>   Still resound in my ears. It would only work
>   If it were sanctioned in a very grand style
>   And conceived as vital
>   To the public good.
>   Then it might work.
>   (*To* SNYDER.) Are there many Bible shops like this one?
>   Since you are needed, Mauler—

SNYDER Yes.

MAULER How are they doing?

SNYDER Badly.

MAULER Doing badly, but there are many of them.
>   If we promoted the cause of the Black Straw Hats
>   In a really big way—if you were equipped
>   With lots of soup and music
>   And suitable Bible quotations, even with shelter
>   In great emergencies—would you then speak
>   On our behalf, saying everywhere that we are good people?
>   Planning good things in bad times? For only
>   By taking extremist measures—measures that might seem harsh
>   Because they affect some people, quite a few really,
>   In short: most people, nearly everybody—
>   Can we preserve this system now, the system
>   Of buying and selling which is here to stay
>   And also has its seamy side.

SNYDER For nearly everybody. I understand. We would.

MAULER (*to the* PACKERS) I have merged your packing plants
>   As one ring and am taking over
>   Half of the stocks.

PACKERS A great mind!

MAULER (*to the* STOCKBREEDERS) My dear friends, listen!
    They whisper.
    The difficulty which oppressed us is lifting.
    Misery, hunger, excesses, violence
    Have one cause only and the cause is clear:
    There was too much meat. The meat market was
    All stuffed up this year and so the price of livestock
    Sank to nothing. Now, to maintain it,
    We, packers and stockbreeders, have formed a united front
    To set some limits to this unbridled breeding:
    To restrict the livestock coming into market
    And eliminate excess from the current supply. This means
    Burning one-third of the livestock total.
ALL Simple solution!
SNYDER (*saluting*) Might it not be possible—if all that cattle
    Is so worthless that it can be burned—
    Just give it to the many standing out there
    Who could make such good use of it?
MAULER (*smiling*) My dear Snyder, you have not grasped
    The root of the situation. The many
    Standing out there—*they are the buyers!*
    (*To the* OTHERS) It's hardly credible.
    (ALL *smile for a long time.*)
    They may seem low, superfluous,
    Indeed, burdensome sometimes, but it cannot elude
    Profounder insight that *they* are the buyers!
    Likewise—there are very many who do not understand this—it is
        essential
    To lock out a third of the workers.
    It is also work that has clogged our market and therefore
    It must be limited.
ALL The only way out!
MAULER And wages lowered!
ALL Columbus' egg!
MAULER All this is being done so that
    In gloomy times of bloody confusion
    Dehumanized humanity
    When there is no end to the unrest in our cities
    (For Chicago is again upset by talk of a general strike)
    The brute strength of the short-sighted people
    May not shatter its own tools and trample its own bread-baskets
        underfoot,

But peace and order may return. That is why we are willing
To facilitate by generous contributions
The work by which you Black Straw Hats encourage order.
It's true that there ought to be people among you again
Like that girl Joan, who inspires confidence
By her mere appearance.

A BROKER (*rushing in*)   Glad tidings! The threatened strike has been suppressed. They've jailed the criminals who impiously troubled peace and order.

SLIFT   Breathe freely now! The market's getting well!
Again the doldrums have been overcome.
The difficult task has once again been done
And once again a plan is finely spun
And the world resumes the way we like it run.
Organ.

MAULER   And now, open wide your gates
Unto the weary and heavy laden and fill the pot with soup.
Tune up some music and we will sit
Upon your benches and be the first
To be converted.

SNYDER   Open the doors! (*The doors are flung wide open.*)

BLACK STRAW HATS (*singing, eyes on the door*)   Spread the net far out:
they're bound to come!
They've just abandoned the last redoubt!
God's driving cold on them!
God's driving rain on them!
So they're bound to come! Spread the net far out!
Welcome! Welcome! Welcome!
Welcome to our humble home!

Bolt everything tight so that none will escape!
They're on their way down to us all right!
If they've no work to do
If they're deaf and blind too
Not one will escape! So bolt everything tight!
Welcome! Welcome! Welcome!
Welcome to our humble home!

Whatever may come, gather everything in!
Hat and head and shoe and leg and scamp and scum!
Its hat has gone sky-high
So it comes right in to cry!

Gather everything in, whatever may come!
Welcome! Welcome! Welcome!
Welcome to our humble home!

Here we stand! Watch them coming down!
Watch their misery drive them like animals to our hand!
Look, they're bound to come down!
Look, they're coming down!
They can't get away from this spot: here we stand!
Welcome! Welcome! Welcome!
Welcome to our humble home!

Stockyards. Environs of Graham's Warehouse. The yards are almost empty. Only a few groups of WORKERS *are still passing by.*

JOAN (*coming up to ask*)   Did three men go by here asking for a letter? (*Shouting from rear, spreading toward front. Then enter five* MEN *escorted by* SOLDIERS: *the two from the union central office and the three from the power stations. Suddenly one of the two stands still and speaks to the* SOLDIERS.)

MAN   If you're taking us to jail now, there's something you ought to know. We did what we did because we are for you.

SOLDIER   Keep moving, if you're for us.

MAN   Wait a little!

SOLDIER   Getting scared, eh?

MAN   Yes, that too, but that's not what I'm talking about. I just want you to stand still a little so I can tell you why you have arrested us, because you don't know.

SOLDIERS (*laughing*)   O.K., tell us why we arrested you.

MAN   Without property yourselves, you help men of property because you don't yet see any possibility of helping men without property.

SOLDIER   That's fine. Now let's move on.

MAN   Wait, I haven't finished the sentence: on the other hand, the working people in this town are starting to help the people without work. So the possibility is coming nearer. Now worry about that.

SOLDIER   I guess you want us to let you go, eh?

MAN   Didn't you understand me? We just want you to know that your time's coming soon too.

SOLDIERS   Can we go on now?

MAN   Yes, we can go on now. (*They move on.* JOAN *stays where she is, watching the arrested* MEN *go. Then she hears two* PEOPLE *talking beside her.*)

FIRST MAN   Who are those people?

SECOND MAN   Not one of them
        Cared only for himself.
        They ran without rest
        To get bread for strangers.
FIRST MAN   Why without rest?
SECOND MAN   The unjust man may cross the street in the open, but the
        just man hides.
FIRST MAN   What's being done to them?
SECOND MAN   Although they work for low wages and are useful to many
        men
        Not one of them lives out the years of his life,
        Eats his bread, dies contented
        Or is buried with honors, but
        They end before their time,
        Struck down and crushed and covered with earth in shame.
FIRST MAN   Why don't we ever hear about them?
SECOND MAN   If you read in the papers that certain criminals have been
        shot or thrown into prison, they're the ones.
FIRST MAN   Will it always be like that?
SECOND MAN   No. (*As* JOAN *turns to go, she is accosted by the* REPORTERS.)
REPORTERS   Isn't this Our Lady of the Stockyards? Hi there! Things
        have gone wrong! The general strike was called off. The stockyards
        are opening up again, but only for two-thirds of the personnel and
        only at two-thirds' pay. But meat prices are going up.
JOAN   Have the workers accepted this?
REPORTERS   Sure. Only a part of them knew a general strike was being
        planned, and the cops drove that part out of the yards by force.
        (JOAN *falls to the ground.*)

11. Death and Canonization of Saint Joan of the Stockyards

The BLACK STRAW HATS' *house is now richly furnished and decorated. Its
    doors are flung wide open; in ordered groups, the* BLACK STRAW
    HATS *with new flags, packers, stockbreeders and wholesalers stand
    waiting for the Gloombs and Luckerniddles.*

SNYDER   Thus our task meets happy ending:
        God's foothold has been found again.

For the highest good contending,
We have faced the depths of pain.

Both our mounting and descending
Show what we can mean to you:
Lo, at last the happy ending!
Look, at last we've put it through!
(*Enter a mass of* POOR PEOPLE, *with* JOAN *at their head, supported by two* POLICEMEN.)

POLICEMAN   Here is a homeless woman
We picked up in the stockyards
In a sick condition. Her
Last permanent residence was
Allegedly here.
(JOAN *holds her letter high as though still anxious to deliver it.*)

JOAN   The man who has perished will never
Take my letter from me.
Small enough service to a good cause, the only service
Demanded of me my whole life long!—
And I did not perform it.
(*While the* POOR PEOPLE *sit down on the benches to get their soup,* SLIFT *consults with the* PACKERS *and* SNYDER.)

SLIFT   It's our own Joan. Why, her coming is like an answer to our prayers. Let's cover her with glory; by her philanthropic work in the stockyards, her championship of the poor, and even her speeches against us, she helped us over some really difficult weeks. She shall be our Saint Joan of the Stockyards! We will cultivate her as a saint and refuse her no jot of respect. The fact that she is shown under our auspices will prove that we hold humaneness in high regard.

MAULER   May the pure and childlike soul
Ever figure on our roll;
May our humble choir delight
In her singing clear and glad;
May she damn whatever's bad
And defend our every right.

SNYDER   Rise, Joan of the stockyards,
Champion of the poor,
Comforter of the lowest depths!

JOAN   What a wind in the depths! What is that shrieking
The snow is trying to hush?
Eat your soup, you!

Don't spill your last bit of warmth, you
Good-for-nothings! Eat your soup! If only I had lived
As tranquilly as a cow,
And yet delivered the letter that was entrusted to me!
BLACK STRAW HATS (*going up to her*)   Sudden daylight makes her ache
After nights of stupefaction!
Only human was your action!
Only human your mistake!
JOAN (*while the* GIRLS *dress her in the Black Straw Hat uniform again*)
The roar of the factories is starting again, you can hear it.
Another chance to stop it—wasted.
Again the world runs
Its ancient course unaltered.
When it was possible to change it
I did not come; when it was necessary
That I, little person, should help,
I stayed on the sidelines.
MAULER   Alas, that man cannot abide
In his distress the earthly bond,
But with swift and haughty stride
Rushes past the everyday
Which he thinks will turn him gray
Past his target and beyond
Into worlds outside his ken,
Endless worlds too high for men.
JOAN   I spoke in every market place
And my dreams were numberless but
I did harm to the injured
And was useful to those who harmed them.
BLACK STRAW HATS   Alas! All effort, sages write,
Achieves but patchwork, void of soul,
If matter make not spirit whole.
PACKERS   And ever 'tis a glorious sight
When soul and business unite!
JOAN   One thing I have learned and I know it in your stead,
Dying myself:
How can I say it—there's something inside you
And it won't come out! *What* do you know in your wisdom
That has no consequences?
I, for instance, did nothing.
Oh, let nothing be counted good, however helpful it may seem,
And nothing considered honorable except that

Which will change this world once for all: that's what it needs.
Like an answer to their prayers I came to the oppressors!
Oh, goodness without consequences! Intentions in the dark!
I have changed nothing.
Vanishing fruitless from this world
I say to you:
Take care that when you leave the world
You were not only good but are leaving
A good world!

GRAHAM   We'll have to see to it that her speeches only get through if they
are reasonable. We mustn't forget that she has been in the stockyards.

JOAN   For there is a gulf between top and bottom, wider
Than between Mount Himalaya and the sea
And what goes on above
Is not found out below
Or what happens below, above
And there are two languages, above and below
And two standards for measuring
And that which wears a human face
No longer knows itself.

PACKERS *and* STOCKBREEDERS (*very loud, so as to shout* JOAN *down*)   Top
and bottom must apply
For the building to be high
That's why everyone must stay
In the place where they belong
Day after day
Man must do what suits his stature
For if he forgets his nature
All our harmonies go wrong.
Underdogs have weight below,
The right man's right when up you go.
Woe to him who'd rouse that host—
Indispensable but
Demanding, not
To be done without
And aware of that—
Elements of the nethermost!

JOAN   But those who are down below are kept below
So that the ones above may stay up there
And the lowness of those above is measureless
And even if they improve that would be
No help, because the system they have made

Is unique: exploitation
And disorder, bestial and therefore
Incomprehensible.

BLACK STRAW HATS (*to* JOAN) Be a good girl! Hold your tongue!

PACKERS Those who float in boundless spaces
Cannot rise to higher places,
For to climb you need a rung,
And to reach for things aloft
You must make a downward tread!

MAULER Action, alas, may break a head!

BLACK STRAW HATS Though your shoe is stained with gore

PACKERS Do not try to pull it off!
You will need it more and more.

BLACK STRAW HATS Keep conduct high and spirit young.
But do not forget to rue it!

PACKERS Do anything!

BLACK STRAW HATS But always do it
With a twinge of conscience, for—
Being given to contemplation
And to self-vituperation—
Your conscience will be sore!
Men of trade, be informed:
You cannot afford
To forget the splendid
Quite indispensable
Word of the Lord
Which is never ended
And ever transformed!

JOAN Therefore, anyone down here who says there is a God
When none can be seen,
A God who can be invisible and yet help them,
Should have his head knocked on the pavement
Until he croaks.

SLIFT Listen, people, you've got to say something to shut that girl up.
You must speak—anything you like, but loud!

SNYDER Joan Dark, twenty-five years old, stricken by pneumonia in the
stockyards of Chicago, in the service of God: a fighter and a
sacrifice!

JOAN And the ones that tell them they may be raised in spirit
And still be stuck in the mud, they should have their heads
Knocked on the pavement. No!
Only force helps where force rules,
And only men help where men are.

(*All sing the first verse of the chorale in order to stop* JOAN's *speeches from being heard.*)

ALL   Fill the full man's plate! Hosanna!

Greatness to the great! Hosanna!

To him that hath shall be given! Hosanna!

Give him city and state! Hosanna!

To the victor a sign from Heaven! Hosanna!

(*During these declamations loudspeakers begin to announce terrible news:*

POUND CRASHES! BANK OF ENGLAND CLOSES FOR FIRST TIME IN 300 YEARS! EIGHT MILLION UNEMPLOYED IN U.S.A.! FIVE YEAR PLAN A SUCCESS! BRAZIL POURS A YEAR'S COFFEE HARVEST INTO OCEAN! SIX MILLION UNEMPLOYED IN GERMANY! THREE THOUSAND BANKS COLLAPSE IN U.S.A.! EXCHANGES AND BANKS CLOSED DOWN BY GOVERNMENT IN GERMANY! BATTLE BETWEEN POLICE AND UNEMPLOYED OUTSIDE FORD FACTORY IN DETROIT! MATCH TRUST, BIGGEST IN EUROPE, CRASHES! FIVE YEAR PLAN IN FOUR YEARS!

Under the impression of this news those not engaged in declamation scream abuse at one another, as: "You slaughtered too much livestock, you rotten hog-butchers!" "You should have raised more stock, you lousy stockbreeders!" "You crazy money-grubbers, you should have employed more labor and handed out more paychecks! Who else will eat our meat?" "It's the middleman that makes meat expensive!" "It's the grain racket that raises livestock prices!" "The railroads' freight rates are strangling us!" "The banks' interest rates are ruining us!" "Who can pay those rents for stables and silos?" "Why don't you start plowing under?" "We did, but you aren't!" "The guilt is yours and yours alone!" "Things won't improve until you're hanged!" "You should have been in jail years ago!" "How come you're still at large?" ALL *sing second and third verses of chorale.* JOAN *is now inaudible.*)

Pity the well-to-do! Hosanna!

Set them in Thy path! Hosanna!

Vouchsafe Thy grace, Hosanna!

And Thy help to him that hath! Hosanna!

Have mercy on the few! Hosanna!

(JOAN's *talk is noticeably stopping.*)

Aid Thy class, which in turn aids Thee, Hosanna!

With generous hand! Hosanna!

Stamp out hatred now! Hosanna!

Laugh with the laugher, allow, Hosanna!

His misdeeds a happy end! Hosanna!

(During this verse the girls have been trying to pour some soup down JOAN's *throat. Twice she has pushed the plate back; the third time she seizes it, holds it high and then tips the contents out. Then she collapses and is now lying in the* GIRLS' *arms, mortally stricken, with no sign of life.* SNYDER *and* MAULER *step toward her.)*

MAULER   Give her the flag! *(The flag is presented to her. It drops from her hands.)*

SNYDER   Joan Dark, twenty-five years of age, dead of pneumonia in the stockyards in the service of God, a fighter and a sacrifice!

MAULER   Something pure
Without a flaw,
Uncorrupted, helpful, whole—
It thrills us common folk to awe!
Rouses in our breast a newer,
Better soul!
(All stand in speechless emotion for a long time. At a sign from SNYDER, *all the flags are gently lowered over* JOAN *until she is entirely covered by them. A rosy glow illumines the picture.)*

THE PACKERS *and* STOCKBREEDERS   The boast of man is that he owns
Immemorial desires
By which toward the higher zones
His spirit constantly aspires.
He sees the stars upon their thrones,
Senses a thousand ways to heaven,
Yet downward by the flesh is driven;
Then in shame his pride expires.

MAULER   A twofold something cuts and tears
My sorely troubled inward state
Like a jagged, deep-thrust knife:
I'm drawn to what is truly great,
Free from self and the profit rate,
And yet impelled to business life
All unawares!

ALL   Humanity! Two souls abide
Within thy breast!
Do not set either one aside:
To live with both is best!
Be torn apart with constant care!
Be two in one! Be here, be there!
Hold the low one, hold the high one—
Hold the straight one, hold the sly one—
Hold the pair!

COMMENTARY

Saint Joan of the Stockyards (1930)   *Saint Joan of the Stockyards*, written in a Germany beset by unemployment, hunger, and confrontations between strikers and police, a Germany about to turn to Nazism, dramatizes the conditions that create communist revolution in the West. Set in Chicago, its milieu is not American but abstract: an industrial city in a capitalist country. A Marxist, though apparently not a member of the Communist Party, Brecht dramatically explores a communist revolution that fails.

In all his plays, Brecht aims to do more than make reality recognizable: he wants to reveal what is beneath the surface of life. Once the people understand why they suffer, he believes, they will be able to rid themselves of their persecutors. Theatre, says Brecht, should communicate this understanding. "Listen to no one, believe nothing," he tells his audience in *Saint Joan of the Stockyards*, "But test every proposal/That leads to genuine change." To help create "genuine change" is Brecht's goal.

The world of capitalism, says Joan, is "a world like a slaughterhouse." Set in the stockyards and the livestock market, the play focuses on the workings of capitalism. Within a system characterized by "exploitation/And disorder, bestial," riven by class conflict, "The givers and the takers of work/Confront one another:/Warring fronts: irreconcilable." From a Marxist viewpoint, *Saint Joan of the Stockyards* demonstrates how the stock market moves, why it moves that way, and its effects on both capitalists and workers. Using exalted language more appropriate to the choruses of Greek tragedy and to the lyric passages of Schiller's and Goethe's plays (which it parodies) than to stock market manipulators, Brecht belittles the notion that economic forces are natural, eternal, inscrutable, or unchangeable. The very absurdity of such noble language as

> *Unshakeable above our heads*
> *Stands economic law, the not-to-be-known.*
> *Terrible is the cyclic recurrence*
> *Of natural catastrophes!*

or of such Biblical patches as "And silence fell upon the waters and/Bankruptcy among the wholesalers" and "For unto prices it was given/To fall from quotation to quotation," makes it difficult for us to take seriously the assertions of the speakers. "It was given," Brecht demonstrates, not by God but by man.

Although Brecht draws two vivid characters in *Saint Joan of the*

Stockyards, the salvationist Joan Dark (a pun on Joan d'Arc) and the comic capitalist Pierpont Mauler, his emphasis is not on individuals but on society. He brings to the foreground the stock market and the stockyards—the home of the capitalists and the prison of the workers. Foils to each other, masses of workers and capitalists, the poor and the rich, sometimes face each other but rarely confront each other, for to deal with the workers the capitalists use surrogates, such as religious institutions, which attempt to draw the workers' teeth. Urging the workers to put their thoughts on heavenly things rather than on improving their lot on earth, the Black Straw Hats do not explain that capitalists create and derive profit from the workers' unhappiness. Instead, they tell them that misery comes "like the rain, no one knows where from, and that they are destined to suffering and there's a reward for it shining at the end of the road."

Offstage are the communists, who only occasionally appear. Sometimes an explicit solution, often a presence waiting in the wings, they represent an alternative whose appearance we anticipate. The anticipation is not fulfilled. Brecht writes not about success but about the need for success. He dramatizes not a classless society but the need for a classless society. His play is not rounded with a happy ending. If there is to be such an ending, he implies, the audience must create it in their world.

A didactic play, *Saint Joan of the Stockyards* revolves around a character whose attitudes, values, and knowledge may resemble those of Brecht's audience in the West. Brecht does not identify Joan's class origins (though she seems middle class), but clearly they are not proletarian. In the course of the play she comes to understand the economic bases of capitalist society, the relationship between capitalism and religion, the cause of human suffering, and the need for force in order to change the world. To two social questions, Brecht provides Marxist answers. What is the cause of the misery of the workers? Neither divine justice nor human nature, Joan learns, but capitalism. How can a better world be created? The Black Straw Hats offer not solutions but palliatives: pious phrases and watery soup. Mauler, who is interested in preventing such a world from being created, insists that "Before the world can change, humanity/Must change its nature." At first an apostle of nonviolence and divine intervention, Joan comes to believe the reverse: "Only force helps where force rules,/And only men help where men are."

The premises of the play derive from a Marxist analysis of capitalism. Its episodic structure is based on two interrelated patterns, one financial (four shifts in economic relationships, precipitated by the four letters which Mauler receives from his New York friends), the other emotional (Joan's three stages of disillusion and learning when she descends "into the depths," that is, into the world of the workers).

Mauler's Wall Street associates fulfill several dramatic functions. First, they suggest that beyond the Chicago stockyards and livestock market is a larger world which affects that market and which they influence. Second, they determine the play's financial crises and dictate its final resolution. Their first letter announces overproduction and tariffs, which have removed markets. Prudently, Mauler sells his cattle at high prices before others learn of the situation. As a result, Lennox is destroyed, plants are closed, and unemployment is created. The second letter announces the probability that tariffs will be removed and new markets therefore opened. Prudently, Mauler buys cattle at low prices. Because of the surplus created by overproduction, however, the plants remain closed and the workers unemployed. The third letter announces that Congressmen have been influenced to remove tariffs. Because Mauler has cornered the meat market, the others have none to sell in the new market. To get meat to sell, they must buy from Mauler at high prices. Many owe Mauler the meat he previously bought from them. Those who cannot deliver must buy from him at high prices in order to sell to him at the low prices they previously agreed upon. Speculators and plant owners are ruined. The fourth letter advises Mauler to reach a settlement with the stockbreeders and limit the quantity of livestock offered for sale—i.e., to create a cartel and stabilize the market by selling a limited amount of the product at controlled, high prices. Acting upon this advice, Mauler absorbs the other plant owners in a giant merger, has a third of the meat burned (rather than give it to the poor, since they are potential customers), locks out a third of the workers (since to maintain high prices the plants will operate at two-thirds capacity), and lowers the wages of the other two-thirds (who must accept his terms because there are three men to every two jobs and their strike has been broken).

A ruthless and selfish man, Mauler deludes himself that his motives are wholly compassionate. Rather, they are conveniently ambiguous. Mauler never permits his compassion to interfere with profits. Sympathetic toward suffering animals, he is usually callous toward his fellow man. "Human beings do not affect me," he admits, though he does pity Joan. His heart swells when a dying ox shrieks, but he tells businessmen on the verge of ruin, "Though you should all go begging, I must have/My money!" As for the poor, "I feel no obligation in any way/And sleep extremely well."

The four letters from New York precipitate the play's economic crises. The play's other major line of development revolves around Joan's personal crises, particularly her three descents into the depths, all of which roughly follow the same pattern. Each time, Joan has a readymade interpretation of why the workers suffer; during each descent, she examines the evidence, learns that the interpretation is wrong, interprets the facts anew, resolves upon a course of action, and then acts, or—after the last descent—is prevented from acting.

When Joan first descends into the depths, she wants "to reintroduce God" as a powerful force. Subscribing to the doctrines of the Black Straw Hats, she preaches to the workers that poverty is ordained by God and urges nonviolence, acceptance of the status quo, and concentration upon God rather than upon such material things as improved economic conditions. The workers themselves know better. Not God, they tell her, but the capitalist Mauler has created mass unemployment. Having come to teach the workers, Joan learns from them. She resolves to act: she visits Mauler, the source of their misery.

By the time she next descends into the depths, Mauler has given her a different readymade interpretation of the cause of poverty: not Heaven, but the poor themselves, who are "wicked and gross . . . full of treachery and cowardice." To demonstrate their wickedness, Mauler's man Slift takes her to the stockyards. To the widow of a worker who was killed in a meat-packing plant, he offers free lunches in the company canteen for three weeks—on condition that she not pursue justice. He offers a worker food and money if he wears the dead man's clothes and tells the widow where he got them. Both the worker and the widow, who has not eaten for two days, accept Slift's offer. To the unemployed Gloomb, whose hand was caught in a tin-cutting machine, he offers the job of foreman in place of the man whose speed-up methods were responsible for his injury—if Gloomb persuades Joan to take his old job. On the basis of Slift's evidence, however, Joan reaches a different conclusion: "Not the wickedness of the poor/Have you shown me, but/*The poverty of the poor.*" To prove to Mauler that poverty is to blame for wickedness, she resolves to take the poor to the livestock exchange, which she does in the next scene, wherein she tries to persuade the capitalists to help them. If man must battle his fellow man merely in order to subsist, she asks, "how can the sense of higher things help being stifled in the human heart?" Adopting an economic metaphor for morality, she urges the capitalists to "think of helping [their] neighbor simply as serving a customer" and to give the poor "moral purchasing-power . . . that is, money, wages."

By bringing grace to the rich, Joan hoped to persuade them to help the poor. But she realizes, "I was a prize fool there," and expels the businessmen from the Black Straw Hat Mission. Since the priests of God serve the priests of Mammon, the Black Straw Hats expel her from the temple for her action. Though Mauler convinces her that religion and capitalism have the same interests, Joan refuses to ally herself with either, even though Mauler promises financial assistance to the Black Straw Hats. She will take her stand, she tells him, in the stockyards among the unemployed, for whom Mauler's offer "does not mean real help. And to whom/Nothing is offered." Until the factories reopen, she vows, she will eat nothing but what they eat, and if they eat only snow, then she will eat only snow.

For a third time, Joan descends into the depths, but although she has determined to make the workers' cause her own, she has not yet shared their experiences and has not yet reached their conclusions. She still feels that one can believe the capitalists and that force is not good. She believes the rumor that employment will resume, for she wants to believe it: she is hungry and afraid, it is cold ("It wasn't as cold as this in my dream"), and the timely news seems symbolically appropriate to the weather ("The ice has thawed in their hearts"). She therefore fails to deliver news of a general strike in support of the stockyard workers and therefore causes the strike to fail. Without a united front, the workers cannot resist their antagonists. Ironically, it is only when the capitalists themselves create a united front—a corporate merger under Mauler—that they (but only they) are able to survive the economic crisis.

The poor will receive help, Joan comes to realize, only "Out of cannon and machine guns." She perceives that under capitalism the few on top keep the many below in order that they themselves may remain above. But it is too late for Joan to translate her new knowledge into action. Her former "goodness," she realizes, did not help those who needed help. During her second descent, she had pitied the widow and Gloomb, but though she went hungry four times longer than the widow, she refuses to pity herself, for pity, she realizes, is not a virtue: it is an excuse for inaction. Because of this, she explains, she "did harm to the injured/And was useful to those who harmed them." Nothing should be counted good, concludes Joan, "except that/Which will change this world once for all. . . ." Turning atheist, the erstwhile salvationist demands that anyone who believes in God "Should have his head knocked on the pavement/Until he croaks." Embracing violence, the proponent of non-violence and persuasion shouts, "Only force helps where force rules. . . ."

But the capitalists use her death as they used her life. To show that they "hold humaneness in high regard," they and the Black Straw Hats canonize her as Saint Joan of the Stockyards. With such Biblical hosannas as "To him that hath shall be given," the capitalists and salvationists drown her out. Although loudspeakers interrupt them to announce the collapse of capitalism, clashes between the unemployed and the police, and the success of Russia's five-year plan, they like Joan are drowned out by the hypocritical litany of the salvationists and capitalists, who add her name to their possessions. The play ends on a note not of triumph but of futility and cynicism, which the audience is left to ponder.

Bibliography

A. Other Plays about Communist Revolution in Europe:

Bertolt Brecht, *The Mother*, 1931
Mikhail Bulgakov, *The Days of the Turbins*, 1926
Karl Herbert Rostworowski, *The Antichrist*, 1925
Ernst Toller, *Man and the Masses*, 1921
Stanisław Ignacy Witkiewicz, *The Water Hen*, 1921
Bernard Zimmer, *The Beautiful Red Danube*, 1931

B. Works about Brecht and Saint Joan of the Stockyards:

Bentley, Eric. *The Playwright as Thinker*. New York: Meridian Books, 1955.

Dukore, Bernard F. and Daniel C. Gerould. *Avant-Garde Drama: Major Plays and Documents*. New York: Bantam Books, 1969.

Esslin, Martin. *Brecht: A Choice of Evils*. London: Eyre and Spottiswoode, 1959.

Ewen, Frederic. *Bertolt Brecht: His Life, His Art, and His Times*. New York: Citadel Press, 1967.

Spalter, Max. *Brecht's Tradition*. Baltimore: Johns Hopkins Press, 1967.

Weideli, Walter. *The Art of Bertolt Brecht*. New York: New York University Press, 1963.

Willett, John. *The Theatre of Bertolt Brecht*. London: Methuen, 1959.

The
Irish
Revolution

THE PLOUGH AND THE STARS
Sean O'Casey

THE PLOUGH AND THE STARS

A Tragedy In Four Acts

Sean O'Casey

CHARACTERS

JACK CLITHEROE *(a bricklayer), Commandant in
    the Irish Citizen Army*
NORA CLITHEROE, *his wife*
PETER FLYNN *(a labourer), Nora's uncle*
THE YOUNG COVEY *(a fitter), Clitheroe's cousin*
BESSIE BURGESS *(a street fruit-vendor)*
MRS. GOGAN *(a charwoman)*
MOLLSER, *her consumptive child*
FLUTHER GOOD *(a carpenter)*

*Residents in
the Tenement*

LIEUT. LANGON *(a Civil Servant), of the Irish Volunteers*
CAPT. BRENNAN *(a chicken butcher), of the Irish Citizens Army*
CORPORAL STODDART, *of the Wiltshires*
SERGEANT TINLEY, *of the Wiltshires*
ROSIE REDMOND, *a daughter of "the Digs"*
A BAR-TENDER
A WOMAN
THE FIGURE IN THE WINDOW

ACT I.—The living-room of the Clitheroe flat in a Dublin tenement.
ACT II.—A public-house, outside of which a meeting is being held.
ACT III.—The street outside the Clitheroe tenement.
ACT IV.—The room of Bessie Burgess.

TIME.—Acts I and II, November 1915; Acts III and IV, Easter Week,
    1916. A few days elapse between Acts III and IV.

Act I

SCENE—*The home of the* CLITHEROES. *It consists of the front and back drawing-rooms in a fine old Georgian house, struggling for its life against the assaults of time and the more savage assaults of the tenants. The room shown is the back drawing-room, wide, spacious and lofty. At back is the entrance to the front drawing-room. The space, originally occupied by folding doors, is now draped with casement cloth of a dark purple, decorated with a design in reddish-purple. One of the curtains is pulled aside, giving a glimpse of the front drawing-room, at the end of which can be seen the wide, lofty windows looking out into the street. The room directly in front of the audience is furnished in a way that suggests an attempt towards a finer expression of domestic life. The large fireplace on* L. *is of wood, painted to look like marble (the original has been taken away by the landlord). Below the fireplace, on the wall, is a small mirror. On the mantelshelf are two candlesticks of dark carved wood. Between them is a small clock. Over the clock, on wall, is a picture of "The Sleeping Venus."*[1] *On the right of the entrance to the front drawing-room is a copy of "The Gleaners,"*[2] *on the opposite side a copy of "The Angelus." Underneath "The Gleaners" is a chest of drawers on which stands a green bowl filled with scarlet dahlias and white chrysanthemums. Near to the fireplace is a couch which at night forms a double bed for* CLITHEROE *and* NORA. *Near the end of the room opposite to the fireplace is a gate-legged table, covered with a cloth. On top of the table a huge cavalry sword is lying. To the* L. *above fireplace is a door which leads to a lobby from which the staircase leads to the hall. The floor is covered with a dark green linoleum. The room is dim except where it is illuminated from the glow of the fire.* FLUTHER GOOD *is repairing the lock of door,* L. *A claw hammer is on a chair beside him, and he has a screwdriver in his hand. He is a man of 40 years of age, rarely surrendering to thoughts of anxiety, fond of his "oil"*[3] *but determined to conquer the habit before he dies. He is square-jawed and harshly featured; under the left eye is a scar, and his nose is bent from a smashing blow received in a fistic battle long*

---

[1] By Giorgione (*c.* 1478–1510).
[2] Novelette by Clara Elizabeth Laughlin.
[3] Ale.

ago. He is bald, save for a few peeping tufts of reddish hair around his ears; and his upper lip is hidden by a scrubby red moustache, embroidered here and there with a gray hair. He is dressed in a seedy black suit, cotton shirt with a soft collar, and wears a very respectable little black bow. On his head is a faded jerry hat, which, when he is excited, he has a habit of knocking farther back on his head, in a series of taps. In an argument he usually fills with sound and fury, generally signifying a row. He is in his shirt sleeves at present, and wears a soiled white apron, from a pocket in which sticks a carpenter's two-foot rule. He has just finished the job of putting on a new lock, and, filled with satisfaction, he is opening and shutting the door, enjoying the completion of a work well done. Sitting at the fire, airing a white shirt, is PETER FLYNN. *He is a little, thin bit of a man, with a face shaped like a lozenge; on his cheeks and under his chin is a straggling wiry beard of a dirty-white and lemon hue. His face invariably wears a look of animated anguish, mixed with irritated defiance, as if everybody was at war with him, and he at war with everybody. He is cocking his head in such a way that suggests resentment at the presence of* FLUTHER, *who pays no attention to him, apparently, but is really furtively watching him.* PETER *is clad in a singlet, white whipcord knee-breeches, and is in his stockinged feet. A voice is heard speaking outside of door* L. *(it is that of* MRS. GOGAN *talking to someone).*

MRS. GOGAN (*Outside door* L.) Who are you lookin' for, sir? Who? Mrs. Clitheroe? . . . Oh, excuse me. Oh ay, up this way. She's out, I think: I seen her goin'. Oh, you've somethin' for her. Oh, excuse me. You're from Arnott's. . . . I see. . . . You've a parcel for her. . . . Righto. . . . I'll take it. . . . I'll give it to her the minute she comes in. . . . It'll be quite safe. . . .Oh, sign that. . . . Excuse me. . . . Where? . . . Here? . . . No, there; righto. Am I to put Maggie or Mrs. What is it? You dunno? Oh, excuse me.

(MRS. GOGAN *opens the door and comes in. She is a doleful-looking little woman of 40, insinuating manner and sallow complexion. She is fidgety and nervous, terribly talkative, has a habit of taking up things that may be near her and fiddling with them while she is speaking. Her heart is aflame with curiosity, and a fly could not come into nor go out of the house without her knowing. She has a draper's parcel in her hand, the knot of the twine tying it is untied.* MRS. GOGAN *crosses in front of* FLUTHER, *behind the couch, to the table* R., *where she puts the parcel, fingering it till she has the paper off, showing a cardboard box.* PETER, *more resentful of this intrusion than of* FLUTHER's *presence, gets up from the chair, and without looking around, his head carried at an angry cock, marches into the room at back. He leaves the shirt on the back of the chair.*)

(*Removing the paper and opening the cardboard box it contains*) I wondher what's this now? A hat! (*She takes out a hat, black, with decorations in red and gold*) God, she's goin' to th' divil lately for style! That hat, now, cost more than a penny. Such notions of upperosity she's getting. (*Putting the hat on her head*) Swank! (*Turning to* FLUTHER) Eh, Fluther, swank, what! (FLUTHER *looks over at her, then goes on opening and shutting the door*)

FLUTHER She's a pretty little Judy, all the same.

MRS. GOGAN Ah, she is, an' she isn't. There's prettiness an' prettiness in it. I'm always sayin' that her skirts are a little too short for a married woman. An' to see her, sometimes of an evenin', in her gladneck gown would make a body's blood run cold. I do be ashamed of me life before her husband. An' th' way she thries to be polite, with her "Good mornin', Mrs. Gogan," when she's goin' down, an' her "Good evenin', Mrs. Gogan," when she's comin' up. But there's politeness an' politeness in it.

FLUTHER They seem to get on well together, all th' same.

MRS. GOGAN Ah, they do, an' they don't. The pair o' them used to be like two turtle doves always billin' an' cooin'. You couldn't come into th' room but you'd feel, instinctive like, that they'd just been afther kissin' an' cuddlin' each other. . . . It often made me shiver, for, afther all, there's kissin' an' cuddlin' in it. But I'm thinkin' he's beginnin' to take things more quietly; the mysthery of havin' a woman's a mysthery no longer. . . . She dhresses herself to keep him with her, but it's no use—afther a month or two, th' wondher of a woman wears off. (MRS. GOGAN *takes off the hat, and puts it back in the box; going on to rearrange paper round box, and tie it up again*)

FLUTHER I dunno, I dunno. Not wishin' to say anything derogatory, I think it's all a question of location: when a man find th' wondher of one woman beginnin' to die, it's usually beginnin' to live in another.

MRS. GOGAN She's always grumblin' about havin' to live in a tenement house. "I wouldn't like to spend me last hour in one, let alone live me life in a tenement," says she. "Vaults," says she, "that are hidin' th' dead, instead of homes that are sheltherin' th' livin'." "Many a good one," says I, "was reared in a tenement house." Oh, you know, she's a well-up little lassie, too; able to make a shillin' go where another would have to spend a pound. She's wipin' th' eyes of th' Covey an' poor oul' Pether—everybody knows that—screwin' every penny she can out o' them, in ordher to turn th' place into a babby-house.[4] An' she has th' life frightened out o' them; washin' their face, combin' their hair, wipin' their feet, brushin' their clothes, thrimmin' their nails, cleanin' their teeth—God Almighty, you'd think th' poor men were undhergoin' penal servitude.

FLUTHER (*With an exclamation of disgust*) A-a-ah, that's goin' beyond th' beyonds in a tenement house. That's a little bit too derogatory.
PETER *enters from room, back, head elevated and resentful fire in his eyes; he is still in his singlet and trousers, but is now wearing a pair of unlaced boots—possibly to be decent in the presence of* MRS. GOGAN. PETER *comes down* C. *and crosses, front of settee, to chair in front of fire; he turns the shirt which he has left to air on the back of the chair, then goes, front of couch, to the chest of drawers, back* L., *opens drawer after drawer, looking for something; as he fails to find it, he closes each drawer with a snap. He jerks out things neatly folded, and shoves them back into the drawers any way.*

PETER (*In anguish, snapping a drawer shut*) Well, God Almighty, give me patience. (PETER *returns, front of couch, to the fireplace, gives the shirt a vicious turn on the back of the chair, and goes back, front of couch, to room, back,* FLUTHER *and* MRS. GOGAN *watching him furtively all the time.*)

MRS. GOGAN (*Curiously*) I wondher what is he foostherin' for now?
FLUTHER (*Coming* C.) He's adornin' himself for the meeting to-night. (*He pulls a handbill from one of his pockets, and reads.*) "Great Demonsthration an' Torchlight Procession around places in the City sacred to th' memory of Irish Pathriots to be concluded be a meetin', at which will be taken an oath of fealty to th' Irish Republic. Formation in Parnell Square at eight o'clock." Well, they can hold it for Fluther. I'm up th' pole; no more dhrink for Fluther. It's three days now since I touched a dhrop, an' I feel a new man already. (*He goes back to door* L.)

MRS. GOGAN Isn't oul' Peter a funny-lookin' little man? . . . Like somethin' you'd pick off a Christmas Tree. . . . When he's dhressed up in his canonicals, you'd wonder where he'd been got. God forgive me, when I see him in them, I always think he must ha' had a Mormon for a father! He an' th' Covey can't abide each other; th'

---

[4] A baby house.

pair o' them is always at it, thryin' to best each other. There'll be blood dhrawn one o' these days.

FLUTHER How is it that Clitheroe himself, now, doesn't have anythin' to do with th' Citizen Army? A couple o' months ago, an' you'd hardly ever see him without his gun, an' th' Red Hand[5] o' Liberty Hall[6] in his hat.

MRS. GOGAN Just because he wasn't made a Captain of. He wasn't goin' to be in anything where he couldn't be conspishuous. He was so cocksure o' being made one that he bought a Sam Browne belt,[7] an' was always puttin' it on an' standin' at th' door showing it off, till th' man came an' put out th' street lamps on him. God, I think he used to bring it to bed with him! But I'm tellin' you herself was delighted that that cock didn't crow, for she's like a clockin' hen if he leaves her sight for a minute. (*While she is talking she takes up a book from the table, looks into it in a near-sighted way, and then leaves it back. She now lifts up the sword, and proceeds to examine it.*) Be th' look of it, this must ha' been a general's sword. . . . All th' gold lace an' th' fine figaries on it. . . . Sure it's twiced too big for him.

(FLUTHER *crosses from door* L. *behind couch, back of table, where* MRS. GOGAN *is examining the sword, and looks at it, standing to* L. *of* MRS. GOGAN.)

FLUTHER (*Contemptuously*) Ah, it's a baby's rattle he ought to have, an' he as he is, with thoughts tossin' in his head of what may happen to him on th' Day of Judgement.

(PETER *appears at the curtained door, back, sees* MRS. GOGAN *with the sword, and a look of vexation comes on to his face. He comes down* C. *to the table, snatches the sword out of* MRS. GOGAN's *hands, and bangs it back on the table. He then returns into room, back, without speaking.*)

MRS. GOGAN (*To* PETER, *as he snatches the sword*) Oh, excuse me. (*To* FLUTHER.) Isn't he the surly oul' rascal, Fluther? (*She wanders from the table, back of the couch, to the chest of drawers, where she stops for a few moments, pulling out drawers and pushing them in again.*)

FLUTHER (*Leaning against left side of the table*) Take no notice of him. . . . You'd think he was dumb, but when you get his goat, or he has a few jars up,[8] he's vice versa. (FLUTHER *coughs.* MRS. GOGAN,

---

[5] The coat of arms of Ulster, adopted as a union emblem.
[6] Labor headquarters, also the home of the Citizen Army.
[7] A leather belt with a strap over the right shoulder.
[8] A few drinks in him.

who has wandered from the chest of drawers, down L. *to the fire-place, where she is fingering* PETER's *shirt, turns to look at* FLUTHER, *as soon as she hears the cough.*)

MRS. GOGAN (*With an ominous note in her voice*)   Oh, you've got a cold on you, Fluther.

FLUTHER (*Carelessly*)   Ah, it's only a little one.

MRS. GOGAN   You'd want to be careful, all th' same. I knew a woman, a big lump of a woman, red-faced an' round-bodied, a little awkward on her feet; you'd think, to look at her, she could put out her two arms an' lift a two-storied house on th' top of her head; got a ticklin' in her throat, an' a little cough, an' th' next mornin' she had a little catchin' in her chest, an' they had just time to wet her lips with a little rum, an' off she went. (*She begins to look at and handle the shirt.*)

FLUTHER (*A little nervously*)   It's only a little cold I have; there's nothing derogatory wrong with me.

MRS. GOGAN (*Warningly*)   I dunno; there's many a man this minute lowerin' a pint, thinkin' of a woman, or pickin' out a winner, or doin' work as you're doin', while th' hearse dhrawn be th' horses with the black plumes is dhrivin' up to his own hall door, an' a voice that he doesn't hear is muttherin' in his ear, "Earth to earth, an' ashes t' ashes, an' dust to dust."

FLUTHER (*Faintly, affected by her talk*)   A man in th' pink o' health should have a holy horror of allowin' thoughts o' death to be festherin' in his mind, for (*With a frightened cough*) be God, I think I'm afther gettin' a little catch in me chest that time—it's a creepy thing to be thinkin' about. (FLUTHER *sits weakly in chair* L. *of table.*)

MRS. GOGAN   It is, an' it isn't; it's both bad an' good. . . . It always gives meself a kind o' thress-passin' joy to feel meself movin' along in a mournin' couch, an' me thinkin' that, maybe, th' next funeral'll be me own, an' glad, in a quiet way, that this is somebody's else's.

FLUTHER (*Very frightened*)   An' a curious kind of a gaspin' for breath— I hope there's nothin' derogatory wrong with me.

MRS. GOGAN (*Examining the shirt*)   Frills on it, like a woman's petticoat.

FLUTHER (*Panic-stricken*)   Suddenly gettin' hot, an' then, just as sudden-ly, gettin' cold.

MRS. GOGAN (*Holding out the shirt towards* FLUTHER)   How would you like to be wearin' this Lord Mayor's nightdhress, Fluther?

FLUTHER (*Vehemently*)   Blast you an' your nightshirt! Is a man fer-mentin' with fear to stick th' showin' off to him of a thing that looks like a shinin' shroud?

MRS. GOGAN (*Startled at* FLUTHER's *vehemence*)   Oh, excuse me.
> (PETER *appears at curtained door, back. Sees his shirt in* MRS.
> GOGAN's *hand, comes rapidly down* C., *goes front of couch to* MRS.
> GOGAN, *snatches shirt from her, and replaces it on the back of the
> chair; he returns the same way to room, back.*)

PETER (*Loudly, as he goes to room, back*)   Well, God Almighty give
me patience!
> (*There is heard a cheer from the men working outside on the street,
> followed by the clang of tools being thrown down, then silence.*)

PETER (*Running into the back room to look out of the window*)   What's
the men repairin' the streets cheerin' for?

FLUTHER (*Sitting down weakly on a chair*)   You can't sneeze but that
oul' one wants to know th' why an' wherefore. . . . I feel as dizzy
as bedamned! I hope I didn't give up th' beer too suddenly.
> *The* COVEY *comes in by door* L. *He is about 25, tall, thin, with lines
> on his face that form a perpetual protest against life as he con-
> ceives it to be. Heavy seams fall from each side of nose, down
> around his lips, as if they were suspenders keeping his mouth from
> falling. He speaks in a slow, wailing drawl; more rapidly when he
> is excited. He is dressed in dungarees, and is wearing a vividly
> red tie. He comes down* C. *and flings his cap with a gesture of
> disgust on the table, and begins to take off his overalls.*

MRS. GOGAN (*To the* COVEY, *as she runs back into the room*)   What's after
happenin', Covey?

THE COVEY (*With contempt*)   Th' job's stopped. They've been mobilized
to march in th' demonstration to-night undher th' Plough an' th'
Stars. Didn't you hear them cheerin', th' mugs. They have to renew
their political baptismal vows to be faithful in *seculo seculorum.*[9]

FLUTHER (*Sitting on the chair* L. *of table, forgetting his fear in his indignation*)   There's no reason to bring religion into it. I think we ought
to have as great a regard for religion as we can, so as to keep it
out of as many things as possible.

THE COVEY (*Pausing in the taking off of his dungarees*)   Oh, you're one
o' the boys that climb into religion as high as a short Mass on
Sunday mornin's? I suppose you'll be singin' songs o' Sion[10] an'
songs o' Tara[11] at th' meetin', too.

FLUTHER   We're all Irishmen, anyhow; aren't we?

---

[9] For ever and ever.
[10] Zion.
[11] In County Meath, the home of the high kings of Ireland from ancient times
to the sixth century. During the nineteenth century, a favorite rallying place of
political factions.

THE COVEY (*With hand outstretched, and in a professional tone*) Look here, comrade, there's no such thing as an Irishman, or an Englishman, or a German or a Turk; we're all only human bein's. Scientifically speakin', it's all a question of the accidental gatherin' together of mollycewels an' atoms.

(PETER *comes in from room, back, with a stiff collar in his hand, comes down* C., *crosses, in front of couch, to the mirror on the wall* L., *below the fireplace. He stands before the mirror and tries to put on his collar.* FLUTHER *gets up from the chair, goes* C. *and stands to* R. *of the* COVEY.)

FLUTHER Mollycewels an' atoms! D'ye think I'm goin' to listen to you thryin' to juggle Fluther's mind with complicated cunundhrums of mollycewels an' atoms?

THE COVEY (*Rather loudly*) There's nothin' complicated in it. There's no fear o' th' Church tellin' you that mollycewels is a stickin' together of millions of atoms o' sodium, carbon, potassium o' iodide, etcetera, that, accordin' to th' way they're mixed, make a flower, a fish, a star that you see shinin' in th' sky, or a man with a big brain like me, or a man with a little brain like you!

FLUTHER (*More loudly still*) There's no necessity to be raisin' your voice; shoutin's no manifestin' forth of a growin' mind.

(FLUTHER *and the* COVEY *turn to look at* PETER.)

PETER (*Struggling with his collar*) God give me patience with this thing. . . . She makes these collars as stiff with starch as a shinin' band of solid steel! She does it purposely to thry an' twart me. If I can't get it on to the singlet, how in the name of God am I goin' to get it on the shirt!

(FLUTHER *and the* COVEY *face each other again.*)

THE COVEY (*Loudly*) There's no use o' arguin' with you; it's education you want, comrade.

FLUTHER (*Sarcastically*) The Covey an' God made th' world I suppose, wha'?

THE COVEY (*Jeering*) When I hear some men talkin' I'm inclined to disbelieve that th' world's eight-hundhred million years old, for it's not long since th' fathers o' some o' them crawled out o' th' sheltherin' slime o' the sea.

MRS. GOGAN (*From room at back*) There, they're afther formin' fours, an' now they're goin' to march away.

FLUTHER (*Scornfully taking no notice of* MRS. GOGAN) Mollycewels! (*He begins to untie his apron*) What about Adam an' Eve?

THE COVEY Well, what about them?

FLUTHER (*Fiercely*) What about them, you?

THE COVEY   Adam an' Eve! Is that as far as you've got? Are you still think-in' there was nobody in th' world before Adam an' Eve? (*Loudly*) Did you ever hear, man, of th' skeleton of th' man o' Java?

PETER (*Casting the collar from him*)   Blast it, blast it! (PETER *angrily picks up the collar he has thrown on the floor, goes up* C., *right of couch, to the chest of drawers, and begins to hunt again in the drawers.*)

FLUTHER (*To the* COVEY, *as he viciously folds apron*)   Ah, you're not goin' to be let tap your rubbidge o' thoughts into th' mind o' Fluther.

THE COVEY   You're afraid to listen to th' thruth!

FLUTHER (*pugnaciously*)   Who's afraid?

THE COVEY   You are!

FLUTHER (*With great contempt*)   G'way, you wurum!

THE COVEY   Who's a worum?

FLUTHER   You are, or you wouldn't talk th' way you're talkin'.
(MRS. GOGAN *wanders in from room, back, turns* L., *sees* PETER *at the chest of drawers, turns back, comes down* C., *goes, front of couch, to the fireplace.*)

THE COVEY   Th' oul', ignorant savage leppin' up in you, when science shows you that th' head of your god is an empty one. Well, I hope you're enjoyin' th' blessin' o' havin' to live be th' sweat of your brow.

FLUTHER   You'll be kickin' an' yellin' for th' priest yet, me boyo. I'm not goin' to stand silent an' simple listenin' to a thick like you makin' a maddenin' mockery o' God Almighty. It 'ud be a nice derogatory thing on me conscience, an' me dyin', to look back in rememberin' shame of talkin' to a word-weavin' little ignorant yahoo of a red flag Socialist!

MRS. GOGAN (*At the fireplace, turning to look at the disputants*)   For God's sake, Fluther, dhrop it; there's always th' makin's of a row in the mention of religion. (*She turns her head, and looks at the picture of "The Sleeping Venus," hanging over the mantelpiece. She looks at it intently and a look of astonishment comes on her face.*) God bless us, it's the picture of a naked woman. (*With a titter*) Look, Fluther.
(FLUTHER *looks over at the fireplace; comes slowly to the fireplace; looks steadily at the picture.* PETER, *hearing what was said, leaves the chest of drawers, and comes down, standing a little behind* FLUTHER *and* MRS. GOGAN, *and looks at the picture. The* COVEY *looks on from* C.)

FLUTHER   What's undher it? (*Reading slowly*) "Georgina:[12] The Sleeping Vennis." Oh, that's a terrible picture. . . . Oh, that's a shockin' picture! (*Peering into it with evident pleasure*) Oh, the one that got that taken, she must ha' been a prime lassie!

PETER   (*Laughing in a silly way, with head tilted back*)   Hee, hee, hee, hee, hee!

FLUTHER   (*Indignantly, to* PETER) What are you hee, hee-in' for? (*Pointing to the picture*) That's a nice thing to be hee, hee-in' at. Where's your morality, man?

MRS. GOGAN   (*Looking intently at it*)   God forgive us, it's not right to be lookin' at it.

FLUTHER   It's nearly a derogatory thing to be in th' room where it is.

MRS. GOGAN   (*Giggling hysterically*)   I couldn't stop any longer in th' same room with three men, afther lookin' at it! (MRS. GOGAN *goes upstage* L., *and out by door* L. *The* COVEY, *who has taken off his dungarees, seeing* PETER's *shirt on the chair, throws dungarees over it with a contemptuous movement.*)

PETER   (*Roused by the* COVEY's *action*)   Where are you throwin' your dungarees? Are you thryin' to twart an' torment me again?

THE COVEY   Who's thryin' to twart you?
(PETER *takes the dungarees from the back of the chair and flings them violently on floor.*)

PETER   You're not goin' to make me lose me temper, me young covey!
The COVEY, *in retaliation, takes* PETER's *white shirt from the back of the chair, and flings it violently on the floor.*)

THE COVEY   If you're Nora's pet aself, you're not goin' to get your own way in everything. (*The* COVEY *moves to the back end of the table, enjoying* PETER's *anger.*)

PETER   (*Plaintively, with his eyes looking up at the ceiling*)   I'll say nothin'. . . . I'll leave you to th' day when th' all-pitiful, all-merciful, all-lovin' God'll be handin' you to th' angels to be rievin' an' roastin' you, tearin' an' tormentin' you, burnin' an' blastin' you!

THE COVEY   Aren't you th' little malignant oul' bastard, you lemon-whiskered oul' swine!
(PETER *rushes to the table, takes up the sword, draws it from its scabbard, and makes for the* COVEY, *who runs round the table* R., *followed by* PETER.)

THE COVEY   (*Dodging round the table—to* FLUTHER)   Fluther, hold him, there. It's a nice thing to have a lunatic, like this, lashing round

---

[12] A mispronunciation of Giorgione (see note 1).

with a lethal weapon! (*The* COVEY, *after running round the table, rushes up* C., *and runs back of couch, out of door* L., *which he bangs to behind him in the face of* PETER. FLUTHER *remains near the fireplace, looking on.*)

PETER   (*Hammering at the door—to the* COVEY, *outside*)   Lemme out, lemme out. Isn't it a poor thing for a man who wouldn't say a word against his greatest enemy to have to listen to that Covey's twartin' animosities, shovin' poor, patient people into a lashin' out of curses that darken his soul with th' shadow of th' wrath of th' last day!

FLUTHER   Why d'ye take notice of him? If he seen you didn't, he'd say nothin' derogatory.

PETER   I'll make him stop his laughin' an' leerin', jibin' an' jeerin' an' scarifyin' people with his corner-boy insinuations! . . . He's always thryin' to rouse me: if it's not a song, it's a whistle; if it isn't a whistle, it's a cough. But you can taunt an' taunt—I'm laughin' at you; he, hee, hee, hee, hee, heee!

THE COVEY   (*Jeering loudly through the keyhole*)   Dear harp o' me counthry, in darkness I found thee, The dark chain of silence had hung o'er thee long—[13]

PETER   (*Frantically to Fluther*)   Jasus, d'ye hear that? D'ye hear him soundin' forth his divil-souled song o' provocation? (*Battering at door* L.)   When I get out I'll do for you, I'll do for you, I'll do for you!

THE COVEY   (*Through the keyhole*)   Cuckoo-oo!

(NORA *enters by door* L. *She is a young woman of 23, alert, swift, full of nervous energy, and a little anxious to get on in the world. The firm lines of her face are considerably opposed by a soft, amorous mouth, and gentle eyes. When her firmness fails her, she persuades with her feminine charm. She is dressed in a tailor-made costume, and wears around her neck a silver fox fur.*)

NORA   (*Running in and pushing* PETER *away from the door*)   Oh, can I not turn me back but th' two o' yous are at it like a pair o' fightin'-cocks! Uncle Peter . . . Uncle Peter . . . UNCLE PETER!

PETER   (*Vociferously*)   Oh, Uncle Peter, Uncle Peter be damned! D'ye think I'm goin' to give a free pass to th' young Covey to turn me whole life into a Holy Manual o' penances an' martyrdoms?

THE COVEY   (*Angrily rushing into the room*)   If you won't exercise some sort o' conthrol over that Uncle Peter o' yours, there'll be a funeral, an' it won't be me that'll be in th' hearse!

NORA   (C. *back, between* PETER *and the* COVEY, *to the* COVEY)   Are yous

[13] Poem by Thomas Moore (1779–1852).

always goin' to be tearin' down th' little bit of respectability that a body's thryin' to build up? Am I always goin' to be havin' to nurse yous into th' habit o' thryin' to keep up a little bit of appearance?

THE COVEY   Why weren't you here to see th' way he run at me with th' sword?

PETER   What did you call me a lemon-whiskered oul' swine for?

NORA   If th' two o' yous don't thry to make a generous altheration in your goin's on, an' keep on thryin' t' inaugurate th' customs o' th' rest o' th' house into this place, yous can flit into other lodgin's where your bowsey[14] battlin' 'ill meet, maybe, with an encore.
(*The* COVEY *comes down, back of couch to the fire, and sits down in the chair where* PETER's *shirt had hung; he takes a book from a pocket and begins to read.*)

PETER   (*To* NORA)   Would you like to be called a lemon-whiskered oul' swine?
(NORA *takes the sword from* PETER, *goes to the table, puts it back in the scabbard, goes to the chest of drawers, back* L., *and leaves it on the chest of drawers.*)

NORA   (*To* PETER)   If you attempt to wag that sword of yours at anybody again, it'll have to be taken off you, an' put in a safe place away from babies that don't know the danger of them things. (NORA *goes across back, taking off her hat and coat, which she leaves.* PETER *comes down* C., *takes up the shirt from the floor, and goes back* C. *towards room, back.*)

PETER   (*At entrance to room, back*)   Well, I'm not goin' to let anybody call me a lemon-whiskered oul' swine! (PETER *goes into room, back.* FLUTHER *moves from the fireplace,* L. *of couch, to door* L., *which he begins to open and shut, trying the movement.*)

FLUTHER   (*Half to himself, half to* NORA)   Openin' an' shuttin' now with a well-mannered motion, like a door of a select bar in a high-class pub.
(NORA *takes up the hat and coat from the table, carries them into the room, back, leaves them there, comes out, goes to the dresser, above table* R., *and puts a few tea things on the table.*)

NORA   (*To the* COVEY, *as she lays table for tea*)   An', once for all, Willie, you'll have to thry to deliver yourself from th' desire to practice o' provokin' oul' Pether into a wild forgetfulness of what's proper an' allowable in a respectable home.

THE COVEY   Well, let him mind his own business, then. Yestherday, I

---

[14] Drunken.

caught him hee-hee-in' out of him an' he readin' bits out of Jenersky's *Thesis on th' Origin, Development an' Consolidation of th'
Evolutionary Idea of th' Proletariat.*

NORA   Now, let it end at that, for God's sake; Jack'll be in any minute,
an' I'm not goin' to have th' quiet of his evenin' tossed about in an
everlastin' uproar between you an' Uncle Pether. (NORA *crosses
back to* FLUTHER L., *and stands on his* R.)

NORA   (*To* FLUTHER)   Well, did you manage to settle the lock yet, Mr.
Good?

FLUTHER   (*Opening and shutting the door*)   It's betther than a new one,
now, Mrs. Clitheroe; it's almost ready to open and shut of its own
accord.

NORA   (*Giving him a coin*)   You're a whole man. How many pints will
that get you?

FLUTHER   (*Seriously*)   Ne'er a one at all, Mrs. Clitheroe, for Fluther's on
th' wather waggon now. You could stan' where you're stannin'
chantin', "Have a glass o' malt, Fluther; Fluther, have a glass o'
malt," till th' bells would be ringin' th' ould year out an' th' New
Year in, an' you'd have as much chance o' movin' Fluther as a tune
on a tin whistle would move a deaf man a' he dead.

(*As* NORA *is opening and shutting the door,* MRS. BESSIE BURGESS
*appears at it. She is a woman of 40, vigorously built. Her face is a
dogged one, hardened by toil, and a little coarsened by drink. She
looks scornfully and viciously at* NORA *for a few moments before
she speaks.*)

BESSIE   Puttin' a new lock on her door . . . afraid her poor neighbours ud
break through an' steal. . . . (*In a loud tone*)   Maybe, now, they're
a damn sight more honest than your ladyship . . . checkin' th'
children playin' on th' stairs . . . gettin' on th' nerves of your ladyship. . . . Complainin' about Bessie Burgess singin' her hymns at
night, when she has a few up. . . . (*She comes in halfway on the
threshold, and screams*)   Bessie Burgess 'll sing whenever she damn
well likes!

(NORA *tries to shut the door, but* BESSIE *violently shoves it in, and,
gripping* NORA *by the shoulders, shakes her.*)

BESSIE   (*Violently*)   You little overdhressed throllope, you, for one pin,
I'd paste th' white face o' you!

NORA   (*Frightened*)   Fluther, Fluther!

FLUTHER   (*Breaking the hold of* BESSIE *from* NORA)   Now, now, Bessie,
Bessie, leave poor Mrs. Clitheroe alone; she'd do no one any harm,
an' minds no one's business but her own.

BESSIE   Why is she always thryin' to speak proud things, an' lookin' like a mighty one in th' congregation o' th' people!
(*The* COVEY *looks up from his book, watches the encounter, but does not leave his seat by the fire.* NORA *sinks down on back of the couch.* JACK CLITHEROE *enters by door,* L. *He is a tall, well-made fellow of 25. His face has none of the strength of* NORA's. *It is a face in which is the desire for authority, without the power to attain it.*)

CLITHEROE   (*Excitedly*)   What's up? What's afther happenin'?

FLUTHER   Nothin', Jack. Nothin'. It's all over now. Come on, Bessie, come on.

CLITHEROE   (*Coming to couch and bending over* NORA—*anxiously*)   What's wrong, Nora? Did she say anything to you?

NORA   (*Agitatedly*)   She was bargin' out of her, an' I only told her to go up ower that to her own place; an' before I knew where I was, she flew at me, like a tiger, an' tried to guzzle me.
(CLITHEROE *goes close to* BESSIE, *standing in front of the chest of drawers, and takes hold of her arm to get her away.*)

CLITHEROE   Get up to your own place, Mrs. Burgess, and don't you be interferin' with my wife, or it'll be th' worse for you. . . . Go on, go on!

BESSIE   (*As* CLITHEROE *is pushing her out*)   Mind who you're pushin', now. . . . I attend me place of worship, anyhow. . . . Not like some of them that go neither church, chapel or meetin' house. . . . If me son was home from the threnches, he'd see me righted.
(FLUTHER *takes* BESSIE *by the arm, and brings her out by the door* L. CLITHEROE *closes the door behind them, returns to* NORA, *and puts his arm around her. The* COVEY *resumes his reading.*)

CLITHEROE   (*His arm around her*)   There, don't mind that old bitch, Nora, darling; I'll soon put a stop to her interferin'.

NORA   Some day or another, when I'm here be meself, she'll come in an' do somethin' desperate.

CLITHEROE   (*Kissing her*)   Oh, sorra fear of her doin' anythin' desperate. I'll talk to her to-morrow when she's sober. A taste o' me mind that'll shock her into the sensibility of behavin' herself!
(NORA *gets up, crosses to the dresser* R., *and finishes laying the table for tea. She catches sight of the dungarees on the floor and speaks indignantly to* COVEY. CLITHEROE *leaves his hat on the chest of drawers, and sits, waiting for tea, on the couch.*)

NORA   (*To* COVEY)   Willie, is that the place for your dungarees?

COVEY   (*Irritably rising, and taking them from the floor*)   Ah, they won't do the floor any harm, will they? (*He carries them up* C., *into room back, comes back again, down* C., *and sits by fire.* NORA *crosses from the table to the fire, gets the teapot from the hob, and returns to the table.*)

NORA (*To* CLITHEROE *and* COVEY) Tea's ready.

(CLITHROE *and* COVEY *go to the table and sit down* L. *of same,* COVEY *nearest the audience.* NORA *sits down on* R. *of table, leaving the chair for* PETER *below, on same side.*)

NORA (*Calling towards room, back*) Uncle Peter, Uncle Peter, tea's ready!

(PETER *comes in from room back.* PETER *is in the full dress of the Irish National Foresters: bright green, gold-braided coat, white breeches, black top boots and frilled, white shirt. He carries a large black slouch hat, from which waves a long white ostrich plume, in his hand. He puts the hat on the chest of drawers beside the sword, he comes down* C., *goes round front end of table, and sits on the vacant seat facing* COVEY *on opposite side of the table. They eat for a few moments in silence, the* COVEY *furtively watching* PETER *with scorn in his eyes;* PETER *knows this, and is fidgety.*)

THE COVEY (*Provokingly*) Another cut o' bread, Uncle Peter? (PETER *maintains a dignified silence.*)

CLITHEROE It's sure to be a great meetin' to-night. We ought to go, Nora.

NORA (*Decisively*) I won't go, Jack; you can go if you wish.

(*A pause.*)

THE COVEY (*With great politeness, to* PETER) D'ye want th' sugar, Uncle Peter?

PETER (*Explosively*) Now, are you goin' to start your thryin' an' your twartin' again?

NORA Now, Uncle Peter, you mustn't be so touchy; Willie has only assed you if you wanted th' sugar.

PETER (*Angrily*) He doesn't care a damn whether I want th' sugar or no. He's only thryin' to twart me!

NORA (*Angrily, to the* COVEY) Can't you let him alone, Willie? If he wants the sugar, let him stretch his hand out an' get it himself!

THE COVEY (*To* PETER) Now, if you want the sugar, you can stretch out your hand and get it yourself!

(*A pause.*)

CLITHEROE To-night is th' first chance that Brennan has got of showing himself off since they made a Captain of him—why, God only knows. It'll be a treat to see him swankin' it at th' head of the Citizen Army carryin' th' flag of the Plough an' th' Stars. . . . (*Looking roguishly at Nora*) He was sweet on you, once, Nora?

NORA   He may have been. . . . I never liked him. I always thought he
     was a bit of a thick.

THE COVEY   They're bringin' nice disgrace on that banner now.

CLITHEROE   (*To* COVEY, *remonstratively*)   How are they bringin' disgrace
     on it?

THE COVEY   (*Snappily*)   Because it's a Labour flag, an' was never meant
     for politics. . . . What does th' design of th' field plough, bearin'
     on it th' stars of th' heavenly plough, mean, if it's not Communism?
     It's a flag that should only be used when we're buildin' th' barri-
     cades to fight for a Workers' Republic!

PETER   (*With a puff of derision*)   P-phuh.

THE COVEY   (*Angrily, to* PETER)   What are you phuhin' out o' you for?
     Your mind is th' mind of a mummy. (*Rising*) I betther go an' get a
     good place to have a look at Ireland's warriors passin' by. (*He
     goes into room* L., *and returns with his cap.*)

NORA   (*To the* COVEY)   Oh, Willie, brush your clothes before you go.

THE COVEY   (*Carelessly*)   Oh, they'll do well enough.

NORA   Go an' brush them; th' brush is in th' drawer there.
     (*The* COVEY *goes to the drawer, muttering, gets the brush, and
     starts to brush his clothes.*)

THE COVEY   (*Reciting at* PETER, *as he does so*)

> *Oh, where's the slave so lowly,*
> *Condemn'd to chains unholy,*
> *Who, could he burst his bonds at first,*
> *Would pine beneath them slowly?*
> *We tread th' land that . . . bore us,*
> *Th' green flag glitters . . . o'er us,*
> *Th' friends we've tried are by our side,*
> *An' th' foe we hate . . . before us!*

PETER   (*Leaping to his feet in a whirl of rage*)   Now, I'm tellin' you, me
     young Covey, once for all, that I'll not stick any longer these titther-
     in' taunts of yours, rovin' around to sing your slights an' slandhers,
     reddenin' th' mind of a man to th' thinkin' an' sayin' of things that
     sicken his soul with sin! (*Hysterically; lifting up a cup to fling at
     the* COVEY) Be God, I'll—

CLITHEROE   (*Catching his arm*)   Now then, none o' that, none o' that!

NORA   (*Loudly*)   Uncle Pether, Uncle Pether, UNCLE PETHER!

THE COVEY   (*At the door* L., *about to go out*)   Isn't that th' malignant oul'
     varmint! Lookin' like th' illegitimate son of an illegitimate child of a
     corporal in th' Mexican army! (*He goes out door* L.)

PETER   (*Plaintively*)   He's afther leavin' me now in such a state of agitation that I won't be able to do meself justice when I'm marchin' to th' meetin'.

(NORA *jumps up from the table, crosses back end of table to the chest of drawers, back, and takes up* PETER's *sword.*)

NORA   Oh, for God's sake, here, buckle your sword on, an' go to your meetin', so that we'll have at least one hour of peace.

PETER *gets up from the chair, goes over to* NORA, *and she helps him to put on his sword.*

CLITHEROE   For God's sake, hurry him up out o' this, Nora.

PETER   Are yous all goin' to thry to start to twart me now?

NORA   (*Putting on his plumed hat*)   S-s-sh. Now, your hat's on, your house is thatched; off you pop! (*She gently pushes him from her, towards door* L.)

PETER   (*Going and turning as he reaches the door* L.)   Now, if that young Covey—

NORA   Go on, go on. (*He goes out door* L.)

(CLITHEROE *goes from the table to the couch and sits down on end nearest the fire, lights a cigarette, and looks thoughtfully into the fire.* NORA *takes things from the table, and puts them on the dresser. She goes into room, back, and comes back with a lighted shaded lamp, which she puts on the table. She then goes on tidying things on the dresser. Softly speaking over from the dresser, to* CLITHEROE.) A penny for them, Jack.

CLITHEROE   Me? Oh, I was thinkin' of nothing.

NORA   You were thinkin' of th' . . . meetin' . . . Jack. When we were courtin' an' I wanted you to go, you'd say, "Oh, to hell with meetin's," an' that you felt lonely in cheerin' crowds when I was absent. An' we weren't a month married when you began that you couldn't keep away from them.

CLITHEROE   (*Crossly*)   Oh, that's enough about th' meetin'. It looks as if you wanted me to go th' way you're talkin'. You were always at me to give up the Citizen Army, an' I gave it up: surely that ought to satisfy you.

NORA   (*From dresser*)   Aye, you gave it up, because you got the sulks when they didn't make a captain of you. (*She crosses over to* CLITHEROE, *and sits on the couch to his* R.)

NORA   (*Softly*)   It wasn't for my sake, Jack.

CLITHEROE   For your sake or no, you're benefitin' by it, aren't you? I didn't forget this was your birthday, did I? (*He puts his arms around her*) And you liked your new hat; didn't you, didn't you? (*He kisses her rapidly several times.*)

NORA (*Panting*)   Jack, Jack; please, Jack! I thought you were tired of that sort of thing long ago.

CLITHEROE   Well, you're finding out now that I amn't tired of it yet, anyhow. Mrs. Clitheroe doesn't want to be kissed, sure she doesn't? (*He kisses her again*) Little, little red-lipped Nora!

NORA (*Coquettishly removing his arm from around her*)   Oh, yes, your little, little red-lipped Nora's a sweet little girl when th' fit seizes you; but your little, little red-lipped Nora has to clean your boots every mornin', all the same.

CLITHEROE (*With a movement of irritation*)   Oh, well, if we're goin' to be snotty! (*A pause.*)

NORA   It's lookin' like as if it was you that was goin' to be . . . snotty! Bridlin' up with bittherness, th' minute a body attempts t'open her mouth.

CLITHEROE   Is it any wondher, turnin' a tendher sayin' into a meanin' o' malice an' spite!

NORA   It's hard for a body to be always keepin' her mind bent on makin' thoughts that'll be no longer than th' length of your own satisfaction.
(*A pause.*)

NORA (*Standing up*)   If we're goin' to dhribble th' time away sittin' here like a pair o' cranky mummies, I'd be as well sewin' or doin' something about th' place.
(*She looks appealingly at him for a few moments; he doesn't speak She swiftly sits down beside him, and puts her arms around his neck.*)

NORA (*Imploringly*)   Ah, Jack, don't be so cross!

CLITHEROE (*Doggedly*)   Cross? I'm not cross; I'm not a bit cross. It was yourself started it.

NORA (*Coaxingly*)   I didn't mean to say anything out o' th' way. You take a body up too quickly, Jack. (*In an ordinary tone as if nothing of an angry nature had been said*) You didn't offer me evenin' allowance yet.
(CLITHEROE *silently takes out a cigarette for her and himself and lights both. Trying to make conversation.*)
How quiet th' house is now; they must be all out.

CLITHEROE (*Rather shortly*)   I suppose so.

NORA (*Rising from the seat*)   I'm longin' to show you me new hat, to see what you think of it. Would you like to see it?

CLITHEROE   Ah, I don't mind.
(NORA *hesitates a moment, then goes up* C. *to the chest of drawers, takes the hat out of the box, comes down* C., *stands front of the*

couch, looks into the mirror on the wall below the fireplace, and fixes hat on her head. She then turns to face CLITHEROE.)

NORA Well, how does Mr. Clitheroe like me new hat?

CLITHEROE It suits you, Nora, it does right enough. (*He stands up, puts his hand beneath her chin, and tilts her head up. She looks at him roguishly. He bends down and kisses her.*)

NORA Here, sit down, an' don't let me hear another cross word out of you for th' rest o' the night. (*The two sit on the couch again,* CLITHEROE *nearest the fire.*)

CLITHEROE (*His arms round* NORA) Little red-lipped Nora.

NORA (*With a coaxing movement of her body towards him*) Jack!

CLITHEROE (*Tightening his arms around her*) Well?

NORA You haven't sung me a song since our honeymoon. Sing me one now, do . . . please, Jack!

CLITHEROE What song? "Since Maggie Went Away"?

NORA Ah, no, Jack, not that; it's too sad. "When You Said You Loved Me."

(*Clearing his throat,* CLITHEROE *thinks for a moment, and then begins to sing.* NORA, *putting an arm around him, nestles her head on his breast and listens delightedly.*)

CLITHEROE (*Singing verses following to the air of "When You and I Were Young, Maggie"*)

Th' violets were scenting th' woods, Nora,
  Displaying their charm to th' bee,
When I first said I lov'd only you, Nora,
  An' you said you lov'd only me!
Th' chestnut blooms gleam'd through th' glade, Nora,
  A robin sang loud from a tree,
When I first said I lov'd you, Nora
  An' you said you lov'd only me!
Th' golden-rob'd daffodils shone, Nora,
  An' danc'd in th' breeze on th' lea;
When I first said I lov'd only you, Nora,
  An' you said you lov'd only me!
Th' trees, birds an' bees sang a song, Nora,
  Of happier transports to be,
When I first said I lov'd only you, Nora,
  An' you said you lov'd only me!

(NORA *kisses him. A knock is heard at the door,* R.; *a pause as they listen.* NORA *clings closely to* CLITHEROE. *Another knock, more imperative than the first.*)

I wonder who can that be, now?

NORA (*A little nervous*)   Take no notice of it, Jack; they'll go away in a minute.

(*Another knock, followed by the voice of* CAPTAIN BRENNAN.)

THE VOICE OF CAPT. BRENNAN   Commandant Clitheroe, Commandant Clitheroe, are you there? A message from General Jim Connolly.

CLITHEROE (*Taking her arms from round him*)   Damn it, it's Captain Brennan.

NORA (*Anxiously*)   Don't mind him, don't mind, Jack. Don't break our happiness. . . . Pretend we're not in. . . . Let us forget everything to-night but our two selves!

CLITHEROE (*Reassuringly*)   Don't be alarmed, darling; I'll just see what he wants, an' send him about his business.

NORA (*Tremulously—putting her arms around him*)   No, no. Please, Jack; don't open it. Please, for your own little Nora's sake!

CLITHEROE (*Taking her arms away and rising to open the door*)   Now don't be silly, Nora. (CLITHEROE *opens door, and admits a young man in the full uniform of the Irish Citizen Army—green suit; slouch green hat caught up at one side by a small Red Hand badge; Sam Browne belt, with a revolver in the holster. He carries a letter in his hand. When he comes in he smartly salutes* CLITHEROE. *The young man is* CAPTAIN BRENNAN. *He stands in front of the chest of drawers.*)

CAPT. BRENNAN (*Giving the letter to* CLITHEROE)   A dispatch from General Connolly.

CLITHEROE (*Reading. While he doing so,* BRENNAN's *eyes are fixed on* NORA, *who droops as she sits on the lounge*)   "Commandant Clitheroe is to take command of the eighth battalion of the I.C.A. which will assemble to proceed to the meeting at nine o'clock. He is to see that all units are provided with full equipment: two days' rations and fifty rounds of ammunition. At two o'clock A.M. the army will leave Liberty Hall for a reconaissance attack on Dublin Castle.—Com.-Gen. Connolly."

CLITHEROE (*In surprise, to* CAPT. BRENNAN)   I don't understand this. Why does General Connolly call me Commandant?

CAPT. BRENNAN   Th' Staff appointed you Commandant, and th' General agreed with their selection.

CLITHEROE   When did this happen?

CAPT. BRENNAN   A fortnight ago.

CLITHEROE   How is it word was never sent to me?

CAPT. BRENNAN   Word was sent to you. . . . I meself brought it.

CLITHEROE   Who did you give it to, then?

CAPT. BRENNAN (*After a pause*)   I think I gave it to Mrs. Clitheroe, there.

CLITHEROE   Nora, d'ye hear that? (NORA *makes no answer. Standing* C.—
there is a note of hardness in his voice) Nora . . . Captain Brennan
says he brought a letter to me from General Connolly, and that he
gave it to you. . . . Where is it? What did you do with it?
(CAPT. BRENNAN *stands in front of the chest of drawers, and softly
whistles "The Soldiers' Song".*[15])

NORA   (*Running over to him, and pleadingly putting her arms around him*)
Jack, please Jack, don't go out to-night an' I'll tell you; I'll explain
everything. . . . Send him away, an' stay with your own little red-
lipp'd Nora.

CLITHEROE   (*Removing her arms from around him*)   None o' this nonsense, now; I want to know what you did with th' letter? (NORA
goes slowly to the couch and sits down again. Angrily) Why
didn't you give me th' letter? What did you do with it? . . . (*Goes
over and shakes her by the shoulder*) What did you do with th'
letter?

NORA   (*Flaming up and standing on her feet*)   I burned it, I burned it!
That's what I did with it! Is General Connolly an' th' Citizen
Army goin' to be your only care? Is your home goin' to be only a
place to rest in? Am I goin' to be only somethin' to provide merry-
makin' at night for you? Your vanity 'll be th' ruin of you an' me
yet. . . . That's what's movin' you: because they've made an officer
of you, you'll make a glorious cause of what you're doin', while
your little red-lipp'd Nora can go on sittin' here, makin' a companion of th' loneliness of th' night!

CLITHEROE   (*Fiercely*)   You burned it, did you? (*He grips her arm*)
Well, me good lady—

NORA   Let go—you're hurtin' me!

CLITHEROE   You deserve to be hurt. . . . Any letther that comes to me
for th' future, take care that I get it. . . . D'ye hear—take care that
I get it! (*He lets her go, and she sinks down, crying on the couch.
He goes to the chest of drawers and takes out a Sam Browne belt,
which he puts on, and then puts a revolver in the holster. He puts
on his hat, and looks towards* NORA. *At door* L., *about to go
out*) You needn't wait up for me; if I'm in at all, it won't be before
six in th' morning.

NORA   (*Bitterly*)   I don't care if you never came back!

CLITHEROE   (*To* CAPT. BRENNAN)   Come along, Ned.
(*They go out; there is a pause.* NORA *pulls the new hat from her*

[15] Popular song among the rebels, became the national anthem of the Republic
of Ireland. Its first verse goes: "Soldiers are we, whose lives are pledged to Ireland,/
Some have come from a land beyond the wave,/Sworn to be free, no more our ancient
sireland/Shall shelter the despot or the slave."

head and with a bitter movement flings it to the other end of the
room. There is a gentle knock at door L., *which opens, and* MOLLSER
comes into the room. She is about 15, but looks to be only about 10,
for the ravages of consumption have shrivelled her up. She is
pitifully worn, walks feebly, and frequently coughs. She goes over
and sits down L. *of* NORA.)

MOLLSER (*To* NORA) Mother's gone to th' meetin', an' I was feelin'
terrible lonely, so I come down to see if you'd let me sit with you,
thinkin' you mightn't be goin' yourself. . . . I do be terrible afraid
I'll die sometime when I'm be meself. . . . I often envy you, Mrs.
Clitheroe, seein' th' health you have, an' th' lovely place you have
here, an' wondherin' if I'll ever be sthrong enough to be keepin' a
home together for a man.
(*The faint sound of a band playing is heard in the distance outside*
in the street.)

MOLLSER Oh this must be some more of the Dublin Fusiliers flyin' off
to the front.
(*The band, passing in the street outside, is now heard loudly play-*
ing as they pass the house. It is the music of a brass band playing
a regiment to the boat on the way to the front. The tune that is
being played is "It's a Long Way to Tipperary"; as the band comes
to the chorus, the regiment is swinging into the street by NORA's
house, and the voices of the soldiers can be heard lustily singing
the chorus of the song.

It's a long way to Tipperary, it's a long way to go;
It's a long way to Tipperary, to th' sweetest girl I know!
Good-bye, Piccadilly, farewell Leicester Square.
It's a long way to Tipperary, but my heart's right there!

NORA *and* MOLLSER *remain silently listening. As the chorus ends,*
and the music is faint in the distance again, BESSIE BURGESS *appears*
at the door L., *which* MOLLSER *has left open.*)

BESSIE (*Speaking in towards the room*) There's th' men marchin' out into
th' dhread dimness o' danger, while th' lice is crawlin' about feedin'
on th' fatness o' the land! But yous'll not escape from th' arrow that
flieth be night, or th' sickness that wasteth be day.[16] . . . An' ladyship an' all, as some o' them may be, they'll be scatthered abroad,
like th' dust in th' darkness! (BESSIE *goes away;* NORA *steals over*
and quietly shuts the door. She comes back to the lounge and
wearily throws herself on it beside MOLLSER.)

MOLLSER (*After a pause and a cough*) Is there anybody goin', Mrs.
Clitheroe, with a titther o' sense?

[16] Misquotation of Psalms, 91:5-6.

Act II

SCENE—*A public-house at the corner of the street in which the meeting is being addressed from Platform No. 1. One end of the house is visible to the audience. Part of the counter at the back, L., extending out towards L., occupies one-third of the width of the scene from R. to L. On the counter are glasses, beer-pulls, and a carafe filled with water. Behind the counter, on the back wall, are shelves containing bottles of wine, whiskey and beer. At back C. is a wide, high, plate-glass window. Under the window is a seat to hold three or four persons seated. L. are the wide swing-doors. At wall, R., is a seat to hold two persons. A few gaudy-coloured show-cards on the walls. A band is heard outside playing "The Soldiers' Song," before the* Curtain *rises, and for a few moments afterwards, accompanied by the sounds of marching men. The* BARMAN *is seen wiping the part of the counter which is in view.* ROSIE REDMOND *is standing at the counter toying with what remains of a half of whisky in a wine-glass. She is a sturdy well-shaped girl of 20; pretty and pert in manner. She is wearing a cream blouse, with an obviously suggestive glad neck; a grey tweed dress, brown stockings and shoes. The blouse and most of the dress are hidden by a black shawl. She has no hat, and in her hair is jauntily set a cheap, glittering, jewelled ornament. It is an hour later.*

BARMAN (*Wiping counter*)   Nothin' much doin' in your line to-night, Rosie?

ROSIE   Curse o' God on th' haporth,[1] hardly, Tom. There isn't much notice taken of a pretty petticoat of a night like this. . . . They're all in a holy mood. Th' solemn-lookin' dials on th' whole o' them an' they marchin' to th' meetin'. You'd think they were th' glorious company of th' saints, an' th' noble army of martyrs thrampin' through th' streets of Paradise. They're all thinkin' of higher things than a girl's garthers. . . . It's a tremendous meetin'; four platforms they have— there's one o' them just outside opposite th' window.

BARMAN   Oh, ay; sure when th' speaker comes (*Motioning with his hand*) to th' near end, here, you can see him plain, an' hear nearly everythin' he's spoutin' out of him.

---

[1] Contraction of halfpennyworth.

ROSIE   It's no joke thryin' to make up fifty-five shillin's a week for your
keep an' laundhry, an' then taxin' you a quid[2] for your own room if
you bring home a friend for th' night. . . . If I could only put by a
couple of quid for a swankier outfit, everythin' in th' garden ud look
lovely—
(*In the window, back, appears the figure of a tall man, who, standing on a platform, is addressing a crowd outside. The figure is
almost like a silhouette. The* BARMAN *comes to* L. *end of counter to
listen, and* ROSIE *moves* C. *to see and listen too.*)

BARMAN   (*To* ROSIE)   Whisht, till we hear what he's sayin'.

THE VOICE OF THE MAN   It is a glorious thing to see arms in the hands of
Irishmen. We must accustom ourselves to the thought of arms, we
must accustom ourselves to the sight of arms, we must accustom
ourselves to the use of arms. . . . Bloodshed is a cleansing and
sanctifying thing, and the nation that regards it as the final horror
has lost its manhood. . . . There are many things more horrible than
bloodshed, and slavery is one of them!
(*The figure, moving towards* L., *passes the window, and is lost to
sight and hearing. The* BARMAN *goes back to wiping of the counter.*
ROSIE *remains looking out of the window.*)

ROSIE   It's th' sacred thruth, mind you, what that man's afther sayin'.

BARMAN   If I was only a little younger, I'd be plungin' mad into th'
middle of it!

ROSIE   (*Who is still looking out of the window*)   Oh, here's th' two gems
runnin' over again for their oil!
(*The doors* L. *swing open, and* FLUTHER *and* PETER *enter tumultu-
ously. They are hot and hasty with the things they have seen and
heard. They hurry across to the counter,* PETER *leading the way.*
ROSIE, *after looking at them listlessly for a moment, retires to the
seat under the window, sits down, takes a cigarette from her
pocket, lights it and smokes.*)

PETER   (*Sputteringly to the* BARMAN)   Two halves . . . (*To* FLUTHER)   A
meetin' like this always makes me feel as if I could dhrink Loch
Erinn dhry!

FLUTHER   You couldn't feel anyway else at a time like this when th'
spirit of a man is pulsin' to be out fightin' for th' thruth with his feet
thremblin' on th' way, maybe to th' gallows, an' his ears tinglin'
with th' faint, far-away sound of burstin' rifle-shots that'll maybe
whip th' last little shock o' life out of him that's left lingerin' in
his body!

---

[2] Slang for a pound.

PETER   I felt a burnin' lump in me throat when I heard th' band playin' "The Soldiers' Song," rememberin' last hearin' it marchin' in military formation, with th' people starin' on both sides at us, carrin' with us th' pride an' resolution o' Dublin to th' grave of Wolfe Tone.[3]

FLUTHER   Get th' Dublin men goin' an' they'll go on full force for anything that's thryin' to bar them away from what they're wantin', where th' slim thinkin' counthry boyo ud limp away from th' first faintest touch of compromization!

PETER   (*Hurriedly to the* BARMAN)   Two more, Tom! . . . (*To* FLUTHER) Th' memory of all th' things that was done, an' all th' things that was suffered be th' people, was boomin' in me brain. . . . Every nerve in me body was quiverin' to do somethin' desperate!

FLUTHER   Jammed as I was in th' crowd, I listened to th' speeches pattherin' on th' people's head, like rain fallin' on th' corn; every derogatory thought went out o' me mind, an' I said to meself, "You can die now, Fluther, for you've seen th' shadow-dhreams of th' last leppin' to life in th' bodies of livin' men that show, if we were without a titther o' courage for centuries, we're vice versa now!" Looka here. (*He stretches out his arm under* PETER's *face and rolls up his sleeve.*) The blood was *boilin'* in me veins!
(*The silhouette of the tall figure again moves into the frame of the window, speaking to the people.*)

PETER   (*Unaware, in his enthusiasm, of the speaker's appearance, to* FLUTHER)   I was burnin' to dhraw me sword, an' wave it over me—

FLUTHER   (*Overwhelming* PETER)   Will you stop your blatherin' for a minute, man, an' let us hear what he's sayin'!
The BARMAN *comes to* L. *end of the counter to look at the figure in the window;* ROSIE *rises from the seat, stands and looks.* FLUTHER *and* PETER *move towards* C. *to see and listen.*

THE VOICE OF THE MAN   Comrade soldiers of the Irish Volunteers and of the Citizen Army, we rejoice in this terrible war. The old heart of the earth needed to be warmed with the red wine of the battlefields. . . . Such august homage was never offered to God as this: the homage of millions of lives given gladly for love of country. And we must be ready to pour out the same red wine in the same glorious sacrifice, for without shedding of blood there is no redemption!

---

[3] Theobald Wolfe Tone (1763–98), one of the leaders of the United Irishmen, led them in 1798 in an unsuccessful rising against the British.

(*The figure moves out of sight and hearing.* FLUTHER *runs back to the counter and gulps down the drink remaining in his glass;* PETER *does the same, less rapidly; the* BARMAN *leaves the end of the counter;* ROSIE *sits on the seat again.*)

FLUTHER (*Finishing drink, to* PETER) Come on, man; this is too good to be missed! (FLUTHER *rushes across the stage and out by doors* L. PETER *wipes his mouth and hurries after* FLUTHER. *The doors swing open, and the* COVEY *enters. He collides with* PETER C. PETER *stiffens his body, like a cock, and, with a look of hatred on his face, marches stiffly out by doors* L. *The* COVEY *looks scornfully after* PETER, *and then crosses to the counter.* ROSIE *sees possibilities in the* COVEY, *gets up and comes to the counter, a little to the* L. *of the* COVEY.)

THE COVEY (*To* BARMAN) Give us a glass o' malt, for God's sake, till I stimulate meself from the shock of seeing the sight that's afther goin' out.

ROSIE (*Slyly, to the* BARMAN) Another one for me, Tommy; the young gentleman's ordherin' it in the corner of his eyes.

(*The* BARMAN *gets a drink for the* COVEY, *leaves it on the counter;* ROSIE *whips it up. The* BARMAN *catches* ROSIE's *arm, and takes glass from her, putting it down beside the* COVEY.)

BARMAN (*Taking the glass from* ROSIE) Eh, houl' on there, houl' on there, Rosie.

ROSIE (*Angrily, to the* BARMAN) What are you houldin' on out o' you for? Didn't you hear th' young gentleman say that he couldn't refuse anything to a nice little bird? (*To the* COVEY) Isn't that right, Jiggs? (*The* COVEY *says nothing*) Didn't I know, Tommy, it would be all right? It takes Rosie to size a young man up, an' tell th' thoughts that are thremblin' in his mind. Isn't that right, Jiggs? (*The* COVEY *stirs uneasily, moves a little farther away, and pulls his cap over his eyes. Moving after him*) Great meetin' that's gettin' held outside. Well, it's up to us all, anyway, to fight for our freedom.

THE COVEY (*To the* BARMAN) Two more, please. (*To* ROSIE) Freedom! What's th' use o' freedom, if it's not economic freedom?

ROSIE (*Emphasizing with extended arm and moving finger*) I used them very words just before you come in. "A lot o' thricksters," says I, "that wouldn't know what freedom was if they got it from their mother." . . . (*To the* BARMAN) Didn't I, Tommy?

BARMAN I disremember.

ROSIE (*To the* BARMAN) No, you don't disremember. Remember you said, yourself, it was all "only a flash in th' pan." Well, "flash in th' pan, or no flash in th' pan," says I, "they're not goin' to get Rosie

Redmond," says I, "to fight for freedom that wouldn't be worth winnin' in a raffle!"

THE COVEY (*Contemptuously*) There's only one freedom for th' workin' man: conthrol o' th' means o' production, rates of exchange an' th' means of disthribution. (*Tapping* ROSIE *on the shoulder*) Look here, comrade, I'll leave here to-morrow night for you a copy of Jenersky's *Thesis on the Origin, Development an' Consolidation of the Evolutionary Idea of th' Proletariat.*

ROSIE (*Throwing off her shawl on to the counter, and showing an exemplified glad neck, which reveals a good deal of a white bosom*) If y'ass Rosie, it's heartbreakin' to see a young fella thinkin' of anything, or admirin' anything, but silk thransparent stockin's showin' off the shape of a little lassie's legs! (*The* COVEY *is frightened, and moves away from* ROSIE *along the counter, towards* R. ROSIE *follows, gliding after him in a seductive way. Following him*) Out in th' park in th' shade of a warm summery evenin', with your little darlin' bridie to be, kissin' an' cuddlin' (*She tries to put her arm around his neck*) kissin' an' cuddlin', ay?

THE COVEY (*Frightened*) Ay, what are you doin'? None o' that, now; none o' that. I've something else to do besides shinannickin' after Judies! (*The* COVEY *turns to* L. *and moves slowly to* L., *away from* ROSIE; *she turns with him, keeping him facing her, holding his arm. They move this way to* C.)

ROSIE Oh, little duckey, oh, shy little duckey! Never held a mot's[4] hand, an' wouldn't know how to tittle a little Judy! (*She clips him under the chin*) Tittle him undher th' chin, tittle him undher th' chin!

THE COVEY (*Breaking away and running out by doors* L.) Aye, go on, now; I don't want to have any meddlin' with a lassie like you!

ROSIE (*Enraged—returning to the seat at the window*) Jasus, it's in a monasthery some of us ought to be, spendin' our holidays kneelin' on our adorers, tellin' our beads an' knockin' hell out of our buzzums!

(*The voice of the* COVEY *is heard outside doors* L. *calling in a scale of notes,* "Cuckoo-ooooo." *Then the swing-doors open, and* PETER *and* FLUTHER, *followed by* MRS. GOGAN, *come in.* MRS. GOGAN *carries a baby in her arms.*)

PETER (*In plaintive anger, looking towards the door* L.) It's terrible that young Covey can't let me pass without proddin' at me! Did you hear him murmurin' "cuckoo" when he were passin'?

FLUTHER (*Irritably—to* PETER) I wouldn't be everlastin' cockin' me ear to hear every little whisper that was floatin' around about me! It's

---

[4] Mot, slang for girl.

my rule never to lose me temper till it would be dethrimental to keep it. There's nothin' derogatory in th' use o' th' word "cuckoo," is there?

(MRS. GOGAN, *followed by* PETER, *go up the seat under the window and sit down,* PETER *to the R. of* MRS. GOGAN. ROSIE *after a look at those who've come in, out by doors* L.)

PETER (*Tearfully*)   It's not the word, it's the way he says it! He never says it straight, but murmurs it with curious quiverin' ripples, like variations on a flute.

FLUTHER (*Standing in front of the seat*)   A' what odds if he gave it with variations on a thrombone? (*To* MRS. GOGAN) What's yours goin' to be, maam?

MRS. GOGAN   Ah, half a malt, Fluther.

FLUTHER *goes from the seat over to the counter.*

FLUTHER (*To the* BARMAN)   Three halves, Tommy.

(*The* BARMAN *gets the drinks, leaves them on the counter.* FLUTHER *pays the* BARMAN; *takes drinks to the seat under the window; gives one to* MRS. GOGAN, *one to* PETER, *and keeps the third for himself. He then sits on the seat to the* L. *of* MRS. GOGAN.)

MRS. GOGAN (*Drinking, and looking admiringly at* PETER's *costume*)   The Foresthers' is a gorgeous dhress! I don't think I've seen nicer, mind you, in a pantomime. . . . Th' loveliest part of th' dhress, I think, is th' osthrichess plume. . . . When yous are goin' along, an' I see them wavin' an' noddin' an' waggin', I seem to be lookin' at each of yous hangin' at th' end of a rope, your eyes bulgin' an' your legs twistin' an' jerkin', gaspin' an' gaspin' for breath while yous are thryin' to die for Ireland!

FLUTHER (*Scornfully*)   If any o' them is ever hangin' at the end of a rope, it won't be for Ireland!

PETER   Are you goin' to start th' young Covey's game o' proddin' an' twartin' a man? There's not many that's talkin' can say that for twenty-five years he never missed a pilgrimage to Bodenstown!

FLUTHER (*Looking angrily at* PETER)   You're always blowin' about goin' to Bodenstown. D'ye think no one but yourself ever went to *Bodenstown?* (FLUTHER *emphasizes the word* "Bodenstown".)

PETER (*Plaintively*)   I'm not blowin' about it; but there's not a year that I go there but I pluck a leaf of Tone's grave, an' this very day me prayer-book is nearly full of them.

FLUTHER (*Scornfully*)   Then Fluther has a vice-versa opinion of them that put ivy leaves into their prayer-books, scabbin' it on th' clergy, an' thryin' to out-do th' haloes o' th' saints be lookin' as if he was wearin' around his head a glittherin' aroree boree allis! (*Fiercely*) Sure, I don't care a damn if you slep' in *Bodenstown!* You can take your breakfast, dinner an' tea on th' grave, in Bodenstown, if you like, for Fluther!

MRS. GOGAN   Oh, don't start a fight, boys, for God's sake; I was only sayin' what a nice costume it is—nicer than th' kilts, for, God forgive me, I always think th' kilts is hardly decent.

FLUTHER (*Laughing scornfully*)   Ah, sure when you'd look at him, you'd wondher whether th' man was makin' fun o' th' costume, or th' costume was makin' fun o' th' man!

BARMAN (*Over to them*)   Now, then, thry to speak asy, will yous? We don't want no shoutin' here.

(*The swing-doors open and the* COVEY, *followed by* BESSIE BURGESS, *come in. They go over and stand at the counter. Passing,* BESSIE *gives a scornful look at those seated near the window.* BESSIE *and the* COVEY *talk together, but frequently eye the group at the window.*)

COVEY (*To the* BARMAN)   Two glasses o' malt.

(*The* BARMAN *gets the drinks; leaves them on the counter. The* COVEY *puts one beside* BESSIE *and keeps the other. He pays the* BARMAN.)

PETER (*Plaintively*)   There he is now—I knew he wouldn't be long till he folleyed me in.

BESSIE (*Speaking to the* COVEY, *but really at the other party*)   I can't for th' life o' me undherstand how they can call themselves Catholics when they won't lift a finger to help poor little Catholic Belgium.

MRS. GOGAN (*Raising her voice*)   What about poor little Catholic Ireland?

BESSIE (*Over to* MRS. GOGAN)   You mind your own business, maam, an' stupify your foolishness be gettin' dhrunk.

PETER (*Anxiously—to* MRS. GOGAN)   Take no notice of her; pay no attention to her. She's just tormentin' herself towards havin' a row with somebody.

BESSIE (*In a quiet anger*)   There's a storm of anger tossin' in me heart, thinkin' of all th' poor Tommies, an' with them me own son, dhrenched in water an' soaked in blood, gropin' their way to a shatherin' death, in a shower o' shells! Young men with th' sunny lust o' life beamin' in them, layin' down their white bodies, shredded into torn an' bloody pieces, on th' altar that God Himself has built for th' sacrifice of heroes!

MRS. GOGAN (*Indignantly*)   Isn't it a nice thing to have to be listenin' to a lassie an' hangin' our heads in a dead silence, knowin' that some persons think more of a ball of malt than they do of th' blessed saints.

FLUTHER (*Deprecatingly*)   Whisht; she's always dangerous an' derogatory when she's well oiled. Th' safest way to hindher her from
havin' any enjoyment out of her spite, is to dip our thoughts into
the fact of her bein' a female person that has moved out of th' sight
of ordinary sensible people.

BESSIE (*Over to* MRS. GOGAN, *viciously*)   To look at some o' th' women
that's knockin' about, now, is a thing to make a body sigh. . . . A
woman on her own, dhrinkin' with a bevy o' men is hardly an
example to her sex. . . . A woman dhrinkin' with a woman is one
thing, an' a woman dhrinkin' with herself is still a woman—flappers
may be put in another category altogether—but a middle-aged
married woman makin' herself th' centre of a circle of men is as a
woman that is loud an' stubborn, whose feet abideth not in her own
house.

THE COVEY (*To* BESSIE—*with a scornful look at* PETER)   When I think
of all th' problems in front o' th' workers, it makes me sick to be
lookin' at oul' codgers goin' about dhressed up like green-ac-
coutered figures gone asthray out of a toyshop!

PETER (*Angrily*)   Gracious God, give me patience to be listenin' to that
blasted young Covey proddin' at me from over at th' other end
of th' shop!

MRS. GOGAN (*Dipping her finger in the whisky, and moistening with it
the lips of her baby*)   Cissie Gogan's a woman livin' for nigh on
twenty-five years in her own room, an' beyond biddin' th' time o'
day to her neighbours, never yet as much as nodded her head in
th' direction of other people's business, while she knows some
(*With a look at* BESSIE) as are never content unless they're standin'
senthry over other people's doin's!

(*Again the figure appears, like a silhouette, in the window, back,
and all hear the voice of the speaker declaiming passionately to the
gathering outside.* FLUTHER, PETER *and* MRS. GOGAN *stand up, turn,
and look towards the window. The* BARMAN *comes to the end of
the counter;* BESSIE *and the* COVEY *stop talking, and look towards
the window.*)

THE VOICE OF THE SPEAKER   The last sixteen months have been the most
glorious in the history of Europe. Heroism has come back to the
earth. War is a terrible thing, but war is not an evil thing. People
in Ireland dread war because they do not know it. Ireland has not
known the exhilaration of war for over a hundred years. When
war comes to Ireland she must welcome it as she would welcome
the Angel of God!

(*The figure passes out of sight and hearing,* L.)

THE COVEY (*Towards all present*) Dope, dope. There's only one war worth havin': th' war for th' economic emancipation of th' proletariat.

BESSIE (*Referring to* MRS. GOGAN) They may crow away out o' them; but it ud be fitther for some o' them to mend their ways an' cease from havin' scouts out watchin' for th' comin' of th' Saint Vincent de Paul man, for fear they'd be nailed lowerin' a pint of beer, mockin' th' man with an angel face, shinin' with th' glamour of deceit an' lies!

MRS. GOGAN (*Over to* BESSIE) An' a certain lassie standin' stiff behind her own door with her ears cocked listenin' to what's being said, stuffed till she's sthrained with envy of a neighbour thryin' for a few little things that may be got be hard sthrivin' to keep up to th' letther an' th' law, an' th' practices of th' Church!

PETER (*To* MRS. GOGAN) If I was you, Mrs. Gogan, I'd parry her jabbin' remarks be a powerful silence that'll keep her tantalizin' words from penethratin' into your feelin's. It's always betther to leave these people to th' vengeance o' God!

BESSIE (*At the counter*) Bessie Burgess doesn't put up to know much, never havin' a swaggerin' mind, thanks be to God, but goin' on packin' up knowledge accordin' to her conscience: precept upon precept, line upon line; here a little, an' there a little. (BESSIE, *with a vigorous swing of her shawl, turns, and with a quick movement goes* C., *facing* MRS. GOGAN. *Furiously*) But, thanks be to Christ, she knows when she was got, where she was got, an' how she was got; while there's some she knows, decoratin' their finger with a well-polished weddin' ring, would be hard put to it if they were assed to show their weddin' lines!

(MRS. GOGAN *springs up from the seat and bounces to* C., *facing* BESSIE BURGESS. MRS. GOGAN *is wild with anger.*)

MRS. GOGAN (*With hysterical rage*) Y' oul' rip of a blasted liar, me weddin' ring's been well earned be twenty years be th' side o' me husband, now takin' his rest in heaven, married to me be Father Dempsey, in th' Chapel o' Saint Jude's, in th' Christmas Week of eighteen hundred an' ninety-five; an' any kid, livin' or dead, that Jinnie Gogan's had since, was got between th' bordhers of th' Ten Commandments! . . .

BESSIE (*Bringing the palms of her hands together in sharp claps to emphasize her remarks*) Liar to you, too, maam, y' oul' hardened thresspasser on other people's good nature, wizenin' up your soul in th' arts o' dodgeries, till every dhrop of respectability in a female is dhried up in her, lookin' at your ready-made manœuverin' with th' menkind!

BARMAN (*Anxiously leaning over the counter*)   Here, there; here, there; speak asy there. No rowin' here, no rowin' here, now.

(FLUTHER *comes from the seat, gets in front of* MRS. GOGAN, *and tries to pacify her;* PETER *leaves the seat, and tries to do the same with* BESSIE, *holding her back from* MRS. GOGAN. *The positions are:* BARMAN *behind the counter, leaning forward;* BESSIE R., *next* PETER; *next* FLUTHER; *next* MRS. GOGAN, *with baby in her arms. The* COVEY *remains leaning on the counter, looking on.*)

FLUTHER (*Trying to calm* MRS. GOGAN)   Now, Jinnie, Jinnie, it's a derogatory thing to be smirchin' a night like this with a row; it's rompin' with th' feelin's of hope we ought to be, instead o' bein' vice versa!

PETER (*Trying to quiet* BESSIE)   I'm terrible dawny, Mrs. Burgess, an' a fight leaves me weak for a long time afterwards. . . . Please, Mrs. Burgess, before there's damage done, thry to have a little respect for yourself.

BESSIE (*With a push of her hand that sends* PETER *tottering to the end of the counter*)   G'way, you little sermonizing, little yella-faced, little consequential, little pudgy, little bum, you!

MRS. GOGAN (*Screaming and struggling*)   Fluther, leggo! I'm not goin' to keep an unresistin' silence, an' her scatherin' her festherin' words in me face, stirrin' up every dhrop of decency in a respectable female, with her restless rally o' lies that would make a saint say his prayer backwards!

BESSIE (*Shouting*)   Ah, everybody knows well that th' best charity that can be shown to you is to hide th' truth as much as our thrue worship of God Almighty will allow us!

MRS. GOGAN (*Frantically*)   Here, houl' th' kid, one o' yous; houl' th' kid for a minute! There's nothin' for it but to show this lassie a lesson or two. . . . (*To* PETER) Here, houl' th' kid, you. (MRS. GOGAN *suddenly rushes over to* PETER, *standing, trembling with fear, between the end of the counter and the seat under the window. Bewildered, and before he's aware of it,* MRS. GOGAN *has put the baby in his arms.* MRS. GOGAN *rushes back* C. *and puts herself in a fighting attitude in front of* BESSIE. *To* BESSIE, *standing before her in a fighting attitude*)   Come on, now, me loyal lassie, dyin' with grief for little Catholic Belgium! When Jinnie Gogan's done with you, you'll have a little leisure lyin' down to think an' pray for your king an' counthry!

BARMAN (*Coming from behind the counter, getting between the women, and proceeding to push* BESSIE *towards the door*)   Here, now, since yous can't have a little friendly argument quietly, yous'll get out o' this place in quick time. Go on, an' settle your differences somewhere else—I don't want to have another endorsement on me licence. (*The* BARMAN *pushes* BESSIE *towards the doors* L., MRS. GOGAN *following.*)

PETER (*Anxiously calling to* MRS. GOGAN) Here, take your kid back ower this. How nicely I was picked now for it to be plumped into my arms!

THE COVEY (*Meaningly*) She knew who she was givin' it to, maybe.
(PETER *goes over near to the* COVEY *at the counter to retort indignantly, as the* BARMAN *pushes* BESSIE *out of the doors* L. *and gets hold of* MRS. GOGAN *to put her out too.*)

PETER (*Hotly to the* COVEY) Now, I'm givin' you fair warnin', me young Covey, to quit firin' your jibes an' jeers at me. . . . For one o' these days, I'll run out in front o' God Almighty an' take your sacred life!

BARMAN (*Pushing* MRS. GOGAN *out after* BESSIE) Go on, now; out you go.

PETER (*Leaving the baby down on the floor* C.) Ay, be Jasus, wait there, till I give her back her youngster! (PETER *runs to the door* L., *opens it, and calls out after* MRS. GOGAN.)

PETER (*Calling at the door* L.) Eh, there, eh! What about the kid? (*He runs back in,* C., *and looks at* FLUTHER *and the* COVEY) There, she's afther goin' without her kid—what are we goin' to do with it now?

THE COVEY (*Jeering*) What are *you* goin' to do with it? Bring it outside an' show everybody what you're afther findin'.

PETER (*In a panic—to* FLUTHER) Pick it up, you, Fluther, an' run afther her with it, will you?

FLUTHER (*With a long look at* PETER) What d'ye take Fluther for? You must think Fluther's a right gom.[5] D'ye think Fluther's like yourself, destitute of a titther of undherstandin'?

BARMAN (*Imperatively to* PETER) Take it up, man, an' run out afther her with it before she's gone too far. You're not goin' to leave th' bloody thing there, are you?

PETER (*Plaintively, as he lifts up the baby*) Well, God Almighty, give me patience with all th' scorners, tormentors, an' twarters that are always an' ever thryin' to goad me into prayin' for their blindin' an' blastin' an' burnin' in the' world to come! (PETER, *with the baby, goes out of the door* L. FLUTHER *comes from the front of the window to the counter and stands there, beside the* COVEY.)

FLUTHER (*With an air of relief*) God, it's a relief to get rid o' that crowd. Women is terrible when they start to fight. There's no holdin' them back. (*To the* COVEY) Are you goin' to have anything?

THE COVEY Ah, I don't mind if I have another half.

FLUTHER (*To the* BARMAN) Two more, Tommy, me son. (*The* BARMAN *gets the drinks,* FLUTHER *pays.*)

---

[5] Dolt.

FLUTHER (*To the* COVEY)   You know there's no conthrollin' a woman when she loses her head.

(ROSIE *appears at the doors* L. *She looks over at the counter, sees the two men, then crosses over to the* L. *end of the counter, where she stands, with a suggestive look towards* FLUTHER.)

ROSIE (*To the* BARMAN)   Divil a use o' havin' a thrim little leg on a night like this; things was never worse. . . . Give us a half till to-morrow, Tom, duckey.

BARMAN (*Coldly*)   No more to-night, Rosie; you owe me for three already.

ROSIE (*Combatively*)   You'll be paid, won't you?

BARMAN   I hope so.

ROSIE   You hope so! Is that th' way with you, now?

FLUTHER (*With a long glance at* ROSIE, *to the* BARMAN)   Give her one— it'll be all right.

(*The* BARMAN *gets a drink, and puts it on the counter before* ROSIE; FLUTHER *pays for it.*)

ROSIE (*Clapping* FLUTHER *on the back*)   Oul' sport!

FLUTHER (*To* COVEY)   Th' meetin' should be soon over, now.

THE COVEY (*In a superior way*)   Th' sooner th' betther. It's alla lot o' blasted nonsense, comrade.

FLUTHER   Oh, I wouldn't say it was all nonsense. After all, Fluther can remember th' time, an' him only a dawny chiselur,[6] bein' taught at his mother's knee to be faithful to th' Shan Vok Vok![7]

THE COVEY   That's all dope, comrade; th' sort o' thing that workers are fed on be th' Boorzwawzee.

FLUTHER (*A little sharply*)   What's all dope? Though I'm sayin' it that shouldn't: (*Catching his cheek with his hand, and pulling down the flesh from the eye*) d'ye see that mark there, undher me eye? . . . A sabre slice from a dragoon in O'Connell Street! (*Thrusting his head forward towards* ROSIE) Feel that dint in th' middle o' me nut!

ROSIE (*Rubbing* FLUTHER's *head, and winking at the* COVEY)   My God, there's a holla!

FLUTHER (*Putting on his hat with quiet pride*)   A skelp from a bobby's baton at a Labour meetin' in th' Phœnix Park!

THE COVEY (*Sarcastically*)   He must ha' hitten you in mistake. I don't know what you ever done for th' Labour movement.

---

6 A puny child.

7 Mispronunciation of the Shan Van Vocht: the poor old woman, i.e., Ireland. The title of a revolutionary song of 1798 (see Act II, note 3), whose refrain is: "Yes! Ireland shall be free/From the center to the sea!/Then hurrah for liberty!/Says the Shan Van Vocht."

FLUTHER (*Loudly*) D'ye not? Maybe, then, I done as much, an' know as much about th' Labour movement as th' chancers[8] that are blowin' about it!

BARMAN (*Over the counter*) Speak easy, Fluther, thry to speak easy.

THE COVEY (*Quietly*) There's no necessity to get excited about it, comrade.

FLUTHER (*More loudly*) Excited? Who's gettin' excited? There's no one gettin' excited! It would take something more than a thing like you to flutther a feather o' Fluther. Blatherin', an', when all is said, you know as much as th' rest in th' wind up!

THE COVEY (*Emphatically*) Well, let us put it to th' test, then, an' see what you know about th' Labour movement: what's the mechanism of exchange?

FLUTHER (*Roaring, because he feels he is beaten*) How th' hell do I know what it is? There's nothin' about that in th' rules of our Thrades Union!

BARMAN (*Protesting*) For God's sake, thry to speak easy, Fluther.

THE COVEY What does Karl Marx say about th' Relation of Value to th' Cost o' Production?

FLUTHER (*Angrily*) What th' hell do I care what he says? I'm Irishman enough not to lose me head be folloyin' foreigners!

BARMAN Speak easy, Fluther.

THE COVEY (*Contemptuously*) It's only waste o' time talkin' to you, comrade.

FLUTHER Don't be comradin' me, mate. I'd be on me last legs if I wanted you for a comrade.

ROSIE (*To the* COVEY, *taking* FLUTHER's *part*) It seems a highly rediculous thing to hear a thing that's only an inch or two away from a kid, swingin' heavy words about he doesn't know th' meanin' of, an' uppishly thryin' to down a man like Misther Fluther here, that's well flavoured in th' knowledge of th' world he's livin' in.

THE COVEY (*Bending over the counter—savagely to* ROSIE) Nobody's askin' you to be buttin' in with your prate. . . . I have you well taped, me lassie. . . . Just you keep your opinions for your own place. . . . It'll be a long time before th' Covey takes any insthructions or reprimandin' from a prostitute!

(ROSIE, *wild with humiliation, bounds from the end of the counter to* C. *and with eyes blazing, faces towards the* COVEY.)

ROSIE You louse, you louse, you! . . . You're no man . . . You're no man . . . I'm a woman, anyhow, an' if I'm a prostitute aself, I have me feelin's. . . . Thryin' to put his arm around me a minute ago, an'

[8] Liars.

givin' me th' glad eye, th' little wrigglin' lump o' desolation turns on me now, because he saw there was nothin' doin'. . . . You louse, you! If I was a man, or you were a woman, I'd bate th' puss o' you!

BARMAN   Ay, Rosie, ay! You'll have to shut your mouth altogether, if you can't learn to speak easy!

(FLUTHER, *with a dignified walk, goes over to* ROSIE C. *and puts a hand on her shoulder.*)

FLUTHER (*To* ROSIE)   Houl' on there, Rosie; houl' on, there. There's no necessity to flutther yourself when you're with Fluther. . . . Any lady that's in th' company of Fluther is goin' to get a fair hunt. . . . This is outside your province. . . . I'm not goin' to let you demean yourself be talkin' to a tittherin' chancer. . . . Leave this to Fluther —this is a man's job. . . . (*He turns from* ROSIE, *comes back, crosses the* COVEY, *then turns and faces him. To the* COVEY) Now, if you've anything to say, say it to Fluther; an' let me tell you, you're not goin' to be pass-remarkable to any lady in my company.

THE COVEY   Sure I don't care if you were runnin' all night afther your Mary o' th' Curlin' Hair, but, when you start tellin' luscious lies about what you done for th' Labour movement, it's nearly time to show y'up!

FLUTHER (*Fiercely*)   Is it you show Fluther up? G'way, man, I'd beat two o' you before me breakfast!

THE COVEY (*Contemptuously*)   Tell us where you bury your dead, will you?

FLUTHER (*With his face stuck into the face of the* COVEY)   Sing a little less on th' high note, or, when I'm done with you, you'll put a Christianable consthruction on things, I'm tellin' you!

THE COVEY   You're a big fella, you are.

FLUTHER (*Tapping the* COVEY *threateningly on the shoulder*)   Now, you're temptin' Providence when you're temptin' Fluther!

THE COVEY (*Losing his temper, knocking* FLUTHER's *hands away, and bawling*)   Easy with them hands, there, easy with them hands! You're startin' to take a little risk when you commence to paw the Covey!

(FLUTHER *suddenly springs into the* C. *of the shop, flings his hat into the corner, whips off his coat, and begins to paw the air like a pugilist.*)

FLUTHER (*Roaring*)   Come on, come on, you lowser; put your mitts up now, if there's a man's blood in you! Be God, in a few minutes you'll see some snots flyin' around, I'm tellin' you. . . . When Fluther's done with you, you'll have a vice-versa opinion of him! Come on, now, come on!

(*The* COVEY *squares up to* FLUTHER.)

BARMAN (*Running from behind the counter and catching hold of the* COVEY) Here, out you go, me little bowsey. Because you got a couple o' halves[9] you think you can act as you like. (*He pushes the* COVEY *to the doors* L.) Fluther's a friend o' mine, an' I'll not have him insulted.

THE COVEY (*Struggling with the* BARMAN) Ay, leggo, leggo there; fair hunt, give a man a fair hunt! One minute with him is all I ask; one minute alone with him, while you're runnin' for the priest an' th' doctor!

FLUTHER (*To the* BARMAN) Let him go, let him go, Tom: let him open th' door to sudden death if he wants to!

BARMAN (*Grappling with the* COVEY) Go on, out you go an' do th' bowsey somewhere else. (*The* BARMAN *pushes the* COVEY *out by doors* L., *and goes back behind the counter.* FLUTHER *assumes a proud air of victory.* ROSIE *gets his coat, and helps him to put it on; she then gets his hat and puts it on his head.*)

ROSIE (*Helping* FLUTHER *with his coat*) Be God, you put th' fear o' God in his heart that time! I thought you'd have to be dug out of him. . . . Th' way you lepped out without any of your fancy sidesteppin'! "Men like Fluther," says I to myself, "is gettin' scarce nowadays."

FLUTHER (*With proud complacency*, C.) I wasn't goin' to let meself be malignified by a chancer. . . . He got a little bit too derogatory for Fluther. . . . Be God, to think of a cur like that comin' to talk to a man like me!

ROSIE (*Fixing on his hat*) Did j'ever!

FLUTHER He's lucky he got off safe. I hit a man last week, Rosie, an' he's fallin' yet!

ROSIE Sure, you'd ha' broken him in two if you'd ha' hitten him one clatther!

FLUTHER (*Amorously, putting his arm around* ROSIE) Come on into th' snug,[10] me little darlin', an' we'll have a few dhrinks before I see you home.

ROSIE Oh, Fluther, I'm afraid you're a terrible man for th' women.

(FLUTHER *leads* ROSIE *to the seat with the round table in front*, R. *She sits down on the seat. He goes to the counter.*)

FLUTHER (*To the* BARMAN) Two, full ones, Tommy.

(BARMAN *gets the drinks.* FLUTHER *brings them over to seat* R., *leaves them on the table, and sits down beside* ROSIE. *The swing-doors* L. *open and* CAPTAIN BRENNAN, COMMANDANT CLITHEROE, *and*

[9] Half pints of ale inside you.
[10] A small private room in a public house.

LIEUTENANT LANGON *enter, and cross quickly to the counter.* CAPT. BRENNAN *carries the banner of The Plough and the Stars, and* LIEUT. LANGON *a green, white and orange Tricolour.*[11] *They are in a state of emotional excitement. Their faces are flushed and their eyes sparkle; they speak rapidly, as if unaware of the meaning of what they say. They have been mesmerized by the fervency of the speeches.*)

CLITHEROE (*Almost pantingly to the* BARMAN)   Three glasses o' port!
The BARMAN *brings the drinks,* CLITHEROE *pays.*

CAPT. BRENNAN   We won't have long to wait now.

LIEUT. LANGON   Th' time is rotten ripe for revolution.

CLITHEROE (*To* LIEUT. LANGON)   You have a mother, Langon.

LIEUT. LANGON   Ireland is greater than a mother.

CAPT. BRENNAN (*To* CLITHEROE)   You have a wife, Clitheroe.

CLITHEROE   Ireland is greater than a wife.

LIEUT. LANGON   Th' time for Ireland's battle is now—th' place for Ireland's battle is here.
(*The tall, dark figure again appears in the window. The three men stiffen to attention. They stand out from the* L. *of the counter,* BRENNAN *nearest counter, then* CLITHEROE, *then* LIEUT. LANGON. FLUTHER *and* ROSIE, *busy with each other, take no notice.*)

THE VOICE OF THE MAN   Our foes are strong, but strong as they are, they cannot undo the miracles of God, who ripens in the heart of young men the seeds sown by the young men of a former generation. They think they have pacified Ireland; think they have foreseen everything; think they have provided against everything; but the fools, the fools, the fools!—they have left us our Fenian[12] dead, and, while Ireland holds these graves, Ireland, unfree, shall never be at peace!

CAPT. BRENNAN (*Lifting up the Plough and the Stars*)   Imprisonment for th' Independence of Ireland!

LIEUT. LANGON (*Lifting up the Tri-colour*)   Wounds for th' Independence of Ireland!

CLITHEROE   Death for th' Independence of Ireland!

THE THREE (*Together*)   So help us God!
(*They lift their glasses and drink together. The "Assembly" is heard on a bugle outside. They leave their glasses on the counter, and*

---

[11] The flag of the Irish Volunteers, now the flag of the Irish Republic.

[12] Members of the Irish Revolutionary Brotherhood (organized in both Ireland and the United States in 1858), usually called "Fenians," which derives from the Fianna, the army of the legendary Irish hero Fionn mac Cumhaill (pronounced Finn MacCool). In 1867 the Fenians staged an unsuccessful rising against the English.

hurry out by doors L. *A pause. Then* FLUTHER *and* ROSIE *rise from the seat, and start to go* L. ROSIE *is linking* FLUTHER, *who is a little drunk. Both are in a merry mood.*)

ROSIE Are you afraid or what? Are you goin' to come home, or are you not?

FLUTHER Of course I'm goin' home. What ud ail me that I wouldn't go?

ROSIE (*Lovingly*) Come on, then, oul' sport.

OFFICER'S VOICE (*Giving command outside*) Irish Volunteers, by th' right, quick march!

ROSIE (*Putting her arm round* FLUTHER *and singing to the air "Twenty-four Strings to My Bow"*)

I once had a lover, a tailor, but he could do nothin' for me,
An' then I fell in with a sailor as strong an' as wild as th' sea.
We cuddled an' kissed with devotion, till th' night from th' mornin' had fled;
An' there, to our joy, a bright bouncin' boy
Was dancin' a jig in th' bed!
Dancin' a jig in th' bed, an' bawlin' for butther an' bread.
An' there, to our joy, a bright bouncin' boy
Was dancin' a jig in th' bed!
(*They go out with their arms round each other.*)

CLITHEROE'S VOICE (*In command outside*) Dublin Battalion of the Irish Citizen Army, by th' right, quick march!

Act III

SCENE—*A corner house of a street of tenements; exterior of house in which the Clitheroes lived. It is a tall, gaunt five-storey tenement. Its brick front is dull from weather and age. It juts out from* L. *more than half-way across stage, showing part of the front elevation, with wide, heavy door, having windows above and on both sides. The windows on* L., *looking into the rooms of the Clitheroes, are hung with good casement cloth. The others are draped with grimy lace curtains. Stone steps lead from the door to the path on the street. From these steps, on each side of the door are railings to prevent anyone from falling down the area. To the extreme* R. *the front of another house is merely indicated by the side aspect of a wall with steps leading from the door, on which the wounded*

LANGON *rests later on in the scene. Between the two runs a lane which, upstage, turns to the* R. *At the corner of the lane, nearest the house shown almost full front, is a street lamp. As the house is revealed,* MRS. GOGAN *is seen helping* MOLLSER *to a chair, which stands on the path beside the railings, at the* L. *side of the steps. She then wraps a shawl around* MOLLSER'S *shoulders. It is some months later.*

MRS. GOGAN (*Arranging shawl around* MOLLSER)   Th' sun'll do you all th' good in th' world. A few more weeks o' this weather, an' there's no knowin' how well you'll be. . . . Are you comfy, now?

MOLLSER (*Weakly and wearily*)   Yis, ma; I'm all right.

MRS. GOGAN (*Bending over her*)   How are you feelin'?

MOLLSER   Betther, ma, betther. If th' horrible sinkin' feelin' ud go, I'd be all right.

MRS. GOGAN   Ah, I wouldn't put much pass on that. Your stomach maybe's out of ordher. . . . Is th' poor breathin' any betther, d'ye think?

MOLLSER   Yis, yis, ma; a lot betther.

MRS. GOGAN   Well, that's somethin' anyhow. . . . With th' help o' God, you'll be on th' mend from this out. . . . D'your legs feel any sthronger undher you, d'ye think?

MOLLSER (*Irritably*)   I can't tell, ma. I think so. . . . A little.

MRS. GOGAN   Well, a little aself is somethin'. I thought I heard you coughin' a little more than usual last night. . . . D'you think you were?

MOLLSER   I wasn't, ma, I wasn't.

MRS. GOGAN   I thought I heard you, for I was kep' awake all night with th' shootin'. An' thinkin' o' that madman, Fluther, runnin' about through th' night lookin' for Nora Clitheroe to bring her back when he heard she'd gone to folly her husband, an' in dhread any minute he might come staggerin' in covered with bandages, splashed all over with th' red of his own blood, an' givin' us barely time to bring th' priest to hear th' last whisper of his final confession, as his soul was passin' through th' dark doorway o' death into th' way o' th' wondherin' dead. . . . You don't feel cold, do you?

MOLLSER   No, ma; I'm all right.

MRS. GOGAN   Keep your chest well covered, for that's th' delicate spot in you . . . if there's any danger, I'll whip you in again. . . . (MRS. GOGAN *crosses to* R., *goes up the lane, turns and looks* R., *as if looking down the street*) Oh, here's the Covey an' oul' Peter hurryin' along. (*She comes down the lane, and crosses to* MOLLSER) God Almighty, sthrange things is happenin' when them two is pullin' together. (*The* COVEY *and* PETER *come into the lane* R., *come down, and stand* R.C. MRS. GOGAN *stands* C., *near the steps. The two men are breathless and excited. To the two men*) Were yous far up th' town? Did yous see any sign o' Fluther or Nora? How is things lookin'? I hear they're blazin' away out o' th' G.P.O. That th' Tommies is sthretched in heaps around Nelson's Pillar an' th' Parnell Statue, an' that th' pavin' sets in O'Connell Street is nearly covered be pools o' blood.

PETER   We seen no sign o' Nora or Fluther anywhere.

MRS. GOGAN   We should ha' held her back be main force from goin' to look for her husband. . . . God knows what's happened to her— I'm always seein' her stretched on her back in some hospital, moanin' with th' pain of a bullet in her vitals, an' nuns thryin' to get her to take a last look at th' crucifix!

THE COVEY   We can do nothin'. You can't stick your nose into O'Connell Street, an' Tyler's is on fire.

PETER   An' we seen th' Lancers—

THE COVEY (*Interrupting*)   Throttin' along, heads in th' air; spurs an' sabres jinglin', an' lances quiverin', an' lookin' as if they were assin' themselves, "Where's these blighters, till we get a prod at them," when there was a volley from th' Post Office that stretched half o' them, an' sent th' rest gallopin' away wondherin' how far they'd have to go before they'd feel safe.

PETER (*Rubbing his hands*)   "Damn it," says I to meself, "this looks like business!"

THE COVEY   An' then out comes General Pearse[1] an' his staff, an', standin' in th' middle o' th' street, he reads th' Proclamation.

MRS. GOGAN   What proclamation?

PETER   Declarin' an Irish Republic.

MRS. GOGAN (*With amazement*)   Go to God!

PETER   The gunboat *Helga's* shellin' Liberty Hall, an' I hear that people livin' on th' quays had to crawl on their bellies to Mass with th' bullets that were flyin' around from Boland's Mills.

MRS. GOGAN   God bless us, what's goin' to be th' end of it all!

BESSIE (*Opening and looking out of a window*)   Maybe yous are satis-fied now; maybe yous are satisfied now! Go on an' get guns if yous are men—Johnny get your gun, get your gun, get your gun! Yous are all nicely shanghaied now; th' boyo hasn't a sword on his

---

[1] Padraic (Patrick) H. Pearse (1879–1916), one of the leaders of the Easter Rebellion, executed by the British after his surrender.

thigh, now! Oh, yous are all nicely shanghaied now! (*She shuts down the window viciously.*)

MRS. GOGAN (*Warningly to* PETER *and the* COVEY)   S-s-sh, don't answer her. She's th' right oul' Orange[2] bitch! She's been chantin' "Rule, Britannia" all th' mornin'.

PETER   I hope Fluther hasn't met with any accident, he's such a wild card.

THE COVEY   Fluther's well able to take care of himself.

MRS. GOGAN (*Dolefully*)   God grant it; but last night I dreamt I seen gettin' carried into th' house a sthretcher with a figure lyin' on it, stiff an' still, dhressed in th' habit of Saint Francis. An' then, I heard th' murmurs of a crowd no one could see sayin' th' litany for th' dead; an' then it got so dark that nothin' was seen but th' white face of th' corpse, gleamin' like a white wather lily floatin' on th' top of a dark lake. Then a tiny whisper thrickled into me ear, sayin', "Isn't the face very like th' face o' Fluther," an' then, with a thremblin' flutther, th' dead lips opened, an', although I couldn't hear, I knew they were sayin', "Poor oul' Fluther, afther havin' handin' in his gun at last, his shakin' soul moored in th' place where th' wicked are at rest an' th' weary cease from throublin'."

While MRS. GOGAN *is speaking,* PETER *wanders up the lane, looks* R., *then stares; then puts on spectacles and looks again. He turns and shouts at* MRS. GOGAN *and the* COVEY.

PETER (*Shouting*)   Here they are, be God, here they are; just afther turnin' the corner—Nora an' Fluther!

(*The* COVEY *runs up the lane and looks* R. *with* PETER.)

COVEY   She must be wounded or something—Fluther seems to be carryin' her.

(FLUTHER, *half carrying* NORA, *comes in* R.; NORA's *eyes are dim and hollow; her face pale and strained-looking; her hair is tossed and her clothes are dusty. They pass by* COVEY *and* PETER, *come down the lane, and cross over to the door of the house* C. PETER *and the* COVEY *follow, and stand* R. MRS. GOGAN *goes over solicitously to* NORA. NORA *wears a brown mackintosh.*)

MRS. GOGAN (*Running over to them*)   God bless us, is it wounded y'are, Mrs. Clitheroe, or what?

FLUTHER (*Confidently*)   Ah, she's all right, Mrs. Gogan; only worn out from thravellin' an' want o' sleep. A night's rest, now, an' she'll be as fit as a fiddle. Bring her in, an' make her lie down.

---

[2] Pro-English Protestant.

MRS. GOGAN (*To* NORA) Did you hear e'er a whisper o' Mr. Clitheroe?

NORA (*Wearily*) I could find him nowhere, Mrs. Gogan. None o' them would tell me where he was. They told me I shamed my husband an' th' women of Ireland be carryin' on as I was. . . . They said th' women must learn to be brave an' cease to be cowardly. . . . Me who risked more for love than they would risk for hate. . . . (*Raising her voice in hysterical protest*) My Jack will be killed, my Jack will be killed! . . . He is to be butchered as a sacrifice to th' dead! (NORA *sinks down on the steps at the door.* BESSIE BURGESS *opens the window, and shouts at them. They do not look at her.*)

BESSIE Yous are all nicely shanghaied now! Sorra mend the lassies who have been kissin' an' cuddlin' their boys into th' sheddin' of blood. Fillin' their minds with fairy tales that had no beginnin', but, please God, 'll have a bloody quick endin'! (*She shuts the window with a bang.*)

FLUTHER (*Losing control*) Y' ignorant oul' throllope, you!

MRS. GOGAN (*Coaxingly, to* NORA) You'll find he'll come home safe enough to you, Mrs. Clitheroe. Afther all, there's a power o' women that's handed over sons an' husbands, to take a runnin' risk in th' fight they're wagin'.

NORA I can't help thinkin' every shot fired 'll be fired at Jack, an' every shot fired at Jack 'll be fired at me. What do I care for th' others? I can think only of me own self. . . . An' there's no woman gives a son or a husband to be killed—if they say it, they're lyin', lyin', against God, Nature, an' against themselves! . . . One blasted hussy at a barricade told me to go home an' not be thryin' to dishearten th' men. . . .

PETER (*Unctuously*) You'll have to have patience, Nora. We all have to put up with twarthers an' tormentors in this world.

THE COVEY If they were fightin' for anything worth while, I wouldn't mind.

FLUTHER (*To* NORA) Nothin' derogatory 'll happen to Mr. Clitheroe. You'll find, now, in th' finish up, it'll be vice versa.

NORA Oh, I know that wherever he is, he's thinkin' of wantin' to be with me. I know he's longin' to be passin' his hand through me hair, to be caressin' me neck, to fondle me hand an' to feel me kisses clingin' to his mouth. . . . An' he stands wherever he is because he's brave? (*Vehemently*) No, but because he's a coward, a coward, a coward!

MRS. GOGAN Oh, they're not cowards anyway.

NORA (*With denunciatory anger*) I tell you they're afraid to say they're afraid! . . . Oh, I saw it, I saw it, Mrs. Gogan. . . . At th' barricade in North King Street I saw fear glowin' in all their eyes. . . . An' in th' middle o' th' sthreet was somethin' huddled up in a horrible tangled heap. . . . An' I saw that they were afraid to look at it. . . . I tell you they were afraid to look at it. . . . I tell you they were afraid, afraid, afraid!

MRS. GOGAN (*Lifting her up from the steps*) Come on in, dear. If you'd been a little longer together the wrench asundher wouldn't have been so sharp.

NORA (*Painfully ascending the steps, helped by* MRS. GOGAN) Th' agony I'm in since he left me has thrust away every rough thing he done, an' every unkind word he spoke; only th' blossoms that grew out of our lives are before me now; shakin' their colours before me face, an' breathin' their sweet scent on every thought springin' up in me mind, till, sometimes, Mrs. Gogan, sometimes I think I'm goin' mad!

MRS. GOGAN You'll be a lot bedther when you have a little lie down.

NORA (*Turning toward Fluther as she is going in*) I don't know what I'd have done, only for Fluther. I'd have been lyin' in th' sthreets, only for him. . . . (*As she goes in*) They have dhriven away th' little happiness life had to spare for me. He has gone from me for ever, for ever. . . . Oh, Jack, Jack, Jack!

(*As* NORA *is led in,* BESSIE *comes out. She passes down the steps with her head in the air; at the bottom she stops to look back. When they have gone in, she takes a mug of milk from under a shawl she is wearing and gives it to* MOLLSER *silently.* MOLLSER *takes it from her.*)

FLUTHER (*Going from* C. *to the* COVEY *and* PETER, R.) Which of yous has the tossers?

THE COVEY I have.

(BESSIE *crosses from* MOLLSER *to* R. *She pauses at the corner of the lane,* R., *to speak to the two men.*)

BESSIE (*Scornfully, to* FLUTHER *and the* COVEY) You an' your Leadhers, and their sham-battle soldiers has landed a body in a nice way, havin' to go an' ferret out a bit o' bread, God knows where. . . . Why aren't yous in the G.P.O., if yous are men? It's paler an paler yous are gettin'. . . . A lot of vipers—that's what the Irish people is! (BESSIE *goes up the lane, turns* R., *and goes out.*)

FLUTHER (*Warningly*) Never mind her. (*To the* COVEY) Make a start, an' keep us from th' sin of idleness. (*He crosses from* R. *to* MOLLSER *and speaks to her*) Well, how are you to-day, Mollser, oul' son? What are you dhrinkin'? Milk?

MOLLSER Grand, Fluther, grand, thanks—yes, milk.

FLUTHER (*To* MOLLSER) You couldn't get a betther thing down you. . . .
This turnup has done one good thing, anyhow; you can't get
dhrink anywhere, an' if it lasts a week I'll be so used to it that I
won't think of a pint. (FLUTHER *returns and joins the two men* R.
The COVEY *takes from his pocket two worn coins and a thin strip of
wood (or tin) about four inches long. He puts the coins on the
strip of wood and holds the strip out from him.*)

THE COVEY What's the bettin'?

PETER Heads, a juice.[3]

FLUTHER Harps,[4] a tanner.[5]

(*The* COVEY *flips the coins from the wood into the air. As they
jingle on the ground the distant boom of a big gun is heard. They
leave the coins where they are and listen intently.*)

FLUTHER (*Awed*) What th' hell's that?

THE COVEY (*Awed*) It's like the boom of a big gun!

FLUTHER Surely to God, they're not goin' to use artillery on us!

THE COVEY (*Scornfully*) Not goin'! (*Vehemently*) Wouldn't they use
anything on us, man?

FLUTHER Aw, holy Christ, that's not playin' th' game!

PETER (*Plaintively*) What would happen if a shell landed here now?

THE COVEY (*Ironically*) You'd be off to heaven in a fiery chariot.

PETER In spite of all th' warnin's that's ringin' around us, are you goin'
to start your pickin' at me again?

FLUTHER Go on, toss them again, toss them again. . . . Harps, a tanner.

PETER Heads, a juice.

(*The* COVEY *tosses the coins as before; they fall on the ground and
roll a little.* FLUTHER *waves the other two back as they bend over
the rolling coins.*)

FLUTHER Let them roll, let them roll—heads be God!

(BESSIE *runs in* R., *runs down the lane towards the three men. She
is breathless with excitement. She has a new fox fur round her
neck over her shawl, a number of new umbrellas under one arm,
a box of biscuits under the other, and she wears a gaudily trimmed
hat on her head. She speaks rapidly and breathlessly.*)

BESSIE They're breakin' into th' shops, they're breakin' into th' shops!
Smashin' th' windows, batterin' th' doors an' whippin' away everything! An' th' Volunteers is firin' on them. I seen two men an' a lassie
pushin' a piano down th' street, an' th' sweat rollin' off them thryin'
to get it up on th' pavement; an' an oul' wan that must ha' been
seventy lookin' as if she'd dhrop every minute with th' dint o' heart

[3] Deuce (apparently two pence).
[4] Tails (the tail side of an Irish coin has the picture of an Irish harp).
[5] Sixpence.

beatin', thryin' to pull a big double bed out of a broken shop
window! I was goin' to wait till I dhressed meself from th' skin out.

MOLLSER (*To* BESSIE, *as she is going into the house* C.)   Help me in,
Bessie; I'm feelin' curious.

(BESSIE *leaves the looted things in the house, and, rapidly returning,
helps* MOLLSER *in.*)

THE COVEY (*To* FLUTHER)   Th' selfishness of that one—she waited till
she got all she could carry before she'd come to tell anyone!

FLUTHER (*Running over to the door of the house and shouting in to*
BESSIE)   Ay, Bessie, did you hear of e'er a pub gettin' a shake up?

BESSIE (*Inside*)   I didn't hear o' none.

FLUTHER (*In a burst of enthusiasm*)   Well, you're goin' to hear of one
soon!

THE COVEY (*To* FLUTHER, *excitedly*)   Come on, man, an' don't be wastin'
time.

PETER (*Calling to them as they run up the lane*)   E, eh, are yous goin' to
leave me here, alone?

(FLUTHER *and* COVEY *halt in middle of lane, and turn to look and
reply to* PETER.)

FLUTHER   Are you goin' to leave yourself here?

PETER (*Anxiously*)   Didn't yous hear her sayin' they were firin' on them?

THE COVEY AND FLUTHER (*Together*)   Well?

PETER   Supposin' I happened to be potted?

FLUTHER   We'd give you a Christian burial, anyhow.

THE COVEY (*Ironically*)   Dhressed up in your regimentals.

PETER (*To the* COVEY, *passionately*)   May th' all-lovin' God give you a
hot knock one o' these days, me young Covey, tuthorin' Fluther
up now to be tiltin' at me, an' crossin' me with his mockeries an'
jibin'!

(FLUTHER *and* COVEY *run up the lane, and go off* R. PETER *looks after
them and then goes slowly into the house,* C. *After a slight pause,*
MRS. GOGAN *appears at the door of the house* C., *pushing a pram in
front of her. As she gets the pram over the threshold* BESSIE *appears,
catches the pram, and stops* MRS. GOGAN'S *progress.*)

BESSIE (*Angrily*)   Here, where are you goin' with that? How quick you
were, me lady, to clap your eyes on th' pram. . . . Maybe you don't
know that Mrs. Sullivan, before she went to spend Easter with
her people in Dunboyne, gave me sthrict injunctions to give an
occasional look to see if it was still standin' where it was left in th'
corner of th' lobby.

MRS. GOGAN (*Indignantly*)   That remark of yours, Mrs. Bessie Burgess,
requires a little considheration, seein' that th' pram was left on our
lobby, an' not yours; a foot or two a little to th' left of th' jamb

of me own room door; nor is it needful to mention th' name of th' person that gave a squint to see if it was there th' first thing in th' mornin', an' th' last thing in th' stillness o' th' night; never failin' to realize that her eyes couldn't be goin' wrong, be sthretchin' out her arm an' runnin' her hand over th' pram, to make sure that th' sight was no deception! Moreover, somethin' tellin' me that th' runnin' hurry of an inthrest you're takin' in it now is a sudden ambition to use th' pram for a purpose, that a loyal woman of law an' ordher would stagger away from! (MRS. GOGAN *pushes the pram violently down the steps, pulling* BESSIE *with her, who holds her up again when they reach the street.*)

BESSIE (*Still holding the pram*)   There's not as much as one body in th' house that doesn't know that it wasn't Bessie Burgess that was always shakin' her voice complainin' about people leavin' bassinettes in th' way of them that, week in an' week out, had to pay their rent, an' always had to find a regular accommodation for her own furniture in her own room. . . . An' as for law an' ordher, puttin' aside th' harp an' shamrock,[6] Bessie Burgess 'll have as much respect as she wants for th' lion an' unicorn![7]

PETER (*Appearing at the door of the house,* C.)   I think I'll go with th' pair of yous an' see th' fun. A fella might as well chance it, anyhow.

MRS. GOGAN (*Taking no notice of* PETER, *and pushing the pram on towards the lane*)   Take your rovin' lumps o' hands from pattin' th' bassinette, if you please, ma'am; an', steppin' from th' threshold of good manners, let me tell you, Mrs. Burgess, that it's a fat wondher to Jennie Gogan that a lady-like singer o' hymns like yourself would lower her thoughts from sky-thinkin' to sthretch out her arm in a sly-seekin' way to pinch anything dhriven asthray in th' confusion of th' battle our boys is makin' for th' freedom of their counthry!

PETER (*Laughing and rubbing his hands together*)   Hee, hee, hee, hee, hee! I'll go with th' pair o' yous an' give yous a hand.

MRS. GOGAN (*With a rapid turn of her head as she shoves the pram forward*)   Get up in th' prambulator an' we'll wheel you down.

BESSIE (*To* MRS. GOGAN *as she halts the pram again*)   Poverty an' hardship has sent Bessie Burgess to abide with sthrange company, but she always knew them she had to live with from backside to breakfast time; an' she can tell them, always havin' had a Christian kinch on her conscience, that a passion for thievin' an' pinchin' would find her soul a foreign place to live in, an' that her present intention is

---

[6] Symbols of Ireland. The Irish harp is pictured on the arms of Ireland. St. Patrick is said to have used a shamrock, symbol of the Trinity, to drive the snakes into the sea.

[7] Symbols of England, pictured on England's royal arms.

quite th' lofty-hearted one of pickin' up anything shaken up an' scatthered about in th' loose confusion of a general plundher!

(MRS. GOGAN, BESSIE *and the pram run up the lane and go off* R. PETER *follows, but as he reaches the corner of the lane the boom of the big guns brings him to a sudden halt.*)

PETER (*Frightened into staying behind by the sound of the gun*)   God Almighty, that's th' big gun again! God forbid any harm would happen to them, but sorra mind I'd mind if they met with a dhrop in their mad endeyvours to plundher an' desthroy. (*He looks down the street from the lane for a moment, then runs to the hall door of the house,* C., *which is open, and shuts it with a vicious pull; he then goes to the chair in which* MOLLSER *had sat, sits down, takes out his pipe, lights it and begins to smokes with his head carried at a haughty angle. The* COVEY *comes in* R. *and down the lane, staggering with a tenstone sack of flour on his back. He goes over to the door, pushes it with his head, and finds he can't open it; he turns slightly in the direction of* PETER.)

THE COVEY (*To* PETER)   Who shut th' door? . . . (*He kicks at it*) Here, come on an' open it, will you? This isn't a mot's hand-bag I've got on me back.

PETER   Now, me young Covey, d'ye think I'm goin' to be your lackey?

THE COVEY (*Angrily*)   Will you open th' door, y'oul'—

PETER (*Shouting*)   Don't be assin' me to open any door, don't be assin' me to open any door for you. . . . Makin' a shame an' a sin o' th' cause that good men are fightin' for. . . . Oh, God forgive th' people that, instead o' burnishin' th' work th' boys is doin' to-day, with quiet honesty an' patience, is revilin' their sacrifices with a riot of lootin' an' roguery!

THE COVEY (*Sarcastically*)   Isn't your own eyes leppin' out o' your head with envy that you haven't th' guts to ketch a few o' th' things that God is givin' to His chosen people? . . . Y'oul' hypocrite, if every one was blind you'd steal a cross off an ass's back!

PETER (*Very calmly*)   You're not goin' to make me lose me temper; you can go on with your proddin' as long as you like; goad an' goad an' goad away; hee hee, heee! I'll not lose me temper.

(*Somebody opens door and the* COVEY *goes in.*)

COVEY (*Inside house, to mock* PETER)   Cuckoo-oo!

(PETER *gets up from chair in a blaze of passion, and follows the* COVEY *in, shouting.*)

PETER (*Shouting*)   You lean, long, lanky lath of a lowsey bastard. (*Going in door of house,* C.) Lowsey bastard, lowsey bastard!

(MRS. GOGAN *and* BESSIE, *pushing the pram, come in* R., *come down lane to front of the house,* C. BESSIE *is pushing the pram, which is filled with loot.* MRS. GOGAN *carries a tall standard lamp, topped with a wide and bright-coloured shade. The pram is filled with fancy-coloured dresses, and boots and shoes. They are talking as they appear* R.)

MRS. GOGAN (*Appearing* R.)   I don't remember ever havin' seen such lovely pairs as them with the pointed toes an' the cuban heels.

BESSIE (*They are now* C., *lifting one of the evening dresses from the pram, holding it up admiringly*)   They'll go grand with th' dhresses we're afther liftin', when we've stitched a sthray bit o' silk to lift th' bodices up a little bit higher, so as to shake th' shame out o' them, an' make them fit for women that hasn't lost themselves in th' nakedness o' th' times.

PETER (*At door, sourly to* MRS. GOGAN)   Ay, you. Mollser looks as if she was goin' to faint, an' your youngster is roarin' in convulsions in her lap.

MRS. GOGAN (*Snappily*)   She's never any other way but faintin'! (MRS. GOGAN *runs into the house with her arm full of things. She comes back, takes up the lamp and is about to go in, when a rifleshot very near is heard.* MRS. GOGAN, *with lamp, and* BESSIE, *with pram, rush to the door which* PETER, *in a panic, has shut.*)

MRS. GOGAN (*Banging at the door*)   Eh, eh, you cowardly oul' fool, what are you thryin' to shut the door on us for? (MRS. GOGAN *pushes the door open and runs in, followed by* BESSIE *dragging in the pram. They shut the door. A pause. Then* CAPT. BRENNAN, *supporting* LIEUT. LANGON, *comes in* L., *along the street in front of the house,* C. *As* BRENNAN *and* LANGON *reach* C. *going* R., CLITHEROE, *pale and in a state of calm nervousness, appears at* L., *walking backwards or looking back in the direction from which they've come; he has a rifle held at the ready in his hands.* LANGON *is ghastly white and now and again his face is twisted in agony.*)

CAPT. BRENNAN (*Back to* CLITHEROE)   Why did you fire over their heads? Why didn't you fire to kill?

CLITHEROE   No, no, Bill; bad as they are, they're Irish men an' women. (BRENNAN *gently lets* LANGON *recline on the steps of the house indicated to the extreme* R., *holding him by an arm.* CLITHEROE *is* C., *watching* LANGON.)

CAPT. BRENNAN (*Savagely*)   Irish be damned! Attackin' an' mobbin' th' men that are riskin' their lives for them. If these slum lice gather at our heels again, plug one o' them, or I'll soon shock them with a shot or two meself!

LIEUT. LANGON (*Moaningly*)   My God, is there ne'er an ambulance knockin' around anywhere? . . . Th' stomach is ripped out o' me; I feel it—o-o-oh, Christ!

CAPT. BRENNAN   Keep th' heart up, Jim; we'll soon get help, now.
> (*Door of house* C. *opens and* NORA *rushes out, dashes down steps into* CLITHEROE's *arms at bottom. She flings her arms around his neck. Her hair is down, her face haggard, but her eyes are agleam with happy relief.*)

NORA (*To* CLITHEROE)   Jack, Jack, oh, God be thanked. Kiss me, kiss me, Jack; kiss your own Nora.

CLITHEROE (*Kissing her, and speaking brokenly*)   My Nora; my little, beautiful Nora, I wish to God I'd never left you.

NORA   It doesn't matter—not now, not now, Jack. It will make us dearer than ever to each other. . . . Kiss me, kiss me again.

CLITHEROE   Now, for God's sake, Nora, don't make a scene.

NORA (*Fervently*)   I won't, I won't; I promise, Jack—honest to God.
> (BESSIE *opens window of house to the* R., *puts out her head, and shouts at* CLITHEROE *and* BRENNAN.)

BESSIE (*At window*)   Has th' big guns knocked all th' harps out of your hands? General Clitheroe'd rather be unlacin' his wife's bodice now than standin' at a barricade. (*To* BRENNAN) An' the professor of chicken butcherin', there, finds he's up against something a little tougher than his own chickens, an' that's sayin' a lot!

CAPT. BRENNAN (*Over to* BESSIE)   Shut up, y'oul' hag!

BESSIE (*Down to* BRENNAN)   Choke th' chicken, choke th' chicken, choke th' chicken!

LIEUT. LANGON   For God's sake, Bill, bring me some place where me wound 'll be looked afther. . . . Am I to die before anything is done to save me?

CAPT. BRENNAN (*To* CLITHEROE)   Come on, Jack. We've got to get help for Jim, here—have you no thought for his pain an' danger?

BESSIE   Choke th' chicken, choke th' chicken, choke th' chicken!

CLITHEROE (*To* NORA)   Loosen me, darling, let me go.

NORA (*Clinging to him*)   No, no, no, I'll not let you go! Come on, come up to our home, Jack, my sweetheart, my lover, my husband, an' we'll forget th' last few terrible days! . . .

LIEUT. LANGON (*Appealingly*)   Oh, if I'd kep' down only a little longer, I mightn't ha' been hit! Every one else escapin', an' me gettin' me belly ripped asundher! . . . I couldn't scream, couldn't even scream. . . . D'ye think I'm really badly wounded, Bill? Me clothes seem to be all soakin' wet. . . . It's blood . . . My God, it must be me own blood!

CAPT. BRENNAN (*To* CLITHEROE)   Go on, Jack, bid her good-bye with another kiss, an' be done with it! D'ye want Langon to die in me arms while you're dallyin' with your Nora?

CLITHEROE (*To* NORA)   I must go, I must go, Nora. I'm sorry we met at all. . . . It couldn't be helped—all other ways were blocked be th' British. . . . Let me go, can't you, Nora? D'ye want me to be unthrue to me comrades?

NORA   No, I won't let you go. . . . I want you to be thrue to me, Jack. . . . I'm your dearest comrade; I'm your thruest comrade. (*Tightening her arms around* CLITHEROE) Oh, Jack, I can't let you go!

CLITHEROE (*With anger, mixed with affection*) You must, Nora, you must.

NORA   All last night at the barricades I sought you, Jack. I asked for you everywhere. I didn't think of the danger—I could only think of you. They dhrove me away, but I came back again.

CLITHEROE (*Ashamed of her action*) What possessed you to make a show of yourself, like that! What are you more than any other woman?

NORA   No more, maybe; but you are more to me than any other man, Jack. . . . I couldn't help it. I shouldn't have told you. . . . My love for you made me mad with terror.

CLITHEROE (*Angrily*) They'll say now that I sent you out th' way I'd have an excuse to bring you home. . . . Are you goin' to turn all th' risks I'm takin' into a laugh?

LIEUT. LANGON   Let me lie down, let me lie down, Bill; th' pain would be easier, maybe, lyin' down. Oh, God, have mercy on me!

CAPT. BRENNAN (*Encouragingly to* LANGON) A few steps more, Jim, a few steps more; thry to stick it for a few steps more.

LIEUT. LANGON   Oh, I can't, I can't, I can't!

CAPT. BRENNAN (*To* CLITHEROE) Are you comin', man, or are you goin' to make an arrangement for another honeymoon? . . . If you want to act th' renegade, say so, an' we'll be off!

BESSIE (*From window*) Runnin' from th' Tommies—choke th' chicken. Runnin' from th' Tommies—choke th' chicken!

CLITHEROE (*Savagely to* BRENNAN) Damn you, man, who wants to act th' renegade? (*To* NORA) Here, let go your hold; let go, I say!

NORA (*Clinging to* CLITHEROE, *and indicating* BRENNAN) Look, Jack, look at th' anger in his face; look at th' fear glintin' in his eyes. . . . He, himself's afraid, afraid, afraid! . . . He wants you to go th' way he'll have th' chance of death sthrikin' you an' missin' him! . . .

CLITHEROE (*Struggling to release himself from* NORA) Damn you, woman, will you let me go!

CAPT. BRENNAN (*Fiercely, to* CLITHEROE) Break her hold on you, man; or go up an' sit on her lap!

(CLITHEROE *tries to break her hold with his right hand (he's holding rifle in the other), but* NORA *clings to him.*)

NORA (*Imploringly*) Jack, Jack, Jack!

LIEUT. LANGON (*Agonizingly*) Brennan, a priest; I'm dyin', I think. I'm dyin'.

CLITHEROE (*To* NORA) If you won't do it quietly, I'll have to make you! (*To* BRENNAN) Here, hold this gun, you, for a minute. (*He hands the gun to* BRENNAN.)

NORA (*Pitifully*) Please, Jack. . . . You're hurting me, Jack. . . . Honestly. . . . Oh, you're hurting . . . me! . . . I won't, I won't, I won't! . . . Oh, Jack, I gave you everything you asked of me. . . . Don't fling me from you, now! (*He roughly loosens her grip, and pushes her away from him.* NORA *sinks to the steps at the door, and lies there.*)

NORA (*Weakly*) Ah, Jack. . . . Jack. . . . Jack!

CLITHEROE (*Taking the gun back from* BRENNAN) Come on, come on. (CLITHEROE *hurries over to* BRENNAN, *catches hold of* LANGON's *other arm; they both lift him up from steps, and supporting him, turn into the lane and go off* R. BESSIE *looks at* NORA *lying on the street, for a few moments, then, leaving the window, she comes out, runs over to* NORA, *lifts her up in her arms, and carries her swiftly into the house. A short pause, then down the street is heard a wild, drunken yell; it comes nearer, and* FLUTHER *enters, frenzied, wild-eyed, mad, roaring drunk. In his arms is an earthen half-gallon jar of whisky; streaming from one of the pockets of his coat is the arm of a new tunic shirt; on his head is a woman's vivid blue hat with gold lacing, all of which he has looted. The evening begins to darken.*)

FLUTHER (*Singing in a frenzy, as he comes down the lane*)

Fluther's a jolly good fella . . .
Fluther's a jolly good fella . . . up th' rebels!
. . . that nobody can deny!

(*He reels across to* L., *staggers up the steps of the house,* C., *and hammers at the door*) Get us a mug, or a jug, or somethin', some o' yous, one o' yous, will yous, before I lay one o' yous out! (*Rifle firing is heard some distance away and the boom of the big gun.* FLUTHER *turns from the door, and looks off* R.) Bang an' fire away for all Fluther cares. (*He beats at the door*) Come down an' open th' door, some o' yous, one o' yous, will yous, before I lay some o' yous out! . . . Th' whole city can topple home to hell, for Fluther. (*Inside the house,* C., *is heard a scream from* NORA, *followed by a moan. Singing frantically*) That nobody can deny, that nobody can deny.

For Fluther's a jolly good fella,
Fluther's a jolly good fella,
Fluther's a jolly good fella . . . up th' rebels!
. . . that nobody can deny!

(*His frantic movements cause him to spill some of the whisky out of the jar. Looking down at jar*) Blast you, Fluther, don't be spillin' th' precious liquor! (*He kicks at the door*) Give us a mug, or a jug, or somethin', one o' yous, some o' yous, will yous, before I lay one o' yous out!

(*The door suddenly opens, and* BESSIE, *coming out, grips him by the collar.*)

BESSIE (*Indignantly*)   You bowsey, come in ower o' that. . . . I'll thrim your thricks o' drunken dancin' for you, an' none of us knowin' how soon we'll bump into a world we were never in before!

FLUTHER (*As she is pulling him in*)   Ay, th' jar, th' jar, th' jar. *Mind th' jar!*

(*A short pause, then again is heard a scream of pain from* NORA. *The door opens and* MRS. GOGAN *and* BESSIE *are seen standing at it. The light gets dim.*)

BESSIE   Fluther would go, only he's too dhrunk. . . . Oh, God, isn't it a pity he's so dhrunk! We'll have to thry to get a docthor somewhere.

MRS. GOGAN   I'd be afraid to go. . . . Besides, Mollser's terrible bad. I don't think you'll get a docthor to come. It's hardly any use goin'.

BESSIE (*Determinedly*)   I'll risk it. . . . Give her a little of Fluther's whisky. . . . It's th' fright that's brought it on her so soon. . . . Go on back to her, you. (MRS. GOGAN *goes into the house, and* BESSIE *softly closes the door. She comes down steps, and is half-way across to* R., *when rifle-fire and the tok-tok-tok of a machine gun bring her to a sudden halt. She hesitates for a moment, then tightens her shawl round her, as if it were a shield. Softly*) O God, be Thou my help in time o' throuble; an' shelther me safely in th' shadow of Thy wings.[8] (*She goes forward, goes up the lane, and goes off* R.)

CURTAIN

Act IV

SCENE—*The living-room of* BESSIE BURGESS. *It is one of two small attic rooms (the other, used as a bedroom, is on the* L.), *the low ceiling slopes down towards the back. There is an unmistakable air of*

---

[8] Combination and misquotation of several psalms, particularly 17:8, 20:1, 57:1, 59:16.

poverty about the room. The paper on the walls is torn and soiled. On the R., *downstage is a door. A small window* C. *back. To* L. *of window, a well-worn dresser, with a small quantity of Delft. On the* L. *wall, upstage is a door leading to a bedroom. The door on* R. *leads to the rest of the house and street. Below door on* L. *wall, the fireplace. Inside fender is a kettle and saucepan. On the hob a teapot. In front of fire a well-worn armchair. In front of window, back, a little to* R., *an oak coffin stands on two kitchen chairs. On floor, front of coffin, is a wooden box, on which are two lighted candles in candlesticks. In front of coffin, a little to* L., *a small kitchen table. At* R. *end of table, a kitchen chair. In corner where* R. *and back walls meet, the standard lamp, with coloured shade, looted in Third Act, stands; beside the lamp, hanging from nail in wall, back, hangs one of the evening dresses. There is no light in the room but that given from the two candles and the fire. The dusk has well fallen, and the glare of the burning buildings in the town can be seen through the windows in the distant sky. The* COVEY, FLUTHER *and* PETER *have been playing cards, sitting on the floor by the light of the candles on the box near the coffin. When the* Curtain *rises the* COVEY *is shuffling the cards,* PETER *is sitting in a stiff, dignified way opposite him, and* FLUTHER *is kneeling beside the window, back, cautiously looking out into street. It is a few days later.*

FLUTHER (*Furtively peeping out of the window*)   Give them a good shuffling. . . . Th' sky's gettin' reddher an' reddher. . . . You'd think it was afire. . . . Half o' th' city must be burnin'.

THE COVEY (*Warningly*)   If I was you, Fluther, I'd keep away from that window. . . . It's dangerous, an', besides, if they see you, you'll only bring a nose on th' house.

PETER (*Anxiously*)   Yes; an' he knows we had to leave our own place th' way they were riddlin' it with machine-gun fire. . . . He'll keep on pimpin' an' pimpin' there, till we have to fly out o' this place too.

FLUTHER (*Ironically to* PETER)   If they make any attack here, we'll send you out in your green an' glory uniform, shakin' your sword over your head, an' they'll fly before you as th' Danes flew before Brian Boru![1]

---

[1] King of Munster who with Malachy, King of Meath, defeated and expelled the Norse invaders of Ireland in 1014, after their 183-year occupation. Died on April 23, Good Friday, at the Battle of Clontarf.

THE COVEY (*Placing the cards on the floor, after shuffling them*) Come on, an' cut. (FLUTHER *creeps* L. *end of table, over to where* COVEY *and* PETER *are seated, and squats down on floor between them. Having dealt the cards*) Spuds up again.[2]

(NORA *moans feebly in room on* L. *They listen for a moment.*)

FLUTHER There, she's at it again. She's been quiet for a good long time, all th' same.

THE COVEY She was quiet before, sure, an' she broke out again worse than ever. . . . What was led that time?

PETER (*Impatiently*) Thray o' Hearts, Thray o' Hearts, Thray o' Hearts.

FLUTHER It's damned hard lines to think of her dead-born kiddie lyin' there in th' arms o' poor little Mollser. Mollser snuffed it, sudden too, afther all.

THE COVEY Sure she never got any care. How could she get it, an' th' mother out day and night lookin' for work, an' her consumptive husband leavin' her with a baby to be born before he died.

VOICES (*In a lilting chant to the* L. *in an outside street*) Red Cr . . . oss, Red Cr . . . oss! . . . Ambu . . . lance, Ambu . . . lance!

THE COVEY (*To* FLUTHER) Your deal, Fluther.

FLUTHER (*Shuffling and dealing the cards*) It'll take a lot out o' Nora —if she'll ever be th' same.

THE COVEY Th' docthor thinks she'll never be th' same; thinks she'll be a little touched here. (*He touches his forehead*) She's ramblin' a lot; thinkin' she's out in th' counthry with Jack; or, gettin' his dinner ready for him before he comes home; or, yellin' for her kiddie. All that, though, might be th' chloroform she got. . . . I don't know what we'd have done only for oul' Bessie: up with her for th' past three nights, hand runnin'.

FLUTHER (*Approvingly*) I always knew there was never anything really derogatory wrong with poor Bessie. (*Suddenly catching* PETER's *arm as he is taking a trick*) Eh, houl' on there, don't be so damn quick—that's my thrick!

PETER (*Resentfully*) What's your thrick? It's my thrick, man.

FLUTHER (*Loudly*) How is it your thrick?

PETER (*Answering as loudly*) Didn't I lead th' deuce!

FLUTHER You must be gettin' blind, man; don't you see th' ace?

BESSIE (*Appearing at door of room,* L.; *in a tense whisper*) D'ye want to waken her again on me, when she's just gone asleep? If she wakes will yous come an' mind her? If I hear a whisper out o' one o' yous again, I'll . . . gut yous!

---

[2] Spud is the name of a card game.

THE COVEY (*In a whisper*)   S-s-s-h. She can hear anything above a whisper.

PETER (*Looking up at the ceiling*)   Th' gentle an' merciful God 'll give th' pair o' yous a scawldin', an' a scarifyin' one o' these days!

(FLUTHER *takes a bottle of whisky from his pocket, and takes a drink.*)

THE COVEY (*To* FLUTHER)   Why don't you spread that out, man, an' thry to keep a sup for to-morrow?

FLUTHER   Spread it out? Keep a sup for to-morrow? How th' hell does a fella know there'll be any to-morrow? If I'm goin' to be whipped away, let me be whipped away when it's empty, an' not when it's half-full! (BESSIE *comes in a tired way from door of room* L., *down to armchair by fire, and sits down. Over to* BESSIE) Well, how is she now, Bessie?

BESSIE   I left her sleeping quietly. When I'm listenin' to her babblin' I think she'll never be much betther than she is. Her eyes have a hauntin' way of lookin' in instead of lookin' out, as if her mind had been lost alive in madly minglin' memories of th' past. . . . (*Sleepily*) Crushin' her thoughts . . . together . . . in a fierce . . . an' fanciful . . . (*She nods her head and starts wakefully*) idea that dead things are livin', an' livin' things are dead. . . . (*With a start*) Was that a scream I heard her give? (*Reassured*) Blessed God, I think I hear her screamin' every minute! An' it's only there with me that I'm able to keep awake.

THE COVEY   She'll sleep, maybe, for a long time, now. Ten here.

FLUTHER (*Gathering up cards*)   Ten here. If she gets a long sleep, she might be all right. Peter's th' lone five.

THE COVEY (*Suddenly*)   Whisht! I think I hear somebody movin' below. Whoever it is, he's comin' up.

(*A pause. Then the door,* R. *opens, and* CAPT. BRENNAN *comes timidly in. He has changed his uniform for a suit of civies. His eyes droop with the heaviness of exhaustion; his face is pallid and drawn. His clothes are dusty and stained here and there with mud. He leans heavily on the back of a chair* R. *end of table.*)

CAPT. BRENNAN   Mrs. Clitheroe; where's Mrs. Clitheroe? I was told I'd find her here.

BESSIE   What d'ye want with Mrs. Clitheroe?

CAPT. BRENNAN   I've a message, a last message for her from her husband.

BESSIE   Killed! He's not killed, is he!

CAPT. BRENNAN (*Sinking stiffly and painfully on to a chair*)   In th' Imperial Hotel; we fought till th' place was in flames. He was shot through th' arm, an' then through th' lung. . . . I could do nothin' for him—only watch his breath comin' an' goin' in quick, jerky gasps, an' a tiny sthream o' blood thricklin' out of his mouth down over his lower lip. I said a prayer for th' dyin', an' twined his Rosary beads around his fingers. . . . Then I had to leave him to save meself. . . . (*He shows some holes in his coat*) Look at th' way a machine-gun tore at me coat, as I belted out o' th' buildin' an' darted across th' sthreet for shelter. . . . An' then, I seen The Plough an' th' Stars fallin' like a shot as th' roof crashed in, an' where I'd left poor Jack was nothin' but a leppin' spout o' flame!

BESSIE (*With partly repressed vehemence*)   Ay, you left him! You twined his Rosary beads round his fingers, an' then, you run like a hare to get out o' danger!

CAPT. BRENNAN (*Defensively*)   I took me chance as well as him. . . . He took it like a man. His last whisper was to "Tell Nora to be brave; that I'm ready to meet my God, an' that I'm proud to die for Ireland." An' when our General heard it he said that "Commandant Clitheroe's end was a gleam of glory." Mrs. Clitheroe's grief will be a joy when she realizes that she has had a hero for a husband.

BESSIE   If you only seen her, you'd know to th' differ.

(NORA *appears at door,* L. *She is clad only in her nightdress and slippers; her hair, uncared for some days, is hanging in disorder over her shoulders. Her pale face looks paler still because of a vivid red spot on the tip of each cheek. Her eyes are glimmering with the light of incipient insanity; her hands are nervously fiddling with her nightgown. She halts at the door for a moment, looks vacantly around the room, and then comes slowly in. The rest do not notice her till she speaks.* BESSIE *has fallen asleep in chair.* PETER, COVEY *and* FLUTHER *stop their card-playing and watch her.*)

NORA (*Roaming slowly towards* R. *to back of table*)   No . . . not there, Jack . . . I feel very, very tired . . . (*Passing her hand across her eyes*) Curious mist on my eyes. Why don't you hold my hand, Jack. . . . (*Excitedly*) No, no, Jack, it's not: can't you see it's a goldfinch? Look at the black satiny wings, with the gold bars, an' th' splash of crimson on its head. . . . (*Wearily*) Something ails me, something ails me. . . . (*Frightened*) You're goin' away, an' I can't follow you! (*She wanders back to* L. *end of table*) I can't follow you. (*Crying out*) Jack, Jack, Jack!

(BESSIE *wakes with a start, sees* NORA, *gets up and runs to her.*)

BESSIE (*Putting arm round* NORA)   Mrs. Clitheroe, aren't you a terrible woman to get out o' bed. . . . You'll get cold if you stay here in them clothes.

NORA (*Monotonously*)   Cold? I'm feelin' very cold . . . it's chilly out here in the counthry. (*Looking around, frightened*) What place is this? Where am I?

BESSIE (*Coaxingly*)   You're all right, Nora; you're with friends, an' in a safe place. Don't you know your uncle an' your cousin, an' poor oul' Fluther?

PETER (*Rising to go over to* NORA)   Nora, darlin', now—

FLUTHER (*Pulling him back*)   Now, leave her to Bessie, man. A crowd 'll only make her worse.

NORA (*Thoughtfully*)   There is something I want to remember, an' I can't. (*With agony*) I can't, I can't, I can't! My head, my head! (*Suddenly breaking from* BESSIE, *and running over to the men, and gripping* FLUTHER *by the shoulders*) Where is it? Where's my baby? Tell me where you've put it, where've you hidden it? My baby, my baby; I want my baby! My head, my poor head. . . . Oh, I can't tell what is wrong with me. (*Screaming*) Give him to me, give me my husband!

BESSIE   Blessin' o' God on us, isn't this pitiful!

NORA (*Struggling with* BESSIE)   I won't go away for you; I won't. Not till you give me back by husband. (*Screaming*) Murderers, that's what yous are; murderers, murderers!

(BESSIE *gently, but firmly, pulls her from* FLUTHER, *and tries to lead her to room,* L.)

BESSIE (*Tenderly*)   Ss-s-sh. We'll bring Mr. Clitheroe back to you, if you'll only lie down an' stop quiet. . . . (*Trying to lead her in*) Come on, now, Nora, an' I'll sing something to you.

NORA   I feel as if my life was thryin' to force its way out of my body. . . . I can hardly breathe . . . I'm frightened, I'm frightened, I'm frightened! For God's sake, don't leave me, Bessie. Hold my hand, put your arms around me!

FLUTHER (*To* BRENNAN)   Now you can see th' way she is, man.

PETER   An' what way would she be if she heard Jack had gone west?[3]

THE COVEY (*To* PETER, *warningly*)   Shut up, you, man!

BESSIE (*To* NORA)   We'll have to be brave, an' let patience clip away th' heaviness of th' slow-movin' hours, rememberin' that sorrow may endure for th' night, but joy cometh in th' mornin'. . . . Come on in, an' I'll sing to you, an' you'll rest quietly.

NORA (*Stopping suddenly on her way to the room*)   Jack an' me are goin' out somewhere this evenin'. Where I can't tell. Isn't it curious I can't remember. . . . (*Screaming, and pointing* R.) He's there, he's there, an' they won't give him back to me!

BESSIE   Sh-s-sh, darlin', s-ssh. I won't sing to you, if you're not quiet.

---

[3] Died.

NORA (*Nervously holding* BESSIE) Hold my hand, hold my hand, an' sing to me, sing to me!

BESSIE Come in an' lie down, an' I'll sing to you.

NORA (*Vehemently*) Sing to me, sing to me; sing, sing!

BESSIE (*Singing as she leads* NORA *into room,* L.)
> Lead, kindly light, amid th' encircling gloom,
>> Lead Thou me on.
> Th' night is dark an' I am far from home,
>> Lead Thou me on.

(*Leading* NORA, BESSIE *goes into room* L. *Singing softly inside room,* L.)
> Keep thou my feet, I do not ask to see
> The distant scene—one step enough for me.

THE COVEY (*To* BRENNAN) Now that you've seen how bad she is, an' that we daren't tell her what has happened till she's bether, you'd best be slippin' back to where you come from.

CAPT. BRENNAN There's no chance o' slippin' back now, for th' military are everywhere: a fly couldn't get through. I'd never have got here, only I managed to change me uniform for what I'm wearin'. . . . I'll have to take me chance, an' thry to lie low here for a while.

THE COVEY (*Frightened*) There's no place here to lie low. Th' Tommies 'll be hoppin' in here, any minute!

PETER (*Aghast*) An' then we'd all be shanghaied!

THE COVEY Be God, there's enough afther happenin' to us!

FLUTHER (*Warningly, as he listens*) Whisht, whisht, th' whole o' yous. I think I heard th' clang of a rifle butt on th' floor of th' hall below. (*All alertness*) Here, come on with th' cards again. I'll deal. (*He shuffles and deals the cards to all*) Clubs up. (*To* BRENNAN) Thry to keep your hands from shakin', man. You lead, Peter. (*As* PETER *throws out a card*) Four o' Hearts led. (*Heavy steps are heard coming up stairs, outside door* R. *The door opens and* CORPORAL STODDART *of the Wiltshires enters in full war kit—steel helmet, rifle, bayonet and trench tools. He stands near door* R., *looks around the room, and at the men who go on silently playing cards. A pause. Gathering up cards, and breaking the silence*) Two tens an' a five.

CORPORAL STODDART 'Ello. (*Indicating the coffin*) This the stiff?

THE COVEY Yis.

CORPORAL STODDART Who's gowing with it? Ownly one allowed to gow with it, you knaow.

THE COVEY I dunno.

CORPORAL STODDART You dunnow?

THE COVEY I dunno.

BESSIE (*Coming into the room*)   She's afther slippin' off to sleep again, thanks be to God. I'm hardly able to keep me own eyes open. (*To the soldier*) Oh, are yous goin' to take away poor little Mollser?

CORPORAL STODDART   Ay; 'oo's agowing with 'er?

BESSIE   Oh, th' poor mother, o' course. God help her, it's a terrible blow to her!

FLUTHER   A terrible blow? Sure, she's in her element now, woman, mixin' earth to earth, an' ashes t'ashes, an' dust to dust, an' revellin' in plumes an' hearses, last days an' judgements!

BESSIE (*Falling into chair by the fire*)   God bless us! I'm jaded![4]

CORPORAL STODDART   Was she plugged?

COVEY (*Shortly*)   No; died of consumption.

CORPORAL STODDART (*Carelessly*)   Ow, is that all—thought she might 'ave been plugged.

COVEY (*Indignantly*)   Is that all! Isn't it enough? D'ye know, comrade, that more die o' consumption than are killed in the war? An' it's all because of th' system we're livin' undher.

CORPORAL STODDART   Ow, I know. I'm a Socialist, myself, but I 'as to do my dooty.

COVEY (*Ironically*)   Dooty! Th' only dooty of a Socialist is th' emancipation of th' workers.

CORPORAL STODDART   Ow, a man's a man, an' 'e 'as to fight for 'is country, 'asn't 'e?

FLUTHER (*Aggressively*)   You're not fightin' for your counthry here, are you?

PETER (*Anxiously, to* FLUTHER)   Ay, ay, Fluther, none o' that, none o' that!

THE COVEY   Fight for your counthry! Did y'ever read, comrade, Jenersky's *Thesis on the Origin, Development an' Consolidation of th' Evolutionary Idea of the Proletariat?*

CORPORAL STODDART (*Good-humouredly*)   Ow, cheese it, Paddy, cheese it!

BESSIE (*Sleepily*)   How is things in th' town, Tommy?

CORPORAL STODDART   Ow, I think it's nearly over. We've got 'em surrounded, an' we're closing in on the blighters. It was only a bit of a dorg-fight.

(*Outside in the street is heard the sharp ping of a sniper's rifle, followed by a squeal of pain.*)

VOICES (*To the* L. *in a chant, outside in street*)   Red Cr . . . oss, Red Cr . . . oss! Ambu . . . lance, Ambu . . . lance!

---

[4] Worn out.

CORPORAL STODDART (*Going up* R. *and looking out of window, back*) Christ, there's another of our men 'it by the blarsted sniper! 'E's knocking abaht 'ere somewheres. (*Venomously*) Gord, wen we gets the blighter, we'll give 'im the cold steel, we will. We'll jab the belly aht of 'im, we will!

(MRS. GOGAN *enters tearfully by door* R.; *she is a little proud of the importance of being connected with death.*)

MRS. GOGAN (*To* FLUTHER) I'll never forget what you done for me, Fluther, goin' around at th' risk of your life settlin' everything with th' undhertaker an' th' cemetery people. When all me own were afraid to put their noses out, you plunged like a good one through hummin' bullets, an' they knockin' fire out o' th' road, tinklin' through th' frightened windows, an' splashin' themselves to pieces on th' walls! An' you'll find, that Mollser in th' happy place she's gone to, won't forget to whisper, now an' again, th' name of Fluther.

(CORPORAL STODDART *comes from window down* R. *to door* R., *and stands near the door.*)

CORPORAL STODDART (*To* MRS. GOGAN) Git it aht, mother, git it aht.

BESSIE (*From the chair*) It's excusin' me you'll be, Mrs. Gogan, for not stannin' up, seein' I'm shaky on me feet for want of a little sleep, an' not desirin' to show any disrespect to poor little Mollser.

FLUTHER Sure, we all know, Bessie, that it's vice versa with you.

MRS. GOGAN (*To* BESSIE) Indeed, it's meself that has well chronicled, Mrs. Burgess, all your gentle hurryin' to me little Mollser, when she was alive, bringin' her somethin' to dhrink, or somethin' t'eat, an' never passin' her without lifting up her heart with a delicate word o' kindness.

CORPORAL STODDART (*Impatiently, but kindly*) Git it aht, git it aht, mother. (*The men rise from their card-playing;* FLUTHER *and* BRENNAN *go* R. *to* R. *end of coffin;* PETER *and* COVEY *go* L. *of table to* L. *end of coffin. One of them takes box and candles out of way. They carry coffin down* R. *and out by door* R., CORPORAL STODDART *watching them.* MRS. GOGAN *follows the coffin out. A pause.* CORPORAL STODDART, *at door* R., *turns towards* BESSIE. *To* BESSIE, *who is almost asleep*) 'Ow many men is in this 'ere 'ouse? (*No answer. Loudly*) 'Ow many men is in this 'ere 'ouse?

BESSIE (*Waking with a start*) God, I was nearly asleep! . . . How many men? Didn't you see them?

CORPORAL STODDART Are they all that are in the 'ouse?

BESSIE (*Sleepily*) Oh, there's none higher up, but there may be more lower down. Why?

CORPORAL STODDART   All men in the district 'as to be rounded up. Somebody's giving 'elp to the snipers, an' we 'as to tike precautions. If
I 'ad my wy I'd mike 'em all join up an' do their bit! But I suppose
they an' you are all Shinners.[5]

BESSIE   (*Who has been sinking into sleep, waking up to a sleepy vehemence*)   Bessie Burgess is no Shinner, an' never had no thruck
with anything spotted be th' fingers o' th' Fenians. But always made
it her business to harness herself for Church whenever she knew
that God Save The King was goin' to be sung at t'end of th' service;
whose only son went to th' front in th' first contingent of the Dublin
Fusiliers, an' that's on his way home carryin' a shatthered arm
that he got fightin' for his King an' counthry!

(BESSIE's *head sinks slowly forward again. Door,* R., *opens and* PETER
*comes in, his body stiff, and his face contorted with anger. He goes
up* R., *to back, and paces angrily from side to side.* COVEY, *with a
sly grin on his face, and* FLUTHER *follow* PETER. FLUTHER *goes to* L.
and COVEY *goes to* R. *end of table.* BRENNAN *follows in and slinks to
back of table to* L. *corner between dresser and door,* L. CORPORAL
STODDART *remains standing a little in from door* R.)

FLUTHER   (*After an embarrassing pause*)   Th' air in th' sthreet outside's
shakin' with the firin' o' rifles, an' machine-guns. It must be a hot
shop in th' middle o' th' scrap.

CORPORAL STODDART   We're pumping lead in on 'em from every side, now;
they'll soon be shoving up th' white flag.

PETER   (*With a shout at* FLUTHER *and* COVEY)   I'm tellin' you either o'
yous two lowsers[6] 'ud make a betther hearseman than Peter!
proddin' an' pokin' at me an' I helpin' to carry out a corpse!

FLUTHER   (*Provokingly*)   It wasn't a very derogatory thing for th' Covey
to say that you'd make a fancy hearseman, was it?

PETER   (*Furiously*)   A pair o' redjesthered, bowseys pondherin' from
mornin' till night on how they'll get a chance to break a gap through
th' quiet nature of a man that's always endeavourin' to chase out
of him any sthray thought of venom against his fellaman!

THE COVEY   Oh, shut it, shut it, shut it!

PETER   (*Furiously*)   As long as I'm a livin' man, responsible for me
thoughts, words an' deeds to th' Man above, I'll feel meself insti-

[5] Members of Sinn Fein (pronounced Shin Fain), meaning We Ourselves
Alone, founded in 1905 by Arthur Griffith, dedicated to Irish independence. To the
British, and to many of the Irish, Sinn Fein became the name for the entire inde-
pendence movement.

[6] Scoundrels.

tuted to fight again' th' sliddherin' ways of a pair o' picaroons, whisperin', concurrin', concoctin' an' conspirin' together to rendher me unconscious of th' life I'm thryin' to live!

CORPORAL STODDART (*Dumbfounded*)   What's wrong, Paddy; wot 'ave they done to you?

PETER (*Savagely to the* CORPORAL)   You mind your own business! What's it got to do with you, what's wrong with me?

BESSIE (*In a sleepy murmur*)   Will yous thry to conthrol yourselves into quietness? Yous'll waken her . . . up . . . on . . . me . . . again. (*She sleeps.*)

FLUTHER (*Coming* C.)   Come on, boys, to th' cards again, an' never mind him.

CORPORAL STODDART   No use of you going to start cards; you'll be going aht of 'ere, soon as Sergeant comes.

FLUTHER (*In surprise*)   Goin' out o' here? An' why're we goin' out o' here?

CORPORAL STODDART   All men in district 'as to be rounded up, an' 'eld in till the scrap is over.

FLUTHER (*Concerned*)   An' where're we goin' to be held in?

CORPORAL STODDART   They're puttin' them in a church.

COVEY (*Astounded*)   A church?

FLUTHER   What sort of a church? Is it a Protestan' church?

CORPORAL STODDART   I dunno; I suppose so.

FLUTHER (*In dismay*)   Be God, it'll be a nice thing to be stuck all night in a Protestan' church!

CORPORAL STODDART   If I was you, I'd bring the cards—you might get a chance of a gime.

FLUTHER (*Hesitant*)   Ah, no, that wouldn't do. . . . I wondher. . . . (*After a moment's thought*) Ah, I don't think we'd be doin' anything derogatory be playin' cards in a Protestan' church.

CORPORAL STODDART   If I was you I'd bring a little snack with me; you might be glad of it before the morning. (*Lilting.*)

Oh, I do like a snice[7] mince pie,
Oh, I do like a snice mince pie.

Again the snap of the sniper's rifle rings out, followed by a scream of pain. CORPORAL STODDART *goes pale, runs up* R. *to near window,* C., *with his rifle at the ready.*

VOICES (*In street to* R., *chanting*)   Red Cr . . . oss . . . Red Cr . . . oss! Ambu . . . lance . . . Ambu . . . lance!

---

[7] Nice.

(*The door* R. *is dashed open, and* SERGEANT TINLEY, *pale, agitated and angry, comes rapidly in. He stands inside the door, glaring at men in the room.* CORPORAL STODDART *swings round at the ready as* TINLEY *enters and lets his rifle drop when he sees the* SERGEANT.)

CORPORAL STODDART (*To* SERGEANT)   One of our men 'it again, Sergeant?

SERGEANT TINLEY (*Angrily*)   Private Taylor: got it right through the chest, 'e did; an 'ole in front as ow you could put your 'and through, an' arf 'is back blown awy! Dum-dum bullets they're using. Gang of assassins potting at us from behind roofs. That's not plying the gime: why don't they come into the open and fight fair?

FLUTHER (*Unable to stand the slight, facing* SERGEANT)   Fight fair! A few hundhred scrawls o' chaps with a couple o' guns an' Rosary beads, again' a hundhred thousand thrained men with horse, fut an' artillery. . . . (*To others in room*) An' he wants us to fight fair! (*To* SERGEANT) D'ye want us to come out in our skins an' throw stones?

SERGEANT TINLEY (*To* CORPORAL)   Are these four all that are 'ere?

CORPORAL STODDART   Four; that's hall, Sergeant.

SERGEANT TINLEY (*Roughly*)   Come on, then, get the blighters aht. (*To the men*) 'Ere, 'op it aht! Aht into the street with you, an' if another of our men goes west, you go with 'im. (*He catches* FLUTHER *by the arm*) Go on, git aht!

FLUTHER (*Pulling himself free*)   Eh, who are you chuckin', eh?

SERGEANT TINLEY (*Roughly*)   Go on, git aht, you blighter.

FLUTHER (*Truculently*)   Who're you callin' a blighter to, eh? I'm a Dublin man, born an' bred in th' City, see?

SERGEANT TINLEY   Oh, I don't care if you were Bryan Buroo; git aht, git aht.

FLUTHER (*Pausing as he reaches door* R., *to face the* SERGEANT *defiantly*) Jasus, you an' your guns! Leave them down, an' I'd beat th' two of yous without sweatin'!

(*Shepherded by the two soldiers, who follow them out,* PETER, COVEY, FLUTHER *and* BRENNAN *go out by door* R. BESSIE *is sleeping heavily on the chair by the fire. After a pause* NORA *appears at door* L., *in her nightdress. Remaining at door for a few moments she looks vaguely around the room. She then comes in quietly, goes over to the fire, pokes it and puts the kettle on. She thinks for a few moments, pressing her hand to her forehead. She looks questioningly at the fire, and then at the press at back. She goes to the dresser* L., *back, opens drawer, takes out a soiled cloth and spreads it on the table. She then places things for tea on the table.*)

NORA   I imagine th' room looks very odd, somehow. . . . I was nearly forgetting Jack's tea. . . . Ah, I think I'll have everything done before he gets in. . . . (*She lilts gently, as she arranges the table.*)

> *Th' violets were scenting th' woods, Nora,*
>   *Displaying their charms to th' bee,*
> *When I first said I lov'd only you, Nora,*
>   *An' you said you lov'd only me.*
> *Th' chestnut blooms gleam'd through th' glade, Nora,*
>   *A robin sang loud from a tree,*
> *When I first said I lov'd only you, Nora,*
>   *An' you said you lov'd only me.*

(*She pauses suddenly, and glances round the room. Doubtfully.*) I can't help feelin' this room very strange. . . . What is it? . . . What is it? . . . I must think. . . . I must thry to remember. . . .

VOICES (*Chanting in a distant street*)   Ambu . . . lance, Ambu . . . lance! Red Cro . . . ss, Red Cro . . . ss!

NORA (*Startled and listening for a moment, then resuming the arrangement of the table*)

> *Trees, birds an' bees sang a song, Nora,*
>   *Of happier transports to be,*
> *When I first said I lov'd only you, Nora,*
>   *An' you said you lov'd only me.*

(*A burst of rifle-fire is heard in a street near by, followed by the rapid tok-tok-tok of a machine-gun. Staring in front of her and screaming*) Jack, Jack, Jack! My baby, my baby, my baby!

BESSIE (*Waking with a start*)   You divil, are you afther gettin' out o' bed again! (*She rises and runs towards* NORA, *who rushes to the window, back* L., *which she frantically opens.*)

NORA (*At the window, screaming*)   Jack, Jack, for God's sake, come to me!

SOLDIERS (*Outside, shouting*)   Git awoy, git awoy from that window, there!

BESSIE (*Seizing hold of* NORA)   Come away, come away, woman, from that window!

NORA (*Struggling with* BESSIE)   Where is it; where have you hidden it? Oh, Jack, Jack, where are you?

BESSIE (*Imploringly*)   Mrs. Clitheroe, for God's sake, come away!

NORA (*Fiercely*)   I won't; he's below. Let . . . me . . . go! You're thryin' to keep me from me husband. I'll follow him. Jack, Jack, come to your Nora!

BESSIE   Hus-s-sh, Nora, Nora! He'll be here in a minute. I'll bring him to you, if you'll only be quiet—honest to God, I will. (*With a great effort* BESSIE *pushes* NORA *away from the window, the force used causing her to stagger against it herself. Two rifle-shots ring out in quick succession.* BESSIE *jerks her body convulsively; stands stiffly upright for a moment, a look of agonized astonishment on her face, then she staggers forward, leaning heavily on the table with her hands. With an arrested scream of fear and pain*) Merciful God, I'm shot, I'm shot, I'm shot! . . . Th' life's pourin' out o' me! (*To* NORA) I've got this through . . . through you . . . through you, you bitch, you! . . . O God, have mercy on me! . . . (*To* NORA) You wouldn't stop quiet, no you wouldn't, you wouldn't, blast you! Look at what I'm afther gettin', look at what I'm afther gettin' . . . I'm bleedin' to death, an' no one's here to stop th' flowin' blood! (*Calling*) Mrs. Gogan, Mrs. Gogan! Fluther, Fluther, for God's sake, somebody, a doctor, a doctor!
(BESSIE, *leaving* R. *end of table, staggers down towards door* R., *but, weakening, she sinks down on her knees,* R.C., *then reclining, she supports herself by her right hand resting on floor.* NORA *is rigid with her back to wall,* L., *her trembling hands held out a little from her sides; her lips quivering, her breast heaving, staring wildly at the figure of* BESSIE.)

NORA   (*In a breathless whisper*)   Jack, I'm frightened. . . . I'm frightened, Jack. . . . Oh, Jack, where are you?

BESSIE   (*Moaningly*)   This is what's afther comin' on me for nursin' you day an' night. . . . I was a fool, a fool, a fool! Get me a dhrink o' wather, you jade, will you? There's a fire burnin' in me blood! (*Pleadingly*) Nora, Nora, dear, for God's sake, run out an' get Mrs. Gogan, or Fluther, or somebody to bring a doctor, quick, quick, quick! (*As* NORA *does not stir*) Blast you, stir yourself, before I'm gone!

NORA   Oh, Jack, Jack, where are you?

BESSIE   (*In a whispered moan*)   Jesus Christ, me sight's goin'! It's all dark, dark! Nora, hold me hand! (BESSIE's *body lists over and she sinks into a prostrate position on the floor*) I'm dyin', I'm dyin' . . . I feel it. . . . Oh God, oh God! (*She feebly sings*)

     I do believe . . . I will believe
     That . . . Jesus . . . died . . . for . . . me,
     That . . . on . . . the . . . cross He . . .
       shed . . . His . . . blood
     From . . . sin . . . to . . . set . . . free.

(*She ceases singing, and lies stretched out, still and rigid. A pause; then* MRS. GOGAN *runs hastily in by door* R. *She halts at door and looks round with a frightened air.*)

MRS. GOGAN (*Quivering with fear*) Blessed be God, what's afther happenin'! (*To* NORA) What's wrong, child, what's wrong? (*She sees* BESSIE, *runs to her and bends over the body.*) Bessie, Bessie! (*She shakes the body*) Mrs. Burgess, Mrs. Burgess! (*She feels* BESSIE's *forehead*) My God, she's as cold as death. They're afther murdherin' th' poor inoffensive woman!

(SERGEANT TINLEY *and* CORPORAL STODDART, *in agitation, enter by door* R., *their rifles at the ready.*)

SERGEANT TINLEY (*Excitedly*) This is the 'ouse! (*They go rapidly to window, back,* C.) That's the window!

NORA (*Pressing back against the wall*) Hide it, hide it; cover it up, cover it up!

(SERGEANT TINLEY, *looking round room, sees body. He comes from window to* BESSIE, *and bends over her.*)

SERGEANT TINLEY (*Bending over body*) 'Ere, wot's this? Oo's this? Oh, God, we've plugged one of the women of the 'ouse!

CORPORAL STODDART (*At window*) W'y the 'ell did she go to the window? Is she dead?

SERGEANT TINLEY Dead as bedamned. Well, we couldn't afford to tike any chances.

(SERGEANT TINLEY *goes back to window, and looks out.*)

NORA (*Screaming, and putting her hands before her face*) Hide it, hide it; don't let me see it! Take me away, take me away, Mrs. Gogan! (MRS. GOGAN, *who has been weeping softly over* BESSIE, *rises, and crosses by front of table to room,* L., *goes in and comes out with a sheet in her hands. She crosses over and spreads the sheet over* BESSIE's *body.*)

MRS. GOGAN (*As she spreads the sheet*) Oh, God help her, th' poor woman, she's stiffenin' out as hard as she can! Her face has written on it th' shock o' sudden agony, an' her hands is whitenin' into th' smooth shininess of wax.

NORA (*Whimperingly*) Take me away, take me away; don't leave me here to be lookin' an' lookin' at it!

MRS. GOGAN (*Going over to* NORA *and putting her arm round her*) Come on with me, dear, an' you can doss in poor Mollser's bed, till we gather some neighbours to come an' give th' last friendly touches to Bessie in th' lonely layin' of her out. (MRS. GOGAN *puts her arms round* NORA, *leads her across from* L. *to* R., *and they both go slowly out by door* R. CORPORAL STODDART *comes from window to table, looks at tea-things on table; goes to fireplace, takes the teapot up in his hand.*)

CORPORAL STODDART (*Over to* TINLEY, *at window*) Tea here, Sergeant; wot abaht a cup of scald?

SERGEANT TINLEY Pour it aht, pour it aht, Stoddart—I could scoff anything just now.

(CORPORAL STODDART *pours out two cups of tea.* SERGEANT TINLEY *comes from window to table, and sits on* R. *end;* CORPORAL STODDART *sits on opposite end of table, and they drink the tea. In the distance is heard a bitter burst of rifle and machine-gun fire, interspersed with the boom, boom of artillery. The glare in the sky seen through the window* C., *back, flares into a fuller and a deeper red.*)

SERGEANT TINLEY There gows the general attack on the Powst Office.

VOICES (*In a distant street*) Ambu . . . lance, Ambu . . . lance! Red Cro . . . ss, Red Cro . . . ss!

The voices of soldiers at a barricade outside the house are heard singing.

They were summoned from the 'illside,
They were called in from the glen,
And the country found 'em ready
At the stirring call for men.
Let not tears add to their 'ardship,
As the soldiers pass along,
And although our 'eart is breaking
Make it sing this cheery song.

SERGEANT TINLEY *and* CORPORAL STODDART *join in the chorus as they sip the tea.* SERGEANT TINLEY *and* CORPORAL STODDART *singing.*

Keep the 'ome fires burning,
While your 'earts are yearning.
Though your lads are far away,
They dream of 'ome;
There's a silver lining
Through the dark cloud shining,
Turn the dark cloud inside out,
Till the boys come 'ome!

THE END

COMMENTARY

The Plough and the Stars (1926)   Armed revolution against English oppression has been a recurrent feature of Irish history. In 1641, an Ulster rebellion precipitated nine years of ferocious fighting. To crush the rebels, England's new Puritan government in 1649 dispatched Oliver Cromwell, who had thousands of Irishmen killed, sent women in slavery to Barbados and Jamaica, and confiscated thousands of acres of land. Wolfe Tone led the United Irishmen in an unsuccessful uprising in 1798. At his court martial he declared that while Ireland was cursed by her servile ties to England she could neither be happy nor free. In 1803, Robert Emmet led another unsuccessful revolution. His address at his court martial was, like Tone's, quoted over a century later by Irishmen still chafing under English rule. Calling England a tyrant and Ireland a slave, Emmet compared his efforts in behalf of Irish independence and liberty to those of George Washington. The Fenians (the Irish Revolutionary Brotherhood) rose against England in 1867 and, like the earlier rebels, failed.

In the late nineteenth century, England's parliament defeated two bills that would have provided home rule for Ireland. In 1912 a third such bill passed the House of Commons and in 1914 the King approved it, but with the outbreak of World War I that year, he suspended home rule until hostilities ceased. Two years later, while English soldiers—and some Irish as well[1]—were fighting the Germans, another rising took place. Variously called the Easter Rising, the Easter Rebellion, the 1916 Rebellion, and Easter Week, it began on Monday, April 24, 1916 at noon, when rebels seized the General Post Office and proclaimed an Irish Republic. It ended on Saturday, April 29 at 3:45 P.M. when Padraic (Patrick) Pearse, their leader and provisional President of the Republic, surrendered unconditionally. Although the Easter Rising did not receive popular support, its aftermath resulted in a shift of sympathy in favor of the rebels, for the English, like their ancestors who dealt with Tone and Emmet, executed the fifteen leaders (their trials averaged five minutes each) and imprisoned over two thousand suspected rebels (more than participated in the Dublin rising). As the English thus radicalized the Irish people, Easter Week, in Sean O'Casey's words, "became the Year One in Irish history and life."

The Plough and the Stars resonates the events of the Easter Rebellion, including bombardment by the British, sniper fire by the rebels,

---

[1] Such as the son of Bessie Burgess in The Plough and the Stars.

385

and looting by the Dubliners. Instead of applauding this dramatization of Ireland's Year One, however, Dubliners rioted when the play was first produced at the Abbey Theatre. The irate audience shouted, cursed, whistled, and booed; threw vegetables and shoes onto the stage; set off stink bombs in the audience. A group of women climbed on stage to debate morality and patriotism with the actors. Some men scrambled to the stage and started a fight with the actors. Barry Fitzgerald, who was playing Fluther, socked one on the jaw and sent him crashing into the orchestra pit. The curtain was closed and the police sent for. William Butler Yeats— poet, playwright, Director of the Abbey, and also a member of the Irish Senate—confronted the crowd. "You have disgraced yourselves again," he castigated them. "Is this to be an ever-recurring celebration of the arrival of Irish genius? . . . From such a scene in this theatre went forth the fame of Synge. Equally the fame of O'Casey is born here tonight. This is his apotheosis."[2]

Why was the audience moved to riot? According to the enraged Dubliners, O'Casey's obscene and sexually degrading play ridiculed patriotism. They objected to such obscenities as "bitch" and to such near blasphemies as Mrs. Gogan's assertion that each of her children "was got between th' bordhers of th' Ten Commandments!" They regarded the love scene of Act I as too passionate. Some were appalled at the playwright's presentation of an Irish girl as a prostitute, which they considered unthinkable. Confronted with evidence of prostitution in Dublin, they declared that Dublin had no prostitutes until the English soldiers brought them. Objectors who were less naive about the facts of Dublin life were shocked that O'Casey presented a prostitute on stage. But prurience alone does not account for the vehemence of the Dubliners' responses. O'Casey's apparent lack of patriotism also angered them. Instead of eulogizing the rebels of Easter Week, he emphasized their vanity and fear; instead of praising the Dubliners' patriotism, he portrayed them as looters who mocked the soldiers. Furthermore, he dared to allow the tricolored flag of Ireland to be brought into a pub (a common occurrence, said the play's defenders).[3]

[2] Riots attended John Millington Synge's *The Playboy of the Western World* in 1907. Yeats might have added his own name to the list, for riots also greeted his first play, *The Countess Cathleen*, which was part of the first production (1899) of the Irish Literary Theatre, precursor of the Abbey.

[3] Before the play went into rehearsal, members of the company had similar objections. F. J. McCormack called the dialogue indecent and refused to say "snotty." One actress insisted that as a Catholic she could not speak Mrs. Gogan's line about the Ten Commandments, and withdrew from the role. Ria Mooney, playing Rosie, was advised that if she did not withdraw from the role she might not be considered respectable; she resisted such pressure. Gabriel Fallon asked that he play not Peter

O'Casey dramatized what he had observed in Dublin during Easter Week: the shooting and the shelling, the fear and the dying, the looting and the lack of sympathy toward the rebels. Instead of composing a patriotic anthem, he portrayed realistically and compassionately the condition of people caught up in revolution. His focus, however, is dual: not only the political turmoil but also, and primarily, the accidentally involved bystanders, the witnesses to revolution.

Although the preparations for the battle, and the battle itself, spill onstage—rousing speeches by an orator[4] and rifle fire, for example—it is not the soldiers but the Dublin tenement dwellers caught in the crossfire who are the chief characters of *The Plough and the Stars*. Victims of poverty, these slumdwellers are also victims of war. But O'Casey, himself born and bred in Dublin's slums, does not sentimentalize them. Pompous, foolish, jealous, frightened, belligerent, and thoughtless, they are also humane, loyal to each other, and courageous. Fluther risks his life to find Nora Clitheroe, then risks it again to make funeral arrangements for Mollser. Even the Covey and Peter, enemies during the first two acts, join forces during the shooting and risk their lives to find Nora and Fluther. Like the Covey and Peter, the women sink their differences in the face of a common danger. Bessie Burgess, who had fought Mrs. Gogan in the second act, helps her daughter in the third. Both Bessie and Mrs. Gogan, who were hostile toward Nora in Act I (Bessie almost hit her), help her in Act IV. In the last analysis, these Dublin slumdwellers value people more than principles, life more than war. Practical and apparently unheroic, they are actually more noble and heroic than the rebel soldiers, who would be (and have been) the heroes of conventional plays. In this play, it is the revolutionist Captain Brennan who demonstrates fear ("Thry to keep your hands from shakin', man," Fluther warns him in Act IV). Motivated as much by pride as by patriotism, the insurgents subscribe to romantic cant about war and glory. Until they face real bullets, their view of bloodshed is operatic.

The Plough and the Stars divides into two parts. Acts I and II occur before the Easter Rising, Acts III and IV during it. The first two acts reveal the illusions and ideals of revolution, the final two—in ironic contrast—the reality. "Bloodshed is a cleansing and sanctifying thing," de-

---

but Captain Brennan (a respectable patriot). In deference to the company, O'Casey agreed to some cuts, including the excision of Rosie's song at the end of Act II ("obscene," it was charged). For fuller accounts of the company's objections and of the riots, see Krause, Lady Gregory, and O'Casey (in bibliography following introduction).

4 Derived from actual speeches by rebel leader Padraic Pearse. For an analysis of O'Casey's use of Pearse's speeches, see Armstrong (in bibliography).

clares the offstage orator in the second act, "and the nation that regards it as the final horror has lost its manhood." Calling upon his audience to "rejoice in this terrible war," he fervently commands, "When war comes to Ireland she must welcome it as she would welcome the Angel of God!" By the time the play ends, the bloodshed has become a reality, but it is neither cleansing nor sanctifying, neither a cause for rejoicing nor an occasion of welcome. The rebel soldiers mimic the orator's warped rhetoric in phrases that by the end of the play turn grotesquely against them. "Imprisonment for th' Independence of Ireland!" cries Captain Brennan in Act II; in the last act he is taken away by the British. "Wounds for th' Independence of Ireland!" cries Lieutenant Langon after him; in Act III he is wounded. "Death for th' Independence of Ireland!" shouts Clitheroe next; in Act IV his death is reported. Langon calls Ireland "greater than a mother" and Clitheroe calls her "greater than a wife." In choosing the "greater," they leave lesser mothers and wives to suffer; in Act IV Bessie Burgess is shot and Nora Clitheroe goes mad. This contrast is vividly encapsulated in Act IV. When Captain Brennan declares that Nora's grief at her husband's death will turn to joy when she realizes he died a hero, Bessie corrects him: "If you only seen her, you'd know to th' differ."

Act I parodies romantic patriotism. Peter Flynn's peacocky uniform—bright green with gold braids, a frilled white shirt, white breeches, black boots, and a white ostrich plume in his hat—resembles, says Mrs. Gogan, "a woman's petticoat" and "[the] Lord Mayor's nightdhress." The Covey declares that it makes him look like a fugitive from a toy shop. Clitheroe, vain about his Citizen Army uniform, shows it off on every possible occasion, according to Fluther and Mrs. Gogan, who also exclaims, "God, I think he used to bring it to bed with him!" Brennan, no less conceited about his captain's uniform, will, says Clitheroe, be 'swankin' it at th' head of the Citizen Army carryin' th' flag of the Plough an' th' Stars." In the fourth act, however, Brennan—in order to evade the British—wears civilian clothes, the uniform of reality.[5]

Act II contrasts idealism and reality. The immediate results of the orator's patriotic cant about the beauty of bloodshed and the wonder of war are imitative barroom rhetoric (the empty bombast of the boozers comments cynically on the orator's language) and orders for ale. "A meetin' like this," says Peter, "always makes me feel as if I could dhrink Loch Erinn dhry!" Fluther is so inspired that he unhesitatingly jumps off

---

[5] Before the Easter Rising, O'Casey unsuccessfully tried to persuade the Citizen Army and the Irish Volunteers (the two major groups that were to participate in the rebellion) not to wear uniforms but instead to wear civilian garb. He advocated guerilla warfare rather than open warfare.

the water wagon. Symbolic of the revolutionary battle of the third and fourth acts is the fracas between Bessie Burgess and Mrs. Gogan, who defending her honor and dignity hands her baby to Peter so she can fight: an innocent victim (the baby/the tenement dwellers) is deemed less important than dignity and idealism (Mrs. Gogan's honor/Ireland's honor). Also, since Mrs. Gogan and Bessie have by this time, because of their political sympathies, become identified with Ireland and England, respectively, their fight parodies the political battle.

Although O'Casey does not deride the ideal of a free, independent Ireland, he does not in this play show the Easter Rebellion to have been worth the suffering it caused, and *The Plough and the Stars* might even imply that the rebels fought the wrong revolution.[6] The Young Covey states this explicitly: "There's only one war worth havin': th' war for th' economic emancipation of th' proletariat." But while he may speak for the author, O'Casey mocks him no less than he does the other idealists. Aggressively socialist, the Covey wears another "uniform," that of a socialist laborer, dungarees and a vivid, red tie. Cowardly, smart alecky, inhibited with women, and as bombastic as the orator, he apparently confines his revolutionary activities to words. He reads (or claims to have read) economic treatises and he talks a great deal, but nowhere does O'Casey suggest he does anything. Nor does his counterpart in the British Army do anything about the same professed ideals.

> COVEY *D'ye know, comrade, that more die o' consumption than are killed in the war? An' it's all because of th' system we're livin' undher.*
>
> CORPORAL STODDART *Ow, I know. I'm a Socialist, myself, but I 'as to do my dooty.*
>
> COVEY (Ironically) *Dooty! Th' only dooty of a Socialist is th' emancipation of th' workers.*
>
> CORPORAL STODDART *Ow, a man's a man, an' 'e 'as to fight for 'is country, 'asn't 'e?*

Though the socialism of the Covey and the Corporal is, like the uniform of Peter Flynn, decorative, and though the Covey is hardly an exemplary figure, it does not follow that his ideas are worthless.

The play's action suggests these ideas. In Act III, for instance,

---

[6] O'Casey, who helped organize the Citizen Army, did not join the Easter Rising. He had withdrawn from the Citizen Army because of its increasing collaboration with the Irish Volunteers, whose nationalism he felt would relegate his own socialist goals to second place—as it later did those of James Connolly, one of the leaders of the Rising and one of the founders of the Irish Socialist Republican Party. In joining the rebels, Connolly agreed to hold his socialist ideals in abeyance until Ireland achieved independence.

Mollser is dying of tuberculosis while people kill each other for nationalist goals. In Act IV, her coffin dominates the setting, a striking image of the killers the rebels are not fighting: poverty, slums, capitalism. Mollser had less of a chance than the rebels. "Sure she never got any care," says the Covey. "How could she get it, an' the mother out day and night lookin' for work, an' her consumptive husband leavin' her with a baby to be born before he died." No sooner are these words spoken than a voice outside calls for a Red Cross ambulance—not for a diseased slum child but for a wounded soldier. Implicit is the question of value. For what cause should men give their lives?

The title of the play is therefore ironic. The Plough and the Stars, flag of the Citizen Army—a workers' army, founded so that workers could protect themselves against strikebreaking police—is the flag of labor. Against a blue background, a golden-brown plough stands beneath a group of stars—symbols of the reality and the ideals of labor. But the flag of labor is raised in the cause of a nationalist revolution, not in the cause of the workers. Perhaps the author agrees with the Covey, who maintains, "They're bringin' nice disgrace on that banner now. . . . Because it's a Labour flag, an' was never meant for politics. . . . What does th' design of th' field plough, bearin' on it th' stars of th' heavenly plough, mean, if it's not Communism? It's a flag that should only be used when we're buildin' the barricades to fight for a Worker's Republic!"

Bibliography

A. Plays about the Irish Revolution:

G. P. Gallivan, Decision at Easter, 1959.

Denis Johnston, The Old Lady Says "No," 1929; The Scythe and the Sunset, 1958.

Sean O'Casey, Juno and the Paycock, 1925; The Shadow of a Gunman, 1922.

Lennox Robinson, The Big House, 1926; The Dreamers, 1915.

William Butler Yeats, Cathleen Ni Houlihan, 1902.

B. Works about Sean O'Casey and The Plough and the Stars:

Armstrong, W. A. "The Sources and Themes of The Plough and the Stars," Modern Drama, IV (December, 1961).

Hogan, Robert. *The Experiments of Sean O'Casey.* New York: St. Martin's
      Press, 1960.
Krause, David. *Sean O'Casey: The Man and His Work.* New York: Macmillan,
      1960.
Lady Gregory's Journals, 1916–1930. Edited by Lennox Robinson. New York:
      Macmillan, 1947.
O'Casey, Sean. *Inishfallen Fare Thee Well.* New York: Macmillan, 1949.

The Chinese Communist Revolution

THE LONG MARCH
Chen Chi-tung

THE LONG MARCH
Chen Chi-tung

CHARACTERS

CHAO CHIH-FANG *aged 21, Commander, First Company, First Battalion of the Red Army; later Acting Battalion Commander, and Battalion Political Instructor.*

LO SHUN-CHENG *aged 31, Deputy Commander, later Commander, First Battalion.*

LI YU-KUO *aged 27, Political Instructor, First Battalion.*

HUANG *aged 27, Commander, First Regiment.*

WANG TEH-CHIANG *aged 21, Commander, Second Company.*

WU *aged 18, Propaganda Group Leader, First Division.*

LI FENG-LIEN *aged 18, member of Propaganda Group, LI YU-KUO's younger sister, betrothed to CHAO CHIH-FANG.*

CHENG LI *aged 16, member of Propaganda Group.*

TIGER CUB *aged 18, runner, First Battalion; later Squad Leader.*

LITTLE WAN *aged 17, HUANG's bodyguard.*

LITTLE CHIN *aged 17, runner, First Company.*

LITTLE TANG *aged 17, runner, First Battalion.*

CHANG TEH-MING *aged 21, organizer, Political Department, First Division.*

PEASANTS' ASSOCIATION CHAIRMAN

WOMEN'S ASSOCIATION CHAIRMAN

CHIEN KUEI-HSI *aged 21, Red Guard; later scout, First Battalion.*

YOUNG CHOU *aged 16, peasant lad; later runner, First Battalion.*

MOTHER CHOU *over 50.*

AN OLD PEASANT

POLITICAL INSTRUCTOR HSIEH

NURSE CHANG *aged 16, chief nurse of a Red Army field hospital.*

CHU *Commander, Third Company, First Battalion.*

A YI *aged 25, local Yi leader (Yi—one of China's minority peoples).*

FIVE OTHER RED ARMY OFFICERS OF COMPANY RANK

A SCORE OF RED ARMY MEN

PEASANT MEN AND WOMEN *young and middle-aged.*

AN OLD BOATMAN

AN OLD TIBETAN *member of one of the committees of the district government.*

395

HIS WIFE *over 50.*
SHANA WURSE *aged 16, his daughter.*
SHALU CHODENG *aged 18, his son.*
TIBETANS AND LAMAS
On the enemy side:

> COMPANY COMMANDER NIU
> SQUAD LEADER HU
> A DEPUTY SQUAD LEADER
> SOLDIERS

Act I

TIME *A moonlit night in mid-February 1935.*

PLACE *The Shens' ancestral temple, at the foot of Loushankuan Pass, which commands the gateway to Tsunyi in Kweichow Province. The large room, at the rear of the temple, had been, for the last four weeks or so, the township government centre set up by the Red Army. Then it had been retaken by a battalion of Chiang Kai-shek's militia.*

SCENE *There is a large round window, centre, back. Left, a gate opens on to a covered path leading to the main hall. Right, a door opens on to a small path that runs up the hill. Through the round window can be seen stone steps, leading to the Pass, dotted with clumps of bamboo and banana plants here and there. On the wall are two pictures, the God of Culture and the God of War, pasted on either side of a maxim: "A good parent must teach his sons the classics." There is some furniture—an old square table with an oil lamp, tea-cups and long tobacco pipes on it, two big chairs, and a bamboo settee and tea-table, but all is in disorder, following the Kuomintang's panic-stricken flight.*

> *There are signs of the recent changes. Kuomintang slogans "Down with the Communists!" and "Wipe out the Reds!" are still on the wall, roughly pasted across the Communist slogans: "Long live the Chinese Communist Party!" and "Long live Chairman Mao!" Below, the words "Propaganda Department, First Division, Red Army, 6 January 1935" can just be seen.*

The moonlight is bright. The oil lamp in the room flickers from time to time, and shows us a peasant, CHIEN KUEI-HSI, *roped up to an overhead beam, struggling to free himself. Shots are heard offstage in rapid succession. A shell whines overhead and explodes. Then the Deputy Commander of First Battalion,* LO SHUN-CHENG, *is seen running up the stone steps.*

LO   Come on, comrades! Charge! Capture the Pass!
    (*A group of Red Army men rush up the steps.*)
LO (*shouting*)   Company Commander Wang! Company Commander Wang! Tiger Cub!
TIGER CUB (*offstage*)   Coming!
LO   Tell Company Commander Wang to hurry up, quick.
TIGER CUB (*offstage*)   Right!
LO   Comrades, charge! Capture the Pass! We've got the enemy on the run!
    (*They follow him up the steps, out of sight.*)
CHIEN (*shouting*)   Get them! Comrades, get the brutes!
    (LI YU-KUO, *Political Instructor of First Battalion,* TIGER CUB, *a runner, and* WANG TEH-CHIANG, *Commander of Second Company, First Battalion, rush up the hill following the group of Red Army men.* COMMANDER CHAO CHIH-FANG *of First Company and* LITTLE CHIN, *a runner, enter, guns in hand.*)
CHAO (*to* CHIEN)   Hands up!
CHIEN   I can't move. Get these ropes off me, can't you? It's all right, comrades, we're all on the same side.
CHAO   Who are you?
CHIEN   A Red Guard. Chien Kuei-hsi's my name. Look, Company Commander Chao, you know me really. It's not a month since you put up at my house for a week.
CHAO (*untying the ropes*)   Well! Chien Kuei-hsi! How did you get in this fix?
CHIEN   Oh, it's a long story. . . .
CHAO   Where's the enemy got to now?
    (CHIEN *is freed.*)
CHIEN   They've all fled, to Loushankuan Pass. Hey, lend me your bayonet! (*Grabs* CHAO's *bayonet without waiting for an answer and dashes out of the room.*) Forward, comrades!
LITTLE CHIN   Phew! What a firebrand!
CHAO (*calling after* CHIEN)   Chien Kuei-hsi, hold on there, what. . . .
    (LI FENG-LIEN, *a girl worker in the Propaganda Group, comes on stage.*)
FENG-LIEN (*interrupting*)   Who are you talking to?

CHAO (*surprised*)   What on earth are you doing here? Go away!

FENG-LIEN   I've come to see what I can do, of course.

CHAO   Where's your group leader?

FENG-LIEN   He's gone off with the Chairman of the Peasants' Association to get hold of some stretcher-bearers. There you are! That's the Peasant Chairman talking now.
(*Offstage, distant shouting "Come on, everybody, come on . . ."* *can be heard, as the* PEASANT CHAIRMAN *and the peasants spread the news that the Red Army is back.*)

CHAO   Oho! So you've already found the Chairman of the Peasants' Association! And you're getting hold of stretchers?

TIGER CUB (*runs in*)   Company Commander Chao! Deputy Battalion Commander Lo and Third Company are attacking the Pass, but they've been surrounded. The supporting Second Company got there a bit late.

CHAO   H'm. What can we do now, I wonder. Our orders are to stand by, really. Where's the Political Instructor?

TIGER CUB   He's fallen back. He's coming down now with one of the platoons.

CHAO   Go and tell him that I'm coming with reinforcements. (*Shouting out of the window.*) First Platoon there! Fix bayonets! Follow me!
(*Just as* CHAO *is leaving,* POLITICAL INSTRUCTOR LI YU-KUO *comes on.*)

LI   I say, Lao Chao, Second Company were much too slow off the mark today. Lo and his men are surrounded up there. We tried to get the platoon up the hill but we couldn't make it. Second, Third and Fourth Regiments are mounting an all-out attack on the Pass now. (*Shooting is heard in the distance.*)

CHAO   I propose to take First Company up, and make a frontal attack, while you attack the flanks with Second.

LI   Thought you were reserves?

CHAO   Not much sense in calling ourselves reserves, when our main force is right behind us.

LI   But who'll look after the prisoners?

CHAO   The Propaganda Group can do it, can't they?
(*The runner* LITTLE TANG *runs in.*)

LITTLE TANG   Political Instructor! Second, Third and Fourth Regiments have come up, and a frontal attack's starting. Commander Lo's men are fighting hand-to-hand now, with bayonets.

CHAO   D'you agree, Political Instructor?

LI   All right. I agree.

CHAO (*runs out, right, and is seen on the stone steps*)   First Company! Follow me!

(CHAO *and Red Army men dash off, followed by* LITTLE TANG. WU, *the Propaganda Group Leader, the Chairman of the Peasants' Association, and a dozen or so young peasants with stretchers enter.*)

WU   Political Instructor, here's the Chairman of the Peasants' Association, and his stretcher-bearers.

LI   (*greeting them with great warmth*)   You're a welcome sight—all of you. (*To* PEASANT CHAIRMAN.) How's life been treating you since I saw you last?

PEASANT CHAIRMAN   No time to tell you all that now! I've got more than twenty men here with me. We can give you a hand—act as guides, stretcher-bearers, guard the prisoners. . . . We're at your disposal, Political Instructor!
(LITTLE WAN *runs on.*)

LITTLE WAN   Political Instructor, the Regimental C.O. wants you immediately.

LI   (*to* PEASANT CHAIRMAN)   Will you come with me? (*Goes off with* LITTLE WAN.)

PEASANT CHAIRMAN   Right you are! (*To the peasants.*) Come on, mates. (*All follow.*)

WU   Aiya! I remember we put up in this room four weeks ago. Didn't we stick some slogans up here? (*Strips off the Kuomintang slogans.*) I thought so! Here they are still.
(*A distressed woman's voice is heard offstage:* "Oh, comrades! Comrades!")

WU   Sounds like a woman. (*To* FENG-LIEN.) Can you organize some cooked food for all of us? If enough people turn up, we can get the township government set up again right away. I'm going to see who that is calling. (*Goes off.*)

FENG-LIEN   All right. (*Goes off.*)
(TIGER CUB, *coming down the steps outside, meets* REGIMENTAL COMMANDER HUANG *climbing up.*)

TIGER CUB   Regimental Commander! Company Commander Chao has taken the hill. His men've got the enemy licked! They're on the run.

HUANG   (*on the stone steps*)   Fine! Little Wan! Tell Third Battalion to get ahead quick and cut off their retreat. Tell Regimental HQ to move up. (*Goes off.*)

LITTLE WAN   (*offstage*)   Right!
(*The shooting dies down.* WU *comes back, helping the* WOMEN'S CHAIRMAN *along. She is dishevelled and exhausted.*)

WU   There you are—rest here, now.
(FENG-LIEN *returns on stage.*)

FENG-LIEN   Comrade Wu, the township turned up to greet us directly they heard the shooting! (*Sees the* WOMEN'S CHAIRMAN.) Oh, my dear comrade! Whatever have they done to you?

WOMEN'S CHAIRMAN (*bursting into tears*)   We had a terrible time after you went away. All the local bullies and the landlords came back. They hunted us night and day. We tried to hide, of course, and fled from place to place. We got our clothes torn to shreds, lost our shoes and had no food most of the time. I'd made up my mind to go and get hold of Chien Kuei-hsi, and join our village guerillas. But I've no experience in this sort of thing and walked straight into their hands the moment I entered Chien's house. They dragged me up to the temple here, and they've been at me, beating me and bullying, to make me give our Chairman away. But I didn't tell them a thing. Oh, comrades, we'd all have been done for if you hadn't come now! (*Breaks down into a storm of tears.*)

FENG-LIEN   What sort of outfit occupied this place after we went?

WOMEN'S CHAIRMAN   They had a regimental headquarters here. They only fled when your attack started.
(CHENG LI, *one of the Propaganda Group, enters, beaming, and greets* WU *and the* WOMEN'S CHAIRMAN.)

WOMEN'S CHAIRMAN   Oh, Cheng Li! I've had a terribly narrow escape!

WU   What is it, Cheng Li? Tell me quickly.

CHENG LI   As soon as they heard the shooting the villagers came back. They're all out in force to welcome us. They've brought us no end of gifts—not forgetting to send up half a dozen captured landlords! They're demanding a public trial for the beasts!

WU (*with deep feeling*)   The people have risen!
(*A crowd of excited peasants swarm in, left. Greetings to* WU *are shouted as they see him. "Comrades, you're back!" "We have had a bad time since we saw you last!" etc., etc. The hubbub dies down as an old peasant comes forward carrying a bottle of Maotai.*)

OLD PEASANT   Comrade Wu, do you remember me? Your Political Instructor Li once stayed at my house. In the land distribution, when you were here last month, we settled accounts with our local bullies and confiscated their things. You gave me clothes and rice, and two rooms to live in. I went out then to buy a bottle of Maotai to give all of you a drink, in gratitude. But when I got back with it, you'd gone! (*Wipes away a tear.*) Oh, you don't know how the White army fiends beat me up. Oh, comrades! But I managed to keep the Maotai, all right. Here it is—it's for you.

WU (*doesn't know how to refuse*)   Well. . . .
(YOUNG CHOU, *a young peasant lad, pushes through the crowd, manhandling a 50-year-old landlord in front of him.*)

YOUNG CHOU (*edging his way in*) Make way, please! (*To the landlord.*) Keep still, you! Group Leader Wu!

WU Who's this?

YOUNG CHOU My name's Chou. When you were here before, my dad was put on the district government, and when you left he didn't get away in time. And then this old bastard (*shakes the landlord*) came back and beat my dad till he died. When I heard the shooting this evening, I rushed straight round to his house with a meat chopper and got him. I demand a trial for him quick—My dad's death must be avenged!

WU Right! We'll see to it for you when we hold the public trial.
(*The crowd stirs and murmurs. "That's fine." "Let's try him now." "Good." "Justice will be done!" etc., etc. A young lad comes forward with a bundle, followed by a girl.*)

YOUNG LAD (*to* WU) Comrade, this is for you!

YOUNG GIRL This, too!

WU Comrades, the army thanks you for your gifts. We'll hold a trial, but first we have to set up the township government again.

CROWD That's right. Where're the people we elected last month?
(*The old peasant sees the* WOMEN'S CHAIRMAN, *and pulls her forward.*)

OLD PEASANT Here's one, surely. Wasn't she the Chairman of the Women's Association?
(*Crowd murmurs in sympathy at her distraught appearance.*)

WOMEN'S CHAIRMAN Neighbours, this room's too small for us to hold a meeting in. Let's go to the main hall. I've got a lot to tell you and our Red Army comrades.
(*Peasants shout agreement, and start to move off.*)

WOMEN'S CHAIRMAN Come on, comrades.

WU All right. (*To* FENG-LIEN.) Can you take these gifts over to Battalion HQ? (*Turns to* CHENG LI.) You can come along, too.
(*All go off except* FENG-LIEN. *Stretcher-bearers are seen on the stone steps, carrying the wounded down. Offstage,* LO's *voice is heard addressing his men. His words are punctuated with shouts of approval. "Comrades!" he says, "we've fought a good battle this evening. Now get a bite quick and snatch a bit of rest. We've got another battle ahead of us, to do as well in!" With another roar of approval the men are heard marching off, laughing and cheering.* LO *comes on stage.*)

LO Phew, I'm dead beat.

FENG-LIEN (*picking up the gifts*) Deputy Battalion Commander Lo, is it all over?

LO Just about. We've knocked out a militia detachment, and two and a half regiments of Wang Chia-lieh's regulars—*and* three more of his regiments are on the run. (*His voice rises with enthusiasm.*) I can tell you, the men did a magnificent job tonight. *And* a quick one—it only took us about twenty minutes.

FENG-LIEN   Our Artillery Company did their stuff, too.

LO   You're right. They got their two rounds bang on, and smashed the fortifications to smithereens just when we wanted it. (*Sees the eggs and wine on the table.*) What's this? Gifts from the peasants? Can I have some?

FENG-LIEN (*passing over the wine*)   Of course—here you are. (*In a changed tone.*) Are there many stretcher cases this time?

LO   Only a few. (*Drinks.*) That goes down well! Feng-lien, one more big victory like this will turn the situation completely in our favour. (*Wistfully.*) This area seems to me to have everything we need for a revolutionary base.

FENG-LIEN (*sticking to her enquiries*)   Were any of the officers wounded?

LO (*in his dream of a base right here*)   M'm! (*Has another drink.*) This Maotai smells wonderful!

FENG-LIEN (*alarmed and impatient*)   What's that?

LO   I said, if we win another victory we'll probably settle down right here and turn it into a base. Or perhaps we can even go back to our old base in Kiangsi. Don't you want to go back, too?

FENG-LIEN   Can't you answer my question? I asked if any of the officers were wounded?

LO   I think so—some.

FENG-LIEN   Have you seen my brother since?

LO   Yes, he's gone to see the wounded. He'll be back in a minute.

FENG-LIEN   Company Commander Chao was in quite a state about you, you know, when he heard you were surrounded.

LO   Chao's fine, I can tell you. He was fine. . . . He makes up his mind quickly and acts on it. If he hadn't brought his men up, I don't know what would have happened to us. He's as brave as a tiger, too, when it comes to actual fighting.

FENG-LIEN   D'you know where he is now?

LO (*playing dumb*)   Where who is?

FENG-LIEN   Chao Chih-fang, you stupid, Chao Chih-fang!

LO (*teasingly*)   D'you think I didn't know what you were after? Of course you're worried about him because he comes from your home town, and he's an old friend of your brother's. . . . Funny how you miss him the moment he's out of your sight.

FENG-LIEN   Oh, shut up! Can't you say whether he was wounded or not?

LO (*still joking*)   Well, yes, he was, I'm afraid. Rather seriously, too.

FENG-LIEN (*nettled at* LO's *joke*) It's a glorious thing for us to be wounded in battle, fighting for the revolution. And he was fighting for the sake of impetuous fools like you, too.

LO (*bursts out laughing*) All right, all right. Don't get excited. Your precious Chao Chih-fang didn't even get a scratch.

FENG-LIEN (*proudly, but relieved*) Well, as a matter of fact, it isn't so easy for the enemy to hit a brave man. (*Picks up the gifts, and turns to go.*)

LO Where are you off to?

FENG-LIEN I'm going to take this stuff to the wounded.

(LI YU-KUO, CHAO CHIH-FANG, WANG TEH-CHIANG *and* TIGER CUB *enter.*)

LI Comrades, we've done a good job tonight and Regimental HQ is very pleased. The comrades there are coming in to see us soon.

LO Hello, here you all are! (*Turns to* FENG-LIEN, *to tease her in front of the others.*) Well, as I was saying, comrade, I'm glad to say your Chao Chih-fang got off without a scratch. (*Leaves the subject and returns to business.*) You chaps hurry up with your meal. We've only got two hours, and we must squeeze in an hour's rest before we get going again.

FENG-LIEN (*with a smile*) Battalion Commander, guess who sent this Maotai over.

LO Peasants who support the Red Army, of course. Who else could it be?

FENG-LIEN You're wrong. It was a special gift from the old peasant friend you stayed with before. Don't forget to thank him for it. (*Goes off.*)

LO (*surprised*) Oh, it must be from Lao Sun! All right, I'll look in on him tomorrow and give him something in return. Come on, let's all have a drink. (*Turns to* TIGER CUB.) Can you get us some drinking water? And get us whatever you've got in the way of food.

TIGER CUB Right away! (*Fishes biscuits, cigarettes, etc. out of his ration bag.*) Try these. It's part of the victory. (*Goes off.*)

LI The little devil knows where to look for food. (*Starts in on a biscuit.*) Biscuits! Help yourselves, comrades. Only mind you leave some for the Regimental Commander!

LO Right. Have an egg . . . here. (*Hands round the eggs and raises his cup.*) But let's have a drink first.

LI Now, Company Commander Wang, what held you up this evening?

LO He doesn't seem half as bright as he used to be. He can be as quick as a rabbit. But sometimes he dawdles, just when what you're looking for is a little quick action.

WANG I wasn't being slow on purpose, you know. I'd have liked to catch up with you, or even outstrip you. But as soon as we got up the hill, the damned militiamen fled in all directions, and my men went after them. It took me some time to get my company into shape again. There wasn't much else I could do.

LO   That shows you haven't kept your men under strict discipline. They're still acting like a bunch of guerillas! Seriously, you ought to admit you were to blame.

WANG   But those militiamen ran helter-skelter the moment we charged. If I'd let them escape, you'd have blamed me for that!

LO   No, Wang! Didn't I tell you clearly before we went into battle that Loushankuan Pass was the essential thing? I don't know what's the matter—you don't seem to be half as bright as you were. All I can say is that you'd better not make the same sort of mistake again, or you'll catch it from me. Come on now, have an egg.

WANG   D'you really want me to put in a self-criticism?

LO   Well, have an egg, anyway.

WANG   Just wait and see whether I'm quick next time.

(*The* PEASANT CHAIRMAN *enters.*)

PEASANT CHAIRMAN   Battalion Commander! Political Instructor! We've just finished seeing to the wounded. Anything else you want us to do?

LO (*pulls* PEASANT CHAIRMAN *over*)   No, thanks. You've been fine. Come on now, sit down and have a drink.

LI (*filling his cup*)   Chairman, let's drink to the victory. It's over a month since we saw you last.

PEASANT CHAIRMAN   We missed you badly, you know.

LI   I know. You must have had a rough time after we went.

PEASANT CHAIRMAN   I couldn't tell you how bad it was if I had three nights and days to do it in. They burnt my house down and killed my father. I went into the hills with a dozen or so others. We only had weeds and cold water to live on. Aiya! Still, the enemy never managed to lay a finger on us!

(LI FENG-LIEN *enters.*)

FENG-LIEN   Oh, here you are, Chairman! You've been elected the township government chairman. The people are looking for you, because they want to start the public trial. Can you come at once?

PEASANT CHAIRMAN   Eh! Chairman of the township government! No, no, comrades. I've promised the others that I'd join the Red Army with them tomorrow.

(LO *and* WANG *exclaim in welcome.*)

LI (*reconsidering it*)   No. We welcome all of them, *except* the chairman of the township government. The people are waiting for you to preside over the trial. You'd better go now.

PEASANT CHAIRMAN   All right. I'll go now, but I'll talk it over with you
again later.
FENG-LIEN   I'm coming with you.
      (PEASANT CHAIRMAN *and* FENG-LIEN *go out.* HUANG *and* LITTLE WAN
      enter.)
HUANG   Aha, you've got quite a party on here, I see. You'll have to hurry
up, though. We've got some new combat orders.
LI   We're ready any time. (*Hands* HUANG *a drink.*) Regimental Com-
mander, a cup of wine for you, a gift from the peasants.
HUANG   Great! (*Holding up his cup.*) To our first victory under the
leadership of Chairman Mao since the Tsunyi Conference. *Kanpei!*
LO   (*holds out a couple of eggs*)   Want some eggs?
HUANG   Thanks. (*Eating.*) The peasants here have always been poor
and the war must have made things even worse. And we take their
gifts. . . .
WANG   We must win more battles!
HUANG   You're right, comrade. Now let's get down to business. (*Turning
to* LITTLE WAN.) Shut the door, will you?
LITTLE WAN   Right! (*Closes the door.*)
      (TIGER CUB *comes up with a kettle of boiled water and pours out a
      bowl for each.*)
WANG   I must be getting back to my men now.
CHAO   Yes. I must be moving too.
HUANG   Company Commander Chao, stay behind a minute, will you?
I've got something to say to you.
CHAO   Right!
      (WANG *goes off.*)
HUANG   Comrades, I've got two bits of good news for you. First, with
Second, Third and Fourth Regiments, we have succeeded in taking
Loushankuan Pass and Tsunyi City, wiped out two and a half
Wang Chia-lieh regiments and routed three others. Divisional HQ
has congratulated us on this, and wishes us even greater successes.
(*Offstage, but near by, in the adjoining temple, shouting can be
heard: "Long live the Chinese Workers' and Peasants' Red Army!
Long live the Chinese Communist Party!"*)
HUANG (*continuing*)   Second, we've had the essentials of the report of
the Tsunyi Conference.
      (LO, LI *and* CHAO *stir, and murmur approval* "Good." "Can we hear
      it?" *and so on.*)
HUANG   The Conference severely criticized military adventurism and
accepted the line advocated by Chairman Mao as correct—that is,
to march north to resist Japanese aggression.

(*His listeners turn to one another enthusiastically: "March north to resist the Japanese!"*)

HUANG   The present situation is like this. The Japanese invaders have seized the three Northeastern provinces and the whole country is demanding that they should be resisted. But Chiang Kai-shek has infuriated the people by wanting to wage a civil war instead. As Chairman Mao points out, there's another high tide of revolution approaching. Our army, the Workers' and Peasants' Red Army, has won the support of the whole people. The strength of our forces in various parts is growing daily. The units we've left behind in the kiangsi base are also growing, while those in the Hupeh-Honan-Anhwei border region are triumphantly moving towards northern Shensi. The Second and Fourth Front Red Armies are this very moment fighting and winning battles. They have a rousing welcome in store for us. They are looking forward to joining forces with us north of the Yangtse.

(*There are further shouts offstage, "Long live Chairman Mao!"*)

LO   What are we going to do? Head north all the way?

HUANG   First we'll cross the Yangtse, and join up with the Fourth Front Army.

(*LO, LI and CHAO are really excited. "That'll be some force!"*)

HUANG (*warningly*)   Yes, but Chiang Kai-shek is still sticking to his treachery and his policy of civil war. He'll try to stop us going north. In fact, our immediate enemy at present is. . . .

ALL   Chiang Kai-shek!

(*Shouts offstage: "Down with traitor Chiang Kai-shek!"*)

HUANG   Comrades. It's still touch and go. (*Spreads a map out.*) Look here. To our west, we've got the warlord forces in Szechuan and Yunnan Provinces building fortifications to block our way, while Chiang Kai-shek's troops are hot on our heels. And Chiang Kai-shek himself flew to Kweiyang yesterday to direct the operations.

LO   The bastard!

LI   We'll let him have it!

CHAO   We'll finish him off first!

HUANG   Chairman Mao's laid down the line for us. We're to concentrate our forces and wipe out the two enemy divisions who are pursuing us. Then we'll drive straight to the River Wu, making a feint at Kweiyang, so as to shake Chiang's nerve. Then when we've got them foxed as to what we're going to do, we'll wheel and advance at top speed to Yunnan and Szechuan.

CHAO (*thinking aloud*)   M'm—yes . . . that means we shall be keeping clear of their main forces.

HUANG   That's right. In order to preserve our main forces we must keep away from the enemy where he's strong. And we must avoid letting the enemy pin us down to battles; we must pick out his weak points, and then strike hard.

LO *and* LI   Right!

CHAO   That's the way to lick 'em!

HUANG   But it's not going to be plain sailing. Where we're going we shall be the first people to try and cross these hills and mountains, let alone get through some of the wilder regions. We've got to get to Yunnan by a roundabout way, cross the Golden Sand River, and enter Szechuan. Then we'll have to get through the Yi area and cross the Tatu before we can join forces with the Fourth Front Army.

CHAO *and* LI   We'll do it.

LO   Which are the Yi areas?

HUANG   (*points to the map*)   Here, see? On the borders here, between Yunnan, Szechuan and Sikang.

LO   Man alive! Look at those gradients! How on earth are we going to get through there?

HUANG   There's no doubt it'll be difficult, breaking through two cordons, getting over that dangerous Golden Sand, and scaling mountains thousands of feet high. But it's the road to victory. What d'you say? Confident that we can do it?

(LI *and* CHAO *assent warmly, but* LO *keeps quiet. Then he says.*)

LO   When do we leave—tonight? Or can we get a bit of rest?

HUANG   We'll get no rest here. For strategic considerations, we must start straight away for the Yunnan-Szechuan border. Orders have come through, and our job's to be the advance guard. This is a great honour, as well as a hard job.

LO   (*sticking to it*)   If we succeed in routing the enemy troops in our way, then maybe we can go back to Kiangsi to build up our bases.

HUANG   Lao Lo, you don't seem to have much confidence, do you?

LO   It's not that I'm afraid of difficulties. But the men are worn out. They've had no rest at all since we left Kiangsi last October.

HUANG   That's true. But it's also true that if we leading comrades keep our spirits up, our men will forget their exhaustion.

LO   I'm feeling pretty low myself these days—wounded three times and then doing all the Battalion C.O.'s work since he was killed.

HUANG   Yes, I know. We haven't forgotten we've got to send you another officer.

LO   I should like to recommend Chao Chih-fang as commander of our battalion. I'm willing to be deputy under him.

CHAO   No, no. I'm not good enough for the job!

HUANG   Lao Lo, you've not been happy about your work lately, have you?

LO   But really I'm telling you the truth!

HUANG   Yes, but only a part of it. Aren't you still hankering after your old base in Kiangsi?

LO   Yes, I don't deny that. But I've never refused to accept orders.

(LI FENG-LIEN *enters.*)

FENG-LIEN   Regimental Commander! (*To* LI YU-KUO.) Brother! I've come to say goodbye. We've just got our new orders—to return to Divisional HQ. (*To* COMMANDER HUANG.) Could you tell us whether we've worked well?

HUANG   You've done excellent work with us. I only hope you'll come to work in our regiment more often.

LI   Feng-lien, tell us how the mass meeting went. Has the township government been set up?

FENG-LIEN   More than two hundred peasants came to the meeting. They've elected the township government and punished seven criminal landlords. This evening the peasants are going to open the landlords' granaries and distribute rice to those who need it. They've formed a Red Guard of twenty too. Six young peasants have joined the Red Army.

LI   Where are they now?

FENG-LIEN   They've gone to say goodbye to their people. They'll be back tomorrow.

ALL   Excellent! Good work! Fine!

FENG-LIEN   I must go now. See you again. (*Goes off.*)

HUANG   See you tomorrow. (*Looking at his watch.*) It's time we got moving.

LO   Tiger Cub, pass word round that the whole battalion's to get moving.

TIGER CUB   Right! (*Picks up the tea things briskly and goes off.*)

CHAO   Regimental Commander, we're going now.

LO   I'm coming too, to look after the men.

(*They go out.*)

HUANG   Lao Li, how has Lao Lo been feeling about his work lately?

LI   All right, I think.

HUANG   All right? He seems a bit conservative, doesn't he?

LI   H'm.

HUANG   H'm? Lao Li, you've got to try to help straighten him out.

LI   I'll do my best. Regimental Commander, how about the resolutions of the Tsunyi Conference? Have you got the full text yet?

HUANG   No. It'll arrive in a few days, I expect. (*Taking out a notebook.*) But I've got the notes I took, if you'd like to have a look at them.

(YOUNG CHOU, *the peasant lad who captured the landlord, comes on with his mother.*)

MOTHER CHOU   Is Political Instructor Li here?

LI (*greeting them*)   Hello, mother. It's more than a month since I saw you last. How's life been treating you?

MOTHER CHOU   Well, you can hardly call it life. Ever since you left, it's been nothing but Kuomintang soldiers coming to take away our men and steal our things, almost every day. And now I've nothing but a pair of empty hands to greet your army with. (*Wiping away tears.*) It's all too dreadful. . . .

YOUNG CHOU   Let's get down to business, mum.

LI (*rubbing his hand over the lad's hair*)   And how's life with you, little brother?

MOTHER CHOU (*answering her boy*)   Yes, son. Comrade Li, he's my youngest, now turned sixteen. Before you came here a month ago, he was in the Young Pioneers. Then you left us and he went to hide at his uncle's. The enemy came and took away his dad, and they . . . killed him. Now you're here again, my son wants to go with you and avenge his father's death. He wants to join the Red Army. I give him to you, Political Instructor! (*Bursts into violent sobs.*)

LI   Mother, it's our duty to see that justice is done. Never fear. But don't you think it'd be better if you kept your son with you?

MOTHER CHOU (*in a firm tone*)   No, I shan't do that. He'll never be able to settle down here. You must take him into your army. Look— this very evening he killed a landlord! (*She tries to fall on her knees and clutches* LI's *hands.* LI *hastily raises her and reassuringly helps her to her chair.*) Please, I beg you, I beg you, take him with you. That's the only way to save him.

LI (*deeply touched*)   All right, mother. We'll take him.

MOTHER CHOU   Thank you. Now my mind can be at rest. (*Taking her son's hand.*) Come home now and get your things. (*Turns back at the door.*) Political Instructor, don't forget, this poor child has just lost his father. Treat him as if he were your own son. You will won't you? (*Goes off.*)

HUANG   There you have it: class hatred. It's the motive force of the revolution.

(PEASANT CHAIRMAN *hurries on.*)

PEASANT CHAIRMAN   Are you really planning to go away immediately? You mustn't leave us on our own again.

LI   You've been elected chairman of the township government, haven't you?

PEASANT CHAIRMAN   Yes, I have. But what can we do on our own?

HUANG   You can pick up a rifle and organize the peasants to go into the hills and be guerilla fighters. (*To* POLITICAL INSTRUCTOR LI.) Can I have two of the rifles we captured from the enemy?

LI   All right. (*Goes out.*)

PEASANT CHAIRMAN   But we've never done anything like that. We're peasants. We can work the land, but we've never gone in for fighting.

HUANG   You learn how to do things by doing them. I once worked the land, too—

PEASANT CHAIRMAN   If only you could stay on with us. Are you *all* going tonight?

HUANG   Yes. Our regiment's moving tonight.

   (*Marching is heard off.*)

HUANG   (*goes over to the window to look out*)   Look, Chairman. You and your neighbours here have all had some experience in fighting for the revolution. I know you, in particular, aren't doing it for the first time. You'll have to work fast and get your people organized. Get a Party branch going and set up your own local armed force. If you get trouble from small enemy forces, wipe them out; if they come in any number, keep clear of them for the time being. You know your people and you know these parts well. You've got nothing to worry about. We've got guerillas on the border of Yunnan and Kweichow. Try and get in touch with them in the next few days. Don't worry, the Divisional Political Department is going to send someone to help you.

LI   (*comes back carrying two rifles*)   Regimental Commander! Let's go.

HUANG   (*taking the rifles and giving them to* PEASANT CHAIRMAN)   Here you are—a couple of presents. I hope when we meet next time you'll have a strong Red Army unit of your own here. Goodbye! Goodbye!

   (HUANG *and* LI *go out.*)

PEASANT CHAIRMAN   (*taking the rifles and almost breaking down*)   Right you are! When we meet next time, we will!

   (*The troops can be heard marching past. The* WOMEN'S CHAIRMAN *dashes in.*)

WOMEN'S CHAIRMAN   Chairman, the Red Army has gone again. What *are* we going to do now?

   (CHIEN KUEI-HSI *and other peasants rush up.*)

CHIEN   Who's here? Where has the Red Army gone?

WOMEN'S CHAIRMAN   They've gone to fight.

CHIEN   What, gone already? I'm nearly too late, then. (*Hurriedly reporting.*) Look, Chairman, I finished off that local bully Shen all right.

PEASANT CHAIRMAN   That's good.

CHIEN   Chairman, I *must* go now.

PEASANT CHAIRMAN   Go? Where?

CHIEN   I'm going to catch up with the Red Army—I'm going to join it. Goodbye! (*He runs off. Several young peasants run after him, shouting: "Wait a minute, we want to go too.")*

(YOUNG CHOU *runs on, his blanket roll on his back.*)

YOUNG CHOU   Political Instructor! Oh, he's gone already. (*Calling after* CHIEN KUEI-HSI.) Hey, brother, wait for me! (*Runs off.*)

WOMEN'S CHAIRMAN   What's our plan now?

(LI YU-KUO, CHANG TEH-MING *and* TIGER CUB *enter.*)

LI   Hello, Chairman, I've got someone for you. (*To* CHANG TEH-MING.) This is the chairman of the township government. (*To* CHAIRMAN.) This is Comrade Chang Teh-ming. Comrade Chang's from the First Division's Political Department. He's going to work with you. He's a Party member, and does organizational work in the Political Department. He's been a guerilla leader.

(*Peasants welcome him with cheers.*)

LI   (*giving* PEASANT CHAIRMAN *a letter and two pamphlets*)   Our Regimental Commander asked me to give you these. This one's on organizing local armed forces in the countryside; this one's the Party Constitution, and this letter's to introduce you to the County Party Committee. You should get in touch with them right away— do it tomorrow. Comrade Chang can tell you all about everything. I've got to go now. Goodbye, dear friends! Goodbye, all!

(*Peasants surround him to say goodbye, and urge him to come back soon.*)

LI   You can depend on it! We'll be back here some day. Goodbye! (*Goes out quickly.*)

PEASANT CHAIRMAN   Goodbye—goodbye till then.

(*They watch him go and then turn to* CHANG *to ask what they should do now.*)

CHANG   (*in centre of stage*)   Comrades! Friends! Take up your arms and get organized! Follow the lead of the Communist Party! Unite as one! Fight the enemy as one man!

ALL   We will! We will!

CURTAIN

Act II

TIME   *May 1935.*

PLACE   *Outside the ruins of Peach Castle, in an area where a minority people, the Yis, live—on the border of Szechuan and Sikang in Southwest China.*

SCENE   *The landscape of Southwest China is distinguished by hills and mountains that rise sharply one upon another and small footpaths that wind in and out of green pine woods. Here, in this area where the Yis live, the landscape is further enriched by old castles built with giant boulders above the mountain brooks, and stone-slab huts by the little streams. Peach Castle is the outer stronghold of the Yi people, built as protection against those who came to kill, rob and exploit them. Standing on a mass of rocks between two hills, this impregnable fortress commands the natural pass to their country. In ancient times if they were attacked they put up resistance before the castle, or if the situation was against them, they stood fast in it. Individual acts of heroism were done here, and a peach tree was always planted to mark each victory. As time went on, the neighbourhood became, to all intents and purposes, a peach garden. That was how the castle got its name.*

They were not always successful, however. On several occasions the enemy succeeded in taking the castle. To allow for such emergencies, the Yis built two other fortresses behind it, called the Front and Rear Castles. Peach Castle was popularly known as the main castle. In our day, all that is left of these three castles are ruins.

On May 14, 1935, advance units of the Red Army—First and Second Companies of First Battalion—took the ruins of Peach Castle in a lightning move, in order to give cover to the main force that was to pass that way. Not knowing who had come into their territory or why they had come, the Yis hastily rallied several hundred of their people at the Front and Rear Castles, and made ready to put up a stiff resistance.

It is a spring afternoon. The sunlight, filtering through the branches of the old pine trees, falls upon DEPUTY BATTALION COMMANDER LO's *long lean face, and makes him look more serious than usual. Beside him, a runner and a battalion bugler stand watching.*

From the Rear Castle can be heard the shouting of the Yi people, the sound of drums, the blare of trumpets and the clatter of musket and rifle fire.

LO (*shouting*) First Company Commander! Chao Chih-fang! (*Then muttering to himself.*) Can't hear me. Young Chou!

YOUNG CHOU Coming!

LO Tell Company Commander Chao to take a platoon up and take the hill in front of us.

YOUNG CHOU Just which hill d'you mean, Battalion Commander?

LO Look here, young fellow, you've been a runner with us for two months, yet you've still no idea how things are done in the army. Listen! A runner must always be on the alert, and anticipate his commander's movements and decisions. You've been standing here watching with me all this time, yet you can't guess which hill I mean. I'll have to get Tiger Cub back to take your place if you can't do better than that.

YOUNG CHOU I understand now. (*Points.*) You mean that hill.

LO Be off with you, then. No, half a minute—ask Company Commander Chao to come over here.

YOUNG CHOU Right! (*Goes out.*)

LO (*swearing at the Yis*) Blast you! I'll be damned if I don't bloody well wipe you out completely today.
      (LITTLE WAN *enters.*)

LITTLE WAN Deputy Commander! Order from the Regimental C.O.: "Keep the Yis off the road—both sides. Our main force will be passing here shortly."
      (YOUNG CHOU *comes back with* CHAO CHIH-FANG.)

LO (*interrupting*) Right! I am sure that we can finish them off within half an hour.

LITTLE WAN (*continues with the order*) "Don't shoot unless they come within 50 meters. If you must shoot, fire over their heads. If a charge is made bayonets are not to be used. Aim at frightening them off. That's all that's needed."

LO (*scandalized*) What? Where on earth do such orders come from?

LITTLE WAN They're from Regimental HQ.

LO Phew! Anything more?

LITTLE WAN Yes. The Regimental C.O. says the Chief-of-Staff, Liu Po-cheng, is parleying with Hsiao Yehtan, the leader of the Yi people, right now. That's our policy, and not to be violated.

LO Is that what the order says? (*To himself.*) What the hell policy is this?

LITTLE WAN (*overhears*) It's our policy towards national minorities. I was told to pass this on to you.

LO All right, all right. Get along now.

LITTLE WAN But I haven't finished yet.

LO Finish it then!

LITTLE WAN Regimental C.O. wants to know whether all your men have arrived, and about the situation here.

LO Report to him that First and Second Companies have come up, but Third Company and the Political Instructor are still on their way. We got here barely twenty minutes ago and took the hill within ten minutes of arrival. There are still two more hills to be occupied, one at the head of the road and the other on the right. There must be some six or seven hundred Yis on these hills, armed with muskets, swords and spears, bows and arrows, and a few rifles. They're blocking our way. That's all I can report now.

LITTLE WAN Nothing else?

LO No. That's all. You can go now.

LITTLE WAN Right. (*Goes off.*)

(*There is another uproar from the Yis. They seem to be getting closer. Small-shot rattles through the pine trees and an arrow hits a branch.*)

LO Lao Chao, what on earth's this business of fighting without shooting? I never heard of such nonsense. Really, I'm beginning to. . . .

CHAO Battalion Commander! You've heard before of the policy towards national minorities, haven't you? Here, in Southwest China, there are so many brother nationalities. It's supremely important for us to carry out this Party policy.

LO Pooh! as if I don't know what this national policy is all about! Respect their customs and habits, pay them with silver dollars for anything we buy, take care not to look down on them, do away with the idea that the Hans[1] are a master race, etc., etc. I can recite the whole blasted thing, chapter and verse, if you like. But I'm damned if there's any mention of not fighting back even when you're attacked! And whoever heard of such a thing as fighting without being allowed to shoot! You call that fighting? Eh?

(NURSE CHANG *runs on.*)

NURSE CHANG Are you the units covering the advance of the main force?

LO Yes, we are. Who are you?

NURSE CHANG I'm the head nurse of the field hospital. Our chief wants to know when you're clearing the enemy off the hills.

---

[1] The Hans, descended from the original Chinese, constitute an overwhelming majority of the population and are the dominant racial and cultural group in China.

LO   You can just tell your chief that we've got orders not to shoot or use
      bayonets. Not being in a position to fight, we can hardly be ex-
      pected to drive 'em off at once. I dare say you could have a bit
      of a rest over there, and continue your march after the Yis have
      withdrawn of their own accord.
NURSE CHANG (*taken aback*)   But they might stay on a whole year!
LO   Then you just have to wait a whole year. It's our policy towards
      national minorities, you know.
NURSE CHANG   And you call yourselves a combat unit!
LO   Why not? We are the Workers' and Peasants' Red Army, the army
      which has just forced two river crossings! That's what we are, if
      you really want to know!
CHAO (*averting a quarrel*)   It's all right, comrade, you can tell your
      chief and patients that our Chief-of-Staff's having a meeting with
      the Yis' leader right now, and we have orders not to launch an
      attack. You could try taking a roundabout way if you like. You'd
      only have another five *li*[2] to do anyway.
NURSE CHANG   Easy enough for you to talk! How do we know if there is
      a roundabout way? The patients have found it bad enough already,
      believe me. These little hill paths are so steep and thorny, and
      crutch cases can't climb anyway, nor can the stretcher-bearers.
LO (*thoroughly irritated*)   All right. Go and tell your chief I'll open a
      path for you within ten minutes.
NURSE CHANG   We could easily wait ten minutes, or half an hour, come
      to that. But I must say it seems rather odd that if you can't even
      deal with a handful of Yis you should have the nerve to lecture
      me on Party policy! (*About to go out.*)
LO   Get out of here! Go away!
NURSE CHANG (*imitating him, good-naturedly*)   Get out of here! Go
      away! You can't scare me. What's the idea, picking a quarrel with
      me? I tell you, if the Yis don't go away in ten minutes, I'll be back
      —see if I'm not. (*Goes out.*)
LO   Silly girl! (*Turns to* CHAO.) Lao Chao, take two platoons and attack
      the Rear Castle. Second Company can go for the Front Castle.
      Leave one platoon with me on guard here. We can make a feint
      of attacking, firing into the air, and see if it works. If it doesn't . . .
      well, to hell with it! Carry on!
CHAO   All right. I'll guarantee not to hurt a single Yi. (*Goes out.*)
      (CHENG LI *enters.*)
CHENG LI   Are you the units covering the advance of the main force?
LO (*is still looking out, and does not turn round*)   Yes. What do you

---

[2] A *li* is approximately one-third of a mile.

want now? (*Looks up. His tone changes.*) Oh, it's you, Cheng Li. What have you come here for?

CHENG LI Have you heard anything about Comrade Wu, our group leader?

LO Why? What has happened?

CHENG LI There's a rumour he's in trouble.

LO Oh, well, the Political Instructor and Third Company haven't arrived yet. Why should you worry about Comrade Wu?

CHENG LI The rumour is that he's been kidnapped by the Yis. The last we heard was about three o'clock, when he went off to sing to the wounded—but we've nothing definite about it.

LO Oh. All right—I'll send out some scouts.

CHENG LI Good, I must get back now. (*Goes out.*)

LO What a life! One queer thing after another. Queer orders and a queer battle! And all these queer things coming together at the same time! (*Shouts.*) Young Chou!

YOUNG CHOU Coming!

LO Tell Second Company Commander Wang to bring a platoon here, double quick. Fetch Chien Kuei-hsi, too.

YOUNG CHOU Right! (*Goes out.*)

LO (*muttering to himself*) Policy towards national minorities indeed! This is simply sticking out your neck at the enemy. No! for the sake of the revolution, I'm not going to do it; I'll not carry out policy mechanically. All right! All right! If I'm not allowed to kill any of them, I'll take them alive. I can fight them with my fists if not with bayonets.

(COMPANY COMMANDER WANG *enters.*)

WANG What's up, Deputy Battalion Commander? New orders for me?

LO Look here, Lao Wang. (*Pointing to the hill in front of him.*) If we leave that hill in the Yis' hands, they'll not only be in the way of our main force, but be a constant menace to our lot. So I'm ordering you to take the hill with a platoon, quick. There's no time to lose.

WANG I'll guarantee to take it. I'll guarantee to be quick.

LO H'm. There's another thing, though. You're not to shoot anyone or use your bayonets.

WANG What on earth do you mean? How are we to take the hill then? What kind of battle will that be?

LO You'll have to try it like this. See if you can scare them away by shouting and swearing at them, and firing a few shots into the air. You can throw a few grenades if you're sure there are no people about. That's our policy towards national minorities. It's not to be violated by anybody. Is that quite clear?

WANG   Is that all we can do? Can't we retaliate if they fire at us? D'you mean we've just got to stick our necks out and let the enemy do as he likes?

LO   You've got hands, haven't you? Take them prisoner! Really, you're not getting any brighter these days. Use your brains, and think up something. Anyhow, your orders are to take that hill in ten minutes without violating our policy.

WANG   All right. I'll try. But I must say this is the damnedest battle I ever heard of, in the damnedest place! (*Goes out.*)

LO   (*mutters to himself*)   All very well for you. You can moan at me. Who've I got to moan at?
     (CHIEN KWEI-HSI *comes in.*)

CHIEN   Did you send for me, Deputy Battalion Commander?

LO   Yes. I want you to take a squad out and scout along the road we came by. They say Group Leader Wu of Divisional HQ and several stretcher cases have been picked up by the Yis. Try the place where we rested at noon today. Make a thorough investigation and let me know at once what you find.

CHIEN   I'll report back as soon as I can.
     (*Yi battle cries are heard.*)

LO   Runners' Squad, get ready for an assault.
     WANG TEH-CHIANG *and two soldiers come up, very excited, escorting* (*a Yi prisoner.*)

WANG   Deputy Battalion Commander! We've taken the hill in the front and the enemy has fallen back on another hill beyond it. Our main force has started moving up. (*Pointing to the prisoner.*) He's a brave chap. He was the last to run away, and we captured him with his gun and sword. Quick enough for you this time, isn't it?

LO   (*not willing to admit it, went off pretty well*)   Any casualties? Ours or theirs?

WANG   Three Yis wounded. We've got two lightly injured men—and I got several punches from this fellow! (*Pointing to his prisoner.*) But what a bloody silly battle! If they had been Chiang Kai-shek's men, I wouldn't have allowed a single one of them to escape.

LO   (*to the prisoner*)   Do you speak Chinese? (*No answer.*) You don't? Are you dumb?

YI   Let me go, quick. Give me back my weapons. Get out of here, otherwise my people will come back and kill you all!

LO   So you do speak Chinese, then.
     (TIGER CUB, *now a squad leader of First Company, enters.*)

TIGER CUB   Deputy Commander! About eight or nine hundred Yis are advancing on us with homemade guns.

LO   I knew it! We'll have to wipe them out if we don't want to be wiped out ourselves. (*Turns to* WANG.) See what's happened? You've driven them from that hill, and now they're coming back here.
(*Fierce battle cries ring through the air:* "*You Han people, we want our leader! Give us back our leader! Set him free, or we'll wipe you out!*")

YI   Let me go! Let me go quick. (*Struggles to get away.*)

LO   (*to* WANG) Company Commander Wang, call up the machine-gunners.

WANG   Right! (*Goes out.*)
(CHAO CHIH-FANG *rushes on.*)

CHAO   Deputy Commander, it doesn't look as if we can press on with a frontal attack.

LO   You're saying this because your heart isn't on hitting the enemy.

CHAO   No, we've tried two charges, one right after the other, and fired into the air, and they just stayed put.

LO   Well, that's because you didn't go all out with my orders.

CHAO   If we charge them there'll be casualties.

LO   Can't have war without 'em, can you?

CHAO   But the orders from the Regimental C.O. said. . . .
Yi battle cries mount again.

LO   I'm giving orders here! I'll take the responsibility. Company Commander Wang, put the machine-guns over here!

CHAO   I'm sure the Yis are just shouting to frighten us. They're not going to attack. A few shots into the air will be enough to stop them.

LO   To hell with it! We haven't got the cartridges to waste like that. See that! They're swarming up this side of the hill. Looks like over three hundred of them!
(WANG TEH-CHIANG *rushes on with the machine-gunners.*)

WANG   Deputy Commander, machine-gunners reporting.

LO   Very good. Place machine-guns at the front gate of the castle and be ready for action.

WANG   Right.

YI   (*upset at the sight of the machine-guns*) Don't shoot! Don't shoot! Let me go! I tell you, let me go.

LO   Look out, they're coming now! Like a flock of ducks! Machine-gunners and riflemen, get ready.

CHAO   Deputy Commander, can't we just shoot into the air only, and frighten them away?

LO   As you like! as you like. Shoot into the air! (*The machine-guns bark and the battle cries die down.*) Stop! They're pulling back. They do seem to be afraid of machine-guns.

(*The Yis start their shouting again.* LO *loses his temper and exposes himself. Just in time,* CHAO *rushes out and drags him back, as a shell bursts right where he stood.*)

LO   Damn it! (*Fists to his face, he frantically tries to get the dust out of his eyes.*) Take over, Lao Chao, my eyes are blurred with dust. Damn it!

CHAO   (*quite calm*)   First Platoon of First Company! Take the mound 50 metres ahead. Lao Wang, tell the machine-gunners to fire another burst into the air.

WANG   Right!

(*As he gives orders, the machine-guns clatter.*)

CHAO   They're falling back, you see.

LO   Yes, yes, but they'll only come back again. I tell you, this is our chance to wipe them out. Lao Chao, take one platoon and get ready for a charge. This time turn the machine-guns on them.

CHAO   If you say so. (*He is about to go, but turns back.*) The order for a charge will be strictly carried out. But I want to say that I don't agree we should fire at them.

LO   This is a battle, not a debate. (*Calls out.*) Machine-gunners, get ready.

(REGIMENTAL COMMANDER HUANG *appears at the castle gate.*)

CHAO   (*turns to go, but comes back again*)   Deputy Commander, as I see it, our job is to ensure the safe passage of the main force—not to annihilate several hundred people of a fraternal nationality. We've taken the front hill; our main force can already pass. I can't agree with your plan for annihilating the Yis.

LO   You don't seem to be half as bright as you used to be. Those Yis are enemies as far as I'm concerned unless they lay down their arms. (*Produces his pistol and gives orders.*) First Platoon of First Company, get ready to charge! Machine-gunners, be prepared. And you, bugler, get ready to sound the charge! Runners' Squad, get ready to follow me.

HUANG   (*authoritatively*)   Stop all this! No shooting and no charge while our Chief-of-Staff is still negotiating with the Yi leader. (*To* LO *and* CHAO.) Come over here. Let's have a look at the situation. (*They all go up and look out.*) Let them shout as much as they want, it won't do us any harm. Let's deal with this problem first. (*Looks at the prisoner.*) This the prisoner I've heard about? (*Pats the* YI *on the shoulder.*) Sorry you had to put up with this. (*Turns to* LO *and* CHOU.) Do you know who he is? He's one of the Yi leaders here. A brave fellow; he's fought the Kuomintang militia several times. Last winter he led several hundred men in an attack against Anshunchang on the bank of the Tatu. And he speaks Chinese. (*Addressing the* YI.) Got you right, haven't I?

YI   Yes. How did you know?

HUANG   Your uncle told me all about it.

YI   (*agitated*)   What! You've got him too? (*He is instinctively about to go for* HUANG *with his bare hands, but thinks better of it.*)

HUANG   No, he's not a prisoner. He came to ask us to free you. He's gone back now.

YI   And what are you going to do with me? Skin me? Bury me alive? You Hans! (*It again looks as though he'll hit* HUANG.)

HUANG   What are you up to? Don't get excited! Look here! We're the Workers' and Peasants' Red Army, and we're Communists. Our army is on your side. Just now we're passing through your bit of country on our way north to resist the Japanese invaders. We shan't stay here long. We won't take even a needle and thread from you. If you'll sell us rice, we'll pay in silver dollars. We'll be gone by tomorrow.

YI   This is all lies—I know you. You Hans always deceive us.

HUANG   No, we're not deceiving you. Look, couldn't we have wiped you out yesterday if we had wanted to? There's no reason why we should have waited till now. After all, we're not afraid of hundreds of thousands of Chiang Kai-shek's regular troops. Do you expect us to cower before your muskets and spears, or your bows and arrows? I tell you again: we're the Workers' and Peasants' Red Army and we'll treat you as we would our own brothers.

YI   (*doubtfully*)   But who ever heard of Hans treating us like that!

HUANG   Look at it this way, then. Couldn't we easily have got rid of you? We've got machine-guns and grenades. But we only fired into the air, and threw grenades where they would do no harm. Isn't that so?

YI   Are you really going to let me go?

HUANG   Yes, right now.

YI   Honest? (*Stands up, to see if this is true.*) That's fine. I'm going, then.

HUANG   Wait a moment. (*Turns to* LO.) Give him back all his things.

LO   (*handing over the captured weapons*)   Here you are. Take your gun and sword.

HUANG   (*picks up the gun and inspects it*)   It's not loaded.

LO   No. It was like that when we captured him.

HUANG   Young Chou, fetch me two rounds.

LO   D'you think it's all right to release him? He has seen quite a lot here, you know.

HUANG   Never mind. The more he has seen the better. (*Hands over cartridges.*) Here's a little present for you. Let's be friends. You're a brave fellow. (*Shaking his hand.*) Go on—you can go home now.

YI (*takes the cartridges. He is deeply moved*) You are good people, good people! (*Bowing.*) Thank you. We are now friends— members of the same family. We Yis will never fight you again. (*The Yis offstage start shouting again.*)

YI (*waving in their direction and shouting*) It's all right! Go back! Go Back! (*Goes off.*)

HUANG   There goes a brave chap. For years there's been bad blood between the Hans and the Yis. We can only convince them of our goodwill by the way we behave. (*Going back to routine matters.*) And now let's take up the second matter. Lao Lo, has Third Company come up yet?

LO   No. Only First and Second Companies and the Scouts' Squad so far.

HUANG   All right. Tell the men that except for the sentries, everyone should clean up, get some food, and doss down early. We've got a new job ahead.

LO *and* CHOU   New job? What is it?

HUANG   Send your runner to tell the men what I've just said, first.

LO   Young Chou, pass on the C.O.'s orders. Company Commander Wang, go and post sentries!
(YOUNG CHOU *and* WANG *run out.*)

HUANG   You runners can all go out for a bit.
(*Runners, bugler and scouts go off.*)

CHAO (*feels that he is not wanted here*) Regimental Commander, I should get back to my men now.

HUANG   No, wait here. We must talk things over. I don't want any report on the situation here; I'm well up on it already. (*Looking at his wrist-watch.*) It'll have to be quick. I've another meeting at Divisional HQ. Lao Lo, you may speak first.

LO   There's not really much to say. Regimental Commander, my health's not been good, you see. As usual, my old wound began bothering me as soon as it was spring.

HUANG   Any other ailments?

LO   There's something wrong with my head.

HUANG   Do you get dizzy spells, or what?

LO   Yes, I do. Regimental Commander, some time ago I asked if Comrade Chao Chih-fang could be made battalion commander. I hope you'll give it further consideration. I don't feel I'm up to it!

HUANG   What else is bothering you?

LO   Nothing.

HUANG (*dryly*)   That sounds better. I was afraid you were going to ask for sick leave. (LO *keeps silent.*) Comrade Chao Chih-fang, have you got anything to say?

CHAO (*thinks it over, and seems agitated*)   I'm quite ready to take my punishment for refusing to carry out Deputy Commander Lo's order today.

HUANG   Look! forbidding you to shoot or use bayonets means that we protect and sympathize with these brother nationalities, and not wipe them out as if they were reactionaries—that's the spirit of the order. The Yis may not understand us now, but they will eventually, you know. And Deputy Commander Lo failed to carry out this order in the right spirit.

LO (*stubbornly*)   It was very difficult, Regimental Commander. The enemy weren't only threatening us. They were actively attacking. I couldn't stick my neck out for them to hack at!

HUANG (*criticizing him sternly*)   The order never asked you to. My order was that you should keep the enemy from attacking us. Who told you to go for them? What happened was that you captured one of the Yi leaders, and his mates raised a hell of a noise, in order to rescue him. But you ignored this. You only wanted to wipe them out, to machine-gun them. That was wrong, because it ran counter to the Party's policy towards national minorities. Company Commander Chao was right. His conduct cannot be looked on as an act of insubordination in the proper sense of the word.

(LITTLE WAN *enters.*)

LITTLE WAN (*to* HUANG)   The Political Commissar wants you urgently for the Divisional HQ meeting.

HUANG   All right. (*To* LO.) Well, think it over and try to find out where you've gone wrong. As I see it, you don't really understand the policy towards our brother nationalities, nor realize how things are going as a whole. Chew it over, and if you like, we can have another talk later on this evening. (*Looks down towards the valley.*) Look, the Yis have stopped coming. They'll soon withdraw altogether.

(LO *follows his gaze, but obviously doesn't trust his own eyes.*)

HUANG   Now, about the question which Lao Lo has raised, about the battalion commander. There's a Divisional HQ order through. Commander Chao Chih-fang of First Company has been appointed Acting Commander of First Battalion. Lao Lo is to announce this to the whole battalion.

CHAO (*earnestly*)   Regimental Commander, compared with Deputy Commander Lo, I'm just a raw lad.

HUANG   Well, we were all raw lads once, come to that. (*Glancing at his*

watch.) All officers down to battalion commanders are to meet at
Divisional HQ to listen to a report by a comrade from the Central
Committee. Which of you will go?

LO   Lao Chao can go.

CHAO   No. Better if Lao Lo went. He knows the general situation in the
battalion better than I do.

HUANG   One of you has to attend the meeting, I don't care which. I'll
leave it to you. You still seem browned off, Lao Lo. What's the
matter? Comrade, when a battalion commander receives orders,
what do you think he should do? Carry them out strictly, or just
ignore them? And what about the Party's national policy? Should
you support it, or just ignore it? Think it all over. I must get along
to the meeting now. I'll be back again tonight. (*Goes out.*)

CHAO   Deputy Commander, will you go to the meeting?

LO   No.

CHAO   (*rather at a loss—goes hesitantly up to him, and speaks in a warm,
friendly way*)   Deputy Battalion Commander!

LO   (*suddenly notices* CHAO *has no cap on*)   Where's your cap?

CHAO   Lost somewhere, I suppose.

LO   (*taking off his own cap and putting it on* CHAO's *head*)   Take mine.
(CHAO *goes out.*)

LO   (*broods unhappily. He feels he has been wronged*)   It's a hard thing,
being a revolutionary. I want to do good work, but I just make a
mess of it every time. Today it's this mistake, and tomorrow it's
that. Today it's this policy that I don't understand and tomorrow
another. What's the matter with me? Did I or didn't I want to
carry out the Party's national policy? You are told to fight, but to
do it without shooting. Is that what you mean by national policy?
Lao Chao is more capable than I. But was it right for him to disobey orders? I dunno, I dunno. . . . You are a damned fool, Lao Lo.
Poor old Lo Shun-cheng, you've lagged behind.
(YOUNG CHOU *slips in.*)

YOUNG CHOU   Deputy Commander, I've boiled some water and cooked
you a meal. Where would you like it? Here, or on the river bank?
Better at the bank, perhaps. There's a clean slab of stone you can
sit on.

LO   Oh, I'm full already.

YOUNG CHOU   (*with concern*)   Full? What with? When did you eat last?
How could you have eaten without me knowing?

LO   Don't fiddle around! When I say I've had enough, I mean it. Give
me a match, I want a smoke.

YOUNG CHOU   (*passes over a box of matches*)   Won't you try to eat a bit?

I've got some pork cooked with peppers. It's very good. Shall I bring it here?

LO   No. Eat it yourself if you want to. Fetch Battalion Commander Chao Chih-fang's things here, and find a clean corner for him to sleep in. And don't forget to keep some hot water and food for him, too.

YOUNG CHOU (*guessing what this means and overjoyed at the news*) Aha, so he has been appointed our Battalion C.O.! Wonderful! I'll fetch his things at once. (*Goes off.*)

(*In the distance the Yis are shouting again.*)

LO   There they are, at their tricks again. I'll teach them a lesson or two if they dare come round here again. (*Then he punches his own head.*) What am I so mad about? (*Throws himself down on the ground in a fit of temper.*)

(WANG TEH-CHIANG *enters.*)

WANG   Good, I see you're turning in already. I've posted the sentries, and the men are all settled. They've cleaned up and eaten. (LO *keeps silent.* WANG *sits down beside him.*) The Yis have moved back again two *li*. Nobody knows what dirty schemes they are cooking up. (*Still no answer from* LO.) Has the Regimental C.O. gone?

LO   Yes!

WANG   What did he say about First Company Commander refusing to obey orders?

LO   What did he say? He said . . . he was right.

WANG   Right? Who was right?

LO   Drop it. Some other time. That's just what I've been wondering.

WANG   I've just had an argument with Political Instructor Hsieh.

LO   What about?

WANG   About the question of "Left" and Right deviations.

LO   (*suspects that* WANG *is referring to himself*) Who are you getting at?

WANG   I'll tell you how the whole thing came about. When we were attacking the hill in front . . . (LO *jumps at this*) one of the soldiers ahead, in First Squad, threw a grenade—not into empty space, as required—and wounded two Yis. They ran away in panic. We took the hill in no time, and captured a prisoner. Well, I thought the man deserved a citation for his action.

LO   I should bloody well think so, too.

WANG   But Political Instructor Hsieh said that he wounded two Yis and this was against Party policy, as well as disobeying your orders. A grave mistake, he said. Do you think Hsieh was right?

LO   What? A grave mistake? Violating *my* orders? . . . Oh, yes, I see what you mean. . . . The political instructor was right.

WANG   Right? How d'you mean, right? Are we supposed not to hurt anybody in a battle? Are Yi lives more precious than ours? Why should a brave deed be condemned as a mistake?

LO   Leave it at that. I'll explain later. All right?

WANG   Just tell me why Hsieh was right.

LO   He was right. Why? I am not very clear about it myself. We go into a battle, but we're not supposed to kill anyone. But it *was* a battle, all the same, and your political instructor was right. Let's leave it at that for now. I'm just about sick of the whole thing.

WANG   All right, we won't talk about it. There's something else.

LO   I've had enough, I tell you, enough! Take your troubles to Political Instructor Li when he turns up. It's more in his line. Let me alone, I've got a headache.

WANG   (*with immediate sympathy*)   A headache? You must have caught cold. Let me get one of the medicos.

LO   Don't trouble about me.

WANG   Why don't you take some hot pepper water and have a good sweat?

LO   I've caught it hot enough already.

WANG   You have? Really?

LO   Oh damn, I need some sleep. And you, too.

WANG   I don't feel like settling down without a good talk. There's something else I want to say. (LO *feigns sleep.*) All right, let's have it after a snatch of sleep. (*Goes out.*)

LO   To hell with it. I've had enough. Get Political Instructor Li to listen to you. (*Lies down to sleep.*)

    (LI YU-KUO *comes in, walks quietly up to* LO, *looks at him and is about to turn away.*)

LO   (*still awake*)   Is that you, Lao Li? Sit down. Have all our men turned up now?

LI   Yes. They're all safe and sound.

LO   Did you see Scout Chien Kuei-hsi?

LI   No. Where has he gone?

LO   About four o'clock Comrade Cheng Li of the Propaganda Group came round to say that their group leader had been carried off by the Yis. So I sent Chien and his squad to look for him. They're not back yet, then.

LI   I don't suppose there's anything to worry about. The comrades at Divisional HQ didn't mention it when I saw them a while ago.

LO   Have you been to Divisional HQ?

LI   Yes, I looked in on my way here. I met the Regimental C.O. and the Divisional Political Commissar there.

LO   Did you see Lao Chao too?

LI   Yes. He was trying to dissuade Division's leading comrades from making him Acting Battalion Commander.

LO   Why should he fuss about that? I won't be insubordinate, even if he is made Battalion C.O.

LI   The Regimental Commander told me what happened here today. He said you weren't happy, and that I ought to come and see you.

LO   To see me? Lecture me rather. H'm, I know. I'm the most backward man in the whole army now.

LI   Don't try to take a rise out of me like that. Get up, and let's have a talk.

LO   (*gets up*)   All right. Go ahead, let's talk.

LI   Got any tobacco on you?

LO   (*handing him his pouch*)   Well. . . .

LI   Let's have a puff at the pipe first.

LO   Take your time. You can lecture me while you smoke. I'll just look on and listen and see what you can do.

LI   That damned tongue of yours! I'll find a way of changing it some-how, somewhere.

LO   It's how it has always been. Where d'you suppose you can change it?

LI   If I can't change it in Szechuan, I will in Kansu. And if not in Kansu, in Shensi, or in Peking or Nanking. I'll do it by hook or by crook.

LO   H'm. Kansu? Shall we ever reach Kansu?

LI   Why not? Eh?

LO   Lao Li, lecture me if you must. But don't beat about the bush.

LI   I'd rather you spoke first.

LO   All right. I'll fire away. Sit down. Lao Li, we've been together for a good many years and you know me as well as I know you. I joined the revolution of my own free will and I'm ready to fight anybody who's against it. I think it's a bit queer, to say the least, that we didn't regard the Yi troops as enemies and fight them as such.

LI   I find it clear enough. The Yis, old friend, have always suffered at the hands of their Han oppressors. They've had to fight to defend themselves against outsiders. We ought to have a fellow-feeling for them, oughtn't we?

LO   O, Heaven help us! But the fact remains that even though we didn't come to fight them, they attacked us.

LI   That is merely because we are new to them and they don't yet know that we're any different from the Kuomintang soldiery. Once they do know they'll not only stop attacking us, but they'll become part of the revolutionary forces.

LO   But they don't understand our policy. They're a backward lot.

LI You call them backward! (*Sits down beside him and speaks in an affectionate tone.*) How shall I put it to you, Lao Lo? We've worked together so many years. I've always looked on you as an elder brother. You're honest, courageous and sincere. The comrades, myself—we've all learnt a lot from you. You've always been a good worker for the Party. The Party trusts you. But why don't you listen to the Party's instructions?

LO No! You can't say that. I've never showed myself unwilling to do what the Party said—whatever it was.

LI Then why did you refuse to carry out the Party's policy towards national minorities?

LO The Yis wouldn't co-operate even when we carried it out.

LI That's because they didn't understand us yet.

LO They'll never understand us. They're backward.

LI Now, Lao Lo, we must get a grip on ourselves, and really learn. The Party trusts us and wants us to lead the whole battalion forward. But what do we know about our jobs really? We were poor lads. Did we mean anything to the ruling class? No, we were lower than dogs in their eyes. In the same way they say our brother nationalities are backward. Are we to do the same? The revolution is advancing and all the comrades are making steady progress. It really won't do for us to fall behind.

LO But I do seem to be lagging behind! Why can't I understand things?

LI Which do you think is the better way: to move safely through the Yi area or to fight our way through?

LO Don't say any more. Talk it over with Lao Wang. He looks at things the same way as I do.

(WANG TEH-CHIANG *and* POLITICAL INSTRUCTOR HSIEH *enter.*)

HSIEH *and* WANG Hello, Lao Li, good to see you again. (*Turn to* LO.) Deputy Commander, all the Yis have withdrawn.

LO All gone! (*His face lights up with joy.*) They're all gone!

WANG Deputy Commander, have you got the thing straightened out? My argument with Hsieh has flared up again.

LI What's that?

LO (*to* WANG) You'd better talk to Lao Li about it.

(CHIEN KUEI-HSI *comes on.*)

CHIEN (*reporting to* LO) We've found out what really happened.

LO Tell us! What did happen?

(*At this moment* WU *comes on.*)

WU (*cutting in*) I can tell you myself.

(*Delighted cries from all:* "Wu, you're back. What happened?" *etc., etc.*)

(LI FENG-LIEN *enters.*)

FENG-LIEN   I came back with him too. (*Waves cheerfully to her brother. Then turns to* LO.)   Deputy Commander, we must have given you a lot to worry about.

LO   Yes. But I'm not worried any more. Tell us what happened? (*To* CHIEN.)   You can go and have a rest now.

CHIEN   Right you are. (*Goes out.*)

FENG-LIEN   It was like this. Around three o'clock in the afternoon we met a group of our wounded in a mountain gully. They stopped us and asked us to sing for them.

WU   So we started up a clapper rhyme and a dance.

FENG-LIEN   And followed it with "March North to Fight the Japanese!" Every one was having a good time, shouting "more!" "more!"

WU   And then suddenly scores of Yis, men and women, rushed down from the hill.

FENG-LIEN   They were all armed—spears and swords, and even Mausers.

WU   They grabbed us before we knew what had happened.

FENG-LIEN   Aiya, it was maddening! We couldn't understand a word they said. Of course we refused to go with them, but after the first shock we saw they were all smiling at us. It was a relief! You could see they meant well.

WU   Finally they got us up the hill, helping us with our things and carrying the wounded.

FENG-LIEN   You'll never guess what they did then when we got there.

ALL   Tell us then, tell us, quick!

FENG-LIEN   Gave us food and asked for songs and dances. Then one of them who spoke Chinese came up and told us that the talk between our Chief-of-Staff and their leader had turned out a success, and that they had become sworn brothers.

ALL   Sworn brothers! That's marvellous! (*An outburst of laughter.*)

WU   It wasn't till then that I realized we had been invited to celebrate the occasion.

FENG-LIEN   And they asked us to sing and dance too.

ALL   Did you?

FENG-LIEN   You bet we did. What's more, they wanted a special song about two leaders becoming sworn brothers.

ALL   But there isn't such a song, is there?

WU   No. We had to make up one on the spot.

FENG-LIEN   We had hardly finished it when Chien Kuei-hsi turned up. The Yis gave back our things and saw us home.

LI (*to* LO)   Now can you see that the Party's national policy works!

LO (*quite won over*)   I certainly can. The policy's right, sure enough!

WANG (*chiming in*)   Yes, it's dead on.

WU   Can anyone tell us where Divisional Political Department Office is? We've got to rush back for new orders.

ALL   Wait a bit. Sing us a song first.

WU   All we have is old stuff. There's nothing new.

LI   What about that new piece you made up?

ALL (*eagerly*)   Yes, yes.

> (COMPANY COMMANDER CHU *arrives with a group of Red Army men.*)

WU   Come on, Feng-lien, sing up.

FENG-LIEN   All right.

> (*They start singing.*)[3]

> *The month of March is full of bloom,*
> *Fresh grass and peach blossoms too.*
> *Fighter Liu and Hsiao Yehtan clasp their hands in love.*
> *How oppress'd were the Yis for ages long!*
> *Suddenly from out the blue came their saving star,*
> *Ai ai ai, ai ai, came their saving star.*
> *Brother peoples, let's unite!*
> *Revolution comes to flow'r.*
> *Dig new wells for water and plant new groves of peaches.*
> *Plant the peach trees, quickly grows the fruit.*
> *Follow the Communist Party, if you would be happy!*
> *Revolution needs the help of all.*
> *Hands are clasped in brotherly love,*
> *Peaches bloom o'er all the land.*
> *Hands are clasped in brotherly love,*
> *And the peach trees bloom o'er all the happy land.*

> (*The song is greeted with laughter and applause, and calls for more.*)

WU   No, I'm not going to sing any more. I've got something else to do. (*Chalks "Long live Chairman Mao!" on the stone wall.*)
(*All present cheer and applaud.* CHAO CHIH-FANG *rushes on, out of breath, almost bursting with joy about something.*)

LI   Here's Lao Chao.

LO   Lao Li, here's an order from the Regimental C.O. Please announce it to the men.

LI (*reads from a paper*)   Comrades! Comrade Chao Chih-fang, Commander of First Company, is hereby appointed Acting Commander of First Battalion.

---

[3] Music for the songs in *The Long March* follows the text of the play.

ALL (*clapping their hands*)   Hurrah! Hurrah!

WU   So Chou's been promoted Battalion Commander. Good, very good indeed!

CHAO   Keep your cheers till the next victory.

FENG-LIEN   We'll take victories for granted!

(CHENG LI *enters.*)

CHENG LI (*to* GROUP LEADER WU)   Ah, here you are. I've been looking for you. We must leave at once. The Director of the Political Department said that we were to go with First Battalion as part of the advance unit.

WU   Very good. I'm coming. Company Commander—oh, no—Battalion Commander Chao, is your battalion leaving at once?

CHAO   Yes, at once. We've a long way to go tonight, you know.

FENG-LIEN   Don't worry. If you can manage a hundred *li*, we shan't stop short at ninety-nine.

CHAO   The difference will be that you'll take several hours longer, eh?

FENG-LIEN   Just you wait and see. (*Goes off.*)

WU   So long, everybody! (*Goes out.*)

ALL   Goodbye! Goodbye!

LO   Lao Chao, tell us about your meeting at Divisional HQ.

CHAO   Well, comrades! I've good news for you. We've been given a glorious task. Go and get your kit ready. Company commanders and political instructors, stay behind for a minute.

(*All go out except company commanders and political instructors.* LITTLE WAN *enters with a* YI, *the late prisoner.*)

LITTLE WAN   Battalion Commander Chao, here's a guide sent round by the Yi leader. Regimental Commander wants your battalion to move off sharp on time. (*Goes out.*)

CHAO   Certainly we will.

YI   Congratulations! So you've been promoted.

CHAO   Thank you for coming to help us. Let's introduce ourselves. This is Political Instructor Li and this is Deputy Commander Lo.

YI (*looking at* LO)   Thank you for setting me free just a while ago.

LO (*smiling uneasily*)   Thank you for coming to help us.

CHAO   Young Chou, take this comrade (*pointing to the Yi guide*) to the mess and give him his supper.

YOUNG CHOU (*beckoning to the* YI)   Come along. (*Turns to* LI, CHAO *and* LO.) When are you going to eat?

CHAO *and* LO   We'll let you know later.

LI   Young Chou, tell the cook to make two more dishes in honour of our guest and our new Battalion Commander.

YOUNG CHOU   Yes, I'll see to it.

YI   Thank you.

(YOUNG CHOU *and the* YI *go off*.)

CHAO   Now let's get down to business. The Engineers' Company originally attached to Divisional HQ has been transferred to our battalion. Regimental Commander's instructions are that it'll come under you, Lao Lo. Our job is to start moving at 7:30 p.m. on a forced march of 140 *li*, reach and occupy Anshunchang by 9 o'clock tomorrow morning. At 6 in the evening we shall force the crossing of the River Tatu.

CURTAIN

Act III

TIME   *The afternoon of May 16, 1935.*

PLACE   *Anshunchang, on the bank of the River Tatu, Sikang.*

SCENE   *The Tatu, a tributary of the Yangtse, runs between perilously high mountains, with a steep drop from cliff top to water. At this point it is more than a thousand metres wide and ten metres deep, and it sweeps down like a torrent.*

The Red Army's advance unit—First Battalion of the First Division—reached Anshunchang at noon after a forced march of 140 li. Almost as soon as they arrived, they knocked out an enemy platoon stationed there, and captured its company commander. No sooner had the engagement ended than the Red Army commanders grappled with their second difficult job—the forced crossing of the Tatu. Battalion HQ was set up on a stone embankment, tucked into the foot of the cliffs, where there was a small stone hut between two huge rocks, and behind it an old, withered pine tree. The scenery is particularly magnificent when looked at from these rocks. Below, the waves roll like galloping horses and roar, filling the hills on both sides with endless reverberations. High above, white fleecy clouds scurry over the sky. The enemy's defence works on the opposite bank can just be made out.

When the curtain rises, DEPUTY BATTALION COMMANDER LO *and* COMPANY COMMANDER WANG *are sitting on a rock waiting for* BATTALION COMMANDER CHAO CHIH-FANG. YOUNG CHOU *is heating water on a fire. Red Army men are hurrying past the stone hut, carrying boards, planks and bamboo poles—materials for making rafts. Two guards are on patrol in front of the stone hut, their rifles slung over their shoulders. Sporadic enemy gunfire is heard from time to time.*

CHAO (*comes on among a group of Red Army men*) Comrades, we shall have to get a move on! Get those boards down to the bank and don't waste any time about it.

SOLDIERS Never you fret, Commander. We'll finish in no time. We'll get it done, etc. (*They run past.*)

CHAO (*shouting*) Company Commander Chu! Hey, you there, of Third Company! Ask your C.O. to come over! Chien Kuei-hsi!
(CHIEN *shows up in the crowd.*)

CHAO Come here!

CHIEN (*hands over his timber to another soldier*) Yes? What's the matter, Commander?

CHAO How're you feeling? You must be pretty tired, after marching 140 *li* and then having that skirmish this morning.

CHIEN No, I'm not too bad.

CHAO Well, I've got a new job for you.

CHIEN What's that?

CHAO Look here. I want you to do a recce up that hill. (*Pointing to hill.*) What I want to know is if there's any way down to the river there, if there're any peasant homes, and what defence works the enemy has on the opposite bank. I shall also want an estimate of the depth of water and the swiftness of the current just there. Got that?

CHIEN Right, Commander, I've got all that.

CHAO Get along then. You've got an hour to do it in.

CHIEN Right. (*Goes off.*)

CHAO (*walking up to* LO) Lao Lo, we need boats badly. How many have you been able to find?

LO They've taken all the boats with 'em. I've only been able to find one that'll only take 20 men—and damaged at that!

CHAO Good enough. Can't it be repaired?

LO The boat belongs to an old chap—over sixty. I've done everything I could to persuade him to lend it to us—begged and pleaded, but he'll have none of it. I don't know what more can be done with him. And we can't just take it, that's certain. We can't do a thing like that, it's against our principle of working with the people.

CHAO   M'm; an old man, eh? (*Turns to* WANG TEH-CHIANG.) What about the rafts? Are we going to be able to make forty in time?

LO   Ha! we're short of planks, nails, and ropes, not to mention time. . . .

CHAO   Lao Wang, what about the pontoons?

WANG   There's just one blame difficulty after another. The river's both wide and deep, and the current flows so fast. We're short of material, too. . . .

CHAO   What's the rate of flow, d'you know?

WANG   Fast enough to sweep a water-buffalo away.

LO   We've measured it. It's 3 metres a second. It makes it a job to get pontoons across.

CHAO   M'm. Well, we'd better drop the pontoon idea and concentrate on making rafts.

WANG   That still doesn't give us logs or planks.

CHAO   You can send your men into the hills for trees, can't you?

WANG   What about the ropes we shall need?

CHAO   Can't you use belts and leggings?

WANG   And nails?

CHAO   Use your head, man! Use sharpened bamboo splinters instead.

WANG   And time?

CHAO   Ah, time! You've got me there. Time's more precious than gold. There's no time to lose—not even a fraction of a second. We shall start crossing at 6 p.m. (*Looks at watch.*) Nearly three now. There's still three hours to get ready in.

WANG   I'll do my best, Commander. (*Dashes off.*)

LI   (*emerging from the crowd*) Lao Chao, how is it going?

CHAO   Oh, there you are. I've been wanting to talk things over with you. We're up against an enemy battalion the other side. I don't know what their defences are like yet. Orders from above say the crossing is a matter of life and death to the whole army and demand that we should cross today, at any cost. But it's a hell of a job. The current is swift, we can't put a pontoon across, and we haven't any boats.

LO   A pontoon's out of the question, no boats can be found, and we've got no rafts made yet.

LI   In that case we'll have to hurry up and get a move on making them.

CHAO   That's it. It's clear what we've got to do: one, find boats; two, make rafts; three, pick out the ferry points; four, get some local boatmen as guides; five, pick out a hundred men who know how to use rafts; and six, since the men must be feeling it after the engagement at noon, mobilize the whole battalion for action. And we've got to get all this done in about three hours.

LI   That means we should start right away. I'll call a Party branch meeting immediately and talk to the men, pick out the rowers and see to the logs. Will you ask the propaganda comrades to try and get hold of the local boatmen?

LO   I'll go and see to the raft-making. (*Starts to go.*)

CHAO   Lao Lo, see if you can get the old boatman to come and talk to me, will you?

LI   What's that? *Is* there a boat, then?

CHAO   Yes. But the owner doesn't want to lend it.

LI   I'll talk him round.

LO   (*mumbling to himself*)   Oh yes, easy as you like. You have a try.

(LO *and* LI *go their separate ways, leaving* CHAO *in deep thought. The surging song of Red Army men comes to his ears.* CHAO *drops his head to one side to listen.*)

First Front Army's made its name!
Our mighty force is led by Chairman Mao Tse-tung.
No mountain peaks can deflect our course,
No great flood, deep and wide, bar our way!
On and on we march! On and on we march!
   On and on we march!

CHAO   (*calling out*)   Tiger Cub! Tiger Cub!

TIGER CUB   (*runs up*)   Yes, Commander.

CHAO   Has the propaganda unit turned up?

TIGER CUB   Yes. I tell you what, Commander, they kept right up with us all yesterday evening. They were fine! They spent half the night teaching us songs, too.

CHAO   Where is Group Leader Wu now?

TIGER CUB   Busy with his group on the hillside.

CHAO   Tell him I want to see him, will you?

TIGER CUB   Right you are. (*Goes off.*)

(COMPANY COMMANDER CHU *enters.*)

CHU   (*reporting*)   Commander, I've got the full report now on that platoon our company cleaned up. We took 23 prisoners, including the company commander, 25 rifles, 1 light machine-gun and 1 revolver.

CHAO   Send the company commander over right away.

CHU   Right you are. (*Goes out.*)

LO (*running on*) Lao Chao!

CHAO Where's the old boatman?

LO Right behind me. Lao Chao, I think. . . .

(*The boatman enters. He looks old and poor, but strong.*)

BOATMAN Good day to you, officer.

LO Sit down here, please.

BOATMAN (*slightly deaf*) What did you say? My poor old boat's a complete wreck, you know.

LO (*brusquely to* BOATMAN) Sit down! I'll leave you two to talk. I'm going.

CHAO No, wait a bit, Deputy Commander, I want to have a word with you. (*Turns to* BOATMAN.) Well, grandad, how old are you?

BOATMAN Nigh on sixty-two, officer. My poor wrecked boat is old too. (*Takes a good look at* CHAO *for the first time.*) You be one of Chairman Mao's generals, I reckon?

CHAO I'm just one of Chairman Mao's comrades. Call me comrade. I'm not a general, and we don't call ourselves officers.

BOATMAN Hee, hee. Comrade. (*Breaks out into an old man's laugh.*) I've heard tell about that, come to think of it. They do say that Chairman Mao's generals and men call one another comrade. You was wanting to ask me about crossing the river?

CHAO That's right. Can you tell me, grandad, if there's anywhere we can get pontoons across from, or if there's anywhere we can swim over?

BOATMAN No. Nay, it be too broad for that, and that current's too strong. A pontoon won't do you. Only a boat and someone who knows the river can get you over.

LO You know the river yourself, don't you?

BOATMAN Ay, but there's no place to land at t'other side. You wouldn't have forgot that, officer—er—comrade?

CHAO Just tell me, shall we be able to find boats and boatmen on this side?

BOATMAN They pressganged all our men and took 'em to the other side, you know. Yesterday afternoon the Kuomintang army took all the boats from here, and a score of our boatmen with them—that's all the men we had round here. My boat got stove in on a hidden rock, and it's not been mended proper since. Then, this morning, before you came, those Kuomintang robbers came round to me and made as if to destroy my boat with a hand-grenade and take me with them, too. But I threw myself into my boat, and told them they'd have to kill me first, I was going to stay here with my boat. They didn't kill me, but they kicked me around and cracked me over the head. Then later on that officer (*pointing to* LO)—no, that comrade—comes and says he wants to repair my boat. But I said it couldn't be done, it's been out of use too long and it's in too bad a state. But he wouldn't believe me. (*Doggedly.*) You gentlemen don't understand that my boat's the only thing I can earn my family's rice with.

CHAO Can you cross the river by raft?

BOATMAN You'd never do it, comrade. This here river's not like other rivers. Do one thing wrong and your life's forfeit. You'd never cross it.

CHAO Supposing we had a boat, how long would it take us to get to the other side?

BOATMAN Two full hours at least, and you'd need a good man at the oars. The current's very swift here, you know.

CHAO Couldn't it be done in one hour?

BOATMAN One hour? Impossible! Impossible!

CHAO Would it be quicker if we crossed where the water flows fastest? (*Points to the swirling currents.*) Do you think we could cross there?

BOATMAN There? No, too dangerous! D'you see the eddies there? That's where I wrecked my boat last month. This place of all places you can't cross at. Comrade, may I ask how many of you want to get across?

CHAO How many of us?

BOATMAN Just a few of you, I suppose?

CHAO A few? (*Breaks out into a laugh.*) No! Hundreds of thousands of us!

BOATMAN Hundreds of thousands of you! How on earth do you think you going to cross the river?

LO Well, what about your boat?

BOATMAN Even suppose I gave you my boat, how can so many people get across? Have you got any motor boats?

CHAO No.

BOATMAN Then you'll have to fly.

CHAO Human beings can't fly without wings, can they?

BOATMAN Then there's only one thing to say: (*with great emphasis*) You never will get across!

CHAO Yes, we will. (*Firmly.*) We'll find a way out.

BOATMAN (*with a laugh*) Comrade from the Red Army, don't be angry with an old man if he tells you plainly—not even the gods could hope to get to that other bank safe and sound, if there was even one man defending it. Think of yourself, floating on the water, completely at the enemy's mercy. He could pick you off as he pleased from behind his defences.

CHAO   I do know a bit about it, as a matter of fact. We crossed the Wu and the Golden Sand. They weren't exactly easy. I am not bragging, you know.

BOATMAN   I never heard naught about the River Wu. But the Golden Sand River is tamer than this one.

LO   (*has lost patience*)   Why the hell can't you lend us your boat and leave the rest to us? Come on, now!

(LI YU-KUO *comes on.*)

BOATMAN   Now, don't keep on at me! Comrades, let me tell you a story, if you're in no hurry.

LO   Lao Chao, let's get back to business.

LI   Lao Chao, a meeting is being held and they're going to pick out men for the oars. All our comrades are in high spirits. (*Sees the old man.*) What's the matter with him?

LO   (*fed up*)   He's got a boat, and yet he won't let us use it. We've been talking to him for hours.

BOATMAN   My boat is damaged, you see.

CHAO   Lao Li, we'll leave the boat business to you. Lao Lo and I'll go down to the riverside and have a look around.

LI   All right. Don't you worry. We'll find a way out. I'll talk to grandad here.

(CHAO *and* LO *go off.*)

BOATMAN   You're all very busy, I see. But it's nothing to do with me. I'll be getting along now.

LI   No, don't do that. Sit down again and let's have a chat.

BOATMAN   I've got nothing to chat with you about. My boat is damaged and no amount of talking can mend it again.

LI   Didn't I hear you say, just when I came, that you'd a story to tell us?

BOATMAN   Would you like to hear it?

LI   You bet. Go ahead.

BOATMAN   My father used to tell me that in the Ching Dynasty, there was a famous general of the Taiping Heavenly Kingdom called. . . .

LI   Shih Ta-kai.

(YOUNG CHOU *enters.*)

BOATMAN   You know about him, I see. Well, Shih Ta-kai and several hundred thousand of his men were all killed by the Manchu troops when they tried to cross this river. And in those days the Manchu troops only had home-made guns, but now there's these new-fangled guns with a lot more power to them. (*Imitates the rattle of a machine-gun.*) I think you'd better give your idea up. Let an old man tell you for your own good. (*Looks up at the darkening sky.*) You know, if it starts to rain. . . .

LI (*breaks in*)   Grandad, we're quite different from General Shih Ta-kai and his troops, you know.

BOATMAN (*shrewdly*)   Are you going to work miracles like the gods? Is that it?

LI   No. We don't expect miracles.

BOATMAN   Then what do you propose to do, pray?

LI   We can trust to the Communist Party and Chairman Mao. Led by them, we know we can make a success of the crossing.

BOATMAN   Why is it so important to you to cross? What's behind it?

YOUNG CHOU (*interrupting*)   No use talking to him. He'll never be able to understand.

BOATMAN   What's that, young fellow?

LI   Nothing important. Do you know that our country's been sold by a traitor? Chiang Kai-shek has sold our three Northeastern provinces to the Japanese! D'you know that the Japanese are murdering our brothers there? We've got to save our people. We've got to cross this river and get to the north. We can't sit idle here, and let the Japanese slaughter people at their leisure, can we?

BOATMAN   Aiya! The Japanese are slaughtering our countrymen in the Northeast?

LI   Yes, and it's not only that. We've also got to help the people get rid of Chiang Kai-shek. His forces have been burning down houses and killing people. We must avenge all the people's wrongs. Haven't you ever wondered why you have so little to eat and so little to wear, after a life-time of hard work?

BOATMAN   Ah, I was born under an unlucky star, surely. I reckon I must have committed some awful sins in my former life to be punished like this.

LI   Unlucky star my foot! It's quite simple. You've just been exploited.

BOATMAN (*quite at a loss*)   What's that? Been exploited?

LI   Yes. Look, year in, year out, you sweat away. Isn't it reasonable to have something to show for it? At least you ought to have enough to eat, and clothes to your back. (*Plucks at the boatman's thin, ragged shirt, which shows bare flesh through the holes.*) Doesn't look as if you do, though, does it? How do you account for that?

BOATMAN   Oh, that's a long story, to be sure. What with all these wars our trade's been completely off for many years now. All we get now is Kuomintang officers and soldiers, but we never see the shadow of their money. Then, you see, my boat got damaged. I couldn't repair it—I never had a penny to spare. I tried renting a bit of land from a landlord, but barely got enough from it to pay the rent and taxes. You can see how it all goes—the twenty-fourth year of the Republic, but we have already paid the grain tax for the thirtieth! What kind of a world is this? We're just robbed, right and left. The likes of us can never hope to have enough to live on. (*Sighs.*)

LI   That's just what I mean. That's just what we mean by "exploitation." That's why we're for the revolution, so that we can get rid of exploiters, avenge the poor and set the people free.

BOATMAN (*reflectively*)   General Shih Ta-kai tried to do the same thing —or so they say—yet he was defeated.

LI   Who else is there in your family?

BOATMAN   My married son was with me. But the Kuomintang troops took him and his wife away yesterday. (*Tears come to his eyes.*)

LI   Where are they, d'you think? Just over there?

BOATMAN   Just over there. . . . But I don't know whether they're dead or alive. Oh, Heaven! Why are you blind to our misery? Why don't you punish these devils! Why don't you strike them down!

LI   Never fear, grandad. We'll save your son and his wife yet, if we succeed in crossing the river tonight.

BOATMAN   I should be everlastingly grateful to you, if you can! May the gods help you!

LI (*with a grin*)   You can help us more than the gods can. And not only our army, but the whole people of China will be grateful to you! (CHAO CHIH-FANG *and* LO SHUN-CHENG *enter.*)

BOATMAN (*after hard thought*)   Very well, comrades. I can't help you in any other way. I'll try to mend the boat and you can have it.

CHAO (*excitedly*)   Are you sure you can mend it?

BOATMAN   Ah, you don't have to worry about that! (*Rather shame-faced when he looks at* LO, *but speaking directly to him.*) Don't blame me for not lending you my boat when you first asked me. It's as dear to me as my own life.

CHAO   Thank you! We'll get you a much better boat when we reach the other side.

LO   Have you got the nails and stuff you need to mend it with?

BOATMAN   What do you think? A boatman that knows his job always has nails! You should have explained it to me properly before. Mustn't waste any more time—I know you want to get across in a hurry. I'll get on with it. (*Bustles off.*)

LI Lao Chao, I'll go and have a look at it myself. (*Goes off.*)

CHAO (*in high spirits*) We've got a boat at last!

LO Lao Chao! The river is wide and swift and we can't rig up a pontoon. The enemy's well entrenched on the other side. Even if we mend this wretched boat, it only holds twenty. And what can twenty men do over there? Not much, I'm afraid. We'll still have to hurry up and build some rafts.

CHAO M'm—yes, still the boat's the main thing. But press on with the rafts as well.

(WANG TEH-CHIANG *rushes on.*)

WANG Battalion Commander, the river's rising.

CHAO How much so far?

WANG About a centimetre, but it's still going up.

(LITTLE WAN *runs on.*)

LITTLE WAN Battalion Commander, here's a note from the Regimental Commander.

CHAO (*jumps with astonishment as he reads*) Oho! When's he coming, d'you know? (*Takes out a slip of paper from his notebook and begins writing.*)

LITTLE WAN Any minute now, he said.

CHAO Give him this. (*Handing over note.*)

LITTLE WAN Yes, Commander. (*Goes out.*)

CHAO Comrades, the Regimental C.O. tells us the situation's changed. Six enemy regiments are pushing up to intercept us. They'll probably be here by tomorrow morning. Orders are to force the crossing earlier, and wipe out the enemy on the opposite bank. The tactic is to lay a snare for these regiments! Comrades! It's not easy, I grant you that, but what a chance for a glorious victory!

WANG When's the crossing put on to then?

CHAO 4:30 p.m. An hour and a half earlier.

WANG Phew! How on earth are we going to be ready at such short notice?

CHAO Is there still time to make fifteen rafts?

WANG Dunno, I'm sure. We can only try. (*Turns to go.*)

LO What's that?

CHAO (*with determination*) Come back there! Just trying's not good enough. You've got to *do* it. I shall expect no less than fifteen rafts by half past four.

WANG Yes, Commander. (*Goes off.*)

(LI YU-KUO *enters.*)

LI Lao Chao, I have just had a look at that boat. I think it can be repaired all right. What's the matter with Lao Wang?

LO He doesn't really believe we can get across the river.

LI   So that's the trouble. I'll catch him up and have a word with him. (*Goes out.*)

CHAO   If we've got that boat I'll make do with only ten rafts.

LO   Well, I'll go and see to making them.

CHAO   Wait a minute, Deputy Commander. How d'you think it would be if we started crossing from here?

LO   Didn't the old boatman say this was a bad place, what with the current and the width?

CHAO   How are we off for machine-gun ammo?

LO   There's not much—about a hundred rounds for each gun. (*Goes out.*)

(TIGER CUB *enters.*)

TIGER CUB   Commander, one of the Propaganda Group comrades is here.

CHAO   Who? Group Leader Wu?

TIGER CUB   No. Comrade Feng-lien.

CHAO   (*thoroughly put out*)   What the devil are they sending me a woman for?

(LI FENG-LIEN *hears him say this as she comes in.*)

FENG-LIEN   Hey! Are you looking down on women comrades?

CHAO   (*very much taken aback*)   No . . . I mean . . . I mean I was surprised because I was expecting your group leader to discuss an important matter.

TIGER CUB   D'you want me for anything else, Commander?

CHAO   No. You can go back now.

TIGER CUB   Yes, Commander. (*Goes out.*)

CHAO   (*very ill at ease*)   Er . . . sit down, please, you must be tired. (*Turns to* YOUNG CHOU.) Fetch her some water, Young Chou.

FENG-LIEN   No, thanks! I didn't come here for water or rest. I'd better go immediately since you look down on women. Don't try this polite stuff on me, please.

CHAO   I had a difficult task in mind that means a lot of heavy physical work. I was afraid that. . . . But you aren't so bad, though. You kept up with the best of us in yesterday's march.

FENG-LIEN   I *told* you that if you walked a hundred *li* I wasn't going to stop at ninety-nine.

CHAO   Have some water, do! What is Wu doing now?

FENG-LIEN   He's busy with our propaganda unit and writing a song about the crossing, so he can't come. Just tell me what you want. You can't muck around with me like this; I've got work to do if you haven't.

CHAO   Very well then. Look, the enemy's kidnapped most of the people from here and they're on the other side of the river. We shall need a dozen boatmen who know this stretch of river, but so far we haven't found any. We can't speak the local dialect, so I sent for Comrade Wu to see if he can help us.

FENG-LIEN All right. (*Rises to go.*)

CHAO What, going already?

FENG-LIEN You have finished talking, haven't you?

CHAO D'you mean you think *you* can get them?

FENG-LIEN Certainly. We'll get you your boatmen within an hour. (*Starts off.*)

CHAO That's fine! To go off like that before we've even finished talking. A fine girl you are!

FENG-LIEN (*turning round in a proper rage*) Hey, Black Ox, you ought to have learnt how to behave by now. Where d'you think we are— still herding cattle in the countryside? You don't learn a thing— there's no sign you ever will! You'd better stop thinking you can stick to your old ways. It's more than time you stopped looking down on me. (*Goes out, leaving him flabbergasted.*)

CHAO What a spitfire! And only yesterday she was a little girl. . . .
    (COMPANY COMMANDER CHU *comes in with the captured officer.*)

CHU Commander, here's the prisoner we captured.

CHAO (*glancing at the prisoner's badge of rank*) Ah yes—a company commander, eh! (*To the prisoner.*) Your name?

PRISONER (*cringingly*) Feng Teh-chang. I was only made company commander last year, sir, and I've never done any harm to the people. If you let me go I'll. . . . (*Fumbles in his pocket.*)

CHAO Have you lost something?

PRISONER No. Look, here's a watch, three gold rings and twenty silver dollars. Please accept them, officer.

CHAO (*coldly disgusted*) Red Army men never take loot from prisoners. You need have no fear of losing your personal belongings. No one here wants them.

PRISONER (*completely out of his depth*) Oh. . . .

CHAO Now I'm going to ask you some questions, and I shall expect honest answers. We'll let you go if your answers turn out to be correct. (*Takes out his notebook.*)

PRISONER I swear to tell you everything I know, officer.

CHAO What exactly is the strength on the opposite bank? How many machine-guns? What artillery?

PRISONER (*hesitates*) Well. . . .

CHAO (*sternly*) Answer me, you—quick!

PRISONER (*hastily*) There's one battalion—that's four companies. Each company's got four light machine-guns. Then there's one extra company with six heavy machine-guns and one extra platoon with three mortars.

CHAO (*points across the river, at the place where the current flows swiftest*)   What about that area? What's the set-up there?

PRISONER   There's only a platoon there. You see, the current's too strong. Nobody could ever cross there.

CHAO (*pointing to the lower reaches*)   And down there?

PRISONER   That's the Old Ferry. That's the only place you can get across by boat. There's two companies there.

CHAO (*pointing to the village on the opposite bank*)   Your Battalion HQ there?

PRISONER   Yes. Guarded by one heavy machine-gun company and one mortar platoon.

CHAO   When did your battalion reach here?

PRISONER   We had one battalion here to fight the Yis. The heavy machine-gun company and the mortar platoon were sent here the day before yesterday.

CHAO   Did you know that we were driving up here?

PRISONER   No. It was a fluke. According to the stories we heard, Generalissimo Chiang planned to intercept you in south Szechuan. No one expected you'd be here so quick. You seemed to drop from the skies.

CHAO   When *were* you expecting us?

PRISONER   Our Intelligence reckoned you'd take at least a month and a half.

CHAO   You herded all the people here across, too? And you seized their boats?

PRISONER   We seized all their boats, yes. (*Hesitates.*) As far as the people here are concerned. . . . As a matter of fact, we took everyone we could lay hands on. I was just carrying out orders, you know. . . .

CHAO   Why did you take the women too?

PRISONER   Well. . . . You see. . . . Our officers haven't got their wives with them. . . .

CHAO (*grinding his teeth*)   Swine! Oh, may those bastards rot!

PRISONER   I swear I was only doing what my orders made me do. It's not my fault really.

CHAO (*contemptuously*)   I'll not hold you responsible for it, if you come out with the truth now. Why didn't you leave a boat for yourself?

PRISONER   We did have two boats on this side. But we used them to send the loot over, when we heard this morning that you were still in the Yi area, and there was no hurry. Then you swooped down on us.

CHAO   You did quite a bit of plundering the people here, I see.

PRISONER   Yes. The orders were that all local property should be transferred to the other bank.

CHAO   Young Chou, take him away.

PRISONER   Mercy, mercy, officer, let me go! I won't go back to the army to risk my life again! I'll go back to my land.

CHAO   You can go after we've won the battle, if your statements turn out to be correct. (*Turns to* YOUNG CHOU.) Young Chou, take him to the Runners' Squad.

YOUNG CHOU   Right! Hey, you, follow me.

PRISONER   And I can't go till the battle's won?

YOUNG CHOU   (*to prisoner*)   Come on. (*Turns to take prisoner away.*)

CHAO   (*turns back abruptly to the prisoner, and points again to the swirling current*)   Stop! How many troops are stationed across there? Quick!

PRSIONER   I told you the truth. Only one platoon.

CHAO   (*pointing to the Old Ferry*)   And there?

PRISONER   Two companies. That's the only place you can get across by ferry.

CHAO   Take him away now, Young Chou, and give him something to eat.

YOUNG CHOU   Go on! I'll give you some food.

PRISONER   Some food?

YOUNG CHOU   Yes. The Red Army never ill-treats prisoners. (*Goes out with the prisoner.*)

CHAO   (*to* CHU)   Send a platoon into the hills to cut timber. Lay on two platoons to keep close watch across the river.
(COMPANY COMMANDER CHU *goes out.* LI YU-KUO *enters, his coat blood-stained.*)

CHAO   (*startled to see the stains*)   What's happened, Political Instructor?

LI   Nothing to worry about. A scratch from a sniper. Look, I've had a word with Company Commander Wang. He's all right, I think. He is the sort who's always got a moan on, but he's perfectly sound when it comes to the pinch. (*Comes back to the present attack.*) Now, you've got your boat. What else do you need?

CHAO   We've got to pick out three points where we can cross. I need more ammunition and something heavy. Any chance of a mortar?

LI   Where d'you reckon to make your main crossing?

CHAO   It's risky, but—
(*They exchange silent glances and turn back again to the turbulent river.*)

CHAO   (*takes* LI's *elbow*)   Lao Li, I'm more than half inclined to say we should make the crossing here. Just because it's so devilish dangerous here, it's the least heavily defended landing. What d'you say?

LI   M'm. D'you thing there's a fair change of doing it?

CHAO   Can't be sure. Look at those rapids.

LI   Well?

CHAO   It means there are hidden rocks.

LI   No, the waves are behind the rocks.

CHAO   (*with a gasp of relief*)   Is that so? Lao Li!

LI   Yes. (*With great seriousness.*) I think you've made the right choice. I'm with you on it.

CHAO   You'll back it? (*Immensely cheered.*) You think it's the best way? I knew you'd understand! Can you pick twenty men, swimmers, handy with an oar, and brave and quick? If you can get chaps who were in the Golden Sand crossing, so much the better.

LI   You're going to lead the job yourself?

CHAO   (*matter-of-factly*)   Yes, of course.

LI   I can see to the men, I think. But what about guides?

CHAO   Your sister's seeing to that now.

LI   Good. I'll be off, then. I'll make myself personally responsible for putting it across properly to all the comrades, so that they can put all their spirit into it. (*Goes out.*)

CHAO   (*can't resist looking at the rapids*)   As the waves swirl behind the reefs we'll be able to get round them. Good. The enemy will be concentrating their fire on the less turbulent part of the river. Right, right . . . (*smiles to himself*) good! (*His face lightens as he becomes more and more convinced of the chances of success. He jumps up on to a higher rock to get a better view.*) They'll never dream we are planning to cross here.

   (WANG TEH-CHANG *and* COMPANY COMMANDER CHU *rush on.*)

CHU   Commander, there's rain blowing up from the northwest—the river's rising.

CHAO   How much?

WANG   Fifteen or sixteen centimetres, I'm afraid.

CHAO   Now listen! I know that we're up against difficulties, but there's victory ahead of us! The Tatu is our enemy, but it's also our life-line. To overcome such difficulties is like overpowering the enemy: it means victory. We're *going* to cross the river, even if we have to crawl over it! Understand? If we fail, it's not only a setback for us, but for the whole revolution.

WANG *and* CHU   Yes.

CHAO   You'd better get back now, and hurry up with those rafts. The more rafts we have, the better our chances. Jump to it, you fellows!

WANG *and* CHU   Yes, Commander. (*Go off.*)

CHAO   (*looks defiantly at the sky, then turns back to the turbulent water*) Oh, you Tatu. . . .

   (TIGER CUB *rushes on.*)

TIGER CUB Commander, my C.O. sent me to report that the river is still rising.

CHAO How much this time?

TIGER CUB Another thirty centimetres.

CHAO Tell your C.O. he must hurry up with the rafts.

TIGER CUB Yes, Commander. (*Goes out.*)

(*There is a loud roll of thunder.*)

CHAO (*glares at the sky and turns back to his map*) Damn the weather. Go ahead! Pour! Flood! I'm going to beat you! I'll be damned if we don't cross the river.

(TIGER CUB *comes back.*)

TIGER CUB Battalion Commander! It's still rising.

CHAO How much?

TIGER CUB Thirty centimetres more.

CHAO (*with a shout*) Tell your C.O. that as long as it doesn't reach the sky, we're crossing that river.

TIGER CUB (*rather apprehensively*) Right, Commander!

CHAO (*with a grin, and more calmly*) You can tell him as well that a boat rises with the water—there's nothing to worry about. It'll be all right. Don't come and report again, not even if it goes up three metres!

TIGER CUB Right! (*Goes off.*)

(CHAO *sits down again, thinking hard.* YOUNG CHOU *enters with hot water and a bowl.*)

YOUNG CHOU (*pours out a bowl of water*) Hadn't you better have a drink and a bite of food?

CHAO (*abstractedly*) What's that?

YOUNG CHOU (*fishing something out of his ration bag*) Eat something, do, or I'll be in trouble again for not taking proper care of you.

CHAO No. Not now.

YOUNG CHOU That's all very well, but you haven't had anything since you got up. You're not busy now—why don't you eat something?

CHAO (*letting his pent-up feelings out on* YOUNG CHOU) Stop fussing, for Heaven's sake! Get out of here!

(LI YU-KUO *comes in and stops short.*)

CHAO (*who hasn't seen* LI) Tell the Political Instructor that I've gone to help out with the rafts.

LI Hey, Lao Chao, wait a minute.

CHAO Yes?

LI I've got something to say.

CHAO (*still worked up*) All right, go ahead and say it.

LI (*warmly and sincerely*) Anything the matter with you, Lao Chao?

CHAO   Me?

LI   Yes. What's made you so angry?

CHAO   You know how things are!

LI   Well?

CHAO   How many rafts have we made?

LI   There'll be ten rafts ready in time.

CHAO   What about the boat?

LI   It's repaired now.

CHAO   How many swimmers have you found?

LI   Over a hundred in the battalion.

CHAO   What about the rain? Is it going to stop soon?

LI   Can't guarantee the weather, I'm afraid.

CHAO   That damned river's rising, you know. It's no good, I must go.

LI   Where?

CHAO   To help make the rafts.

LI   (*interrupts*)   Come off it. You're a commander, not a sapper. Calm
   down.

CHAO   (*in cold desperation*)   All right then. Supposing we take it that
   one boat and ten rafts will be ready in time. The river's still wide,
   and the rapids dangerous. What's more, it's raining and the water's
   rising! Work it out for yourself. The boat can take twenty men, say,
   and the ten rafts about a hundred. Let's suppose there won't be
   any losses during the crossing. That means that at the utmost we
   can only get a hundred and twenty men across for the initial assault.
   And they'd have no support, and no artillery. There's not even
   enough ammunition for the machine-guns. And how are we going
   to bring up the rest of the men? These are the odds against me—
   the raw lad. See?

LI   The Party's put you in command of the battalion. You should have
   more faith in yourself—more faith that you can do the job the
   Party gave you to do. No good flying into a rage, you know!

CHAO   What should I do then?

LI   Report to Regimental C.O. what the difficulties are. We must have
   HQ's help in a situation like this.
   (REGIMENTAL COMMANDER HUANG *comes in with* LO SHUN-CHENG.
   *The C.O. is covered with mud, and has evidently come straight
   from the riverside.*)

HUANG   How are the preparations going?

LI   They're well under way.

HUANG   (*giving* CHAO *a searching look*)   Bit worried about the odds,
   aren't you? Well, you shouldn't be. Buck up! You've got to be bold
   if you're in command. I think your plan's a good one.

CHAO   You think we can go ahead, Commander?

HUANG   Why, certainly! Go ahead with your plan. Hello, here's Group Leader Wu and one of his propaganda comrades coming.

(WU *and* LI FENG-LIEN *come in, greet everybody with "We're here to wish a victorious crossing of the Tatu!"*)

WU   Victory is certain, isn't it?

HUANG   It certainly is. Everything's under control. All we need is your inspiration.

WU   Well, that's why we've come. (*Fetching a note from his pocket.*) This is a note from Divisional HQ wishing you luck. There're a lot of comforts coming up. And we've got fifteen local boatmen arriving soon.

HUANG   Fine, comrades! Thank you. That's splendid.

WU   We must get back to our unit now. Goodbye! See you after the attack. (*Goes out with* FENG-LIEN.)

ALL   Goodbye! So long. Be seeing you. See you on the other side, etc.

HUANG   I've got some more good news. I've rustled up 1,000 rounds for your machine-guns, 200 grenades, and ten rafts. Third Battalion's sending all this up any minute now. And best of all, there's a mortar and a field gun with two rounds coming!

CHAO   A mortar and a field gun! That's great.

HUANG   You've got our whole army behind you, you see. How d'you feel about it now?

CHAO   Not a doubt in the world!

LI   It's going to be all right!

HUANG   Now then, Lao Chao, let's go over your plan for the actual crossing.

(LITTLE WAN *runs on.*)

LITTLE WAN   (*his face alight, he is bubbling over with something, and bursts out*) Regimental Commander! Chairman Mao himself, Commander-in-Chief Chu Teh and the Commander of the Army Corps have arrived at Regimental HQ. The Political Commissar wants you and Battalion Commander Chao to go there!

(*A roar of excitement and joy goes up from the whole stage.*)

CHAO   (*thinks of the implications and says immediately*) Go quick and tell them they shouldn't come here. There are snipers about.

HUANG   (*to* CHAO) Come on, Lao Chao. Come on, and bring your confidence in victory with you. Let's go! Leave everything for the moment to Lao Lo. (*Seizes* CHAO *by the elbow and pulls him off.*)

CHAO   Hey, just a sec. Here you are. (*Hands* LO *a note.*) This is the note from Divisional HQ. (*Goes off with* HUANG.)

LO   Lao Li, will you hold the fort? I'm off to see how the sappers are doing. (*Goes out.*)

LI   Young Chou, if you want me, I'm at First Company. (*Goes out.*)

YOUNG CHOU   (*can't keep still with excitement; climbs up a rock and sings out*)   Everyone's really on their toes, now Chairman Mao's here! (TIGER CUB *enters.*)

TIGER CUB   Hello, Young Chou, anything special to look at? (*Begins to climb after him.*)

YOUNG CHOU   (*stops him*)   Stop. What d'you want here?

TIGER CUB   I want the C.O. We want him to let us go with the shock force, me and the Youth Leaguers of my company.

YOUNG CHOU   Me, too!

TIGER CUB   No. You're not coming.

YOUNG CHOU   Why ever not? They let me join the Youth League last week.

TIGER CUB   No good trying that on me. I'm not taking you. (*Makes as if to climb the rock.*)

YOUNG CHOU   (*imperiously*)   Don't move! Stay where you are!

TIGER CUB   Show-off! Quite the little battalion commander, aren't you? Let me tell you I was a battalion runner myself once.

YOUNG CHOU   And let *me* tell you, you're not getting on this rock if you don't let me join your old shock force.

TIGER CUB   All right, then, you can come.

YOUNG CHOU   Fine. Now you can get up here.

TIGER CUB   (*gets up on the rock*)   What were you looking at anyway?

YOUNG CHOU   Chairman Mao and Commander-in-Chief Chu Teh!

TIGER CUB   Go on! Where?

YOUNG CHOU   They've gone now.

TIGER CUB   Beast! See if I don't punch your head.

YOUNG CHOU   Hey, don't fool around. Here come the chiefs.
        (*They scramble hastily down, and straighten up smartly as* HUANG *and* CHAO *enter, all smiles.*)

TIGER CUB   Battalion Commander, representing the Communist Youth League members of First Company, I would like to ask your permission to join the shock force.

YOUNG CHOU   Me too, Commander!

CHAO   Let's see. Tiger Cub, how many of you are there?

TIGER CUB   Forty-five, without Young Chou.

YOUNG CHOU   (*promptly*)   Forty-six, with Young Chou.

HUANG   That's rather a lot.

CHAO   I'll let sixteen of you join the shock force.

TIGER CUB   Yes, Commander. (*Rushes off to tell the others.*)

YOUNG CHOU   What about me, Commander?

CHAO   You run and ask all company leading comrades to come here.

YOUNG CHOU   At once! (*Goes out.*)

CHAO Why hasn't that scout returned yet, I wonder.

(LO SHUN-CHENG *comes on.*)

LO Lao Chao, Regimental Commander, everything's ready. The Divisional HQ's message has been read to all the comrades and the comforts distributed. The men are full of beans.

HUANG So are you, Lao Lo!

LO (*with a grin*) Rather!

HUANG Think the crossing's going to be a success?

LO Sure of it!

(*Old boatman enters.*)

BOATMAN I been thinking, Red Army comrades. Why don't you go by the Iron Chain Bridge on the Luting? I can take you there if you like.

HUANG It's good of you to think of it, but we've already sent some of our people to take that bridge.

BOATMAN Have you now? You think of everything, to be sure. I think you'll do all right here. You'll get across, I can see that.

(CHIEN KUEI-HSI *comes in.*)

CHIEN Report to Commander. . . .

CHAO Here you are. What's your news?

CHIEN We can climb that hill all right—there's no one living there. The river there's worse than here—I shouldn't think anyone could swim it. But there's no sign of the enemy the other side at all.

CHAO (*to* BOATMAN) Do *you* think it would be possible for anyone to swim the river at that point?

BOATMAN Never—no one could do it.

HUANG What about the weather, boatman? How long's the rain going to keep on?

BOATMAN I reckon it'll stop quite soon. You know what we say in these parts: Black sky overhead, expect more rain; light overhead, the shower will pass. And it's light overhead now, isn't it? Never fear, Heaven will help you. (*Looks skyward again.*) This rain won't keep on long.

CHIEN Do you want me for anything else, Commander?

CHAO No. You can get back to your unit.

CHIEN Commander, can I go with the shock force?

CHAO All right. Go and get ready.

CHIEN Right! (*Runs off.*)

BOATMAN Red Army comrades, are you going to let me help? I should like to help with the boat, if I may.

CHAO No, thanks all the same. There's no need. We've got boatmen now.

BOATMAN Young fellow, d'you think I'm too old to be useful? Eh? You may be good at war, but when it comes to managing a boat on this river. . . .

LO   You're an old hand, we know.

BOATMAN   I am as good as the next man, I dare say. I know the whole river by heart. I could tell you the exact number of rocks in it.

CHAO   Grandad, we're going to cross just where the current is worst.

BOATMAN   You can't fool me on my river. I can swim under water if necessary.

HUANG (*smiling at the old chap*)   Here's a real old hero, Lao Chao. Let him go with you and welcome.

CHAO (*can't keep it up any longer. Bursts into a loud laugh*)   Come along, come along, by all means. We can't do without you.

BOATMAN   You like your little joke, I see. I can't stay here, though. I'm off to my boat to see if everything's ready. (*Goes off, chuckling.*)

CHAO (*contentedly*)   Nothing like having a really knowledgeable old man like that with us.

(*All the company commanders and the political instructors come in, for briefing. They wait expectantly to hear what their orders are.* LI YU-KUO *enters.*)

LI   Regimental Commander! Lao Chao! We're all ready now. I've picked out the boatmen you want. They'll be here in a minute for you to look them over.

CHAO   Fine. (*Turns to* HUANG, *and says formally.*) Regimental Commander, will you give the orders?

HUANG   No, you carry on, Battalion Commander!

CHAO   All right. You correct me if I make any mistakes.

HUANG   Go ahead.

CHAO   Comrades, the orders we have had through our Regimental Commander are: our battalion is to lead the attack. Second Battalion will be in support and cover our rear. Now, what's the situation facing us? The enemy across the river is in battalion strength. Their HQ's in the little village there. Their river defences are concentrated at the safest places for crossings. There's very little opposite here, where the current is at its strongest. So we're choosing to make the key crossing right there, where we'll be least expected. Now the actual battle order will be like this. There'll be two crossings. Political Instructor Li and Company Commander Wang will take First and Second Companies on rafts, and force a crossing at the Old Ferry. Deputy Commander Lo will be in charge of the sappers and Third Company, and cover the Old Ferry crossing. His orders are to act as the situation demands. The Old Ferry attack will start at 4:30 p.m. The enemy will certainly concentrate all their forces there. I shall be taking the boat, with seventeen men, and cross here, where the rapids are, and catch them unawares. They'll have to turn back to stop us. When that happens, our Artillery Company will use the field gun at the grestest concentration of the enemy that they can see. I'll force the crossing in the confusion. Then we will execute a pincer movement, and crush them. . . . (*Pauses a moment.*) Well, comrades, that's our plan. Any comments?

WANG   You think the best chance is to attack where the current is strongest?

CHAO   Yes, because that's the most poorly defended. It'll be a tricky job, but the boat can get across faster just because the current's so swift. We'll dupe the enemy and win our victory! (*Pauses for further questions.*) Do you want to add anything, Regimental Commander?

HUANG   Comrades, we consider Commander Chao's plan to be a very good one. It's been examined and fully approved by Divisional HQ. We're going to win this battle, because the enemy will never dream that we're taking the most dangerous course. Furthermore, you don't have to worry about your rear or flanks. Advance boldly, comrades. We have full confidence that you can do it.

Shout of agreement from all on stage: "We know we can do it."

HUANG   The crossing of the Tatu is a matter of life and death to the Red Army. And both Chairman Mao and Commander-in-Chief Chu Teh have said how much they are counting on it.

ALL   Yes, Commander. We know. We'll make a success of it.

HUANG   More than one regiment will be thrown into it. The whole action will start from three directions simultaneously. Second Division will attack at the Luting bridge, Fourth Regiment will advance along the west bank, while our Regimental Political Commissar will lead Second Battalion to attack the lower bend. When our regiment has crossed the river and wiped out the enemy opposite, we shall turn east immediately and join up with the east column. Then we shall proceed to spring the trap on six regiments the enemy is sending up. This strategy is Chairman Mao's, and it's the right one. Although the enemy forces confronting us are rather weak, we must not underestimate them. Attack fearlessly, forcefully and quickly. Fearlessly, so as to strike terror into them, forcefully, so as to make it impossible for them to put up any resistance, and quickly, so as to win time.

ALL   We will.

HUANG   Immediately after victory we shall join up with the Fourth Front

Red Army. (*Everyone cheers. He pauses, looks at watch.*) Comrades, the general offensive will start in twenty minutes. Go back to your own units and get ready.

(*Company commanders and political instructors straighten up. They go out, followed by* LO *and* LI. TI7ER CUB *and fifteen young Red Army men rush on.*)

TIGER CUB (*to* CHAO)   Commander, we have been chosen to man the boat.

(CHIEN KUEI-HSI *runs on.*)

CHIEN   Me too. (*Falls into the line with the others.*)

CHAO   Good chaps! How many of you are Communists?

(*Five salute.*)

CHAO   And Youth League members?

(*Seven salute.*)

CHAO   Can you all swim and handle an oar?

ALL   Yes.

CHAO   How many of you were at the other river crossings?

ALL   All of us.

CHAO (*turns to* HUANG)   Any instructions, Regimental Commander?

HUANG   Comrades, you are seventeen tigers! You know yours is a most glorious task! You are going to force a crossing in the only boat we've got and open the way for the whole army. The whole Party and the whole army give you their support and look forward to your success! Now go ahead. The time has come.

ALL   We'll guarantee to do the job!

CURTAIN

Act IV

TIME   *A sunny morning in early July 1935.*

PLACE   *Near a lama temple in Maoerhkai, on the border of Sikang and Chinghai Provinces.*

SCENE   *Outside the house of a Tibetan family where* POLITICAL INSTRUCTOR LI *is lodged. The Red Army successfully crossed the River Tatu, and after seven days' forced march reached Chiachin Mountain, on the Szechuan-Sikang border. The mountain peaks lie under eternal snows anything up to thirty metres deep. On the heights the air is rarefied, so that the higher a traveller climbs the harder it is for him to breathe. Many lives have been lost here. Sudden tempests arise, strong enough to knock man and beast into a snowy grave. But the Red Army has passed by still more dangerous routes elsewhere.*

The First and Fourth Front Armies joined forces in the middle of June, at the foot of Chiachin Mountain. By July 9 they were at Maoerhkai—the gateway to the steppelands. With the Great Snow Mountains to the southeast and the uninhabited steppelands beyond the ridge to the northwest, Maoerhkai is a lonely little hamlet with some two hundred Tibetan households. A big lama temple, which looks like a palace, towers over the humbler dwellings of the people. The ordinary houses are like pigmy fortresses, built of stones as protection against bandits and wild animals. Some of these houses have three or four storeys, but they are usually two-storey affairs, with the people living upstairs, and the cattle kept on the ground floor. An outside stairway made of a tree trunk gives access to the upper storey.

POLITICAL INSTRUCTOR LI is lodged with a Tibetan family on the first floor of one of these houses. From the balcony which runs round the house, looking towards the north, stretch the boundless, hazy steppelands, to the west the magnificent lama temple, and southwards, the Great Snow Mountains. Two old cypresses stand in the yard, with goat heads and yak horns hanging on the branches. Under the cypresses is a pile of building stones, and a wooden scaffold for slaughtering cattle, slung with lamb skins and yak hides. The house stands a little high and only the heads and shoulders of travellers can be seen along the nearby road. Tibetans have been coming in twos and threes to the farewell party given in honour of the Red Army. Lamas also come in groups, carrying ancient musical instruments. They all pass by LI's lit-up room.

The curtain rises at daybreak.

SHANA WURSE, the daughter of the house, comes down the steps with a water jar. She pauses halfway down, and looks offstage. Her brother, SHALU CHODENG, is coming.

SHALU CHODENG (*offstage*)   The farewell meeting will begin soon. Come along, everyone, come along.
Comes on.

SHANA WURSE   Really, brother? Is the meeting to begin so soon?

SHALU CHODENG   Yes. Have you got the *tsamba*[4] ready yet?

SHANA WURSE   The barley's parched and mother's busy at the millstone now.

SHALU CHODENG   Oh, you must hurry up. (*Goes out.*)

(*Their father, an oldish man, comes on.*)

FATHER   Shana Wurse!

SHANA WURSE   Yes, father.

FATHER   How's the Political Instructor today?

SHANA WURSE   No better. You know you said that you would keep him with us? Did they agree?

FATHER   No. But I'll try my best to persuade them to let him stay. You keep watch over him. Don't let him go out. I'm going to the meeting first.

SHANA WURSE   But, father, I want to go to the meeting too. . . .

FATHER   Nonsense, daughter. You stay here and look after the Political Instructor. Don't let him go out. (*Goes out.*)

SHANA WURSE   Mother!

MOTHER   (*comes out on to the balcony*)   What's the matter?

SHANA WURSE   May I go to the meeting?

MOTHER   No. I want you to fetch me some water.

SHANA WURSE   How ever many helpers do you need to make a bit of *tsamba* and boil a kettle of water?

MOTHER   A kettle of water and a bit of *tsamba* indeed! There's two catties of butter and five catties of barley flour in it. Don't you call that just "a bit of *tsamba*"! Go and get me some water at once. Think how nice it will be for you to go to the meeting with the *tsamba*! Run along now. There's no time to lose, you know. (*Goes into the house.*)

SHANA WURSE   All right, mother.

(YOUNG CHOU *comes out of* LI's *room and tears down the stairs holding a water jar.*)

YOUNG CHOU   Shana Wurse, give me your jar, I'll get the water for you. Then you can go to the meeting.

SHANA WURSE   (*pulls* YOUNG CHOU *away from the house*)   It's all right, thank you. (*In a whisper, so that her mother can't hear.*) Are you leaving today, too?

YOUNG CHOW   Yes, of course.

---

[4] Parched flour made from *chingko*, a kind of barley, which the Tibetans mix with a churned emulsion of butter and tea to make their staple food.

SHANA WURSE   Why can't you stay here?

YOUNG CHOU   We've got to fight the Japanese invaders, see? There aren't any Japanese here, are there? There's no sense in our staying on.

SHANA WURSE   What about your Political Instructor? Is he going too? He's still very ill.

YOUNG CHOU   Well, he's packed all his things up. He's determined to go.

SHANA WURSE   I'm sure that's not right. You'd better try and talk him out of it. (*Pulling* YOUNG CHOU's *sleeve.*) Look, it's all steppe from here on—just a huge stretch of barren land. You can go for days and find nothing to eat.

YOUNG CHOU   We're going to take our rations with us.

SHANA WURSE   Where will you shelter for the night? Not a soul lives on the steppes.

YOUNG CHOU   We'll have to sleep wherever we happen to find ourselves. In the Red Army we're used to such hardships.

SHANA WURSE   You can sleep on the dry grass, maybe, but what about where it's all swampy? There's often pouring rain, and snowstorms, and then it's just a mess of mud. Once you begin to sink into it, you're done for. (YOUNG CHOU *listens, rather alarmed.*) Besides, (*points dramatically at* YOUNG CHOU) there are devils who attack travellers. . . .

YOUNG CHOU (*in astonishment*)   Devils? What do you mean?

SHANA WURSE   Man-eating devils! Once there was an Iron-Rod Lama in these parts who set out with about a hundred young men on horseback to hunt wild yaks on the steppelands. On the marshes they met those devils, who called up a violent tempest and struck them dead!

YOUNG CHOU   What do the devils look like?

SHANA WURSE   Silly! Devils are invisible. They breathe on you and you drop dead. The bodies of their victims don't even rot.

YOUNG CHOU   Oh, I don't believe in such nonsense. People don't die because a devil's got poisonous breath, but because the air's rarefied. Before we crossed the Great Snow Mountains, we heard the same old yarn about man-eating devils.

SHANA WURSE   Did you?

YOUNG CHOU   But we never saw a single devil all the way across six great snowy mountains.

SHANA WURSE   Yet many of you *were* blinded and crippled.

YOUNG CHOU   Yes. But it was the glare of the snow that blinded them and frost-bite that crippled them.

SHANA WURSE   Anyway, it's hard going. (*Naively.*) You'd much better stay here. The steppelands are far more dangerous than the Great

Snow Mountains. For one thing, you haven't got any horses. Even if you had, they'd be no use in the swamps.

MOTHER (*inside the house*)   Shana Wurse!

SHANA WURSE   Yes, mother.

MOTHER (*on balcony*)   Why, still here, gossiping! Go and get me the water, quick. (*Goes in again.*)

SHANA WURSE   Yes, mother.

(HUANG *and* LITTLE WAN *come up.*)

HUANG   Hello, Young Chou.

YOUNG CHOU   Good morning, Regimental Commander!

HUANG (*hushing them*)   Easy there!

SHANA WURSE (*taking* YOUNG CHOU's *water jar from him*)   Let me get the water for you. (*Goes off.*)

HUANG   Young Chou, is the Political Instructor any better today?

YOUNG CHOU   No. he's still feverish.

(NURSE CHANG *comes out of* LI's *room.*)

NURSE CHANG   Young Chou!

HUANG (*beckoning to the nurse*)   Come here, Nurse Chang.

NURSE CHANG (*halfway down the stairs*)   Hello, Regimental Commander.

HUANG   Tell me frankly just how the Political Instructor is.

NURSE CHANG   He's got a bad chill, and his temperature's right up. His old wounds are infected. He's just dozed off.

(WANG TEH-CHIANG, CHAO CHIH-FANG, LO SHUN-CHENG *and* LI FENG-LIEN *come on. They all greet* HUANG.)

HUANG   Not so much noise, please, everybody.

(LI FENG-LIEN, *a bundle in her hand, begins to climb the stairs.*)

HUANG   Feng-lien, come down. I want to talk things over before we wake him. (FENG-LIEN *comes back.*) It's an unusually difficult job, you know, to cross the steppelands. There's no end to them and they're completely uninhabited. Bad weather and bad going are much more difficult for a sick man to stand up to. And every day's a forced march for advance units like ours. What d'you think we ought to do about him?

NURSE CHANG   I think it would be better for him to wait here for the rear units. His fever will be over in a few days.

LO   Suppose he doesn't pick up before the last unit goes by here?

NURSE CHANG   He's not well enough to move now, anyway.

HUANG   What do you think, Feng-lien?

FENG LIEN (*on the verge of tears*)   Oh, Commander Huang!

HUANG   What about you, Lao Lo?

LO   It's up to you to decide, really. (*Suddenly, as the idea comes to him.*) Can't we find a horse for him?

HUANG   There were plenty here, but they mostly got stolen by the enemy before we came. The few that are left are worth their weight in gold to the Tibetans. They need them for breeding. They wouldn't sell them and we couldn't very well ask them to.

CHAO   (*sighing—almost a groan*)   Ah!

HUANG   (*struck by the depth of sorrow in* CHAO's *face*)   Can you think of any way, Lao Chao?

(CHAO *looks at him but can say nothing.*)

HUANG   (*making up his mind*)   We'll take him along on a stretcher.

NURSE CHANG   I can't guarantee at all that he won't get worse.

HUANG   Well, it's worth trying. Let's see. We'll need eight men, I should think.

SHANA WURSE   (*comes back with her filled water jar*)   Young Chou, here's your water. (*Realizes what they are saying.*) What! You're planning to take the Political Instructor away from us? Father! Father! (*Hands jar to* YOUNG CHOU *and makes a dash for the square where the meeting is being held.*)

HUANG   What's the matter with her?

YOUNG CHOU   She wants the Political Instructor to stay behind with them, so she's gone to fetch her father.

HUANG   Nurse Chang, let me come with you and see how Lao Li is. (*Goes up the stairs with the nurse.*)

(SHANA WURSE *comes on with her father, and goes up the stairs.*)

FATHER   Good day to you, comrades. Where's your Regimental Commander?

LO   He's gone up to see the Political Instructor.

(HUANG *and the nurse come down.*)

LO   How is he?

HUANG   (*heavily*)   He looks very feverish still. He's asleep now.

FATHER   (*very seriously*)   Regimental Commander, I pray you, leave him with us. I ask you on behalf of all of us local people. Why must you insist on taking him? Don't you trust us to look after him?

HUANG   No, friend, it's not that. But we think we can take him along by stretcher.

FATHER   By stretcher, eh? How many men d'you reckon that will take?

HUANG   Eight would be able to do it, I think.

FATHER   I tell you, not even eighty would be enough. Look, after you've crossed that ridge, a day's journey from here, you'll reach the swamps. Its difficult enough for anybody to get across that soft mud and not be sucked down. Stretcher-bearers with a load on their shoulders would never do it.

HUANG   I know the difficulties. We're prepared to meet them.

FATHER   You'll find no food on the steppes, you know.

HUANG   We're carrying our rations.

FATHER   And there's no shelter for the night.

HUANG   We're used to sleeping in the open.

FATHER   That's all very well for those in health. But the Political Instructor's a sick man. (HUANG *listens thoughtfully, without answering.*)
Why don't you leave him with us? We need people to lead us in the
revolution, too.

   (LITTLE WAN *comes in.*)

HUANG   Well, I'll talk it over with the Regimental Political Commissar,
and get instructions from Divisional HQ.

LITTLE WAN   Regimental Commander, the send-off meeting has begun
and the Political Commissar has sent me to get you. He's expecting
you to make a speech.

HUANG   Right, I'm coming.

FATHER   Comrades, rest assured we shall take good care of him. After
you've gone, my son shall take him to my elder brother's. We'll give
him Tibetan clothes and he shall ride on my own horse. When he
has recovered, a young fellow like him, with a rifle and a horse,
will have nothing to fear at all.

HUANG   We thank you for your goodness. You really have a heart of gold.
But. . . .

FATHER   (*interrupts*)   You don't know how much we Tibetans owe to
the Communist Party and all of you. In the past we were always
looked down on. We were called barbarians, savages, and worse.
You never harm us, or cheat us. Your doctors treat us for nothing,
and you pay in silver dollars for whatever you buy from us. You
let us run our own government and choose our own leaders. We'll
never forget the help you've given us, never!

HUANG   Well. . . . Whether he will stay or not can be decided later.

FATHER   You must remember the Political Instructor's a very sick man.
Otherwise we wouldn't ask you to let him stay on at all.

HUANG   Well, we'll talk about it again after the meeting. Come, Nurse
Chang.

   (HUANG, LO, NURSE CHANG, CHAO, WANG *and* LITTLE WAN *go off.*)

FATHER   What is it? Don't they trust me? I'm not letting him go, anyway.
(*Calls out.*) Shana Wurse!

SHANA WURSE   (*runs down the steps*)   Yes, father?

MOTHER   (*comes out after her daughter*)   Where are you running off
now, Shana Wurse? You'll make me late with the *tsamba*.

FATHER   Look, wife, the Political Instructor is going to stay on with us.
Tidy up the back room a bit and put some carpets on the floor.

Shana Wurse, run over to your uncle's and fetch me my new fur coat.

SHANA WURSE   Yes, father. (*Goes off.*)

MOTHER   Good, I'm glad of that. I'll see to the room. (*Goes into house.*) (SHALU CHODENG *enters.*)

SHALU CHODENG   Father, come to the meeting at once. Everybody's waiting for your speech. (*Goes off again.*)

FATHER   Coming! Coming! Wife! (MOTHER *comes on the balcony.*)

MOTHER   Goodness, what's the matter now? You've been calling me all the morning.

FATHER   I'm off to the meeting. I'll leave the Political Instructor in your hands. Don't let him go away. (*Goes out.*)

MOTHER   Never you worry about that. (*Goes quietly to the door of* LI'S *room and listens. Hearing nothing, she goes round the balcony to her own room.*) (LI YU-KUO *himself comes feebly out of his room, carrying his kit on his back.*)

LI   Young Chou, it's time we were off, I suppose. (*Sees his sister.*) You're in good time, Feng-lien. Young Chou, take my kit for me. (*Throws down his kit.*) Let's go. (*Walks to the stairs but staggers and is on the point of fainting. They rush up the stairway.*)

FENG-LIEN   Oh brother, be careful. (*She and* YOUNG CHOU *help to steady him.*)

LI   I'm all right. Time's up, isn't it? Let's go.

YOUNG CHOU   The Regimental Commander and the others were here just now.

LI   Where have they gone?

YOUNG CHOU   Everyone's at the farewell meeting.

LI   Good. Let's go there, too. (*Reels again before he has taken two steps.*)

YOUNG CHOU   Political Instructor!

FENG-LIEN   Brother!

MOTHER   (*rushes down the steps when she hears* LI'S *voice*)   Why are you going out like this? (*Feels his forehead.*) You have a high fever. It fairly burns my hand! Go in, quickly!

LI   Well, mother, I'm afraid I've given you a lot of trouble while I've been here. Now the army is going, and I must go with it. I'm most grateful for all your kindness.

MOTHER   No, you can't go. It's been decided that you're to stay on at our house. (*Tries to drag him in.*)

LI   What! Is that true?

FENG-LIEN   Nothing's been decided yet. Sit down here for a bit. (*Helps him to sit down.*)

LI (*taken aback and worried*) What's all this about? Tell me, quick.

YOUNG CHOU It's like this. The Regimental Commander said you can be carried by stretcher, with eight bearers. The old man here insisted that you must stay on with them. The Commander said he'd think it over.

LI I see. (*Gets up and tries to walk, but has to stop short, unable to go any further.*) Eight men to carry me? That is . . . Young Chou, tell the Battalion Commander I'd like to see him.

YOUNG CHOU Right away! (*Goes off.*)

MOTHER Won't you come back in, Political Instructor?

LI No, I'd like to stay outside for a while.

MOTHER All right. I'll go and tidy up your room, while I have the chance. But you mustn't go away. Eighty men wouldn't be able to carry you through the swamps, let alone eight. (*Goes back up the steps, taking* LI's *kit and ration bag with her.*)

FENG-LIEN (*anxiously watches* MOTHER *take* LI's *things away*) Are you giving up the idea of going, brother?

LI Is there any choice? I don't want the Party to have to worry about me. There's a danger even of normal, fit people being sucked into the swamps. I can't allow myself to be a burden to my comrades—it would mean risking their lives! No. I can't let them do anything like that. We've got to get every man through that we can. Each one is precious; each one carries the seed of revolution, and each one will be added strength to the revolution and victory. I'm going to ask permission to stay behind. Can't you understand how I feel?

FENG-LIEN Yes, I do.

LI You'd better go now. They'll be moving on at any moment.

FENG-LIEN I shall ask the Party if I can stay behind, too.

LI What ever for?

FENG-LIEN To look after you. We can set out later.

LI Don't be silly! You're not a little girl now. Did you join the revolution because of me?

FENG-LIEN Well . . . it was you who brought me out here. (*Begins to cry.*)

LI But it's not your job to stay on with me. . . .

FENG-LIEN I can ask for permission.

LI I won't let you do that. Aiya! You don't understand at all.

FENG-LIEN It's up to the Party to say. I'm going to ask now. (*Starts up.*)

LI No, hold on! I won't have it. You're no sister of mine if you act like that. You. . . .

FENG-LIEN You can't frighten me. No, I'm not a little girl now! (*Rushes out.*)

LI Feng-lien! Feng-lien!

(SHANA WURSE *runs on, carrying a fur cap and a red fur coat over one arm, and holding a horse whip.*)

SHANA WURSE Political Instructor, this is the new wedding coat my father bought for brother. Come on, try it on. It'll make you feel lovely and warm. (*Tries to make* LI *put it on.*)

LI Thank you, little sister. Put it down for the moment. I'll put it on later.

SHANA WURSE You feel shy about it, don't you? I've always heard that you young Hans are bashful with girls. Is it true?

LI (*doesn't know quite how to take this*) No, it's not that.

SHANA WURSE All right, then. You can put it on later yourself. You know, I brought father's favourite horse for you, too. When you're better I should love to go for a ride with you. (*Abruptly.*) Can you ride? (*No answer from* LI.) Oh, you are shy! You're blushing!

LI (*an idea flashing into his mind*) How many horses has your family got?

SHANA WURSE We did have fourteen, but last spring several of them died of disease. Then the counter-revolutionaries came and stole some, just before you came. We've only got three now: two old mares, and this stallion. Father loves this one so much that he wouldn't even let us ride it—that's why he sent it over to my uncle's. (*All of a sudden.*) Oh, I forgot to bring the boots. (*Calling to her mother inside.*) Mother!

MOTHER (*offstage*) What do you want?

SHANA WURSE I only wanted to tell you I'm going back to uncle's for the boots.

MOTHER All right. But mind you come straight back.

SHANA WURSE (*looking* LI *up and down*) M'm. If you'd got proper clothes and boots on—like ours—you'd be as good looking as my brother. You wait here. I'll get the boots for you. (*Starts to hurry off again, stops short to cast one more glance at him and goes.*)

(CHAO CHIH-FANG, *looking worried, comes in with* YOUNG CHOU.)

YOUNG CHOU Political Instructor, here's the Battalion Commander.

LI Hello, Lao Chao. Come and sit down. (CHAO *doesn't answer. He just looks at* LI's *face.*) Well, don't you recognize me? (*Still no answer.*) Why don't you say something? You understand why I want to stay behind, don't you?

CHAO What did you want to see me for?

LI Is the army ready to move now?

CHAO Yes.

LI All the preparations made?

CHAO Yes.

LI How do the comrades feel?

CHAO All in high spirits, all determined to beat the steppelands.

LI   That's fine. That will mean another victory.

CHAO   Did you send for me to talk about these things?

LI   Yes and no. I'm all mixed up, old chap. Of course I want to go with you, but I don't want to be carried. And we can't get hold of a horse. It seems there's no choice but to stay behind.

CHAO *(despairingly)*   How can you say that?

LI   But I give you my word: wherever I am, I'll remain a true Communist and your loyal comrade.

CHAO *(bursts out)*   No! I can't leave you like that! You've little chance to recover here. I'll help you through the steppelands, even if I have to carry you on my back. I won't leave you here alone. It's a crazy idea even to think of staying behind.

LI   Crazy? *(Suddenly clasping* CHAO's *shoulders.)* You do think I can go, don't you? And that I won't be a burden? To tell the truth, I'd never dream of parting company with you. I want to go. But the Party wants eight men to carry me. Everybody's up against it. Why should I be an exception? Why should I be carried through the steppelands? What have I done to deserve that? No! I'm going, but I shall carry myself. You understand? *(Gets up resolutely and walks a few steps forward. Then exclaims with joy.)* Look, Lao Chao, I *can* walk! I *can* walk!

   (HUANG, LO, WANG, CHIEN, NURSE CHANG *and* LITTLE WAN *comes on.)*

HUANG   Hello there, Lao Li!

LI *(standing firmly before* HUANG*)*   Regimental Commander, I can walk, you see. I can go with you on my own two feet.

HUANG   But. . . .

LI *(with fierce determination)*   I can't leave our army, not even for a moment. I've got work to do. I'd be utterly helpless, cut off from the Party. I can't fight, separated from the army. I must go with you, on my own legs!

HUANG   How did all this come about?

SHANA WURSE *(comes back with a pair of new boots, still holding the riding whip. She sees* LI *up and about, and is startled)*   Political Instructor, what ever are you doing?

   (SHALU CHODENG *comes on with his father.)*

FATHER *and* SHALU CHODENG   Hey, what's up?

MOTHER *(comes out on the stairway)*   What are you letting him do!

CHAO   Regimental Commander, I think he should go with us. In fact, we can't go without him. I'll carry him myself, on my back, all the way through the steppelands, if necessary.

YOUNG CHOU, CHIEN, LO, WANG *(together)*   I can carry him.

HUANG   Who told you that we were going to leave him behind? We've decided to take him. We're organizing stretcher-bearers, and Nurse

Chang, Young Chou and Chien Kuei-hsi have been detailed to look after him.

LI   I don't want people to carry me. I can walk by myself. I'm not going to be carried . . . I'll, I'll . . .

SHANA WURSE (*interrupts*)   Please leave him with us, Regimental Commander. We'll take good care of him. I'll see that no harm comes to him. (*Touches the stiletto which hangs from her belt.*)

FATHER   What's all this about? Don't you trust us with him?

HUANG   No, no, of course it's not that. To tell the truth, his comrades can't bear to part with him.

LI (*picks up the fur cap and coat*)   Dear father, mother, little sister! For a month I've lived with you like one of the family. Now I've got to go, for the sake of the revolution and the liberation of all the nationalities of China. It was just the same, I remember, when I left home many years ago. My father and mother were reluctant to see me go, just as you are now. (*Gives the cap and coat back to* SHANA WURSE.)

FATHER   During your stay here you have treated us as if we were your own people. Every day you told us of the revolution. It was our fondest hope that you would stay here. Regimental Commander, it was my idea to keep the Political Instructor here. (*Turns to* LI.) But if you are determined to go, I suppose I must give in. (*Turns to his daughter.*) Shana Wurse, fetch me my stallion.

SHANA WURSE   I have, already.

FATHER (*takes the whip from her*)   Political Instructor, since your comrades must have you with them, I'll have to let you go. Look, I want to give you a present, one of my horses. (*Handing him the whip.*) Shalu Chodeng, go and saddle the horse and put the Political Instructor's things in the saddle bags.

LI (*resolutely*)   No. Thank you, father, but I can't take it.

FATHER   Look here, the counter-revolutionaries took away most of my horses before you came. This is the only stallion I've got left. Now you're to have it as a gift. You must accept it. Otherwise I can only think that you despise me and my horse, and I'll kill it, that I will. (*Notices at this moment that his son hasn't gone to saddle the horse, and gets angry.*) Shalu Chodeng, why haven't you gone to saddle the horse? If you don't hurry, I'll kill you, too!

SHALU CHODENG   I'm going, aren't I? (*Goes out with* LI's *kit.*)

FATHER   Wife, bring out the *tsamba* and give it to the Political Instructor.

MOTHER   All right. (*Goes in.*)

(*Offstage, the Red Army units have started moving. The lamas begin their music.*)

HUANG   Young Chou, give me those forty silver dollars.

YOUNG CHOU   Here they are.

HUANG   (*silver dollars in hand*)   Father, we have accepted your horse as a gift. You must take our gift in return. It's not much.

FATHER   (*refuses to take the money*)   Regimental Commander, you do despise me! I'm not selling the horse, you know.

HUANG   Nor am I buying it. If you don't accept the money, I can only assume you're despising *me*! I'll throw it away if you don't want it.

FATHER   All right. (*Takes twenty dollars.*) I'll take half.

MOTHER   (*comes down with the tsamba*)   Political Instructor, there's really nothing in these parts, and we've got nothing much in the house to give you either. Here is some *tsamba* I made myself. You can eat it on your way. Please take it.

HUANG   Thank you. We accept your gift. (YOUNG CHOU *takes the bag from her.*) But you must take ours in return. (*Gives her the other twenty silver dollars.*)

MOTHER   No, I can't. I'm not going to take it.

HUANG   (*in mock anger*)   Young Chou, give her back her *tsamba*.

MOTHER   Oh!

FATHER   We'll take it, Regimental Commander. You're exactly like our own people. (*Moved to tears.*)

MOTHER   (*also in tears*)   Oh, they are good, these Red Army men! Oh, why can't you stay longer?

(SHALU CHODENG *enters.*)

SHALU CHODENG   The stallion's ready, father.

HUANG   Very good. Let's go now.

FATHER   Shalu Chodeng, go with them part of the way. (*Grasps* LI'S *hand.*) Come to see us again when the revolution's successful.

SHALU CHODENG   (*slings his rifle over his shoulder and sticks his stiletto in his belt*)   Come on then.

LI   Goodbye, father, goodbye, mother, and you, little sister! I'll come to see you after the revolution.

(*The Red Army units march away from the meeting place in good order, singing the song "Three Rules of Discipline and Eight Points for Attention."*[5] *They are followed by the lamas playing music and*

---

[5] The "Three Rules of Discipline" are: 1. Obey orders in all circumstances; 2. Do not take a single needle or piece of thread from the people; 3. Hand in all property captured in battle to the government. The "Eight Points for Attention" are: 1. Talk to the people courteously; 2. Observe fair dealing in all business transactions; 3. Return everything you borrow; 4. Pay for anything you damage; 5. Do not swear at people or beat them; 6. Be careful not to damage crops; 7. Respect women; 8. Do not ill-treat prisoners of war.

the Tibetans shouting slogans, "Long live the Chinese Workers' and Peasants' Red Army!" and "Long live the Chinese Communist Party!" There is a sea of waving hands and a chorus of "goodbyes.")

CURTAIN

Act V

TIME   *The afternoon of August 15, 1935.*

PLACE   *The steppelands.*

BACKGROUND   *The steppelands spread for thousands of* li *over the plateau which lies on the Chinghai-Sikang border. They are practically uninhabited and the climate is appalling, heavy rain and snow-storms alternating in rapid succession. In summer, a white pall of fog and drizzle hangs over them for weeks at a time. Rank grass grows a metre high, and then quickly wilts and decays in autumn. The accumulation of layers of rotten grass forms a deceptive surface. Large areas are unsafe, and the ground gives way under-foot. Here and there only a quick dash will get a man over it. Any attempt at walking would mean certain death. It is on these terrible steppelands that our heroes of the Red Army wrestle with the forces of nature. By day they struggle with the swamps, and at night have to sleep in the open, on the wet ground. When their rations run out, they eat weeds. When their clothes wear out, they wrap them-selves in their bedding and undressed sheepskin. Hunger and disease are their constant companions. Are there any whose coats are not torn, whose shoes are not worn out? Are there any who are not emaciated and exhausted? Their journey seems endless; yet dauntless, indomitable, they plod on day and night for four weary weeks until they beat the odds against them and finally get out of these dreadful steppes.*

SCENE   *A cypress grove on a little rise where First Battalion HQ is en-camped. Though damp, the ground is comparatively firm. Through the branches of the cypress which surrounds the place, a thick fog can be seen shrouding the steppelands. Occasionally a gust of wind clears the fog momentarily, and affords a glimpse of the surrounding desolation.*

The sky is overcast. There is no way of getting one's bearings, except by compass—and the army hardly possessed any—unless it clears at noon, and there is a sight of the sun. At 3 p.m., when the scene opens, there is rarely any sun, but today, as luck would have it, a strong wind has sprung up and there is a shaft of sunshine through a gap in the clouds. Such afternoon radiance is brief and ominous. It often portends approaching hail or snow.

When the curtain rises, a few Red Army stragglers are seen battling through the wind and fog. YOUNG CHOU *is sheltering from the wind behind a tree. Violent gusts are shaking his improvised shelter—made from his bedding. His wash-basin, strung on a tree, clatters against the branches.*

TIGER CUB (*comes in through the grove. He is taken aback at seeing* YOUNG CHOU's *huddled figure, thinking he has collapsed*) Young Chou! Young Chou! Whatever's the matter with you?

YOUNG CHOU (*gasping*) Heavens, what a wind! It knocks the breath out of you.

TIGER CUB Where's the Political Instructor?

(*The wind drops.*)

YOUNG CHOU He'll be here any minute. Well, fancy that! the wind's dropped as suddenly as it rose. How queer!

TIGER CUB Phew! You gave me a turn. I thought you were done for.

YOUNG CHOU What a thing to say! I'm going to do my bit and build socialism in China. Catch me ending up here! (*Straightens his "tent."*)

TIGER CUB Don't you look too far ahead. Count yourself lucky if you get through this place alive, and pass away in the first Han area you reach.

YOUNG CHOU I like that! If I didn't look far into the future I wouldn't be here talking. Why, only the day before yesterday, I fell into one of the bogs. "Now then, Young Chou," I says to myself, "pull yourself together, you've got to get out of this! You can't die here! You must live to do your bit in building socialism."

TIGER CUB (*changes his tune*) The same sort of thing's happened to me. That's just the way I feel about it, really. What d'you think socialism or communism's going to be like?

YOUNG CHOU It'll be much the same as it is in the Soviet Union, the Political Instructor told me once.

TIGER CUB   And what's that like?

YOUNG CHOU   There aren't any landlords, or warlords or foreign op-pressors in the Soviet Union. All the children go to school, and there's work for everybody. No one goes short of food and clothes. The land is worked by machines, and the people live in proper houses. . . .

TIGER CUB (*musingly*)   I see. . . . Well, we'll make it like that here, in our own China. We'll follow Chairman Mao out of the steppelands, get to the Northwest and wipe out the Japanese invaders and Chiang Kai-shek's troops. (*Comes back to the present with a jerk.*) I say, Young Chou, is the Political Instructor any better?

YOUNG CHOU (*sadly*)   No. He's still got his fever and his wounds are bothering him again.

TIGER CUB   I thought he said he was better.

YOUNG CHOU   Pooh! He talks and laughs when there's anyone around, but, I tell you, when he's alone he clenches his teeth and groans.

TIGER CUB   I've never heard him groan.

YOUNG CHOU   'Course you haven't. He'd take good care never to show anything like that in front of people. I'm probably the only soul who knows about it. Look at him, when his horse died the day before yesterday. What did he say? "Young Chou," he said, "now that I've lost my horse, I'll challenge you to a walking race." And sure enough, the moment he started walking, the whole battalion was inspired to get a move on, more than ever before. Not a single man dropped behind that day. When the Battalion C.O. came up and suggested that we should get a stretcher for him, he flew into a proper rage—the first time I've ever seen him lose his temper. Come to think of it, I'm darned if he's marched together with the Battalion C.O. since. (*Begins to get worried about today.*) You know, I'm beginning to wonder why he asked me to leave him alone today and come on ahead by myself.

(LO SHUN-CHENG *comes on, worn and haggard, his uniform wet and bedraggled. He drags himself along with the help of a stick.*)

LO   I thought you were with your unit. What are you doing here, Tiger Cub?

TIGER CUB   My company C.O. sent me to help Young Chou look after the Political Instructor.

LO   Where *is* the Political Instructor, Young Chou?

YOUNG CHOU   He's behind a bit.

LO   What! He's not with you? Why on earth did you leave him behind? That's a fine way to look after him!

YOUNG CHOU   Well, you see, he told me to go ahead to see how you were.

He said you were ill, that you felt dizzy and that you'd got something the matter with your stomach.

LO I thought you had more sense! You let him send you away, you little fool? H'm. You don't seem to be half as bright as you were. And now he's lost, what are you going to say for yourself? Don't you know he's a sick man? Have you forgotten that it's your special duty to take care of him?

YOUNG CHOU He said you'd been unwell since yesterday. Stomach trouble, he said. He *ordered* me to come to look after you. Ought I to have disobeyed him?

LO Now listen, you. Boil some water and get some food ready, and find a good place so that he can sleep. I've got to go and see how the men are. Where's the nurse?

YOUNG CHOU She's ill too. She's gone back to the Medical Department.

LO (*rather shocked*) What? She's not with the Political Instructor? Is the Battalion Commander about?

YOUNG CHOU He's gone to a meeting at Regimental HQ.

LO (*going back to his worry about the Political Instructor*) You little rascal, I just don't know what to do with you. If I give you a piece of my mind, you sulk. If I don't, well. . . . What will you do if something happens to the Political Instructor?
(*Goes out.*)

YOUNG CHOU I know I was a fool to leave him. (*Breaks down in complete misery.*) Tiger Cub, come with me. Let's go and find him.

TIGER CUB Cheer up! He'll show up in a bit. He won't get lost that easy. Hadn't we better do as the Deputy C.O. said and boil some water and get some food ready for him? If we start on it he'll have something to eat and drink when he gets here. (*Picking up a basin.*) I'll go and get some water. You make a fire and get the place ready.

YOUNG CHOU (*stops crying*) All right. Get running water, though—the stagnant water's poisonous.
(*Sets to work on making a fire with twigs, starting it with a piece of oiled cloth.*)

TIGER CUB I know. (*Goes out.*)

YOUNG CHOU (*getting out the ration bag*) It's empty! There's nothing left anywhere! (*Buries his face in his hands and bursts out crying again.*)

TIGER CUB (*coming back with the water*) Gosh, what a windy, rainy, stinking place this is! Can't even get clear water! Do you think this is safe to use? (*Looks at* YOUNG CHOU.) You crying again?

YOUNG CHOU (*sheepishly*) What d'you mean?

TIGER CUB What I say? Just look at your face!

YOUNG CHOU (*throws him the empty ration bag*) Look at this! Not a grain left. How can we cook a meal with no rice?

TIGER CUB (*depressed himself*) Our company's got no rice left either. What are we going to do now? (*Starts to cry too.*)

(LI YU-KUO, *helped by* CHIEN KUEI-HSI, *comes up. He is in rags, drawn and sallow, his feet showing through his straw sandals. It is all he can do to shuffle along, with help, against the wind and rain.*)

YOUNG CHOU *and* TIGER CUB (*they are struck dumb by his sudden appearance, then jump up and call out joyfully*) Political Instructor! You're here!

LI (*puts a bold face on it*) Well, you beat me today, I must say. I dropped behind. (*Manages to laugh.*) You must have arrived a good hour before me. Nice to see a fire and have a tent. This is wonderful! Anything for me to sit on?

YOUNG CHOU *and* TIGER CUB (*pulling a log over between them*) Sit here, and warm your hands over the fire. (*Help him on to it.*) You're soaked to the skin!

LI What's up with you two? You look so down in the mouth! Been quarrelling?

YOUNG CHOU No.

TIGER CUB The Deputy C.O. ticked Young Chou off for deserting you.

LI Oho, that's what's the matter, is it? It's not Young Chou's fault, but mine, for not listening to him. Where is the Deputy C.O.?

TIGER CUB He went to Company HQ.

LI To inquire about me, I suppose. Tiger Cub, run and tell him I'm here, will you?

TIGER CUB Yes. (*Goes out.*)

LI Chien Kuei-hsi, go and have a bit of a rest. Thanks for your help.

CHIEN Right! (*Goes off.*)

LI Young Chou, I'm sorry that you got into trouble because of me. It was my fault entirely. Where's the Battalion C.O.?

YOUNG CHOU Gone to a Regimental HQ meeting. The Deputy C.O. told me to get a meal ready for you. But look! (*Showing him the empty bag.*) We've absolutely nothing left. I kept a little parched flour this morning, so that there'd be something for you to eat in the evening, but you went and gave it to that comrade who's ill. What shall we do now?

LI Oh well, I couldn't have done anything else, could I? We'll just have to set our teeth, that's all, Young Chou! If we can tide over today, things will be better tomorrow, when we arrive in Panyu. It's a wonderful place! They eat *tsamba* with butter there! And there are great herds of yaks, queer yaks with great long hair and big horns, that bellow like thunder. Yak meat's very good eating. And they're so big that one of them would make a square meal for a whole company. They've got huge sheep there, too. Ever seen them?

YOUNG CHOU   Big sheep like the Paotso ones?

LI   Oh, no, much bigger than them. Panyu sheep are as big as our cows. Their tails alone weigh ten catties or so. And can they move!—faster than horses on the steppelands. They've got a bleat like the roar of a tiger, too. Have you ever set eyes on houses made of yak dung?

YOUNG CHOU   No, never.

LI   You will tomorrow.

YOUNG CHOU   That's all very well, but what are we going to eat today?

LI   Oh, today . . . oh well, we'll manage. What have we been eating the last few days?

YOUNG CHOU   Nothing but weeds.

LI   Well, why can't we get some of them?

YOUNG CHOU   Because up till now we had some flour to cook them with. Now there's none left! How can you eat just weeds? Both the C.O. and the Deputy Commander have had dizziness and stomach trouble since yesterday. If we eat nothing but weeds today. . . .

LI   We'll have to think up something else then. (*Picks up the rice bag and examines it minutely.*) Look here, little rascal, there's quite a bit of flour left, stuck on to the bag. If we wash the whole bag carefully, we'll get the flour off into the water, and then we can boil weeds in it. That'll make a fine meal, won't it? Full of resource, aren't we?

YOUNG CHOU   (*suddenly changing the subject*)   Why didn't you have a walking race with me again today?

LI   Well, we'll have a go tomorrow, if you like. I don't see how I can let a young beggar like you beat me.

YOUNG CHOU   You made an awful fuss the other day when your horse dropped under you and the Battalion Commander sent people to carry you. Were you *really* angry?

LI   Of course I was. Why? Was the C.O. mad, too?

YOUNG CHOU   No, not exactly. But he was so upset that he broke down the moment you went away.

(LO SHUN-CHENG *and* TIGER CUB *enter.*)

LO   (*excitedly*)   Political Instructor! Here at last!

LI   Phew! You made me jump!

LO   You had me just about worried to death! Now about our battalion. . . .

LI   (*interrupting him*)   Young Chou, you go and get some more firewood, and you, Tiger Cub, go and pick some green stuff. We are going to have a good meal today.

YOUNG CHOU *and* TIGER CUB   Yes. (*Go out.*)

LO   How are those wounds of yours, Lao Li?

LI   Nothing serious. Look here, you got on to Young Chou for leaving me behind, didn't you? I must tell you I had to plead with him and the men—in fact I actually had to order them not to worry about leaving me behind, but to march ahead. (*Changes the subject suddenly.*) You're losing weight, Lao Lo. How's the stomach trouble?

LO   Don't try to put me off. I was asking about your wounds.

LI   Oh, I'm all right.

LO   Come down to brass tacks, please.

LI   Get along—I'm perfectly all right, you see. Why do you all bother about me so much? I won't have it!

LO   From now on, you're not to go round to the Company HQ or go about on your own. I'm not going to let you walk tomorrow.

LI   Am I allowed to open my mouth?

LO   Well, yes. But you're not to talk so much.

LI   Really, I think you'd better leave all this to me to decide.

LO   (*smoking his pipe*)   Bah!

LI   Why do you smoke that stuff? Give it up!

LO   When I give it up, I long for it again; then, when I try it, it tastes and smells awful.

LI   Now tell me about the battalion.

LO   Eleven men of First and Third Companies dropped out today.

LI   (*very disturbed*)   What's the feeling among the men?

LO   We can talk about that later. The most serious thing at present is food. We haven't a single grain left and round here it's difficult even to get weeds. The men are so desperate that they've been boiling their rifle-straps.

(*A despairing cry comes from the nearby woods.*)

LI   That sounds like Company Commander Wang. (*Makes an effort to get up but is too weak.*) Go and see, quick! (*Falls.*)

LO   Yes, it does. Stay here. I'll go and see what's the matter. (*Goes out.*)

LI   (*heavily, now he is by himself*)   It's not an easy trial we are undergoing.

YOUNG CHOU (*comes back with a bundle of firewood*)   Political Instructor, Tiger Cub told me he couldn't find any weeds round here fit to eat.

LI   Well, any weeds will have to do. Have you got anything made of leather on you?

YOUNG CHOU   Yes. What for?

LI You'll see. (*Undoing his own belt.*) You can eat belts at a pinch, you know.

YOUNG CHOU (*unfastens his rifle-strap*) Really?

LI First warm it up by the fire, so as to soften it. Then cut it into little bits and simmer it in water. (*Smacks his lips.*) Weeds and leather done with flour soup! Delicious! Mind you do as I tell you.

YOUNG CHOU All right. (*Starts getting busy with the belts.*)

LI Give me a strip of something. I've got to keep my trousers up!

YOUNG CHOU (*tears a strip off the quilt*) Here you are. Let me tie it round.

LI No, it's all right. I can do it myself. (*Stands up, but feels giddy and staggers.*)

YOUNG CHOU Political Instructor! You *must* let me help you.

LI It's terrible! I'm like a three-year-old—can't even tie up my own trousers.

YOUNG CHOU What about your wounds?

LI They're all right.

YOUNG CHOU You always say that. Do you think I don't know they're bothering you again? You can hide the truth from the others, maybe, but not from me. When the Battalion Commander comes I'm going to tell him.

LI Why bother him with it? Look here, Young Chou, the Commander's already got too much to do. We mustn't pile more trouble on him! Don't tell him anything. I promise to go with you tomorrow. Young Chou! Do you hear what I've said?

(LO SHUN-CHENG *comes on, helping* WANG TEH-CHIANG, *who looks a wreck.*)

WANG Political Instructor!

LI Come and sit down here, Lao Wang. Was it you I heard calling out just now?

WANG No. It was one of the men from Second Squad. I never cry out.

LI Feeling a bit queer, aren't you?

WANG Yes. I haven't been well for the last three days. My head's bad and I've got stomach trouble. I've got stars dancing before my eyes. I don't think I shall last much longer.

LI Stuff and nonsense! People in the prime of life don't die so easily. Haven't you ever had to eat chaff during a famine?

WANG Yes, of course.

LI Well, then, weeds are no more indigestible than chaff.

WANG Don't let's talk about me now. I'll get out of these steppelands, even if I have to crawl on my hands and knees. But the comrades. . . .

LI How many in your company dropped out today?

WANG   Six. . . .

LI   (*unable to hide his alarm*)   Oh!

WANG   Not a day passes without somebody falling ill, and we've got no medicines at all. The weather's just foul in this damned place. If it's not wind and rain, it's hail and snow. The whole place is a stinking swamp. One of the Third Company comrades fell into the bog today. Two others dropped dead just a moment ago while they were warming themselves before the fire and talking. Others have died with their bellies swollen from eating these weeds. The dead are dead, but those that are left. . . .

LI   (*with determination*)   . . . have got to find their way out.

WANG   Yes, that's right.

LI   When men with guts come up against serious difficulties, they try to overcome—not brood about death. We must overcome our difficulties, just as we overcome our enemies.

WANG   Yes, but if my ammunition runs out in a real battle, I use my bayonet, and don't feel at all sorry when enemy soldiers drop dead one after another. But I can't stand seeing my own comrades fall like this. I've got a heart, Political Instructor.

LI   Well, we're none of us stones, I suppose.

WANG   Think of the years I've been with these comrades in the revolution! We joined the Red Army together, we fought together against the White troops, and marched together from our base in Kiangsi. We have all worked together, one . . . two . . . three . . . five years together, for the success of the revolution and never dreamt of giving up. . . .

LI   Oh come, Lao Wang, the cause isn't lost, however bad our present circumstances.

WANG   No, of course it isn't. But look how many comrades have given their lives for it! I shall never forget the last words of the leader of Second Squad as he lay dying: "Company Commander," he said, "you go ahead and work hard. I'm dying. As for me, my revolutionary task's over, here and now. When we've won, go to my home and look my people up. If my mother's still alive, tell her that though I died, the revolutionary cause will never die. It will succeed, and then there'll be no more local bullies or landlords to oppress us, and our lives will be as happy as in the Soviet Union. I'm sure my mother will smile when she hears this." (WANG *himself is on the verge of tears.*) Then he died, and died needlessly! Needlessly!

LI   No! He didn't die needlessly at all. And he was right when he said that though he died the revolutionary cause would never die. We shall win in the end, and then those bullies, the landlords, the warlords, the imperialists, will no longer dare oppress us. His death, like his comrades' deaths, is the price we pay for the future happiness of the Chinese people. We can learn much from the example of the leader of Second Squad, who saw our bright future and was sure of the coming victory.

WANG   But at present we have no food and no water. The weather's foul. How can we hold out till victory comes?

LI (*winces, but fights to hide the torturing pain of his wounds*)   Keep a grip on yourself, and hold out to the bitter end. If you believe in our cause, it'll give you strength. (*Defiantly.*) When we came to the river crossings and the Great Snow Mountains the enemy called down curses on us, and prophesied that we'd never get through. We'd freeze to death, they said, or starve, or die of exhaustion. But did we? No! We survived! Of course the enemy can never understand how, but you and I can. We survive because we are the Communist-led Red Army of the Chinese working class; we're tempered and steeled by fire. We're as strong as steel! If you can't endure hardship you're not fit to do revolutionary work. Revolution doesn't *come* from comfortable living, though it does lead to comfort and all the good things in life in the future.

WANG   You're right, of course. But d'you think we'll be able to reach Panyu tomorrow?

LI   Don't you trust our leaders' judgment? It's only a two days' journey from Panyu to the foot of Mount Min. And then we'll have plenty of food.

LO   That's true.

WANG   When d'you reckon we'll be out of the steppelands, then?

LI   It'll take another two weeks.

WANG   If only we hadn't chosen to come this way, through these damned steppelands.

LI   Did we have any choice? They tried to cut us off in Szechuan and Sikang and at the Chinghai border, and to drive us into a trap. It never dawned on them that we'd dare to cross the steppelands and make our way to Kansu like this! So when, in a few days, we suddenly appear deep in their rear they'll be completely out of their depth. And before they even find out where we are, we'll have built a base and reinforced our army. There we'll be able to take the initiative, and strike back. And by that time the whole nation will be on the move. The people will rise to join us in the fight against the Japanese aggressors. (*His wounds forgotten, his voice rises to a shout.*) Comrades, the fame of the invincible

Chinese Workers' and Peasants' Red Army will spread all over the world. (*Winces again.*) It's true that we're facing great difficulties now. But what are they due to? It's part of the struggle.

WANG Political Instructor, I make a vow never to complain about difficulties again. But I will remember the hardships we've gone through, and mark them up as a score to be settled.

LI You're right there. We'll certainly pay off the old scores! Lao Lo, old friend, why are you so quiet?

LO I've been thinking. I want to say how deep your words sink home, and how much I appreciate all the help you've given me. Yes, really! You've been very patient. D'you remember what you said to me when we were making our way through the Yi area? You said I must change that tongue of mine, or you'd find a way of making me. You've succeeded, you know. You've made everything clear to me.

WANG (*notices the belts boiling in the cooking pot*) Are you cooking belts, too?

LI Yes, of course. Belts are meat of a sort, aren't they? Quite nice to have a bit of meat in this back of beyond!

TIGER CUB (*comes on with a bundle of green stuff*) All that's any good has already been picked, I'm afraid. I only found the leavings.

LI Let's see. (*Picks out a few sprigs and chews them.*) Oh, well, they'll do.

WANG (*also tasting some*) Gosh! They're bitter, aren't they? What is this stuff? D'you think it's fit to eat?

LI Yes. They are bitter, but never mind. They'll be better if you cook them a bit longer. You know the saying: You really know sweetness when you've first tasted bitterness. Bitterness always comes before sweetness, you know.

WANG Yes, but these are just *too* bitter. You better stop cooking 'em. The stuff we got for Company HQ is fennel, which isn't so bad as this. Send Young Chou over to get some of ours.

(LI FENG-LIEN *enters, and asks generally.*)

FENG-LIEN Is this First Battalion camp?

LO Hello, Comrade Feng-lien, come along. Your brother's here.

FENG-LIEN (*greatly alarmed at* LI YU-KUO's *appearance*) Oh heavens, brother, what on earth's happened to you?

LI Happened to me? I'm all right. I could ask what's happened to you?

FENG-LIEN (*at a loss*) Me?

LI Yes. What are you doing here?

FENG-LIEN Divisional HQ have been worried about your wounds getting worse. So they sent me round to see. Aren't you pleased to see me?

LI   Of course I am! That's very thoughtful of them. I'm very pleased to
see you, really I am.

FENG-LIEN (*digging in her kit-bag*)   And here's two and a half pounds of
parched flour and a packet of that Yunnan "White Powder" stuff.

LI (*carried away by emotion*)   Just like a real father and mother, always
thinking of their children. Oh, dear Party! You're always thinking
of your comrades! They've thought of everything, haven't they—
even to sending my sister. Class love and sisterly love all at one
time.

FENG-LIEN   The doctor said you were to use the powder for your wounds,
and afterwards cover them with a clean cloth. Come on, let me
do it. (*A clapper rhyme wafts in from the nearby woods*):

> *Wide, boundless, far as eye can see*
> *Extend the lovely plains—*
> *Now bitter cold, now burning heat,*
> *Now snow, now driving rains.*
> *And everywhere grow flowers bright*
> *Which spread a fragrance sweet,*
> *And everywhere the wild herbs grow,*
> *Wild herbs that man may eat. . . .*

> *The steppelands once beaten,*
> *The victory nears.*
> *The Red Army's valour*
> *Shall reach all men's ears.*

LI   Who made that up?

WANG   The propaganda unit must have come up. Look, I must go now.
Don't forget to come and fetch that green stuff, Young Chou.

LO   I'm coming with you.
(WANG *and* LO *go out.* TIGER CUB *and* YOUNG CHOU *make their way
towards the nearby woods.*)

FENG-LIEN   Brother, let me dress your wounds now.

LI   They can wait. Sit down here. (*They sit down together. Suddenly* LI
asks.) Feng-lien, you're nineteen now, aren't you?

FENG-LIEN   Yes.

LI   You are fond of your "Black Ox," aren't you?

FENG-LIEN (*shyly*)   Who d'you mean?

LI   You know who I mean! Lao Chao, the Battalion C.O. We used to
call him "Black Ox," didn't we?

FENG-LIEN   Oh!

LI   You were only ten years old when you were betrothed to him. Mother
used to say, I remember, "That Black Ox is a good boy, clever,

good-hearted and capable." We know now, for ourselves, that he really is a sterling fellow.

FENG-LIEN He's not so bad. But, brother, this is no time to talk about marriage.

LI No, of course not. But when times are bad, it cheers you up to think that there's a happy life ahead. Do you feel we're having a pretty hard time now?

FENG-LIEN Yes, we certainly are. But thanks to our Party and Chairman Mao, we'll get through our troubles.

LI By the way, what do you want to do with your life? D'you mean to go on doing propaganda work?

FENG-LIEN Well, I'll do any work the Party wants me to—I don't mind, as long as it's for the revolution. But I'd like to go on with this work.

LI How are your studies going?

FENG-LIEN I study whenever I get the chance.

LI Good girl—make the best use of your time. After we get out of these steppelands, you know, and take Latsekou Pass, the revolutionary situation will be completely different. We'll have no end of new jobs, that'll take every bit of knowledge we've been able to gain.

FENG-LIEN (*earnestly*) Don't worry, brother, I'll do my best.

LI (*affectionately*) Good, you've come on amazingly. I'm very happy today.

(LO SHUN-CHENG *and* WANG TEH-CHIANG *come on. They walk confidently and are obviously feeling much more cheerful.*)

LO How right it is, Lao Li. "The steppelands once beaten. The victory nears." The propaganda comrades are doing a fine job. They've cheered everybody up tremendously.

WANG (*enthusiastically*) Political Instructor! "The steppelands once beaten, The victory nears."

(CHAO, *thin but in high spirits, comes on briskly, grinning broadly. His breast pocket is bulging.*)

CHAO Lao Li, we've really got a good place to camp in tonight. Much better than last! Nice big cypresses you've got here!

LI (*matching his grin*) Your coming makes it better still! But you've overlooked something, though, haven't you? See who's here! (*Nods towards* FENG-LIEN.)

CHAO Oh, it's you, Feng-lien! Sorry, I didn't see you.

FENG-LIEN H'm. You didn't look very hard.

LI Any new orders for us?

CHAO Yes. Our battalion's been given the job of taking Latsekou Pass. Isn't that grand?

LI   But it's another week's going, isn't it?

CHAO   No. This morning Divisional HQ ran across a fellow who knows
these parts like the palm of his hand—he collects medicinal herbs
hereabouts. He was tremendously useful. . . .

WANG   How? Found us some food?

CHAO   No! Told us a short cut to Panyu. We can be there by tomorrow
afternoon. We're practically out of the steppelands.

LO   Oh, so that accounts for these cypresses.

WANG   Hurrah! We're going to get out of the steppelands!

(*Murmurs and exclamations of joy from all.*)

(TIGER CUB *and* YOUNG CHOU *come in.*)

CHAO   There's better news still. We thought it would take ten days to
reach Latsekou from Panyu. But the man says the short cut will
save three days. Moreover, three days after Panyu we'll be at the
foot of Mount Min. That's quite an inhabited place, and it'll mean
the end of our troubles about food.

(*The listeners burst into cheering.*)

CHAO   This herb-gatherer comes from Latsekou. He says the place's very
lightly defended—just a few local regiments under Lu Ta-chang.
Chiang Kai-shek's troops and the northwestern warlords' troops are
stationed well away, at Tienshui and Pikou; they'll never believe
that we've made our way to Latsekou.

LI   That's it! Just what the Central Committee expected! (*Joyously.*)
Comrades, we shall reach Latsekou Pass in a week. That means
we'll have beaten both the steppelands and the Great Snow Mountains! (*Carried away with excitement.*) It means more than that.
We're not only rid of the steppelands, but we'll be jumping on the
enemy where he's weak. Once through Latsekou, we'll be like tigers
loosed from their den. The enemy'll be in complete panic, and
we'll smash him to smithereens. What a victory for the Chinese
people, and the Party that leads them! And that victory will be the
result of the correct policy laid down by our Central Committee.

CHAO   (*equally joyful*)   Aha! They thought we'd freeze to death on the
Great Snow Mountains, or die of starvation on the steppelands! But
we're coming through, despite everything.

LI   We proved that there's no difficulty we can't overcome and no hardship we can't bear. However powerful the enemy, he can't stop us
going where we wish. (*An excruciating pain shoots through his
wounds.*) Ah!

CHAO   What's the matter, Lao Li?

LI   Nothing. Got worked up a bit, that's all. Any more news for us?

CHAO   Here's what the Regimental C.O. says: We are not far from

Mount Min now. There's some active enemy cavalry quite close, on our left flank. Divisional HQ believes they are out on reconnaissance.

LO We'll wipe them out!

OTHERS Just in time! Let's wipe them out! Fine! etc.

WANG The bastards! They've turned up just when I want to settle scores with them.

CHAO Yes. The Regimental C.O. ordered us to send two companies to ambush them. We'll not only knock them out, but capture their horses and have a square meal.

ALL Very nice too! Now we know where supper and breakfast're coming from. Apparently they want to do us a good turn, etc.

WANG Battalion Commander, put me on the job!

LO (*in high spirits*) Have you finished reporting? If you have, I think I'd better begin making preparations.

CHAO All right. Go ahead! Lao Lo, you take First and Second Companies to the woods so as to trap them. Hold your fire till they're really close. We've got to save our ammunition for Latsekou. I'll be along in a minute.

LO Right you are! Come on, Lao Wang, let's get a move on.

YOUNG CHOU Deputy Commander, the food's ready. Won't you have a bite before you're off?

LO Better wait. There'll be something worth eating after the battle. (*Goes out.*)

LI Young Chou, warm the parched flour up—we'll all have some.

CHAO No, you don't! You're to warm it up specially for the Political Instructor.

LI Young Chou, do as you're told. Meanwhile, go off for a bit with the runners. I have something to talk over with the Commander. (*To* FENG-LIEN.) You, too, sister. (*Suddenly.*) No, half a minute. (*Produces some very dog-eared documents from his pocket.*) Can you take these and mend them for me? They're nearly in bits.
(YOUNG CHOU, TIGER CUB *and* FENG-LIEN *go off.*)

LI Lao Chao, come over here. Sit down with me and talk a bit. We've hardly seen one another since the Long March began. Do sit down. You look a bit done up—you're much thinner than you were. Working too hard, eh?

CHAO I haven't completely outgrown my bad habit of spending too much time on routine work.

LI And I've given you hardly any help.

CHAO What ever do you mean?

LI (*changing the subject abruptly*)   I hope you weren't too upset when
      I lost my temper with you the other day when my horse died.

CHAO   D'you think I didn't realize why you were so angry?

LI   That's all right then. Well, we're up against terrible odds. For weeks
      our comrades have been tramping through wind and rain, snow and
      mud, with nothing to eat but wild stuff. . . .

CHAO   How many have we lost today?

LI   Eleven.

CHAO   Murdered by the enemy! (*Shaking his fist in the air.*) The
      bastards!

LI   Come closer, Lao Chao. (*Purposely changing the subject.*) D'you
      remember that winter of '28 when we first joined the revolutionary
      army? We'd been together before that, working for that bloody
      landlord as farm labourers. One day—the twenty-third of the
      twelfth month it was, I never forgot that date—he kept on and on
      at me for not fetching enough water. And we lost our tempers,
      gave him a sound thrashing, and got away quick. (*Musing.*)
      That's how we came across the Communist Party and threw in our
      lot with the revolution. . . . A common destiny you might call it.
      We've always done everything together, grown up, carried out our
      work . . . even saw Chairman Mao together. I've lost count of the
      battles we went through, how many *li* we've tramped. (*Suddenly
      clasps* CHAO's *shoulder.*) Old comrade-in-arms!

CHAO (*choking back tears*)   Why do you bring all this up, today of all
      days?

LI   No particular reason. I was just thinking of the first time we saw
      Chairman Mao. You remember what he said? "We must put all
      we've got into the fight. The enemy is strong. We'll have to bear
      all sorts of hardships before we beat him." Remember? (*His mus-
      ing tone changes as he comes back to the present.*) It'll be a great
      victory if we get safely out of the steppelands. How are the
      comrades at Supreme HQ?

CHAO   Fine. I saw them this morning. (*A pause.*) But how is it with you?
      Be honest.

LI   I won't lie to you. My wounds have festered. My head swims and my
      whole body aches. I passed out three times today.

CHAO   Oh, why didn't you tell me before! I didn't realize you were so
      bad when you refused to be carried on a stretcher yesterday. You
      got into such a rage when I tried to insist! I blame myself for not
      taking proper care of you—I'm always saying I will, but I don't.
      You're not walking any more. It's the stretcher from now on.

LI   Everyone else is just as exhausted. I'm not going to be a burden, tiring out my comrades. You'll never get me on a stretcher!

CHAO (*passionately*)   I'll carry you myself. I told you long ago that I'd get you out of the steppelands, even if I had to carry you on my back.

LI   Don't forget the Party trained you to do useful work, not to make unnecessary sacrifices.

CHAO   No good trying that line on me! I'm still quite fit, you see. No. It's waste of breath arguing. You'll listen to me this time. (*Opens his bulging pocket and takes out a package.*) Lao Li, you're to have this. I didn't give it to you before because I was afraid you'd say again, "Put it in the pot and we'll all have some!" This is a present from Divisional HQ to *you*, and you can't pass it on.

LI (*taking the package*)   From Divisional HQ? I bet you're lying! It's yours that you saved to give to me. (*Opens it.*) Oh, beef! Where did you get it?

CHAO   It's not beef. Supreme HQ killed a horse and sent Divisional HQ a portion. They knew you were ill and asked me to bring you some.

LI   What? Supreme HQ killed a horse? (*With unusual fright in his eyes.*) Is that a fact?

CHAO   Yes. . . .

LI   Then we're right out of food! Even Chairman Mao must have been trudging through these damned bogs on an empty stomach. (*Breaks down completely, and then faints.*)

CHAO   Lao Li! Lao Li! What's the matter?

LI (*comes to himself*)   That really hurt, you know. I felt almost as if somebody had stabbed me to the heart.

TIGER CUB (*rushing on*)   Battalion Commander! Enemy cavalry approaching!

CHAO (*whips out his field-glasses*)   Yes! There they are! Report back to your own company.

LI   Tiger Cub, try to bring back a live horse!

TIGER CUB   You bet! (*Rushes off.*)

(YOUNG CHOU *comes on.*)

YOUNG CHOU   Battalion Commander! Three columns of enemy cavalry approaching!

CHAO   All right. Don't get too worked up.

FENG-LIEN (*runs on*)   It's true! It's true! They're coming.

LO (*hurries on, all grins*)   Lao Chao, this is really too good to be true! The enemy is sending us up horse meat! There's about six hundred of 'em. Can we attack now? Supper's in sight!

CHAO   Better wait. Wait till they get right up to the woods.

LI   Agreed! Let them come nearer. We can take some of their horses alive.

LO   Suppose they turn round and run? Look, they're coming to a halt. They're thinking of pulling back!

CHAO   Tell First Company to prepare for a charge, Third Company to use their machine-guns, rifles and grenades, and Second Company to outflank the enemy and cut off their retreat.

LO   Right! (*Goes off.*)

CHAO   Look, they're deploying. Let's wait till they get still nearer!
(*The enemy cavalry can be heard now, obviously quite close. Cries and galloping horses can be heard.*)

LI   (*sits up briskly, gets out his revolver, and is quite calm, as if he were in normal health*)   Lao Chao, we'd better attack at once. Our Party leaders are with us here. We can't allow the enemy to come too close.

CHAO   Right. Buglers! Stand by to sound the charge. First Company! Machine-guns and rifles, at the ready!

LI   Fire now!
(*He and* CHAO *climb up the highest point, and stand there side by side.*)

CHAO   (*firing in the direction of the enemy*)   Fire! First Company, charge from the flank!
(*There is a pandemonium of bugle calls, battle cries and firing.*)

LI   They're on the run! After them!

CHAO   First Company, charge!

CHIEN   Charge! (*Runs across stage with several others, rifles at the ready.*)

LI   We're doing all right, Lao Chao. The enemy's done for. The whole battalion should charge now.

CHAO   Right! Second and Third Companies, charge!
(*The noise fades as the fight moves away.* POLITICAL INSTRUCTOR HSIEH *comes on, with Third Platoon of Second Company.*)

LI   Phew! That cavalry can go! Our men'll never be able to catch up with them.

CHAO   Right. Buglers! Sound the "Fall in." Young Chou, run and tell the Deputy C.O. to cease pursuit and clear the field.

YOUNG CHOU   Yes, Commander. (*Dashes off.*)

LI   We did all right, even if we didn't wipe them out completely.

CHAO   We killed a lot of 'em anyway. Here comes Lao Lo.

LO   (*comes on with* YOUNG CHOU)   Here are the results so far: twenty odd killed, thirty wounded.

WANG (*comes on*) Battalion Commander! A detailed report's being prepared. Can we distribute the dead horses straight away to the battalion?

LI No. To the whole army. (*His strength is ebbing fast now that the stimulus of battle is over.*)

WANG Tiger Cub and a squad of the men have gone to round up the loose horses. Maybe they'll be able to get a few alive.

LI (*battling with his weakness*) What? Live horses? Send them to Supreme HQ.

CHAO Right!

LI Let the revolution advance on horseback!
(*Slumps down, unconscious.*)

LO Right, Lao Li! (*Looks sharply at* LI.) Here, what's the matter with you?

CHAO Lao Li, Lao Li, what's wrong?
Everyone stands still. A chill comes over them all.

CHAO Can he really be gone?

LO Lao Li!

YOUNG CHOU *and* WANG Political Instructor!

FENG-LIEN Oh, brother! brother!

TIGER CUB (*dashes on, full of joy, his arms loaded with horse-gear*) Political Instructor, I've captured three horses! (*Notices the horror-stricken silence, and sees now that the Political Instructor is dead.*) Comrade Political Instructor!

CHAO (*unable to believe the truth*) Lao Li, have you really gone? (*Cradles him in his arms.*) My old comrade-in-arms, what can I say to you now? (*Gently lays him down under a tree.*)
(*The men come on from all directions. They are all near to tears. Snow begins to fall.* REGIMENTAL COMMANDER HUANG *comes up with a parcel of parched flour for* LI. *When he finds that he is too late, he stands before the body and takes off his cap. The others do likewise.*)

HUANG You can rest in peace now, old fighter. You are a worthy fighter for the Party, a true son of the working people. You've set a good example of revolutionary perseverance. The things you stood for . . . we'll make them come true. Soon Latsekou will be freed, and your comrades-in-arms will free it.
(CHAO CHIH-FANG *pulls down the white bedding and spreads it over the dead body.*)

CURTAIN SLOWLY DESCENDS

Act VI

TIME   *A moonless night early in September 1935.*

PLACE   *Latsekou Pass in Minhsien County, Kansu Province.*

SCENE   *High up on Mount Min, the stronghold of Latsekou towers hundreds of metres above its surroundings. The slopes are precipitous. Only one footpath leads to it, and that is narrow and steep and strewn with great rocks. Apart from this path, the mountain is almost unscalable. As the old saying goes: "To pass through Latsekou is like passing through a tiger's den."*

The enemy has made some makeshift defences in the caves which open on to the path. Commanding the only entrance, these constitute their outer defence line. On each side fall precipices. Great peaks rise above them. On a rock facing the audience is scrawled four lines of doggerel:

Latsekou can never be taken!
Its peaks touch the clouds;
One man with a lance
Can stop a million.

When the curtain rises, the sharp crack of stray shots can be heard, ricocheting through the ravines. NIU, *an enemy company commander, looks downwards to the foot of the hill. His men are shouting and running about.*

ENEMY DEPUTY SQUAD LEADER *(running on)*   Company Commander! The Reds are charging up the hill.

NIU   Second Platoon—deploy! *(His men go off in different directions. He has another good look downwards. Nose in the air he says.)* They really *are* coming! So much the better. We'll show them! *(Shouts.)* Now, listen, all of you. The battle has begun. You mustn't get windy, you mustn't look back. You're all to put your hearts into it, for General Lu's sake. Fire! Throw your grenades!

ENEMY SOLDIERS   Yes, Commander.

(There is an outburst of shooting. Two enemy soldiers fall, screaming.)

NIU   Don't get the wind-up. We've got the terrain on our side, our own units on the hill-top to cover us, and cliffs below to keep the enemy from ever getting here. No one can take Latsekou—even if the Red Army does get near us. Fire away!

AN ENEMY SOLDIER (*panicking*) Ah, the Reds are coming!

NIU Damn you. Where d'you think you're going? (*Shoots the man down. Grandiloquently.*) No one runs away in front of *me*. (*To the others.*) Now, you, keep on with it. You'll get your cash bonus at the end of the battle. No retreat. That's an order. Anyone who tries to run away will be shot on the spot, and his whole family executed for good measure.

(*More enemy soldiers fall.* HU, *a squad leader, comes up, left, in retreat, with two of his men.*)

NIU (*to* HU) Hold out, there! Don't be scared. I'll send down reinforcements.

HU Yes, Commander. As long as I'm here, the Reds will never get past.

NIU Very good. I'll see that you get the credit if the enemy's halted. I'll recommend you for promotion as soon as the battle's won.

HU (*picking up two grenades*) Follow me for a charge! (*He and several enemy soldiers rush off, left.*)

(*Suddenly,* CHAO CHIH-FANG, YOUNG CHOU *and* TIGER CUB *appear, centre, back, from a rock behind* NIU. *They are carrying grenades and hooked spears.*)

CHAO (*shouting at* NIU) Don't move. Hands up!

(LO *and another group of Red Army men appear over the rocks, right. They go up the hill, right.*)

LO Come on, men. Forward!

TIGER CUB (*jumps down from a rock and seizes* NIU, *just as he is aiming at* CHAO) Hands up, you bastard! (*Gets* NIU's *rifle in the scrimmage.* NIU *gets away and hides behind a rock.*)

YOUNG CHOU (*drags* HU *out of a cave*) No, you don't! You're not getting off that easy.

(*Several Red Army men come over to collect the prisoners. A hand-to-hand fight is going on between* WANG TEH-CHIANG *and* CHIEN KUEI-HSI *and some enemy soldiers.*)

CHIEN Bastard! I'll show you! (*Pursues.*)

CHAO (*to his men*) Comrades, occupy this pathway, quick. And watch out for any counter-attack by the enemy. Shove the prisoners in that cave.

SOLDIERS Yes, Commander.

(CHIEN *and several Red Army men go off, right.*)

LO (*comes back, right, with* LITTLE CHIN) Lao Chao, the entrance to the pathway is under enemy machine-gun fire. Our reinforcements can't get up. The advance units are pinned down too. What shall we do?

CHAO   Collect all the hooked spears and leggings we've got. Give them to First Company and tell them to get up over that hill there.

LO   Right. (*Goes out with* LITTLE CHIN.)

CHIEN (*comes on*)   Battalion Commander! The enemy has started a counter-attack.

CHAO   Let them go ahead. We're not starting the assault till Second Company turns up.

CHIEN   Right. (*Goes out.*)

LITTLE CHIN (*comes on*)   Commander, the Deputy C.O. has sent me to report that the enemy's got that hill under machine-gun fire, so First Company can't get up.

CHAO   Tell him to hold the attack for the time being.

LITTLE CHIN   Yes. (*Goes off.*)

NIU (*comes out from under his rock*)   You've got yourselves into a jam now. There are precipices above your head and deep gullies below. You can't get forward or back. You'd better let me go, and give me my rifle back, and I'll let you go back the way you came.

CHAO   Who the hell are you?

NIU   I've been one of General Lu's men for years, and I'm the Commander of his Tiger Company.

CHAO   Are you that bandit chief Niu?

NIU   That's me. You can let me go, or lay down your arms and surrender. If you surrender, I can personally put in a word for you to General Lu, for a platoon leader's job. I mean it—you can take my word for it.

YOUNG CHOU (*enraged at such impudence*)   None of your cheek, or I'll do for you.

CHAO (*stopping* YOUNG CHOU)   Take it easy. (*To* NIU.) If you tell me all about your defences up there, I'll let you go after we've won.
(LO SHUN-CHENG *enters.*)

NIU   What's the good of talking about winning, when death is staring you in the face? If you don't want to surrender, you'd better at least set me free. I'll let you go if you do.

YOUNG CHOU (*can't control himself—pokes* NIU *with his rifle*)   Any more of this and you've had it!

NIU (*actually very frightened but putting a bold face on it*)   Don't you dare threaten me! You'll be skinned alive if you fall into my General's hands. Set me free, or surrender!

CHAO   You tell me the truth about your defences, and I'll let you go as soon as we get to the top of the hill.

NIU   You're dreaming, man. You're in a blind alley. You'll never reach the top of the hill. On the right, we've got a company with three mortars *and* three heavy machine-guns covering the entrance to the pathway. You'd never get past them.

LO   H'm. Anything there, on the left?

NIU   A machine-gun company with five light machine-guns.

CHAO   And on the hill-top itself?

NIU   Two regiments—the First and Fourth.

LO   Any other units?

NIU   Well, no. But don't worry—you'll never get there.

CHAO   That all? Where are your Second, Third, Fifth and Sixth Regiments?

NIU   They're on their way here. They'll be here tomorrow. I tell you again, you'll never get to the top. I'll let you go, if you let me go. Let's make a deal. How about it?

CHAO   Young Chou, take this fool to the cave. Let him watch and see how the Red Army gets to the top.

YOUNG CHOU   Get on, you, into the cave, quick!

NIU   (*taken aback*)   You spurn my offer? You'll *never* reach the top! Tell you what, if you do, you can chop my head off! I'm speaking the truth, you know.

YOUNG CHOU   (*giving him a shove*)   Stop your rot! Get a move on! No one's going to bother with your head. (*Hauls* NIU *to the cave.*)

LO   Lao Chao, what shall we do now? We're rather up against it, you know. Both these paths—this one and that rocky one—are under fire. A direct frontal attack would be asking for heavy casualties. What shall we do?

CHAO   What shall we do? Think of some way of getting round the difficulties.

WANG   (*arriving*)   Commander Chao, we've held the attack.
　　　　(COMPANY COMMANDER CHU *enters.*)

CHU   Commander, so far we've beaten back two counter-attacks.

CHAO   The first thing we've got to do is to get rid of those machine-gun nests.

WANG   Yes. Till we've done that we'll never get to the top.

CHU   What about an all-out frontal attack?

WANG   Sure, why not! We've met more ferocious enemies than these bandits, and fought on worse ground. Yes, I'm all for an all-out frontal attack, Commander.

CHAO   An all-out frontal attack? No. Our men would just be pinned down on this narrow path. The casualties would be too heavy.

LO   I think I've got the way to crush them.

CHAO *and* WANG   What's that?

LO   Let's try a sort of double action.

CHAO *and* WANG   What do you mean?

LO   There's a cave up there. Keep some of our men hidden in that cave. When they start attacking again, let them come right past the cave, up to where we are now.

CHAO *and* WANG   Until they reach this point!

LO   Yes. The cave party lies completely quiet. After they've passed the cave, Company Commander Chu will take two squads, each man with a rifle and three grenades, and make straight up the hill to the machine-gun positions. I'll take a platoon right behind Chu's men and get up the hill to the right to cut off any reinforcements. Meanwhile Company Commander Wang should take a platoon over those rocks and get the machine-gun company on the left. Understand? If we're sharp enough, we'll be up on top with our red flag before the enemy knows where he is!

CHU, WANG, *and* CHAO   That's great. That's a good plan. That ought to do it.

CHAO   What about the enemy who come straight to the cave?

LO   You can easily settle their hash with Tiger Cub's squad and a machine-gun.

CHAO (*has worked it out and realizes its potentialities*)   Yes . . . yes

WANG   D'you think a squad's enough for the job?

CHAO   Plenty. They'll be hidden in the cave, so the enemy'll have no idea of their strength.

LO   Right.

CHAO   Another thing. If they turn round and start retreating, Company Commander Chu, you mustn't fail to intercept them.

LO   Yes. Got that, Lao Chu?

CHU   Yes.

LO   Lao Chao, have you anything more to say?

CHAO   Don't think so. I agree with the battle order. Go ahead with it, Lao Lo. Give me the word when you're ready. (*Turns to* CHU *and* WANG.) Take good cover, and set about it calmly. But move quickly when it comes to a charge. We can go and get ready now, I think.

ALL   Yes.

(LO *and* WANG *go out.*)

CHAO   Young Chou, you heard what the Deputy C.O. said just now, didn't you?

YOUNG CHOU   Yes.

CHAO   You try to go back down the hill the way we came, find the Regimental C.O. and report on our plan of action. Tell the Commander and Political Instructor Hsieh of Third Company too that they should advance quickly straight up to the top the moment they hear our bugler sound the charge.

YOUNG CHOU   I'll go right away, Commander.

CHAO   Be careful, Young Chou.

YOUNG CHOU   Don't worry about me, Commander. (*Goes out over the rocks, left.*)

CHAO   Tiger Cub, a lot depends on us now. Let's get ready.

TIGER CUB   Just tell me how to start. I've been looking forward to this for a long time!

CHAO   How many are there in your squad?

TIGER CUB   Ten altogether.

CHAO   Right. Put two men on patrol duty and bring the others here. Get Chien Kuei-hsi and the machine-gunners too.

TIGER CUB   Yes, Commander. (*Goes out and comes back immediately with his group of soldiers. Goes off again and returns with* CHIEN KUEI HSI.)

CHIEN   Battalion Commander!

TIGER CUB   Except the patrol men, the whole squad's here, Commander.

CHAO   Comrades, there are eighteen of us here altogether. I'm sure we can make a good job of it. We're Red Army men. We have crossed the Tatu, the Great Snow Mountains and the steppelands. I'm going to tell you exactly how we're going to set about it. The Deputy Battalion Commander and Company Commander Wang will let the enemy come right up to the cave, so that we can deal them a crushing blow. We'll have to be both calm and alert. We're not going to move, though, till they come close to us. If they start to turn back, give chase. Now then, let's put the machine-guns here. Chien Kuei-hsi and Tiger Cub, take your mates and hide behind that rock. The runners and myself will give you cover and be your reserves. All right, comrades?

ALL   Yes, Commander.

CHAO   Get into position then.

ALL   Yes. (*They get into their respective positions.*)

LITTLE CHIN   (*climbs down over rocks, right*)   Commander, the Deputy C.O. sent me to say they're all ready. But it's absolutely quiet on the enemy side.

CHAO   Absolutely quiet, eh?

LITTLE CHIN   Yes. There's a complete lull. Maybe they're scared after what we've done to them already.

CHAO   Oh no, I don't think so. They'll come sooner or later. Tell the Deputy C.O. that's all the more reason to keep a sharp look-out.

LITTLE CHIN   Yes. (*Goes out.*)
> (REGIMENTAL COMMANDER HUANG *enters with* LITTLE WAN *and* YOUNG CHOU.)

HUANG   Well, Lao Chao, how goes it?

CHAO   We're ready for 'em. . . . Did you get my message from Young Chou? It's Lao Lo's plan, you know.

HUANG   Yes, I got it. And I fully approve.

CHAO   I'm expecting them to attack again after their last two failures.

HUANG   I think you're right. (*Turns to the men.*) Well, comrades, d'you think we can take Latsekou tonight?

TIGER CUB   *We're* already planning what we're going to do afterwards.

CHAO   It's queer, though, the enemy keeping quiet like this.

HUANG   Don't let's get impatient. It's still quite early. We've got time for a bit of a talk. (*Takes a good look at the summit and goes on with a grin.*) Comrades, Chiang Kai-shek will go green when he hears we're at Latsekou. But what can he do about it? It's too late for anything now. And tomorrow we'll be out of our bad patches and marching straight on to the rich Tao valley. We can stop there for a time, regroup, and get back to strength. After that we'll continue our march north, until we join our brothers in the Red Army in northern Shensi, and build up an anti-Japanese base.

MEN   (*enthusiastically*)   Join the comrades in northern Shensi! That'll be fine! Great! etc.

HUANG   HQ says we may expect a high tide of revolution when victory crowns our Long March.

LO   (*comes in, right*)   Lao Chao! Regimental Commander! There's still no sign of any enemy activity.

HUANG   Never mind. Lao Chao, Lao Lo, let's go and look over our preparations for the coming attack. Let's give 'em another twenty minutes. If the enemy still hasn't made a move, we'll take the offensive.

CHAO   All right. Come on, Lao Lo. (HUANG, CHAO *and* LO *go off.*)

TIGER CUB   Coo! Victory, and a high tide of revolution, both together!

CHIEN   Comrades, did you hear what the Regimental Commander said just now? That this was the last battle before we joined our Red Army brothers in northern Shensi!

TIGER CUB   Do you know where northern Shensi is?

CHIEN   (*flummoxed by this*)   Well, northern Shensi is the north of Shensi, isn't it?

TIGER CUB   It'll take us a good twenty days to get there. Forget it for now. Better talk about the battle just ahead.

MACHINE-GUNNER   I can tell you what I'm going to be doing twenty minutes from now. (*Holds forth with great gusto.*) I tell you, once my gun starts clattering, all the good things we've been dreaming about—you know, the revolutionary high tide, the war of resistance against the Japanese, proper houses and high buildings, electric light and telephones, a flood of recruits to our Red Army—they'll all be in sight. And to top it all, (*smacking his lips*) there'll be a good meal for all of us tomorrow morning!

TIGER CUB We'll have to smarten up a bit then—can't go about in rags! I reckon we ought to chuck our old clothes away. It won't be cold at the top, once we're over this bit, anyhow.

MACHINE-GUNNER You're right. After we've wiped out the enemy here, we'll be going down the hill again. And you'll see houses with tiled roofs again, like we're used to, in the villages at the foot. Oh, we'll be able to get rice and flour and meat there, and eat as much as we want!

TIGER CUB No. We ought to clean up a bit first, wash our clothes and get ourselves a hair-cut, so that we can swank through the villages all smart and dapper.

CHIEN Swank? Give ourselves airs towards our fellow countrymen?

TIGER CUB You know I don't mean that! What I want to say is, we've swept through eleven provinces, smashed four hundred enemy regiments on the way and taken two rivers in our stride, forced the Tatu, scaled the Great Snow Mountains, tramped through the steppelands, and here we are at Latsekou. We're the Chinese Workers' and Peasants' Red Army led by the Communist Party. Nothing got us down. We don't fear anybody! So we must look smart!

MACHINE-GUNNER That's right. And when they see us the villagers will all exclaim: "Fine boys! How smart these Red Army men look!" And they'll invite us into their houses. We may strike up some friendships, you know.

TIGER CUB (*rather sternly*) The first thing to do after you go into a village is to hold a mass meeting and call on the peasants to overthrow the landlords and redistribute the land. You're not supposed just to gad about.

MACHINE-GUNNER (*meekly*) You're quite right. And none of us should forget to try to get young volunteers for our army.

TIGER CUB Of course. It's only a question of getting them to understand what the Red Army stands for. If we do that we'll get plenty.

CHIEN And then when our ranks are swelled with new comrades, Squad Leader Tiger Cub will be made a platoon leader!

TIGER CUB I'm damn well not going to let you call me by my nickname any longer! Haven't I got a proper name? If anyone tries using my nickname again, don't say you haven't been warned!

CHIEN Have you got another name besides Tiger Cub?

TIGER CUB (*indignantly*) Of course! It's Wang Erh-hu.

(HUANG, CHAO and WANG *come back. As they enter* HUANG *is muttering:* "What's this 'tiger this—tiger that' about?" *Meanwhile a group of Red Army men come on.*)

HUANG Company Commander Wang, do you see that cleft between the rocks over there? Do you think we can get through it?

WANG Well, Regimental Commander, if *you* think it's possible, then I can do it.

HUANG No ifs, now!

WANG I'll try, if. . . .(*Then, resolutely.*) Yes, I can.

HUANG Good. You get up through it with a couple of squads and on to that hill-top, then give it to them hot and strong from there. They'll be caught unawares and thrown into a panic, thinking we must have descended from the skies. That'll give us a chance to rush up from here, along the path.

WANG Yes, Commander.

HUANG Get going, then, and take a Very pistol with you. Give us two red flares when you've got to the top.

WANG Yes, Commander. (*Goes off.*)

HUANG Little Wan, you keep an eye open for the signals.

LITTLE WAN Yes, Commander. (*Goes off.*)

HUANG I think we should wait another ten minutes.

CHAO Right.

HUANG (*to* CHAO) I say, to go by Lao Lo's work nowadays, he's come on wonderfully.

CHAO He certainly has. He's doing very well. I'm going to suggest that he takes over the battalion and I act as his deputy. I'm also going to ask HQ to appoint a new political instructor to the battalion.

HUANG Come to that, now, your new political instructor's already here.

CHAO Where? Who?

HUANG You!

CHAO Me?

HUANG Yes. (*Turns towards the men.*) Divisional HQ has decided to make Lao Lo Commander of First Battalion and Lao Chao the Political Instructor. (*Takes a paper out of his notebook.*) Here's the order.

(*There is general rejoicing.*)

HUANG Lao Chao, tomorrow we must see that everyone gets a good clean-up and hair-cut.

CHAO   Yes. I can do with one myself!
(*There is a sudden outburst of gunfire.*)
TIGER CUB (*runs over*)   Commander! Here they come!
CHAO (*jumping up*)   And there we go! The attack's begun! Steady now, comrades. All ready? Machine-guns? Grenades? Keep cool. We'll let 'em come close . . . come very close. . . .

THE STAGE TURNS DARK

Epilogue

TIME   *Shortly after Act VI.*

PLACE   *On the hill-top. The fortifications stand left and far below spreads the boundless plain. The hill is in Red Army hands. Hordes of prisoners being escorted down the hill pass Red Army men climbing joyfully up. It is morning, and broad daylight. The world seems particularly wide to those who come to it from the murk of battle. On a wall, LATSEKOU, in bold characters, shows still among the ruins.*

   Bursts of song ring out all around, as the Red Army reserves come up. Those at the top, who include the propaganda unit, shout down "Get a move on, comrades! You'll get here in the end!" and are cheerfully answered: "You bet! We'll get there all right!"

   When the curtain rises, CHAO CHIH-FANG, LO SHUN-CHENG, WANG TEH-CHIANG, LI FENG-LIEN *and* WU *stand looking over the plain.* CHAO *has been wounded in the left arm.*

CHAO   Well, we've come through! And now look at the houses in the valley—we're in sight of victory!
FENG-LIEN (*looking at* CHAO's *arm*)   You're wounded! (*Starts to dress it.*) Does it hurt much?
WU (*winking at the others, so as to leave* CHAO *and* FENG-LIEN *alone together*)   Ahem! Shall we go over there and, er—look at the others coming up?
LO   All right—come on.
(*They all go off.*)

CHAO (*lost in admiration of the military advantages of the place*) Just see what a narrow path!

FENG-LIEN You mean what a narrow escape! It only just missed your chest!

CHAO What on earth do you mean?

FENG-LIEN I'm talking about your wound.

CHAO I'm talking about Latsekou.

FENG-LIEN (*has almost finished dressing the wound*) Don't you feel any pain?

CHAO (*absently*) Not a thing!

FENG-LIEN Not a thing! You don't feel anything but warfare!

CHAO (*still oblivious of anything but the battle*) Feng-lien, looking at it, you'd never have expected us to make it, would you?

FENG-LIEN Of course I would! You'd have done it if it was even harder! But, you know, I managed to get up here, too!

CHAO Yes, I know you did; we're all victors together. If only your brother could have lived to see this with us! (*Tears spring to his eyes.*) Oh, Lao Li, my dear comrade-in-arms!

FENG-LIEN (*her face speaking of tender memories*) My brother . . . he still lives, in a way.

CHAO How do you mean? Where?

FENG-LIEN Right here. You're like him—in many ways, you know. (*She pulls out the documents her brother gave her.*) These were his. They're for you.

CHAO (*takes the papers reverently*) Oh, my old comrade!

FENG-LIEN (*drying her eyes*) We must go on.

(FENG-LIEN *and* CHAO *go off.* WU, LO *and the others come back on. One of the climbing groups leads the way with a red flag, which flutters in the morning breeze. The air is full of laughter, singing, greetings, exultation. . . .* REGIMENTAL COMMANDER HUANG *climbs up and comes on stage. He is on top of the world. He greets the men warmly, and shakes hands all round. Then he stops to look over the plain which stretches before them, seemingly boundless.*)

HUANG Comrades, it's good to see you all! Here we are, indeed—as victors! Look over there, comrades. See how fertile the land is, and how wide the plain! What a long way we've travelled! What a vast motherland we have! (*Calls down to the soldiers still coming up the hill.*) Pull up, comrades. We'll soon be walking on broad roads! Get a move on!

(*Cheerful shouts answer him: "We're coming, all right!"*)

(CHAO *and* FENG-LIEN *come back.*)

CHAO Good morning, Regimental Commander!

FENG-LIEN *(handing* HUANG *a spray of flowers she has just picked)*
Flowers for you, Regimental Commander.

HUANG *(taking them)* Flowers, eh? Where did you find them?

FENG-LIEN They're growing all over these hills.

HUANG What's their name?

FENG-LIEN We call them Red-All-over-the-Hill.

HUANG Red-All-over-the-Hill? Pretty name! Look at the fresh green leaves and red petals! Comrades, I think we'll rename them. They should be Red-All-over-the-Land! Red-All-over-the-Land, shining as brightly as the sun.
(In the distance is heard more laughter. The peasants are greeting the Red Army and shouting slogans. The noise increases as they draw nearer.)

YOUNG CHOU Regimental Commander, the peasants have all turned out to greet us. Listen to their gongs and drums!
(The peasants burst on. They shake hands eagerly with HUANG *and the others.)*

LITTLE WAN *(breathless with excitement)* Regimental Commander! Regimental Commander! Here's Chairman Mao coming!

HUANG *(shouts at the top of his voice)* Comrades, comrades! Our Chairman Mao is coming!
(There is a great outburst of singing and cheering:)

Nothing daunted by our trials on the Long March,
O'er rolling rivers and great mountains high,
The surging waves of Gold Sand River.

We crossed the Tatu though no boats were there,
The snowy mountains where no birds are flying.
We crossed the steppelands where no men build their homes.

Red Army of the workers and peasants,
Steeled people's army conqu'ring many towns,
Four hundred reg'ments we have put to rout.

Led by the Party we are marching forth!
The mighty people stand by our side.
Led by our Party we go forward,

From victory to vict'ry, ever forward!
Led by our Party we go forward
To victory, forward to victory!

CURTAIN

Songs From
"THE LONG MARCH"

THE MONTH OF MARCH IS FULL OF BLOOM

(for Act II)

Music by Shih Lo-meng

The month of March is full of bloom, fresh____ grass and peach blos-soms too.

Fight-er__ Liu and Hsiao Yeh-tan clasp their hands in__ love. How op-press'd

were the Yis for a - ges__ long! Sud-den-ly from out the blue

came their sav-ing__ star. Ai ai ai, ai ai, came their sav-ing star.

Broth-er peo-ples, let's_ u - nite! Rev-o-lu-tion comes__ to flow'r.

Dig new wells for wa - ter and plant new groves of___ peach-es plant the peach trees,
Fol - low the Com-mun-ist Par - ty, if you would be hap-py! Rev - o - lu - tion

quick - ly___ grows the fruit needs the help of all. Hands are clasp'd in bro-ther-ly love,

Peach - es bloom o'er all___ the___ land. Hands are clasp'd in bro - ther - ly

love, And the peach trees___ bloom o'er all the___ hap - py___ land.

500

CROSS THE TATU RIVER!

(for Act III)

Music by Shih Lo-meng

River Ta - tu we now ap - proach: Tum - bling flood so

cra - ven___ flows! Broad though it be we fear it not,

No more than peaks or un - told foes! Ta - tu shall be cross'd!___

Ta - tu shall be cross'd!___ Ta - tu shall be cross'd!___

First Front Ar - my's made its___ name! Our___ might - y force is led by

Chair - man __ Mao Tse - tung. No moun - tain peaks can de - flect our

course, No great flood, deep and wide, bar our way! On and on we

march! __ On and on we march! __ On and on we march!

FORWARD WE MARCH!

(for Epilogue)

Music by Shih Lo-meng

No - thing daun - ted by our— tri - als on the Long— March,—

O'er roll - ing riv - ers and great moun - tains high, The surg - ing waves of

Gold Sand Riv - er. We cross'd the Ta - tu though no— boats were there,

The snow - y moun - tains where no birds are fly - ing. We cross'd the

steppe-lands where no men build their homes. Red Ar - my of the work - ers and peas -

ants, Steel'd peo-ple's ar - my con-qu'ring ma - ny towns, Four hun-dred reg'-ments

we have put to rout.___ Led by the Par - ty we are march-ing forth!

The might - y peo - ple stand by our side. Led by our Par - ty we go for-ward

from vic-to - ry to vic - t'ry, ev - er for - ward! Led by our Par - ty

we go for - ward to vic - to - ry,___ for - ward to vic-to - ry!___

COMMENTARY

The Long March (1954)   A throwback to the didactic, realistic drama of the late nineteenth century, the drama of Red China is for that reason reactionary. Realistic in form and communist in theme, these plays are intended to be comprehensible to audiences of workers and peasants. Unlike Bertolt Brecht, who dramatizes a complex social reality in complex ways, Red Chinese playwrights dramatize a complex social reality in the simplistic terms of Socialist Realism.

Opposing literature and art that do not promote the cause of communism, the Red Chinese demand that writers and artists "fit well into the whole revolutionary machine as a component part." Since the Communist Party determines the goals and tactics of "the whole revolutionary machine," this means, in the words of Mao Tse-tung, that artistic works must conform to "the stand of the Party, keeping to the Party spirit and Party policy." To expose "the aggressors, exploiters and oppressors and the evil influences they have on the people" and to praise "the masses of the people, their toil and their struggle, their army and their Party" are the tasks of Red Chinese writers and artists. Educative and propagandist in goal, the drama of mainland China is elementary in technique.

In this unsophisticated drama, plots demonstrate the forging of communism and the benefits of communism; dialogue praises the leadership, wisdom, and inspiration of Chairman Mao and the Party; characters are divided into single-dimensional heroes and villains. Often, Americans are portrayed as the villains. In *Raid on the White Tiger Regiment*, for example, an operatic drama about the Korean War, the Americans are portrayed as hypocritical cowards who wantonly shoot pro-Chinese civilians. Such statements as "We'll make the U. S. imperialists repay the debts of blood they owe the people!" pepper the play. Songs, important in Chinese communist drama, are propagandistic. Communism, rather than romantic love, is usually the subject of these songs, as in *Taking the Bandits' Stronghold*, where a Red Army soldier sings, "A Communist always heeds the party's call . . ./I want only to smash the chains of a thousand years/And open a freshet of endless happiness for the people." To introduce passages that point morals, Chairman Mao's name is frequently invoked, as in *On Guard Beneath the Neon Lights*:

> Chairman Mao said that "some Communists, who were not conquered by enemies with guns . . . will be defeated by sugar-coated bullets." I've learned a lot from the things that have happened during the last three days. I've gradually come to understand the truth of this statement of Chairman Mao Tse-tung's made at the Second Plenary Session of the Seventh Central Committee of the Party.

505

Quotations from Chairman Mao introduce, underlie, and summarize the themes of entire scenes. At the beginning of a scene about the relationship between Red Chinese soldiers and Korean civilians in *Raid on the White Tiger Regiment*, for instance, is the quotation "The army must become one with the people so that they see it as their own army. Such an army will be invincible."

The Long March, which is typical of Red Chinese drama, is based on one of the major events in the history of communist China. By 1934, Japanese troops had captured China's three northeastern provinces. To battle the Japanese invaders, the Red Army, which was engaged in civil war with the forces of Chiang Kai-shek, marched in October, 1934 from Fukien and Kiangsi in the southeast, eastward to Yunnan, and then north to Shensi. Pursued, intercepted, and attacked by enemy troops, particularly those of Chiang Kai-shek, they marched more than eight thousand miles and overcame enormous difficulties before they reached northern Shensi, where they fought the Japanese in October, 1935. A remarkable achievement in itself, the march was also important politically and as propaganda, for it brought the principles and presence of Chinese communism to a large part of the nation. Chen Chi-tung, author of the play *The Long March*, participated in the march.

In *The Long March*, the principal villain (offstage) is Chiang Kai-shek, leader of the Kuomintang. "Down with the traitor Chiang Kai-shek!" someone cries. Upon hearing his name, another character automatically exclaims, "The bastard!" Just as every reference to Generalissimo Chiang is maledictory, every reference to Chairman Mao is reverential. "But thanks to our Party and Chairman Mao, we'll get through our troubles," exclaims a character. At the news of Chairman Mao's arrival in the area, "*A roar of excitement and joy goes up from the whole stage.*" Attacking the enemies of the Chinese Communists and praising the people, the Red Army, the Communist Party, and Chairman Mao, *The Long March* employs such devices as slogans ("Long live the Chinese Workers' and Peasants' Red Army! Long live the Chinese Communist Party!"), inspirational songs ("Follow the Communist party, if you would be happy!/Revolution needs the help of all."), didactic dialogue (as a soldier converts an incredulous Boatman to the cause of the Red Army, he feeds anti-Kuomintang and pro-communist propaganda to the audience as well), and sermons ("He didn't die needlessly at all. And he was right when he said that though he died the revolutionary cause would never die. We shall win in the end, and then those bullies, the landlords, the warlords, the imperialists, will no longer dare oppress us. His death, like his comrades' deaths, is the price we pay for the future happiness of the Chinese people."). Each act dramatizes one or two propagandist points: the Red

Army's victory over the enemy troops of Chiang and its friendly dealings with the peasants (I), the Communist Party's successful policy toward national minority races (II), the Red Army's success in converting skeptical proletarians to its cause (III), self-sacrificing Red Army soldiers and political instructors who travel with the army (IV), the heroism of starving soldiers as they cross dangerous terrain (V), and a victorious battle with the enemy (VI and Epilogue).

Beginning in February, 1935 with the Red Army's first victory under the leadership of Mao Tse-tung and ending in September, 1935 with the imminent arrival of Chairman Mao after a victorious battle in the mountains of northeast China, *The Long March* dramatizes the heroism and self-sacrifice of the soldiers, the successful application of the policies of the Communist Party under Chairman Mao, and the mutual friendship between the Red Army and the Chinese people. Condemning the enemies of the Communist Party, particularly Chiang Kai-shek and the Japanese invaders, and eulogizing the people, the army, the Party, and its leader, *The Long March* follows the precepts that guide revolutionary drama in Communist China.

Bibliography

A. *Plays about the Chinese Communist Revolution:*

Ho Ching-chih and Ting Yi, *The White-Haired Girl*, 1945 (musical version, based on play, 1944)

Lao Sheh, *Dragon Beard Ditch*, 1950

Shen Hsi-meng, Mo Yen, and Lu Hsing-chen, *On Guard Beneath the Neon Lights*, c. 1955

Tuan Cheng-pin and Tu Shih-tsun, *Taming the Dragon and the Tiger*, c. 1960

Wong Ou-hung and Ah Chia, *The Red Lantern*, 1965 (publication date)

B. *Works about Theatre in Communist China:*

Meserve, Walter J. and Ruth I. Introduction to *Modern Drama from Communist China*. New York: New York University Press, 1970.

Scott, A. C. *Literature and the Arts in Twentieth Century China*. Garden City, N. Y.: Doubleday Anchor, 1963.

————. "Hung Teng Chi: *The Red Lantern*: An Example of Contemporary Dramatic Experimentation," *Modern Drama*, IX (February, 1967).

Tung, Constantine. "The Communist Anxiety: A Study of Two Chinese Plays," *Modern Drama*, XII (September, 1969).

Yang, Daniel S. P. "Peking Drama with Contemporary Themes," *The Drama Review*, XIII (Summer, 1969).

———. "The Peking Theatre Under Communism," *Theatre Annual*, XIV (1968).

Third
World
Revolution

CANDAULES, COMMISSIONER
Daniel C. Gerould

CANDAULES, COMMISSIONER

A Dramatic Fable in Four Scenes
Daniel C. Gerould

CHARACTERS

CANDAULES, *High Commissioner of Economic Assistance to Lydia*
GYGES, *his native Lydian bodyguard*
NYSSIA, *Candaules' wife*
The names are pronounced: Căndō'lēs, Gī'jēz, and Nī'ssĭa

Scene One

Sardis, capital of Lydia. The stage represents a dusty dirt road which winds through the bazaar and by the shacks along the river. This is the route to the airport. A cardboard cut-out of a big black diplomatic limousine bumps slowly along. GYGES is driving, and CANDAULES sits in the back seat, holding an attaché case on his lap.

GYGES is dressed in a chauffeur's uniform: high boots, black suit, gloves, and cap. CANDAULES is wearing morning clothes: striped pants, tailcoat, grey vest, boiled shirt, silk tie, and top hat.

They bump along in silence for a few moments; CANDAULES looks straight ahead. Then the car stops. CANDAULES speaks to GYGES by means of a microphone which he holds in his hand, and his voice is heard amplified through a speaker in the front seat. GYGES replies without turning around, with the result that they never look at one another.

CANDAULES *speaks in a serious, dignified manner throughout the play.*

GYGES, *an Oriental, speaks with an accent, in tense, staccato tones, but is always most agreeable and friendly.*

CANDAULES   Gyges?

GYGES   Yes, Mr. High Commissioner.

CANDAULES   Why have we stopped?

GYGES   I apologize, sir. There are goats in the road.

CANDAULES   Goats? I don't see any goats.

GYGES   They are too low for you to see. You are too high up.

CANDAULES   We've no time for goats, Gyges. Make them get out of the way. Honk the horn.
(GYGES *honks the horn which emits an unusually loud blare. The car starts to bump along again.*)
We mustn't be late, Gyges. (CANDAULES *pulls out from his vest pocket a huge pocket watch the size of a saucer and examines it carefully.*)
It is now exactly twelve minutes past two. We should reach the airport in approximately nineteen minutes. It will take four minutes to walk to the landing area. The reception will begin at exactly 2:36. The ambassador is precise. Never forget that, Gyges! The plane will first appear in the sky at 2:31. It will seem a tiny speck; then it will gradually grow larger. It will land at 2:35. The photographers will be there, and we shall all shake hands and look grave or smile, depending on the circumstances.

GYGES   Yes, Mr. Commissioner.

CANDAULES (*after a pause during which the journey continues*)   Gyges, are you following the route precisely as I instructed you?

GYGES   Yes, sir, just as you say. We now are passing through the New Bazaar. Look, Mr. Commissioner, there is the café where the plastic bomb was thrown last week!

CANDAULES   I look neither to the right, nor to the left. I only look straight ahead. I do not wish to dignify such wanton acts of violence by looking at them.

GYGES   Oh, there is a hole in the ground where the bomb went off!

CANDAULES   I refuse to look at that hole. I refuse to acknowledge that such a hole exists.

GYGES   But look, sir! Tables and chairs have been arranged again—around the hole!

CANDAULES   I am glad, Gyges, I am very glad. I love order—I abhor anarchy. And Gyges, are there people sitting at the cafe again, drinking coffee?

GYGES   Yes, sir, yes, sir. There are many people. An old waiter with a white bandage on his head is carrying glasses of orange sherbet on a tray.

CANDAULES   Good, Gyges, good! Terrorist gangs cannot stop civilization. The war is improving every day. Believe me, Gyges, it's a much better war today than it was five years ago, and it will be an even better war five years from today!

GYGES   Yes, Mr. Commissioner.

CANDAULES   Gyges, I predict that in five years time all these roads will be paved. (*The car bumps along.*) Oh, my back! What a wonderful world it will be! You will be driving me along over paved roads, Gyges! Your children will enjoy a better life!

GYGES   Oh, thank you, sir!

CANDAULES   You don't have any children, do you, Gyges?

GYGES   Unfortunately not. I am sorry, sir.

CANDAULES   There's no reason at all to apologize. You're not even married, are you, Gyges?

GYGES   No, sir. I regret to say so, sir.

CANDAULES   In that case, it's just a figure of speech about your children. There will be a better future for you and for all your people. Every one will be happier. (*pause*) I have a lovely wife. We have two wonderful children. We're very proud of them.

GYGES   And they must be proud of you, sir.

CANDAULES   We hardly see them any more. It's been years, years, years. We have their photographs. We look at them. (*a pause as the car bumps along*)

This is the seventeenth anniversary of the beginning of the war. It's hard to believe that it was only seventeen years ago to this very day that the war began. Gyges, can you remember back that far?

GYGES   Yes sir, I think I can. I shall try.

CANDAULES   How old were you then, Gyges?

GYGES   Two years old, sir.

CANDAULES   A two-year-old can't remember the beginning of a war. It's not possible.

(CANDAULES *continues to speak through the microphone, although what he says next is not addressed to any one in particular.*)

We're on our way to the airport to meet the Prince. The Prince has flown back to Lydia to declare his unwavering determination to prosecute the war until the enemy is utterly annihilated. The Prince will remain in the country for an hour. As High Commissioner of Economic Assistance, representing a friendly foreign government, my presence is always required at welcoming ceremonies at the airport. Our two countries are allies in this great struggle, indissolubly linked by the closest ties of everlasting friendship and military aid.

Since Gyges, this native lad here, entered my service forty-three days ago, I've felt safer—he has a revolver and he knows how to use it to protect me in case of incidents.

(GYGES *removes his revolver from his body holster and displays his gun.*)

Then too, he seems to understand me. I can tell him anything, about myself—or about my children—or about my wife. (GYGES *smiles deeply.*) Everything that I have interests him. He listens so sympathetically. His whole face lights up.

You see, I'm always surrounded by barriers—interpreters and bullet-proof glass. I spend all my days with generals and statisticians. I speak officially—I issue or receive orders; I dictate into dictaphones. It's my work. I love the economy of this country.

But there's no one I can talk to—about myself. Busy as I am, I'm lonely sometimes. Before Gyges came into my life, I'd settle down into the back seat of the limousine and draw into myself. When I'd catch a glimpse of my face in the rearview mirror, I looked old and tired and drawn.

Now when I come out of a meeting, Gyges is there holding the door open for me, smiling. Then off we go together, and I can talk with him as we drive along. All during the meetings I look forward to our rides. I think of things to tell him about myself.

If I ever seem cross with him, it's just a game, the master and the servant. It doesn't really mean anything. He understands that. (*pause*)

What was that noise, Gyges? Was that gunfire?

GYGES   No, Mr. Commissioner. Only an insignificant backfire. No need to worry, sir.

CANDAULES (*after a pause in which the car bumps along*)   What's that yelling, Gyges?

GYGES   A group of happy peasants. They are cheering; they're waving flags. You know, sir, the little flags given out for spontaneous demonstrations.

CANDAULES   But is it a friendly spontaneous demonstration?

GYGES   They're smiling. You may smile back at them, sir. (CANDAULES *smiles.*) You may wave at them, sir. (CANDAULES *waves, looking straight ahead all the while.*)

CANDAULES   Should I put on my peasant hat, Gyges? Is this the right moment?

GYGES   Yes, sir. A friendly crowd likes a peasant hat. It indicates you are one of us, one of the people.

(GYGES *hands* CANDAULES *a large basket-shaped straw hat.* CANDAULES *takes off his top hat and puts on the peasant hat. He smiles and waves and looks straight ahead. After a pause during which the journey continues, he takes off his peasant hat and puts on his top hat again.*)

CANDAULES   It's quiet here. Where are we, Gyges, where are we?

GYGES   An old dump heap, Mr. High Commissioner. Full of old rubble, old junk, old shacks.

CANDAULES   Why don't we stop here, Gyges? (CANDAULES *pulls out his watch and looks at it.*) We can spare exactly three minutes. The thermos, Gyges, the thermos!

(*The car bumps to a stop.* GYGES *hands back to* CANDAULES *a large picnic thermos bottle.* CANDAULES *unscrews the top and pours out some warmed milk into the cup contained in the cover. He puts his little finger into the cup to test the temperature.*)

The milk's not warm enough, Gyges! Did you heat it yourself, Gyges?

GYGES   No, sir, Cook did. I told Cook exactly how you like it, sir. I said it must be warm enough, or else there'd be trouble.

CANDAULES   I didn't think that you'd forget to warm it properly, Gyges. After all, you like it too. We both like it the same way. Here's your cup. (CANDAULES *passes a cup of warmed milk to* GYGES.)

Try it and see what you think. You don't think it's warm enough, do you, Gyges?

(*They both drink their warmed milk, sampling it, rolling it around in their mouths, and making faces.* CANDAULES *smiles faintly in a prissy, disappointed way.* GYGES *imitates his smile, and, for* CANDAULES' *benefit makes a polite face indicating mild disapproval of the warmth of the milk. For the audience,* GYGES *gags on the milk and spits it out on the ground.*)

GYGES   You're right, sir, not quite warm enough.

CANDAULES   We'll have to drink it anyhow. Warm milk is good for the stomach. I must have something soothing in my stomach, or I begin to feel nauseated driving over these bumpy dirt roads. (*pause*) What's that noise, Gyges? What's that thumping noise?

GYGES   That bump-bump, sir?

CANDAULES   It's a kind of slapping. Or it's more a rubbing. What is that noise, Gyges?

GYGES   Oh, I see now, sir. It's just a group of children. They're gathered round the car and now they're running their hands all over the fenders.

CANDAULES   How big are they, Gyges? How old are they, Gyges? How many of them are there, Gyges?

GYGES   Ten years old, just little boys, not more than a dozen, sir. No need to fear.

CANDAULES   They don't have to be stopped, do they, Gyges? They're not rubbing disrespectfully, are they?

GYGES   No, Mr. High Commissioner, they stroke it like a dog.

CANDAULES   I should like to permit them to continue thumping as long as they do it properly and do no damage to government property. The poor little rascals, they're probably all war orphans. The war's been going on so long, war orphans are fathering war orphans now. You're a war orphan yourself, Gyges.

GYGES   Yes, sir.

CANDAULES   They don't get enough to eat. Get out the box of candy, Gyges. (GYGES *produces a huge colored candy box the size of a suitcase.*)

Distribute the candy, Gyges. (GYGES *distributes the candy.*) Give them all they want, Gyges, all they want. No stinting! This is personal diplomacy. (*pause*) Well, do they seem pleased? Are they smiling?

GYGES   They keep rubbing the car, sir. Bumpety-bumpety-bump. Thump, thump, thump.

CANDAULES   It's beginning to make me nervous. God knows, I'm sympathetic, I feel for them. I want them to thump. But they've thumped enough. It's making me nervous. Thump, thump, thump. Why don't they stop? Why don't they go away? We gave them candy, didn't we? Start the car, Gyges. Warn the children first. I don't want any one to get hurt. I abhor any kind of violence. Honk the horn, Gyges. Make them get out of the way.

(GYGES *honks the horn which emits an unusually loud blare.* CANDAULES *removes his top hat and puts on his peasant hat; he smiles and waves and looks straight ahead. The car starts to bump along again.*)

Once the war is won, the children in your country will lead a better life. There will be better roads, there will be elections every year. There will be a better future for every one.

Someday, Gyges, your son may drive along this same way over a four lane highway—chauffering my son!

GYGES Yes, sir. I hope so. I hope so.

CANDAULES (*after a pause in which the car bumps along*) Gyges, where are we now? I thought I heard shouting.

GYGES We're driving through a slum. There are many dirty people.

CANDAULES Drive faster, Gyges. I abhor unpleasantness. It serves no useful purpose.

GYGES I apologize, sir. I cannot drive faster. There are too many people in the street, Mr. Commissioner.

CANDAULES Be careful. I want no one run over. I want no blood on my wheels.

GYGES (*The car comes to a stop.*) We cannot proceed, sir. A crowd is gathering around the car.

CANDAULES (CANDAULES *holds his hands at the side of his eyes like blinders.*) Is it an ugly crowd, Gyges? Is it menacing?

GYGES I apologize, sir. But I have to say they jeer, they hoot. They beat on the windows and try to look in at you.

CANDAULES I refuse to recognize that their hostility exists.

GYGES Some begin to spit, sir.

CANDAULES Spitting! Spitting on a government car! How terrible! Quick, Gyges, give me your golden ring!

(GYGES *passes back to* CANDAULES *a large gold ring about two feet in diameter to which is attached a long, black bag capable of containing a person.*)

I refuse to acknowledge that they exist. I'll put on your ring and become invisible. Then they'll let the car pass. Help me on with the ring, Gyges!

(GYGES *lowers the ring and black bag down over* CANDAULES' *head, still wearing his top hat, and then down over his body until he is invisible. As the bag is lowered over* CANDAULES *and he disappears, wooden clappers are beaten against a board, as in the Kabuki drama. In fact, the person who beats the clappers can appear at the edge of the stage in full view of the audience. The sound continues until the curtain.*)

GYGES You are now invisible, sir.

CANDAULES (*speaks in a muffled voice from within the ring*) Straight ahead, Gyges, straight ahead!

CURTAIN

Scene Two

CANDAULES' *dressing room. Various dress suits, including some expensive oriental robes, hang from hooks which come down from the ceiling. There is also a table with hair brushes, a full-length mirror in a stand, and a special shoeshine chair with a foot rest and other shining equipment.*

GYGES *has his chauffeur's jacket off and is in his shirt-sleeves; he has a revolver strapped under one arm.* CANDAULES *is in full evening dress. The suit which he has worn during the day is hanging up one one of the hooks.* GYGES *is brushing it with a clothes-brush, and then he brushes the pants and tailcoat which* CANDAULES *is now wearing.* GYGES *brushes alternatingly the two costumes. Finally* GYGES *pulls down a clothesbag over the earlier suit. In* CANDAULES' *dressing room, everything is kept clean and orderly and put in its proper place.*

CANDAULES   I'm thinking of something, Gyges. . . .

GYGES   Yes, sir.

CANDAULES   Tell me something, Gyges.

GYGES   Yes, Mr. High Commissioner.

CANDAULES   You're a typical Lydian. Tell me, what do you think of my charming wife, Nyssia?

GYGES   I think that she is a great lady. She is the sponsor of the Girl Scout movement, she is an honorary General in the Women's Militia.

CANDAULES   But Gyges, do you find her attractive?

GYGES   Oh, yes, sir! So much I cannot say how much! She is a great lady.

CANDAULES   You know what, Gyges, I think my wife is absolutely beautiful! I think that my wife is the most beautiful woman in the world. Gyges, what do you really think of my beautiful wife? Truthfully, man to man?

GYGES   Yes sir, yes sir. I agree.

CANDAULES   Gyges, I don't think you're being sincere with me. You're not telling the truth. I don't want you to say just what you think I want to hear. I want you to be honest with me, Gyges. I'm not sure you really believe that my wife is beautiful!

What do you think of her color?

GYGES   Her color, sir?

CANDAULES   Do you think that she's too white?

GYGES   Too what, sir?

CANDAULES   Too white.

GYGES   No, Mr. Commissioner. She is just right. White is the right color. White is the ideal color.

CANDAULES   Oh, you dont have to pretend with me, Gyges. After all, we don't have the same color skins. Hold out your hand. (CANDAULES *compares their hands.*)

Perhaps you think that I'm not sensitive to these things and that I don't notice what you're thinking. I'm watching you carefully, Gyges.

GYGES   Oh, thank you, sir, thank you! (GYGES *giggles and covers his face with his hands, and peers between his fingers.*) I watch you too, sir. (*He laughs again.*)

CANDAULES   That's good, Gyges! We're watching each other!

Now tell me the truth, Gyges: you don't think that my wife's skin is too white.

GYGES   I swear it, sir! (GYGES *bows, almost kneels.*) We respect white. In pictures, our gods are white.

CANDAULES   Listen, Gyges, I know how all you natives feel. You are intensely patriotic; your country is small, but strategically located. You are a proud people. Am I right, Gyges? (GYGES *bows and scrapes.*) I thought that you might like the color of your own skins.

GYGES   On the contrary, sir, we prefer your skins. I wish I had your skin, I wish I were in your skin!

CANDAULES   I'm glad you're not prejudiced, Gyges. Small countries are often so skin-conscious. It's ridiculous! (*a slight pause*) Tell me, Gyges, how much of her skin have you seen?

GYGES   O, nothing, sir, nothing! Only what is shown to the whole world, Mr. Commissioner.

CANDAULES   Ankles, hands, arms, face, neck! Is that all?

GYGES   (*respectfully ingenuous*)   I should not want the High Commissioner to think that I am unappreciative! I have eyes, sir, I have eyes. Sometimes when I wait on the table, I see her bare shoulders.

CANDAULES   Gyges, you know, she's much taller than you are. That doesn't bother you, does it?

GYGES   No, Mr. High Commissioner! How can you think that of me? I should never dare criticize her height! I am happy that she is so tall. In that way I can always look up to her. (GYGES *bows.*)

CANDAULES   (*confiding*)   She's taller than I am too. (*explaining*) But we're both of the same race. It's not so noticeable.

GYGES   You must be joking, Mr. High Commissioner. You are taller than she! I am sure, I am sure.

CANDAULES   Of course, different countries have different tastes in beauty. That's as it should be. Men of different nations like completely different things in their women. Take you. You are completely indifferent to a woman's breasts, aren't you?

GYGES   Oh, yes, yes, you are right, Mr. Commissioner! You are always right. How did you know? How did you find out? You know everything, everything, Mr. Commissioner. We have no secrets from you. You know us, you know us. (GYGES *laughs and bows.*)

CANDAULES   In fact, I don't imagine that you find my wife's breasts particularly attractive.

GYGES   I never said that, Mr. High Commissioner, I never said that!

CANDAULES   Of course, you haven't really seen them yet, but they're too big for you.

No need to deny it, Gyges. Each country has a right to self-determination. We're not here to try to force our tastes on you, but merely to protect your right to choose for yourself.

(CANDAULES *sits down in the shoe-shine chair.*)   Shine my shoes, Gyges.

(GYGES *squats down on his haunches and begins to shine* CANDAULES' *shoes. First he applies saddle soap and washes them, then he puts on the polish, and continues shining throughout the rest of the scene between the two.*)   Gyges, what do you think of my wife's body?

GYGES   Mr. Commissioner, how could I form an opinion on such a subject? I ask you, sir?

CANDAULES   You don't have to pretend with me, Gyges. Confess. You have ways of forming an opinion of her body.

GYGES   (*shining furiously*)   For example, sir, how?

CANDAULES   Well, for example, what does my wife's maid tell you? She help my wife dress and undress. She's seen everything. What does she tell you?

GYGES   She says nothing, Mr. Commissioner. She doesn't tell me anything!

CANDAULES   If I were in your position, I'd have seen things.

GYGES   Excuse me, sir. Seen things? What things, sir?

CANDAULES   Well, for example, what about through a window—or a partly open door? You're in and out of the house all day long. As bodyguard, you're free to come and go as you wish. Perhaps you saw her one day coming out of the shower. Or perhaps the maid hid you in a closet late at night. Tell the truth, Gyges: what have you seen?

GYGES (*brushing energetically on* CANDAULES' *shoes*)   Nothing, Mr. Commissioner, nothing—except her clothes! The maid opened all her closets one day and showed me all her dresses hanging side by side.

CANDAULES   Did you touch them?

GYGES   We went into the closet, sir. I could not help brushing against her dresses. We saw shoes too, row after row of shoes.

CANDAULES   You've seen her shoes too. Is that all you saw?

GYGES   Mr. High Commissioner, I saw gloves. Hundreds of pairs of gloves.

CANDAULES   Did you try them on, Gyges? Did you put your hands in her gloves? Did you try putting your feet in her shoes?

GYGES   No, sir! (*He polishes frantically.*)

CANDAULES   Why not, Gyges, why not? You've got small feet. You could get into her shoes. Your feet are no bigger than hers.

GYGES   I swear, sir! I never wore her shoes!

CANDAULES   There's no need to deny anything, Gyges. I want to prove to you how much I trust you; I'd like to show you how much I respect you and understand you. You don't have to believe me about how beautiful my wife is—I'd like to show you, take you completely into my confidence, make a total revelation to you.

Gyges, how would you like to see my wife stark naked?

GYGES   Stark naked?

CANDAULES   Stark naked!

GYGES   But Mr. High Commissioner . . . (*He polishes with the cloth at high speed.*) Your Excellency!

CANDAULES   Oh, don't try to thank me, Gyges! I'm not doing you a favor; you're doing me a favor. Quite frankly, Gyges, I want to be your friend. I've been thinking about this for a long time. Don't you think that this will bring us closer together?

GYGES   Oh, Mr. High Commissioner, you are kind! You are good! But I am too small, I am too low! I do not deserve such generosity.

(GYGES *bows.*)

GANDAULES   Gyges, this is no longer a question of personal preference; it's a matter of duty! Look at this telegram which I have just received from headquarters overseas.

(CANDAULES *pulls a telegram out of his pocket, unfolds it and hands it to* GYGES.)

You can see for yourself.

GYGES (*reading with difficulty*)   Bfzit Gklop Brrtra . . .

CANDAULES (*taking back the telegram*)   Oh, I forgot, it's in code, of course. You can't read it. Here's what it says, after it's been decoded. "Show your wife's private parts to natives." I tried decoding it several ways, but that's the only way that it made any sense. "Show your wife's private parts to natives." We have no choice, Gyges. But even if I hadn't received these instructions, it was something that I'd been thinking about for some time. I kept asking myself what I could do to bring us closer together.

Then it came to me, one night as I was lying awake, looking out through the mosquito netting at the moon. "Candaules," I said to myself, "The least that you can do is to show Gyges your beautiful wife—absolutely naked."

Gyges! (CANDAULES *puts his arm around* GYGES' *shoulder.*) Never forget that this is essentially a struggle for the minds and hearts of men! This war will not ultimately be won on the battle-fields; but by the side which can best satisfy men's longings for the truth and a better way of life. Gyges, I offer you a glimpse of my wife, naked! I want to make you happy, Gyges! (*making an official declaration*) To win the war, we must win the people. To win the people, we must give them what they want. And Gyges, you want what I want. My wife is beautiful, and you want to see her naked tonight. We can't wait any longer. If we don't act now, the enemy may get the idea and start making similar offers with their own wives. We must be first, Gyges!

GYGES (*snapping to attention*) Mr. High Commissioner, there is nothing I would not do for my country!

CANDAULES Don't worry, Gyges, there's no danger. I've gone over the plan night after night, as I've lain awake in my bed. My wife won't even know that you've seen her. It will be between the two of us.

You know, Gyges, how you always stand guard outside my bedroom door to protect me—while I sleep—against attacks by terrorists?

GYGES Yes, Mr. Commissioner, I'm always there. I sit on a chair right out-side your bedroom door.

CANDAULES That's all right, Gyges, you're allowed to sit down while you stand guard. Now, tonight, Gyges, after you've driven us back from the Ambassador's dinner party . . .

GYGES Yes, sir?

CANDAULES Tonight, Gyges, tonight instead of sitting outside my door, sit outside the door to my wife's room! (CANDAULES *reaches in his pocket and produces a whistle.*) Gyges, do you see this whistle?

GYGES Yes, sir!

CANDAULES When my beautiful wife has taken off her clothes, I'll blow the whistle—then you come in! Do you understand, Gyges: when I blow the whistle!

(CANDAULES *puts the whistle in his mouth and blows it with vigor.*

The sound he produces is insinuating, lilting, even goatish. As he blows the whistle, CANDAULES *looks at* GYGES *rapturously, and* GYGES' *look of astonishment gradually turns into a broad grin of recognition. At this moment* NYSSIA *opens the door and enters the room. She has heard nothing, but she may have been secretly and magically drawn by the whistle.*)

NYSSIA (*She appears to be in her early forties, but is still quite beautiful. She is wearing a gold brocaded evening gown, tight and low-cut. It is slit up the front to her calves and discloses her gold slippers and flesh-colored mesh stockings. Over her shoulders she has a golden-brown sable jacket. Her dyed golden-brown hair is piled high on her head, and she wears matching yellow-diamond neck-lace, earrings, bracelet, and ring. She has on beige gloves with buttons that come up above her elbows, and she carries a small, gold handbag. Her face, lips, eyes, eyebrows are elegantly made up like a model's so that she seems to wear a beautiful inexpressive mask.*)

      Aren't you ready to go yet, Candaules? It takes you longer to get dressed than it does me. You know the ambassador can't stand lack of punctuality.

She never looks at GYGES, *as though he weren't there.*

CANDAULES (*He puts his hand around her waist.*) My lovely Nyssia! Isn't she lovely, Gyges?

GYGES Yes, sir, lovely.

CANDAULES Doesn't she dress beautifully?

GYGES Yes, sir, beautifully.

CANDAULES (*He strokes her sable coat.*) Nyssia, you're gorgeous, but you can't wear that coat, my love. (*He shakes his head disapprovingly.*)

NYSSIA What do you mean, I can't wear my sable coat? What's the matter with it? Don't you like it?

CANDAULES It isn't a question of liking it or not. It's simply that given present conditions neither of us can go through the streets looking the way we do now.

NYSSIA (*She looks at herself in the large mirror.*) What's the matter with the way we look? I like the way I look.

CANDAULES My dear lady, do you happen to realize that there's a war going on here?

NYSSIA Oh, I'm sick and tired of hearing about your war! What do you want me to do, rip off all my clothes and go around stark naked just because there's a war?

CANDAULES (*He sneaks a look at* GYGES.) Nyssia, my dear, try to understand. There's a tense atmosphere in the capital. There have already been bombings and rioting again this week. We're on the brink of another crisis. It's not safe to be seen wearing such expensive clothes. Remember, they threw mud on the Ambassador's wife only last month.

NYSSIA It wasn't mud. It was shit they put on the rice fields, and you know it!

CANDAULES Nyssia! You know I don't like you to talk that way. It's not pleasant.

(CANDAULES *speaks as though giving a report or proposing a program.*)

In the light of the strained situation existing in the capital, I suggest that you wear the following over your own clothes: one, an old straw hat; two, a dirty old coat; and three, an old pair of sandals.

NYSSIA What's the point of owning nice clothes, if no one can ever see them?

CANDAULES Please, Nyssia. Don't argue. Gyges, get the rags.

GYGES Yes, Mr. Commissioner.

CANDAULES You know, Gyges, your old coat, your old hat, your old shoes —all your old clothes. They were all you had when we first found you.

GYGES Yes, sir.

CANDAULES Now look at the nice uniforms you have!

GYGES Yes, sir.

CANDAULES We're going to wear some of your old clothes. We'll be inconspicuous that way—we'll seem to be just ordinary people. Don't forget the brown coat with the torn sleeve and the holes in the back. I particularly like that coat. It fits me very well; it's very comfortable.

GYGES Yes, sir. I'll go get the rags now. (GYGES *bows and goes out of the room.*)

CANDAULES Now try to be reasonable, Nyssia. I don't like sneaking around in disguise. I don't like this any better than you do. Here, sit down beside me. (CANDAULES *and* NYSSIA *sit down in the two seats of the shoe shine stand, side by side.*)

Isn't Gyges wonderful? He makes you love all these people, he's so friendly. He makes you feel that the war is all right after all, that it really is worth fighting and spending all that money. If we can only make people like him see that we're fighting the war for them; if we can only make a better future for him and his people. Well, what do you think of Gyges, Nyssia? Do you like him as much as I do?

NYSSIA   He doesn't seem to eat a great deal—some of them eat so much. It's hardly worth keeping servants if all they do is eat.

CANDAULES   I'll never forget when we first saw him! That photograph in *Vacation Magazine* we just happened to see, showing him as a homeless, starving war orphan. He was looking up at us with those big, imploring eyes. I've still got that picture here in my wallet. (*He gets it out.*) Here, remember! I cut it out and kept it. So we sent ten dollars, and they sent him food and clothing. Our name was on the box.

NYSSIA   You were working at the Institute for Lydian Studies as a government research specialist then. I hated that.

CANDAULES   I was becoming an expert on the economy of the country, on the production and distribution of rice. And there he was looking at me in that picture! It seemed only right that we send him rice!

NYSSIA   We didn't have so much ourselves.

CANDAULES   We adopted him, as it were—we kept sending him money for his education. He's our orphan, we adopted him. I remember the first letters we got from him, thanking us. His handwriting was such a scrawl.

NYSSIA   And he made so many mistakes in grammar and spelling!

CANDAULES   But he learned so fast. I think he must have come from the aristocracy. But we'll never know for sure. All his family had been killed. His father and mother and all his twelve brothers and sisters. His whole village had been burned down, and they found him alone, crying in the burning rubble.

NYSSIA   They don't value human life the way we do.

CANDAULES   Then when I was assigned here, we looked him up right away, to see what he was doing.

NYSSIA   Driving a garbage truck! After all the money we'd poured into his education!

CANDAULES   I got him the job as my chauffeur and bodyguard and valet.

NYSSIA   It was a big step up for him.

CANDAULES   He has proved that he was worthy of my faith in him.

NYSSIA   You treat him like a friend.

CANDAULES   He practically is a friend. He's almost like one of the family. I take out some of his pay every month for his retirement.

NYSSIA   But what makes you think you can trust him? If there's an uprising, what makes you think he'll be so true to you? You can't trust any of them. I'm afraid of being raped every time I set foot out-of-doors. They hate me—they're jealous of my clothes, of my house, of my looks, of my body. And then, they're so short. They

don't even have hair on their chests. Just look at us! We don't dare
set foot in the streets, as we really are! And we have to have an
armed guard around the house to protect us. I know Gyges has
got that big gun; I can see it under his coat. But he's one of them.
Don't forget that. How do you know he wouldn't turn against you
if he had a chance? If there's a rebellion, you just watch. He'll
turn that gun on us. I'm afraid of him, he's so little. And the way
he looks at me all the time. His eyes are strange. He's always
staring at my breasts.

CANDAULES But he's only that tall, Nyssia! He can't help it. I can trust
Gyges. Gyges will always be true to us, no matter what happens.
After all, he's our orphan.

NYSSIA You're awfully interested in Gyges. Without that big gun, he's
just like millions of others of these people!

CANDAULES Look at it this way, Nyssia. I've been sitting behind Gyges,
looking at the back of his head for 8,783 miles, as of four o'clock
this afternoon. That's a lot of miles. It's made me think! I've always
wondered what is going on inside that head of his. I've asked myself: what does Gyges think of me? I've devoted my life to the study
of his country. I'm a career Lydia man. But I discovered that I
didn't know the people or what they thought. I didn't know what
one simple, ordinary man thinks. I didn't even know what my
chauffeur thinks. I want to know how the people here really feel
about us. My whole understanding of this country depends on one
man. Gyges is that man. I've gained his trust, I want him to like me,
to understand what I'm trying to do for them and why I'm here.
I want to make them happy. I want to make Gyges happy. Do you
know what he really thinks of us?

NYSSIA He hates us; he's jealous of everything that we have and that he
doesn't.

CANDAULES That shows how little you know him, Nyssia. Now I've been
watching him, asking myself what he's thinking.

NYSSIA And what is he thinking?

CANDAULES He's thinking how he can be like me! He wants to be me!
He wishes he had skin the color of my skin; he wishes he were in
my skin. He wishes he could have a wife like you! It's that simple.
And I want to help him, to share with him. I want to be his friend.
I haven't had a real friend like Gyges, since I was a boy.

NYSSIA You never were a boy.

CANDAULES Yes, I was. I must have been.

NYSSIA You've always been an official; an official boy, an official son, an
official husband. Our marriage has always been official.

CANDAULES Marriage is official. That's the whole point of it. Now with Gyges, I feel young again. There's something to look forward to each day. I haven't really looked forward to anything for years. I want to help him. I want to show him!

NYSSIA Show him what?

GYGES (*He returns carrying a large bundle of old clothes.*) Here are the old clothes, Mr. High Commissioner.

(*Both* CANDAULES *and* NYSSIA *rise from their shoeshine chairs, as though they were thrones.*)

CANDAULES Thanks, Gyges, thanks. (CANDAULES *picks out his favorite coat.*) Here's the coat I like. Help me on with it, Gyges. (GYGES *helps him into the brown coat with the torn sleeve and holes in the back.*)

It's so comfortable!

(*He rummages in the pile of old clothes.*)

Here's a good one for you, Nyssia. (*He holds up a ragged coat.*) It's not half bad! It's really not bad looking. (*He gives it to* GYGES.) Here Gyges, help her on with this coat.

(GYGES *tries to help* NYSSIA *into the old coat. She pulls and twists.*)

NYSSIA Be careful, can't you? You'll wrinkle my dress. You're crushing my bodice! Watch what you're doing! You've disarranged my décolletage! You're so clumsy with your hands! He keeps touching me!

GYGES (*bowing*) I apologize, Lady. I did not mean to, Lady.

NYSSIA Look what he's done to my dress with those filthy old rags!

(*She looks at herself in the mirror and adjusts her breasts in her gown so that they are prominently displayed.*)

CANDAULES Nyssia! Really! You're talking about Gyges' clothes! Try to be a little more polite!

NYSSIA I'm sick and tired of them! His clothes smell! I hate all those smelly old rags! I won't wear them!

CANDAULES Please, Nyssia, these are Gyges' clothes. (*to* GYGES, *as though he were thanking a child*) Gyges, I like my coat very much. It's comfortable. Thank you, Gyges.

NYSSIA Well, I hate it, do you hear, hate it! I'm not going to lie and be a hypocrite all the time. When am I going to be able to wear my nice clothes again?

CANDAULES But you are wearing them.

NYSSIA I mean, wear them so that every one can see them, and not have to put filthy rags over them.

CANDAULES When the war's over, my dear, when the war's over! Soon! In five or ten years! (CANDAULES *caresses her cheek.*)

NYSSIA I'm sick and tired of your war! I hate it! It's ruining my life.

What's the point of being young and beautiful if you can't show others!

CANDAULES   No more arguments, my love! Put on this hat. (*He hands her a lopsided, dilapidated straw hat.*)

NYSSIA   It will ruin my hair!

CANDAULES   It'll fit right over your hair. (*She puts on the hat like a petulant child.*) Now, off with those gold shoes and put them in this paper bag, and put on these straw sandals. (*He gives her a paper bag and a pair of huge floppy straw sandals.*)

NYSSIA   I won't, I won't!

CANDAULES   Yes, you will. (*She angrily takes off her gold shoes, puts them in the paper bag, and shoves her feet into the huge floppy straw sandals.*)

Now look, I'm putting on my coolie hat. (CANDAULES *puts on his coolie hat.*)

Now Gyges, on with your coat. (GYGES *puts on his chauffeur's jacket.*) On with your hat, Gyges. (GYGES *puts on his chauffeur's hat.* CANDAULES *pulls out his gigantic pocket watch.*) It is now exactly 7:37. We must be at the Ambassador's at 8:15. We've no time to lose. The Ambassador demands punctuality. Let us go. Nyssia, Gyges. Straight ahead!

(CANDAULES *directs* NYSSIA *to lead the way; he follows, taking the whistle out of his pocket and putting it in his mouth and blowing it softly and suggestively, like a satyr's flute.* GYGES *follows. As they all march out, the wooden clappers are beaten rapidly against the board, as at the end of the first scene.*)

CURTAIN

Scene Three

Later that night in NYSSIA's *dressing room. There is a large dressing table with an attached mirror. Bottles of perfumes, jars, lotions, powder boxes, lipsticks, creams, and ointments cover the table. There are several photographs in gold frames and snapshots stuck around the edge of the mirror. There are two small dressing table chairs.*

CANDAULES *and* NYSSIA *have just returned from the Ambassador's and are still wearing their evening clothes, but they have dis-*

carded GYGES' *rags. Both stand, as though discussing a play at
intermission.*

CANDAULES   That was one of the most enjoyable evenings we've ever
spent at the Ambassador's! I enjoyed myself immensely.

NYSSIA   His wife serves such good native dishes.

CANDAULES   The rice was wonderful. I had three helpings.

NYSSIA   She knows how to make her cooks do what she tells them. I wish
we did.

CANDAULES   And then the view is wonderful.

NYSSIA   The location is ideal.

CANDAULES   The house high up on the hill overlooking the valley and the
river with the whole plain stretching out beneath you.

NYSSIA   We certainly got a magnificent view from the dining room.

CANDAULES   What a marvelous outlook through that big window!

NYSSIA   We could see the whole battle.

CANDAULES   You didn't even have to get up from the table.

NYSSIA   How was your seat? Could you see well?

CANDAULES   Perfectly! I had the best seat in the house! It was spectacular.
The whole sky was lighted up.

NYSSIA   It was hard to tell which side was which. I was confused.

CANDAULES   The idea of giving the guests binoculars was a good one. And,
of course, if you wanted to get up from your seat, you could look
through the Ambassador's high power telescope.

NYSSIA   I didn't want to get up and spoil the dinner. After all, it was a
dinner party, not really a battle-watching party. I wish we had a
view like that!

CANDAULES   You know we can't afford it. Not on my salary.

NYSSIA   Well, it's embarrassing! I don't like entertaining any more. All the
other diplomats' wives have battle-watching. People expect you to
have it. If you don't, they grow restless after dinner. Just talking
about the war isn't enough. It leads to unpleasant arguments about
the number of people killed. People don't want to just talk about
the war, they want to see it.

CANDAULES   Unfortunately there's been a lot of running away recently.

NYSSIA   After some of those supposedly big battles, it turns out that only
three or four people have been killed. Only three or four people
killed, and they call that a big battle!
(NYSSIA *sets down her fur coat and takes off her gloves.*) I'm
going to get undressed, Candaules. I'm tired and I'm going to get
ready for bed.

CANDAULES (*He fumbles in his pocket for the whistle which he looks at on the sly to make sure he has it.*) That's a splendid idea!

NYSSIA Well, aren't you going?

CANDAULES Mayn't I stay and talk a moment while you're getting ready for bed? We can talk about the war.

NYSSIA (*detached, in a flat voice*) Certainly, if you wish, you may stay your usual fifteen minutes—your usual time.

CANDAULES (*He pulls out his huge pocket watch.*) Fifteen minutes—it's now almost 1:17. That gives me until 1:32.

NYSSIA Why don't you sit down? (*She indicates the other gold chair. She is still standing.*)

CANDAULES May I? (*He sits down and looks at* NYSSIA *as though he were a spectator at a play, in a very special seat in the first row.*) It's such a nice chair!

NYSSIA If you're going to stay, why don't you take off your tail-coat? You'll be more comfortable that way.

CANDAULES No thank you. I wouldn't feel quite right. I couldn't be more comfortable than I am now.

NYSSIA You always were modest.

CANDAULES It's just that I'm more at ease fully dressed. I sometimes wish that it were possible for me to be fully dressed all the time. I'd like to go to bed fully-dressed.

NYSSIA I'm going to get out of my evening gown. I don't want to soil it. It soils so easily I'm afraid to perspire in it. (*She takes off her jewelry: the earrings, necklace, bracelet, and ring—and puts them in a special box on the dressing table.*) Here, help me undo the hooks. It's hard to get out of.

CANDAULES (*He goes up to her and undoes the hooks.*) I've undone the hooks. What's next?

NYSSIA Now it goes up over my head. (*She puts her hands up and* CANDAULES *starts to pull the gown over her head. When it covers her face and head, he stops and holds it frozen there. With the other hand, he gets the whistle out of his pocket and blows it gently. It makes chirping, cooing bird noises. The door opens and* GYGES *looks in.* CANDAULES *gestures to him not to come in yet, but to be ready.* GYGES *looks mysterious and closes the door again. Then* CANDAULES *continues to pull the gown over* NYSSIA's *head. She acts as though there had been no immobile pause.* NYSSIA *is wearing a hand-made French chemise and bra. She hands the gown to* CANDAULES.) Here, please hang my gown up.

CANDAULES (*He holds the gown expectantly, talking with the whistle still in his mouth. It sputters slightly as he talks.*) Hang the gown up?

NYSSIA   Yes, hang it up and get me my dressing gown.

CANDAULES   Your dressing gown? Did I hear you correctly?

NYSSIA   Yes, my dressing gown. I'm going to take my make-up off and get ready for bed. I always wear my dressing gown while I take my make-up off.

CANDAULES   That's irresponsible! Don't do it! Take all your clothes off right now!

NYSSIA   What would I want to do that for? I intend to sit down at my dressing table and take my make-up off. Can't you understand that? Get me my dressing gown and don't just stand there!

CANDAULES   (*He sinks down on his little stool in shock and astonishment.*) You're not going to undress all the way! I can't believe it!

NYSSIA   Be careful, you'll wrinkle my dress! What's got into you? Did you drink too much champagne tonight? Why in the world would I parade around naked here in front of you? After all, we haven't had sexual intercourse for seventeen years.

CANDAULES   Has it been that long! It seems more like eight years. How did it happen? Why did it happen that way?

NYSSIA   Oh, I don't remember any more.

CANDAULES   I don't either. It just slipped my mind. I knew there was something I'd forgotten. I've been so busy with my work. And you've been busy . . . shopping, with your fashion shows, your trips to the dressmaker and all of that. Oh, I'm glad you reminded me! I must have completely forgotten. I'm at fault, I'll admit it. But Nyssia, it's not too late, is it? I want our relationship to be a meaningful one. I want our relationship to be rich and rewarding. Undress. Take your clothes off, right now. I beg you. We'll start over again. (*He starts to kneel.*)

NYSSIA   You're dragging my brocaded gown on the floor! Can't you see you're getting it dirty!

CANDAULES   (*He gets up.*)   Don't worry, Nyssia. We're safe here. We're alone. Gyges is sitting outside the door. (CANDAULES *goes to the door and opens it.* GYGES *looks in, and* CANDAULES *makes a gesture indicating that the time has not yet come.*) He's got his hand on his gun. We're safe. Take all your clothes off! Undress! Let's start to build a meaningful relationship!

NYSSIA   No, I'm tired. Give me my old red bathrobe.

CANDAULES   (*He goes to the closet and hangs up the brocaded evening gown. Then he brings out an old red bathrobe, which he brings over to* NYSSIA.)   Try to be reasonable, Nyssia. You're making a terrible mistake. Don't put that red bathrobe on.

NYSSIA   (*She grabs the bathrobe out of his hand and puts it on.*)   Of course, I'll put it on. (*She sits down at the dressing table and starts to take off her make-up. For the rest of the scene, she applies all kinds of creams, lotions, eye preparations, and totally removes her present face in a series of stages and transformations. When she turns around at various intervals, she appears as a different person or several different people. She gradually looks more natural, older, and for the first time, human. Her face undergoes a series of metamorphoses.*)

CANDAULES (*He sits down again on his little stool and clasps his knees with his hands and rocks gently.*)   Perhaps you're right, Nyssia; something has gone out of our marriage. It's possible that with the passing of the years we've grown a little apart. God knows, I've worked hard to make our marriage a challenging and rewarding experience. (*He smiles sweetly as he speaks.*) Oh, we've had our difficulties, our moments of trial. But I think that I can truthfully say that our marriage has brought both my wife and me great happiness.

NYSSIA   But I am your wife.

CANDAULES   Yes, of course, that's true. That's important.

NYSSIA   And you didn't ever make me happy. (*As she says that, she looks at him. The make-up is now off one half of her face, leaving her with two different faces.*)

CANDAULES   Why didn't I? Why haven't you been happy? Why haven't I made you happy? I've spent my whole life trying to make you happy—you and the people in this country. If I could only make all of you happy! (*He gets to his feet and waves his arms in an expansive gesture of good will.*) There's no other way, but absolute nakedness!

NYSSIA   I remember, you wanted to photograph me naked on our wedding night! You brought your camera and all that photography equipment—your enlarger and your developer.

CANDAULES   If you'd only let me! I wish I had those photographs now!

NYSSIA   What's so interesting about seeing me naked? I don't even look at myself naked any more. I like my clothes.

CANDAULES   It could be the beginning of a new life, a new understanding. Our marriage could be so rewarding. We could have such a meaningful relationship.

NYSSIA   You have your mistresses, don't you?

CANDAULES   That's preposterous! Do I look like a man who has mistresses? And risk ruining my career? If some one even claimed that I had a mistress, it could finish my career. It could set back the program of Economic Aid for years! There are people here—and back home—

who would like nothing better than to catch me in a scandal. There are groups intriguing here—right now! I have chosen sexual frustration rather than risk my career. I consider it my duty to be frustrated. I'm glad I'm frustrated. It furthers the program of Economic Assistance. It furthers the war effort. And furthermore, there's nothing wrong with being sexually frustrated! Many great men have been sexually frustrated.

NYSSIA   What about a native girl? Not even once?

CANDAULES   A native girl! That would be the worst of all! I don't know how you can suggest such a thing. If it were discovered that I'd been involved with a native girl, even once, even quickly, I'd be dragged down into the mud. I've weighed the consequences. Momentary pleasure is simply not worth it. Our whole influence here would be discredited, the friendly government might be toppled, then all our military and economic aid would be stopped —think of it, it's frightening! The war would end! There'd be a truce with the enemy! I've not thought of myself, but of the war. I've put the war before my personal pleasure. I'm delighted to be frustrated for the sake of the war!

NYSSIA   (*She looks around at* CANDAULES. *More of her make-up is off, and she is beginning to look not only older and more human, but slightly demented.*)   I saw the prisoners going by again today. I watched the trucks go by for an hour. Their hands were tied behind their backs. Some of them were quite young and handsome. There was one—I swear, he didn't look over fifteen! As they went by, he winked at me obscenely—like this. (*She winks obscenely at* CANDAULES.) He looked at me obscenely and winked. (*She winks again.*)

CANDAULES   Don't do that, Nyssia. It's not ladylike. You're imagining things, anyhow. Prisoners don't wink. They don't feel like winking.

NYSSIA   Why? What happens to the prisoners?

CANDAULES   Most of them go directly into the government army.

NYSSIA   And what about the government soldiers who are taken prisoner by the enemy?

CANDAULES   Most of them go directly into the enemy army.

NYSSIA   It's all right then?

CANDAULES   What do you mean?

NYSSIA   Nothing's essentially changed—they're still fighting each other.

CANDAULES   That's right.

NYSSIA   What about killing?

CANDAULES   Of course, there's some killing—it's a war! That's the whole point.

NYSSIA   But do our military advisors help the government forces do the killing?

CANDAULES   No, our people don't do any of the actual killing.

NYSSIA   What do we do?

CANDAULES   We watch.

NYSSIA   What do we watch?

CANDAULES   We watch them killing.

NYSSIA   Oh, we watch them killing one another.

CANDAULES   Yes, we're here simply as observers. When we're asked, we can give advice.

NYSSIA   About what?

CANDAULES   About how to do the killing.

NYSSIA   Why are they killing one another? I forget.

CANDAULES   It's a civil war.

NYSSIA   Oh, I see! But it still isn't very nice to watch, is it? Shouldn't we turn our heads away?

CANDAULES   Oh, we try not to look—but you see, first we train them to kill one another, and then we have to watch to see how well they do it.

NYSSIA   Is that pleasant?

CANDAULES   Nobody said it was pleasant.

NYSSIA   Then it's not pleasant.

CANDAULES   It's not pleasant for me. I've got feelings, I'm sensitive. After all, I love this country and its people. I've spent years studying its economy. I know all about its soil. I wrote a book—*The Rice Economy of Lydia* which has become the standard work in the field. I want to feed people, not kill them or see them killed. You know I have a gentle disposition. I abhor violence. In all the years we've been married, I've never once raised my voice. I never struck you, or the children, or even the dog. I wouldn't be here now, if I didn't think my work would make life better for the people here. I want to make them happy. I want universal happiness! There are just certain unpleasant things you have to reconcile yourself to. For the sake of a greater good.

NYSSIA   What about torturing?

CANDAULES   What about torturing?

NYSSIA   Is there torturing?

CANDAULES   Perhaps a little. There has to be some.

NYSSIA   Do we teach them how to torture? Do we train them in torturing?

CANDAULES   We don't need to. Remember, their civilization is even older than ours. They don't need any instructions about torturing.

NYSSIA   And what kinds of tortures are there? (*She asks her questions in a very matter-of-fact way.*)

CANDAULES Well, I don't really know . . .

NYSSIA You know. Just tell me what kinds of tortures there are.

CANDAULES It embarrasses me to say. There's something very intimate about torture. It's like matters of personal hygiene. I find it difficult to talk about, especially to one's wife.

NYSSIA Tell me one torture. Please! Just one! (*As a child begs for one more story before going to bed.*)

CANDAULES I've heard that they apply electric charges on the breasts.

NYSSIA Do we do that?

CANDAULES No, we just supply the current. We generate the current with our generators. But the government forces actually apply the wires.

NYSSIA What's it like? I wonder what it feels like?

CANDAULES Really, Nyssia! I don't think that you're showing good taste. It doesn't make sense to try to put yourself in someone else's place.

NYSSIA Tell me what it's like.

CANDAULES Well, they say, it's like the shock you get if you accidentally put your finger in a light socket or touch bare electrical wires— except it's more prolonged.

NYSSIA And breasts are very sensitive.

CANDAULES They say they even twitch a little.

NYSSIA How do you know? Have you watched? Have you watched them torturing?

CANDAULES Heavens no! God forbid! We always turn the other way. Torturing is even more personal than killing. I want to be as considerate and discreet and quiet as possible. After all, I've got humanitarian feelings. I can't bear to think of any one being hurt, not even animals. I don't like the thought of killing and torturing any better than any one else does. No one likes it.

NYSSIA Do you try to stop them? Do we try to stop them?

CANDAULES I wish we could. Don't think I condone this. It made me sick for two days the first time I was in the field and heard the moans. But there are powerful arguments for torturing. Both sides torture. Even if the government forces stopped, the enemy would continue. And then the government says they have to get the information. They say hundreds would be killed instead of just one being tortured. They say that torture is actually more humane than letting hundreds be ambushed and murdered.

NYSSIA Do they do that to women?

CANDAULES Not often. It's expensive. They can't afford to torture indiscriminately. It costs too much. Only spies and students.

NYSSIA (*She looks around with a strange, thoughtful look.*) I can imagine what it would be like. I can imagine it happening to me. And are there any other things?

CANDAULES Yes, there are other things. But I'd rather not talk about them just before going to bed.

NYSSIA I can imagine what they'd all be like. I can imagine them all happening to me.

CANDAULES Don't be morbid, Nyssia. Try to get a grip on yourself. There are some things in life that you have to get used to. Like beggars and cripples and all the sick people in hospitals all over the world. It's not pleasant either.

    In the same way, you have to reconcile yourself to people killing one another and torturing one another. People have been killing one another for centuries; it's been going on ever since the world began. And there's always been torturing. I'd never torture any one myself, but there's always been torturing. It has to be. But it's morbid to dwell on it; a healthy person can't afford to think that way. All a healthy person can do is to try to lead his own life as decently as he can, and try to help others to be happy. I'm doing the best I can. I have nothing to reproach myself for. I get up at six o'clock. I work twelve to fourteen hours a day trying to improve the rice economy of this country. More people are getting more to eat because of my efforts. That gives me peace of mind.

NYSSIA What if they tortured you? How would you feel about that? Would that change your views?

CANDAULES That question is absolutely inadmissible. I don't permit myself that kind of thinking. A healthy mind doesn't think that way. I'm afraid you're showing signs of instability, Nyssia. Get a grip on yourself. Snap out of it! Don't give in to such morbid thoughts. Think of our children instead. Think of them back home, safely in their houses, sleeping securely with their own children asleep there too.

NYSSIA I'm trying to think of them, but I can't seem to visualize them. I can't remember what they look like.

CANDAULES Well, look, there's their picture on your dressing table right in front of you!

(CANDAULES *picks up a large framed photograph from the dressing table.*) What's this? This isn't the children's picture! It's a picture of a burned native child being carried out of a burning village by his father!

NYSSIA Yes, there are burns all over his body.

CANDAULES What's going on here? What have you done with all the family pictures? (*He picks up another picture in a frame.*) Look, that isn't me! Instead of my picture, there's a horrible picture of a prisoner hanging from a wall by his hands!

NYSSIA (*She hands him another framed picture.*)   Here's another picture
of a burning village . . .

CANDAULES (*looking at the picture in astonishment*)   You used to have
my mother's picture in that frame, Nyssia! What's wrong with you?
And look, what are all these pictures around your mirror, where
you used to keep the snapshots of our nephews and nieces? (*He
takes down a snapshot from around the mirror.*) Look at that! A
prisoner with his hands tied dragged along on a rope through a
rice field!

NYSSIA He isn't more than twelve years old, is he?

CANDAULES But what's he to you? Why should you collect these hideous
pictures?

NYSSIA I cut them out of newspapers and magazines. Then I put them
in my picture frames and around my mirror. I collect them.

CANDAULES But why? Why? Nyssia, what have you done with the
pictures of me and the children and of my mother and all our
relatives? Tell me, what have you done with them?

NYSSIA I forget. I think I threw them away. I tore them up and burned
them in my big ashtray.

CANDAULES What's wrong with you, Nyssia? Don't look at me that way!
What are you doing this for? Don't you feel well?

NYSSIA It gives me something to do. You have Gyges; I have my pictures.
Both bring us closer . . . to the people. I have my pictures. I collect
them. Pictures of burning villages, of prisoners, of torturings, whenever I can find them. They're hard to find. (*She smiles vacantly.*)
And especially of children, burned children. I cut them out and put
them up here on my dressing table where I can look at them
whenever I feel like it. I like collecting.

CANDAULES You must be joking! People collect matchbook covers, not
pictures of tortures! You're out of your mind! What do you think
about these pictures of burning villages?

NYSSIA I don't think anything. It has to be.

CANDAULES Doesn't it upset you?

NYSSIA No. I don't believe them. I don't believe they're true. People
don't really do such things to one another. Nothing like that really
happens. It's only a joke. People don't really set one another on fire
or put electric wires on people's breasts. It's not credible. They
don't really burn one another or torture one another. It's not
possible. From childhood we're taught not to hurt one another, not
to burn one another. We're taught not to! It's only a joke. (*She
laughs insanely, not a stage laugh, but a deranged laugh.*)
(*She lets down her hair which falls around her shoulders.*) I'm

naked now. Look at me, Candaules. Look at my face. I'm naked now. (*She takes the shade off the small lamp on her dressing table and holds the bright bulb under her face. She looks mad. Then she unscrews the bulb from the lamp and removes it. The stage is partly darkened.*)

CANDAULE (*in fear*)   What are you doing? Why did you take the light bulb out of the lamp?

NYSSIA (*She pulls down her bra and holds the lamp socket over one breast which she squeezes into it.*)   I'm sticking my breast into the light socket. I'm sticking my breast into the light socket! (*She starts to scream and moan.*)

CANDAULES (*He reaches in his pocket and gets out the whistle which he blows loudly.*)   Gyges! Gyges! Come quickly! (*As* CANDAULES *continues to blow the whistle,* GYGES *comes in through the door. He is covered by the black bag of the invisible ring; since it comes down over his feet, he seems to glide along the floor. The light from the open door illuminates the moving black shape, while the rest of the stage remains in semi-darkness. The stage-manager beats the wooden clappers on the board at the side of the stage.* GYGES *floats slowly towards* NYSSIA *who continues to moan and hold the lamp on her breast, as* CANDAULES *blows his whistle. It makes shrill, insistent sounds—almost a call for help or for attention.*)

CURTAIN

Scene Four

The following day, in the indoor garden on the first floor where NYSSIA *is finishing her breakfast. She is wearing an oriental house-coat as a negligée. It is made of lemon-yellow brocade, lined with café-au-lait silk; it has a high collar and is in the style of a straight column, unfitted and fastened with frogs all the way down the front. It is split up to the calf on either side.* NYSSIA *wears gold sandals on her feet, and her hair is in a chignon on top of her head, fixed with two tortoise shell pins ornamented with gold. Her eyes are made up to have a slightly slanting oriental look. On the table before her are the remains of her breakfast. Various magazines and newspapers are piled in front of her. From time to time she puts on chic*

*slanted glasses and looks through the papers; occasionally she cuts
out something for her clippings with a pair of gold sewing scissors.
She cuts very carefully. She drinks coffee now and then as she
continues to study her paper.*

GYGES *stands a little behind the table, like an attentive but
not too obtrusive waiter. He wears a waiter's coat, instead of his
chauffeur's jacket. He looks off into space, and at the same time
notices when* NYSSIA *is ready for more coffee.*

Although outwardly GYGES *remains most respectful towards*
NYSSIA *throughout the following dialogue between the two, he
looks at her with contempt, as though she were merely a thing
that he had used with distaste and quickly discarded.* NYSSIA *continues to dominate with words, but she cringes in actual fact, as*
GYGES *holds up the various silver coffee implements before her face
in a manner that is both sinister and threatening in its cold pre-
cision and indifference.* NYSSIA *seems hypnotized by his hidden
authority.*

GYGES (*approaching the table and holding up the silver coffee container*)
More coffee, Lady?

NYSSIA (*Without looking up, she nods yes and* GYGES *pours the coffee. As
he is finishing pouring, she looks at him.*)   Gyges, tell me again
how much you used to hate me.

GYGES   Cream, Lady?

NYSSIA (*She nods yes, and he pours the cream into her coffee.*)   Tell me
all the thoughts you used to have about me.

GYGES   Sugar, Lady? (*He opens the sugar container, and holds the tongs
as though they were pincers used for torturing.*)

NYSSIA (*She makes a negative gesture, and* GYGES *closes the sugar container and sets down the tongs.*)   Gyges, tell me how much you
hated me!

GYGES (*He stands again a little behind the table, and speaks without
looking directly at* NYSSIA, *as a waiter does when he talks with
those he is serving.*)   I thought awful thoughts about you, Lady.
I imagined bad things about you, Lady. (*GYGES' accent has changed
and is less pronounced now.*)

NYSSIA   What awful things? What kinds of awful things? Tell me!

GYGES   I imagined degrading things—things humiliating for you, Lady.

NYSSIA   What things?

GYGES   I imagined that you were married to me; that we lived together
in my native village in a thatched hut. There was no running water,
no electric lights. It was very degrading for you, Lady.

NYSSIA   Is that all?

GYGES   No, Lady, there is worse. You had to wait on me and cook my dinner on a little charcoal stove and wash my dishes in a wooden bucket. You had to sweep the floor with a grass broom. You had to sew for me and mend my old clothes and put patches on the holes in my old coat.

NYSSIA   And what about Candaules? What did you imagine about him?

GYGES   He had to draw water from the well and carry it across his shoulders in buckets on a yoke.

NYSSIA   Yes, and what else?

GYGES   He had to feed the pigs and weed all day in the hot sun and work in the rice field all day long in the hot sun.

NYSSIA   And what else? Didn't you imagine anything else?

GYGES   No, Lady, that is all.

NYSSIA   Tell me, didn't you ever want to torture us?
(GYGES *shakes his head negatively.*)
     Didn't you ever want to torture me? Not even once? Not even a little?
(GYGES *says nothing and looks straight ahead in silence.*)
     You're my master now. You can do anything to me you want. I've dressed like this for you, to be like one of your women. You can do anything you like with me.
After a moment's silence, CANDAULES *comes in. He is dressed officially, as in the first scene, except without a hat.*

CANDAULES   Good morning, Nyssia, my dear. (*He takes out his huge pocket watch and looks at it.*) Having breakfast at 12:07? You must have slept well.
(*As he passes by* NYSSIA, *she puts her foot out and causes* CANDAULES *to trip and fall to the floor. At the same time she is peeling and eating an orange.* CANDAULES *falls and rolls in pain on his side on the floor.* NYSSIA *looks at him casually, and continues peeling and eating her orange.* GYGES *stands behind* NYSSIA's *table correctly, without any expression on his face.*)

CANDAULES   Oh, I've hurt my back! You should be more careful, Nyssia. You know my back is bad. I fell over your foot. (CANDAULES *even when complaining does not raise his voice, but speaks in a reasonable tone.*)

NYSSIA   You didn't fall. I tripped you.

CANDAULES   You tripped me! That doesn't make any sense at all, Nyssia. Why would you want to trip me?

NYSSIA   I wanted to see you fall.

CANDAULES   You wanted to see me fall! That isn't possible!

NYSSIA   I wanted to see you fall. I've always wanted to see you fall.

CANDAULES   Nyssia, this is no time for joking. Gyges and I must be at the Council meeting by one o'clock. (*He tries to get up, but cannot.*) Oh, my back is hurt. You know my back is weak. I can't get up. Help me get up, please.

NYSSIA   No.

CANDAULES   Your joking is in very poor taste, Nyssia. Gyges, help me. Help me up.

GYGES   Yes, Mr. High Commissioner. (GYGES *goes to* CANDAULES *and starts to help him up.* GYGES *gets* CANDAULES *about halfway up;* CANDAULES *has his arm around* GYGES' *neck.*)

CANDAULES   Thanks, Gyges. There, that's better. Easy, easy. Oh, my back! It still hurts. That's it, Gyges. Gently, gently, Gyges.

NYSSIA   Let him go, Gyges. Drop him, Gyges.

(GYGES *hesitates a moment, and then drops* CANDAULES *suddenly.* GYGES *resumes his previous position behind the table.*)

CANDAULES   (*in pain*)   Oh, my back! Gyges, that's not like you! You're usually so thoughtful! Nyssia, that's your fault; you've confused him.

Gyges! We've got to be at the Council meeting. Don't you remember? Today there'll be the Delegation from the locomotive engineers.

NYSSIA   Gyges, clear the table.

(GYGES *picks up her breakfast plate, which contains orange peels, egg shells, and crusts of toast.*) Stop. (GYGES *stops just over* CANDAULES' *body.*) Dump the garbage on him. (GYGES *dumps the garbage in* CANDAULES' *face.*)

CANDAULES   Nyssia! I am *not* pleased. We'll talk about this later. Gyges, this is not your fault. I won't hold you responsible. You're just doing what you are told. But from this moment on, you're to do only what I tell you, and not what she tells you. My beautiful, charming wife is engaging in a little joke, which you don't understand. Now, help me up, Gyges, this minute, or we'll be late. (*He pulls out his watch.*) It's already 12:29!

NYSSIA   Gyges, go get a can of gasoline.

CANDAULES   (*holding up his hand, imploring*)   Gyges, your hand! Give me your hand!

GYGES   (*after looking impassively at* CANDAULES' *outstretched hand*)   Yes, Lady, I'll get the gasoline for you.

(GYGES *turns and starts to go into the house.*)

CANDAULES   (*calling after him, in a controlled, quiet way*)   Gyges, Gyges!

You're making a mistake, Gyges. You're showing poor judgment. You're behaving rashly. You'll regret it later.

(*after* GYGES *has left*) Now listen to me, Nyssia. I am very displeased with you. Your behavior is inexcusable. Don't you know that that's the way to spoil servants—to give them contradictory orders? You've hopelessly confused Gyges.

(*Throughout the rest of the scene,* CANDAULES *continues to lie on the floor.*)

NYSSIA   I want to read you a story in the morning paper. It just came. (*She picks up the newspaper.*) This is from the front page of the official government foreign language paper.

"BOMB KILLS SIX CHILDREN, MAIMS DOZENS." That's the headline.

CANDAULES   Good God! How horrible!

NYSSIA   Here's the story. "This morning at a special matinée movie performance for the children of foreign military advisers and diplomats, an enemy terrorist threw a plastic bomb in the middle of the audience, instantly killing six children and seriously injuring scores of others."

CANDAULES   Good God! Our own children! How terrible!

NYSSIA   "When the bomb was thrown, the children, ages six to fourteen, were laughing uproariously at an animated cartoon. The vicious terrorist had carefully planned his attack. He threw the home-made bomb in the center section of the theatre where the children of the highest ranking foreign military advisers and diplomats were sitting."

CANDAULES   How ghastly!

NYSSIA   "The theatre was suddenly filled with screams and cries. Many children were trampled in the stampede to get out of the theatre."

CANDAULES   Were the children of any of our friends killed or hurt?

NYSSIA   Yes, several. The Director of Information's son was killed.

CANDAULES   How terrible! And we just had dinner with him last night at the Ambassador's!

NYSSIA   And the white-haired Colonel in Counter-Intelligence—his daughter had both her legs blown off.

CANDAULES   Oh, no! This is terrible!

NYSSIA   Be quiet! Let me finish reading the story. "Wounded and dying children were rushed to the hospital by ambulances and in taxis. Many still remain on the critical list. The foreign community is stunned and outraged by this hideous crime which reveals the indescribable savagery of the enemy and makes more necessary than ever prosecution of the war with renewed vigor until we have brought about the absolute annihilation of every last man, woman, and child responsible for such atrocities."

CANDAULES   Such brutality cries out for a just revenge!

NYSSIA   Shut up: (*She gives him a kick.*) I haven't finished yet. "The enemy terrorist is still at large. He must be destroyed. Military and civilian police are conducting a thorough search to apprehend the brutal criminal and bring him to speedy and stern justice. Many suspects have already been arrested, and a large number of students have been interrogated and held in special compounds. The foreign community can rest assured that the government will exact swift vengeance."

CANDAULES   What a monstrous crime!

NYSSIA   I only wish there were photographs.

CANDAULES   Photographs!

NYSSIA   Yes, I could add them to my collection. But there weren't any photographs.

CANDAULES   To your collection!

NYSSIA   Yes, my pictures of the other bombings and burnings. The ones I showed you last night. The burned children . . .

CANDAULES   But you can't think that they're the same thing!

NYSSIA   Why aren't they?

CANDAULES   One is a senseless and perverted inhuman crime. The other is the unfortunate but unavoidable consequence of a legitimate war. Our intentions are good. We don't mean to burn little children. Don't you understand? The enemy is hiding in those villages. We have to get the enemy out.

NYSSIA   The children get burned, don't they?

CANDAULES   Yes, unfortunately they sometimes do. But no one wants them to. That's not the same thing as this wanton, barbarous murder of our own children.

NYSSIA   (*taking her scissors and cutting out the article*)   Children's corpses are children's corpses.

CANDAULES   Nyssia, I've been watching you carefully for some time now. I'm afraid that you're not well. The stresses of being here have been too much for you. Living in constant danger like this! Your sensitive nature hasn't been able to endure the hardships. Your sense of perspective is gone. You're starting to see things in a morbid and unhealthy light. I'm going to send you back home for a rest.

(GYGES *comes back in the room, carrying a can of gasoline which he sets down on the table in front of* NYSSIA. GYGES *again stands behind the table.*)

Thank goodness you're back, Gyges! Gyges, my wife is feeling a little sick. She needs our help. Put that gasoline line down, and come here. I'll explain it to you.

You see, Gyges, there's been a terrible atrocity this morning. A terrorist threw a bomb into a theatre full of children, the children of the highest ranking foreign military advisers and diplomats. The children of some of our friends. Gyges! Some of them were badly burned! My wife's been disturbed by this awful crime; she's not herself. Think of it! What fiendish mind could have conceived such a crime? What mind warped by hatred could have thought of such an atrocity?

NYSSIA   I did.

CANDAULES   You see, Gyges, she's out of her mind. We'll have to call a doctor.

NYSSIA   I thought of it last night when I was in bed, naked with Gyges. His breathing suggested it to me.

CANDAULES   Don't be morbid, Nyssia. You might have thought of something that horrible, but you didn't do it.

NYSSIA   No, Gyges did it. Gyges threw the bomb.

CANDAULES   I refuse to lose my temper. Gyges, do something like that? It isn't possible. Gyges, say it isn't so.

NYSSIA   Take his clothes off, Gyges.

(GYGES *begins to take off* CANDAULES' *clothes, having to roll him from side to side to get his arms and legs free.*)

You've always been interested in others' nakedness. (GYGES *pulls off his coat first.*) Now it's your turn to be stripped.

CANDAULES   Gyges, I'm giving you one more chance. I'm warning you. Don't pull my pants off. You'll regret it. (GYGES *pulls off his pants.*) Gyges, how could you do that? We drank our warmed milk together only yesterday! And after all I've done for you!

GYGES   You murdered my parents, sir.

CANDAULES   What do you mean I murdered your parents? That's absurd.

GYGES   I saw you do it, sir.

CANDAULES   That's simply not true. You're not making sense, Gyges. Try to talk sense. I saved you from the burning village. I saved you from starvation. Get me my wallet. It's in my coat pocket. (*pointing to his coat*)

GYGES   Yes, Mr. High Commissioner. (GYGES *gets the wallet out of* CANDAULES' *coat and hands it to him.*)

CANDAULES   (*getting the folder of pictures out of the wallet and turning to the one of* GYGES *as a child in the magazine advertisement*)   Look at that, you ungrateful boy! That's you as a child. You were nothing but a starving orphan. Look what it says under the picture. "Help feed little Gyges. He's never had a full meal in his life. His mother and father and twelve brothers and sisters were all killed in the war. He lives in a dump and has to beg. Adopt him, and let him love you for only ten dollars a month."

    I sent my check in. Remember all those years I bought your food. Where's your gratitude?

GYGES   Mr. High Commissioner, as I ate my rice and saw your name printed on the box, I hated you.

CANDAULES   You hated me! What gave you the right to hate me? All I've ever tried to do is to help you and your country. We come over here and risk getting blown up at any moment, and then you think you are entitled to hate us. What selfishness! What ingratitude! You'd have starved to death if it weren't for me!

GYGES   (GYGES *picks up one of the pictures from* NYSSIA's *collection on the table.*)   There's my picture.

CANDAULES   That's one of Nyssia's pictures. That burned child again. Take it away. That's not you, Gyges. Stop lying.

GYGES   (*He rolls up the sleeve of his waiter's jacket.*)   Look, there are the burns on my arms. I'm scarred for life.

CANDAULES   Get me the telephone.

GYGES   Yes, sir. (GYGES *brings* CANDAULES *the telephone. The wire is obviously cut although* CANDAULES *cannot see this.*)

CANDAULES   (*attempting to telephone*)   "Hello, hello, this is Candaules, the Commissioner of Economic Assistance. Candaules. C-A-N-D-A-U-L-E-S. Get me the Ambassador. Hello, hello. I've been undressed! (*As* CANDAULES *is attempting to talk on the telephone,* GYGES *continues to roll* CANDAULES *back and forth and pull his shirt off.*) They're taking my clothes off. I've been stripped! Hello! Get me the Ambassador! Get me the military police! They've taken my pants off! I'm the High Commissioner of Economic Assistance and they've taken my pants off."

NYSSIA   (*As* CANDAULES *talks on the telephone,* NYSSIA *holds the cut ends of the wires in her hand and looks at them curiously.*)   You can stop talking now.

    (CANDAULES *pulls the cord until he has the end in his hand; he looks at it in surprise.*)

    There's been an uprising. The palace has been attacked and the government's been overthrown.

CANDAULES   You don't think you're telling me anything new, do you? I knew this was going to happen. The Ambassador told me last night. He whispered it to me. We planned it. We were tired of the old ruling clique. They were corrupt. They were inefficient. They had to go. You're not telling me anything I didn't know!

NYSSIA   But it went further than expected. The embassy's been looted. The Ambassador's in hiding. Bands of students are swarming the streets attacking foreigners, setting fire to their cars.

CANDAULES   Setting fire to cars! How terrible!

NYSSIA   The students are in a violent mood. The police threw acid into a crowd. Some students were blinded and several were disfigured. There's rioting. They stormed and burned the police headquarters. And they set fire to a hospital and clubbed the patients as they tried to run out.

CANDAULES   If only the war doesn't end! Think of all we have invested in this war. All the suffering and tears! And then it would all go for nothing! For nothing!

GYGES   (*as he unties* CANDAULES' *shoes*)   Hold still, please, sir, so that I can untie your shoes. (GYGES *removes* CANDAULES' *shoes and stockings. He has now removed all of* CANDAULES' *clothes except his underwear.* CANDAULES *wears fancy knee-length shorts and an elbow-length undershirt.*)

NYSSIA   Stop, Gyges. I don't want to see any more of his body. His soft, pale skin makes me feel sick. He's too white. We'll darken his skin for him. Let's char him a bit. Pour the gasoline over him.
(GYGES *picks up the can of gasoline.*)

CANDAULES   Gyges, I'm warning you for the last time. I'll have to write up an unfavorable report about you. It will go in your personnel file. It will go on your permanent record. You'll not be promoted to Chauffeur Grade Four.

NYSSIA   Now pour, Gyges. (GYGES *pours the gasoline over* CANDAULES' *body, very carefully as though he were watering flowers.*)

CANDAULES   Gyges!

GYGES   (*getting out a box of matches*)   Shall we light him in here, Lady? (GYGES *lights a match.*)

NYSSIA   No, in the street. I don't want to smoke up the house. Throw him out into the street.

CANDAULES   I refuse. I'd never set foot in the street in only my underwear! It's undignified! It's unprofessional! It's contrary to diplomatic protocol and to my instructions as an ambassador of good will. "Friendly but dignified" are the key words. I won't budge!

NYSSIA   Throw him out!

CANDAULES   Please don't raise your voice, Nyssia. Don't shout. We can all hear you.

NYSSIA   (*feeling his underwear*)   Is that all the gasoline? He's barely

damp! (*She shakes the gasoline can up and down over his body
in order to get out the last drops.*)

CANDAULES   Don't shake it in my eyes, Nyssia. Try to be more careful!

NYSSIA   (*looking out the window into the street*)   Throw him out into the
street, Gyges. There's a mob of students out there now. Let them
have him.

CANDAULES   The students are my friends. I'm not afraid of the students.
They won't hurt me. They respect me. I've been given an honorary
degree from the University. I've given lectures there. The students
won't hurt me. At least not if I have my clothes on. But if I don't
have my clothes on, they won't know who I am. I won't be anybody
if I don't have my clothes on. Let me put my clothes back on.

NYSSIA   Throw him out, Gyges.

GYGES   (*attempting to drag* CANDAULES *along the floor by his legs*)   Could
you help, Lady? Pick up his hands, please, Lady. He keeps dragging
and holding on to the floor with his fingernails.

NYSSIA   I'll step on his fingers. (*She steps on his fingers as he attempts
to hold onto the floor while* GYGES *drags him slowly across the
room.*)

CANDAULES   I don't want the native population to see me in my underwear. Let me put my pants back on! As a favor, let me put my
pants on. Gyges, if you have any sense of humanity, let me at least
put my bathrobe on. I can't go out into the street in my underwear.
What will people think? What will all those students think? Gyges,
I appeal to you, as one man to another. Let me put my pants back
on! Remember, I have devoted my life to working for your country.
I have only tried to make every single person in the entire world
happier. Let me put my pants on! Why do you hate me, Gyges?
Why do you hate me? I gave you my old clothes, my old radio,
razor, and golf clubs; I paid to have your teeth fixed. When you
smile at me like that, Gyges, I can see your gold fillings. I paid for
those fillings. I never thought you'd repay me this way. I like you,
Gyges. I liked you more than any one in the whole world. Why do
you hate me? What have I ever done to deserve your hate? Why
shouldn't I be able to come to your country and work to help you,
without being hated?

NYSSIA   I can't stand to hear him talk that way. It's sickening. Put his
whistle in his mouth. (GYGES *puts* CANDAULES' *whistle in his mouth.*
CANDAULES *keeps talking, but it comes out as a long, soulful whis-
tling.* GYGES *and* NYSSIA *drag* CANDAULES *out the door. The stage is
momentarily empty; then* NYSSIA *returns, followed by* GYGES.)

NYSSIA   What's happening? (*She hands him a pair of opera glasses. As she does so, she strokes his cheek tentatively and pathetically with her hand after she has held the opera glasses up to his eyes.*) Here are my opera glasses.

GYGES (*looking out the window through the opera glasses*) They're kicking him. Now they've stopped. (*Pause*)

NYSSIA   What's happening?

GYGES   Now they're starting to light him. He's beginning to flame. Now he's gone out. He won't stay lighted. He starts to flame, he sputters, and then he goes out.

NYSSIA   I told you we didn't pour enough gasoline over him.

GYGES   His underpants and undershirt have burned off.

NYSSIA   What's he doing?

GYGES   He's just lying there. The whistle's still in his mouth. But he's not blowing it any more. It just wheezes now and then. Oh, now it's stopped. His eyes are closed. Look. (*He hands her the opera glasses.*) Maybe he's dead.

NYSSIA (*looking through the glasses*)   No, he's just pretending. He always does that when he doesn't want to see what's going on around him. I know him. He never could face reality. He simply closes his eyes. He always did that in bed. (*She hands him back the opera glasses, stroking his cheek as before.*)

GYGES (*looking through the glasses*)   He's just lying there, naked, in the street, with his eyes closed. (*He gives her the opera glasses.*)

NYSSIA (*looking through the glasses*)   It's really too bad. I almost feel sorry for him. He devoted his whole life to this country, and there he is, kicked and burned, lying naked in the street.

Gyges, go get all my shoes.

GYGES   Yes, Lady. (*He leaves and goes into the house.* NYSSIA *looks through the opera glasses out the window while* GYGES *is gone. Then she turns and looks through the opera glasses at* CANDAULES' *empty shoes which are sitting on the floor at the front of the stage.* GYGES *returns soon with a blanket full of hundreds of pairs of* NYSSIA's *shoes.*)

There are your shoes, Lady.

NYSSIA   Dump them on the floor there with Candaules'. (GYGES *dumps the shoes out on the floor, and* NYSSIA *now looks at her own shoes through the opera glasses.*) I hate my shoes.

I envy you, Gyges. I admire you. You have a purpose. Your skin is dark. I worship you as my master. You're in charge now. (*She helps* GYGES *put on* CANDAULES' *tailcoat which is lying on the floor. The tails hang down to the floor.*) You throw bombs and kill people. You're going out into the streets—with your gun drawn, ready to shoot. (GYGES *draws his gun.*) I'm just a spectator, an onlooker. Look at me! (NYSSIA *unbuttons and takes off her oriental house coat. She stands stark naked. Her body appears pale and sickly; her skin has a cadaverous greenish hue, and her flesh hangs loosely from her bones as though she were dead.*)

I'm white. I'm nothing. (GYGES *doesn't look at her.*) Look at me! I'm naked. Won't you even look at me! I can see you. But you don't see me. When I take off my clothes, there's nothing underneath. Don't I exist? Gyges, what are you doing with that ring?

GYGES *lowers the ring over her, covering her with the black bag, but without looking at her. The wooden clappers are beaten on the board as at the end of the previous scenes.* GYGES *releases the safety clip on his revolver and prepares to join the revolution outside.* NYSSIA *sensing that he is about to leave, cries out in a muffled voice through the black bag.*)

Gyges! Don't leave me here by myself! Take me with you! (*She staggers about through the heap of her shoes, but only goes in circles.*) Gyges! Gyges! Take me with you! (*She stumbles and falls, collapsing on top of the shoes.* GYGES *steps over her body and strides off purposefully into the street with his gun drawn and the tails of* CANDAULES' *coat dragging the ground.*) Gyges! Gyges! Don't leave me alone!

(*Shots are heard from the street; and then the mob begins to shout:* "GYGES! GYGES!")

CURTAIN

COMMENTARY

Candaules, Commissioner (1965)   As recorded in Plato's *Republic* and Herodotus' *History*, the myth of the ruler Candaules, his wife Nyssia, and the usurper Gyges focuses on sex and revolution. Updating the action to the present day, *Candaules, Commissioner* explores these themes in relation to neurosis and nudity, colonialism and race. Although the play takes place in Lydia (the setting of the myth, an ancient country in Asia Minor), it almost inevitably suggests the American involvement in South Vietnam. In both Lydia and South Vietnam the war has lasted so long that, in Candaules' words, "war orphans are fathering war orphans now." Candaules' pronouncements on the Lydian war echo those of U. S. officials on the Vietnamese: "Never forget that this is essentially a struggle for the minds and hearts of men!" "Each country has a right to self-determination. We're not here to try to force our tastes on you, but merely to protect your right to choose for yourself."

Candaules, the punctilious High Commissioner of Economic Assistance to Lydia, wants "to feed people, not kill them or see them killed." To this end, he has studied and written a book on Lydia's rice economy. "I wouldn't be here now," he adds, "if I didn't think my work would make life better for the people here." But his sincerity is vitiated by his admission, "There are just certain unpleasant things you have to reconcile yourself to. For the sake of a greater good." An agent of a government which orders and supervises the killing and maiming of noncombattants as well as troops, his successful reconciliation to such "unpleasant things" dehumanizes him to a level where he is no better and perhaps worse than those who actually do the deeds. He has, in fact, even managed to be persuaded by what he calls "powerful arguments" in favor of torture. "Both sides torture. Even if the government forces stopped, the enemy would continue. And then the government says they have to get the information. They say hundreds would be killed instead of just one being tortured. They say that torture is actually more humane than letting hundreds be ambushed and murdered." For these reasons, the native Gyges regards him as guilty, though he pulled no trigger, dropped no bomb, and pressed no button. "You murdered my parents, sir," charges Gyges. Although Candaules uncomprehendingly disavows responsibility for their deaths, he inadvertently suggests his responsibility for the creation of war orphans when he remarks to Nyssia, "He's our orphan."

Intentionally, however, Candaules means that Gyges is his and Nyssia's foster child. On both literal and symbolic levels, Candaules' attitude toward Gyges and his country is paternalistic. As a foster father taking up the white man's burden, Candaules is an unsuccessful parent. The advertisement which impelled him to adopt Gyges hints at the basis and method of his paternalism: "Adopt him, and let him love you for only ten dollars a month." The same basis and method underlie his government's treatment of the other natives, and he cannot understand why it is unsuccessful. "Why don't they stop?" he asks of war orphans who refuse to be pacified, "We gave them candy, didn't we?" Unconsciously racist as well, Candaules regards his foster child one way, his blood kin another. "Once the war is won," he tells his oriental chauffeur, "the children in your country will lead a better life. . . . Someday, Gyges, your son may drive along the same way over a four lane highway—chauffeuring my son." His foster son is of a different color, which keeps him and those like him in subservient positions.

Candaules' attitude is partly projective, for he is not only paternalistic, he is childlike as well. "I haven't had a real friend like Gyges, since I was a boy. . . . Now with Gyges, I feel young again." Like a boy with his buddy, he wants to show Gyges his proudest possession, his wife's body, which he expects Gyges to enjoy as much as he. The assumption that the natives should admire what he admires is an underlying aspect of paternalism and colonialism. Although Candaules claims he does not want to force his tastes and values on the Lydians, he expects Gyges to share his tastes and values from warm milk to women to political institutions. Ironically, however, Candaules himself does not "enjoy" his wife. But whereas Gyges rejects Nyssia after having slept with her (like a disappointing toy, she is *"quickly discarded"*), it is she who rejects Candaules, who no longer sleeps with her.

Candaules recognizes none of this. He understands neither himself, his wife, nor his servant, who by extension represents the people of Lydia. Though he thinks he understands Nyssia, his surprise on discovering her collection of torture pictures and her insane desire to be tortured reveal he does not. Though he hopes to understand Gyges and through him Gyges' countrymen, he never does.

"I'm watching you carefully, Gyges," declares Candaules, and Gyges responds, "I watch you too, sir." Nyssia also watches Gyges, but her vision is different from her husband's. To Candaules, Gyges personifies his benevolent hopes for Lydia and exemplifies what it may become. To Nyssia, Gyges is first a threat, then a means of salvation from her arid life.

For all their careful watching, neither sees the real Gyges. Like Ralph Ellison, who in his autobiographical novel *Invisible Man*, about the Negro in the U. S., Gyges might say, "I am an invisible man. No, I am not a spook like those who haunted Edgar Allan Poe; nor am I one of your Hollywood-movie ectoplasms. I am a man of substance, of flesh and bone, fiber and liquids—and I might even be said to possess a mind. . . .

[But people] see only my surroundings, themselves, or figments of their imagination—indeed, everything and anything except me." Invisibility is a major motif of the play. Each character wears the magic ring which makes him invisible. Candaules becomes invisible in Scene 1 so that he will not be seen and also so that he will not see others. To him, the ring is like the bullet-proof glass of his car: a means by which he may insulate himself from reality and make the unpleasant invisible. "I refuse to recognize that their hostility exists," he says of the natives who jeer and hoot at him, and Nyssia observes, "He never could face reality. He simply closes his eyes. He always did that in bed." When Nyssia herself is made invisible in Scene 4, she apparently becomes, like her husband, unable to see. By contrast, Gyges, who makes himself invisible in Scene 3, sees more when he becomes invisible.

Not only the ring but also clothes make one "invisible." Candaules hides himself beneath a peasant's hat in Scene 1. He and Nyssia disguise themselves by wearing rags in Scene 2. Gyges wears a chauffeur's uniform, which conceals his real self. Nudity, on the other hand, reveals. When Nyssia disrobes, she also reveals her hidden desires. Without his formal diplomatic attire, Candaules has no identity: "they won't know who I am. I won't be anybody if I don't have my clothes on." He therefore prefers to be fully dressed at all times, even when he goes to bed. Only once does Gyges, who of the three is the only one who successfully hides his real self, show the man beneath the clothes: when he rolls up his sleeve to reveal his wounds, both physical and psychic.

At all other times, Gyges is clothed—and enigmatic. Is Gyges, who is *"always most agreeable and friendly,"* a revolutionist at the start of the play, cunningly awaiting the right moment to strike? Or does he naively admire his benefactor and only late in the play realize his identity as a revolutionary leader of his people? The play is ambiguous. Did Gyges throw the bomb? Only a neurotic woman says so. Can we believe her? If he did throw the bomb, did he know it would trigger a revolution? Here too the play is ambiguous. Revolution proceeds from both the revolutionist's determination and the ruler's corruption.

In a sense, Candaules precipitates his own downfall by his frustrations, his voyeurism, and his possible impotence. Sexual aberration parallels political oppression, and war perverts all human relationships. Throughout the seventeen-year war, the warped Candaules has not made love. "I have chosen sexual frustration," he boasts. Candaules may be voicing his own sexual fantasies when he asks Gyges, "Did you put your hands in her gloves? Did you try putting your feet in her shoes?" Perverted, Candaules perverts his wife. He has maimed her psychologically; she wants to maim others physically. His actions and her desires lead her to a yearning for self-abasement, a subconscious response of this type of guilt-ridden white when confronted with "colored" people of the third world. A voyeur (*"He sits down and looks at* NYSSIA *as though he were a spectator at a play, in a very special seat in the first row."*), he turns Gyges into a voyeur—and does the same with the audience.

A failure as husband, father, and bureaucrat, Candaules turns his victims against him. He puts Gyges in his place as husband; Gyges then takes his place as ruler. He abandons Nyssia for the war; Nyssia then abandons him for another man. His desires turn against him. He wants Nyssia to strip; she does so, then has him stripped. He wants to bring self-determination to the Lydians; the Lydians, led by Gyges, determine their own destiny by destroying him and what he represents.

In the final scene, revolution erupts. Whereas in the first scene Candaules was sitting higher than Gyges, in the fourth scene he is on the floor and Gyges stands. In the first scene Gyges was in the driver's seat, but he obeyed Candaules' orders. In the fourth scene, he does not obey his former master; and though he begins by obeying his mistress, he rejects her sexual shackles as he rejected Candaules' economic shackles, and ends by disobeying her as well. Gyges and his country achieve independence.

At the end of the play, Gyges, who has slept with the wife of his former master, carries the gun his former master gave him and wears his former master's coat. Will the new master of Lydia, who was raised by the former one, differ from him in any way but color? As Bernard Shaw said in his preface to *The Millionairess*, "The assumption of the more advanced spirits that revolutionists are always right is as questionable as the conservative assumption that they are always wrong." *Candaules, Commissioner* makes neither assumption.

Bibliography

A.   Plays about the Vietnam War:

Terence McNally, *Tour*, 1968.
Megan Terry, *Viet Rock*, 1966.
Peter Weiss, *Vietnam Discourse*, 1968.

B.   Works about Candaules, Commissioner:

Brukenfeld, Dick. "Off-Off," *The Village Voice*, February 12, 1970.
Gerould, Daniel C. "Candaules and the Uses of Myth," *Modern Drama*, XII (December, 1969).
Gussow, Mel. "Gerould's 'Candaules, Commissioner' Bows", *New York Times*, May 29, 1970, p. 15.

The
Black
Revolution

THE SLAVE
LeRoi Jones

THE SLAVE

A Fable in a Prologue and Two Acts

LeRoi Jones

CHARACTERS

WALKER VESSELS, *tall, thin Negro about forty.*
GRACE, *blonde woman about same age. Small, thin, beautiful.*
BRADFORD EASLEY, *tall, broad white man, with thinning hair, about forty-five.*

The action takes place in a large living room, tastefully furnished the way an intelligent university professor and his wife would furnish it. Room is dark at the beginning of the play, except for light from explosions, which continue, sometimes close, sometimes very far away, throughout both acts, and well after curtain of each act.

Prologue

WALKER (*Coming out dressed as an old field slave, balding, with white hair, and an old ragged vest. [Perhaps he is sitting, sleeping, initially-nodding and is awakened by faint cries, like a child's]. He comes to the center of the stage slowly, and very deliberately, puffing on a pipe, and seemingly uncertain of the reaction any audience will give his speech*) Whatever the core of our lives. Whatever the deceit. We live where we are, and seek nothing but ourselves. We are liars, and we are murderers. We invent death for others. Stop their pulses publicly. Stone possible lovers with heavy worlds we think are ideas . . . and we know, even before these shapes are realized, that these worlds, these depths or heights we fly to smoothly, as in a dream, or slighter, when we stare dumbly into space, leaning our eyes just behind a last quick moving bird, then sometimes the place and twist of what we are will push and sting, and what the crust of our stance has become will ring in our ears and shatter that piece of our eyes that is never closed. An ignorance. A stupidity. A stupid longing not to know . . . which is automatically fulfilled. Automatically triumphs. Automatically makes us killers or foot-dragging celebrities at the core of any filth. And it is a deadly filth that passes as whatever thing we feel is too righteous to question, too deeply felt to deny. (*Pause to relight pipe*) I am much older than I look . . . or maybe much younger. Whatever I am or seem . . . (*Significant pause*) to you, then let that rest. But figure, still, that you might not be right. Figure, still, that you might be lying . . . to save yourself. Or myself's image, which might set you crawling like a thirsty dog, for the meanest of drying streams. The meanest of ideas. (*Gentle, mocking laugh*) Yeah. Ideas. Let that settle! Ideas. Where they form. Or whose they finally seem to be. Yours? The other's? Mine? (*Shifts uneasily, pondering the last*) No, no more. Not mine. I served my slow apprenticeship . . . and maybe came up lacking. Maybe. Ha. Who's to say, really? Huh? But figure, still, ideas are still in the world. They need judging. I mean, they don't come in that singular or wild, that whatever they are, just because they're beautiful and brilliant, just because they strike us full in the center of the heart. . . . My God! (*Softer*) My God, just because, and even this, believe me, even if, that is, just because they're *right* . . . doesn't mean anything. The very rightness stinks a lotta times. The very rightness. (*Looks down and speaks softer and quicker*) I am an old man. An old man. (*Blankly*) The waters and wars. Time's a dead thing really . . . and keeps nobody whole. An old man, full of filed rhythms. Terrific, eh? That I hoarded so much dignity? An old man full of great ideas. Let's say theories. As: Love is an instrument of knowledge. Oh, not my own. Not my own . . . is right. But listen now. . . . Brown is not brown except when used as an intimate description of personal phenomenological fields. As your brown is not my brown, et cetera, that is, we need, ahem, a meta-language. We need some thing not included here. (*Spreads arms*) Your ideas? An old man can't be expected to be right. If I'm old. If I really claim that embarrassment. (*Saddens . . . brightens*) A poem? Lastly, that, to distort my position? To divert you . . . in your hour of need. Before the thing goes on. Before you get your lousy chance. Discovering racially the funds of the universe. Discovering the last image of the thing. As the sky when the moon is broken. Or old, old blues people moaning in their sleep, singing, man, oh, nigger, nigger, you still here, as hard as nails, and takin' no shit from nobody. He say, yeah, yeah, he say yeah, yeah. He say, yeah, yeah . . . goin' down slow, man. Goin' down slow. He say . . . yeah, heh . . .

(*Running down, growing anxiously less articulate, more "field hand" sounding, blankly lyrical, shuffles slowly around, across the stage, as the lights dim and he enters the set proper and assumes the position he will have when the play starts . . . still moaning . . .*)

Act I

THE SCENE   *A light from an explosion lights the room dimly for a second and the outline of a figure is seen half sprawled on a couch. Every once in a while another blast shows the figure in silhouette. He stands from time to time, sits, walks nervously around the room examining books and paintings. Finally, he climbs a flight of stairs, stays for a few minutes, then returns. He sits smoking in the dark, until some sound is heard outside the door. He rises quickly and takes a position behind the door, a gun held out stiffly.* GRACE *and* EASLEY *open the door, turn on the light, agitated and breathing heavily.* GRACE *quiet and weary.* EASLEY *talking in harsh angry spurts.*

EASLEY   Son of a bitch. Those black son of a bitches. Why don't they at least stop and have their goddamned dinners? Goddamn son of a bitches. They're probably gonna keep that horseshit up all goddamn night. Goddamnit. Goddamn it! (*He takes off a white metal hat and slings it across the room. It bangs loudly against the brick of the fireplace*)

GRACE   Brad! You're going to wake up the children!

EASLEY   Oh, Christ! . . . But if they don't wake up under all that blasting, I don't think that tin hat will do it. (*He unbuttons his shirt, moves wearily across the room, still mumbling under his breath about the source of the explosions*) Hey, Grace . . . you want a drink? That'll fix us up. (*He moves to get the drink and spots* WALKER *leaning back against the wall, half smiling, also very weary, but still holding the gun, stomach high, and very stiffly.* EASLEY *freezes, staring at* WALKER's *face and then the gun, and then back to* WALKER's *face. He makes no sound. The two men stand confronting each other until* GRACE *turns and sees them*)

GRACE   Sure, I'll take a drink . . . one of the few real pleasures left in the Western world. (*She turns and drops her helmet to the floor, staring unbelievingly*) Ohh!

WALKER   (*Looks over slowly at* GRACE *and waves as from a passing train. Then he looks back at* EASLEY; *the two men's eyes are locked in the same ugly intensity.* WALKER *beckons to* GRACE) The blinds.

GRACE   Walker! (*She gets the name out quietly, as if she is trying to hold so many other words in*) Walker . . . the gun!

WALKER   (*Half turning to look at her. He looks back at* EASLEY, *then lets the gun swing down easily toward the floor. He looks back at* GRACE, *and tries to smile*) Hey, momma. How're you?

EASLEY   (*At* WALKER, *and whatever else is raging in his own head*) Son of a bitch!

GRACE   What're you doing here, Walker? What do you want?

WALKER   (*Looking at* EASLEY *from time to time*) Nothing. Not really. Just visiting. (*Grins*) I was in the neighborhood; thought I'd stop by and see how the other half lives.

GRACE   Isn't this dangerous?
(*She seems relieved by* WALKER's *relative good spirits and she begins to look for a cigarette.* EASLEY *has not yet moved. He is still staring at* WALKER.)

WALKER   Oh, it's dangerous as a bitch. But don't you remember how heroic I am?

EASLEY   (*Handing* GRACE *a cigarette, then waiting to light it*) Well, what the hell do you want, hero? (*Drawn out and challenging*)

WALKER   (*With same challenge*) Nothing you have, fellah, not one thing.

EASLEY   Oh? (*Cynically*) Is *that* why you and your noble black brothers are killing what's left of this city? (*Suddenly broken*) I should say . . . what's left of this country . . . or world.

WALKER   Oh, fuck you (*Hotly*) fuck you . . . just fuck you, that's all. Just fuck you! (*Keeps voice stiffly contained, but then it rises sharply*) I mean really, just fuck you. Don't, goddamnit, don't tell me about any goddamn killing of anything. If that's what's happening. I mean if this shitty town is being flattened . . . let it. It needs it.

GRACE   Walker, shut up, will you? (*Furious from memory*) I had enough of your twisted logic in my day . . . you remember? I mean like

your heroism. The same kind of memory. Or Lie. Do you remember which? Huh? (*Starting to weep*)

WALKER (*Starts to comfort her*) Grace . . . look . . . there's probably nothing I can say to make you understand me . . . now.

EASLEY (*Steps in front of* WALKER *as he moves toward* GRACE . . . *feigning a cold sophistication*) Uh . . . no, now come, Jefe,[1] you're
not going to make one of those embrace the weeping ex-wife
dramas, are you? Well, once a bad poet always a bad poet . . .
even in the disguise of a racist murderer!

WALKER (*Not quite humbled*) Yeah. (*Bends head, then he brings it
up quickly, forcing the joke*) Even disguised as a racist murderer . . . I remain a bad poet. Didn't St. Thomas say that? Once
a bad poet always a bad poet . . . or was it Carl Sandburg, as
some kind of confession?

EASLEY You're not still writing . . . now, are you? I should think the
political, now military estates would be sufficient. And you always
used to speak of the Renaissance as an evil time. (*Begins making
two drinks*) And now you're certainly the gaudiest example of
Renaissance man I've heard of.
(*Finishes making drinks and brings one to* GRACE. WALKER *watches
him and then as he starts to speak he walks to the cabinet, picks
up the bottle, and empties a good deal of it.*)

GRACE (*Looking toward* WALKER *even while* EASLEY *extends the drink
towards her*) Walker . . . you are still writing, aren't you?

WALKER Oh, God, yes. Want to hear the first lines of my newest work?
(*Drinks, does a theatrical shiver*) Uh, how's it go . . .? Oh,
"Straddling each dolphin's back/And steadied by a fin,/Those
innocents relive their death,/Their wounds open again."

GRACE (*Staring at him closely*) It's changed quite a bit.

WALKER Yeah . . . it's changed to Yeats. (*Laughs very loudly*) Yeah,
Yeats. . . . Hey, professor, anthologist, lecturer, loyal opposition,
et cetera, et cetera, didn't you recognize those words as being
Yeats's? Goddamn, I mean if you didn't recognize them . . . who
the hell would? I thought you knew all kinds of shit.

EASLEY (*Calmly*) I knew they were Yeats'.

WALKER (*Tilting the bottle again quickly*) Oh, yeah? What poem?

EASLEY The second part of "News for the Delphic Oracle."

WALKER (*Hurt*) "News for the Delphic Oracle." Yeah. That's right.
(*To* GRACE) You know that, Grace? Your husband knows all about

---

[1] Spanish for *chief.*

everything. The second part of "News for the Delphic Oracle."
(*Rhetorically*) Intolerable music falls. Nymphs and satyrs copulate
in the foam. (*Tilts bottle again, some liquor splashes on the floor*)

EASLEY (*Suddenly straightening and stopping close to* WALKER) Look
. . . LOOK! You arrogant maniac, if you get drunk or fall out
here, so help me, I'll call the soldiers or somebody . . . and turn
you over to them. I swear I'll do that.

GRACE Brad!

WALKER Yeah, yeah, I know. That's your job. A liberal education, and
a long history of concern for minorities and charitable organiza-
tions can do that for you.

EASLEY (*Almost taking hold of* WALKER's *clothes*) No! I mean this,
friend! Really! If I get the slightest advantage, some cracker soldier
will be bayoneting you before the night is finished.

WALKER (*Slaps* EASLEY *across the face with the back of his left hand,
pulling the gun out with his right and shoving it as hard as he
can against* EASLEY's *stomach.* EASLEY *slumps, and the cruelty in*
WALKER's *face at this moment also frightens* GRACE) "My country,
'tis of thee. Sweet land of liber-ty." (*Screams off key like drunken
opera singer*) Well, let's say liberty and ignorant vomiting faggot
professors. (*To* GRACE) Right, lady? isn't that right? I mean you
ought to know, 'cause you went out of your way to marry one.
(*Turns to* GRACE *and she takes an involuntary step backward. And
in a cracked ghostlike voice that he wants to be loud . . .*) Huh?
Huh? And then fed the thing my children.
(*He reaches stiffly out and pushes her shoulder, intending it to be
strictly a burlesque, but there is quite a bit of force in the gesture.*
GRACE *falls back, just short of panic, but* WALKER *hunches his
shoulders and begins to jerk his finger at the ceiling; one eye closed
and one leg raised, jerking his finger absurdly at the ceiling, as if
to indicate something upstairs that was to be kept secret.*)
Ah, yes, the children . . . (*Affecting an imprecise "Irish" accent*)
sure and they looked well enough . . . (*Grins*) and white enough,
roosting in that kennel. Hah, I hope you didn't tell Faggy, there,
about those two lovely ladies. (EASLEY *is kneeling on the floor
holding his stomach and shaking his head*) Ahh, no, lady, let's
keep that strictly in the family. I mean among those of us who
screw. (*He takes another long drink from the bottle, and "threatens"* EASLEY's *head in a kind of burlesque*) For Lawrence, and all
the cocksmen of my underprivileged youth. When we used to
chase that kind of frail little sissy-punk down Raymond Boulevard
and compromise his sister-in-laws in the cloak room . . . It's so

simple to work from the bottom up. To always strike, and know, from the blood's noise that you're right, and what you're doing is right, and even *pretty*. (*Suddenly more tender toward* GRACE) I swear to you, Grace, I did come into the world pointed in the right direction. Oh, shit, I learned so many words for what I've wanted to say. They all come down on me at once. But almost none of them are mine. (*He straightens up, turning quickly toward the still kneeling* EASLEY, *and slaps him as hard as he can across the face, sending his head twisting around*) Bastard! A poem for your mother!

GRACE (*Lets out a short pleading cry*) Ohh! Get away from him, Walker! Get away from him, (*Hysterically*) you nigger murderer!

WALKER (*Has started to tilt the bottle again, after he slaps* EASLEY, *and when* GRACE *shouts at him, he chokes on the liquor, spitting it out, and begins laughing with a kind of hysterical amusement*) Oh! Ha, ha, ha . . . you mean . . . Wow! (*Trying to control laughter, but it is an extreme kind of release*) No kidding? Grace, Gracie! Wow! I wonder how long you had that stored up.

GRACE (*Crying now, going over to* EASLEY, *trying to help him up*) Brad. Brad. Walker, why'd you come here? Why'd you come here? Brad?

WALKER (*Still laughing and wobbling clumsily around*) Nigger murderer? Wowee. Gracie, are you just repeating your faggot husband, or did you have that in you a long time? I mean . . . for all the years we were together? Hooo! Yeah. (*Mock seriously*) Christ, it could get to be a weight after a time, huh? When you taught the little girls to pray . . . you'd have to whisper, "And God bless Mommy, and God bless Daddy, the nigger murderer." Wow, that's some weight.

GRACE Shut up, Walker. Just shut up, and get out of here, away from us, please. I don't want to hear you . . . I don't need to hear you, again. Remember, I heard it all before, baby . . . you don't get me again.

(*She is weeping and twisting her head, trying at the same time to fully revive* EASLEY, *who is still sitting on the floor with legs sprawled apart, both hands held to the pit of his stomach, his head nodding back and forth in pain.*)

Why'd you come here . . . just to do this? Why don't you leave before you kill somebody? (*Trying to hold back a scream*) Before you kill another white person?

WALKER (*Sobering, but still forcing a cynical hilarity*) Ah . . . the party line. Stop him before he kills another white person! Heh. Yeah. Yeah. And that's not such a bad idea, really. . . . I mean, after all, only you and your husband there are white in this house. Those two lovely little girls upstairs are niggers. You know, circa 1800, one drop makes you whole?

GRACE   Shut up, Walker! (*She leaps to her feet and rushes toward him*) Shut your ugly head! (*He pushes her away*)

EASLEY   (*Raising his head and shouting as loud as he can manage*) You're filth, boy. Just filth. Can you understand that anything and everything you do is stupid, filthy, or meaningless! Your inept formless poetry. Hah. Poetry? A flashy doggerel for inducing all those unfortunate troops of yours to spill their blood in your behalf. But I guess that's something! Ritual drama, we used to call it at the university. The poetry of ritual drama. (*Pulls himself up*) And even that's giving that crap the benefit of the doubt. Ritual filth would have been the right name for it.

WALKER   Ritual drama . . . (*Half musing*) yeah, I remember seeing that phrase in an old review by one of your queer academic friends. . . . (*Noticing* EASLEY *getting up*) Oh well, look at him coming up by his bootstraps. I didn't mean to hit you that hard, Professor Easley, sir . . . I just don't know my own strent'.
(*Laughs and finishes the bottle . . . starts as if he is going to throw it over his shoulder, then he places it very carefully on the table. He starts dancing around and whooping like an "Indian".*) More! Bwana, me want more fire water!

EASLEY   As I said, Vessels, you're just filth. Pretentious filth.

WALKER   (*Dances around a bit more, then stops abruptly in front of* EASLEY; *so close they are almost touching. He speaks in a quiet menacing tone*)   The liquor, turkey. The liquor. No opinions right now. Run off and get more liquor, *sabe*?

GRACE   (*Has stopped crying and managed to regain a cynical composure*) I'll get it, Brad. Mr. Vessels is playing the mad scene from Native Son. (*Turns to go*) A second-rate Bigger Thomas.[2]

WALKER   (*Laughs*)   Yeah. But remember when I used to play a second-rate Othello? Oh, wow . . . you remember that, don't you, Professor No-Dick? You remember when I used to walk around wondering what that fair sister was thinking? (*Hunches* EASLEY) Oh, come on now, you remember that. . . . I was Othello . . . Grace there was Desdemona . . . and you were Iago . . . (*Laughs*) or at least between classes, you were Iago. Hey, who were you during classes? I forgot to find that out. Ha, the key to

---

[2] The main character of *Native Son*, a dramatization (1941) by Paul Green and Richard Wright of Wright's novel.

my downfall. I knew you were Iago between classes, when I saw you, but I never knew who you were during classes. Ah ah, that's the basis of an incredibly profound social axiom. I quote: . . . and you better write this down, Bradford, so you can pass it on to your hipper colleagues at the university . . . (*Laughs*) I mean if they ever rebuild the university. What was I saying to you, enemy? Oh yeah . . . the axiom. Oh . . .

GRACE (*Returning with a bottle*)   You still at it, huh, Bigger?

WALKER   Yeah, yeah . . . (*Reaches for bottle*) lemme see. I get it. . . . If a white man is Iago when you see him . . . uhh . . . chances are he's eviler when you don't. (*Laughs*)

EASLEY   Yes, that was worthy of you.

WALKER   It *was* lousy, wasn't it?

GRACE   Look (*Trying to be earnest*) Walker, pour yourself a drink . . . as many drinks as you need . . . and then leave, will you? I don't see what you think you're accomplishing by hanging around us.

EASLEY   Yes . . . I was wondering who's taking care of your mighty army while you're here in the enemy camp? How can the black liberation movement spare its illustrious leader for such a long stretch?

WALKER (*Sits abruptly on couch and stretches both legs out, drinking big glass of bourbon. Begins speaking in pidgin "Japanese"*)   Oh, don't worry about that, doomed American dog. Ha. You see and hear those shells beating this town flat, don't you? In fact, we'll probably be here en masse in about a week. Why don't I just camp here and wait for my brothers to get here and liberate the whole place? Huh? (*Laughs*)

GRACE   Walker, you're crazy!

EASLEY   I think he's got more sense than that.

WALKER (*Starting to make up a song*)   Ohhh! I'll stay here and rape your wife . . . as I so often used to do . . . as I so often used . . .

GRACE   Your mind is gone, Walker . . . completely gone. (*She turns to go upstairs. A bright blast rocks the house and she falls against the wall*)

WALKER (*Thrown forward to the floor, rises quickly to see how* GRACE *is*)   Hey, you all right, lady?

EASLEY   Grace! (*He has also been rocked, but he gets to* GRACE *first*) Don't worry about my wife, Vessels. That's my business.

GRACE   I'm O.K., Brad. I was on my way upstairs to look in on the girls. It's a wonder they're not screaming now.

WALKER   They were fine when I looked in earlier. Sleeping very soundly.

EASLEY You were upstairs?

WALKER (*Returning to his seat, with another full glass*) Of course I
went upstairs, to see my children. In fact, I started to take them
away with me, while you patriots were out. (*Another close blast*)
But I thought I'd wait to say hello to the mommy and step-
daddy.

EASLEY You low bastard. (*Turning toward* WALKER *and looking at*
GRACE *at the same time*)

GRACE No . . . you're not telling the truth now, Walker. (*Voice quaver-
ing and rising*) You came here just to say that. Just to see what
your saying that would do to me. (*Turns away from him*) You're
a bad liar, Walker. As always . . . a very bad liar.

WALKER You know I'm not lying. I want those children. You know that,
Grace.

EASLEY I know you're drunk!

GRACE You're lying. You don't want those children. You just want to
think you want them for the moment . . . to excite one of those
obscure pathological instruments you've got growing in your head.
Today, you want to feel like you want the girls. Just like you
wanted to feel hurt and martyred by your misdirected cause,
when you first drove us away.

WALKER Drove you away? You knew what I was in to. You could have
stayed. You said you wanted to pay whatever thing it cost to stay.

EASLEY How can you lie like this, Vessels? Even I know you pushed
Grace until she couldn't retain her sanity and stay with you in that
madness. All the bigoted racist imbeciles you started to cultivate.
Every white friend you had knows that story.

WALKER You shut up. . . . I don't want to hear anything you've got to
say.

GRACE There are so many bulbs and screams shooting off inside you,
Walker. So many lies you have to pump full of yourself. You're
split so many ways . . . your feelings are cut up into skinny horrible
strips . . . like umbrella struts . . . holding up whatever bizarre
black cloth you're using this performance as your self's image.
I don't even think you know who you are any more. No, I don't
think you *ever* knew.

WALKER I know what I can use.

GRACE No, you never even found out who you were until you sold the
last of your loves and emotions down the river . . . until you
killed your last old friend . . . and found out *what* you were.
My God, it must be hard being you, Walker Vessels. It must be
a sick task keeping so many lying separate uglinesses together

. . . and pretending they're something you've made and understand.

WALKER What I can use, madam . . . what I can use. I move now trying to be certain of that.

EASLEY You're talking strangely. What is this, the pragmatics of war? What are you saying . . . use? I thought you meant yourself to be a fantastic idealist? All those speeches and essays and poems . . . the rebirth of idealism. That the Western white man had forfeited the most impressive characteristic of his culture . . . the idealism of rational liberalism . . . and that only the black man in the West could restore that quality to Western culture, because he still understood the necessity for it. Et cetera, et cetera. Oh, look, I remember your horseshit theories, friend. I remember. And now the great black Western idealist is talking about use.

WALKER Yeah, yeah. Now you can call me the hypocritical idealist nigger murderer. You see, what I want is more titles.

GRACE And saying you want the children is another title . . . right? Every time you say it, one of those bulbs goes off in your head and you think you can focus on still another attribute, another beautiful quality in the total beautiful structure of the beautiful soul of Walker Vessels, sensitive Negro poet, savior of his people, deliverer of Western idealism . . . commander-in-chief of the forces of righteousness . . . Oh, God, et cetera, et cetera.

WALKER Grace Locke Vessels Easley . . . whore of the middle classes.

EASLEY (*Turning suddenly as if to offer combat*) Go and fuck yourself.

GRACE Yes, Walker, by all means . . . go and fuck yourself. (*And softer*) Yes, do anything . . . but don't drag my children into your scheme for martyrdom and immortality, or whatever else it is makes you like you are . . . just don't . . . don't even mention it.

EASLEY (*Moving to comfort her*) Oh, don't get so worried, Grace . . . you know he just likes to hear himself talk . . . more than anything . . . he just wants to hear himself talk, so he can find out what he's supposed to have on his mind. (*To* WALKER) He knows there's no way in the world he could have those children. No way in the world.

WALKER (*Feigning casual matter-of-fact tone*) Mr. Easley, Mrs. Easley, those girls' last name is Vessels. Whatever you think is all right. I mean I don't care what you think about me or what I'm doing . . . the whole mess. But those beautiful girls you have upstairs there are my daughters. They even look like me. I've loved them all their lives. Before this there was too much to do, so I left them with you. (*Gets up, pours another drink*) But now . . . things are changed. . . . I want them with me. (*Sprawls on couch again*) I want them with me very much.

GRACE   You're lying. Liar, you don't give a shit about those children. You're a liar if you say otherwise. You never never never cared at all for those children. My friend, you have never cared for anything in the world that I know of but what's in there behind your eyes. And God knows what ugliness that is . . . though there are thousands of people dead or homeless all over this country who begin to understand a little. And not just white people . . . you've killed so many of your own people too. It's a wonder they haven't killed you.

EASLEY   (*Walks over to* WALKER)   Get up and get out of here! So help me . . . If you don't leave here now . . . I'll call the soldiers. They'd just love to find you. (WALKER *doesn't move*) Really, Vessels, I'll personally put a big hole in that foul liberation movement right now . . . I swear it. (*He turns to go to the phone*)

WALKER   (*At first as if he is good-natured*)   Hey, hey . . . Professor Easley, I've got this gun here, remember? Now don't do that . . . in fact if you take another step, I'll blow your goddamn head off. And I mean that, Brad, turn around and get back here in the center of the room.

GRACE   (*Moves for the stairs*)   Ohhh!

WALKER   Hey, Grace, stop . . . you want me to shoot this fairy, or what? Come back here!

GRACE   I was only going to see about the kids.

WALKER   I'm their father . . . I'm thinking about their welfare, too. Just come back here. Both of you sit on this couch where I'm sitting, and I'll sit in that chair over there near the ice tray.

EASLEY   So now we get a taste of Vessels, the hoodlum.

WALKER   Uh, yeah. Another title, boss man. But just sit the fuck down for now. (*Goes to the window. Looks at his watch*) I got about an hour.

GRACE   Walker, what are you going to do?

WALKER   Do? Well, right now I'm going to have another drink.

EASLEY   You know what she means.

GRACE   You're not going to take the children, are you? You wouldn't just take them, would you? You wouldn't do that. You can't hate me so much that you'd do that.

WALKER   I don't hate you at all, Grace. I hated you when I wanted you. I haven't wanted you for a long time. But I do want those children.

GRACE You're lying!

WALKER No, I'm not lying . . . and I guess that's what's cutting you up . . . because you probably know I'm not lying, and you can't understand that. But I tell you now that I'm not lying, and that in spite of all the things I've done that have helped kill love in me, I still love those girls.

EASLEY You mean, in spite of all the people you've killed.

WALKER O.K., O.K., however you want it . . . however you want it, let it go at that. In spite of all the people I've killed. No, better, in spite of the fact that I, Walker Vessels, single-handedly, and with no other adviser except my own ego, promoted a bloody situation where white and black people are killing each other; despite the fact that I know that this is at best a war that will only change, ha, the complexion of tyranny . . . (*Laughs sullenly*) in spite of the fact that I have killed for all times any creative impulse I will ever have by the depravity of my murderous philosophies . . . despite the fact that I am being killed in my head each day and by now have no soul or heart or warmth, even in my long killer fingers, despite the fact that I have no other thing in the universe that I love or trust, but myself . . . despite or in spite, the respite, my dears, my dears, hear me, O Olympus, O Mercury, God of thieves, O Damballah, chief of all the dead religions of pseudo-nigger patriots hoping to open big restaurants after de wah . . . har har . . . in spite, despite, the resistance in the large cities and the small towns, where we have taken, yes, dragged piles of darkies out of their beds and shot them for being in Rheingold ads, despite the fact that all of my officers are ignorant motherfuckers who have never read any book in their lives, despite the fact that I would rather argue politics, or literature, or boxing, or anything, with you, dear Easley, with you . . . (*Head slumps, weeping*) despite all these things and in spite of all the drunken noises I'm making, despite . . . in spite of . . . I want those girls, very, very much. And I will take them out of here with me.

EASLEY No, you won't . . . not if I can help it.

WALKER Well, you can't help it.

GRACE (*Jumps up*) What? Is no one to reason with you? Isn't there any way something can exist without you having the final judgment on it? Is the whole world yours . . . to deal with or destroy? You're right! You feel! You have the only real vision of the world. You love! No one else exists in the world except you, and those who can help you. Everyone else is nothing or else they're something to be destroyed. I'm your enemy now . . . right? I'm wrong. You are the children's father . . . but I'm no longer their mother. Every one of your yesses or nos is intended by you to reshape the world after the image you have of it. They *are* my children! I am their mother! But because somehow I've become your enemy, I suddenly no longer qualify. Forget you're their mother, Grace. Walker has decided that you're no longer to perform that function. So the whole business is erased as if it never existed. I'm *not* in your head, Walker. Neither are those kids. We are all flesh and blood and deserve to live . . . even unabstracted by what you think we ought to be in the general scheme of things. Even alien to it. I left you . . . and took the girls because you'd gone crazy. You're crazy now. This stupid ugly killing you've started will never do anything, for anybody. And you and all your people will be wiped out, you know that. And you'll have accomplished nothing. Do you want those two babies to be with you when you're killed so they can witness the death of a great man? So they can grow up and write articles for a magazine sponsored by the Walker Vessels Society?

WALKER   Which is still better than being freakish mulattoes in a world where your father is some evil black thing you can't remember. Look, I was going to wait until the fighting was over . . . (*Reflective*) until we had won, before I took them. But something occurred to me for the first time, last night. It was the idea that we might not win. Somehow it only got through to me last night. I'd sort've taken it for granted . . . as a solved problem, that the fighting was the most academic of our problems, and that the real work would come necessarily after the fighting was done. But . . .

EASLEY   Things are not going as well for you as you figured.

WALKER   No. It will take a little longer, that's all. But this city will fall soon. We should be here within a week. You see, I could have waited until then. Then just marched in, at the head of the triumphant army, and seized the children as a matter of course. In fact I don't know why I didn't, except I did want to see you all in what you might call your natural habitats. I thought maybe I might be able to sneak in just as you and my ex-wife were making love, or just as you were lining the girls up against the wall to beat them or make them repeat after you, "Your daddy is a racist murderer." And then I thought I could murder both of you on the spot, and be completely justified.

GRACE   You've convinced yourself that you're rescuing the children, haven't you?

WALKER Just as you convinced yourself you were rescuing them when
  you took them away from me.
EASLEY She was!
WALKER Now so am I.
GRACE Yes (*Wearily*) I begin to get some of your thinking now. When
  you mentioned killing us. I'm sure you thought the whole thing up
  in quite heroic terms. How you'd come through the white lines,
  murder us, and *rescue* the girls. You probably went over that . . .
  or had it go through your head on that gray film, a thousand times
  until it was some kind of obligatory reality. (WALKER *laughs*)
EASLEY The kind of insane reality that brought about all the killing.
WALKER Christ, the worst thing that ever happened to the West was
  the psychological novel . . . believe me.
EASLEY When the Nazis were confronted with Freud, they claimed his
  work was of dubious value.
WALKER Bravo!
GRACE It's a wonder you *didn't* murder us!
WALKER (*Looking suddenly less amused*) Oh . . . have I forfeited my
  opportunity?
EASLEY (*Startled reaction*) You're not serious? What reason . . . what
  possible reason would there be for killing us? I mean I could
  readily conceive of your killing me, but the two of us, as some
  kind of psychological unit. I don't understand that. You said you
  didn't hate Grace.
GRACE (*To press* WALKER) He's lying again, Brad. Really, most times
  he's not to be taken seriously. He was making a metaphor before
  . . . one of those ritual-drama metaphors . . . (*Laughs, as does*
  BRAD) You said it before . . . just to hear what's going on in his
  head. Really, he's not to be taken seriously. (*She hesitates, and
  there is a silence*) Unless there's some way you can kill him.
WALKER (*Laughs, then sobers, but begins to show the effects of the
  alcohol*) Oh, Grace, Grace. Now you're trying to incite your
  husbean . . . which I swear is hardly Christian. I'm really surprised at you. But more so because you completely misunderstand
  me now . . . or maybe I'm not so surprised. I guess you never
  did know what was going on. That's why you left. You thought I
  betrayed you or something. Which really knocked me on my ass,
  you know? I was preaching hate the white man . . . get the white
  man off our backs . . . if necessary, kill the white man for our
  rights . . . whatever the hell that finally came to mean. And
  don't, now, for God's sake start thinking he's disillusioned, he's
  cynical, or any of the rest of these horseshit liberal definitions of

the impossibility or romanticism of idealism. But those things I said . . . and would say now, pushed you away from me. I couldn't understand that.

GRACE   You couldn't understand it? What are you saying?

WALKER   No, I couldn't understand it. We'd been together a long time, before all that happened. What I said . . . what I thought I had to do . . . I knew you, if any white person in the world could, I knew you would understand. And then you didn't.

GRACE   You began to align yourself with the worst kind of racists and second-rate hack political thinkers.

WALKER   I've never aligned myself with anything or anyone I hadn't thought up first.

GRACE   You stopped telling me everything!

WALKER   I never stopped telling you I loved you . . . or that you were my wife!

GRACE   (*Almost broken*)   It wasn't enough, Walker. It wasn't enough.

WALKER   God, it should have been.

GRACE   Walker, you were preaching the murder of all white people. Walker, I was, am, white. What do you think was going through my mind every time you were at some rally or meeting whose sole purpose was to bring about the destruction of white people?

WALKER   Oh, goddamn it, Grace, are you so stupid? You were my wife . . . I loved you. You mean because I loved you and was married to you . . . had had children by you, I wasn't supposed to say the things I felt. I was crying out against three hundred years of oppression; not against individuals.

EASLEY   But it's individuals who are dying.

WALKER   It was individuals who were doing the oppressing. It was individuals who were being oppressed. The horror is that oppression is not a concept that can be specifically transferable. From the oppressed, down on the oppressor. To keep the horror where it belongs . . . on those people who we can speak of, even in this last part of the twentieth century, as evil.

EASLEY   You're so wrong about everything. So terribly, sickeningly wrong. What can you change? What do you hope to change? Do you think Negroes are better people than whites . . . that they can govern a society *better* than whites? That they'll be more judicious or more tolerant? Do you think they'll make fewer mistakes? I mean really, if the Western white man has proved one thing . . . it's the futility of modern society. So the have-not peoples become the haves. Even so, will that change the essential functions of the world? Will there be more love or beauty in the world . . . more knowledge . . . because of it?

WALKER   Probably. Probably there will be more . . . if more people have a chance to understand what it is. But that's not even the point. It comes down to baser human endeavor than any social-political thinking. What does it matter if there's more love or beauty? Who the fuck cares? Is that what the Western ofay[3] thought while he was ruling . . . that his rule somehow brought more love and beauty into the world? Oh, he might have thought that concomitantly, while sipping a gin rickey and scratching his ass . . . but that was not ever the point. Not even on the Crusades. The point is that you had your chance, darling, now these other folks have theirs. (*Quietly*) Now they have theirs.

EASLEY   God, what an ugly idea.

WALKER   (*Head in hands*) I know. I know. (*His head is sagging, but he brings it up quickly. While it is down,* EASLEY *crosses* GRACE *with a significant look*) But what else you got, champion? What else you got? I remember too much horseshit from the other side for you to make much sense. Too much horseshit. The cruelty of it, don't you understand, now? The complete ugly horseshit cruelty of it is that there doesn't have to be a change. It'll be up to individuals on that side, just as it was supposed to be up to individuals on this side. Ha! . . . Who failed! Just like you failed, Easley. Just like you failed.

EASLEY   Failed? What are you talking about?

WALKER   (*Nodding*) Well, what do you think? You never did anything concrete to avoid what's going on now. Your sick liberal lip service to whatever was the least filth. Your high aesthetic disapproval of the political. Letting the sick ghosts of the thirties strangle whatever chance we had.

EASLEY   What are you talking about?

WALKER   What we argued about so many times . . . befo' de wah.

EASLEY   And you see . . . what I predicted has happened. Now, in whatever cruel, and you said it, cruel political synapse you're taken with, or anyone else is taken with, with sufficient power I, any individual, any person who thinks of life as a purely anarchic relationship between man and God . . . or man and his work . . . any consciousness like that is destroyed . . . along with your *enemies*. And you, for whatever right or freedom or sickening cause you represent, kill me. Kill what does not follow.

WALKER   Perhaps you're right. But I have always found it hard to be neutral when faced with ugliness. Especially an ugliness that has worked all my life to twist me.

---

[3] Derogatory term for white man, pig latin for *foe*.

GRACE   And so you let it succeed!

WALKER   The aesthete came long after all the things that really formed me. It was the easiest weight to shed. And I couldn't be merely a journalist . . . a social critic. No social protest . . . right is in the act! And the act itself has some place in the world . . . it makes some place for itself. Right? But you all accuse me, not understanding that what you represent, you, my wife, all our old intellectual cut-throats, was something that was going to die anyway. One way or another. You'd been used too often, backed off from reality too many times. Remember the time, remember that time long time ago, in the old bar when you and Louie Rino were arguing with me, and Louie said then that he hated people who wanted to change the world. You remember that?

EASLEY   I remember the fight.

WALKER   Yeah, well, I know I thought then that none of you would write any poetry either. I knew that you had moved too far away from the actual meanings of life . . . into some lifeless cocoon of pretended intellectual and emotional achievement, to really be able to see the world again. What was Rino writing before he got killed? Tired elliptical little descriptions of what he could see out the window.

EASLEY   And how did he die?

WALKER   An explosion in the school where he was teaching. (*Nodding*)

EASLEY   One of your terrorists did it.

WALKER   Yeah, yeah.

EASLEY   He was supposed to be one of your closest friends.

WALKER   Yeah, yeah.

GRACE   Yeah, yeah, yeah, yeah. (*With face still covered*)

WALKER   We called for a strike to show the government we had all the white intellectuals backing us. (*Nodding*) Hah, and the only people who went out were those tired political hacks. No one wanted to be intellectually compromised.

EASLEY   I didn't go either. (*Hunches* GRACE, *starts to ease out of his chair*) And it was an intellectual compromise. No one in their right mind could have backed your program completely.

WALKER   No one but Negroes.

EASLEY   Well, then, they weren't in their right minds. You'd twisted them.

WALKER   The country twisted 'em. (*Still nodding*) The country had twisted them for so long. (*Head almost touching his chest*)

EASLEY   (*Taking very cautious step toward* WALKER, *still talking*) The politics of self-pity. (*Indicates to* GRACE *that she is to talk*)

WALKER (*Head down*)   Yeah. Yeah.

EASLEY   The politics of self-pity.

GRACE (*Raising her head slowly to watch, almost petrified*)   A murderous self-pity. An extraordinarily murderous self-pity.
(*There is another explosion close to the house. The lights go out for a few seconds. They come on, and* EASLEY *is trying to return to his seat, but* WALKER'S *head is still on his chest.*)

WALKER (*Mumbles*)   What'd they do, hit the lights? Goddamn lousy marksmen. (EASLEY *starts again*) Lousy marksmen . . . and none of 'em worth shit.
(*Now, another close explosion. The lights go out again. They come on;* EASLEY *is standing almost halfway between the couch and* WALKER. WALKER'S *head is still down on his chest.* EASLEY *crouches to move closer. The lights go out again.*)

BLACK
(*More explosions*)

Act II

Explosions are heard before the curtain goes up. When curtain rises, room is still in darkness, but the explosion does throw some light. Figures are still as they were at the end of first act; light from explosions outlines them briefly.

WALKER   Shit.
(*Lights come up.* WALKER'S *head is still down, but he is nodding from side to side, cursing something very drunkenly.* EASLEY *stands very stiffly in the center of the room, waiting to take another step.* GRACE *sits very stiffly, breathing heavily, on the couch, trying to make some kind of conversation, but not succeeding.* WALKER *has his hand in his jacket pocket, on the gun.*)

GRACE   It is self-pity, and some weird ambition, Walker. (*Strained silence*) But there's no reason . . . the girls should suffer. There's . . . no reason.
(EASLEY *takes a long stride, and is about to throw himself at* WALKER, *when there is another explosion, and the lights go out again, very briefly. When they come up,* EASLEY *is set to leap, but*

WALKER'S *head comes abruptly up. He stares drunkenly at* EASLEY, *not moving his hand. For some awkward duration of time the two men stare at each other, in almost the same way as they had at the beginning of the play. Then* GRACE *screams.*)

GRACE   Walker!

(WALKER *looks at her slightly, and* EASLEY *throws himself on him. The chair falls backward and the two men roll on the floor.* EASLEY *trying to choke* WALKER. WALKER *trying to get the gun out of his pocket.*)

GRACE   Walker! Walker!

(*Suddenly,* WALKER *shoves one hand in* EASLEY'S *face, shooting him without taking the gun from his pocket.* EASLEY *slumps backward, his face twisted, his mouth open and working.* WALKER *rolls back off* EASLEY, *pulling the gun from his pocket. He props himself against the chair, staring at the man's face.*)

GRACE   Walker. (*Her shouts have become whimpers, and she is moving stiffly toward* EASLEY) Walker. Walker.

EASLEY   (*Mouth is still working . . . and he is managing to get a few sounds, words, out*)

WALKER   (*Still staring at him, pulling himself up on the chair*)   Shut up, you! (*To* EASLEY) You shut up. I don't want to hear anything else from you. You just die, quietly. No more talk.

GRACE   Walker! (*She is screaming again*) Walker! (*She rushes toward* EASLEY, *but* WALKER *catches her arm and pushes her away*) You're an insane man. You hear me, Walker? (*He is not looking at her, he is still staring down at* EASLEY) Walker, you're an insane man. (*She screams*) You're an insane man. (*She slumps to the couch, crying*) An insane man . . .

WALKER   No profound statements, Easley. No horseshit like that. No elegance. You just die quietly and stupidly. Like niggers do. Like they are now. (*Quieter*) Like I will. The only thing I'll let you say is, "I only regret that I have but one life to lose for my country." You can say that. (*Looks over at* GRACE) Grace! Tell Bradford that he can say, "I only regret that I have but one life to lose for my country." You can say that, Easley, but that's all.

EASLEY   (*straining to talk*) Ritual drama. Like I said, ritual drama . . . (*He dies.*)

(WALKER *stands staring at him. The only sounds are an occasional explosion, and* GRACE'S *heavy brittle weeping.*)

WALKER   He could have said, "I only regret that I have but one life to lose for my country." I would have let him say that . . . but no more.

No more. There is no reason he should go out with any kind of
dignity. I couldn't allow that.

GRACE   You're out of your mind. (*Slow, matter-of-fact*)

WALKER   Meaning?

GRACE   You're out of your mind.

WALKER   (*Wearily*)   Turn to another station.

GRACE   You're out of your mind.

WALKER   I said, turn to another station . . . will you? Another station!
Out of my mind is not the point. You ought to know that. (*Brooding*) The way things are, being out of your mind is the only thing
that qualifies you to stay alive. The only thing. Easley was in his
right mind. Pitiful as he was. That's the reason he's dead.

GRACE   He's dead because you killed him.

WALKER   Yeah. He's dead because I killed him. Also, because he thought
he ought to kill me. (*Looking over at the dead man*) You want
me to cover him up?

GRACE   I don't want you to do anything, Walker . . . but leave here.
(*Raising her voice*) Will you do that for me . . . or do you want
to kill me too?

WALKER   Are you being ironic? Huh? (*He grabs her arm, jerking her
head up so she has to look at him*) Do you think you're being
ironic? Or do you want to kill me, too? . . . (*Shouting*) You're
mighty right I want to kill you. You're mighty god damn right.
Believe me, self-righteous little bitch, I want to kill you.

GRACE   (*Startled, but trying not to show it*)   The cause demands it, huh?
The cause demands it.

WALKER   Yeah, the cause demands it.

GRACE   (*She gets up and goes to* EASLEY, *kneeling beside the body*)   The
cause demands it, Brad. That's why Walker shot you . . . because
the cause demands it. (*Her head droops but she doesn't cry. She
sits on her knees, holding the dead man's hand*) I guess the point
is that now when you take the children I'll be alone. (*She looks up
at* WALKER) I guess that's the point, now. Is that the point, Walker?
Me being alone . . . as you have been now for so long? I'll bet that's
the point, huh? I'll bet you came here to do exactly what you did
. . . kill Brad, then take the kids, and leave me alone . . . to suffocate
in the stink of my memories. (*She is trying not to cry*) Just like
I did to you. I'm sure that's the point. Right? (*She leaps up suddenly at* WALKER) You scum! You murdering scum. (*They grapple
for a second, then* WALKER *slaps her to the floor. She kneels a little
way off from* EASLEY's *body*)

WALKER   Yeh, Grace. That's the point. For sure, that's the point.

GRACE   You were going to kill Brad, from the first. You knew that before you even got here.

WALKER   I'd thought about it.

GRACE   (*Weeping, but then she stops and is quiet for a minute*)   So what's supposed to happen then . . . I mean after you take the kids and leave me here alone? Huh? I know you've thought about that, too.

WALKER   I have. But you know what'll happen much better than I do. But maybe you don't. What do you think happened to me when you left? Did you ever think about that? You must have.

GRACE   You had your cause, friend. Your cause, remember. And thousands of people following you, hoping that shit you preached was right. I pitied you.

WALKER   I know that. It took me awhile, but then I finally understood that you did pity me. And that you were somewhere, going through whatever mediocre routine you and Easley called your lives . . . pitying me. I figured that, finally, you weren't really even shocked by what was happening . . . what had happened. You were so secure in the knowledge that you were good, and compassionate . . . and right, that most of all . . . you were certain, my God, so certain . . . emotionally and intellectually, that you were right, until the only idea you had about me was to pity me. (*He wheels around to face her squarely*) God, that pissed me off. You don't really know how furious that made me. You and that closet queen, respected, weak-as-water intellectual, pitying me. God. God! (*Forcing the humor*) Miss Easley, honey, I could have killed both of you every night of my life.

GRACE   Will you kill me now if I say right here that I still pity you?

WALKER   (*A breathless half-broken little laugh*)   No. No, I won't kill you.

GRACE   Well, I pity you, Walker. I really do.

WALKER   Only until you start pitying yourself.

GRACE   I wish I could call you something that would hurt you.

WALKER   So do I.

GRACE   (*Wearily*)   Nigger.

WALKER   So do I. (*Looks at his watch*)   I've got to go soon.

GRACE   You're still taking the girls. (*She is starting to push herself up from the floor*)
(WALKER *stares at her, then quickly over his shoulder at the stairway. He puts his hand in the pocket where the gun is, then he shakes his head slowly.*)

GRACE   (*Not seeing this gesture*)   You're still taking the children?

(WALKER *shakes his head slowly. An explosion shakes the house a little*)

GRACE   Walker. Walker. (*She staggers to her feet, shaking with the next explosion*) Walker? You shook your head? (WALKER *stands very stiffly looking at the floor*)
(GRACE *starts to come to him, and the next explosion hits very close or actually hits the house. Beams come down; some of the furniture is thrown around.* GRACE *falls to the floor.* WALKER *is toppled backward. A beam hits* GRACE *across the chest. Debris falls on* WALKER. *There are more explosions, and then silence.*)

GRACE   Walker! Walker! (*She is hurt very badly and is barely able to move the debris that is covering her*) Walker! The girls! Walker! Catherine! Elizabeth! Walker, the girls!
(WALKER *finally starts to move. He is also hurt badly, but he is able to move much more freely than* GRACE. *He starts to clear away the debris and make his way to his knees.*)

GRACE   Walker?

WALKER   Yeah? Grace?

GRACE   Walker, the children . . . the girls . . . see about the girls. (*She is barely able to raise one of her arms*) The girls, Walker, see about them.

WALKER   (*He is finally able to crawl over to* GRACE, *and pushes himself unsteadily up on his hands*) You're hurt pretty badly? Can you move?

GRACE   The girls, Walker, see about the girls.

WALKER   Can you move?

GRACE   The girls, Walker . . . (*She is losing strength*) Our children!

WALKER   (*He is silent for a while*) They're dead, Grace. Catherine and Elizabeth are dead.
(*He starts up stairs as if to verify his statement. Stops, midway, shakes his head; retreats.*)

GRACE   (*Looking up at him frantically, but she is dying*) Dead? Dead? (*She starts to weep and shake her head*) Dead? (*Then she stops suddenly, tightening her face*) How . . . how do you know, Walker? How do you know they're dead? (WALKER's *head is drooping slightly*) How do you know they're dead, Walker? How do you . . .
(*Her eyes try to continue what she is saying, but she slumps, and dies in a short choking spasm.*)
(WALKER *looks to see that she is dead, then resumes his efforts to get up. He looks at his watch. Listens to see if it is running. Wipes his face. Pushes the floor to get up. Another explosion sounds very*

close and he crouches quickly, covering his head. Another explosion. He pushes himself up, brushing sloppily at his clothes. He looks at his watch again, then starts to drag himself toward the door.)

WALKER They're dead, Grace! (*He is almost shouting*) They're dead. (*He leaves, stumbling unsteadily through the door. He is now the old man at the beginning of the play. There are more explosions. Another one very close to the house. A sudden aggravated silence, and then there is a child heard crying and screaming as loud as it can. More explosions*)

BLACK
(*More explosions, after curtain for some time.*)

COMMENTARY

The Slave (1964)   In one sense, LeRoi Jones's *The Slave* might be regarded as a sequel to Bertolt Brecht's *Saint Joan of the Stockyards*, since one of Joan's final perceptions, "Only force helps where force rules," is the starting point of *The Slave*.[1] The title of Jones's play looks three ways —to the past at the initial role of the black man in the new world, to the present when ideational shackles enchain him, and to the future when in a national and perhaps international black revolution he sheds both literal and metaphoric slavery.

Since the United States' emergence as a nation, the rights of black Americans have been compromised. Prophetically, the Continental Congress in 1776 made only one substantive change in the draft of the Declaration of Independence presented to them by Thomas Jefferson.[2] In compliance with the wishes of the delegates from South Carolina and Georgia, says Jefferson in his *Autobiography*, the Congress deleted a section that denounced slavery as an "execrable commerce," a "cruel war against human nature itself," and a violation of the "most sacred rights of life and liberty." Although Abraham Lincoln's Emancipation Proclamation of 1863 abolished slavery, economic, social, and political shackles still bound black Americans. Exactly one century later, Martin Luther King, Jr. in his famous "I have a dream" speech testified that his dream of true racial equality was not yet a reality. Whereas Dr. King urged nonviolence to achieve an egalitarian goal in an integrated United States, other blacks rejected both nonviolence and integration. In 1964, one year after Dr. King's speech and the same year *The Slave* was written, Malcolm X urged the people and government of the United States immediately to give black Americans what the Constitution says all Americans should have. "It isn't that time is running out—time has run out!" he exclaimed, and he warned that unless blacks were given the ballot they would use the bullet. *The Slave* takes place after such warnings have been ignored.

Does the title of Jones's play refer only to the Negro? In the Prologue, Walker appears as an old field slave, and the past is not only prologue to the present but also an emblem of the black man's status today. Whereas the Prologue shows a literal slave, the play proper reveals figurative slaves, for its three characters have been shackled to what the

---

[1] C. W. E. Bigsby (see bibliography) relates this passage to Jones's entire dramatic work.

[2] Drafted by a committee consisting of Thomas Jefferson, Benjamin Franklin, John Adams, Robert R. Livingston, and Roger Sherman, the Declaration of Independence is chiefly the work of Jefferson.

author regards as outmoded ideals. Easley and Grace still cling to liberal conceptions of black-white relationships. Only Walker Vessels, who had been in thrall to such liberal ideals as integration and to the apolitical aestheticism of the artist, is able to shed these notions. Recently wed to the white woman and taught by the white man, Walker in destroying them severs his bondage to whites and their culture.[3] As the characters' names suggest, Walker rejects the easy, politically uninvolved life of the liberal man, divorces himself from the condescendingly divine favor (grace) of the white woman, empties his intellectual and emotional vessels of their liberal ideals, and walks away a free man.

Symbolically important in the fabric of this play are Walker's and Grace's children, who do not appear. Each parent wants custody of them, but will either race control the other's future? Offspring of a white mother and a black father, these children are symbols of integration. As such, can they survive in either a white or a black society? In a white society, says Walker, they are "freakish mulattos in a world where [their] father is some evil black thing." Does he believe that in a black society they would be freakish mulattos in a world where their mother is some evil white thing? Their death—if it is true that he killed them—might suggest this, and it does symbolize the death of integration at his hands. But did he murder them? Although he tells his dying ex-wife that their daughters are dead and although she realizes the only way he could know is that he killed them, one of the final stage directions provides a tantalizing ambiguity. After Walker leaves, *"there is a child heard crying and screaming as loud as it can."*

In *The Slave*, the black man's enemy is not the reactionary, overt racist but the liberal, whose ideals, according to Jones, are similarly racist. Jones represents the white liberal as spineless, ineffectual, evasive, and hypocritical. Giving blacks no more than "sick liberal lip service," Walker charges Easley, "You never did anything concrete to avoid what's going on now." Unable or unwilling to act, the liberal "backed off from reality" and immersed himself in "some lifeless cocoon of pretended intellectual

---

[3] It is difficult to avoid identifying Jones's views with those of Walker Vessels. Like Jones, Vessels is a poet, propagandist, and social activist. Like Jones, he was married to a white woman, had two daughters, and then was divorced. Like Jones, he is a militant black nationalist. During the riots (or rebellion) in Newark, New Jersey in July, 1967, the white police arrested Jones and charged him with illegally possessing weapons and resisting arrest. Although Jones was found guilty the following January and was sentenced to two and a half to three years in jail, he appealed for a new trial on the grounds that the judge's charge to the jury was improper and prejudicial. A higher court upheld this appeal. While art imitates life, life also imitates art: it should be noted that Jones's divorce and his activities in Newark occurred *after* he wrote *The Slave*.

and emotional achievement. . . ." To Walker, the refusal of intellectual
white liberals, such as Easley, to back the black liberation program (he
did not agree with all its demands, explains Easley) was evasive nit-
picking that revealed the failure of liberalism to render meaningful, effective assistance to black Americans. Easley argues that the blacks who
backed the liberation program "weren't in their right minds. You'd twisted
them." But Walker refuses to allow the guilt to be transferred from the
oppressors to the oppressed, and counters, "The country twisted 'em."
Having rejected neutrality in the face of "an ugliness that has worked all
my life to twist me," he has also rejected the roles of journalist and social
critic. Instead, he has chosen activism. The play's plot—in which a black
militant confronts his white ex-wife and her white, liberal husband, kills
him, and watches her expire—dramatizes the ineffectuality of liberalism
in dealing with the threat of revolution and the destruction of liberalism
by revolution.

With the death of liberalism and the possible death of integration,
with the execution of middle-class blacks assimilated into white culture
(Walker announces that "we have . . . dragged piles of darkies out of their
beds and shot them for being in Rheingold ads"), the black man, according to Jones, is trying to create his own identity and his own culture. As
the old field slave says in the Prologue, "We . . . seek nothing but ourselves." He admits that blacks may be "liars, and . . . murderers" who
resolutely ignore the "deadly filth" of what they feel and do. Walker confesses that the mutual slaughter of blacks and whites "is at best a war that
will only change, ha, the complexion of tyranny," that "the depravity of
[his] murderous philosophies" has killed his creative impulses, and that
intellectually he has more in common with Easley than with his black
officers "who have never read any book in their lives." Unimportant, claims
Walker, is the question of whether the blacks will necessarily create a
better society. What matters is that the whites who had the opportunity
failed, and that the black revolutionists are an alternative not yet tested:
"The point is that you had your chance, darling, now these other folks
have theirs." Perpetuation of the *status quo* is intolerable and unaccept-
able. Because the black revolution may achieve meaningful social improvement, declares Walker, it supersedes considerations of murder,
artistic creativity, and intellectuality. When Easley laments the destruction of the city, country, or world by the revolutionists, Walker shrilly
asserts that "if this shitty town is being flattened . . . it needs it."

As blacks battle whites, myths battle myths and words are used as
weapons. Implying the myth of Negro inferiority, Easley condescendingly
calls Walker by his last name, without the "Mr." and even addresses him
as "boy." Provoked by Walker, Grace calls him "nigger." With equal

condenscension, Walker addresses Easley as "Brad" and "Mr. Easley." Utilizing the myth of black sexual prowess, he taunts Easley, "I'll stay here and rape your wife" and referring to him as "faggot," "fairy," "closet queen," and "Professor No-Dick," he asserts that Easley is not "among those of us who screw." Although such epithets are vivid metaphors for the liberal's lack of virility, there is no evidence that they are literally true. As anti-white weapons, Walker adapts white racist myths about non-whites and taunts Easley by mimicking three non-whites in a menacing and mocking manner. He dances and whoops like an Indian on the warpath; he demands, mixing clichés about Indians and Africans, "Bwana, me want more fire water"; and imitating a cliché Japanese soldier of World War II, he calls Easley "doomed American dog"—thus suggesting the worldwide scope of the revolution that is the play's background. The New York production employed a visual parody of a racist stereotype: Walker wore an armband with the insignia of the black revolutionary army, a grinning, big-lipped minstrel.

The white couple of *The Slave* often appear to be stereotypes: flabby liberals with thinly disguised racist attitudes. By giving them weak arguments or none at all, Jones appears unfairly to stack the cards against them. When, for instance, Grace explains to her black ex-husband, "Walker, you were preaching the murder of all white people. Walker, I was, am, white. What do you think was going through my mind every time you were at some rally or meeting whose sole purpose was to bring about the destruction of white people?" Walker claims that to do otherwise would be to keep silent in the face of centuries of oppression and that though he did not say so she should have realized his anti-white outcries did not include her. Unfortunately for the sake of dramatic dialectic, Grace makes no reply and Easley's rejoinder is inadequate. Since Jones is certainly familiar with such possible responses as "opposition to whites who oppress blacks is different from opposition to whites generally," he could have but obviously did not wish to give the liberals a better argument. Perhaps, as some critics contend, he accepts black racial myths. Perhaps, as others believe, he is indulging in sadomasochistic fantasies. More likely, I think, is the conclusion that Jones's intent, which is neither understanding nor intellectual exploration, does not permit dramatic dialectic. Instead, he is interested in a particular kind of social drama— through the eyes of black victims of white America, from the viewpoint of a black revolutionist. In creating this type of play, he aims to transform stereotype into archetype and, in the words of the field slave of the Prologue, "[discover] racially the funds of the universe." In presenting the crumbling of liberal white America and the emergence of the colonized black into freedom, Jones tries to create what Easley in his dying words calls "ritual drama," but a ritual of black revolution.

Consonant with Jones's program of a social theatre of and for black Americans, *The Slave* speaks directly to what he conceives to be their needs and aspirations. This theatre echoes Malcolm X's declaration, "I see America through the eyes of the victim. I don't see any American dream; I see an American nightmare." It portrays America through the eyes of black victims, dramatizes their problems in order to make a black audience feel brotherhood with them, and suggests a remedy: a black revolution that will destroy racist America. *The Slave* is a striking example of social theatre, political theatre, black revolutionary theatre.

Bibliography

A. Plays about the Black Revolution:

Kingsley B. Bass, Jr., *We Righteous Bombers*, 1968.
Ben Caldwell, *Family Portrait (or My Son the Black Nationalist)*, 1967; *The Job*, 1968.
Jimmy Garrett, *And We Own the Night*, 1967.
Jean Genet, *The Blacks*, 1958.
LeRoi Jones, *Black Mass*, 1965; *Dutchman*, 1964; *Experimental Death Unit #1*, 1964; *Madheart*, 1966.
Herbert Stokes, *The Man Who Trusted the Devil Twice*, 1969.

B. Works about LeRoi Jones and The Slave:

Bigsby, C. W. E. *Confrontation and Commitment: A Study of Contemporary American Drama 1959–1966*. Columbia: University of Missouri Press, 1968.
Brustein, Robert. *Seasons of Discontent: Dramatic Opinions 1959–1965*. New York: Simon and Schuster, 1967.
Jones, LeRoi. *Home: Social Essays*. New York: Morrow, 1960.
Neal, Larry. "The Black Arts Movement," *Tulane Drama Review, XII* (Summer, 1968).
Richardson, Jack. "Blues for Mr. Jones," *Esquire, LXV* (June, 1966).

The
Brown
Revolution

JUSTICE
Guadalupe de Saavedra

JUSTICE
Guadalupe de Saavedra

CHARACTERS

NARRATOR
OLD FARMER (*Honkie Sam*)
DOG
MADRE (*Mother*)
COMPADRE (*Friend*)
LITTLE GIRL
FIGURE IN BLACK
VILLAGERS

(*Narrator comes on stage.*)

NARRATOR Quihoble, Raza.[1] Les voy a contar un cuento de mi pueblo.[2] I am going to tell you a tale of my village. In the old days, there lived an old, pale, sickly excuse for a human being named Honkie Sam.

(HONKIE *makes his entrance from right. He wears a Texas hat and a sign round his neck: "Honkie Sam." He prances and struts about the stage.*)

Now, Honkie Sam had gotten his entire fortune by stealing and robbing from the pobre.

HONKIE W-aaa-lll, you know how it is. Law of the jungle. And after all, I am the whitest dude in the universe, and you know that *White* is *all pure.*

NARRATOR As always happens to those that are greedy, Sam had spread himself too thin. Sam stood in danger of losing all that he had. He

[1] Greetings, my people [lit., my race].
[2] Translated in next sentence.

couldn't sleep at nights. Y, sabes que,[3] he had developed ulcers. Now, the people of my village had over the years gotten a fill of Honkie Sam.

(SAM *continues pacing on the left of the stage. On the right side,* TWO VILLAGERS *appear and start talking to each other. They wear signs: "Madre" and "Compadre.")*

MADRE   Oye, compadre, el Honkie Sam nos trata como animales. Ayer[4] he demanded all of our corn.

COMPADRE   That's right. Sabes que,[5] yesterday they took most of my plata.[6] There is hardly enough left for us to eat, y menos to have a small tragito de pulque now and then. Que hacemos?[7] (*They drop to their knees.*)

MADRE *and* COMPADRE   Dios nuestro ten piedad de nosotros.[8]

NARRATOR   (*as* VOICE OF GOD)   My children, this is your God talking to you. Over. (*They pray.*) I have only one thing to say to you. Don't waste time! Organize! Over and out.

(MADRE *and* COMPADRE *look at the heavens amazed, then move off stage.*)

NARRATOR   Meanwhile, back at the ranch, Sam was in mortal fear. Honkie bought himself some dogs and trained them.

HONKIE   (*snaps his fingers*).   Here, boy. Here, boy.

(*The* DOG *enters. On his head is a police helmet and round his neck, a sign: "Dog." He licks his master's boots while wagging his tail, then lays himself down at his feet.*)

NARRATOR   The dogs had no mind of their own. They were conditioned to act by remote control.

HONKIE   (*holds* DOG *by collar and snaps his fingers*)   Go, boy, go!

DOG   (*to audience*)   Arf! Arf! *Kill! Kill! Kill! Kill!* Arf! Arf! Arf!

HONKIE   Down, boy, down. Sit, sit. (*Pulls* DOG *to his side and watches over his property.*)

NARRATOR   Honkie sent his dogs to maim and brutalize the populace.

(HONKIE *turns* DOG *loose.* DOG *heads toward backstage. Two sharp, screeching screams are heard.* DOG *returns to master's side.*)
The dogs became known as the *mad dogs.*

---

[3] And, you know . . .
[4] Listen, friend, Honkie Sam treats us like animals. Yesterday . . .
[5] You know . . .
[6] Money.
[7] . . . *much less* to have a small *drink of pulque* [fermented juice of the maguey] now and then. *What shall we do?*
[8] Our God, have mercy on us.

(*The* DOG *then makes mad faces and noises.*)

And the people of the village became more and more concerned, and they sent a delegation to Honkie Sam.

(*Enter* VILLAGERS, *with the* NARRATOR *joining in, marching in a single line, singing.*)

VILLAGERS (*in unison*) De colores,
De colores,
Se pinta los campos en la primavera.[9]

(*The* VILLAGERS *stop in front of* HONKIE SAM. HONKIE *holds the* DOG *by the collar. The* DOG *growls. The* VILLAGERS *recoil, meekly hold their hands in front of them.*)

COMPADRE Mister Sam, we came, señor, to beg you to please tell your pets to be more careful. They have begun to hurt our people. This we beg, please. (*Turns to other* VILLAGERS.) Is that not so?

HONKIE W-aaa-l, now. Le's see, mah little brown brothers. Mah friends, come now, let us reason together. (*Takes out a pot of atole, dips fingers in, and feeds the* VILLAGERS.)[10] Here is one for you. And some for you. And Honkie would never forget you. Go now, mah chillun.

(VILLAGERS *march off stage, with the exception of the* NARRATOR, *who returns to his position.*)

NARRATOR But Honkie was slick. He was lying and he knew it. Honkie did not call his dogs off, but instead unleashed them and gave them free rein.

HONKIE (*chuckling, turns* DOG *loose*) I'll teach them stupid idiots. Dirty Mexicans! (*Walks off stage.*)

(DOG *is roaming in the center of the stage. A* VILLAGE GIRL *starts to walk across the stage. The* DOG *attacks her and kills her, then runs off stage. A* VILLAGER *walks on stage, finds the* GIRL, *and calls out.*)

VILLAGER ¡Auxilio![11] Help! Help! Help!

(*Other* VILLAGERS *enter and gather round the body.*)

SECOND VILLAGER This is too much. I have had it.

THIRD VILLAGER Sí, mano,[12] we must do something ourselves.

SECOND VILLAGER I say that the guilty dog should die.

THIRD VILLAGER Sí, sí, the dog must die.

(VILLAGERS *pick up the body. They chant and march off chanting,*

[9] With colors,/With colors,/The fields are painted in the Spring.

[10] To feed someone *atole* (a thick, corn meal drink) with one's fingers, an expression in the Southwest, means giving him leftovers instead of a full meal.

[11] Help!

[12] Yes, brother [*mano* is a shortened form of *hermano*].

"The dog must die!" *The* DOG *enters and walks around. A hooded* FIGURE IN BLACK *enters and shoots the* DOG. *The* DOG *dies. The hooded* FIGURE IN BLACK *steps to stage left.*)

NARRATOR   That very night the mad Dog was killed by forces unknown.

HONKIE *(heard from off stage)*   Here, boy. Where are you at? Here, boy. *(He enters, sees the dead* DOG, *and kneels beside it, crying, sobbing, broken-hearted, and lost.*)

NARRATOR   And this continued. Every time that a dog attacked a person of the village, the carcass of the dog would be found in the gutter —dead, dead, dead.

*(*HONKIE'S *crying gets louder and louder.*)

And it came to pass that the dogs, stupid as they were, got the message and no longer attacked the village people.

DOG *(half-raising himself to a semi-sitting position)*   Ujule,[13] we may be mad dogs, but we know when to quit. Brother dogs: hell, no, we won't go! *(Starts chanting, stops when* HONKIE *hits him on the head.* HONKIE *is still crying.*)

NARRATOR   The people of the village were proud of their accomplishments. They had met and learned the meaning of Justice.

FIGURE IN BLACK *(uncovers a sign that reads "Justice")*

Yo soy la Justicia.
Soy hijo de la verdad.
Tengo una mano de acero
Para el que no quiera pagar.[14]

(The people of the village come on stage. JUSTICE *walks over to them. The* VILLAGERS *and* JUSTICE *embrace each other.*)

NARRATOR   Justice belongs to the people. In the final analysis, it is the people who administer it. *(Walks over and joins the group.*)

(The group then points their fingers at HONKIE SAM *and begins advancing toward him in slow motion, driving him off the stage while echoing slogans.*)

GROUP IN UNISON   ¡Viva la Justicia!
¡Viva la Verdad!
¡Viva la Causa!
¡Viva la Raza![15]

---

[13] Of course . . .

[14] I am Justice./I am the son of truth [or *daughter—hija*—if an actress plays the role]./I have a fist of steel for he who does not want to pay.

[15] Long live Justice!/Long live Truth!/Long live the Cause!/Long live our people! [*La Causa* (the cause) here refers to the movement for the advancement of Chicano rights in the United States.]

(*After* HONKIE SAM *is driven off the stage, the group faces the audience and with clenched fists shouts:*)

       ¡Orale, raza, no se deje!

       ¡Organise, raza![16]

(*One of the women begins to have labor pains. Everyone gathers round her. Someone calls (to audience):* "Is there a doctor in the house?" *Another cries:* "She's having a baby!" *Then, another cries:* "It's a boy! It's a boy!" *Everyone forms a stage picture of the Nativity scene with the woman who just gave birth cradling a picture (as Mary held Jesus) of Che Guevara.*)

---

[16] Listen to what I'm telling you, my people, do not allow yourselves to be had!/Organize yourselves, my people!

COMMENTARY

Justice (1968) *Justice*, by Guadalupe de Saavedra, derives from and is part of *la Causa*. Literally "the Cause," *la Causa* refers to two causes. One is *la Huelga* (the strike) against the deplorable working conditions of Mexican-American grape pickers on California farms and the accompanying boycott of table grapes grown in the vineyards against whose owners the workers are striking. The other is the struggle by Chicanos (Mexican-Americans) to achieve full civil rights and to maintain their ethnic identity. Their name probably stemming from *Mexicanos* (with *x* given the *ch* pronunciation of the Chihuahua Indians), Chicanos are part of *la Raza* (literally, "the Race," usually translated as "the People"), North and South American *mestizos* (people of mixed Indian and Spanish or Portuguese blood) of Spanish surname and language. *El Día de la Raza* (the Day of *la Raza*), celebrated on both sides of the Rio Grande, is October 12, Columbus Day.

Chicanos are a significant portion of the population of southwestern United States—over two million in California, over a million and a half in Texas, and more than three-quarters of a million in New Mexico, Arizona, and Colorado. In the Treaty of Guadalupe-Hidalgo (1848), the United States acquired land from Mexico and guaranteed the rights of Mexicans living there, including recognition of their language (Spanish) in these southwestern territories. Despite this, Chicanos have been discriminated against and subjected to virtual peonage, and white authorities have attempted to suppress their language. Angry at such treatment and resentful of the stereotype of the Mexican and Mexican-American as a loafer lazily enjoying a siesta beneath a sombrero, Chicanos are also determined to resist pressures to conform to the *Anglo* (white American) way of life. Militant Chicanos demand the immediate end of prejudice and discrimination in all phases of their lives, community control of police and education, the teaching of Spanish as a first language and English as a second, restoration of land taken from the pueblos as well as restitution for mineral and other resources taken from it.

Utilizing theatre to further these goals, Teatro Chicano is one of the more militant and radical manifestations of *la Causa*. In their pamphlet-program, the members of Teatro Chicano declare "the independence of our mestizo nation." Protesting against "the brutal gringo [white man] invasion of our territories," they affirm their unity with all Chicanos in the "struggles against the foreigner gabacho [white man] who exploits our riches and destroys our culture." Aiming to educate, organize, and mobilize *la Raza* in the southwest, their productions include songs, poetry readings, and *actos* (short, one-act plays) that satirically and farcically "present the obstacles that confront *la Raza* in our struggle towards liberation" and "offer solutions and alternatives." Saavedra regards Teatro Chicano as a sower of "seeds of liberation among our peoples" and hopes to have a teatro in every Chicano *barrio* (district or neighborhood) in the southwest.

Although Teatro Chicano derives from and is part of *la Causa*, its inspiration was the Teatro Campesino (Farm Workers' Theatre), which was created in 1965 in Delano, California—the center of the striking grape pickers—by Luis Valdez, who wanted to use theatre to educate the Chicano farm workers about the causes of their condition, unions, and *la Huelga*. In simple scenes performed on picket lines, in farm communities, and at union meetings, such caricatures as noble *Huelgista* (Striker) and villainous *Esquirol* (Scab)—each with an identifying placard hung round his neck—dramatized with broad humor the farm workers' problems. Stimulated by these productions, as well as by their effect on the audiences of farm workers, Saavedra in 1968 founded Teatro Chicano in Los Angeles to deal with the problems of Chicanos in city barrios. Like its forerunner, Teatro Chicano employs masks, caricatures, and simple situations to convey clear messages to unsophisticated audiences.

A theatre for a people whose first (in some cases, only) language is Spanish, Teatro Chicano is bilingual. Dialogue is sometimes delivered in one language, sometimes in the other. Sometimes, Spanish phrases are immediately translated into English. Sometimes, Spanish and English are interlaced in the same sentence. Depending upon the audience, the amount of each language varies from one performance to another. Audience-centered plays, the *actos* of Teatro Chicano, such as *Justice*, contain such easily recognizable references as "mad dogs" (police) and a Texas-accented *Anglo* who implores the people to come and reason together (a phrase of former President Lyndon B. Johnson). Changes in audience dictate changes in performance. In areas where the grape strike is a major issue, Honkie Sam may ad lib, "Buy my grapes." In Los Angeles, where "Protect and Serve" is an emblem on the side of police prowl cars, Sam tells his dogs to protect and serve. In performance, caricatures of gentle Chicanos and their villainous oppressors are played zestfully, broadly, and with as much comedy—often slapstick—as possible. In *Justice*, Honkie Sam struts about the stage, lording it over the meek Chicanos. Urging the dog to intimidate them, the actor, gnashing his teeth, almost growls. When the Narrator says that Sam has ulcers, the actor vomits into his hat, then puts it back on his head.

Portraying godly and diabolical forces in conflict, like medieval morality plays, the *actos* of the Teatro Chicano deal with three general themes: ethnic identity, the need for organization to fight the evils which *Anglo* society perpetrates on Chicanos, and revolution. The assertion of ethnic identity is not merely a matter of affirming what the audience already believes, though this is partly the case. A more important part is helping the audience create a sense of their own identity as Chicanos. In *A Boy Says Goodbye to His Mother*, for example, a racist schoolteacher (wearing a sign, "Angela Anglo") transforms a Chicano boy into an *Agringada* (a Mexican-American who has embraced the *Anglo* way of life), whereupon, instead of treating his *madre* politely, he impolitely talks to his ma. Thinking of himself as an *Anglo*, he is disabused of this fallacy by a brutal, racist policeman. Reeducated by fellow Chicanos into accepting his Chicano heritage, he rebels against Angela Anglo. Graphically symbolizing the stages of his transformation, the placards around his neck are changed from "*Niño*" (Boy) to "American" to "*Hombre*" (Man). Many of the *actos* depict the present problems of Chicanos in *barrios*. In *Welfare*, a whip-wielding social worker (Angela Anglo again) demands that "those dirty little Mexicans" line up and, in order to receive welfare payments, kiss her well-padded butt. This is done by all members of a Chicano family, including a babe in arms. In *Yerba Buena* (slang for marijuana), a white policeman stops a little girl who, frightened, starts to run. Pulling out his gun and shooting her without warning, he then intones, reeling it off by rote, "Halt, halt, halt, stop in the name of the law or I'll fire," and adds in an aside to the audience, "That ought to take care of the Supreme Court." When Chicanos ask each other what they can do to prevent such actions, the Policeman tells them, "There ain't nothing you can do, 'cause you ain't organized."

"Organize!"—as the Voice of God tells the Villagers in *Justice*— is the message of most of the Teatro Chicano's *actos*. Even *The Battle of Puebla*—a historical *acto* about the decisive battle of May 5, 1862, in which the Mexicans, led by General Ignacio Zaragoza and inspired by President Benito Juarez, defeated the invading French armies—has contemporary relevance in the *barrios*, for in dealing with the organized Mexican people's defeat of white outsiders who seek to dominate them, it conveys a militant message to Chicanos who resent *Anglo* efforts to dominate their lives and suppress their aspirations.

Teatro Chicano regards organization as a necessary but not as a sufficient goal. As suggested by the image of the Cuban rebel leader Che Guevara at the end of *Justice*, the next step is revolution: transforming society itself, perhaps along socialist lines. In *Justice*, the Chicanos are exploited by an *Anglo* property owner, Honkie Sam. Discriminated against because they are not white, they are treated like animals by Sam, who takes most of what they produce and keeps them subjugated by force and trickery. The people want to end such abuses. Theoretically, Sam himself might recognize his immorality and reform. An unlikely event in real life, it does not happen in the play. Although Sam might be persuaded by nonviolent means to behave decently, he deceives the people who employ such means and continues acting as before. Since nonviolence has failed, the people solve their problem by organizing and destroying the armed agents of the oppressor, and then a figure—Justice—kills the oppressor himself. In an epilogue, originally a separate *acto* but later added to *Justice*, the birth of Che Guevara implies that the solution was insufficient and suggests revolution to transform the society of which Sam was a part.

Bibliography

A. *Other Plays about the Brown Revolution:*

Guadalupe de Saavedra: *Aggression Gringo Style*, 1969; *The Battle of Puebla*, 1969; *A Boy Says Goodbye to His Mother*, 1968; *Jorge el Chingón*, 1969; *Welfare*, 1968; *Yerba Buena*, 1968.

Luis Valdez: *The Fifth Season*, 1966; *The Shrunken Head of Pancho Villa*, 1965; *The Two Faces of the Boss*, 1966.

B. *Works about the Brown Revolution and Teatro Chicano:*

(1) Although no articles on Teatro Chicano have yet appeared in books or national magazines, the following have useful background information:

Bigart, Homer. "A New Mexican-American Militancy," *The New York Times*, April 20, 1969, Section I.

"The Little Strike that Grew to *La Causa*," *Time*, XCIV (July 4, 1969).

Steiner, Stan. *La Raza: The Mexican Americans*. New York: Harper and Row, 1970.

Valdez, Luis. "Teatro Campesino" (interview), *Tulane Drama Review*, XI (Summer, 1967).

(2) Periodicals of the Chicano movement:

California: *Carta Editorial* (Los Angeles), *El Chicano* (San Bernardino), *Chicano Student Movement* (Los Angeles), *The Forumeer* (San Jose), *La Hormiga* (Oakland), *Inside Eastside* (Los Angeles), *El Malcriado* (Delano), *El Machete* (San Jose), *La Raza* (Los Angeles), *La Verdad* (San Diego), *La Voz* (Los Angeles).

Texas: *Compass* (Houston), *El Deguello* (San Antonio), *Inferno* (San Antonio), *La Raza Nueva* (San Antonio), *La Revolución* (Uvalde), *El Yaqui* (Houston).

Arizona: *Coraje* (Tucson), *El Paisano* (Tolleson).

New Mexico: *El Grito del Norte* (Espanola), *El Papel* (Albuquerque).

Colorado: *El Gallo* (Denver).

Florida: *Nuestra Lucha* (Delray Beach).

Illinois: *Lado* (Chicago).

Wisconsin: *La Voz Mexicana* (Wautoma).

Supplementary Bibliography

For lists of plays dealing with revolutions represented in this volume, see bibliographies following each Commentary. The works listed below concern revolutions not represented in this volume. Unless specifically indicated, the revolutions they dramatize have no historical model.

Robert Ardrey, *Shadow of Heroes*, 1958 (the Hungarian Revolution of 1956).

Robert Montgomery Bird, *The Gladiator*, 1831 (the uprising of Roman gladiators under Spartacus, first century B.C.).

Bertolt Brecht, *The Days of the Commune*, 1949 (the Paris Commune, 1871); *Drums in the Night*, 1920 (the Spartakist uprising in Germany, 1918-19).

Albert Camus, *The Just Assassins*, 1949 (anarchist revolutionists in Russia, 1905).

William DuBois, *Haiti*, 1938 (the Haitian Revolution of the 1790s).

Jack Gelber, *The Cuban Thing*, 1968 (the Cuban Revolution).

Jean Genet, *The Balcony*, 1956; *The Screens*, 1961 (the Algerian Revolution).

Michel de Ghelderode, *Pantagleize*, 1929.

Johann Wolfgang von Goethe, *Götz von Berlichingen*, 1773 (the Peasants' Revolt of 1525).

Gerhart Hauptmann, *Florian Geyer*, 1896 (the Peasants' Revolt of 1525); *The Weavers*, 1892 (the revolt of Silesian weavers in the 1840s).

Henrik Ibsen, *Cataline*, 1849 (the rebellion of the Roman Cataline, first century B.C.).

Zygmunt Krasiński, *The Undivine Comedy*, 1833.

The Living Theatre, *Paradise Now*, 1968.

Jean-Paul Sartre, *The Devil and the Good Lord*, 1951 (the Peasants' Revolt of 1525).

William Shakespeare, *Henry VI* trilogy, 1590-92 (the Wars of the Roses; Part 2 also deals with the Jack Cade Rebellion, 1450); *Julius Caesar*, 1599 (the revolt against Julius Caesar); *Richard II*, c. 1597 (the revolt against King Richard II).

Ernst Toller, *The Machine Wreckers*, 1920 (the Luddite Revolt of 1815).

Stanisław Ignacy Witkiewicz, *The Anonymous Work*, 1921.